"With this handbook, the editors demonstrate that they have a keen eye for identifying and researching issues at the very vanguard of the counter-narratives research field. This handbook will be a reference work for scholars and students alike".

Peter Kastberg, *Professor in the Department of Culture and Learning, Aalborg University, Denmark*

"This book is truly a handbook, being conceptual, empirical, and cross-contextual. First, it is conceptual, containing a broad and firm grounding in counternarrative, including what it is, why it is important, and how it can be useful. Second, its empirical examples can provide a 'how to' guide for others to follow. Third, this book contains a broad range of applications of counternarrative research in a variety of contexts, all in one convenient location. This is sure to be an indispensable bedrock source for this relatively new yet rapidly growing field of counternarrative research".

Grace Ann Rosile, *Professor Emeritus of Management, New Mexico State University, USA*

"The concept of counter-narrative has become valuable in many disciplines. A thorough, critical and yet accessible examination as provided by this handbook is a must-have for both students and scholars of narrative. Recommended!"

Per Krogh Hansen, *Head of Department for the Study of Culture, University of Southern Denmark, Denmark*

Routledge Handbook of Counter-Narratives

Routledge Handbook of Counter-Narratives is a landmark volume providing students, university lecturers, and practitioners with a comprehensive and structured guide to the major topics and trends of research on counter-narratives. The concept of counter-narratives covers resistance and opposition as told and framed by individuals and social groups. Counter-narratives are stories impacting on social settings that stand opposed to (perceived) dominant and powerful master-narratives. In sum, the contributions in this handbook survey how counter-narratives unfold power to shape and change various fields. Fields investigated in this handbook are organizations and professional settings, issues of education, struggles and concepts of identity and belonging, the political field, as well as literature and ideology. The handbook is framed by a comprehensive introduction as well as a summarizing chapter providing an outlook on future research avenues. Its direct and clear appeal will support university learning and prompt both students and researchers to further investigate the arena of narrative research.

Klarissa Lueg, Dr.phil.habil, Associate Professor, is the Head of the Center of Narratological Studies (CNS) at the University of Southern Denmark. She researches themes within narrative inquiry, organization studies, and cultural sociology. She has published in *Studies in Higher Education*, *Innovation*, *The European Journal of Social Science Research*, *Academy of Management, Learning and Education*, and the *Asian Journal of Social Sciences*.

Marianne Wolff Lundholt, PhD, is the Head of the Department of Design and Communication at the University of Southern Denmark. She is the co-author of *Leadership Communication in Theory and Practice* (2019) and *Counter-Narratives and Organization* (2017).

Routledge International Handbooks

The Routledge Handbook of British Politics and Society
Mark Garnett

The Routledge Handbook of Integrated Reporting
Edited by Charl de Villiers, Pei-Chi Kelly Hsiao and Warren Maroun

The Routledge International Handbook of Global Therapeutic Cultures
Edited by Daniel Nehring, Ole Jacob Madsen, Edgar Cabanas, China Mills and Dylan Kerrigan

Routledge Handbook of Street Culture
Edited by Jeffrey Ian Ross

The Routledge International Handbook of Simmel Studies
Edited by Gregor Fitzi

Routledge Handbook of Counter-Narratives
Edited by Klarissa Lueg and Marianne Wolff Lundholt

Routledge Handbook of Art, Science, and Technology Studies
Edited by Hannah Star Rogers, Megan K. Halpern, Kathryn de Ridder-Vignone, and Dehlia Hannah

Routledge Handbook of Bounded Rationality
Edited by Riccardo Viale

Routledge International Handbook of Charisma
Edited by José Pedro Zúquete

Routledge International Handbook of Working-Class Studies
Edited by Michele Fazio, Christie Launius, and Tim Strangleman

Routledge Handbook of Digital Media and Communication in Society
Edited by Leah A. Lievrouw and Brian D. Loader

For more information about this series, please visit: www.routledge.com/Routledge-International-Handbooks/book-series/RIHAND

Routledge Handbook of Counter-Narratives

Edited by Klarissa Lueg and Marianne Wolff Lundholt

Routledge
Taylor & Francis Group
LONDON AND NEW YORK

First published 2021
by Routledge
2 Park Square, Milton Park, Abingdon, Oxon OX14 4RN

and by Routledge
52 Vanderbilt Avenue, New York, NY 10017

Routledge is an imprint of the Taylor & Francis Group, an informa business

British Library Cataloguing-in-Publication Data
A catalogue record for this book is available from the British Library

Library of Congress Cataloging-in-Publication Data
A catalog record has been requested for this book

ISBN: 978-0-367-23403-4 (hbk)
ISBN: 978-0-367-56437-7 (pbk)
ISBN: 978-0-429-27971-3 (ebk)

Typeset in Bembo
by Newgen Publishing UK

Contents

Figures

Tables

Contributors

Adriana Aldana is an assistant professor in the Department of Social Work at California State University, Dominguez Hills. She earned her doctorate from the Joint Doctoral Program in Social Work and Developmental Psychology at the University of Michigan. Her scholarship examines how critical pedagogy and multicultural organizing models help build youth's capacity for social action across difference. Her publications include: *Dialogic Pedagogy for Youth Participatory Action Research: Facilitation of an Intergroup Empowerment Program, Social Work with Groups* and School Racial-Ethnic Socialization: Learning About Race and Ethnicity Among African American Students, *The Urban Review*, (47), 563–576.

Maria Avila is Associate Professor in the Department of Social Work at California State University, Dominguez Hills, in Carson, CA. Her scholarship includes civic engagement and community organizing in higher education, narrative enquiry and community based learning pedagogies. Avila earned a PhD in Adult and Community Education at Maynooth University, in Ireland. Her publications include: *Transformative Civic Engagement through Community Organizing. Sterling, VA: Stylus Publishing* and "Historical and Contemporary Models: An Organizing Approach to Community-Based Research", in *Higher Education and Community Based Research: Creating a Global Vision*. New York, NY: Palgrave Macmillan.

Ann Starbæk Bager, PhD, is an associate professor in Organizational and Leadership Communication at the Department of Design and Communication at the University of Southern Denmark. Ann is Head of the Center for Narratological Studies (CNS) and one of the organizers of an international annual storytelling conference. She is part of defining the field of organizational discourse and storytelling activism concerning how a discourse based narrative framework can assist organizational reflexivity and change. She is currently publishing on matters of storytelling, power and ethics in relation to topics as organizational and leadership communication and organizational change processes. She has published broadly at publishers and journals such as John Benjamins, Palgrave, Communication and Language at Work (CLaW), Tamara: Journal of Critical Organization Inquiry and Journal of Philosophy of management.

Michael Bamberg received his MPhil from the University of York (Linguistics) and PhD from UC Berkeley (Psychology). Previous to his appointment as Professor of Psychology at Clark University (USA), he held teaching positions in Sociology (FU Berlin), in Linguistics at the University of York (UK), Foreign Languages at Tongji University (Shanghai) and Guangdong University of Foreign Studies (Guangzhou), as well as Universität Saarbrücken (Germany). His scholarly interests are in narrative, identity, and qualitative methodology. Michael currently is the

President Elect of the Society for Qualitative Inquiry in Psychology (APA Division 5) with his upcoming term as President for 2021–2022.

David M. Boje, PhD, is a professor at Aalborg's Business College, and Emeritus Regents Professor at New Mexico State University. He teaches qualitative storytelling science methods. He is editor-in-chief of the *Business Storytelling Encyclopedia.* Boje gives invited keynote presentations on storytelling science, water crises, and the global climate crisis, all around the world. He is a member of the editorial board of *The Systemic Change Journal* that is an ongoing conversation about ways of Governing the Anthropocene, and helping to set up a Sustainability Storytelling Lab.

Katherine Borland is Associate Professor of Folklore in the Department of Comparative Studies in the Humanities and Director of the Center for Folklore Studies at The Ohio State University. She is the author of *Creating Community: Hispanic Migration to Rural Delaware* (2001) and *Unmasking Class, Gender and Sexuality in Nicaraguan Festival* (2006). With Abigail E. Adams, she edited the volume, *International Volunteer Tourism: Reflections on Good Works in Central America* (2013). In addition, she has authored several essays on feminist ethnography, narrative, dance and festival. She is a founding member of Be the Street: A Performance Studies Project on Human Mobility and Placemaking, an engaged university-community partnership in the Hilltop area of Columbus, Ohio.

Sören Carlson, Dr. phil., is a research associate at Europa-Universität Flensburg in Germany. His research interests include education, social inequality and transnationalization processes.

Judith Eckenhoff is a lecturer at the Chair for Cognitive Literary Studies at RWTH Aachen University, where she is at present working towards her PhD. In her thesis project she investigates postapocalyptic storyworlds and estranging ecologies in twenty-first century fiction. Further research interests of hers include cognitive narratology, posthumanism and human-animal studies, as well as Gothic and horror studies. In 2018 she coordinated the interdisciplinary RWTH Aachen research project The Apocalyptic Dimensions of Global Climate Change in Contemporary Models and Discourses.

Jette Ernst is Associate Professor at the Department of Social Sciences and Business at Roskilde University Denmark. Her empirically based research focuses on the organization and management of work. She is particularly interested in how organizational change affects people in organizations, how they respond to change and how change is managed. Her current work includes themes such as professional identities in hospitals, health care digitalization, counter-narratives and standardization of work, company privatization and the automatization of work. Her work appeared in journals such as *Organization Studies*, *Scandinavian Journal of Management Culture and Organization*, *Qualitative Research in Organizations and Management* and *International Journal of Public Sector Management.*

Antoinette Fage-Butler is an associate professor at the Department of English, School of Communication and Culture, Aarhus University, Denmark. Her primary research interests are in cultural aspects related to health and public health, health communication, risk communication and methodological aspects of Foucault's works.

Sanne Frandsen is Associate Professor in Organization Studies at Lund University. She uses ethnographic and narrative methods to study identity work at individual and organizational levels in the face of stigmatizing images. She is particularly interested in employee responses such as emotional work, resistance, counter-narratives, cynical distancing, and paranoia. She was the co-editor of the Routledge book *Counter-narratives and Organization*. Her work has been published in, for example, *Management Communication Quarterly*, *Journal of Organizational Ethnography*, *Scandinavian Journal of Management*, *European Journal of Marketing* and in several books.

Angela Graf, Dr. phil., is Postdoc at the Chair of Sociology of Science at the Technical University of Munich. Her research focus is especially on sociology of science, power structure analysis and social inequality. Recently, she has published numerous articles with a focus on organizations and power structure analysis in academia and higher education.

Maria Grafström is Associate Professor in Business Studies at Stockholm Centre for Organizational Research (SCORE), Stockholm University and Stockholm School of Economics. Her research focuses on the mediatization of organizations and how media participate in creating and circulating ideas and shaping organizational agendas. Recently her research has also included analyses of what happens in the intersections of different knowledge domains, such as academia and practice as well as facts and fictions.

Lise-Lotte Holmgreen, PhD, is Associate Professor at the Department of Culture and Learning, Aalborg University, Denmark. Her current research interests include studying various social concepts such as leadership, gender, culture and communication in real-life organizational contexts from a critical (discourse, narrative, metaphor and framing) perspective. The aim of her research is to uncover and discuss discursive practices that contribute to upholding or establishing power and inequality in organizational contexts.

Matti Hyvärinen, PhD, is a research director based at Tampere University, Finland. He has studied the conceptual history of narrative, narrative turns and interdisciplinary narrative theory. He is the co-editor of the volumes *Narrative Theory, Literature, and New Media: Narrative Minds and Virtual Worlds* (Routledge 2015), *The Travelling Concepts of Narrative* (Benjamins 2013), and *Beyond Narrative Coherence* (Benjamins 2010). He has published in *Partial Answers, Qualitative Inquiry, Style, and Narrative Works*, as well as in several edited volumes.

Astrid Jensen is Associate Professor of Organizational Communication at the Department of Language and Communication, University of Southern Denmark. Her research interests include various aspects of organizational communication. Recent work combines theories of metaphor and narratives with a practice-based perspective on organizational change, culture and identity. Projects that she currently works on include, counter-narratives in and around organizations, metaphor and narratives in mergers, strategizing and identity construction. She has published in international journals such as *Organization Studies, English for Specific Purposes, Bulletin Suisse de Linguistique Appliquée, Culture and Organization and Qualitative Research in Organizations and Management*.

Trine Susanne Johansen PhD, is Associate Professor at Aarhus University. Her main research areas include strategic communication, corporate/organizational identity and narrativity. Additional work falls within the areas of branding, CSR and stakeholder relations. She has published in a number of academic journals, including *Corporate Communication: An International Journal, International Journal of Strategic Communication, Journal of Marketing Communications* and *Journal of Communication Management*. Amongst her recent publications are "Countering the 'Natural' Organizational Self on

Social Media" (2017) published in *Counter-Narratives and Organization* edited by Frandsen, Kuhn and Lundholt and "Me, We and Them: Complexity in Employee and Organizational Identity Narration" (2017) published in *Tamara: Journal for Critical Organization Inquiry*.

Lena Kahle, Dr. phil., is a research associate at the Stiftung Universität Hildesheim, Germany. She has a strong interest in biographical research, theories of agency and debates about migration societies.

Reiner Keller, Dr., is Professor of Sociology at Augsburg University (Germany) since 2011. His research centers on sociology of knowledge and culture, discourse studies, sociological theory, qualitative methods, risk and environment, politics of knowledge and knowing, and French sociology. He has published extensively on these areas.

Denise Klinge, Dr. phil., is a research associate at the Universität der Bundeswehr in Munich, Germany. The focal points of her research are parental school choice, the documentary method, practices of technological development and educational logics of algorithmic systems.

Eva Knutz is Associate Professor at University of Southern Denmark, Department of Design & Communication. She works at the intersection of social design, co-design and interaction design within practice-based design research, with a special focus on two large public sectors, health care and criminal care.

Matias Laine works as an academy research fellow at Tampere University. He has been a joint editor of the *Social and Environmental Accountability Journal*, in addition to serving as an editorial board member for several international journals. Matias is interested in examining the interface of business, society and the natural environment, and in exploring the role of private corporations and the business world in the pursuit of a less unsustainable world. In his research, Matias seeks to understand the role of sustainability accounting and reporting in society's struggle with the escalating global environmental challenges. His work has been published in both edited volumes and in various scholarly journals, including *Accounting, Auditing and Accountability Journal*, *Accounting, Organizations and Society*, *European Accounting Review*, *Journal of Business Venturing*, *Journal of Business Ethics*, and *Sustainable Development*.

Klarissa Lueg, Dr. phil. habil. is Associate Professor at, and Director of, the Center for Narratological Studies (CNS), University of Southern Denmark. She researches the nexus of societal narratives, culture, and organization. Klarissa Lueg has published, inter alia, in *Journal of Cleaner Production*; *Academy of Management, Learning and Education; Studies in Higher Education*; *Innovation: The European Journal of Social Science Research*; *Asian Journal of Social Science*.

Marianne Wolff Lundholt, PhD, is the Head of Department of Design and Communication at University of Southern Denmark. She is the co-author of Leadership Communication in theory and practice (Samfundslitteratur 2019) and *Counter-Narratives and Organization* (Routledge 2017).

Cindie Aaen Maagaard is Associate Professor in the Department of Language and Communication at the University of Southern Denmark, where her main fields of research and teaching are within narratives and their uses in organizations and institutions. She is currently part of a team developing a narrative medicine program at her university, and her latest research is on nurses' narrations of diaries for patients in intensive care. She has published widely on narrativity, narrative medicine and organizational communication, and is the coeditor (with Marianne Wolff Lundholt and Daniel Schäbler) of Exploring Fictionality: Conceptions, Test-Cases, Discussions (University Press of Southern Denmark 2020).

Maria Mäkelä, PhD, is Senior Lecturer in Comparative Literature and former Director of Narrare: Centre for Interdisciplinary Narrative Studies (2016–2020) at Tampere University, Finland. In 2018, she was Visiting Professor at the Centre for Fictionality Studies, Aarhus University. In 2019, she was President of the International Society for the Study of Narrative. She was co-editor of *Narrative, Interrupted* (De Gruyter 2012), *Narrative Theory, Literature, and New Media* (Routledge 2015) and *Routledge Companion to Narrative Theory* (with Paul Dawson, 2021). She has published on consciousness, voice and realism across media, the literary tradition of adultery, authorial ethos, critical applications of postclassical narratologies, the storytelling boom and "story-critical" narratology. She is heading three research projects that deal with the contemporary instrumentalization of narratives.

Thomas Markussen is Associate Professor of Social Design at University of Southern Denmark, Department of Design & Communication. Among his research interests are methodologies of practice-based design research and cross-disciplinary exchanges between social design and narrative practice research.

Sonja Mausen is currently pursuing her PhD on the topic of contemporary indigenous novels from Australia and New Zealand at RWTH Aachen University. Her research interests include post-colonial literatures, queer and gender studies, trauma, and narratology. She holds a Master of Arts degree in English Studies and German Literature and is an Alumni of the German-American Fulbright Commission. She serves on the Council of the New Zealand Studies Association and is part of the international Advisory Board of the Journal of New Zealand and Pacific Studies.

Hanna Meretoja is Professor of Comparative Literature and Director of SELMA: Centre for the Study of Storytelling, Experientiality and Memory at the University of Turku (Finland) and in 2019–2020 Visiting Fellow at the University of Oxford (UK). She is a narrative scholar whose monographs include *The Ethics of Storytelling: Narrative Hermeneutics, History, and the Possible* (Oxford University Press 2018) and *The Narrative Turn in Fiction and Theory* (Palgrave Macmillan 2014) and her co-edited volumes include *The Routledge Companion to Literature and Trauma* (Routledge 2020) and *Storytelling and Ethics: Literature, Visual Arts and the Power of Narrative* (Routledge 2018).

Monika Müller is Associate Professor in Organization Studies at Lund University in Sweden. Her research interests cover a range of topics including internal branding and normative control, corporate culture management, identification, and time/space in terms of office design and working times. Her research methods include qualitative case studies, discourse analysis, linguistic analysis, semiotics and psychoanalytic analysis. So far, her work has been published in *Organization Studies*, *Organization*, *Journal of Management Studies*, and *European Management Journal*.

Matias Nurminen, MA, is a PhD student of comparative literature at Tampere University. His thesis maps out how radical masculinity movements use strategic storytelling. First article of the thesis was recently published in *Narrative Inquiry*. He is currently working as a researcher on the project Dangers of Narrative.

Donna Pendergast is Dean of the School of Education and Professional Studies at Griffith University, Australia. Her fields of research expertise are initial teacher education; early and middle years' teacher education and home economics. In 2018, Donna was awarded the Australian Council for Educational Leadership Miller-Grassie award for Outstanding Educational Leadership.

Anke Piekut is an associate professor at the Department for the Study of Culture, University of Southern Denmark. Her main research interests are the study of narratives in and about subjects in upper secondary education, narrative writing in school subjects and the use of narrative and narrative inquiry in educational settings with a focus on student's narratives about education. She has published theoretical and empirical studies on educational narratives, narrative writing and on L1 and L2 subjects in a Nordic and international context. Her methodological interest and experience is within longitudinal ethnographic research. She is a member of the research Center for Narratological Studies (CNS) at the University of Southern Denmark.

Justin J.W. Powell is Professor of Sociology of Education in the Institute of Education & Society at the University of Luxembourg. His comparative institutional analyses chart persistence and change in special and inclusive education, in vocational training and higher education, and in science systems and research policy. Recent books include *The Century of Science: The Global Triumph of the Research University* (Emerald, 2017/2019) and *European Educational Research (Re) Constructed: Institutional Change in Germany, the United Kingdom, Norway and the European Union* (Symposium Books, 2018).

Thore Prien, Dr. phil., Lecturer at the Seminar for Sociology/European University Flensburg, Germany.

Georgii Prokhorov, PhD Dr. Habil. (Doctor of Sciences) in Literary Theory and Textology, from Russian State University for Humanities (RGGU) Moscow. Full Professor, Department of Literature at State University of Humanities and Social Studies (Kolomna, Russia). Currently researching Early Modern travelogues on Russia, and working within the framework of research grant 'Voyages into Russia: Unknown and Obscure Early Modern European Travelogues. Textology. Poetics. Bibliography', supported by Russian Foundation for Basic Research (RFBR/RFFI).

Hanna Sofia Rehnberg is Senior Lecturer in Journalism at Södertörn University, Stockholm. Being a linguist with a professional background in journalism, she focuses on media discourse as well as strategic and organizational communication, especially in the public sector. Her ongoing studies include analysis on narrativity and identity issues in the asylum process.

Michelle Ronksley-Pavia, PhD is a lecturer and Griffith Institute for Educational Research Adjunct Research Fellow in the School of Education and Professional Studies at Griffith University, Australia. Michelle lectures in initial teacher education and specializes in gifted and talented and inclusive education. Her research interests include: educational provision and differentiation for diverse learners through transformative pedagogical approaches; narrative inquiry; twice-exceptional children's lived experiences and, initial teacher education engagement and belongingness.

Sergei Saveliev, PhD (candidate of science) in English Literature, from Moscow Pedagogical State University (MPGU). Associate Professor, Deptment of Modern Languages, State University of

Humanities and Social Studies (Kolomna, Russia). Currently researching Early Modern travelogues on Russia, and working within the framework of research grant 'Voyages into Russia: Unknown and Obscure Early Modern European Travelogues. Textology. Poetics. Bibliography', supported by Russian Foundation for Basic Research (RFBR/RFFI).

Wolf J. Schünemann Dr. phil. is an assistant professor of Political Science with a focus on Internet and Politics at Hildesheim University. His research and teaching cover the fields of Internet Governance, International Relations and European Integration.

Amy Shuman is Professor of Folklore and Narrative in the Department of English at The Ohio State University. She is the author of *Storytelling Rights: The Uses of Oral and Written Texts Among Urban Adolescents* and *Other People's Stories: Entitlement Claims and the Critique of Empathy*. With Carol Bohmer, she has coauthored *Rejecting Refugees: Political Asylum in the 21st Century* (2007) and *Political Asylum Deceptions: The Culture of Suspicion* (2018). With Bridget Haas, she is the coauthor of *Technologies of Suspicion and the Ethics of Obligation in Political Asylum*. Among other awards, she is the recipient of a Guggenheim Fellowship, supporting her ongoing research on the life story narratives of Italian marble carvers.

Abigail Stepnitz is a doctoral candidate in Jurisprudence & Social Policy at the University of California, Berkeley, where she teaches undergraduate Legal Studies, is a Berkeley Empirical Legal Studies Fellow, and a member of the UC Humanities Research Institute research group on the theme of "Truth". She is also affiliate faculty at the University of San Francisco, teaching graduate seminars in Migration Studies. Abigail has more than a decade of experience working with refugees and asylum seekers in Europe and the United States and her research focuses on narrative and credibility, with a particular focus on migrant narratives and the legal process. She also writes about the production and management of information about migrants and migration amid evolving social and political understandings of truth and credibility.

Jeanne Strunck, PhD, is Associate Professor at the Department of Culture and Global Studies, Aalborg University, Denmark. Her research focuses on communication in organizational settings, private as well as public. For the moment, she works on health communication, internal communication in financial institutions and in airports. Among her fields of interest are intercultural communication, gender, leadership, inequality and power. Methodologically, her research includes investigations of oral and written data from a critical perspective using critical discourse analysis as well as narrative, linguistic and rhetorical analysis.

Marita Svane, PhD, is an associate professor at the Department of Business and Management, Aalborg University. Her main research area focuses on storytelling organizations with a specific interest in strategizing and organizing processes. Marita's research areas of interest include leadership, dialogue, power, materiality, culture, ethics, and performativity. Her teaching areas comprise the field of organizational theory and leadership, theory of science, and methodology.

Niels Uhlendorf, PhD, is a research associate (post-doc) at the Department of Educational Sciences at Humboldt-University of Berlin.

Eija Vinnari holds a Chair in Public Financial Management at Tampere University. She is Associate Editor of Critical Perspectives on Accounting, as well as serving on several editorial boards. Eija's academic work covers a range of fields including accounting, public management, and environmental/animal ethics. A cross-cutting theme of her research in critical accounting is non-human animals as a marginalized constituency. She is also keen to explore the potential of agonistic democracy and critical dialogic accounting for facilitating a transition towards a more sustainable world characterized by inter-species justice. In broader terms, Eija is fascinated by ontological, epistemological and methodological questions, actor-network theory and discourse analytical approaches.

Zachary Wipff received his BA in psychology from Clark University with highest honors. In his senior thesis, Activity & Passivity, he formulated a narrative theory of psychological agency. He currently works as a member of the University of Massachusetts Medical School's MIND clinical research team, and is seeking to continue his education through pursuing a graduate degree in psychology. His academic interests include narrative, identity, consciousness, and philosophical metaphysics.

Wafula Yenjela teaches literature at South Eastern Kenya University, Kitui, Kenya. He is also an adjunct lecturer at Africa Nazarene University, Nairobi, Kenya. He holds a BA (Literature and Linguistics) and an MA (Literature) from University of Nairobi, Kenya, and a PhD in literary studies from Stellenbosch University, Cape Town, South Africa.

Michelle Zaragoza is currently an associate clinical social worker at a community mental health organization in Carson, CA. Michelle received a Master of Social Work degree at California State University, Dominguez Hills in 2018. Her Master's thesis, "From the U.S. to Norway: Exploring the Intersection of Sexual, Gender, and Student Identities", examined the narratives and experiences of LGBTQ+ MSW students in the context of social work education and practice. Her research interests include issues related to LGBTQ+ community, the use of narratives, social justice and storytelling.

Acknowledgements

All contributions in this book have been peer-reviewed. We would like to thank all those colleagues that have agreed to review, anonymously, one or more manuscripts. We do appreciate their careful reading of manuscripts and for their many insightful comments and suggestions.

Introduction

What counter-narratives are: Dimensions and levels of a theory of middle range

Klarissa Lueg, Ann Starbæk Bager and Marianne Wolff Lundholt

This handbook aims at presenting, and highlighting, the notion of "counter-narrative". Then again, in a broader context, this handbook is an endeavor meant to show, and bring together, those manifold disciplines and areas which a) employ narrative as a perspective, a theory and a method and b) operate with counter-narrative as a tool. In particular, when drafting the initial call for papers for this rather comprehensive book, we aimed at engaging researchers from manifold disciplines and area studies, in order to show the diversity, and the reach, of narrative inquiry. Also, we set out to lay open current state-of-the-art issues, advancements and problems. This publishing project on (counter-)narratives is being conducted at the Center for Narratological Studies (CNS) at University of Southern Denmark, Kolding. The CNS functions as a research group, with headquarters in Kolding. Simultaneously, center activities serve to maintain, and foster, an extensive network of scholars working together, in order to promote narrative inquiry: by hosting conferences, workshops, seminars, summer schools, as well as pursuing conjoint publishing endeavors – one of those being this handbook's predecessor, the Routledge anthology *Counter-Narratives and Organization* (Frandsen, Kuhn, & Lundholt, 2017). In that work, editors and authors unfolded the concept of counter-narrative with a view to studies into organizations: authors explored diverse takes on counter-narratives as a means of addressing "how some narratives gain dominance over others; how narratives intersect, relate to, challenge and reinforce each other; and how actors 'inside' and 'outside' organizations co-construct narratives" (Frandsen et al., 2017: 2). Counter-narrative, in the 2017 anthology, is presented as an alternative way of re-telling the story about the complexities inherent in organizational life that is increasingly emphasized in contemporary organizational studies. Counter-narratives are introduced as social, organizational practices as organizations are a) constituted by communication and storytelling practices, b) sites of struggle over meaning and identity and c) engaging a polyphony of voices from organizational stakeholders. This 2017 anthology does point to one inherent issue with the then state-of-the-art research into counter-narrative: the existence of a counter-narrative implied the existence of a primary narrative being countered. Logically, this narrative, as countered, would then be a narrative that was there in the first place, that was proposing something, pushing some agenda or alluding to something in a way bound to provoke countering. This logical deduction, though, does evoke the image of a quite static dichotomy: of counter-narratives, namely, on the one hand,

and countered narratives, on the other hand. Questions arising from this binary situation were and still are, inter alia: can a counter-narrative be countered? What shape does it adopt in the process of being countered? Processes of social narrative interaction could not sufficiently be depicted by the notions at hand. The authors referred to master-narratives in order to show the power dynamic between these two notions, however the question as to conceptual inertia remained. This current handbook, the *Routledge Handbook of Counter-Narratives*, connects to its predecessor in taking two steps. First, we take a trans-disciplinary approach to narrative inquiry: this handbook reaches out to disciplines and area studies such as education studies, sociology, literature studies, political science, organization studies and critical accounting. Second, numerous contributions in this handbook focus on the question of processuality in trying to conceptualize the counter-master-narrative dynamics beyond the binary perspective. This introduction is structured as follows: first, we elaborate the eminent notion of "narrative"; and we will comment on one of its possible social effects, that is shaping and stabilizing social power structures. Clearly, narratives may function, and this is the gist of this book, as powerful mental models impacting on various dimensions and levels of human interaction. Thereafter, an explanation of our focusing on counter-narrative, in the handbook, will follow. Ensuing, there will be a discussion of levels and dimensions, which, within narrative research, seem the most vital to us. We do so by referring to social dimensions of narrative, that is *culture*, *organizing* and *sense-making*. We do suggest analyzing these dimensions on three levels of societal investigation: the *macro-level*, the *meso-level* and the *micro-level* (for a similar approach pertaining to narrative and identity, see Loseke, 2007). Subsequently, and finally, we do give an overview of the different themes and chapters of this handbook.

What narratives are

In many settings, and in responding to many research questions, it seems useful to start with analyzing *a* narrative, e.g. a novel or a story. Then again, in such contexts, it would seem useful to know, before starting the investigation, what actually does qualify as *a* narrative.

Various features are commonly adduced when attempting to pinpoint the notion of "narrative". Often it is described as "having" certain characteristics. First, a narrative has temporal order; there is a beginning, a middle, an end. Second, the story has a "teller" (Ewick & Silbey, 1995: 200), one agent mediating the story. Third, the story consists of sundry interconnected episodes or sequences – this is, often with reference to White (1973), called "emplotment". Finally, this cohesion allows for, instead of simply listing sequences or events, explaining their temporal order and thus, allude, by this interpretation to some sort of moral interpretation of the tale (White, 1990). Controlling whether the object a researcher gazes upon fulfills all these criteria can help answering the question: "what is a narrative?" – and: what is a narrative *not*? Though we think that definitory approaches are useful in approaching a research subject, we would like to stray away from these structural questions. What a narrative is or what it is not, will help researchers to a certain extent, but it will not help with observing numerous interesting blind spots that are not being covered by the features as introduced earlier. What if we are out focusing on what is *not* being told? On gaps between two sequences? What if we want to research not the narrative as a whole, but rather some exclusive parts of it? What if the story of our interest is in-the-making, and does lack a proper ending?

What if our narrator is not, in fact, an agent in its classical sense (a human being), but a non-human mediator of a story? What if we detect some tiny wording, indicating a story being told, potentially? What if we, ourselves, are the teller? Questions like these can still be approached by using the above-mentioned definition of a narrative. Yet, such questions testify to the need of extending approaches to narrative: towards, that is, a more processual understanding. Not only do we need to know what a narrative is, we need *narrative inquiry*. In this regard, Liora Bresler, in her 2006 article, has made a valuable conceptual comparison:

> The distinction between narrative and narrative inquiry, I propose, parallels Barthes' distinction between text and textuality (in Csordas, 1999). Text is a material object that occupies space in a bookstore; textuality is a methodological field that is experienced as activity and production (Csordas, 1999, p. 145).
>
> *(Bresler, 2006)*

One understanding of narrative inquiry is that it can be used to investigate how humans negotiate their social actions, their social positioning, their identities (Bamberg, 1997). All these negotiations are social interactions, and they are brought forward as stories. As to the form of these stories, numerous scholars have contested the idea of one clearly identifiable narrative structure, and, especially, its temporal order, including Bamberg (2011) and Boje (2014), who argue for acknowledging the importance of "small stories" (M. Bamberg, 2011) and for the fragmented and living character of narratives, respectively. Regarding the "teller", numerous researchers focus on social interactions between humans. Others consider, in addition, material (Strand, 2014) as well as sociomaterial narratives (Flora, Boje, Rosile, & Hacker, 2016; Lueg, Boje, Lundholt, & Graf, 2019). Also, there is expanding form and state of narrative, and emphasizing embodied narratives, or multimodal narratives (Bager, 2019). The common idea of this social interactionist approach, however, is about narratives impacting on human sense-making and identity-seeking (Loseke, 2007). Narrative inquiry helps researchers understanding social formulas providing value and valuation to interactions between humans (and non-humans). Narrative inquiry, of this kind, does research powerful mental models socially upheld and contested. However, again, as to the characteristics of the research object: not every approach does focus on *a* narrative that is clearly structurally cognizable (such as in the fairy tale). Researchers may also investigate narratives in the making, narratives that are being planned and constructed, and fragments of narratives.

Narrative inquiry researches what people do with narratives, as well as how narratives impact on people. Narratives do hold, in the form of a story told, or a bet on the future taken (Boje, 2001), the potential to reproduce or challenge "existing relations of power and inequity" (Ewick & Silbey, 1995: 197). In this regard, and with a view to their function as condensed figures of thought, narratives carry manifold names, depending on various research areas. James Paul Gee, in his book on discourse analysis, describes:

> These typical stories haven been given many different names. They have been called, "folk theories", "frames", "scenarios", "scripts", "mental models", "cultural models", "Discourse models", "social models" and "figured worlds" (and each of these terms has its own nuances).
>
> *(Gee, 2009: 89)*

We would like to call attention to the first, and to us, most significant, notion in this list of kin: "typical stories", which is, in its most simple form, the core definition of the narrative. As, in our view, all attempts at explaining the manifold notions, mentioned afore, lead back to a "typical story"/ a narrative, we do stand by employing this simple notion. To understand how deeply entangled these narratives are with human cultural and social every-day-life, it is useful to turn to the Holland et al. (1998) description of a "figured world" as a "socially and culturally constructed realm of interpretation in which particular characters and actors are recognized, significance is assigned to certain acts, and particular outcomes are valued over others" (Holland et al., 1998: 52).

What we would like to emphasize, with this book, and with our focus on *counter*-narrative, is the social and normative struggle alluded to in the last part of the Holland et al. definition: certain, particular outcomes, depending on the socio-cultural arena, are being valued over others. Certainly, narratives and counter-narratives are densely interwoven with social rules for "when, what, how, and why stories are told" (Ewick & Silbey, 1995). Understanding how narratives come into and unfold power by creating or benefitting from such contextual social rules is valuable when drawing into question power relations. Understanding a narrative means being able to answer the question how, and by what means, social groups inter-subjectively account for social life and contend over its meanings. Again, moral interpretations of ideal social behavior are densely interrelated with social power structures. Narratives, thus, are instruments, consciously or unconsciously to produce a normatively laden social order: giving ample reason for scholars to investigate their emergence and social anchoring.

Why counter-narrative?

Being observant of narratives represented in the social world, and of the power relations they are embedded in, can contribute to the gathering of insights on marginalized positions. Stories revealing these marginalized views can be called counter-narratives (for a definition of hegemonic narratives s. Lueg, Graf, & Powell, 2020 in this handbook). Counter-narratives resist another narrative (Bamberg & Andrews, 2004, p. 1), this one often being, or being perceived as being, more powerful. This simple rule indicates the assumption of two narratives in confrontation and apprehension. Most affirmatively, counter-narratives can be interpreted as creative, innovative forces fostering beneficial societal change; forces holding productive potential for progress, development, as well as for ethical issues such as justice and accessible resources. From a more dialectic point of view, counter-narratives cannot be reduced to emancipatory, liberating or constructive stories. Instead, they can be hostile, and destabilizing: politics and organized propaganda come to mind, but also phenomena such as the loosely organized misogynist "manosphere" (s. e.g., Matias Nurminen's chapter on the "manosphere" in this handbook). Obviously, the interpretation of a counter-narrative liberating or hostile, even of being "counter" or "master" in the first place, hinges upon the interpreter's social position and belonging. Several chapters in this handbook will touch upon the issue of dialectic potential in counter-narratives (s. e.g., Hyvärinen; Meretoja in this handbook). The dialectic, "living" character of counter-narrative (any narrative, indeed) will be reflected in conceptual contributions, and coherently applied and further developed in empirical work (e.g., Nurminen; Johansen; Svane). Narrative and counter-narrative, as notions, help us naming and categorizing how social groups position their sense-making processes vis-à-vis each other, and help us observing how this "map" of narrative interpretations shift form and position through social negotiations.

On counter-narrative as a theory of middle-range

Within this handbook, "counter-narrative", as a notion, is being employed in combination with numerous other concepts and theoretical frameworks. This leads to questioning what, from a basic epistemological view, researchers are referring to when doing "counter-narrative" research. First, narrative inquiry, in general, is a theoretical *and* methodological approach. Aspects of methodology and theory are understood here as intrinsically tied to each other: applying narrative methods suggests a certain perspective; "narrative inquiry" or "narrative analysis" is not an isolable method or a tool simply to be put to work, on arbitrary assumptions as to how the social world works. Instead, narrative inquiry, always presupposes the research object representing a narrative, to make sense of by means of narrative structuring. The toolkit of narrative inquiry is, as are most "rules" of social science inquiry, in a constant flux of being discussed. In general though, "narrative inquiry", including counter-narrative, does contain theories about how human experience works, and about methodology of exploring the "grande idée" (Bresler, 2006) of narrative. Narrative theory, when being used to explain and understand human experience, can indeed be considered a "grande idée" as a transdisciplinary understanding of the sociological – slightly ironized – term "grand theory". "Grand theory" postulates a universal explanans in order to explain observed phenomena, and has been criticized for suffering from unreachability of empirical verification (Mills, 1959). Narrative inquiry, obviously, makes reference to such a universal explanans: Bruner's fundamental idea of the "narrative construction of reality" has brought about the idea of humans organizing "experience and our memory of human happenings mainly in the form of narrative—stories, excuses, myths, reasons for doing and not doing, and so on" (Bruner, 1991: 4). To quote another dictum, Mark Turner positions narrative as the explanans for functional thought: "Narrative imagining — story — is the fundamental instrument of thought. Rational capacities depend upon it. It is our chief means of looking into the future, or predicting, of planning, and of explaining" (Turner, 1998: 4f). Obviously, as in other grand theories, specifications about explanans and explanandum vary, e.g. between considering narrative structuring as explaining belonging and social moral communalities (Gottschall, 2013), thought (Turner, 1998), experience (Dewey, 1997) or, essentially, being (Bruner, 1991). In assuming "narrative" as a rather abstract grand idea or a grand theory, that is not immediately applicable in empirical research, two questions come to mind: what function, then, does "counter-narrative" have in this theoretical environment and how can it be applied? This handbook, with its large body of empirical applications, might serve to demonstrate that theorizing on counter-narrative is to be subsumed under the label "theory of middle range" (Merton, 1957). Robert Merton has suggested this notion in order to describe such ideas

> that lie between the minor but necessary working hypotheses that evolve in abundance during day-to-day research and the all-inclusive systematic efforts to develop a unified theory that will explain all the observed uniformities of social behavior, social organization and social change.
>
> *(Merton, 1957: 39)*

Though "middle-range theory" has been brought forward to describe (and legitimate) analytical *sociological* research, it is, we argue, applicable to interdisciplinary considerations as well. Middle-range theories are apt to "guide empirical inquiry" (Merton, 1957: 39). Doing research into counter-narrative obviously means trespassing into territory of grand narrative theory; however, it allows for empirical research built on a "relatively simple idea" (Merton, 1957: 43) (here: an account of social life is opposing another account of social life). Three characteristics, of counter-narrative research, may qualify it to be a middle-range theory. It is a) consistent with grand narrative assumptions, but functions b) independent of these axiomatic assumptions, and is thus, c) applicable in congruence with other theories and approaches (Merton, 1957). In this book, counter-narrative, as the relatively simple idea of an account opposing anther account, is being connected to: Bourdieusian field theory, Foucauldian discourse analysis and Bakthinian language philosophy, inter alia. Though it seems counter-intuitive, theories of the middle-range are apt to be employed within discrepant grand theories and schools of thought (Merton, 1957). "Counter-narrative", as a theory of middle-range is apt to guide empirical investigations into the social, and its basic assumptions are abstract enough to be applied to several different settings (e.g. from organizational change to negotiations of manliness and belonging). The conceptual, and methodological, value of counter-narrative research lies exactly here: as a theory of middle-range it does not claim, nor does it need to claim, being an "all-encompassing general theory" (Merton, 1957: 64). It is an intermediate theory to understand and explain specific empirical settings, and it is apt to show similarities in human sense-making and behavior across manifold fields of action. As Boudon has summarized:

> As we all know from our studies in the philosophy and history of the natural sciences, a "scientific theory is a set of statements that organize a set of hypotheses and relate them to segregated observations. If a "theory" is valid, it "explains" and in other words "consolidates" and federates empirical regularities which on their side would otherwise appear segregated.
>
> *(Boudon, 1991: 520)*

Consequently, in addition to being potentially consonant with several grand theoretical approaches, counter-narratives can be explored, empirically, with several different measures, using quantitative, qualitative and mixed-methods data, as long as these data can be consolidated. As to methods and instruments, obviously, and as in every other research tradition, there are some being employed more than others. In general, researching counter-narratives tends to be conducted within the qualitative paradigm, often employing narrative or biographical interviews (Schütze, 2011; see also Klinge et al. in this handbook), as well as observing "small stories" (M. Bamberg & Georgakopoulou, 2008); classic works do focus on subjective construction of how the social world makes sense to sampled social groups. However, scholars, not only scholars subscribing to a narrative "school", have long been using narratives not only as research objects but as a form to mediate their insights: Pierre Bourdieu's famous inaugural speech "Leçon sur la Leçon" (Bourdieu, 1990) at the Collège de France on his own struggles with academic authority and legitimacy being one example (for narratives as a form of research experience and mediation s. also Avila et al. in this handbook).

Levels and areas of (counter-)narrative analysis

(Counter-)narrative theory is a means of understanding social behavior in core-dimensions of social interaction, on the one hand, and of conducting observations on different analytical levels, on the other hand. The three core-dimensions being addressed, here, are culture, organizing and individual sensemaking. The three levels of analysis are the ones known in social science research as macro, meso and micro. These core-dimensions and levels correspond with, and overlap, each other, meaning that any dimension can be analyzed on any level.

Culture, organizing and sense making as macro, meso and micro observation categories

Three levels of society, ideal-typically, may be addressed to refer to different dimensions of social reality. These levels are drafted from a sociological perspective, but are employed here, to frame "observation categories" of an interdisciplinary theory. Counter-narrative and narrative research generate data and gather information that can be observed on the different levels, with interconnections and overlaps. *First*, we look at the so-called *micro level* of analysis. On this level, researchers study tangible interactions between individuals, often in high-grade detail, as done, e.g. in conversation analysis (Sacks, Schegloff, & Jefferson, 1974). Micro-level analysis allows for nuanced analysis of particular dynamics of social phenomena. The micro-level analysis within narrative research is important because it acknowledges that individual identities are created by making use of narratives, and that narrative capability is one important form of self-expression (Loseke, 2007). In consequence, micro-level analysis will often center on the dimension of individual sense-making – this, however, not implying micro-level analysis as being inapt to include cultural narratives (Loseke, 2007). On the contrary: as cultural narratives are vital to individual sense making, these two dimensions are often being considered in unison (s. Piekut in this handbook). As micro-level analysis foregrounds individuals, agency – the belief, that an individual's actions and accounts do have an impact on social development – are often considered as important. As important, whilst social structures are not prominently researched. *Second*, counter-narrative analysis and theory can also be applied at the social *meso-level*: meso-level analysis conducts research in the next "largest" entity, following the individual sphere. Meso-level research examines various types of group processes and interactions, "group" implying communities, societies, any organization or parts thereof, and any encounter of more than one person. This level is most obviously connected to the dimension of organizing, or organization. It is at the meso-level of intersubjective organizing and organizations that institutionalized cultural narratives turn manifest in policies, rules, laws and structures. The notion of organization, just like that of the institution, exceeds the idea of the group-level: in a Durkheimian sense, all beliefs and behaviors "instituted by the collectivity" (Durkheim 1893: 46) are institutions. Akin to institutions, organizations build on specific and durable rules (Senge & Graf, 2017), and thus, exert control over parts of society (Goffman 1961:168). *Third*, there is the *macro-level* analysis. It examines large-scale social processes and phenomena. As an outcome of focusing on society in its entity, and of striving to understand societal processes in larger interrelations, the macro-level is likely to emphasize generous patterns, such as social class or structure (Bourdieu, 1991b; Marx, 1922), systems (Parsons & Shils, 1976) or the power of culture and religion (Simmel, Frisby, & Featherstone, 1997; Weber, 2010). Individual agency does not play a prominent role, though there are, obviously, exceptions. With a view to the dimensions of (counter-)narrative analysis, macro-level analysis is most apt to investigate "large" cultural narratives, that is those narratives which society at large does recognize as important, fights about and reinvents, processually. Taking up our previous assumption of (counter-)narrative theory possibly functioning as a theory of middle-range, we are met with this question: can a theory of middle-range be employed in a macro-level investigation? We do propose that yes, (counter-)narrative theory is able to function as an analytical tool within macro-level-analysis. By way of example, (counter-)narrative theory when harnessed to explore – capitalizing on a contemporary subject of media reports – accounts of a "good refugee", or a "bad refugee", may very well be able to reveal a net of conflicting narratives of what is perceived, by what parts of society, as appropriate refugee behavior (for a relevant discussion, s. Stepnitz in this handbook). However, (counter-)narrative theory, obviously, is more likely to uncover nuances of such narratives, and to provide an appropriate picture of them, altogether, when applied on a smaller scale. Finally, and vitally, all those levels of analysis can be bridged and linked to each other; and this linking is, actually, the hallmark of counter-narrative theory. Discussing conflicting accounts of social life and its morality often means paying attention to cultural narratives (the macro-level), whilst investigating organizations (the meso-level), by means of methods that pay respect to the individual (the micro-level). Counter-narrative research takes an interest in how cultural narratives manifest themselves on the organizational and on the individual level (see Lueg et al. in this handbook). Though dimensions (culture, organizing, sense making) and levels (macro, meso, micro), as outlined earlier, are each important in themselves, integrating them, and analyzing interdependencies and interrelationships between these six items, is paramount. Again, though being a transdisciplinary concept, (counter-)narrative inquiry is highly compatible with earlier sociological attempts to systematically integrate micro- and macro-level research, on the one hand, and "multidimensional" research, on the other hand (Alexander, 1982; Ritzer, 1981). Consequently, it makes good sense to connect counter-narrative as a theory of middle-range to other, less directly applicable, theories pertaining to those different levels and dimensions. At the same time, those grand theories stand to profit from applicable conceptual expansion in order to explain, systematically, micro-macro-interrelations, e.g., Elias' figurations (Elias, 1978), Bourdieu's constructivist structuralism (Bourdieu, 1991a; Bourdieu & Passeron, 1977), Arendt's "space of appearance" (Arendt, 1998).

Overview of chapters

This handbook is presented in seven thematic sections, each section containing various chapters. The first two large sections are dedicated to theoretical ground-laying, and to methodological considerations. Only thereafter, the next five sections turn to considering fields of application: our authors provide work on organizations and professions, on education, on literature and ideology, on identity and belonging, and on the political sphere. In the following, we will briefly summarize and connect the seven sections and their chapters.

Counter-narratives as a theoretical concept

Chapters in this section conceptualize counter-narratives and relate the concept to established traditions and debates. Here, authors discuss diverse takes on how to theorize on matters of narrative-counter-narrative dynamics. The chapters link to previous central texts on counter-narratives and challenge structuralist and merely text- and product-oriented perspectives. The chapters all share interest in dynamic, complex and context-sensitive approaches to narrative studies that challenge the more traditional beginning-middle-end (BME) approaches. *Matti Hyvärinen*, revisiting and rethinking Brunerian narrative theory, is critical of a binary relationship between narrative and counter-narrative. Investigating their different ontological status, as well as potential uses in narrative research, he suggests looking at how narrators draw on diverse master-narratives and counter-narratives as resources.

Hanna Meretoja unfolds a dialogic understanding of counter-narrative from the viewpoint of Bakhtinian and hermeneutic critical theory. She advocates a contemporary approach to theorizing counter-narratives that is sensitive towards its relational embeddedness in power structures, and further, she discusses ethical dimensions. The dialogic framework challenges non-dialogic and structuralist takes on narrative studies.

Marita Svane, equally, draws on Bakhtinian thinking, in combination with Hegel's dialectics, to relate to organizational-managerial tasks. From there, she discusses the connections between narrative and living stories. She proposes the concept antenarrative as connecting narrative and living story, and outlines what she terms the four middles of storytelling. She also indicates implications for management executives. *David Boje* draws on a complex compilation of methodological and theoretical texts relevant to counter-narratives. He proposes six antenarrative inquiry strategies through which he reflects the historical and situated circumstances of the Kolding Pyramid in a sustainability perspective. The contribution of antenarrative inquiry to counter-narrative, is fleshing out the dialectical and dialogical processes pre-constitutive of the narrative-counter-narrative relationalities, as well as highlighting the interplay with untold stories, living stories and counterstories. *Michael Bamberg and Zachary Wipff* elaborate on an approach to narrative practice, and on a preliminary definition of counter-narratives, and its theoretical roots. The authors revisit and refine their definition of counter-narratives by distinguishing it from other types of narrative, such as alternative or conflicting narratives.

Counter-narratives as a methodological perspective

Chapters in this section provide access to theory-based analysis of methods and frameworks potentially applicable when working with a counter-narrative perspective in different empirical settings.

Antoinette Mary Fage-Butler investigates the potential of applying a discourse-based and poststructuralist Foucauldian tool-box to the understanding and study of counter-narratives. She applies two of Foucault's analytical concepts, statement function and subject position, to the study of health narratives from online forums. She concludes that these concepts are particularly well-suited for analyzing counter-narratives that challenge powerful discourses and master-narratives. *Reiner Keller* introduces the sociology of knowledge approach to discourse (SKAD) as a frame to analyze competing narratives such as counter-narratives in and across highly diverse social arenas, ranging from (world, transnational, nation-wide or issue-specific) public spheres to regional, local and organizational contexts and events. He argues for a discourse-oriented approach following Foucault's interest in power/knowledge regimes, informed by and grounded in the interpretive paradigm of sociology. Keller emphasizes "Discourse" as providing general contextualization, supportive to the analysis of narratives and counter-narratives, directing attention to particular issues and features of narrative processes as part of discursive structuration. *Monika Müller and Sanne Frandsen* discuss how three different strategies of counter-narratives analyses can complement traditional categorizing and coding strategies, or what they term "common sense coding" of empirical data. The authors unfold theoretical and methodological implications of a counter-narrative lens and illustrate how that lens enables scholars to handle empirical data in more nuanced ways. Their counter-narrative strategies involve looking at aspects such as untold stories and deconstruction, multiplicity and ambiguity, and tensions and paradoxes. The strategies represent counter-points to Aristoteles' axiomatic laws of identity, non-contradiction and excluded middle. *Matias Laine and Eija Vinnari*, with a view to counter-narrative research in combination with accounting, unfold two different methodological perspectives: counter-accounts as a research method, and counter-accounts as a research topic. They define counter-accounts and explain how they have been studied in accounting literature. As part of their conclusion they propose analyses of counter-accounts as a potent way for researchers to understand and engage with contemporary sustainability debates. *Thomas Markussen* and *Eva Knutz* reflect on a social design perspective contributing, with innovative methods, to studying family storytelling in difficult empirical settings. They study narrative processes involving a board game, set up in Danish maximum-security prisons to help children maintain a relationship with their incarcerated fathers. Notably, the authors propose a theoretical distinction between personal, family and master-narratives.

Counter-narratives in organization and profession

The contributions in this section empirically investigate counter-narratives in and around organizations and professional work contexts. The authors observe tensions between management, groups of employees and representatives of structural change in hospitals, private business and in the media landscape to arrive at their insights. In the first contribution, *Trine Johansen* reports on researching the potential of applying a counter-narrative perspective in investigating craft breweries. Departing from organizational autobiographies, she discusses the collective identity of craft breweries as potentially constituting a counter-narrative. Studying positioning and identity in the making, she concludes that the duality of "counter" and "master" is challenged by the way craft breweries construct identities. She argues that this interplay can more accurately be understood as centripetal and centrifugal processes of counter-narrativizations. *Ann Starbæk Bager* and *Marianne Wolff Lundholt* elaborate on a methodological framework binding together storytelling organization theory and discourse-based small story analysis. They provide a lens through which we can perceive of and analyze organizational storytelling practices ranging from abstract, philosophical dimensions to tangible everyday interaction. Analyzing a change process in a Danish bank, the authors focus on management having implemented a material discursive design for counselling practices, involving a range of new multimodal technologies. Interview data show how counsellors, navigating the new design, express identity-dilemma between the bank's narrative structures and their own professional identities. This provides a lens to study how power and control versus agency mechanisms come alive and are negotiated in a mix of resistive and complicit forces from which organizational reflexivity and change can be fostered. *Lise-Lotte Holmgreen* and *Jeanne Strunck* explore the construction of organizational identity in a Danish bank and building society. The overall research perspective draws on counter-narrative, critical discourse analysis and legitimation. From this wide-ranging perspective the authors analyze recruitment practice, as reported in interviews with mid-level management. Interviews show contesting narratives existing peacefully alongside the master-narrative preferred by bank leadership. Their approach aims at understanding how narratives either impede or support organizational strategies.

Astrid Jensen and *Jette Ernst* explore counter-narratives by combining a temporal-spatial perspective on narratives with Bourdieu's conceptual triad of field, habitus and capital. They analyze data from observations, semi-structured interviews and organizational texts gathered in a post-merger process in a Danish hospital involving nurses of two departments. They conclude that combining narrative with the conceptual triad helps reflecting narrative-time and space in organizational processes. *Hanna Sofia Rehnberg* and *Maria Grafström* focus on discursive struggles in the media landscape in times of radical re-organization, where the meaning of journalism is under negotiation. They analyze articles published in legacy media, and demonstrate counter-narrative not always emerging in opposition to another narrative; rather they posit that a counter-narrative can be positioned in a defensive act performed by those guarding the master-narrative.

Counter-narrative in education

Authors, in this section, introduce counter-narratives catering to the needs and situations of high-ability/dis-ability children and to non-traditional students. It is further shown how university internationalization triggers politically motivated counter-narratives. Finally, counter-narratives are viewed from a didactical perspective and tested as to their applicability in classroom instruction. *Denise Klinge, Sören Carlson* and *Lena Kahle* study educational inequalities in relation to master-narratives of "good parenting", which often favor parents with academic backgrounds. Authors refer to narrative interview data and look at how parents with a non-academic background negotiate the master-narrative. Authors supplement Bamberg's work on counter-narratives with Schütze's text structure analysis, specifically by drawing on Schütze's distinction of text genres: narrative, argumentation, evaluation and description. Thereby, counter-narratives are reconstructed via text structure analysis. *Michelle Ronksley-Pavia* and *Donna Pendergast* study counter-narratives of parental agency. They demonstrate that contested roles and identities are being assigned to parents and children by way of continued medicalization of disability and norming of giftedness prevalent in dominant narratives of educative practices. Polkinghorne's narrative analysis strategy is adduced for inductively organizing involving different experiences into categories. Three parental counter-narratives, extracted from interview data, suggest societies continuing to show limited understanding of both giftedness and disability, as well as, frequently, outright misunderstanding of these two particularities combined in a child. *Maria Avila, Adriana Aldana* and *Michelle Zaragoza* share insights about teaching and learning about social justice via the use of counter-narrative in teaching critical race theory (CRT) in higher education. The authors represent teachers and a student from the program and reflect on how their personal narratives inform experience teaching and learning about CRT, as a form of narrative inquiry.

The authors further explore the extent to which this class, particularly through an assignment that has students reflect about their political, social and economic positionality, leads students to creating counter-narratives that enhance their sense of agency toward creating social change. *Klarissa Lueg, Angela Graf* and *Justin Powell* focus on narratives propounding the value of higher education. In particular, they investigate grand narratives of Bildung (education) connecting to university governance. Contemporary governance discourse is suspended between two poles: the Humboldtian perspective, favoring professorial power and authority relations, and the managerial perspective, subordinating faculty under market considerations. Both positions are introduced as *hegemonic* narratives. In this way, elitism is continuously being reproduced: in-between a time-honored Humboldtian, and a contemporary, yet equally hegemonic managerialist narrative.

Counter-narratives, literature and ideology

This section, dedicated to studies focusing on literature, contains contributions outlining how counter-narratives pose a vital tool for contesting canonicity, and ideological dominance, in fiction. *Georgii Prokhorov* and *Sergei Saveliev*, in their chapter on the genre of travel writing, discuss the narrative structure of books covering travels of Western Europeans to Russia: the chapter presents an analysis of travelers re-evaluating narrative during the voyage, of foreign countries´ self-glorifying narrative, and of travelers depicting and evaluating presentations of folklore. Authors of this chapter also comment on how to perceive such travelogues, partly, as counter-narratives. *Wafula Yenjela* provides a critique of post-2000 Kenyan novelists' counter-narratives. These counter-narratives are presented to have problematic associations to traumatic pasts. Evocations of Mau Mau wars unfold socio-political potency in contemporary Kenya. The chapter highlights the novel as transfiguring histories, but at the same time adduces experiences in Kenya, in wartime, to demonstrate pitfalls, intrinsic in uncritical glorifications of violent memories.

Judith Eckenhoff and *Sonja Mausen* discuss Alexis Wright's 2013 novel *The Swan Book*. They do so by combining indigenous studies, eco-criticism, narratology and cognitive approaches. They argue for *The Swan Book*'s function as a counter-narrative to a "white Western bias". Analysis highlights the novel as integrating indigenous mythology and knowledge systems. Authors suggest Wright's novel formally challenging established conventions of the post-apocalyptic genre. *Cindie Aaen Maagaard* researches the narration of experiences of illness. The chapter outlines different perspectives within the medical humanities and narrative scholarship: one perspective favors patients capable of telling a coherent story about their illness, the other perspective favors emphasizing intervals and episodes. The latter perspective is elaborated, in adducing two literary works: *The Two Kinds of Decay* (2008) by Sarah Manguso and the novel *Transfer Window. Stories About The Mistakes of the Well* (2018) by Maria Gerhardt. The authors of the analyzed texts resist the prescriptive narrative by embracing ambiguities and contradictions about what illness means.

Counter-narratives and their relevance for belonging and identity

This empirical section unites several chapters dedicated to topics that relate to identity: race, class, migration experience, social ascent and masculinity. Authors, in respective chapters, elaborate on insights on how agents construct identity and belonging by spinning, and relating to, counter-stories. This section, especially, reveals the interconnection of this handbook's thematic sections: both educational and organizational context matter as to the narrated experiences of social groups. *Katherine Borland* and *Amy Shuman* contribute a chapter critical towards an Ohio-based heritage project: a Confederate Civil War Memorial and Cemetery. This project is presented by its proponents, as a legitimate counter-narrative: a perspective contested by the authors of this chapter. Employing critical race theory and drawing on narratives of residents, the authors argue that such heritage narratives serve to forestall interracial understanding.

Matias Nurminen dedicates his chapter to examining the "manosphere" an online network for those interested in radical masculinity. Counter-narratives, here, turn out to be misogynist accounts positioned against a perceived narrative of feminism. The empirical study at hand contributes to a conceptual development of counter-narrative by emphasizing that it is not always fabricated for purposes of constructive resistance. In the next chapter, *Anke Piekut*, referring to social relations in an adult education center, shows how mechanisms of othering get in the way of personal and social identification. Data are drawn from interviewing three foreign adult learners of Danish, as a second language. Othering, the author argues, stands in important relation to master and counter-narratives; master-narratives especially are intertwined with othering perspectives. Finally, *Niels Uhlendorf* assigns two purposes to his chapter on self-positioning of German-Iranian students: he elaborates on the functions of master- and counter-narrative in biographical interviews, on the one hand, and presenting empirical insights into a master-narrative of "self-optimization in a context of migration", on the other hand. Empirical data is gathered from interviewing students. Interviewees use master and counter-narratives in order to position themselves within the reconstructed discourse.

Counter-narratives and the political sphere

This section is dedicated to cases of emergence, construction and change of counter-narrative in political movements. The section's first contribution, by *Maria Mäkelä*, centers on social media and the notion of a well-functioning Finnish welfare-system. The author proposes that within social media, counter-narratives have a considerable potential to manipulate users' political consciousness. Empirical observations stem from personal stories in social media profiles and from human-interest journalism countering the alleged master-narrative of a foolproof welfare system in Finland. In these stories, the moral positioning and the ensuing social media virality is based on a caricaturized casting where the deserving individual encounters an inhumane system. These counter-narratives, proposes the author, are highly tellable because they are disruptive; the alleged master-narrative of a well-functioning social system is much more challenging to tell. *Thore Prien*, turns to the theme of food sovereignty, people's right to define their own sustainable and appropriate food systems. The author positions food security as a globally dominant master narrative, against a counter-narrative of agricultural food sovereignty. Departing from Foucault and Ricœur, the author shows how narratives are constitutive for the discourses of truth games. Empirically, he showcases philanthrocapitalist foundations and the international peasant movement La Via Campesina, creating distinct plots, and notions of time and space. *Wolf J. Schünemann* deals with European project in its narrative form: the European project, he argues, has for many years been an uncontested narrative of peace and success. Only disruptions in the form of Brexit or the Euro crisis have made Eurosceptic counter-narratives socially acceptable. The author traces the Eurosceptic counter-narrative to its roots in previous discussions during referendums on EU treaty ratification in France, the Netherlands and Ireland. This section's last chapter by *Abigail Stepnitz* addresses narrative strategies of asylum seekers to the US. Asylum seekers, when claiming politically oppositional, even revolutionary, activity in their countries of origin in order to seek asylum, tend to propose a set of themed counter-narratives in order to legitimize their story. The author analyses 30 asylum claims proposed in the US and how refugees motivate and emplot their relation to law, justice, politics and national values.

References

Alexander, J. C. (1982) *Theoretical Logic in Sociology*. London: Routledge and Kegan Paul.
Arendt, H. (1998) *The Human Condition* (2nd ed.). Chicago: University of Chicago Press.

Bager, A. S. (2019) "A Multimodal Discourse Analysis of Positioning and Identity Work in a Leadership Development Practice". *Communication & Language at Work* 6(1), 40–62.

Bamberg, M. G. W. (1997) "Positioning between Structure and Performance". *Journal of Narrative and Life History*, 7(1–4), 335–342.

Bamberg, M. G. W. (2011) "Who Am I? Narration and Its Contribution to Self and Identity". *Theory & Psychology,* 21(1), 3–24. doi:10.1177/0959354309355852

Bamberg, M., & Andrews, M. (Eds.). (2004). *Considering counter-narratives: Narrating, resisting, making sense (Vol. 4).* Amsterdam: John Benjamins Publishing.

Bamberg, M. G. W., & Georgakopoulou, A. (2008) "Small Stories as a New Perspective in Narrative and Identity Analysis". *Text & Talk,* 28(3), 377–396. doi:10.1515/TEXT.2008.018

Boje, D. M. (2001). What Is Antenarrative. Retrieved from https://business.nmsu.edu/~dboje/papers/what_is_antenarrative.htm

Boje, D. M. (2014) *Storytelling Organizational Practices: Managing in the Quantum Age.* Abingdon, Oxon: Routledge.

Boudon, R. (1991) "What Middle-Range Theories Are". *Contemporary Sociology,* 20(4), 519–522.

Bourdieu, P. (1990) *In Other Words: Essays Towards a Reflexive Sociology.* Stanford: Stanford University Press.

Bourdieu, P. (1991a) "The Social Institution of Symbolic Power". In J. B. Thompson (Ed.), *Language and Symbolic Power.* Cambridge: Polity 105–160.

Bourdieu, P. (1991b) "Social Space and the Genesis of 'Classes'". In J. B. Thompson (Ed.), *Language and Symbolic Power* (pp. 229–251). Cambridge: Polity.

Bourdieu, P., & Passeron, J.-C. (1977) *Reproduction in Education, Society and Culture.* London: Sage.

Bresler, L. (2006) "Embodied Narrative Inquiry: A Methodology of Connection". *Research Studies in Music Education,* 27(1), 21–43. doi:10.1177/1321103X060270010201

Bruner, J. (1991) "The Narrative Construction of Reality". *Critical Inquiry,* 18(1), 1–21. doi:10.1086/448619

Dewey, J. (1997) *Experience and Education* (Reissued.). London: Pocket Books.

Durkheim, É. (1893) "The Division of Labour in Society." pp. 19–38 in Thompson, P. K. (2004). *Readings from emile durkheim* (Revis ed.). London: Routledge Ltd. doi:10.4324/9780203337141

Elias, N. (1978) *What Is Sociology?* London: Hutchinson.

Ewick, P., & Silbey, S. S. (1995) "Subversive Stories and Hegemonic Tales: Toward a Sociology of Narrative". *Law & Society Review,* 29(2), 197–226. doi:10.2307/3054010

Flora, J., Boje, D., Rosile, G. A., & Hacker, K. (2016) "A Theoretical and Applied Review of Embodied Restorying for Post-Deployment Family Reintegration". *Journal of Veterans Studies,* 1(1), 129–162. doi:10.21061/jvs.41

Frandsen, S., Kuhn, T., & Lundholt, M. W. (2017) *Counter-Narratives and Organization* (Vol. 39). London; New York: Routledge, Taylor & Francis Group.

Gee, J. P. (2009) *An Introduction to Discourse Analysis: Theory and Method* (2nd ed.). London; New York: Routledge.

Goffman, E. 1961. *Asylums: Essays on the Social Situation of Mental Patients and Other Inmates.* New York: Doubleday.

Gottschall, J. (2013) *The Storytelling Animal: How Stories Make Us Human.* New York; Boston: Mariner Books.

Holland, D., Lachicotte, W., Jr., Skinner, D., & Cain, C. (1998) *Identity and Agency in Figured Worlds.* Cambridge: Harvard University Press.

Loseke, D. R. (2007) "The Study of Identity as Cultural, Institutional, Organizational, and Personal Narratives: Theoretical and Empirical Integrations". *The Sociological Quarterly,* 48(4), 661–688. doi:10.1111/j.1533-8525.2007.00096.x

Lueg, K., Boje, D., Lundholt, M. W., & Graf, A. (2019) *How an Organizational Narrative Creates a New Doxa in Higher Education: A Case Study of Sociomaterial Construction of Educational Value in a Danish University.* Paper presented at the 35th EGOS Colloquium, Edinburgh, United Kingdom.

Lueg, K., Graf, A., & Powell, J. W. (2020) "Hegemonic University Tales. Discussing Narrative Positioning within the Academic Field between Humboldtian and Managerial Governance". In K. Lueg & M. W. Lundholt (Eds.), *The Routledge Handbook of Counter-Narratives.* Routledge 269–282.

Marx, K. (1922) *Das Kapital: Kritik Der Politischen Ökonomie* (Band 1: 10. Auflage;Band 3: 1–2 Teil, 6. Auflage;Band 2: 7. Auflage; ed.). Hamburg.

Merton, R. K. (1957) *Social Theory and Social Structure.* Glencoe, IL: Free Press.

Mills, C. W. (1959) *The Sociological Imagination.* Harmondsworth: Penguin.

Parsons, T., Shils, E. A. (1976) *Toward a General Theory of Action: Theoretical Foundations for the Social Sciences.* Cambridge: Harvard University Press.

Ritzer, G. (1981) *Toward an Integrated Sociological Paradigm: The Search for an Exemplar and an Image of the Subject Matter.* Boston, MA: Allyn and Bacon.

Sacks, H., Schegloff, E. A., & Jefferson, G. (1974) "A Simplest Systematics for the Organization of Turn-Taking for Conversation". *Language*, 50(4), 696–735. doi:10.2307/412243

Senge, K., & Graf, A. (2017). Institutionen, Organisationen und implizites Wissen. In J. Budde, M. C. Hietzge, A. Kraus, & C. Wulf (Eds.), *Handbuch Schweigendes Wissen: Erziehung, Bildung, Sozialisation und Lernen* (pp. 686–699). Weinheim: Beltz Juventa.

Schütze, F. (2011) "How to Deal with Autobiographical Narrative Interviews in the Euroidentity Research Project". *Przegląd Socjologiczny*, 60(1), 41–91.

Simmel, G., Frisby, D., & Featherstone, M. (1997) *Simmel on Culture: Selected Writings*. London: Sage.

Strand, A. M. (2014) "Material Storytelling. Introduction". In M. Boje & T. L. Henderson (Eds.), *Being Quantum: Ontological Storytelling in the Age of Antenarrative* (pp. 232–248). Newcastle upon Tyne, UK: Cambridge Scholars Publishing.

Turner, M. (1998) *The Literary Mind.* New York; Oxford: Oxford University Press.

Weber, M. (2010). *Die protestantische Ethik und der Geist des Kapitalismus*. München: C.H. Beck.

White, H. (1973) *Metahistory: The Historical Imagination in Nineteenth-Century Europe*. Baltimore: The Johns Hopkins University Press.

White, H. (1990) *The Content of the Form: Narrative Discourse and Historical Representation.* Baltimore: John Hopkins University Press.

Part I

Theoretical discussions and developments

1

Toward a theory of counter-narratives

Narrative contestation, cultural canonicity, and tellability

Matti Hyvärinen

Especially since the publication of *Considering Counter-Narratives* (Bamberg & Andrews, eds. 2004), discussion on counter and master-narratives has been lively in fields ranging from psychology to politics and organizational studies (Ewick & Silbey, 1995; Loseke, 2007; Frandsen et al., eds. 2017; Meretoja, 2018). Recent studies have provided several proposals for master-narratives, but not much in the way of a shared, solid theoretical grounding. This chapter maps some of these proposals, their mutual connection, and – above all – their connection to narrative theory. The perspective of master and counter narratives is relevant for at least three reasons. First, it is one of the most promising ideas for introducing the notions of societal power, resistance, and conventionality into narrative studies. Second, while the methodological work on small stories (Georgakopoulou, 2015) and narrative positioning (Deppermann, 2015) is vibrant, the study of larger narratives urgently needs new analytic perspectives. As Lundholt et al. (2018) note, "counternarratives play a role in storytellers positioning themselves against, or critiquing, the themes and ideologies of master-narratives" (p. 421). Third, the theorization of larger narratives is often based on the analysis of individual, isolated materials, whereas the counter narrative approach immediately positions the stories within a larger narrative contest.

A major purpose of this chapter is to connect these terms more closely to narrative theory and practical narrative analyses instead of using them for mere descriptive or metonymic purposes. Counter narrative theories should not ignore and pass over the relevant definitions of narrative to begin with (Abbot, 2002; Tammi, 2006; Herman, 2009). More specifically, my point of departure is Jerome Bruner's theory of "canonicity and breach" (Bruner, 1990, 1991; Amsterdam & Bruner, 2000; Hyvärinen, 2016). With the help of Bruner, I suggest a clearer distinction between narratives and scripts, and consider just how narrative master or "grand" narratives (Lyotard, 1993) are. Based on this discussion, I also suggest a move in empirical analysis from naming stories as master or counter narratives to analyzing the ways individual stories and storytellers *draw on* different master and counter narratives. Paraphrasing Holstein and Gubrium (2000), a master narrative "is also always a resource for local *use*; it is not automatically invoked" (p. 162). I then consider the relationship between narrative contests and counter narratives, discuss the normative approach to counter narratives, and present history writing as an exceptional case of master and counter narratives.

Metonymic confusion

In a metonymic discourse, "narrative" is used to denote hypotheses, assumptions, theories, or argumentation – i.e., it is used for forms of discourse that are not narrative (Fludernik, 2000; Rimmon-Kenan, 2006, p. 11). Similarly, some academic styles allow the metonymic use of (master-) narrative to substitute such terms as discourse, theory, script, or plan. For the sake of simplicity, I call these forms "metonymic narratives." In such confusing cases, it remains unclear how the definition "Someone telling somebody else that something happened" (Phelan 2005, p. 217) is matched by the material and where there is a narrative text to be analyzed. In other words, the problem concerns narrow versus problematically broad definitions of narrative (Tammi, 2006). Following Ryan (2005, p. 347), I understand narratives exclusively as semiotic objects (or at least as phenomena that encompass such a semiotic facet).

Lyotard's (1993) metonymic "grand narratives" loom large behind the theories of master-narratives. As Chandler and Munday (2016) state, "grand narratives" (metanarratives, master-narratives) is "Lyotard's term for the totalizing narratives or metadiscourses of modernity which have provided ideologies with a legitimating philosophy. For example, the grand narratives of the Enlightenment, democracy, and Marxism." "Metadiscourse" is obviously the most apposite term here. It is easy to imagine vivid theories about the effects of the "master-narrative of the Enlightenment." Yet we are short of the "authoritative text" (Kuhn, 2017) of the Enlightenment, and on closer analysis we might find a striking number of different and even competing versions of this presumed master-narrative (Kurunmäki & Marjanen, 2018, p. 18). Arguably, there is a risk of over-generalizing the homogeneity of master-narratives because few scholars have systematically charted these presumed master-narratives (Kölbl, 2004, p. 28). The existence and characteristics of a master-narrative are more often presumed, invoked, and projected by counter narratives than documented. When they are documented, they are most often in the form of argumentative discourse (Fludernik, 2000).

Some studies seem to equate plans and narratives in the organizational context. For example, Rasmussen (2017) discusses the competition between two different action plans or orientations in marketing the country of Denmark. The article manages to reveal two distinct marketing discourses, yet it fails to demonstrate how "branding" or its bureaucratic alternative is a narrative. The excerpts the author presents are not specifically narrative, and he does not conduct any particular narrative analysis besides using the term "master-narrative." In this way, narrative metonymically substitutes such exact terms as "plan" and "discourse."

Conversely, Mutua's "Counternarrative" primarily portrays broad ideological discourses.

> The expressions of this form of counter-narrative, in which non-Western knowledge forms and epistemologies not only are celebrated but also have emerged as a separate and different way of thinking about and narrating experience, are at the heart of decolonizing and post-colonial works found in virtually all disciplines today.
>
> *(Mutua, 2012, p. 2)*

The aim of the critical discourse above is clear enough, yet the narrative terminology appears to be superfluous, without a proper anchoring in narrative theory. Halverson et al. (2013) similarly suggest "a master-narrative is a transhistorical narrative that is deeply embedded in a particular culture" (p. 14, emphasis removed, MH). Besides being a limited definition (are master-narratives always or ever transhistorical?), it also distances master-narratives from actual stories. The metonymization of the concepts already begins with the authors' proposal that a narrative "is a coherent system of interrelated and sequentially organized stories that share a common rhetorical desire to resolve a conflict by establishing audience expectations according to the known trajectories of its literary and rhetorical form" (Halverson et al., 2013, p. 14, emphases removed). If narratives are "coherent systems of stories," we hardly have empirical access to either master or the counter-narratives, and "narrative" is a metonymical term for the ideology lurking behind the actual narratives.

In critical race research, the terms "master-narrative" and "counter-narrative" are obviously used as rhetorical tools to consider cultural resistance. For example, Stanley (2007) offers a convincing analysis of dominant research ideologies and discourses at work in the review process of an academic journal. As Stanley (2007) maintains,

> [a] master-narrative is in place, and maybe influencing educational journal review board as well. I certainly see evidence that the educational research master-narrative – in which members of editorial review boards are privileged by race, gender, and epistemological paradigms [...] – continues to increase in number, power, and renewed vigor.
>
> *(p. 15)*

The evidence of master-narrative is thus recognizable in the observed privileges of "race, gender, and epistemological paradigms." Stanley then goes on to mention that "[m]aster narratives are often mental models of how voices of the dominant culture have justified systems and rules in educational research, in such a way that makes these models 'the standard'" (Stanley, 2007 p. 15). Temporality never enters into the description of master narratives. The actual reviews Stanley quotes are written in the argumentative mode, not the narrative mode (Fludernik, 2000). Event sequencing, for example, plays no role at all. The terms "master-narrative" and "counter-narrative" work as broad catchwords for dominance and resistance but without any noticeable connection to narrative theory. Ironically, Stanley's article itself constitutes a perfect example of counter-narrative. She recounts the story of writing an article and receiving contradictory and contestable reviews. As a version of master-narrative, the story might have continued: "Then we made the corrections, got the article published, and we were happy with it." All this might have happened, yet the resistance and rejection of the rules of the game (by criticizing the reviews and their expectations) make the story a clear counter-narrative.

Jerome Bruner, canonicity, and the breach

According to my hypothesis, counter-narratives strictly observe the requirements of tellability and exist in discernible textual form, while master-narratives tend to suffer from limited tellability. Labov (1972) raises the issue of tellability (reportability) and expectations with the following question: "What reason would the narrator have for telling us that something did not happen, since he [sic] is in the business of telling us what did happen?" (p. 380) Labov did not theorize this question much further, yet he made it clear that narratives are essentially about expectations. Tannen (1993, pp. 14–50) equally foregrounds the relevance of expectations, and, by referring to Robert Abelson, notes, "it is interesting to talk about scripts when there is a clash between how people behave and how you might expect them to behave" (1993, p. 17). This clash, I argue, is intrinsically linked with master and counter-narrativity. Because of the clashes, people need to give explanations, often in narrative form, in order not to appear folk psychologically insane, as Bruner puts it.

Bruner (1990) incorporates the concept of expectation as an integral part of his theory of narrative: "I shall have to consider the nature of narrative and how it is built around *established or canonical expectations* and the mental management of deviations from such expectations" (p. 35, emphasis added). Narrative indeed "specializes in the forging of links between the exceptional and the ordinary," whereas its conceptual pair, folk psychology, "is invested in canonicality. It focuses upon the expectable and/or the usual in the human condition" (Bruner 1990, p. 47).

The expression "the human condition" may be dangerously broad in this context, and in alignment with Bruner's cultural orientation, we may need to add that this condition is only valid within the limits of particular cultural and institutional contexts. Nevertheless, the similarity between the Brunerian "canonicity" and "master-narratives" described by Michael Bamberg is obvious. According to Bamberg (2004), "master-narratives are setting up sequences of actions and events as routines and as such have a tendency to 'normalize' and 'naturalize'" (p. 360). Bamberg (2004) pays attention to the enabling side of master-narratives, highlighting that they "also give guidance and direction to the everyday actions of subjects; without this guidance and sense of direction, we would be lost" (p. 360). Canonicity and master-narrative thus seem to refer to the very same phenomenon. Accordingly, a master-narrative can be understood as a sequence of culturally expected events. This cultural conventionality has also been theorized in terms of scripts and frames. When counter-narratives – or scholars – invoke master-narratives, they typically outline such scripts instead of proper narratives.

For Bruner (1990, pp. 39–50), narratives are prototypically told only when some constituent beliefs of folk psychology – the canonical course of events – have been violated. This suggests that canonicity and proper narratives exhibit distinct forms of knowledge. Amsterdam and Bruner (2000) specify these conceptual relations further: "We use the term *scripts* to refer to stories that provide walk-through models of culture's canonical expectations, and *narratives* to refer to stories that illustrate what happens when a script is thrown off track or threatened with derailment" (p. 45). Of course, their distinction between stories (scripts understood as stories) and narratives looks somewhat idiosyncratic, yet they draw the decisive distinction between scripts and narratives clearly enough (Abbott, 2002, pp. 12–24).

Amsterdam and Bruner foreground the narrative contestation by analyzing courtroom debates between prosecutors and defendants who are telling divergent narratives. "Narratives [...] are deeply concerned with legitimacy: they are about threats to normatively valued states of affairs and what it takes to overcome those threats" (Amsterdam & Bruner, 2000, p. 121). The writers draw explicitly on the script theory outlined by the psychologists Schank and Abelson (1977). Yet, instead of focusing on the scripts' cognitive role, they importantly introduce a historical perspective on the formation of scripts: "Some situations are ambiguous as to scripting [...] Scripts eventually get established to cope with yesterday's social anomalies. Until they are established, the uncertainty itself provides fertile ground for storytelling" (Amsterdam & Bruner, 2000, p. 121).

The connection between scripts and narratives is intimate and strong, and Amsterdam and Bruner (2000) see the presence of established scripts as "often tacit rather than explicit," since they are "a precondition for narratives" (p. 121). Their view about the tellability of scripts is clear: "You do not tell about a visit to the restaurant unless something not in the script occurs" (Amsterdam & Bruner, 2000, p. 121). The reference, of course, is to the classical restaurant script (Schank & Abelson, 1977, pp. 42–44). If master-narratives are scripts, no one prefers to tell them as such. Bruner's functional theory succeeds in explaining prototypical narratives and passes such non-prototypical cases off as boring stories. However, the theory suggests that the shortage of adequate cultural knowledge induces boring stories – people telling something that all others already know too well.

This discussion suggests that possibly (most) master-narratives are not narratives at all (Nelson, 2001, p. 158 makes a similar observation), not in the rhetorical (Phelan, 2005) or discursive (Ryan, 2005; Herman, 2009) sense of understood narratives. As abstractions, master-narratives do not account for particular events, nor do they have an explicit narrator or a particular narrative text. What the Brunerian narratives do – i.e., deal with violations – is not far from the theoretical descriptions of counter-narratives. Bruner's theory explains why counter-narratives embody a great deal of tellability, while master-narratives seem to suffer from a kind of dullness. Are we then entitled to claim that all proper (Brunerian) narratives are counter-narratives? Hardly, since we need to require something more from counter-narratives. As Bruner (1990) emphasizes, narratives are built around violated expectations but also "the mental management of deviations from such expectations" (p. 35). Amsterdam and Bruner (2000) note explicitly how "narrative has a way of domesticating the breakings themselves" (p. 122). The particular way the story ends and the events and violations are evaluated is thus decisive for the aspect of counter-narrativity. The narrative may either reinforce or, in the case of a counter-narrative, question or reject the original expectations.

Bruner's theory of canonical expectations seems to have some shortcomings. Despite his cultural orientation to psychology, he considers the canonical expectations as almost universally shared within a whole culture. However, most of the canonicities relevant for counter-narratives are contested and more local than Bruner's theory suggests. As Kölbl (2004) writes, "at least 'we' in the western world live in different and internally highly differentiated societies with numerous coexisting and interacting (and often also conflicting) life forms" (p. 28). I have previously analyzed Ian McEwan's (2014) novel *The Children Act* and pointed out the significance of competing cultural and religious canonicities (Hyvärinen, 2018). If we understand the master-narratives as universally shared within nation states, the concepts of master and counter-narrative cannot have relevance in organizational studies (Frandsen et al., 2017) without paying attention to expectations and canonicities within smaller cultural, religious, and institutional contexts.

Secondly, Bruner's discussion only addresses the lower level of tellability. As Norrick (2005) points out, some events "are so intimate (so frightening) that they lie outside the range of the tellable in the current context" (p. 327). In Norrick's (2005) view, the "truly tellable narrative is one which accrues to just the sort of identity a teller wishes to project in the current context" (p. 329). Considering that these upper limits of tellability are equally regulated by cultural and contextual rules, it makes sense to presume that at least some counter-narratives seek to breach precisely these upper limits of tellability.

Narratives in contest

The narratologist James Phelan (2008) has argued that every narrative is contestable by nature. This is mainly because "narrative is not just an object to be interpreted and evaluated but also a way of interpreting and evaluating" (Phelan, 2008, p. 167). Phelan takes a rather Brunerian approach here in emphasizing the necessity of studying narratives in contest instead of focusing on individual narratives in the way classical narratology used to do. Despite the contest, it is premature to presume that all narrative contests are about a struggle between master and counter-narratives (Rassmussen, 2017, p. 174).

For Phelan, the disparity between narratives primarily derives from opposing ways of interpreting experience. "At one end of a wide spectrum are narratives offering thick descriptions," not only providing the contextual details but also "the affective, and ethical dimensions of experience" (Phelan, 2008, p. 167). At the opposite end, there are narrative "means in the service of abstraction and simplification, eschewing thick description for the synoptic view" (Phelan, 2008, p. 167). Meretoja (2018, p. 12) portrays a similar polarity with her terms "subsumptive" and "non-subsumptive" narratives. Fundamentally, both authors suggest that some narratives simplify, reduce, and mythologize experience, while others entertain the contradictions and plurality of experience and are open to the ambiguities of understanding.

"To say that every narrative is contestable," Phelan (2008) adds, is not to say, "that the contest among alternatives will always be carried out on a level playing field" (p. 168). In culture and politics, level playing fields are rare occurrences. Does this uneven ground, the uneven share of generic narrative resources and sites of telling, defend the idea that narrative contestation usually or always consists of a struggle between master and counter-narratives? Such a conclusion would be premature and misleading. In a court session, it would be a serious failure to defend a presumed offender by resorting to a canonical script or only metonymically narrative discourse. A detailed, thickly descriptive, and genuinely narrative account arguably works better in the contest.

Instead of dividing contested empirical narratives into master and counter-narratives, I suggest a different strategy. Ever since Derrida's (1981) contribution to genre theory, several scholars have argued that narrative texts do not primarily "belong" to a particular genre; rather, the case is that authors and tellers draw on different genres (Hyvärinen, 2015). Loseke (2007) points out, similarly, how "[s]ocial members *do* craft their own stories of personal identities, and they *do* use formula stories as a resource to do this" (p. 675). Therefore, it is reasonable to study how different narrators, within the frame of narrative contest, draw on various master and counter-narratives. From this perspective, it is perfectly possible to enforce a master-narrative by drawing substantially – but not exclusively – on it. Therefore, it is possible to analyze empirical narratives as particular articulations of master and counter-narrativity.

Counter or alternative narrative?

Nelson (2001) situates counter-narratives within an explicitly normative frame, maintaining that counter-narratives are "typically told within the moral space of community of choice, are stories of self-definition" (p. 9). These stories of self-definition "refine a past that has been, until now, characterized incorrectly" (Nelson, 2000, p. 18). This normative approach eventually leads to the strict categorization of narratives. "Counterstories set out to *repair* damage to an identity, but the [discussed] teenager's stories don't engage the act of repair" (Nelson, 2001, p. 154). A proper "repair" of an American Irish identity story should include proudness about the family origins. Counter-narratives can never be, in Nelson's theory, malicious or racist in the way that Nurminen suggests in this volume. As Rasmussen (2017) argues, the "claim of an automatic emancipatory potential [of counter-narratives] is largely empirically unwarranted" (p. 175).

Nelson (2001) positions master and counter-narratives within the discourse of oppression and argues "counterstories allow oppressed people to refuse the identities imposed on them by their oppressors and to reidentify themselves in more respectworthy terms" (p. 22). The language of oppression, of course, does radically limit the scope of these concepts, and brings in problematic theoretical presumptions. How, indeed, would a study focusing on master and counter-narratives document oppression? Nelson's primary example comes from a fragmentarily documented professional struggle between physicians and nurses. The professional power hierarchies are obvious, yet a reference to stories told by nurses hardly legitimizes the terminology. "Master-narrative" exists primarily as a projection of the studied counter-narratives. Professions often struggle with each other, thus a collection of stories from one of them hardly warrants talk about oppression (see Skjørshammer, 2002). The field is uneven, yet without proper ethnographic research, one group's identity stories within a narrative contest do not deserve to be called counterstories against oppression.

Countering the master-narratives is arguably a matter of degree. Acevedo et al. (2010) offer one extreme case of the Nation of Islam (NOI), a Black Nationalist group. The article's central concept is "narrative inversion" – i.e., turning everything around. The author's "notion of narrative inversion suggests that certain master-narratives can be challenged by inverting the narrative itself so that commonly held beliefs lead to the creation of completely new ideological systems" (Acevedo et al., 2010, p. 131). The history of political thought knows similar cases, most famously Machiavelli's *The Prince*, which also works through the "upending of widely accepted narratives so that what was once sacred now becomes profane" (Acevedo et al., 2010, p. 131). Ewick and Silbey (1995) similarly establish a radical opposition between "subversive stories" and "hegemonic tales."

Such radical cases of inversion narratives are important, albeit rare, and the Brunerian theory recommends paying attention to the diversity of countering. At the opposite end of the scale of radicalness, personality psychologists suggest a contrast between master and *personal* (Hammack, 2008) or *alternative* narratives (McClean & Syed, 2016). These theories presume a societal-level grand narrative of the good life, and then theorize the process of individualization in terms of construing alternative narratives. At first sight, these theories may seem to be far from actual counter-narratives. Indeed, previous studies have suggested almost the opposite. As Andrews (2004) puts it, "One of the key functions of master-narratives is that they offer people a way of identifying what is assumed to be a normative experience" (p. 1). This is a valid claim and in alignment with Bruner's theory, yet these new studies claim that the mere identification with the normative experience is not quite sufficient for drawing oneself as an individual. Instead, these studies foreground the tensions between individual initiative and action versus narrative structures (master-narratives). Rather than rejecting these ideas directly, it might be useful to ask to what extent all counter-narratives are about finding an individual version or niche in the world as regards the master-narratives and expectations.

Beyond Bruner: contesting history

Some master-narratives do not fit the outlined Brunerian model. The first exception became conspicuous while I was analyzing an interview with a 91-year-old woman from the perspective of master and counter-narratives. Against my previous claim that master-narratives do not textually exist as proper narratives, I encountered the following future narrative. The interviewee, "Aila," talking about her late husband's wartime experiences, says:

> But those who came back from the war in some way, they didn't come back healthy. And this one stayed for five years, as they say in the song, [...] "with a sword we draw the border from Dvina Bay to Ladoga Lake", like this, and Dad spent five years at the bridgehead.

Aila ironically contrasts her own experience-based story about the men returning from the Continuation war against Soviet Union (1941–1944) in poor health with the words of a wartime propaganda song by the Academic Karelia Society (AKS). AKS was an influential nationalist right-wing organization whose "March of Honor" crystallized the propagandist master-narrative of the war. The counter-narrative aptly contrasts the heroic, nationalist future narrative with the grim consequences of the war. However, Aila is not re-telling the past master-narrative as such in her own speech; she is including it intertextually within her counter-narrative speech act.

Historical master-narratives are thus indeed able to exist in narrative form. Political activists tell their versions of past events much before historians enter the field and start working with documents. In particular, competing stories impregnate the political past. In such cases, a counter-narrative sets out to contest a generic master narrative, not any past canonical course of events. Twentieth-century Finnish history witnessed at least one case of a powerful, fictional counter-narrative. During and after the Finnish Civil War of 1918, the victorious Whites framed the war as a "War of Independence" carried out by a "peasant army" against the Russians and traitorous Reds (Alapuro, 1988, pp. 150–218; Hentilä, 2018, pp. 60–86). From 1918 to the 1950s, the victors' story dominated in media, schools, and public life, whereas the communists in particular kept calling the events a "revolt."

Väinö Linna's trilogy *Täällä pohjantähden alla* [Under the North Star] (1959–1962) is a trailblazing counter-narrative that foregrounds the domestic conflict, the emerging labor movement, and the dramatically unfair treatment of tenant farmers before the Civil war. The novels became a topic of heated cultural debate, and consequently a part of the foundational experiences of the political generation in 1960s Finland. According to the historian Seppo Hentilä (2018, p. 244), the trilogy changed the Finnish understanding of early twentieth-century history more radically than any other book. The debate challenged the hegemony of the "War of Independence" story, inspired academic research on the topic, and eventually led to the hegemony of the "Civil war" narrative, which, of course, also revised many elements of Linna's account (Alapuro, 1988). The novel is a work of fiction, yet through its reception and the consequent national debate, it managed to change the relationship between the master and counter-narratives.

What Linna was countering with his novel can aptly be described as "a coherent system of interrelated and sequentially organized stories that share a common rhetorical desire to resolve a conflict by establishing audience expectations according to the known trajectories of its literary and rhetorical form" (Halverson et al., 2013, p. 14). Because political history in particular prefers the narrative form, versions of master-narratives accounting for the past can and will be found in explicit narrative form.

Historiography is not the only area of textual master-narratives. Maagaard and Lundholt (2018) analyze spoof videos as counter-narratives of "humanitarian aid appeals." The critical spoof videos require the prior existence of easily recognizable media genres, such as the "genres of humanitarian communication" (Maagaard & Lundholt, 2018, p. 64) – i.e., touching videos portraying the sufferings of individual children and the immediate need for help. Such examples testify that contested conventionality can indeed reside on two analytically different levels: as canonical and scripted ways of acting, and as conventional genres of telling. Respectively, a counter-narrative may also bring about a new narrative genre. Davis (2002) tells the story of Florence Rush, who in 1971 publically told her story as a victim of child abuse. As Davis maintains, "Rush did not simply share childhood experiences, she also proffered, in schematic form, the plot for a new collective narrative" (p. 108). Notably, this is a case of challenging the *upper* limit of tellability with the consequence of generating a new subgenre of narratives.

A difficult case

The material of my case study comes from a story column "Vaikea tapaus" (A difficult case), published in *Mediuutiset,* a Finnish journal for health professionals. The journal has published the stories since 2009, and according to a recent editor-in-chief, the column is popular and keenly followed. The journal is published weekly and embraces an extensive array of stories. The column emphasizes the aspect of professional identity with a photo of the physician storyteller, who is usually wearing a white coat. A standard introductory text accompanies all stories:

> In this column, a physician recounts a challenging situation from his or her working life, how the issue was solved, and what it was learned from it. At the same time, he or she nominates the narrator of the next difficult case.

The editors of the column conduct a 15-minute phone interview and edit the final story with the help of this material. The doctors and journalists thus jointly produce the stories. The journalists most likely pursue their journalistic interest to guarantee the tellability of the story.

While reading the stories, my first observation concerned the phenomena that doctors identified as difficulties. If we presuppose for a moment that physicians fashion their stories in line with the model of epicrisis, we should obviously expect stories recounting difficult illnesses and injuries, as well as the quest for correct diagnoses and successful treatments. Indeed, there are plenty of examples of such stories focusing on challenging diagnoses and treatments, yet they do not constitute the totality or perhaps even the majority of the stories. Such stories obviously recount the canonical, textbook course of events within the frame of scientific medicine, thus endorsing the corresponding master-narrative.

Numerous early stories foreground an entirely different difficulty. Rather than dramatizing the diagnosis or treatment, the encountered problem resides in the *interaction* between the doctor, nurses, patient, and the family members as the real difficulty requiring resolution. These two major story types seem to reflect the double nature of medicine – on the one hand, it is a strict, biomedical science, and on the other hand, the actual practice of medicine is an interpretative and interactional enterprise. While the first category of stories privileges acquired knowledge and new steps in the command of good medical procedures, occasionally even good intuition, the second category comprises a whole range of stories on the contradictions and absurdities of life.

Montgomery has explored this duality of contemporary medicine as a biomedical science and an interpretative practice. "Physicians draw on their diagnostic skills and clinical experience as well as scientific information and clinical research when they exercise clinical judgement" (Montgomery, 2006, p. 3). However, in a somewhat exaggerated manner, Montgomery reasons that the practical nature of medicine is continually overlooked in medical training, because "work is described – despite the evidence – as an old-fashioned, positivist, Newtonian science" (2006, p. 4). The objective is impossible, as "no matter how solid the science or how precise the technology that physicians use, clinical medicine remains an interpretive practice" (2006, p. 5). Consequently, Montgomery defines medicine as "learned, rational, science-using practice" (p. 36) whose central element is clinical judgement. Judgement is needed because in their practice, doctors face the puzzle of an individual case and not only general biomedical principles. Charon (2006, p. 39) similarly argues that what "distinguishes narrative knowledge from universal or scientific knowledge is the ability to capture the singular, irreplicable, or incommensurable" (p. 45). As mentioned, the column is aptly titled "A Difficult Case," directing the reader's attention to clinical judgment.

The puzzle of the individual case establishes a constant need for narratives and intensifies the tellability of the physicians' stories. The stories foregrounding the interactional problems set out to counter the discourse of medicine-as-science more explicitly than the stories about finding the correct diagnosis and treatment. However, these two categories of story are not in open contest. If they compete for something, it is for recognition, individuality, and tellability. The mere repetition of the expected course of action – diagnoses, treatment, and recovery – without portraying a proper clinical puzzle will poorly serve as a method of individualization.

The interactional paradigm contains plenty of comically humorous encounters. These stories are typically set in the early years of practice and in a distant, northern location. Humor in this and similar stories obviously has a double function, both adding to the tellability and domesticating the potentially damaging consequences of the communicational gap. For Norrick (2005, p. 338), laughter is one method of taming the consequences of approaching or breaking the upper limit of tellability. Humor, it would seem, works similarly in the following story.

The story is provocatively titled "The sore testicles," and the course of events with its repetition resembles folk tales and children's games with a play on (false) expectations. Once again, the story is set decades ago in a small town. Towards the end of a long day, the physician in charge has two patients remaining when he receives a phone call from a man complaining of sore testicles. The doctor promises to see him as his last patient of the day. When, eventually, a third patient comes in, the doctor orders him to undress and palpates his testicles without finding any notable problems. The next morning, a man knocks on the physician's door and comes in, apologizing for not being able to come the previous evening to have his testicles examined (Kuittinen, 2010a). This story, exceptionally, was told about another physician (at the time of the publication, in a leading position in his area) and by a teller who was in the position of a witness and deliverer of the punch line. The long day in the small town, the third man who is not the man expected, and the delicacy attached to the young male doctor's reasons for touching another man's testicles all connect the story to inherited story genres and intensify its tellability. Nevertheless, the story is about clinical judgment – the necessity to check the anamnesis carefully at the beginning of every encounter with a patient.

Stories of communicational impasse continue to foreground the potential absurdity of encounters in the actual work of physicians. While the previous story used humor as a crucial resource, a story titled "The mind-reading device" (Kuittinen, 2010b) emphasizes its darker aspects. Years ago, an elderly female patient comes to a young doctor and announces that she has reported a crime, since someone had implanted a mind-reading device into her head. From the medical records, the doctor learns that the woman refuses to take her prescribed pills for paranoia, and keeps moving from town to town to escape her persecutors. The young physician consults a psychiatrist, who suggests taking the patient's delusion seriously and partly going along with her story. Together with the patient, the doctor begins the search for the device. He orders X-rays of her skull, and later the patient and the doctor study the images together without being able to locate the harmful implant. The patient agrees that an operation is impossible due to the device's invisibility.

To solve the dilemma, the physician suggests a medicine (unbeknownst to the patient, an anti-psychotic medication) that is able to dissolve the device. The patient accepts, and in a few days, the harmful device stops working. However, the victory is only temporary, since the national health insurance service sends an official letter to the patient, informing her that she is entitled to receive a permanent reimbursement for her anti-psychotic medication. The patient stops taking the medicine, and soon disappears.

This story exhibits several aspects of counter-narrative. The medical diagnosis is clear before anything takes place. The trouble is miles away from a standard biomedical problem. The young physician does not invent the interactional strategy himself; instead, he receives the help of a psychiatrist from a nearby mental hospital. Most shockingly, the story resolves with only a transient success, ultimately ending with a failure and enigma. What happened to the woman? Had the doctor any chance of solving the dilemma differently? Even his prescription was legally questionable, since the medicine was misleadingly prescribed for "the dissolution of a mind-reading device." However, he achieved the transitory results only by taking the patient's paranoid story seriously. Eventually, the success was in vain because of a bureaucratic act by the well-meaning authorities, who revealed the true nature of the medication and returned the story to the biomedical discourse on psychosis.

On the other hand, the story corresponds with the emergent "A difficult case" genre in some of its crucial features. These confusing events took place "at the beginning of my career," and in a small municipality in the countryside. The privileged chronotope includes a distant, preferably small or exotic place, and the formative years of the physician's professional identity, the years spent learning clinical judgment. The closer the events of the story come to the time of telling, the more we can expect a story that recounts a success in diagnosis and treatment – i.e., the learning of the medical procedure. The problem in the interactional stories, however, is not about following some correct scientific path pointed out by biomedical research, but the negotiation of the terms and limits of clinical judgment.

The format of the stories – edited interviews published in a professional journal – discriminates against surface-level contestation. The principles of collegial conduct equally restrict expressions of open criticism. The pull of tellability, recognition, and individualization together direct the physicians' attention to paradoxical cases of clinical judgment instead of mere medical success stories. These stories do not employ inversion; they do not struggle against oppression or broad cultural hegemony. However, many of the stories can legitimately be understood as counter-narratives against the narrow and inherited discourse of medicine as a pure biomedical science.

Counter, contested, hegemonic, or alternative narratives?

As the sociologists Jaber F. Gubrium and James A. Holstein (2009) protest, narratives "are considered mainly for their internal organization" (p. vii) in contemporary narrative analysis in social research. As argued earlier, the study of counter and master-narratives works as a useful corrective move in this respect. A characteristic feature in studies on counter-narratives is understanding the stories within a frame of narrative contestation or narratives resisting "master-narratives" or dominant discourses.

Within the suggested frame of the Brunerian narrative theory, most master-narratives – with the exception of historical narratives – can more accurately be theorized as canonical scripts, as expected courses of events, or abstractions from numberless narratives. Master-narratives rather resemble abstractions of narratives than real, tellable, and recognizable stories. Counter-narratives always provide the narrator with more tellability and individuality compared to master-narratives.

For two reasons, I have distanced myself from the Lyotardian heritage of "grand narratives." My first reason is the purely metonymic talk of dominant discourses as narratives. Narrative analysis has little to offer such discourse analyses. Another reason is the limitation on totalizing and trans-historical discourses as master-narratives. The concepts of master and counter-narratives function productively on many different levels of particularity. They may be studied on institutional, organizational, local, or other cultural levels. In a similar way, the aspect of countering should not be understood as a uniform, constant quality. The countering can extend from the radical inversion of cultural values to the search for individualization with the help of alternative narratives. Like positioning, the urge to find individuality with narratives is a constant element of storytelling.

Reaching beyond the Brunerian frame, history offers a different variety of master-narratives. Telling is equally a form of action, and it is under the same processes of conventionalization and canonicity. In representing the contested past, master-narratives can perfectly exist in the form of dominant narratives, or to use the expression by Halverson et al. (2013), "a coherent system of interrelated and sequentially organized stories that share a common rhetorical desire" (p. 14). Master-narratives of the contested past can thus exist textually as a system of different versions, with or without one "authoritative text" (Kuhn, 2017). A question for further research concerns the entitlement to tell (a version of) such master-narratives, to produce a version of "the authoritative text." For example, physicians are likely to tell the story of medicine from the perspective of clinical judgment, while hospital managers may prefer, in public talks and texts, the understanding of medicine as a strict biomedical science that is about solving the most pressing health problems.

Ultimately, the empirical distinction between master and counter-narratives can be challenged. Counternarrativity is by no means an essential, abstract, and totalizing feature of any narrative. An individual narrative may counter a particular dominant discourse while at the same time drawing on some other cultural canonicities. For this reason, I suggest a change in the basic methodology of using these concepts. Instead of dividing empirical narratives into master and counter-narratives, it is far more recommendable to investigate how different narratives and narrators draw on different and contradictory canonical and countering resources. After all, the time of binary concepts should have passed by now. This point also demonstrates the ontological difference between actual narratives and metonymic, abstracted narratives. Metonymic (master or counter-) narratives exhibit pure and fundamental "mastering" or "countering," and they cannot be contradictory in the same way individual narratives told by ordinary people usually are.

Acknowledgments

I am grateful to the Academy of Finland research projects Voices of Democracy (SA 2501308792) and The Literary in Life (285144) for supporting my work on this chapter. Earlier versions of this chapter have been discussed at the ENN Prague (2017) and Narrative Matters (2018) conferences.

References

Abbott, H. P. (2002). *The Cambridge introduction to narrative*. Cambridge: Cambridge University Press.
Acevedo, G. A., Ordner, J., & Thompson, M. (2010). Narrative inversion as a tactical framing device. The ideological origins of the Nation of Islam. *Narrative Inquiry*, *20*(1), 124–152.
Alapuro, R. (1988). *State and revolution in Finland*. Berkeley: University of California Press.
Amsterdam, A., & Bruner, J. (2000). *Minding the law*. Cambridge, MA: Harvard University Press.
Andrews, M. (2004). Opening to the original contributions: Counter-narratives and the power to oppose. In M. Bamberg & M. Andrews (Eds.), *Considering counter-narratives: Narrating, resisting, making sense*. (pp. 1–6) Amsterdam: Benjamins.
Bamberg, M. (2004a). Considering counter narratives. In M. Bamberg & M. Andrews (Eds.), *Considering counter-narratives* (pp. 351–371). Amsterdam: Benjamins.
Bamberg, M. (2004b). Positioning with Davie Hogan. Stories, tellings, and identities. In C. Daiute & C. Lightfoot (Eds.), *Narrative analysis. Studying the development of individuals in society.* (pp. 135–157). Thousand Oaks: Sage.
Bamberg, M., & Andrews, M. (Eds.) (2004). *Considering counter-narratives. Narrating, resisting, making sense.* Amsterdam: Benjamins.
Bruner, J. (1990). *Acts of meaning*. Cambridge: Harvard University Press.
Bruner, J. (1991). The narrative construction of reality. *Critical Inquiry 18*, 1–21.
Chandler, D., & Munday, R. (2016). Grand narratives (metanarratives, master-narratives). In D. Chandler & R. Munday (Eds.), *A dictionary of media and communication*. Oxford: Oxford University Press.
Charon, R. (2006). *Narrative medicine. Honoring the stories of illness*. Oxford: Oxford University Press.
Davis, J. E. (2002). Social Movements and Strategic Narratives: Creating Sexual Abuse Survival Account. In W. Patterson (Ed.), *Strategic narrative. New perspectives on the power of personal and cultural stories* (pp. 107–125). Lanham: Lexington Books.
Deppermann, A. (2013). Positioning in narrative interaction. *Narrative Inquiry*, *23*(1), 1–15.
Deppermann, A. (2015). Positioning. In A. De Fina & A. Georgakopoulou (Eds.), *The Handbook of Narrative Analysis* (pp. 368–387). Malden, MA: Wiley Blackwell.
Derrida, J. (1981). The law of genre. In W. J. T. Mitchell (Ed.), *On narrative* (pp. 51–77). Chicago: University of Chicago Press.
Ewick, P., & Silbey, S. S. (1995). Subversive stories and hegemonic tales: Toward a sociology of narrative. *Law & Society Review*, *29*(2), 197–226.
Frandsen, S., Kuhn, T., & Lundholt, M. W. (Eds.). (2017). Counter-narratives and Organizations. Abingdon: Routledge.
Fludernik, M. (2000). Genres, text types, or discourse modes? Narrative modalities and generic categorization. *Style*, *34*(1), 274–292.
Frank, A. W. (1995). *The wounded storyteller: Body, illness, and ethics*. Chicago: University of Chicago Press.
Gabriel, Y. (2017). Narrative ecologies and the role of counter-narratives. The case of nostalgic stories and conspiracy theories. In S. Frandsen, T. Kuhn, & M. W. Lundholt (Eds.), *Counter-narratives and organizations* (pp. 208–225). Abingdon: Routledge.
Georgakopoulou, A. (2015). Small stories research. Methods - analysis - outreach. In A. De Fina & A. Georgakopoulou (Eds.), *The handbook of narrative analysis* (pp. 255–271). Chichester: John Wiley.
Gubrium, J. F., & Holstein, J. A. (2009). *Analyzing narrative reality*. Los Angeles: Sage.
Halverson, J. R., & Goodall Jr., H. L. (2013). *Master-narratives of Islamist extremism*. New York: Palgrave Macmillan.

Hammack, P. L. (2008). Narrative and the cultural psychology of identity. *Personality and Social Psychology*, *12*(3), 222–247.

Hentilä, S. (2018). *Pitkät varjot. Muistamisen historia ja politiikka.* Helsinki: Siltala.

Herman, D. (2009). *Basic elements of narrative.* Malden, MA: Wiley-Blackwell.

Holstein, J. A., & Gubrium, J. F. (2000). *The self we live by. Narrative identity in a postmodern world.* New York: Oxford University Press.

Hyvärinen, M. (2015). Analyzing narrative genres. In A. De Fina & A. Georgakopoulou (Eds.), *The handbook of narrative analysis* (pp. 178–193). Chichester: Wiley.

Hyvärinen, M. (2016). Expectations and experientiality: Jerome Bruner's "canonicity and breach". *Storyworlds*, *9*(1), 1–25.

Hyvärinen, M. (2018). Toward a geographical socionarratology. *Frontiers of Narrative Studies, 4* (2), 215–231.

Kuhn, T. (2017). Communicatively constituting organizational unfolding through counter-narrative. In S. Frandsen, T. Kuhn, & M. W. Lundholt (Eds.), *Counter-narratives and organizations* (pp. 17–42). Abingdon: Routledge.

Kuittinen, T. (2010a). "Kipeät kivekset" [The sore testicles]. *Mediuutiset* 5.2.2010.

Kuittinen, T. (2010b). "Aivokuuntelulaite" [The thought-reading device]. *Mediuutiset* 21.5.2010.

Kurunmäki, J., & Marjanen, J. (2018). Isms, ideologies and setting the agenda for public debate. *Journal of Political Ideologies, 23*(3), 256–282.

Kölbl, C. (2004). Blame it on psychology? In M. Bamberg & M. Andrews (Eds.), *Considering counter-narratives* (pp. 27–32). Amsterdam: Benjamins.

Labov, W. (1972). *Language in the inner city.* Oxford: Basil Blackwell.

Loseke, D. R. (2007). The study of identity as cultural, institutional, organizational, and personal narratives: Theoretical and empirical integrations. *The Sociological Quarterly*, *48*(4), 661–688.

Lundholt, M. W., Maagaard, C. A., & Piekut, A. (2018). Counternarratives. In R. L. Heath & W. Johansen (Eds.), *The International Encyclopedia of Strategic Communication* (pp. 421–430). Hoboken, NJ: Wiley Blackwell.

Lyotard, J.-F. (1993 [1983]). *The postmodern condition.* Minneapolis: University of Minnesota Press.

Maagaard, C., & Lundholt, M. W. (2018). Taking spoofs seriously. The counter-narrative potential of spoofs as critical discourse. *MedieKultur, 64*, 116–137.

McClean, K. C., & Syed, M. (2016). Personal, master, and alternative narratives: An integrative framework for understanding identity development in context *Human Development*, *58*(6), 318–349.

McEwan, I. (2014). *The children act.* New York: Nan A, Talese/Doubleday.

Meretoja, H. (2018). *The ethics of storytelling. Narrative hermeneutics, history, and the possible.* New York: Oxford University Press.

Montgomery, K. (2006). *How doctors think. Clinical judgement and the practice of medicine.* New York: Oxford University Press.

Mutua, K. (2012). Counternarrative. In L. M. Given (Ed.), *The Sage encyclopedia of qualitative research methods* (p. 132). Thousand Oaks: Sage.

Nelson, H. L. (2001). *Damaged identities, narrative repair.* Ithaca: Cornell University Press.

Norrick, N. R. (2005). The dark side of tellability. *Narrative Inquiry*, *15*(2), 323–343.

Phelan, J. (2005). *Living to tell about it: A rhetoric and ethics of character narration.* Ithaca and London: Cornell University Press.

Phelan, J. (2008). Narratives in contest; or, another twist in the narrative turn. *PMLA*, *123*(1), 166–175.

Rasmussen, R. K. (2017). Rethinking counter-narratives in studies of organizational texts and practices. In S. Frandsen, T. Kuhn, & M. W. Lundholm (Eds.), *Counter-narratives and organizations* (pp. 171–192). Abingdon: Routledge.

Rimmon-Kenan, S. (2006). Concepts of narrative. In M. Hyvärinen, A. Korhonen, & J. Mykkänen (Eds.), *The travelling concept of narrative* (pp. 10–19). Helsinki: Helsinki Collegium for Advanced Studies, University of Helsinki.

Ryan, M.-L. (2005). Narrative. In D. Herman, M. Jahn, & M.-L. Ryan (Eds.), *Routledge encyclopedia of narrative theory* (pp. 344–348). London: Routledge.

Schank, R., & Abelson, R. (1977). *Scripts, Plans, Goals and Understanding.* New York: John Wiley & Sons.

Skjørshammer, M. (2002). Understanding conflicts between health professionals: A narrative approach. *Qualitative Health Research, 12*(7), 915–931.

Stanley, C. A. (2007). When counter narratives meet master-narratives in the journal editorial-review process. *Educational Researcher, 36*(1), 14–24.

Tammi, P. (2006). Against narrative. A boring story. *Partial Answers, 4*(2), 19–40.

Tannen, D. (1993). What's in a frame? In D. Tannen (Ed.), *Framing in discourse* (pp. 14–56). Oxford: Oxford University.

2

A dialogics of counter-narratives

Hanna Meretoja

The purpose of this chapter is to propose a new way of theorizing counter-narratives on the basis of a dialogical conception of narrative, identity, and subjectivity. This theorization draws on dialogical approaches developed in narrative psychology, continental philosophies of narrative, and Bakhtinian and hermeneutic critical theory. That narratives have a dialogical dimension means that they always take shape in relation to culturally mediated narrative models of sense-making, which are inextricably entangled in relations of power. Some narrative models are culturally dominant and can be construed as master-narratives while others provide critical perspectives on such dominant narratives and function as counter-narratives. The chapter shows how acknowledging the dialogical interplay between narrative models and individuals allows us to avoid reification of narratives, to theoretically explain their relationality and intrinsic contestability, and to account for both the agency and the socially conditioned nature of individual subjects engaged in processes of (re)negotiating their narrative identities. This chapter provides a theoretical-analytic framework that addresses the existential-ethical significance of counter-narratives and their importance for narrative agency, which involves the ability of agents to negotiate their narrative sense of self in relation to culturally dominant narrative models (master-narratives) and to produce their own narrative versions that may (counter-narratively) challenge these models.

A dialogical approach to narrative

The most influential narratological approaches theorize narrative as a textual structure (structuralist narratology), cognitive model (cognitive narratology), or an act of communication (rhetorical narratology). They all tend to dismiss the way in which narrative is a socially embedded and culturally mediated interpretative practice of sense-making that has an inextricably dialogical dimension. While postcolonial and feminist approaches to counter-narratives (e.g. Bhabha, 1990; Delgado, 1995; Romero & Stewart, 1999), in the 1990s, acknowledged the ways in which narratives are modes of negotiating identities, a large part of narratology has been dominated by structural and cognitive approaches that tend to neglect the existential, ethical, and political aspects of narratives and their entanglement in relations of power. This is something that the dialogical approach, in contrast, allows us to articulate. Drawing on my earlier theorization of the dialogical approach to narrative (Meretoja, 2014, 2018), I will now outline its three key aspects. First, I will discuss how the dialogical approach to narrative is linked to a *relational ontology* that emphasizes the *reciprocity* between and *interdependence* of the *individual* and *social structures*. Second, I will show how the dialogical approach foregrounds the *existential* and *ethical* dimension of narratives. Third, I will draw attention to how the dialogical approach stresses the embeddedness of narratives in *relations of power*.

First, a key thesis of the dialogical approach to narrative and subjectivity is that cultural webs of narratives only exist through individual interpretations, and individual subjects, in turn, are embedded in and become who they are in relation to cultural narrative webs. The relationship between individuals and narratives is reciprocal. Acknowledging this dialogical reciprocity allows us to articulate both that we have agency in interpreting cultural narratives and that our agency is socially conditioned. Narratives are dialogical in that they always take shape in relation to culturally mediated narrative models of sense-making, which they implicitly or explicitly draw on, perpetuate, or challenge. But instead of doing this automatically, they do this via the interpretative agency of human subjects who use, interpret, and reinterpret the narrative traditions in which they are enmeshed. We can, however, be only partly aware of our own interpretative agency: as historical beings, we can never be fully self-aware or transparent to ourselves (see Gadamer, 1997, p. 302).

A dialogical approach to narrative emerges from a dialogical approach to human existence more broadly, including language and subjectivity, emphasizing that our existence is thoroughly relational. Such an approach has been developed by a range of theorists across the humanities, social sciences, philosophy, and psychology. One of the key theorists of dialogism – of the profoundly dialogical nature of human existence – is the literary theorist Mikhail Bakhtin, who writes:

> Life by its very nature is dialogic. To live means to participate in dialogue: to ask questions, to heed, to respond, to agree, and so forth. In this dialogue a person participates wholly and throughout his whole life .... He invests his entire self in discourse, and this discourse enters into the dialogic fabric of human life, into the world symposium.
>
> *(1984, p. 293)*

Bakhtin has a close affinity with philosophical hermeneutics, which similarly emphasizes the "dialogical structure of thinking" (Gadamer, 2001, p. 57) and that the "crucial feature of human life is its fundamentally dialogical character" (Taylor, 1991, p. 32). Both Bakhtin and philosophical hermeneutics consider language to be intrinsically dialogical: it exists first and foremost contextually and situationally in the form of a conversation embedded in a socio-historical world. An utterance is meaningful only if it is understood as part of a dialogue:

> Each utterance is filled with echoes and reverberations of other utterances to which it is related by the communality of the sphere of speech communication. Every utterance must be regarded primarily as a *response* to preceding utterances of the given sphere.... With meaning I give answers to questions. Anything that does not answer a question is devoid of sense for us.
>
> *(Bakhtin, 1986, pp. 91, 145)*

This conception of language differs fundamentally from the structuralist one, which has been highly influential in variants of narratology. While structuralists believed that language exists primarily in the form of a language system (*langue*), philosophical hermeneutics emphasizes the radically temporal nature of language: language only exists through "conversation," through the intersubjective, temporal process of being used (Gadamer, 1997). It exists in the dialogic interaction between individual embodied subjects in the world – situated individuals with divergent "socio-linguistic points of view" (Bakhtin, 1981, p. 273). The use of the language system can never be mechanical. In applying language to particular situations, we necessarily engage in interpretation. Language and individual subjects are interdependent: the subjects become who they are in and through language, and language exists through individual subjects' continuous interpretative processes. This is why concepts are not fixed and closed but change as they are used and reinterpreted in new contexts. Similarly, cultural narratives exist as models of sense-making, but these models are in a constant process of changing as they are interpreted and reinterpreted, reinforced and challenged, in concrete situations. This process of reinterpretation can perpetuate dominant narrative sense-making models or it can involve various degrees of countering in relation to dominant models.

Second, a dialogical conception of narrative emphasizes that narratives have ethical and existential significance – they shape who we are and what matters to us. Dialogical theories of narrative identity articulate how we become who we are in a dynamic process of constant reinterpretation and reidentification (Ricoeur, 1985, 1992), in an "ongoing conversation" in dialogical frameworks or "webs of interlocution" (Taylor, 1989, pp. 35–36), which are, to an important extent, also webs of narrative:

> We are born into webs of interlocution or narrative—from familial and gender narratives to linguistic ones and to the macronarratives of collective identity. We become aware of who we are by learning to become conversation partners in these narratives.
>
> *(Benhabib, 2002, p. 15)*

These webs are constituted by narrative models of sense-making. We become who we are by engaging with these models – by following and perpetuating them and by resisting and challenging them. These models, however, cannot determine how we use them to make sense of our experiences; our relation to them is a relationship of possibility, and there is always scope for alternative interpretations, creative reinterpretations, and critical contestations. Because they only exist through interpretative practices, narrative models of sense-making can be questioned and changed, even if in practice this can prove difficult, particularly in the case of naturalizing narratives that appear as inevitable, camouflaging themselves as a simple reflection of the order of things. It is easier to tell counter-narratives once it has become explicit what the relevant master-narratives are.

The dialogical dimension of narratives is linked to their performative and existential aspects. Narratives are performative in their ability to not only represent but also create and shape intersubjective reality. They perpetuate and transform social structures, and our activity as narrative agents participates in reinforcing or questioning these structures. The existential dimension of narratives has to do with the way in which narratives are relevant for the understanding of human possibilities. Narratives are dialogical by engaging not only in a dialogue with other narratives but also in a dialogue about the world, interpreting the human possibilities of being in the world. The action and experience narrated in a narrative implies a certain understanding of what is possible for subjects of action and experience in a particular world. Narratives provide different subject positions, and in narrative worlds agents seize certain possibilities that are open to them and dismiss others. Narratives explore these possibilities, and through this exploration, they can provide us with new perspectives on our own world and on how we orient ourselves to our present and future possibilities. Central to the ethical-existential significance of narratives is their relevance for our "sense of the possible," which involves a sense of how things could be otherwise (Meretoja, 2018, pp. 4, 50–52, 90–97).

Third, the dialogical approach to narrative emphasizes the socially embedded nature of narratives and foregrounds the entanglement of narratives in relations of power. This is most evident in the Bakhtinian dialogics of narrative. Bakhtin makes it clear that dialogue is not about harmonious agreement but involves a dimension of strife, contest, and dispute. Dialogue takes place in social relationships that are also relationships of power. Since language lives in and through discourse embedded in social contexts, every word comes to us "from another context, permeated with the interpretations of others," and integral to these social contexts are practices of power (Bakhtin, 1984, p. 202). Bakhtin suggests that we should not stress

> that which takes place within, but that which takes place on the *boundary* between one's own and someone else's consciousness, on the *threshold*. And everything internal gravitates not toward itself but is turned to the outside and *dialogized*, every internal experience ends up on the boundary, encounters another, and in this *tension-filled encounter* lies its entire essence.
>
> *(p. 287, emphasis added)*

Narratives participate in shaping social reality through a dialogue of interpretations – a dialogue that often takes the form of a tension-filled encounter between master and counter-narratives.

The dialogical approach, however, does not see individual subjects as mere effects of power, as some poststructuralist approaches suggest, but emphasizes that power structures exist only through individual interpretations that perpetuate them, and hence there is always the possibility of interpreting otherwise. Judith Butler's approach is similar to the dialogical approach in that it also articulates the dependence of social power structures on repetition and that the subject is constituted through this process of reiteration, which also includes the possibility of repeating otherwise: "the subject is precisely the site of such reiteration, a repetition that is never merely mechanical" (Butler, 1997, p. 16). The poststructuralist idiom, however, tends to efface the agency of those who engage in repetition, for example by privileging the passive form (conditions of power "must be reiterated"). The vocabulary of the dialogical approach, in contrast, makes explicit – through the key notion of (re)interpretation – the subject's role as an agent.

By explicating the role of human subjects who practice their agency in interpreting narrative models, the language of dialogism allows us to avoid the reification of narratives. Reification means that something that is human-made is portrayed and perceived as thing-like, that is, as a natural or inevitable phenomenon, like a force of nature. Peter Berger and Thomas Luckmann (1987, p. 106) define reification as follows:

> [R]eification is the apprehension of the products of human activity *as if* they were something other than human products – such as facts of nature, results of cosmic laws, or manifestations of divine will. [...] The reified world is, by definition, a dehumanized world. It is experienced by man as a strange facticity, an *opus alienum* over which he has no control rather than as the *opus proprium* of his own productive activity.

The hermeneutic notions of (re)interpretation and dialogue provide a non-reifying way of characterizing the relationship between the subject and socio-cultural structures. In speaking and acting, we not only reiterate but also (potentially creatively) reinterpret linguistic and social – including narrative – practices. Since interpretation cannot be mechanical, there is always the possibility of subversive interpretation, of interpreting otherwise. Interpretations are always part of a dialogue of interpretations. As Paul Ricoeur (1991, p. 33) puts it, "the key hypothesis of hermeneutic philosophy is that interpretation is an open process that no single vision can conclude." Because the socio-cultural systems of meaning, including narrative webs of master and counter-narratives, cannot determine how they will be interpreted and all interpretation takes place in different socio-historical situations, ultimately all understanding has the structure of "always-understanding-differently" ("Immer-anders-Verstehen," Gadamer 1993, p. 8). In a similar vein, Bakhtin asserts that all understanding implies "reinterpretation, in a new context" (1986, p. 161).

We should acknowledge the emancipatory significance of the hermeneutic insight that social structures only exist through the temporal process of being interpreted: "Precisely this is the fundamental idea of hermeneutics, namely, that symbolic orders, as opposed to natural laws, are founded in interpretations; hence . . . they can be transformed and transgressed by new projections of meaning" (Frank, 1989, p. 6; see also Gadamer, 1997, p. 334). In other words, hermeneutics acknowledges the role of individual subjects in reinterpreting – and potentially transforming – cultural systems of meaning. The dialogical structure of cultural narrative systems of meaning means that they can be subverted and contested. Counter-narratives are critical reinterpretations of dominant narrative models; they typically question the power structures underlying master-narratives and shed problematizing light on them. At the same time, however, it is important to acknowledge that individuals are largely unaware of the power structures they perpetuate through their narrative interpretations. Power dynamics play an important role in shaping not just the narrative webs in which we are entangled but also us as subjects who exercise our narrative agency by following and (re)interpreting culturally available narrative models. Power not only structures the options we have in constructing our life stories but also shapes the subject who chooses between and negotiates various narratives (see Allen, 2008, p. 165). Even when we engage in telling counter-narratives, we are not outside realms of power.

Instead of being merely constraining, power is productive and an enabler of agency (Foucault, 1975). This Foucauldian perspective allows us to acknowledge that the dialogic dynamic in which we are constituted not only makes us internalize social power structures that then govern us from within but also allows us to become subjects and agents capable of acting in the world. While poststructuralist theories often downplay agency and individualist-humanist theories downplay power and social embeddedness, a dialogical, Foucauldian-hermeneutic approach allows us to rethink narrative subjectivity in nuanced terms that give due attention to both agency and social embeddedness. This is precisely the key strength of the model of dialogical narrativity: it acknowledges the fundamental role played by power in the constitution of subjectivity and identity, while also recognizing the subject's ability to resist and transform prevailing narratives and the power relations in which they are embedded.

Three levels of dialogical narrative subjectivity

I will next summarize a model for differentiating between three levels at which we are dialogically constituted (Meretoja, 2018, pp. 75–83). We are constituted 1) through dialogic social interaction with other people, 2) through internalizing subject positions and voices, and 3) through a dialogue with cultural narrative models of sense-making. These levels are interdependent but can be analytically distinguished from one another.

First, the dialogical process of becoming ourselves in social interaction involves a developmental and performative aspect. Developmental psychologists agree that from the beginning of our lives we become who we are in a dialogic relationship with our significant others. Crucial to this is a collaborative, dialogical process of co-telling and co-construction (see Ochs & Capps, 2001; Schiff, 2017). Parents and other care-givers contribute to their children's narrative competence by scaffolding their emerging narrative skills in ways that reinforce their temporal sense of self (McLean & Mansfield, 2012; Fivush, Haden & Reese, 2006). This involves helping them to make sense of their experiences and to articulate their feelings and thoughts about those experiences, supporting their perspectives and contributions to the practice of sharing stories (McLean & Mansfield, 2012, pp. 436–437). The narrative competence that we acquire through the developmental process involves not only cognitive but also affective and ethical aspects. Our dialogical interaction with our significant others, since early childhood, shapes the "tone" for our future constructions of narrative identity (McAdams, 2006, p. 217) and helps us develop into moral agents who learn to act upon their narrative identities (Lindemann, 2014, pp. 89–95). Narrative identities are *co-authored* with others (McLean, 2015). Practicing to tell about our lives to others in different social situations is also practicing to position ourselves in relation to others and their stories. In this social interaction, we perpetuate and challenge dominant narratives; often it involves finding our own narratives by constructing counter-narratives. The dialogical process of narrating has a performative dimension. Identities take shape in an ongoing process of performing for others in social situations (see Goffman, 1959; Riessman, 2003). Such performances are largely habitual and regulated by narrative models or scripts – socially shared narratives that "govern conduct in specific situations" (Lindemann, 2014, p. 98). These "performative exchanges" between interlocutors "draw on their lived, embodied experience" (Heavey, 2015, p. 430). Counter-narrating involves counter-performing.

Second, the process of socialization involves the internalization of different voices and subject positions; we are dialogical in that we engage in a constant dialogue between these positions within ourselves. The internal dialogue between different voices is a crucial aspect of our subjectivity. Drawing on positioning theory and Bakhtin's views on the polyphonic novel in which different voices enter into a dialogue without any one voice dominating the others (Hermans et al., 1992; Hermans, 2001, 2015; Raggatt, 2006), the Dialogical Self Theory conceptualizes the self "in terms of a dynamic multiplicity of relatively autonomous I positions in an imaginal landscape" (Hermans et al., 1992, p. 28). We are polyphonic in embodying different voices and perspectives. The Dialogical Self Theory argues that an important part of a child's development is "positioning, repositioning, and contrapositioning itself to the world of social relationships," which includes learning to "reverse positions" and "take the perspective of others" (Hermans, 2015, p. 280). The individual sees him or herself as an unstable and often conflictual "product of dialogical relations in a field or landscape of I-positions" as he or she interacts with others in the world via a repertoire of "internalized voices" that embody these I-positions (Raggatt, 2006, p. 18). The internalized voices vary from our constructions of the voices of concrete others (parents, teachers, friends etc.) to our own subject positions ("me as a daughter," "me as a student" etc.). Theorists of the Dialogical Self distinguish between their own decentralized approach (no single I-position dominates the others) and a theory of possible selves, which they take to assume a hierarchical structure (Hermans et al., 1992, p. 30). I have suggested, however, extending the notion of internal dialogue to encompass the *dialogue between different possible selves* – or what Ricoeur (1992, p. 148) calls "imaginative variations" of the self – that indicate different possibilities of thinking, acting, and experiencing (Meretoja, 2018, pp. 78–79). The cultivation of narrative imagination – through literature, for example, and in dialogue with others – can be seen as a way of *expanding the repertoire of subject positions* available to us. We should acknowledge that internalized voices or subject positions are dynamic, constantly shifting, merging into one another, and not separate and stable I-positions as the metaphor of "the self as a society of I-positions" (Hermans, 2015, p. 291) suggests. As we internalize different voices and narrative models that perpetuate or challenge dominant norms, we position ourselves in relation to them, deciding whether we align ourselves with master-narratives or want to challenge them and find alternative – counter-narrative – ways of narrating our experiences and our sense of who we are.

Third, we are constituted in dialogue with cultural models of sense-making, crucial to which are narrative models of sense-making. Just as language in general only exists through the dialogical process of being interpreted, so do all other aspects of intersubjective systems of meaning, such as narrative webs. It is part of "the dialogical structure of all understanding" (Gadamer, 2001, p. 57) that general models of sense-making are interpreted in particular social, cultural, and historical situations, and these interpretations, in turn, participate in shaping the meaning of the general models. While individual subjects are constituted in relation to social structures and social structures depend on a process of being interpreted, the process of interpretation is mostly habitual and automatized; only rarely does it become an object of reflection. As Seyla Benhabib puts it, "we do not choose the webs in whose nets we are initially caught or select those with whom we wish to converse" (1999, p. 344). Even so, we can practice our agency by (re)interpreting differently the cultural narratives in which we are entangled. This involves engagement with their *normativity*, which can be potentially limiting or oppressive. Cultural narrative models, provided by master and counter-narratives, present us with cultural ideals and norms. They suggest that while certain things are possible for us – given our gender, race, class, age, looks – others are impossible or unlikely. But the narrative identities ascribed to us do not automatically determine who we are. We practice our agency in responding to the labels imposed on us. Nevertheless, narrative identity is not something we can simply choose for ourselves. It is shaped in a dialogical, often highly anguished and conflictual process of negotiation that involves both self-interpretation and engagement with the identities into which we have been "interpellated" (Althusser, 2014) and with the ones that are not so readily available to us. It is often painful not to conform to narratives that we anticipate for ourselves on the basis of cultural expectations and "story templates" (see Josselson & Hopkins, 2015, p. 223).

On all three levels, *dialogical interaction* involves *interaction with master and counter-narratives*. In narrative interaction with concrete others we learn to position ourselves in relation to these others and their master and counter-narratives, articulating how we experienced a certain event in relation to others' narrative accounts. As we internalize different voices, we position ourselves in relation to them, deciding whether we align ourselves with dominant narratives or whether we want to challenge and resist them by finding alternative ways of narrating our experiences and identities. This is an ongoing dialogue with cultural models of narrative sense-making. This dialogue is something we *do* – it consists of *acts of perpetuating and countering* – and it is a process embedded in a social and cultural world.

Ontology of counter-narratives

In theorizing counter-narratives, it is important to reflect on what kind of entities counter-narratives are. Do they exist in a similar way to master-narratives or is their ontological status, their mode of being, different? The theorization of master-narratives has been dominated by François Lyotard's (1979) conceptualization of *grand narratives* that have a legitimizing role, such as the narratives of Enlightenment or Marxism. Others have used the notions of *dominant cultural narratives* (Andrews, 2004), *culturally dominant narrative models* (Meretoja, 2018) or *scripts* (Schank & Abelson, 1977; Bruner, 1991) to draw attention to how certain narrative models have normative power to guide people's actions. Counter-narratives are conceptualized in relation to master-narratives, as narratives that resist and challenge them. Scholars have noted, however, that master and counter-narratives seem to exist on different levels of reality. In this section, I propose that the distinction between *explicit and implicit narratives* is useful in making sense of the ontology of master and counter-narratives. I also suggest that the notion of *narrative assumption* may be helpful in theorizing counter-narratives.

Historically, the concept of counter-narrative was first used in the early 1990s predominantly with reference to the stories of marginalized groups who resist hegemonic narratives in which a minority is rendered voiceless or portrayed oppressively. For example, Homi K. Bhabha articulates how counter-narratives of the nation resist essentializing nationalist identities that marginalize those who fail to conform: "Counter-narratives of the nation that continually evoke and erase its totalizing boundaries—both actual and conceptual—disturb those ideological manoeuvres through which 'imagined communities' are given essentialist identities" (1990, p. 300). Scholars have observed that master-narratives are often abstractions that need to be constructed from concrete narratives, as an underlying script that the counter-narrative projects and resists. For example, Matti Hyvärinen argues (in this volume) that master-narratives are not "real narratives": "master-narratives rather resemble abstractions of narrative than real, tellable, and recognizable stories." This reference to "real narratives" is indicative of how the discussion on the ontology of counter-narratives is linked to different conceptions of narrative in general. The conceptual reach of narrative is broad: while in some contexts it refers to concrete, textual accounts of meaningfully connected temporal sequences of actions and experiences, in other contexts it refers to cultural models of sense-making underlying such concrete accounts. It is important to retain conceptual clarity so that narrative is not robbed of its specificity for example by conflating it with experience in general, but it is also necessary to take into account the different meaningful functions of the concept (see Meretoja, 2018, pp. 49–50, 60). I suggest that the notions of implicit and explicit narrative can clarify different aspects of narrative in a way that could be particularly useful for understanding the ontology of master and counter-narratives. More specifically, I argue that both master and counter-narratives range from implicit to explicit narratives, although master-narratives are most often implicit and counter-narratives explicit.

So, what do I mean by saying that master and counter-narratives range from implicit to explicit? *Explicit narratives* are *narrative artifacts*, stories told by someone to someone in a concrete textual or other material form. *Implicit narratives* are *models of sense-making* that underlie specific narratives but may not be anywhere available in a material form. They need to be constructed by interpreters of explicit narratives, which carry implicit narratives within them – as that which they resist or reinforce. Drawing on Roger Schank and Robert P. Abelson's (1977) script theory, Anthony Amsterdam and Jerome Bruner (2000, p. 21) call implicit narratives "scripts" of temporally ordered sequences of actions that guide our actions and expectations: "Established scripts (sometimes called stock scripts) are the hidden cargo of narratives, often tacit rather than explicit, but always there." In addition to scripts of concrete social situations, implicit narratives can be abstract narratives of the good life, for example. Such implicit narratives often function as "providers of meaning for the community that shares and believes in them" (Ritivoi, 2009, p. 35).

A master-narrative is typically implicit because it can be construed from public discourse but it is rarely told in an explicit form. An implicit master-narrative would be, for example, the narrative of the American dream. It is a narrative pattern that underlies many concrete (explicit) narratives in which an individual who works hard succeeds in leading a wealthy and happy life, no matter how challenging the obstacles he or she faces. These narratives are typically ones in which individuals overcome difficulties through their perseverance and diligence. Hyvärinen argues (in this volume) that master-narratives, de facto, lack temporality which is an important reason why they are not, in his view, real narratives. This take, however, can be problematized. The master-narrative of the American Dream, for example, suggests that a person who works tirelessly will become successful, implying a temporal development and a causal link between the action and the outcome. Similarly, the Enlightenment narrative involves a temporal progression in which humankind learns to use reason, leading humankind towards ever greater rationality and overcoming such obstacles as superstition, poverty, and illness through the cures provided by science. The narrative of the Socialist utopia likewise involves a temporal development of humankind progressing towards greater freedom and happiness through the dialectic movement inherent in history. In these last two examples, the narrative's temporality is linked to an overarching narrative explanation of the history of humankind. Hyvärinen suggests that master-narratives exist in a concrete textual form only in history-writing. But there are also other examples of discourse in which master-narratives are fleshed out, such as political speeches that tell a narrative of how society has developed to its current state, possibly accompanied by a utopian vision of where it will or should develop.

Hyvärinen argues that, in contrast to master-narratives, counter-narratives "strictly observe the requirement of tellability and exist in discernible textual form." Although this is typically the case, counter-narratives, too, range from implicit to explicit. For example, we can find implicit anti-immigration counter-narratives underlying populist political discourse and slogans, such as those by representatives of the Finns Party, driven by ethnic nationalism. According to their implicit counter-narrative, a "flood" of immigrants arrived in Finland in order to take advantage of our social welfare system, and this is now leading to a degradation of our traditional culture and threatens the "purity" of our "race" or national identity. This is a counter-narrative because it aims to subvert the dominant success story of the Nordic social welfare system that is committed to universal and inalienable human rights. The counter-narrative is rarely told as a full narrative, nor is there one canonical narrative text; nevertheless, the counter-narrative is recognizable and frequently evoked by the allusions, slogans, and declarations of populist politicians and their supporters.

As this example shows, not all counter-narratives are emancipatory, progressive, or liberating; instead of promoting the rights of repressed minorities, right-wing populist counter-narratives typically reinforce white supremacy. Moreover, counter-narratives can focus on privileged majorities from a (self-)critical perspective without particularly promoting the rights of repressed minorities. Henry Miller's *Death of a Salesman* (1949), for example, challenges the master narrative of the American Dream by telling the story of a regular, white, heterosexual, lower middle class salesman, Willy Loman, who aspires all his life to achieve success, measured in terms of wealth and popularity, but never makes it and ends up living in lies in order to bear his tedious, disappointing everyday life. It shows how the master narrative of the American Dream not only tells a false story of how anyone who works hard will become successful but can also be harmful in suggesting a link between human worth and success.

I propose that the concept of a *narrative assumption* elucidates usefully the logic of master and counter-narratives. Narrative assumptions shape how we assume things to be meaningfully connected. For example, the narrative of the American Dream is based on the narrative assumption that when you work diligently, it will bring you prosperity. Social scientific research does not support the assumption that irrespective of social conditions everyone has an equal chance to gain wealth by working hard; it is hence an ideological assumption. Similarly, the narrative of a "battle" or "war" against cancer suggests that when one fights hard enough, one's cancer will be defeated. The narrative is based on the assumption that "fighting" is causally linked to survival, thereby positing the incurable as "losers" (on the war metaphor, see Hansen, 2018; Sontag, 1978; Bleakley, 2017). There is no scientific evidence to support such an assumption; in fact, research suggests that war metaphors for cancer in fact harm health (Hauser & Schwartz, 2019). It is an ideological assumption linked to *normative optimism*, the pressure to have a positive approach to one's illness, as if cancer patients did not have enough challenges without such additional pressure. Similar problems pertain to the use of the master narrative of war in the context of the coronavirus pandemic (Meretoja 2020a). It is central to the logic of counter-narratives that they challenge the key narrative assumptions underlying master-narratives.

Another set of master and counter-narratives revolves around narratives of love and friendship. The heteronormative master narrative of a nuclear family as the basis of a happy life has been extended in many cultural contexts to accommodate same-sex couples as part of the nuclear family, but the underlying implicit master narrative remains the same: a couple-centred narrative of a fulfilling love relationship. There is a strong assumption underlying this master narrative that the ideal relationship in which people thrive is a monogamous romantic and sexual relationship. One example of a counter-narrative that challenges this assumption is Hanya Yanagihara's novel *A Little Life*, which suggests that sexual couple relationships are not self-evidently more fulfilling than deep friendship. The novel is about four friends who are one another's most important others. Two of them, Willem and Jude, end up living together for years, and their friendship evolves into a love relationship; eventually they decide to leave sex out of the relationship but this does not diminish its significance or profundity. On the other hand, the novel suggests that Willem would experience the love relationship as even more fulfilling if Jude were able to enjoy sex and that Jude's inability to enjoy it results from his traumatic past (sexual abuse throughout his childhood). Hence, the novel can be considered ambiguous in relation to the master narrative of romantic love. This ambiguity leaves room for divergent interpretations. It highlights how meaning is ultimately always produced in a dialogical process of interpretation. Not only is the novel a dialogical interpretation of the cultural narrative model of romantic love but the novel's meaning, in turn, emerges in the dialogical process of being interpreted by readers from divergent backgrounds and with different interpretative horizons (for a more detailed analysis of the novel, see Meretoja, 2020b).

Finally, in thinking about the ontology of counter-narratives, we should acknowledge that counter-narratives are *acts of resistance* and as actions they are about doing, instead of mere artifacts (as representational models of narrative assume). Often it makes more sense to think of counter-narratives in verb-like and processual terms – as a process of *counter-narrating* – than in terms of narrative representations that exist in the mode of objects or artifacts (on the activity aspect and artifactual aspect of narratives, see Meretoja, 2018, 48–49). This is perhaps most evident in the case of conversational storytelling, in which the act of countering involves positioning oneself as one who resists dominant narratives (see Bamberg & Georgakopoulou, 2008; Hyvärinen, this volume), but the same applies to literary narratives. Despite their artifactual dimension, they are also part of a tradition of "writing back" to power or of constructing alternative identities and subject positions. The dialogical approach allows us to account for the interpretative agency involved in actions of *countering* and *perpetuating* dominant cultural narratives.

Ethical evaluation of counter-narratives

The way in which counter-narratives have, historically, functioned as a form of resistance for marginalized and oppressed groups can easily lead us to think that counter-narratives are inherently ethically beneficial. As we have already seen, however, with the example of populism, counter-narratives are not necessarily ethically superior to master-narratives. Climate change deniers and antivaccine activists challenge dominant narratives, but their arguments contest scientific evidence on which the academic community has a strong consensus, and accepting their counter-narratives would be damaging for future lives. How should we, then, differentiate between different forms of counter-narratives?

In my earlier research, I have proposed a heuristic model for analyzing and evaluating the ethical potential and dangers of different kinds of narratives (Meretoja, 2018, Chapter 3). The model provides six evaluative continuums on which narratives can be placed in context-sensitive ethical evaluation of social and cultural narrative practices. These continuums explore whether narratives 1) expand or diminish our sense of the possible, 2) cultivate or distort personal and cultural self-understanding, 3) promote or impair our ability to understand the experiences of others in their singularity, 4) participate in building inclusive or exclusive narrative in-betweens, 5) develop or impede our perspective-awareness, and 6) function as a form of ethical inquiry or dogmatism.

This model is applicable in the ethical evaluation of any cultural narratives, including master and counter-narratives.

In ethically evaluating counter-narratives, particularly important is whether they expand or diminish the repertoire of socially available narrative models of sense-making and thereby our sense of the possible, including our sense of possible ways of living a fulfilling life, without diminishing the possibilities of others. In discussing whether narratives enhance or impair our ability to understand the experiences of others in their singularity, I distinguish between subsumptive and non-subsumptive narratives (Meretoja, 2018, pp. 107–113). While *subsumptive narrative practices* reinforce cultural stereotypes by subsuming singular experiences under culturally dominant narrative scripts, *non-subsumptive narrative practices* challenge such categories of appropriation, inviting us to do justice to the particularity of the experiences or events that we are trying to understand and to acknowledge the need to modify our interpretative categories accordingly. Non-subsumptive understanding is fueled by a non-subsumptive ethos, which is essentially an ethos of dialogue and openness to what evades our preconceptions. Dialogicality is not only something that inevitably pertains to our mode of being as relational beings, it is also an ethical ideal (on the ontological and ethical meanings of dialogicality, see Meretoja, 2018, p. 254). Non-subsumptive narratives that encourage us to engage with the singularity of others' experiences can be considered ethically more sustainable than totalizing, subsumptive narratives that desensitize us to others' experiences. Dialogic narrative interaction requires a willingness and an ability to listen and to learn and – if the situation requires – to be transformed by the dialogic event.

Conclusion

This chapter has outlined a dialogic approach to theorizing counter-narratives. It emphasizes that cultural webs of narratives only exist through individual interpretations – which include the possibility of counter-interpretations – while individual subjects and their identities are constituted in relation to cultural narrative webs. The chapter has elucidated how this approach allows us to avoid reification of narratives and to theoretically explain why all narratives are contestable, due to the way their existence depends on being interpreted and thereby on the narrative agency of the interpreters. This approach has situated counter-narratives in relation to narrative agency – as actions of interpretative agents who negotiate their sense of self in relation to culturally dominant narrative models of sense-making.

This chapter has also sought to clarify the ontology of master and counter-narratives through the distinction between implicit and explicit narratives. That implicit narratives function as models of sense-making, instead of being concrete, textual narratives, does not mean that they are not narratives. They are models of making sense of events and experiences in time, and they embody narrative assumptions. Crudely put, both master and counter-narratives suggest that if you do X, then Y can or is likely to follow. That they often remain untold does not make master-narratives any less real. They are important underlying models of sense-making that guide our actions and expectations. As models, however, they can never determine our actions. Every master narrative lends itself to being subverted by a counter-narrative. Both master and counter-narratives, however, exert their power only when they are interpreted and applied in concrete situations. This process of interpretation is an inescapably dialogical activity, and it often remains fundamentally unpredictable.

Acknowledgement

Work on this chapter has been funded by the Academy of Finland project Instrumental Narratives: The Limits of Storytelling and New Story-Critical Narrative Theory (project number 314769).

References

Allen, A. (2008). *The politics of our selves: Power, autonomy, and gender in contemporary critical theory*. New York: Columbia University Press.

Althusser, L. (2014). *On the reproduction of capitalism: Ideology and ideological state apparatuses* (1995). Trans. G.M. Goshgarian. London: Verso.

Amsterdam, A. & Bruner, J. (2000). *Minding the law*. Cambridge, MA: Harvard University Press.

Andrews, M. (2004). Counter-narratives and the power to oppose. In M. Bamberg & M. Andrews (eds), *Considering counter-narratives: Narrating, resisting, making sense*, pp. 1–6. Amsterdam: Benjamins.

Bakhtin, M. (1981). *The dialogic imagination*. Ed. M. Holquist. Trans. C. Emerson & M. Holquist. Austin: University of Texas Press.

Bakhtin, M. (1984). *Problems of Dostoevsky's poetics*. Trans. C. Emerson. Manchester: Manchester University Press.

Bakhtin, M. (1986). *Speech genres and other late essays*. Trans. V. McGee. Austin: University of Texas Press.

Bamberg, M. & A. Georgakopoulou (2008). Small stories as a new perspective in narrative and identity analysis. *Text & Talk* 28(3), 377–396.

Benhabib, S. (1999). Sexual difference and collective identities: The new global constellation. *Signs: Journal of Women in Culture and Society* 24(2), 335–361.

Benhabib, S. (2002). *Claims of culture: Equality and diversity in the global era*. Princeton: Princeton University Press.

Berger, P. & T. Luckmann (1987). *The social construction of reality: A treatise in the sociology of knowledge* (1966). London: Penguin Books.

Bhabha, H. K. (1990). *Nation and narration*. London: Routledge.

Bleakley, A. (2017). *Thinking with metaphors in medicine: The state of the art*. London: Routledge.

Bruner, J. (1991). The narrative construction of reality. *Critical Inquiry* 18, pp. 1–21.

Butler, J. (1997). *The psychic life of power: Theories in subjection*. Stanford: Stanford University Press.

Delgado, R. (1995). Legal storytelling: Storytelling for oppositionists and others: A plea for narrative. In R. Delgado (ed), *Critical race theory: The cutting edge*, pp. 64–74. Philadelphia: Temple University Press.

Fivush, R., E. Haden & C. A. Reese. (2006). Elaborating on elaborations: Role of maternal reminiscing style in cognitive and socioemotional development. *Child Development* 77(6), 1568–1588.

Foucault, M. (1975). *Surveiller et punir*. Paris: Gallimard.

Frank, M. (1989). *What is neostructuralism? (1984)* Trans. S. Wilke & R. Grey. Minneapolis: University of Minnesota Press.

Gadamer, H.-G. (1993). *Gesammelte Werke 2: Hermeneutik II*. Tübingen: Mohr.

Gadamer, H.-G. (1997). *Truth and method* (1960). Trans. J. Weinsheimer & D. G. Marshall. New York: Continuum.

Gadamer, H.-G. (2001). *Reason in the age of science* (1979). Trans. F. G. Lawrence. Cambridge, MA: The MIT Press.

Goffman, E. (1959). *The presentation of self in everyday life*. New York: Anchor Books.

Hansen, P. K. (2018). Illness and heroics: On counter-narrative and counter-metaphor in discourse on cancer. *Frontiers of Narrative Studies* 4(1), 213–228.

Hauser, D. J. & N. Schwartz (2019). The war on prevention II: Battle metaphors undermine cancer treatment and prevention and do not increase vigilance. *Health Communication*. doi: 10.1080/10410236.2019.1663465.

Heavey, E. (2015). Narrative bodies, embodied narratives. In A. de Fina & A. Georgakopoulou (eds), *The handbook of narrative analysis*, pp. 429–446. Malden, MA: Wiley Blackwell.

Hermans, H. J. M. (2001). The dialogical self: Toward a theory of personal and cultural positioning. *Culture and Psychology* 7, 243–281.

Hermans, H. J. M. (2015). The personal position repertoire (PPR) method as based on dialogical self theory. In J. Martin, J. Sugarman & K. L. Slaney (eds), *The Wiley handbook of theoretical and philosophical psychology*, pp. 277–292. Malden, MA: Wiley Blackwell.
Hermans, H. J. M., H. J. G. Kempen & R. J. P. Van Loon. (1992). The dialogical self: Beyond individualism and rationalism. *American Psychologist*, 47(1), 23–33.
Hyvärinen, M. (in this volume). Toward a theory of counter-narratives: narrative contestation, cultural canonicity and tellability.
Josselson, R. & B. Hopkins (2015). Narrative psychology and life stories. In J. Martin, J. Sugarman & K. L. Slaney (eds), *Wiley handbook of theoretical and philosophical psychology*, pp. 219–233. Malden: Wiley–Blackwell.
Lindemann, H. (2014). *Holding and letting go: The social practice of personal identities*. Oxford: Oxford University Press.
Lyotard, J.-F. (1979). *La condition postmoderne*. Paris: Minuit.
McAdams, D.P. (2006). *The redemptive self: Stories Americans live by*. Oxford: Oxford University Press.
McLean, K.C. (2015). *The co-authored self: Family stories and the construction of personal identity*. Oxford: Oxford University Press.
McLean, K.C. & C.D. Mansfield (2012). The co-construction of adolescent narrative identity: Narrative processing as a function of adolescent age, gender, and maternal scaffolding. *Developmental Psychology* 48(2), 436–447.
Meretoja, H. (2014). *The narrative turn in fiction and theory: The crisis and return of storytelling from Robbe-Grillet to Tournier*. Basingstoke: Palgrave Macmillan.
Meretoja, H. (2018). *The ethics of storytelling: Narrative hermeneutics, history, and the possible*. New York and Oxford: Oxford University Press.
Meretoja, H. (2020a). Stop narrating the pandemic as a story of war. *OpenDemocracy* 19 May 2020 (www.opendemocracy.net/en/transformation/stop-narrating-pandemic-story-war/).
Meretoja, H. (2020b). Philosophies of trauma. In C. Davis & H. Meretoja (eds), *The Routledge companion to literature and trauma*, pp. 23–35. London: Routledge.
Miller, A. (1949). *Death of a salesman*. New York: Viking Press.
Ochs, E. & L. Capps (2001). *Living narrative: Creating lives in everyday storytelling*. Cambridge, MA: Harvard University Press.
Raggatt, P. T. F. (2006). Multiplicity and conflict in the dialogical self: A life-narrative approach. In R.-E. Josselson, D. McAdams & A. Lieblich (eds), *Identity and story: Creating self in narrative*, pp. 15–35. Washington: American Psychological Association.
Ricoeur, P. (1985). *Temps et récit 3*. Paris: Seuil.
Ricoeur, P. (1991). *From text to action: Essays in hermeneutics II* (1986). Trans. K. Blamey & J. B. Thompson. Evanston: Northwestern University Press.
Ricoeur, P. (1992). *Oneself as another* (1990). Trans. K. Blamey. Chicago: The University of Chicago Press.
Riessman, C. K. (2003). Performing identities in illness narrative: Masculinity and multiple sclerosis. *Qualitative Research* 3(1), 5–33.
Ritivoi, A. D. (2009). Explaining people: Narrative and the study of identity. *Storyworlds* 1, 25–41.
Romero, M. & A. J. Stewart (1999). *Women's untold stories: Breaking silence, talking back, voicing complexity*. New York: Routledge.
Schank R. & R. Abelson (1977). *Scripts, plans, goals and understanding: An inquiry into human knowledge structures*. Hillsdale: Lawrence Erllbaum Associates.
Schiff, B. (2017). *A new narrative for psychology*. Oxford: Oxford University Press.
Sontag, S. (1978). *Illness as metaphor*. New York: Farrar, Straus & Giroux.
Taylor, C. (1989). *Sources of the self: The making of the modern identity*. Cambridge, MA: Harvard University Press.
Taylor, C. (1991). *The ethics of authenticity*. Cambridge, MA: Harvard University Press.
Yanagihara, H. (2015). *A little life*. London: Picador.

3

Counter-narratives and counter-stories

The dynamics of dialectical dialogical storytelling

Marita Svane

Introduction

The focus of this chapter is to contribute to the conceptualization of the dynamical forces involved in constitutive and performative organizational storytelling. For decades, storytelling has been acknowledged as both constitutive and performative in bringing forth worlds and realities. The chapter departs from Boje's triad storytelling framework as it distinguishes between narratives and living stories. Furthermore, antenarratives contribute to the conceptual understanding of the dynamic interplay between narratives and living stories in space and time (see Figure 3.1).

The conceptual work of this chapter is rooted in addressing the distinction between the narrative – counter narrative middle and the middle involved in the encounter between living stories and counter-stories. Furthermore, the chapter contributes by enlightening the antenarrative as a third middle that connects the dynamics of the other two middles in space and time. What is the nature of these three middles? How do they differ from each other with regard to the nature of their dynamical forces? The relevancy of these questions is accentuated by the growing academic interest in counter-narratives. Dealing with these questions from a dialectical dialogical perspective, the chapter suggests distinguishing between counter-narratives and counter-stories in order to enrich our understanding of the complexity of storytelling dynamics in organizations.

Boje (2014, p. 67) has, among others, been inspired by Bakhtin's dialogical philosophy. This chapter therefore views the storytelling framework through Bakhtin's perspective. Bakhtin's distinction between dialogue and monologue supports the need to distinguish between narratives and living stories. While some storytelling researchers use narratives and stories interchangeably, Boje argues for their distinction.

Narratives are associated with the single-voiced monologue: "the narrative forms are always encased in a firm and stable monologic framework" (Bakhtin, 1984, p. 17). They tend to be formed through a linear BME structure encompassing a fixed Beginning, fixed Middle, and fixed Ending, each consisting of a pre-structured series of events (Boje, 2014, p. xx). Hence, narratives are constitutive of a ready-made settled world.

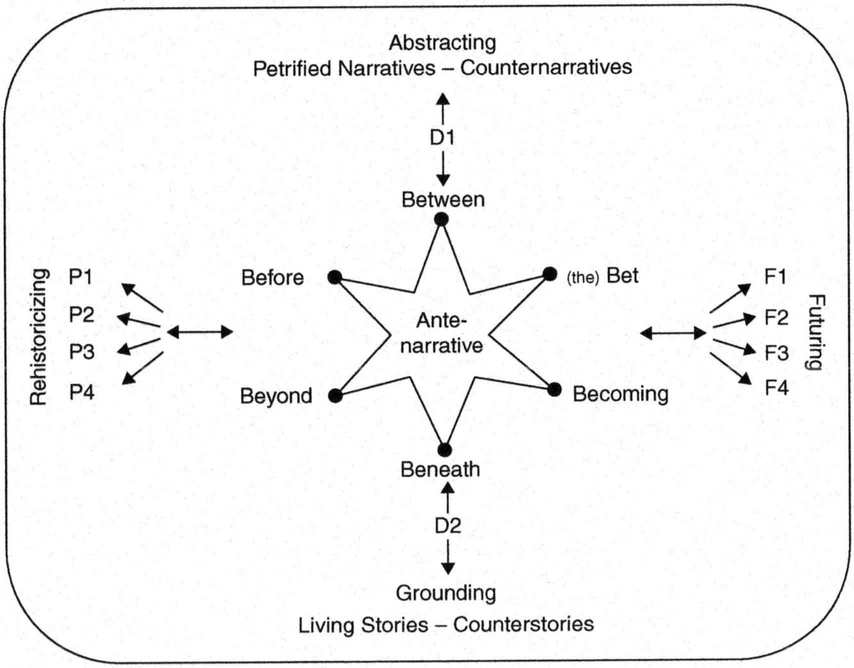

Figure 3.1 The dynamics of storytelling. Developed by David Boje and Marita Svane.

In contrast, living stories are associated with Bakhtin's multi-voiced dialogue and its openness towards diversity, heterogeneity, and alterations. They constitute what Bamberg also refers to as small stories that are told in passing, being unfinalized, fluent, contextual, and situational, as well as embedded in the social realm of interaction. They constitute the real stories of our lived lives (Bamberg, 2004, p. 356); stories that are shared through the living story web of story-tellers and story-listeners (Boje, 2014). Opposing the narrative ready-made world, the dialogical conception implies a world living in dissensus; an incomplete and unfinalized wholeness, albeit still alive and under construction. Living stories are thus the real-life stories of the world of life (Bakhtin, 1999).

Antenarratives work in the tensed middle between narratives and living stories. They are defined as "fragmented, non-linear, incoherent, collective, unplotted, and improper storytelling" (Boje, 2001, p. 1). Boje (2014; 2001, 2008, 2011, 2012) has defined antenarratives in terms of five dimensions: bet, before, beneath, between, and becoming. A sixth dimension (beyond) was added by Svane (2019a). The six dimensions (see Figure 3.1) illuminate how antenarratives operate in the middle *between* narratives and living stories. Going *beyond* the petrified taken-for-grantedness of narratives-counter-narratives, antenarratives grasp, feel, and intuit the future in advance of its arrival. Differing from the retrospective past-oriented temporality of narratives and the now-ness of living stories, antenarratives *bet* on the future through prospective (futuring) sensemaking of what is grasped. By weaving and piecing fragments of the living stories together and repackaging narratives *before* narrative cohesion, antenarratives are performative in resolving the petrified gap *between* narratives-counter-narratives. By being responsive and answerable to the living stories grounded in the real world *beneath* the narrative abstraction, antenarratives care about the well-being of the world of life in its ongoing process of *becoming*.

The conceptual complexity of the storytelling framework increases with the intersection of counter-narratives; a concept that has gained an increasingly firm foothold within the storytelling field (Bamberg & Andrews, 2004; Frandsen, Kuhn, & Lundholt, 2016). According to Andrews and Bamberg (2004), counter-narratives can be identified as positional categories in tension with other categories playing out at multiple layers of positioning. Counter-narratives are thus defined as relational categories that only make sense in relation to that which they are countering.

The intersection of the prefix 'counter' gives rise to new questions such as: What is meant by 'counter'? What is the nature of a counter position? Does the meaning of 'counter' change when the prefix is related to narratives, to living stories, or to antenarratives? Furthermore, the prefix 'counter' is unavoidably associated with the idea of tensions and contradictions appearing in the middle between something. Hence, the prefix seems to foster a natural call for dialectics as a relevant perspective that, in addition to Bakhtin's dialogue, may contribute to shedding more light on the dynamical forces involved in the three middles of the storytelling framework. The use of the prefix 'counter' and its associated middle thus need further scholarly attention.

The chapter will draw on Hegel and Bakhtin as they represent two approaches to the 'middle' that fundamentally differ from each other. Hegel's work on dialectics is chosen as it can be argued that Bamberg's definition of counter-narratives reflects a dialectical relation. Moreover, Hegel's dialectics is already used by Boje to further enlighten storytelling (Boje 2016a, 2016b).

Figure 3.1 illustrates that D1 is related to the *dialectical* middle between narratives – counter-narratives, whereas D2 is related to the *dialogical* middle between exchanged living stories. The dynamics of the dialectical and dialogical middles differ fundamentally from each other as they work with time and space in different ways. As such, they contribute to clarifying the dynamics of storytelling.

By connecting the two middles with each other, the six antenarrative dimensions aim to work with the spatializing (e.g. create, open, polarize, close spaces) and temporalizing (futuring many possible futures and rehistorizing the many forgotten or neglected pasts) processes of storytelling.

The conceptual framework of dialectical dialogical storytelling thus contributes by identifying three types of middles as relevant to the dynamics of storytelling. A fourth one, the excluded middle, can be added in order to address what happens if the dialectics and dialogues cease to work.

The middles of storytelling

1. The dialectical middle of N-CN (narratives – counter-narratives)
2. The dialogical middle of LS-CS (living stories – counter-stories)
3. The antenarrative middle between N-CN and LS-CS
4. The excluded middle

The chapter is structured in three sections. The first section accounts for a dialectical perspective on narratives and counter-narratives. The second section examines a dialogical perspective on living stories and counter-stories. The third discusses the role of antenarratives in connecting narrative – counter-narratives with living stories – counter-stories. At the end of the chapter, the contributions to the academic field, as well as the practical implications to management, are summarized and further research is suggested.

A dialectical perspective on narratives and counter-narratives

Similar to storytelling, dialectics is acknowledged as a constitutive and performative meta-theoretical perspective apt for analyzing the dynamics of contradictions, tensions, paradoxes, and oppositional forces inherent in social and organizational life (Baxter & Montgomery, 1996; Putnam, Fairhurst, & Banghart, 2016).

Dialectic is a method of discussion dating back to ancient Greek philosophers such as Aristotle, Socrates, and Plato. Throughout its long history, many variations of dialectics have emerged, including that of Hegel. Despite their differences, their basic worldviews share some family resemblance as they all deal with contradiction, change, praxis, and totality (unity) (Baxter & Montgomery, 1996, pp. 3–4, 6).

Based on the work of Hegel (1977, 2010) and the literature reviews conducted by Putnam et al. (2016), and Baxter and Montgomery (1996), the main ontological assumptions underlying a dialectical perspective are summarized in Figure 3.2. At the heart of dialectics, we thus find the dynamical interplay between mutually defining contradictory poles, which negate and exclude each other whilst simultaneously being related; each possessing what the other is missing.
In Figure 3.1, dialectics is associated with the encounter between narratives and counter-narratives for two reasons. First, *narratives* and hence also counter-*narratives* are defined as monological by Bakhtin. Both narratives and counter-narratives centripetally orbit around their own center, with clear boundaries between them. Second, narratives and counter-narratives are defined by Andrews and Bamberg (2004) as relational interdependent categories that only make sense in relation to one another. This definition thus assumes a tensed unity of opposing relational entities. Together, the two arguments support the relevancy of applying a dialectical perspective when conceptualizing the dynamical forces of encounters between narratives and counter-narratives. The dynamics of the dialectical middle between narratives – counter-narratives are elaborated on in the following section.

---

1) Contradictory oppositions:
Mutually negating and excluding each other.

2) Unity of oppositions:
One presupposes the other in its very meaning and existence.
Defining and sensemaking each other in terms of:
- Differences
- Sameness

3) The dynamic tensed interplay of oppositions:
The ongoing dynamic interaction occurring between unified oppositions due to their dialectical tensions.
Dialectics deal with the tensions inherent in relating.

4) The 'both/and' quality of the oppositions:
Truth immanent in both of them.

5) The constitutive 'middle' mediating between oppositions:
The middle transforms the contradictory oppositions, as well as their unity, thereby driving organizational and social change.

6) The dialectical forces and processes of relating oppositions:
Defining, excluding and unifying, and negating and mediating.

Figure 3.2 Ontological assumptions of dialectics.

The dialectical middle and its polarized space

Hegel's philosophy is based on the ontological assumption that the aliveness of the world and its movement and actualization is due to the work of dialectics (Hegel, 2010, § 81). Contradiction is the fundamental moving principle of the aliveness of the world and its inhabitants (Hegel, 2010, § 119). In order to understand, intervene, and carry things into effect, we need to become conscious of the ontological contradictions inherent in the world and of the dialectical struggles through which they transform and further develop the world and its inhabitants in their ongoing movement.

In Hegel's account of dialectics, the concepts of unity, diversity, difference, and contradictions play a key role. Using the notion of the world assumes a unity. However, "the unity has to be conceived in the diversity" (Hegel, 2010, § 88). The unity is not fixed and settled but instead always in the process of becoming, unresting, and moving because of its inherent contradictions and struggles (Hegel, 2010, § 88). To understand what dialectic is and how it moves, we need to distinguish between diversity, difference, and contradiction.

Initially, Hegel makes a distinction between diversity and difference. Diversity refers to the fragments of the unity that fall indifferently apart (Hegel, 2001, § 931), whereas difference presupposes a relation between being and its otherness. Difference thus indicates a specific relation where one and the other are mutually defined and determined with regard to their relational differences and similarities. Subsequently, their similarities and differences demarcate their individual uniqueness, as well as their unifying sameness. One is what the other is not. The Hegelian dialectical betweenness is thus composed by two counter centers: the self-center and the other-center (Gurevitch, 2001).

Meaning nothing exists without the other, they presuppose each other in their mutual constitutive process of becoming. Because of their co-constitutive relation, they carry within themselves the immanent potentiality of becoming something else mediated by their relational otherness (Hegel, 2001, § 932). Hence, they are co-emerging and co-developing.

Distinguishing between diversity and difference in this manner, Hegel continues by relating difference to oppositions and contradictions (Hegel, 2001, § 934–935); being different is not enough to form a dialectical relation. The difference needs to form an oppositional contradiction, meaning that one is excluding the other, one being positive and the other negative. Hence, we arrive at the well-known 'thesis' and 'antithesis' proposition of dialectics. Negating the thesis, the antithesis determines what the thesis lacks or has not yet become but potentially could do by merging with the anti-thesis.

The epistemological movement from grasping differences in general to understanding differences as contradictions requires what Hegel calls intelligent reflection and thinking, as opposed to superficial and ordinary thinking remaining indifferent by forgetting about the process of negation and only remembering differences in general (Hegel, 2001, § 961, § 962). Hence, we need to sharpen our critical and reflexive understanding of what is *essentially* different about the difference. This is a process of determining and separating the oppositional poles inherent in the contradiction.

The important point of Hegel's dialectics is this polarizing process of moving from diversity to difference to contradictions, defined as the mutual excluding and opposing poles which still constitute a unity, however unresting, as they only make sense in relation to each other. The diversity of a fragmented world is thus structured and organized in dialectical relations of polarized contradictions.

Having identified and qualified the opposing poles as the thesis and anti-thesis, the dialectical dynamics continue to work across the middle between the two poles. The dialectical dynamics are related to what Hegel refers to as the law of identity-in-difference (Hegel, 2001, § 954) implying three essential features.

First, the acknowledgment that both sides of the contradiction are equally right and equally wrong. Dialectic thus rejects reasonings for true versus false, for the either/or position. Instead, dialectic allows both sides of the contradiction to take part in the self-moving truth (Hegel, 1977, § 780, § 58) and transformation.

Second, the law of identity-in-difference implies that the transformation moves toward a third moment, called synthesis by some, albeit not by Hegel (Pinkard 2011, 6, Hegel 1977: § 65). In the third moment, the identity of the unity is transformed as it now encompasses both the thesis and the anti-thesis. Having resolved the previous contradiction, a new thesis emerges at a higher level only to be contradicted with multiple new anti-theses arising and co-emerging due to the aliveness of the world. Dialectics is thus an ongoing process until no further contradictions appear.

Third, the law of identity-in-difference implies that the dialectical transformation occurs as a merger between thesis and anti-thesis. The dialectical transformation of the thesis encompasses two movements: 1) the preserving and conserving and 2) the vanishing and canceling. Challenged by its anti-thesis, the thesis absorbs from the anti-thesis what it is missing, while at the same time maintaining and preserving its useful parts. Thesis and anti-thesis merge through these two movements.

The excluded middle and its closed space

As long as the encounter is based upon the both-and principle and as long as new contradictory and negating anti-theses emerge, dialectics continue to work in the dynamical middle between the two poles. Without these two dialectical principles, movement ceases to occur and the world turns into a closed, fixed, and mechanical system of relations. Mechanical comparison, contrast, and denial imply the exclusion of dialectics and is referred to as the law of the excluded middle (Hegel, 2001, § 952). The excluded middle is governed by the either/or principle allowing for only one truth. One is right, the other wrong (Hegel, 2010, § 119).

In the excluded middle, the negating and mediating force of the anti-thesis is rejected. Consequently, dialectics cease to work and is replaced by the dualistic positions of opposite poles with clear-cut boundaries, no overlap, and no middle. The middle thus turns into a closed, fixed space where each of the opposite poles arrive at their respective dead-ends. The most essential difference between the dialectical and excluded middle is thus about whether or not otherness is acknowledged.

The dialectical middle between narratives – counter-narratives

The following case study illustrates the dialectical struggle between narratives and counter-narratives. It also reveals the devastating process of moving from the dialectical middle to the excluded middle deadening the in-between dynamics by suppressing otherness.

Case study of D1

This case study is about a fragmented consultancy organization that had passed through a number of horizontal mergers, giving rise to us-them categorizations. "It was like marrying your worst enemy", as stated by one of the organizational members. A new CEO initiated a multi-voiced strategizing process involving the whole of the organization at all levels as an attempt to break down these counter-positions.

At the end of the process, some changes did occur. For instance, several members began to refer to 'we', particularly when speaking about the future of the company. However, all did not move along in this direction. A picture drawn by some members of the company identified the emergence of a new counter position. The picture uncovered the contradiction between the change ready team: those organizational members who were opposed to some of the issues apparent in the new direction. Unflatteringly, they were drawn as dead dinosaurs. The dead dinosaurs referred, among others, to the 30 members of the economic department

After tense discussions and conflicts, the CEO and other organizational members stopped listening to their arguments. Gradually, the voices silenced. The door to the economic department began to stay closed on an everyday basis. Suddenly, on one particular day, all 30 members of the department emailed their resignations to the CEO. Through an organized process, they were hired by a competitor and resigned on the very same day.

The event gave rise to many self-critical reflections such as: Why did we not see it coming? What signals did we overlook? In particular, one interesting reflection came up: Did they do it because they were afraid of losing their job because of their resistance?

The story exemplifies how the dialectic middle, as well as the excluded middle, works in social interactions.

The categorization between us and them as the worst enemy, as well as the contradiction between the change ready team and the dead dinosaurs, exemplifies how narrative and counter-narrative have been co-constructed as oppositional contradicting poles in and through social interactions. The story illuminates how the narrative language is used to label, stereotype, and categorize the many voices of the organization, thereby creating polarized positions. Narratives can therefore be viewed as a constructive mean for "the creation of characters in space and time, which in turn are instrumental for the creation of positions ...", as well being "... aspects of situated language use, employed by speakers/narrators to position a display of contextualized identities" (Bamberg, Georgakopoulou, 2008, p. 379). The language used in the story displays the construction of heroes and villains, enemies and friends, as well as the emerging resistance, which – to begin with – is loudly displayed.

Narratives and counter-narratives are thus co-produced in and through the discursive interaction, as well as forming the context and basis for the ongoing discourse. Because narrative and counter-narrative are discursively rooted in interactions, their relational categories should not be conceived of as static. On the contrary, their dialectical interplay is fluid and ever-changing, thereby potentially transforming the N-CN constructions. Emerging in the presence of each other and through a discursive process, the interactive realm of everyday interactions thus constitutes the ongoing fabric of counter-narratives (Bamberg & Andrews, 2004).

The story illuminates the dialectical dynamics in the sense that the contradiction between us and them is resolved through their merger, developing a sense of 'we'. Moreover, the positional and labelling categories of the change ready team versus the dead dinosaurs illuminate how new oppositional poles emerge through everyday interaction. The resistance of the group of people identifies how resistance against narrative singularity, coherency, and dominance may develop and take the shape of a counter-narrative defined as being in opposition to the grand (master) narrative (Bamberg, 2004; Bamberg & Andrews, 2004; Frandsen et al., 2016).

The dialectical dynamics of N-CN thus seem to be at work at the beginning of the storyline. Its premises, however, seem to change at the end. The silence and the closed door indicate the closing down of the space for speech and action and hence a turn towards the excluded middle where the either/or principle rules. The two groups seem to be orbiting around their own center, getting more and more stuck and cemented in their pre-defined structures and relations. Hence, the resisting group finally exits.

Even though the excluded middle may have been in play, ceasing the dialectical movement in this particular space time frame, this does not imply that dialectics is not at work in other space time frames of the organization. In fact, the exit can be interpreted as the outcome of a dialectical discourse that has moved into the shadows, excluding the rest of the organization from participation, yet includes the competitor, looking for alternative solutions. The exit phenomenon is what Deleuze refers to as lines of flight (Deleuze & Guattari, 1987).

Hegel's polarizing dialectic has been criticized by Deleuze, among others (Henriksen, 2017). By sharpening differences through sensemaking and reflection to such an extent that contradictory poles emerge, numerous small nuances, variations, and alterations may be lost as they are submerged into the antithetic formation of the privileged contradiction. In the ongoing process of transformation, they are overlooked and ignored by the accentuated contradiction. In that sense, the polarized contradiction is constructed as an abstraction of concrete real life without noticing the real emerging differences. In fact, Deleuze's criticism addressing the lost sight of multiplicity resembles Bakhtin's critique against dialectical betweenness (unfolded later in the chapter).

In fact, this criticism constitutes Hegel's contribution as he acknowledges that we tend to comprehend differences and individuality through processes of abstraction, reflection, and sensemaking (Hegel, 1977, § 235, § 305). Hegel conceptualizes the dualist tendency underpinning much of Western thinking producing abstract binary logical relations. The split between us and them, as well as between the change ready team versus the dead dinosaurs, thus decodes a sensemaking process that leads to generalized and stereotyped abstractions reducing the diversity of the organizational life. The apparent consensus among the 30 employees indicates a counter-narrative discursive power guiding and controlling sensemaking whilst demanding allegiance. Subsequently, both narratives and counter-narratives may regress into simplifying abstractions as the straightforward contradictory implies a reduction of the dialectical manifold into the dialectical opposition between counter-positions (Gurevitch, 2001).

The contribution of a dialectical perspective to the triad storytelling framework is summarized in Figure 3.3.

The dialogical middle and its open space

Bakhtin's approach to the middle differs from Hegel's dialectical betweenness. Whilst Hegel's dialectics work across the middle between the two centers, Bakhtin's dialogue works *in* the middle, *on* the boundary of the two centers. Being off-centered, Bakhtin aims to engage a multiplicity of subjects, topics, and voices in order to expand multiplicity and polyphony (Gurevitch, 2001). Bakhtin thus rejects the dialectical betweenness for a number of reasons.

In Bakhtin's view, existence and life cannot be separated from dialogue: "To be is to communicate" (Bakhtin, 1984) or from the act: "to *be* in life, to be *actually,* is to *act,* is to be unindifferent toward the one-occurrent whole" (Bakhtin, 1999, p. 42). Dialogue is thus a live process of being responsive to events with our lives through action and speech (Bakhtin, 1999, p. 2). We are always already in dialogue, there is no entering into dialogue as if there existed other ways of living (Morson & Emerson, 1990). In Bakhtin's understanding, dialogue, not dialectics, constitutes the ontological foundation of life. The opposing contradiction can only work as an abstraction pigeonholing individuals or social entities. In this sense, detaching people from the real world of life, the intimate relation between the person and his or her act, is lost.

Bakhtin therefore conceives of dialogue and dialectic as two different models through which to understand social life. Even though "dialectics was born of dialogue so as to return again to dialogue on a higher level" (Bakhtin, 1987c, p. 162), dialectics fails to comprehensively grasp the infinite contextual meaning or the contact between diverse voices and speaking subjects. By finalizing and systematizing dialogue, dialectic instead leads to a reification of the living dialogue:

- **Middle:**
  - Across the middle
  - Dialectical betweenness
  - Self-center and other-center
  - Polarized
- **Conception of difference and contradiction:**
  - Reducing the dialectical manifold to dialectical oppositions
  - Moving from diversity to difference to polarized contradictions
  - Abstraction
- **Conception of unity:**
  - Unresting, struggling unity
  - Unity of relational contradictory pole
  - Identity of difference
- **Dynamics**:
  - Merging across the middle
  - Resolution
  - Transformation
  - Returning at a higher level
- **Forces:**
  - The negating and mediating middle-term (counter-narrative)
  - The preserving
  - The vanishing
- **The counter:**
  - Defines the oppositional relation
  - Clear-cut boundary
  - To be resolved

Figure 3.3 The dialectical betweenness of narratives – counter-narratives.

> Dialogue and dialectics. Take a dialogue and remove the voices (the partitioning of voices), remove the intonations (emotional and individualizing ones), carve out abstract concepts and judgments from living words and responses, cram everything into one abstract consciousness – and that's how you get dialectics.
>
> *(Bakhtin, 1987a, p. 147)*

In Bakhtin's view, dialectical betweenness thus represents a monological perspective on communication, reducing people to counters by treating individuals or social entities as monads with clear boundaries. In objection, Bakhtin (1984) states that we are always wholly on the boundary, on the threshold between one's own and someone else's consciousness.

An essential difference between dialogue and dialectic is about the process of merging. Dialectics aims to merge through synthesis, whereas dialogue remains open-ended and unmerging. Bakhtin thus stresses the importance of staying on the boundary of unmerged horizons. Although the goal of the synthesizing process is to achieve coherency between merged voices, the dialogical encounter continues to remain open for a plurality of unmerged voices. In dialogue, voices are not to be contained within a single consciousness, as in monologism, or to be reduced to a counter or monad as they are much looser, messier, and more open (Morson & Emerson, 1990). Dialogical understanding is active and continuously creative (Bakhtin, 1987a, p. 142).

The unmerging, infinite, and unfinalized dialogue is thus full of tension, giving rise to the emergence of something new. This shines through in what Bakhtin defines as the great dialogue: "a dialogue where all voices participate with equal rights for which reason the dialogue becomes rich in reference to other voices and their discourses, alternative worldviews, questions, doubts, criticism, counter-arguments, and different interpretations" (Bakhtin 1984, p. 71).

What, then, are the dynamical forces of the dialogical middle, as opposed to the synthesizing forces of dialectics? Bakhtin's notion of heteroglossia and its inherent centripetal and centrifugal forces offer a relevant answer to this question. Heteroglossia refers to the different-speech-ness (Roberts, 2003) of the polyphonic dialogue and embraces different voices of the past, the present, and the future. Moreover, heteroglossia emerges as an outcome from the clashes between the centrifugal forces of decentralization and disunification and the centripetal forces that serve to unify and centralize. If separated from the centrifugal forces, the centripetal forces may result in a closed-structured and schematized space (Svane, 2019b). The ongoing battle between the forces, however, ensures the potential openness of the space. The heteroglossic unfinalized outcome thus differs from the process of merging across the boundary, of producing sameness and eliminating contradictions. Even if agreement occurs among the plurality of voices, Bakhtin warns us not to conceive of the agreement as sameness, but to understand agreement in dissensus as the voices may agree but for different reasons: "...agreement retains its dialogic character, that is, it never leads to a merging of voices and truths in a single impersonal truth, as occurs in the monologic world" (Bakhtin, 1984). On the contrary, "Each retains its own unity and open totality, but they are mutually enriched" (Bakhtin, 1987b, p. 7). The dialogical process therefore educates each side about itself and the other: "I cannot become myself without another; I must find myself in another by finding another in myself (mutual reflection and mutual acceptance)" (Bakhtin, 1984). Relational selves are thus co-constituted not across boundaries but on the boundary itself (Gurevitch, 2001).

Thanks to heteroglossia and its immanent forces, the dialogical encounter is kept open for the countless varieties, alterations, shadings, and gradations of the world of life. To the extent it makes sense to speak of a contradiction, Bakhtin states that these contradictions are not dialectical but spread out, standing alongside or opposite one another but not merging (Bakhtin, 1984).

The following case study illuminates how to work in the middle and off-center from a dialogical perspective.

Case Study of D2

Sarah works as a middle manager at a hospital. In her section, all managers join a leadership group coordinating actions and decision making. About a year ago, a new manager, Peter, entered the group. Very shortly after his entrance as a group member, Sarah experienced conflicts and collaborative problems in their relationship with a devastating effect on not only her leadership performance but also on her personal well-being. She experienced how his decision making, actions, and ways of communication intervened into her areas of responsibility without any pre-given information or warning. Moreover, his dominating behavior violated the norms and conventions of the group, which was used to much more open and democratic leadership practices. She felt that her personal values and leadership integrity was violated by his interference and furthermore that his way of acting was disrespectful towards her position as an equal collegial leader, as well as towards the rest of the group.

Whenever she responded with disagreement or counter-arguments, she ended up in new conflicts, which became more and more severe until the point where she realized that the conflicts had to do with their interpersonal relationship and could not be ascribed to him alone. From then on, she started to reflexively experiment with her own way of speaking and acting in relation to him. Gradually, she got to understand that in the beginning of their relationship, she perhaps communicated in an aggressive and direct way. Direct confrontations, her embodied moods, tone of voice, and use of language revealed her feelings of irritation and anger.

During the next 8 months, she consciously tried to change her own communicative practices. She became aware of controlling her own immediate emotional response. Instead of being the first voice to speak or respond to Peter's ideas, she started to withhold her own viewpoints and asked the other members of the team to share their perspectives and co-inquire into ideas or thoughts raised at the meetings. When developing the agenda for each meeting, she made sure to have each team member be responsible for a topic to be discussed at the meetings. Gradually over the months, it seemed as if the dialogical space was restored. Over time, it also seemed as if Peter began to relax more, listen more, and speak less. The other members gradually shifted from being silent and passive to taking an active part in the discussions. Sometimes, new creative solutions to problems emerged during these discussions which neither Peter nor Sarah had thought of. It was not the case that new incidents of tensed situations between Peter and Sarah did not occur. But according to Sarah's story, it seemed as if she and the leadership group had learned how to handle such incidents in their communicative practices.

Sarah's story discloses how she tries to move herself and Peter away from the self- and other-centered poles towards the off-centered middle. A new space seems to emerge that is more open for multiplicity and polyphony, thereby encouraging the other participants to be answerable in joining the multi-voiced dialogue. Being answerable is about taking ownership and responsibility of one's own actions instead of hiding by being passive or pretending (Bakhtin, 1999, p. 41). Without answerability, the variety, alternations, shadings, and gradations are lost, and the dialogue becomes empty and dead.

Furthermore, the story illuminates Bakhtin's conception of the open ended, unmerging, and creative dialogue. In the beginning of the story, the forces in play seem to sharpen the differences, tighten counter positions, and polarize the relationship resulting in self- and other centering. When Sarah starts to work off-centered, a creative heteroglossic dialogue and understanding seems to emerge as the centrifugal forces continue to disrupt the centripetal ones, thereby preventing the meeting from closing in on Peter's decision without further exploration.

Even though Peter and Sarah have gradually moved off-center, this does not imply the resolution of contradictions and tensions as in the dialectical merger. On the contrary, contradictions continue to emerge and create tensions between them. It therefore makes sense to conceive of their unity and contradictions as "as an eternal harmony of unmerged voices or as their unceasing and irreconcilable quarrel" (Bakhtin, 1984).

Reading Hegel and Bakhtin through each other, an important difference appears that matters to our conception of the prefix 'counter'. In dialectical betweenness, the counter demarcates the contradictions between self and other, which are overcome through the dialectical merger. In dialogue, relational selves emerge on the boundary (Gurevitch, 2001). In fact, there is no counter, no single sovereign territory, and no monads, meaning that the concept of a boundary may be a faulty metaphor (Morson & Emerson, 1990). Still, Bakhtin does speak of contradictions and counter-arguments. In dialogue, it therefore makes sense to conceive of the counter and the boundaries as living, dynamical, and in flux. Integrating this point into the triad storytelling framework, this chapter therefore suggests distinguishing between narratives-counter-narratives and living stories – counter-stories. While dialectics is associated with the encounter between narratives and counter-narratives, it makes sense to associate dialogue with the encounter between living stories and counter-stories as visualized in Figure 3.1.

Dialogical Living Stories – Counter-stories:

- **Middle:**
  - In the middle
  - On the boundary
  - Off-center
  - Expanding multiplicity and polyphony
- **Conception of Difference and Contradiction:**
  - Tensed dissensus
  - Countless varieties, alterations, shadings, and gradations
  - Contradictions are spread out, standing alongside, or opposite one another
  - Agreement and disagreement in dissensus
- **Conception of Unity:**
  - An eternal harmony of unmerged voices
  - An unceasing and irreconcilable quarrel
- **Dynamics:**
  - Unmerging voices
  - Each retains its own unity and open totality
  - Mutually enriched
  - Transgression and Creativity
- **Forces:**
  - Centripetal forces of order and closure
  - Centrifugal forces of disorder and opening
  - Heteroglossic force and the unfinalized, infinite outcome
- **The Counter:**
  - Open, dynamic, living, in flux
- on the boundary
- in the middle
  - Faulty metaphors: boundary, territory, counter
  - No clear-cut boundaries as in dialectical betweenness
  - No sovereign territories or poles as in dialectical betweenness

Figure 3.4 Dialogical living stories – counter-stories.

The contribution of dialogical perspective to the triad storytelling framework is summarized in Figure 3.4.

The antenarrative middle – creating a free space for multiplicity and polyphony

In the triad storytelling framework, the antenarrative process aims to bridge the gap between narratives and living stories: "antenarrative processes perform a transformation of stories into narratives, and narratives into stories, and therefore are in between" (Boje, 2014, p. 71). The concept of antenarratives is thus a way of conceptualizing the dynamic relationship between narratives and living stories. The research ambition of the antenarrative approach is to enlighten how lived experience and living stories are assimilated into narratives, as well as how the rise of struggling counter-narratives and micro living stories are challenging dominant narratives (Rosile et al., 2013).

The dynamic relationship between N-CN and their dialogical realm are also addressed in Bamberg's research. According to Bamberg, the interactive realm constitutes "the territory where counter as well as master-narratives emerge in co-presence and as discursive process" (Bamberg,

2004, p. 353). Narratives and counter-narrative impact everyday interaction, as they are employed to make claims on identities and positions, to give guidance and direction to the everyday actions of subjects, to normalize and naturalize, and to constrain and delineate their agency. Conversely, the interactive realm of everyday interactions, the small stories, constitutes the ongoing fabric of counter-narratives (Bamberg & Andrews, 2004). The interplay gives rise to the construct narratives-in-interaction (Bamberg, 2004, pp. 351, 360).

In order to further enlighten the dynamical relationship between narratives and living stories and the role of 'counter' in these dynamics, this chapter proposes to make a distinction between counter-narratives and counter-stories, which are otherwise used interchangeably (e.g. by Andrews, 2004, p. 2). Viewed from a dialectical dialogical storytelling perspective, the two types of counter are connected to each other through a dynamical antenarrative relationship. On the one hand, antenarratives disrupt the dialectical process leading to narratives – counter-narratives, thereby disentangling the polarized centers of self and other and expanding multiplicity and polyphony. On the other hand, antenarratives simultaneously reweave the appearing fragments and threads of stories and narratives, thereby paving a way for "a future that would not otherwise be" (Boje, 2008, pp. 13–14).

To some extent, Sarah's story reflects an antenarrative approach. What makes it antenarrative is her way of working towards the future through embodied and reflexive sensemaking and experimental actions. Planning her experiments, she has no certain knowledge of how Peter or the other team members would respond but still allows herself to be led by her senses and intuitions. Hence, she is moving *beyond* the petrified narrative-counter-narrative constructions of their relationship. Each experiment is a *bet* on how to improve the relationship between herself and Peter, as well as the work of the leadership group. Because she cares about this, she is determined in carrying out these experiments and thereby actualizing the *becoming* of a better future. To accomplish this, she tries to move *beneath* the narrative – counter-narrative constructions and create a space that is open to the polyphonic voices. Withholding her own as well as Peter's polarizing voices, she uses the voices of the other group members to off-center the interaction. By trying to restore the balance between centripetal and centrifugal forces, she disrupts narrative and counter-narrative coherence and keeps the communicative process open *before* new narrative cohesion. Sarah's approach may therefore reveal how antenarratives can help to bridge the gap *between* N-CN and LS-CS and eventually to transform the relation *between* petrified narratives-counter-narratives.

Viewed through the lenses of the dialectical dialogical storytelling framework, Sarah's story throws some light upon the antenarrative connection between N-CN and LS-CS. If the balance between the centripetal and centrifugal forces of LS-CS is disrupted at the expense of the centrifugal forces, the centripetal forces of everyday interactions may give rise to a polarizing movement, prompting N-CN constructions. These constructions may dominate, restrain, guide, and shape real-life interactions. At the same time, the polarizing movement can be disrupted or broken down if the centrifugal forces move back into play and restore the off-centered dynamics of LS-CS.

The antenarrative approach thus contributes to informing the relationship between dialectics and dialogues with regard to how dialectics is born out of dialogue and returned to dialogue at a higher level (Bakhtin, 1987c, p. 162). Conversely, the dialectical dialogical perspective contributes to enrichening our understanding of the dynamics of the triad storytelling framework, as well as the role of antenarratives.

The aforementioned example of Sarah is limited to its microlevel of interaction, as well as to the single-voiced perspective of Sarah. The case story does not contextualize the political organizational environment or tell the story of Peter's perspective or of other voices. Still, the example may shed some light on the antenarrative interplay between political controlling forces working towards the suppression of otherness, as well as ethical struggles striving for a free space for action, speech, and conversations (Gurevitch, 2001).

The contribution of the chapter

In this chapter, a dialectical dialogical perspective has been applied to storytelling organizations. The dialectical dialogical storytelling perspective contributes to distinguishing between N-CN and LS-CS. The distinction is useful for the purpose of better understanding the complexity of the dynamics of storytelling organizations.

The dialectical betweenness of contradictory N-CN is visualized as D1 in Figure 3.1, whereas the tense dissensus of LS-CS is visualized as D2. The abstract dualistic contradictions of N-CN are transformed through the dialectical merger across the polarized middle. The tensed dissensus of LS-CS emerges in the dialogical middle, which is kept open for potentially expanding multiplicity and polyphony. Without merging, the different horizons are transgressed, thereby giving rise to creativity and to the appearance of something new. In the chapter, it is argued that both types of dynamics contribute to the complex dynamics of a fragmented, diversified, struggling, and unresting organizational whole.

Based upon the work of Bamberg and Boje, N-CN and LS-CS are conceived of as in an interaction with one another. Antenarratives concern the resolution of their gap while shaping and creating the organizational future; they constitute the connecting arc between the two counters. On the one hand, antenarratives unravel and disentangle the N-CN, breaking diversity down into two poles. On the other, antenarratives reweave the various fragments of stories and narratives, thereby antenarrating the future of the organization.

Inspired by Bakhtin, the antenarrative middle is conceived of as working in the midst of the heteroglossic process of balancing the centripetal and centrifugal forces of dialectical dialogue. Subsequently, antenarratives disturb and disrupt the polarizing process, while creating a more open space striving for expanded multiplicity and polyphony. The case study of Sarah provides a practical example of how to approach the antenarrative middle through off-centering.

The main contribution of the chapter is therefore three-fold. First, the distinction between counter-narratives and living counter stories enriches our meta-theoretical conceptualization of the complexity of storytelling dynamics. Second, the conceptualization of the antenarrative middle bridges the gap between N-CN and LS-CS through dialectical dialogical storytelling. Third, the chapter examines the identification of four types of middles, each of which play a role in the dynamics of storytelling organizations: the excluded, dialectical, and dialogical middle, as well as the antenarrative middle. In this chapter, it is suggested that the management of storytelling organizations needs to be conscious of these middles as the nature of their performative and constitutive dynamics differ essentially. In this chapter, it is suggested that managing the four middles is a managerial task.

References

Andrews, M. (2004). Opening to the original contributions. In M. Bamberg, & M. Andrews (Eds.), *Considering Counter-Narratives: Narrating, Resisting, Making Sense* (pp. 1–6). Philadelphia: John Benjamins.

Bakhtin, M. M. (1984). *Problems of Dostoevsky's Poetics*. Minneapolis: University of Minnesota Press.

Bakhtin, M. M. (1987a). From notes made in 1970–71. In M. Holquist (Ed.), *Speech Genre and Other Late Essays* (pp. 132–158). Austin: University of Texas Press.

Bakhtin, M. M. (1987b). Response to a question from Novy Mir. In M. Holquist (Ed.), *Speech Genre and Other Late Essays* (pp. 1–7). Austin, Texas: University of Texas Press.

Bakhtin, M. M. (1987c). Toward a methodology for the human sciences. In M. Holquist (Ed.), *Speech Genre and Other Late Essays* (pp. 159–172). Austin, Texas: University of Texas Press.

Bakhtin, M. M. (1999). *Toward a Philosophy of the Act*. Austin, USA: University of Texas Press.

Bamberg, M. & Georgakopoulou, A. (2008). Small stories as a new perspective in narrative and identity analysis. *Text & Talk, 28*(3), 377–396.

Bamberg, M. (2004). Considering counter-narratives. In M. Bamberg & M. Andrews (Eds.), *Considering Counter-Narratives. Narrating, Resisting, Making Sense.* (pp. 351–371). Philadelphia: John Benjamins.

Bamberg, M., & Andrews, M. (Eds.) (2004). *Considering Counter-Narratives: Narrating, Resisting, Making Sense.* Philadelphia: John Benjamins.

Baxter, L. A. & Montgomery, B. M. (1996). *Relating Dialogues and Dialectics*. New York: The Guilford Press.

Boje, D. (2014). *Storytelling Organizational Practices. Managing in the Quantum Age*. New York: Routledge.

Boje, D. M. (2001). *Narrative Methods for Organizational & Communication Research*. London: Sage Publications.

Boje, D. M. (2008). *Storytelling Organizations*. London: Sage.

Boje, D. M. (2011). *Storytelling and the Future of Organizations: An Antenarrative Handbook* (pp. 1–19). New York: Routledge.

Boje, D. M. (2012). Reflections: What does quantum physics of storytelling mean for change management? *Journal of Change Management, 12*(3), 253–271.

Boje, D. M. (2016a). Dialectical storytelling: Transitioning university into respecting hawk rights to reproduce and have their family in a posthumanist world. Retrieved from http://davidboje.com/hawk/. Accessed on 2016, May 5.

Boje, D. M. (2016b). The dialectic storytelling of the standing conference for management and organization inquiry (sc'MOI) as it dismembers and re-members. *Tamara Journal of Critical Organisation Inquiry*, 14(1), 53–64.

Deleuze, G., & Guattari, P. F. (1987). *A Thousand Plateaus: Capitalism and Schizophrenia* (Vol. 2). Minneapolis, MN: University of Minnesota Press.

Frandsen, S., Kuhn, T., & Lundholt, M. W. (2016). *Counter-narratives and Organization. Counter-Narratives and Organization*. New York: Routledge, Taylor & Francis.

Gurevitch, Z. (2001). Dialectical dialogue: The struggle for speech, repressive silence, and the shift to multiplicity. *The British Journal of Sociology, 52*(52), 87–104.

Hegel, G. W. F. (1977). *Phenomenology of Spirit*. Oxford: Clarendon Press.

Hegel, G. W. F. (2001). Science of logic. Retrieved May 28, 2019, from www.inkwells.org/index_htm_files/hegel.pdf

Hegel, G. W. F. (2010). Encyclopedia of the philosphical sciences in basic outline. *Part One. Science of Logic*. Retrieved May 28, 2019, from http://hegel.net/en/pdf/Hegel-Enc-1.pdf

Henriksen, T. D. (2017). Genveje og vildveje i design af organisatoriske læringsspil. In J. Hanghøj, T. Misfeldt, & M. Bundsgaard (Eds.), *Hvad er Scenariedidaktik?* (pp. 234–258). Århus: Aarhus Universitetsforlag.

Morson, G. S., & Emerson, C. (1990). *Mikhail Bakhtin: Creation of a Prosaics. Comparative Literature* (Vol. 44). Stanford, CA: Stanford University Press.

Pinkard, T. (2011). *Hegels naturalism: Mind, nature, and the final ends of life*. New York, NY: Oxford University Press.

Putnam, L. L., Fairhurst, G. T., & Banghart, S. (2016). Contradictions, dialectics, and paradoxes in organizations: A constitutive approach. *The Academy of Management Annals, 10*(1), 65–171.

Roberts, G. (2003). A glossary of key terms. In P. Morris (Ed.), *The Bakhtin Reader: Selected Writings of Bakhtin, Medvedev, Voloshinov* (pp. 245–252). London: Arnold.

Rosile, G. A., Boje, D. M., Carlon, D. M., Downs, A.& Saylors, R. (2013). Storytelling Diamond: An Antenarrative Integration of the Six Facets of Storytelling in Organization Research Design. *Organizational Research Methods* 16(4), 557–580.

Svane, M. (2009a). Organizational world-creating: being-in-becoming. A quantum relational process philosophy. In D. Boje & M. Sanches (Eds.), *The Emerald Handbook of Quantum Storytelling Consulting* (pp. 245–279). Bingley: Emerald Publishing.

Svane, M. (2019b). Antenarratives and heteroglossia in organizational storytelling: A living medium shaping the future of organizations in the quantum age. *Communication & Language at Work, 6*(1), 63–77.

4

A counter-narrative to the accepted 'Kolding Pyramid 9th Wonder of the World' narrative with some antenarrative process inquiries

David M. Boje

Introduction

After returning from a sabbatical, partly enjoyed in Kolding Denmark, I found myself making plans to build an Earthship Double Greenhouse next to my straw bale blacksmith shop in Las Cruces New Mexico. Just yesterday, my friend Steve Self and I pounded four 16-inch (R235) tires with sand and clay, to being first row of the 300-pound brick foundation walls. An Earthship is a New Mexico invention by Michael Reynolds, a self-contained water treatment system, off-the-grid photovoltaic for electricity, pounded earth into tires to develop high thermal mass, and using recycled tires, aluminum cans, and bottles as a source of building materials. The thermal mass, the recycled material, and collection of rain water in cisterns, allow the residents to farm fish, whose waste feeds the plants in grow beds, whose waste in turn feeds the fish. It's a closed loop survival system that without any fossil fuel can keep humans, animals, plants, and water warm all year round. One recent innovation for colder climates is the double greenhouse structure. Instead of one room with south facing (double panel) windows, there are two adjacent rooms so the sun shines through to heat both greenhouse rooms. Roof windows are opened to allow cool air to enter (or not) from cool tubes coming out the north side, buried several feet below ground. This combination of systems, much of them, form recycled materials, is a possible way for people to get off-grid, not just the electric grid, but the water grid, the food grid, and become self-sufficient instead of dependent upon what the sociologist Lewis Mumford (1934) calls "Carboniferous Capitalism".

Carboniferous Capitalism (aka Fossil Capitalism) is a particular retrospective narrative in various versions: '*there is no alternative to fossil fuel*,' '*there will be a technological fix to the coming energy crisis*,' '*we can all transition to solar energy and drive electric cars*' or '*we can all build Earthships and live off-grid growing aquaponics.*' There are more and more counternarratives to the Carboniferous progress narrative variants. Another counternarrative is that electric cars will be affordable by the rich, and the last time we looked the Earthships are as expensive as McMansions in Taos, New Mexico. Even the smaller version I am building in New Mexico, the double greenhouse, despite using mostly recycled materials, will be expensive. It is a rich man's hobby, but some day, it could become a lifeboat alternative should the sixth extinction bring about the predicted apocalypse (Boje, *in press*) because '*there is no planet B*' and we have all but exhausted fossil fuel, are well past peak oil, and just past peak water, with a result expected that peak food will be upon us all in 2050. Life as we know it is changing radically, and preparations for the future, in management and organization, are a grand progress narrative of '*business-as-usual*' live out the peak oil and peak water, until climate change melts glaciers, seas rise, and weather patterns become increasingly unpredictable. Even the Anthropocene counternarrative to the Carboniferous progress narrative, has its counternarrative. I don't think we have spent much time theorizing or investigating counternarratives to counternarratives. Anthropocene counternarrative is that somehow we will find economic equality, social equality in our use of planetary resources that are finite. However, the wind energy alternative to carbon sources is only 1.1% and photovoltaic only 0.06% of what the fossil fuel economy is supplying (Malm, 2016: 368). Not everyone will have a lifeboat, or an Earthship, to ride out the climate change. And as counternarrative to the Anthropocene counternarrative is the prediction that climate change will continue to intensify, so the rich man's lifeboats will not be a long-term survival approach. Malm is predicting that people in catastrophe continue with a death grip on the capitalism they know, and do not change, until its all too late. In other words, the antenarrative prospective sensemaking, the preparing in advance to bring about a future other than business-as-usual will not happen without lots of suffering, a loss of biodiversity, and if Sixth extinction predictions are correct, the death of most of humanity, most of the mammal and fish species, because climatic conditions will be quite different than today.

You can now perhaps understand, why, when I encountered rumors of the Kolding Pyramid (KP), its water treatment, and using that water from the apartment complex to do aquaponics, to use the power of the sun for photovoltaic production, to have a year-round greenhouse to grow fish and plants ➡ why I was so captivated. Here in the middle of Kolding, in a housing complex (Hollandervej/Fredensgade block), was for me, the ninth wonder of the world: a pyramid greenhouse, and a possible solution to peak oil, peak water, and peak food, and a way to save more humanity from the Sixth Extinction prophecy.

In what follows I will explore my research question: why is KP, the ninth wonder of the world, no longer in operation? No fish or plants are growing. Yet the pyramid glass and its concrete foundations, its fish tank- and plant-grow beds, are intact. One could flip a switch and send photovoltaic energy to open the windows, run the water pumps, flood the grow beds, and let life happen. I will use six antenarrative approaches to explore ways various narratives and counternarratives, and some indigenous living stories are in evidence. The six kinds of antenarrative inquiries include: (1) Benjaminian dialogical foretelling method, (2) Heideggerian dialectic of 'negation of the negation' fore-notions, (3) Bakhtinian architectonic dialogism, (4) Deleuzian rhizomatics, (5) a sociomaterial antenarrative inquiry into actor routines and material actants, and (6) a UN sustainable development goal: quality water for the world. After unpacking the antenarrative inquiries I will return to discuss the counternarrative implications. In short, how antenarrative processes are constitutive of narrative-counternarrative dialectics and in dialogical relation to living stories.

First antenarrative inquiry: Benjaminian dialogical foretelling method

Walter Benjamin (2016, written 1924–1926, first published, 1928), for me, has done the most pioneering work in antenarrative. His book, *One Way Street*, contains 60 vignettes. Each is about the signs and symbols of a German city, following the destruction of World War I. My antenarrative reading is Benjamin looking at the wreckage of history, trying to make sense of 'what's next,' 'what future is arriving.' As yet there is no narrative or counternarrative, only fragments, clues as to which of many futures will befall humanity. The editors re-releasing Benjamin's book, do not give an antenarrative reading, but instead says Benjamin is doing an early surrealism project. For me, the vignettes provide an antenarrative methodology, one we can use to unpack the KP situation. There are signs and symbols present that are clues about the future in a variety of webpages (listed below), Beatley's (2000) book, and a master's thesis by Nelson (2010), and my own visits to the Solgarden (which means, sun court) urban renewal project in Kolding.

Kolding's 'Bioworks' Pyramid is enclosed by a residential block of 129 or so apartments, built in the late 1930s, housing about 250 residents. Beatley (2000: 305) says there are 140 flats, in a block of four- and five-story buildings. During the project two older buildings were demolished, and two new ones constructed, entirely from recycled building materials (ibid.). On the website in the UK, is our first fragment: "The Pyramid 'green' sewage treatment plant is the most spectacular element in the entire project. However, the project comprises":[1]

- Energy savings in the dwellings
- Passive solar heating
- Photovoltaics
- Water saving installations
- Use of rainwater for toilet flushing
- Renewed courtyard
- Use of sustainable materials
- Composting of organic waste
- Recycling of paper, glass etc.

Beatley (2000: 305) says "It comes into sight spectacularly as one enters the courtyard from one of several street entrances." The project resulted in a 50% reduction in fossil fuel consumed by the residents of the block. Newman and Jennings (2012: 113) says its "perhaps the most spectacular of the Danish urban ecology projects" taking a "run-down inner-city block of some 145 apartments (in five-story traditional buildings) with an enclosed courtyard" and creating "a beautiful water recycling system based on a 'glass pyramid.'" "The complex, also has solarized buildings, a slid-waste recycling center womplete with a worm composting unit (which also takes sludge from the treatment process), and a community garden" (p. 114).

One of the original basic ideas was to use the Pyramid as part of the common space for residents in the block. There are old photos of the aquaponics working, the pools of water, with swimming fish, their excrement giving nutrients to a lush munificent green life, as the light of the sun energizes the entire pyramid (See Kolding's Bioworks Pyramid 2003/2015, photo by Tania Wegwitz).[2]

Kolding 'Bioworks' Pyramid is a living sociomaterial mattering aliveness of many species and concrete, glass, and iron materialities. It is social in the community of residents and interspecies relations among plants, fish, microbes, algae, and humans. The bottom floor of the Kolding Bioworks Pyramid is a series of ponds. The blackwater is further filtered in a reed-bed then infiltrated in the ground. Water makes a journey through a hierarchy of living things: algae, plankton, plants, and then fish. In short, there was aquaponics in this pyramid greenhouse.

Needless to say I went to Kolding Bioworks Pyramid with great anticipation, to see cascades of plant, green algae, fish jumping, and lots of activity. Shock. Surprise. The Kolding Bioworks Pyramid is not operative. As I spoke to several residents, I discovered to my amazement it had not been operating for some years. None of the residents I met knew when was the last time the Kolding Bioworks Pyramid had been operative.

Following an online search I discovered that the pyramid was last operational in 1994, but not since then. Residents have moved in who do not remember it ever working. They have no living memory of it producing food. What happened to the storytelling memory? That is my research question. Why is this aquaponics wonder not in operation? In the above photo, you can see signs marking the pyramid, some graffiti, perhaps by local youth, claiming territory. There are these Benjaminian fragments of antenarratives that I think are the beginnings of a counternarrative to Carboniferous capitalism. Is Andreas Malm (2016) correct, that in the face of catastrophe, people forget about alternative solutions, and hang on to dear life, gripping 'business-as-usual'? Keep in mind that ancient Chinese, Middle East, South American cities, and the indigenous tribes around the world, had a working relationship with nature. Lewis Mumford (1961) asserts that the rise of the sky gods initiated a separation from nature's ecosystems, and sustainable ways of living (see Newman & Jennings, 2012: 114, on this point).

Second antenarrative inquiry: Heideggerian dialectic of 'negation of the negation' fore-notions

I have come across this approach before in work with Sabine Trafimow (Boje, 2018a), and with Martia Svane (Svane & Boje, 2014, 2015; Svane, Boje, & Gergerich, 2015; Svane, Gergerich, & Boje, 2017). Sabine is a native German speaker who attended every doctoral course I taught in New Mexico for several years, working out the Heidegger translations of *Ontology – The Hermeneutics of Facticity* (1923/1988/1999), *Being and Time* (1927/1962), and *The Question Concerning Technology* (1977). We worked out a theoretical model of Heideggerian antenarrative with five components: forehaving, foreconception, forestructure, foresight, and forecaring. Recently Marita and I are working out the antenarrative process aspects that are dialectical between narrative-counternarrative and more dialogical to living story. I will next apply this to the Kolding Bioworks Pyramid situation.

There is forehaving in the Transorganization alliances that formed between the City of Kolding, the Municipality, the Ministry of Housing, and the Danish Town Renewal Company and two consulting firms took up the Kolding innovation to demonstrate state of the art demonstration projects. In 1992, before the Kolding Bioworks Pyramid, a leading Danish urban renewal company presented it as an integrated solution.

> The project was built in a collaboration between the city of Kolding and the social housing company Byfornyelsesselskabet Denmark, and funding for the Bioworks project comes from the Danish Green Fund (which provides monies for a variety of pilot environmental projects).
>
> *(Beatley, 2000: 305)*

The pyramid and the infrastructure to create compost fertilizer, roof gardens, and so on was built by the City of Kolding as a pilot project, and given to inhabitants of the block as a gift. Owners of the apartment became responsible for billing for wastewater treatment performed by a landscaping company that looked after the green spaces within the block. Owners were responsible for paying for broken pumps or windows.

Forestructuring the relationships and infrastructure was only partial. As historical records tells us, the Department of Waste Management does not allow residents of the block, or anyone else, to enter the Pyramid without a waste management certificate. The Department of Health does not allow anyone to grow fruits and vegetables in the Pyramid. I want to return to see if this applies to the Community Garden, outside the Pyramid, or even find out if it is still in existence.

Foreconception can be traced to the aquaponics, biology, and waste management sciences, to the concepts and theories that make up that knowledge, in order to even talk intelligently about the Kolding Bioworks Pyramid.

The foresight, the preparing in advance for the future of the Pyramid had some shortcomings. Antenarrative foresight is a prospective sensemaking, and a way of bringing some future into being-in-the-world (Heidegger, 1962), as opposed to the narrative of 'business-as-usual' and resident lifestyles-as-usual.

Forecaring involves the antenarrative process of forehaving, forestructuring, foreconception, and foresight. Forecaring is a kind of ethical answerability for the future. In the case of Kolding Bioworks Pyramid, it's something that reconnects humankind to many other species: fish, algae, and plants of all kinds (except fruit and vegetables, forbidden by the State).

Third antenarrative inquiry: Bakhtinian architectonic dialogism

Mikhail Bakhtin (1990, 1993) distinguished two kinds of answerability: moral and special. Special answerability is cultural because it is about a spectator's interest, while moral answerability is about one's accountability in the life world. Bakhtin (1993) is very definite that what he calls "Culture World" and "Life World" has a gap or block between them, making direct communication near impossible. Bakhtin also writes of a Technology World, which I theorize, in this situation is more directly connected to Culture World than to Life World. For me, Life World is where 'indigenous ways of knowing' (IWOK), the living stories offer story aliveness. Culture World, is where I observe 'western ways of knowing' (WWOK). I have added Future World, to this otherwise Bakhtinian dialogical theory. It is not just any of the dialogisms Bakhtin (1993) is theorizing, but in particular, the architectonic dialogism (defined in Bakhtin, 1981) as the interanimation of three discourses (cognitive, ethical, and aesthetic), see Boje (2008) for more on this topic.

In Figure 4.1 I have drawn in the barrier between World of Culture and World of Life that Bakhtin has acknowledged where there is no possible communication, fusion, or concresence (Bakhtin, 1993: 2). IWOK, living story, is the Being of event "*in its entirety*" and as "a *whole* act [that] is alive" with antenarrative processes constitutive of a path of connectivity between WWOK narrative and IWOK living story. The 'World of Culture,' its 'special answerability' as judgment validity, and the 'World of Life,' its 'moral answerability' has no communication possible except through antenarrative processes. Bakhtin's special answerability actor does not intervene, merely looks on as the passive bystander, while the moral answerability actor in the once-occurring event-ness of Being actually does enter into the constitutive moment as active, complicit, responsible, and ethical participant in Life-World. In and around organizations we need more moral answerability. Bakhtin says that the "aesthetic activity as well is powerless to take possession of the moment of Being which is constituted by the transitiveness and open event-ness of Being" (1993: 1). I take this to mean the retrospective narrative in its aesthetic activity of plots and characters is split off from the living story looking down at present, and in its moments of open event-ness of Being. Antenarrative is an ontology process of becoming ante (before, between, beneath, & bets on the future) by looking forward to many possible futures, and enacting one of them in an historical act or activity. Narrative by itself is "unable to apprehend the actual event-ness of the once-occurrent event" of living story relations (Bakhtin, 1993: 1).

The City of Kolding constructed an impressive decentralized wastewater cleaning technology and an aesthetically-pleasing glass pyramid within a city block of apartments. The project was

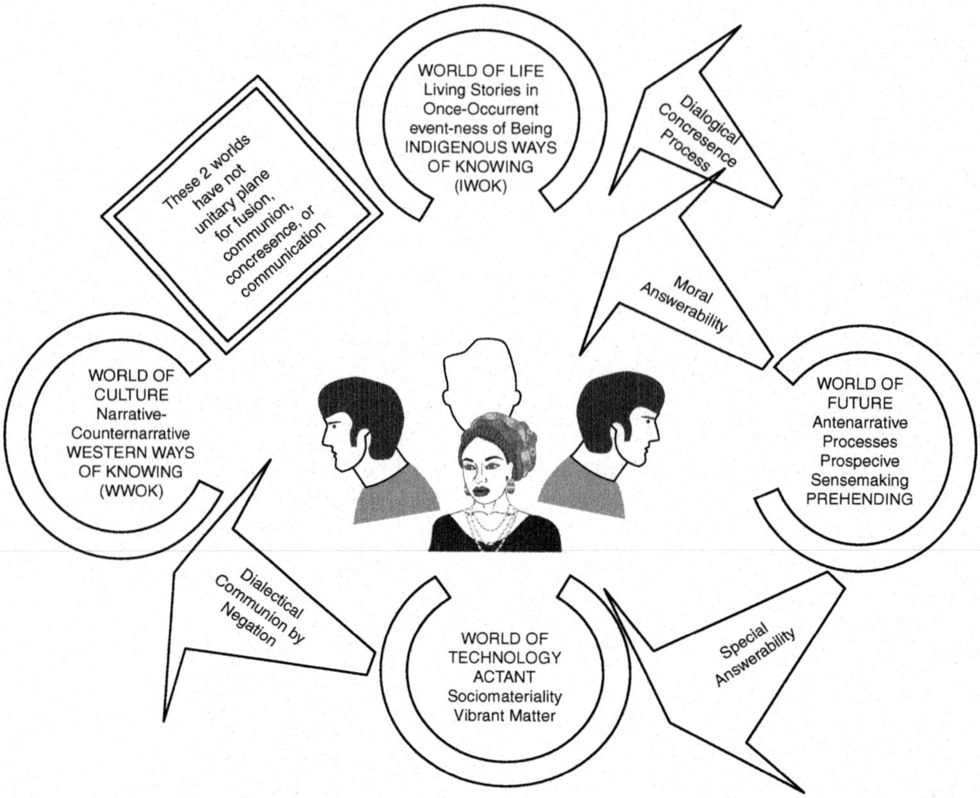

Figure 4.1 A blockage between two worlds and two very different antenarrative processes constitutive of some other worlds (Boje, 2018).

> developed for an ecological wastewater treatment plant as part of an urban renewal project in 1995. It is an older pilot project, so the long-term consequences can be seen.
>
> *(Insideflows.com).*[3]

But, on the contrary, the project lies as dormant as the Egyptian pyramids. Nelson (2010: 22) puts it this way "As part of an urban renewal project in 1995, the City of Kolding constructed an impressive decentralized wastewater cleansing operation and glass pyramid within a city block in downtown Kolding." The Technology World and the Life World of residents could not align, because the Culture World of government (Department of Waste Management, Department of Health) presented a disconnect, a block or severance.

In 1991, the Kolding Municipality, the Ministry of Housing, and the Danish Town Renewal Company and two consulting firms took up the Kolding innovation to demonstrate state of the art demonstration project. The City of Kolding as part of a 1995 urban renewal project constructed the glass pyramid water treatment plant within a city block. Photovoltaic electric cells mounted above a parking area powered it. The World of Technology did not have all the foresight needed. As Nelson (2010: 23) reports, the 846 solar PV panels do not provide enough energy to operate the entire system. PV is also used to charge electric vehicles, but it's not clear how many renters have electric vehicles. The project was part of a larger Denmark set of test cases in integrated ecological urban renewal. Blackwater and greywater are collected inside the block of apartments into a buffer tank where sludge settles and is removed. The wastewater is treated in the neighborhood with a simple fabric filter, and series of aeration reactors, ozone and ultraviolet light, and enters tilapia fishponds. However, all the varied systems of aquaponics have to be operative, to handle all the black and grey water of residents. In other words, if you don't grow the fish or the plants, then the Bioworks does not have the biotic capacity to generate clean and odor free water. Rainwater is harvested from the apartment roofs that collect in a below-ground cistern, purified in a pond, and is pumped to apartments for toilet flushing and washing machines. Finally, the wastewater is infiltrated into surface water. Residents have access to green roofs. I have to check on this when I return to Kolding, to see if these are still operative.

The World of Technology of the Kolding Bioworks Pyramid, includes using the Decentralized Sanitation and Reuse (DESAR) system that uses anerobic digestion of blackwater in a water treatment process to produce energy rather than consume it (Nelson, 2010: 22). DESAR was invented in 1866 by a Dutch engineer named Liernur to convert blackwater and food waste to fertilizer for sandy soil. This reduces the need for synthetic fertilizer and fresh water, which is important to global ecological overshoot. Nelson describes the Kolding DESAR as "environmentally and economically sustainable for over a decade": and "financially, the inhabitants enjoy a 15–20% reduction in tariffs, and new jobs ... created within the community. Furthermore, the value of the decentralized infrastructure belongs to the inhabitants, rather than an endless 'rent' paid for the WWTP through tariffs." (p. 22).

According to the website (insideflows.org, IBID), "The residents continue to use the pyramid to purify their wastewater, but all other functions it was planned to serve has ceased." I have to stress once more, if all the biotic systems are not operating, then it is doubtful that the Bioworks Pyramid, is able to handle the load. Of the 120 (some say 140 or 150) units, owners occupied only 30, and the rest became rental property (Nelson, 2010: 90). That is too few to take moral answerability, leaving most as curious special answerability, bystanders (Bakhtin, 1993).

For a time the Pyramid operated, and a staff member checked all the gauges to ensure the system was working properly, and once a year a local landscaping company checks all the pumps. Currently, not even the wastewater treatment operates. Insideflows.org gives some idea about what can happen. "Operationally, the largest problem is odor, which is a serious nuisance to the inhabitants" (Nelson, 2010: 90). Nelson (2010: 89) adds, "the first rainwater is a bit darker, and almost every time complaints are made." This odor could be, and I suspect it is, the result of not having a fully functioning complex biotic system. There are also structural issues in the technology. The aeration pond is an open system, and continually smells like sewage. The difficulty with the rainwater is when there are periods of no rain, dust settles on the roofs, and the water becomes slightly dirty and clouded. Nevertheless, the four-story Bioworks Pyramid has a strong spatial quality, along with the infiltration pond and community garden, which constitute a green aesthetics.

The Insideflows.com website says the Bioworks Pyramid continues to perform, but as I have said, the greenhouse space is not being used, and the greywater and rainwater catchment no long works. There are no long tilapia fish and no algae growth to support them. Where at one time almost every apartment had a glass-enclosed patio, and grew a variety of plants, now there are very few gardens visible. The website (insideflows.org) and Nelson (2010) offer some advice for future developments:

> ... the pyramid could have been connected to a café which might be interested in using the glasshouse for cultivation of small foods for clients. This is not an option for Kolding, because the pyramid sits within the block with no street front and also no areas that could be turned into a kitchen and dining room.
>
> *(IBID)*

> Cardiff University (UK) offers 'The Kolding Pyramid' as a case study in urban ecology, to create more sustainable cities.[4] The Kolding Pyramid can be seen as a counternarrative to what the Cardiff case study describes as the usual narrative of "top-down, large scale integrated project with emphasis on documentation."The unknown authors give their evaluation of the results, based on an official evaluation in 1997: "All the sewage from the block has been cleaned and infiltrated. The block produced approximately 11000 m3 of sewage per year. The sewage is leaned sufficiently to satisfy the rather strict Danish regulation – except for phosphorus. Approximately 40000 plants have been produced per year ... The quality of the air was corresponding to the quality in a clean room. The energy used for heating was 237 MWh per year ... An important lesson learnt is about the conflicts between visions of sustainability and health hazards. The original vision was that the Pyramid would be used [by] the local residents for growing their own vegetables. Health authorities, however, would only let people with an exam in sewage handling enter the Pyramid. Furthermore, they would not let any kind of human food grow there due to the risk of epidemics (even though the sewage is sterilized before it enters the Pyramid). ... One general lesson learnt is that the persons responsible for the Pyramid have to be very well trained and it takes time before they have sufficient experience in running the facility. ... The residents have accepted the project, but it has proved very difficult to engage them fully in this basically top-down riven project ... it seems like conditions further sought in Europe could be more favorable for the Pyramid project, wth less need for artificial light and heating in wintertime."
>
> *(IBID, Cardiff Case Study)*

Forestructuring – since the construction of the pyramid in 1995 there have been several advances in small-scale anerobic digestion systems. According to Beatley (2012: 251), since the health department has forbidden the growing of vegetables or fish for human consumption, "it may take some confincing of helath officals before it is allows." However, as Nelson (2010 reports "inhabitants have completely lost interest in the pyramid." For a while the four levels of the pyramid were greenhouse space for inhabitants, and after their interest faded, only one hobbyist gardener (at no cost) tended some greenhouse beds. "Interestingly, the Bioworks pyramid has actually one tenant: a commercial plant grower, who pays rent for the space to the city. While there are fish in the lowest level of the structure, they are currently not harvested" (Beatley, 2000: 251) When I visited in August 2018, there were no fish that I could see, and no evidence of either the hobbyists or the commercial plan growers. Today, the greenhouse beds sit empty. Land next to the Pyramid set aside for urban agriculture, sits unused.

> Seen beside the pyramid, where a piece of land was set aside for urban agriculture and now sits unused. At the base of the pyramid, there are three water ponds in a cascade which hosted tilapia fish when it was constructed, but now only support algae.
>
> *(Nelson, 2010: 90)*

> According to the caretaker, the problem is three-fold: firstly, the community has changed from owners to renters, and the renters have no long-term invested interest in utilizing the space provided; second, no professional cultivator can use the greenhouse because it is too small with too many stairs; third, the pyramid is a repetition of service, because almost every apartment is equipped with its own small, glass-enclosured patio in which small plants can also be grown with more convenience. So, until a renaissance, the pyramid will remain sadly under-utilized.
>
> *(Nelson, 2010: 90–1)*

Fourth antenarrative inquiry: Deleuzian rhizomatics

Gilles Deleuze and Felix Guattari (1987) develop rhizomatics, as an alternative to dialectics. While Heidegger sets out to retheorize Hegelian dialectics, for Deleuzians some other kind of ontological process is going on. Rhizomatics is neither dialectical nor dialogical. It is something else (see Boje, 2018a) for differences between these relational process ontologies. Here I want to limit the presentation to how rhizomatics can be used as antenarrative inquiry into the situation of the Kolding Bioworks Pyramid. Rhizomatics, for me, is constitutive of both the living stories of residents and the institutional narratives about the project. There is from the inception, the tearing down of two buildings, and recycling the materials to construct two 'new' buildings, a reterritorialization. And it continues with the gifting of the Bioworks Pyramid to the residents. Many are renters, and only a few are owners (some 30 of the 130–150). The Technology World begins to deterritorialize, and this is helped along by prohibitions by the government departments, to grow food, or to even be able to enter the Pyramid, without getting certified. As the technology systems, one by one, go offline, the aquaponics cannot handle the loan (a hypothesis at this point, in need of more fieldwork to fully answer the question). The promised dissemination to other Denmark cities, the replication of the Kolding Bioworks Pyramid, has not yet happened. But, with the arrival of Peak Oil, Peak Water, and Peak Food (soon to arrive), this could still reterritorialize across Denmark. As noted, the winter months of Denmark are too cold for the current glass pyramid design, more suitable to southern climates. Climate change could actually help. More likely the kind of Earthship Double Greenhouse I am building in New Mexico (and others already built in Taos, New Mexico) could work better than a single layer of glass. Thermal mass is what keeps the greenhouse able to retain heat, and a double greenhouse has more thermal mass capacity to allow year-round aquaponics.

Fifth antenarrative inquiry: sociomaterial actor routines and material actants

The Kolding Bioworks Pyramid is an actant, with many biotic species as actors, and they all interact with the human species, in government, in science, university, and in residence. Here the inquiry turns to the relation of humanistic to posthumanistic concerns. The Sixth Extinction is slated to be the most devastating extinction to the biodiversity of the planet that has ever been (Boje, *in press*). A 2 degree centigrade rise in world temperature will spell the end of most of the mammal species, and many plant species. 'Climate change' is something not being denied by politicians, but not so in the US. While the solutions to climate change are self-evident (develop a post-Carboniferous Capitalism), the way to achieve this new capitalism is not forthcoming. Reasons vary, but among them is the sunk cost of carbon capital, in the infrastructure investments, of business-as-usual, and its legitimating narratives (Boje, *in press*). There are many sociomaterialism theories. For this inquiry, what works for me, is the ecologies of routines (Sele & Grand, 2016). Actants are shaping the human routines. If Kolding Bioworks Pyramid is an actant it is mediating and intermediating by its technological systems, the human routines of not only residents of Kolding officials, and Danish government departments. A local landscape company checks in on the pumps, takes readings once a year. Someone is employed to tend to the grounds, keep checking on the Pyramid week-to-week. This is a kind of forecaring, but its primarily custodial. It takes a village to raise a child, and this innovative Pyramid is a child that is in search of a village, to care for its future. The deeper ecologies of routines, the actant technology of aquaponics, for example, have many generative effects in the routine interactions between the Pyramid and the residents. For Baradians, it's never interaction, but always the sociomaterialism of intra-activity of materiality *with* discourse. It takes human and many nonhuman actors and lots of actants to engage the Pyramid in routine performances. The residents could not adapt their existing routine performances as renters and owners to the routines demanded by the Pyramid. New routines emerged, such as shutting down the aquaponics, not doing renovations to the technologies that would resolve basic problems, such as cloudy water after rain, and the odor from the outdoor filtration ponds. The sociomaterialism literature on ecologies of routines provides insights into the micro-activities that drive the dynamic evolution of Kolding Bioworks Pyramid. It points us to inquiry into the decomposing, the activities into routines and their evolvement over time, to develop antenarratives of new developments to the relations of residents and governments with nature. There are repetitive actions, as bundles of routines evolve and change. Many of the human routines are called forth by that grand actant, the Kolding Bioworks Pyramid. In short, there is a year-by-year, ongoing negotiation process between human actors, biotic actors, and the thing-actant-Pyramid, itself. It is the material arrangement of the Pyramid, its actants that intra-act with the discourse of humans (who are themselves embodied material beings, as well as discourse interlocutors). In short, we can inquire antenarratively, into the actor-actant network of connecting routines, intermediators and mediators that transform, translate, and shape meaning (Sele & Grand, 2016: 724).

Sixth antenarrative inquiry: The United Nations sustainable development goals

UN goal 6 is to ensure availability and sustainable management of water and sanitation for all.[5] In my last semester at New Mexico State University, as I transition to emeritus, and take on a less than full time position at Aalborg University, I am very focused on all 17 UN sustainable development goals (UN SDGs). Water Capitalism is taking over from Fossil Capitalism (see Boje, 2018b). Water is 75% of the earth's surface, but only 2.5% is fresh drinkable water. Where I live, the Rio Grande River is in the death throes of climate change. It does not run all year, and so much of it is diverted to agriculture and city life, not much is left to keep fish and wild plant life alive. Snowpacks in Colorado are not sufficient to sustain our river. The silvery minnow and other species are only 5% their historic level. Since water is not running like it once did in the Rio Grande, groundwater is being pumped at ever increasing rates out of the aquifers. Aquifer water is precious, since 39% of it is fresh and drinkable, yet so rare that it is only 1.69% of all water on the planet. Water affects all 17 UN SDGs, but I will not go down that path. Our bodies are 55% to 75% water, more so when we are young than when we are old. Some part of us, like the lungs are 83% water, the skin only 64% water, and our blood a mere 20%. In New Mexico, the water rights are more expensive than the land value, and soon it will be so everywhere, because beneath the surface, often there are aquifers.

Water treatment has been a demonstration project in constructing the Kolding Bioworks Pyramid, but soon the project may be in high demand. Perhaps, the City of Kolding can make it a UN SDG project. All this concern about water, has put me in the mood, to repair our own rainwater barrels, and embark on building a water catchment system, that feeds the fish and plants in the Earthship double greenhouse, which I am constructing day-by-day. It is not yet, for the survival of my family, rather it's a way to keep connecting my human routines to nature, to give a participatory role to my lifestyle. There needs to be pioneering projects, or the mainstream will be left high, dry, and thirsty.

Discussion and conclusion

The six antenarrative inquiries I chose to study about the Kolding Bioworks Pyramid can be helpful when the project is taken out of mothballs, and put back on line. If I was a resident of Kolding, I would move there in a flash, take the wastewater treatment courses seriously, and get my official certification. There is nothing I would rather do, than enter that Pyramid. I believe it is possible for the City of Kolding and the Danish government as a whole, to revitalize the project.

Can there be a Kolding Bioworks Pyramid renaissance? My answer is a resounding 'yes.' We have the technology, and only need the will to proceed. To me, it's a question of transforming special answerability of the spectator into a moral answerability of the enthusiast. It will take a new community of residents to raise the Kolding Pyramid, to make it a generative routine, which yields results in the ecologies of routines we will need to survive Sixth Extinction.

Operational efficiency could be improved by changing the spatial position of the grow tanks to reduce the number of pumps (and electricity) used. There are improvements to blackwater treatment since 1995 that can address the odor problem. Instead of an open system, a closed system blackwater treatment system is common practice in New Mexico, for example. The rainwater from the building roofs can go through a first-flush pre-collection of the first 200 gallons or so, the dust can be separated from the usable water for greywater purposes.

This chapter makes several contributions to the theme of counternarratives. In particular, I have argued that there are dialectical aspects to narrative-counternarrative, as well as between various counternarratives. Second, there are not just dialectical, but dialogical and rhizomatic kinds of interplay between the various narratives and counternarratives, as well as the stories, and counterstories. Third, and for me, most important, I have attempted to show that antenarrative processes, all six of them, are pre-constitutive of narratives and counter-narratives, as well as living stories and counter-stories (the difference is between WWOK narratives & IWOK living stories). Finally, water is alive, in IWOK, a lining and spiritual being, and one that our human lives depend upon. The Kolding Bioworks Pyramid is important to our future. As water becomes more scarce than it is today, and becomes the commodity of choice of Water Capitalism, it will be of great necessity to do more demonstration projects of the sort that Kolding pioneered so boldly.

Notes

1 Cardiff cases of sustainability, accessed Aug 26 2018 at www.cardiff.ac.uk/archi/research/cost8/case/watersewerage/kolding.html
2 Water, water everywhere: sustainable redevelopment in Kolding, Denmark by Tania Wegwitz, October 4, 2015, She originally wrote story for *Momentum Magazine in 2003,* accessed Aug 29 2018 at www.connectdots.ca/community/kolding-redevelopment/
3 Insideflows.com Kolding Bioworks Pyramid, by Pollyane Brasilino, with photo and schematic, accessed Nov 2 2018 at www.insideflows.org/project/kolding-bioworks/ The article includes a summary of the Nels Nelson report on three case sites in Northern Europe, accessed Nov 2 2018 at www.nelsonelson.com/sustainable_implant_erasmusveld.pdf
4 Cardiff University Kolding Pyramid Case Stuy, accessed Nov 2 2018 at www.cardiff.ac.uk/archi/research/cost8/case/watersewerage/kolding.html
5 UN Sustainable Development Goal 6, accessed Nov 2 2018 at https://sustainabledevelopment.un.org/sdg6

References

Bakhtin, M. M. (1981). *The Dialogical Imagination: Four Essays*. M. Holquist (Ed.), trans. C. Emerson and M. Holquist. Austin, TX: University of Texas Press.

Bakhtin, M. M. (1990). *Art and Answerability: Early Philosophical Essays* (Vol. 9). Foreword by M. Holquist, and trans. V. Liapunov. Austin, TX: University of Texas Press.

Bakhtin, M. M. (1993). *Toward a Philosophy of the Act.* Written as unpublished notebooks written between 1919–1921, first published in the USSR in 1986 with the title K *filosofii postupka*; 1993 English, trans. V. Liapunov; V. Liapunov & M. Holquist (Eds.). Austin, TX: University of Texas Press.

Beatley, T. (2000). *Green Urbanism: Learning From European Cities.* Island Press.

Beatley, T. (2012). *Green urbanism: Learning from European cities.* Washington D.C.: Island Press.

Benjamin, W. (2016). *One-way street.* Traslated by Edmund Jephcott, Edited and intro by Michael W. Jennings, preface by Greil Marcus. Cambridge, Massachuetts: Harvard University Press.

Boje, D. M. (2008). *Storytelling organizations.* Thousand Oaks, CA: Sage.

Boje, D. M. (2018a). *Organizational Research: Storytelling in Action.* London/NY: Routledge.

Boje, D. M. (2018b). True storytelling of New Mexico Water. Proceedings paper for the 8th annual Quantum Storytelling Conference, Las Cruces New Mexico, December 14–16, 2018. Accessed Nov. 2, 2018 at https://davidboje.com/quantum

Boje, D. M. (2019). Storytelling in the global age: There is no Planet B. Singapore: *World Scientific Books.*

Deleuze, G. & Guattari, F. (1987). *A Thousand Plateaus: Capitalism and Schizophrenia.* Foreword and trans. Brian Massumi. Minneapolis: University of Minnesota Press.

Heidegger, M. (1923/1988/1999). *Ontology – The Hermeneutics of Facticity.* Trans. J. van Buren. Lecture given 1923/German publication 1988/ English publication 1999. Bloomington & Indianapolis: Indiana University Press. Accessed https://docs.google.com/file/d/0BylvcBG7_xG_bzVkQUxSbnk1ODg/edit

Heidegger, M. (1927/1962). *Being and Time.* Trans. J. Macquarrie & E. Robinson. NY: Harper Row. 1927 in German publication, 1962 English translation.

Heidegger, M. (1977). *The Question Concerning Technology.* Trans. W. Lovitt. NY: Harper and Row. Also accessed online www.psyp.org/question_concerning_technology.pdf

Malm, A. (2016). *Fossil Capital: The Rise of Steam-Power and the Roots of Global Warming.* London/NY: Verso.

Mumford, L. (1934). Technics and Civilization. Accessed Oct 31 2018 at *https://monoskop.org/images/f/fa/Mumford_Lewis_Technics_and_Civilization.pdf*

Mumford, L. (1961). *The City in History: its Origins, its Transformations, and its Prospects.* NY: Houghton Mifflin Harcourt.

Nelson, N. (2010). Sustianable investigation into an implant in the erasmusveld neighborhood. The Hague. Masters Thesis, Rotterdam, the Netherlands, accessed Nov. 2, 2018 at www.nelsonelson.com/sustainable_implant_erasmusveld.pdf

Newman, P. & Jennings, I. (2012). *Cities as Sustainable Ecosystems: Principles and Practices.* Washington D.C.: Island Press.

Sele, K.; Grand, S. (2016). Unpacking the dynamics of ecologies of routines: Mediators and their generative effects in routine interactions. *Organization Science, 27*(3), 722–738.

Svane, M., & Boje, D. (2014). Merger strategy, cross-cultural involvement and polyphony. Between Cultures and Paradigms, IACCM 2014, University of Warwick, UK. Conference Proceeding. To be published in: *European Journal of Cross-Cultural Competence and Management.*

Svane, M. S., & Boje, D. M. (2015). Tamara land fractal change management: in between managerialist narrative and polyphonic living stories. In Standing Conference for Management and Organizational Inquiry (Sc'Moi). http://vbn.aau.dk/files/225730097/Tamara_Land_Fractal_Change_Management_Las_Vegas_Paper.pdf

Svane, M., Boje, D. & Gergerich, E. M. (2015). Counternarrative and antenarrative inquiry in two cross-cultural contexts. Accepted for publication in Special Issue on counternarrative, European Journal of Cross-Cultural Competence.

Svane, M., & Gergerich, E. M. (2017). Fractal change management and counter-narrative in cross-cultural change. Pp. 129–154 in Frandsen, S.; Kuhn, T.; Wolff Lundholt, M. (Eds). *Counter-Narratives and Organization.* NY: Routledge.

5

Reconsidering counter-narratives

Michael Bamberg and Zachary Wipff

Introduction

In this chapter, we shall review and follow up on the history of analytic work with master and counter-narratives through the narrative practice approach, beginning about 15 years ago (Bamberg & Andrews, 2004). Initial work with these constructs through the methodological lens of narrative practices tried to disentangle two potentially misleading assumptions that had surfaced throughout many contributions discussing counter-narratives: (1) that 'counter' and 'master' were two clearly definable and opposed territories, and (2) 'master' typically as coinciding with 'collective' and 'culturally-shared', in contrast to 'counter' as voiced by few – typically in the form of *personal* (and oppressed) narratives of experience. In contrast, it was argued (Bamberg, 2004, pp. 353 and 368f.) that countering and doing 'being complicit' (both as discursive activities) go hand-in-hand and emerge in co-presence; and that the role of the individual and personal as the center for suffering and agency for self-reflection (and change) had largely been overestimated.

In the years since, a number of important contributions have presented a more complex landscape within which counter-narratives play an important role. To name just two – and we will follow up on them – the first consisting of Frandsen, Kuhn and Lundholt (2017), who expanded and enriched the analysis of counter-narratives in personal storytelling by turning our attention to the public domain of organizational identity formation. They also deserve credit for complexifying the original and somewhat naïve strict opposition of counter-narratives to dominant, hegemonic, or master-narratives (Frandsen, Lundholt & Kuhn, 2017; Kuhn, 2017). A second major turn was facilitated by discussions around what would empirically qualify as 'narrative'; and here it was particularly Georgakopoulou's (2007) continuous promotion of the 'small story approach' which later turned into a more integrative approach under the header of 'narrative practices' (cf. Bamberg 2020; Georgakopoulou, 2015). The importance of these moves cannot be underestimated, since they signify a shift from the analysis of narratives as texts or personal memories (i.e., as parts of people's or organizations' interior resources) to empirically analyzable discursive activities taking place in interactive activities.

In the following, we start with a brief presentation of advances made with the development of an integrated approach to the analysis of narratives termed 'narrative practices'. This will give opportunity to qualify what narratives (better: storytelling practices) consist of, where and how to locate them empirically, and how to approach them analytically. To clarify: this implies shifting the unit of analysis from people's interiorities, where they are said to HAVE memories, and where stories are assumed to guide peoples' lives, to the ethnographic study of the contexts in which people share stories in interaction. Thereafter, we will re-address the relationship between master/hegemonic and counter-narratives and attempt to clarify how alternative narratives fit into the larger picture.

Narrative practices

Recent events unveiled more clearly the promise and confusion that co-exist when it comes to how widespread, but simultaneously how diverse, we make use of the term 'narrative'. For instance, when the *Social and Behavioral Sciences for National Security* summoned leading US-scholars in 2018 "to explore featured state-of-the-art narrative studies to examine cutting-edge questions relevant to national security and intelligence analysis" (National Academies of Sciences, Medicine and Engineering, 2018), we found little agreement as to what the term narrative meant, and which approach ultimately would have more potential regarding making decisions for national security and foreign affair purposes. Although we all seemed to be in some sort of agreement that well-established cultural or communal storylines have a certain organizing power for individuals' and organizational experience and decision making, what exactly would count as narrative or story, but even more so, what formed our 'unit of analysis' for analytical purposes, seemed to remain up for grabs (National Academy of Sciences, Medicine and Engineering, 2018). While some of us seem to trust that the study of narratives may grant access to the interiority of subjective experience and memory (e.g. Pennebaker, 2011), especially to so-called "autobiographical memories" (Smorti, 2011), others confine the study of narratives to texts – usually in the form of transcripts (e.g. Franzosi, 2010). Another distinction that crisscrosses the domain of narrative studies is the investigation of unfolding or developing stories, such as in breaking news or new revelations that require adjustment to existing, larger sense-making units (Georgakopoulou, 2013). And last, but definitely not least, there is the use of the term 'narrative' for pre-existing and often dominant sense-making and framing strategies, as for instance national narratives positioning 'others' as foreigners or immigrants. In one storyline they may be positioned as an enrichment to '*our* nation-state', and as such are constructed as important characters in a continuing line with our (US-)forefathers; in another storyline they are positioned as a threat to national security that interrupts temporal continuity and threatens well-being.

It is our aim with this chapter to sort through some of the existing ambiguities and forge a path that connects the study of personal and organizational/institutional narrative – as well as what can be considered counter and master-narratives – and across existing disciplines and contrasting methodologies. To do this effectively within the boundaries of this chapter, we start with two points of divergence from traditional narrative theorizing and their methodologies, and specify from where we enter. The first challenges the assumption that individual selves (people) and social systems or organizations (such as institutions or nation states) HAVE a story, and that this story can be explored through interviews. The second challenges the study of narratives as texts or products – where we will make the argument to study narrative as process. Let us briefly outline our line of argument that will be clarified and made relevant throughout the rest of this chapter.

First, the approach presented in this chapter, labelled 'the narrative practice approach' (laid out in detail in Bamberg, 2020), works from the assumption that the same methodology applies to work with stories of individual storytellers as to stories of organizations. In both cases, we study the 'small' stories of people who share accounts of events that happened, are unfolding and about to happen, or as imagined for distant futures. These stories are communicatively situated and shared for a (relational/social) purpose vis-à-vis others and typically occur in mundane, everyday encounters. In addition, these stories are shared in a vis-à-vis relationship to culturally shared background assumptions. And in terms of why they are called 'stories', we principally follow traditional formal/structural assumptions that storied accounts create characters in a there-and-then of a story-world, woven into a temporal beginning, middle, and ending. However, we additionally include in our analysis stories that are alluded to, are not well-formed, or incomplete. And, in contrast to theories that consider narratives or stories as representations of reality, we claim that storytelling always incorporates fictional elements into story-making processes; the question only becomes: to what degree. Finally, we include all kinds of stories – thereby countering the traditional privilege of story-analytic approaches to self-reflective stories, in which tellers thematize themselves as the topic of reflection (cf. Bamberg & Wipff, in press). What already shines through the approach we are advocating is an emphasis on storytelling as an interactive activity in contrast to stories or narratives as textual products (Georgakopoulou, 2007, 2015). Thus, neither individual selves nor social systems or organizations are said to HAVE a story that can be studied independently from actual storytelling interactions. Consequently, the analysis of storytelling activities cannot be carried out independently from their local context, revealing where, how, and why stories are told. Thus, individuals and organizations cannot be reduced to 'walking stories', and they also are more than the stories *they* tell or the stories that are told about them.

Our second point of divergence considers narrative practices as situated processes. Traditional approaches typically consider stories as representations of (subjective) experience or memories, for which psychologists developed the term 'autobiographical memories', hoping that particular elicitation techniques[1] can 'dig into' the interiority of story-tellers and 'unearth' the narratives they HAVE – thereby gaining access to their deep-seated convictions, beliefs, and values (cf. Smorti, 2011). Interestingly, these traditional approaches simultaneously work with the assumption that these deep-seated convictions and values are the motivating forces for what people say and do; and as such, people's engagement in storytelling activities are at best performative 'expressions' of their interiority – clouded and impaired by the interactive situation and the actual language used. In stark contrast, our narrative practice approach urges us to investigate storytelling processes, i.e., to interrogate the contextual embeddedness as the analytic starting point for how meaning and identity are regularly constituted and continually under construction. Methodologically, this approach favors culturally sensitive, ethnographic perspectives – including the analysis of microgenetic, moment-by-moment navigations of the processes in which narrative practices are being conducted and 'small stories' emerge.

Counter narratives – a preliminary definition

A counter narrative has the illocutionary force to *counter*; i.e., in one or another way, it not only contrasts with, but opposes, another narrative – just as counterstatements or counterintelligence counter other statements or another intelligence. As put lucidly in a recent opinion piece by David McCraw, the deputy counsel of the NYT: when coming to the defense for doctors who botched surgeries, or greedy industrialists, he argues,

> I try to look for the counter-narrative that they could (and their lawyers will) build from what supposedly is the same set of facts. It's a counterintuitive form of reading. It's looking for the innocent explanation or the possibility that what appears to all the rest of the world to be nefarious may in fact just be a mistake made in good faith.
>
> *(McCraw, 2019)*

In other words, a counter-narrative starts as a counter-piece, *a vis-à-vis*, to which it can be viewed as a reaction – usually, but not necessarily, crafted to come across as intended – and bearing some similarity by seemingly following the same line of factual statements, though most likely constructing events and happenings differently in terms of their relevance to the unfolding storyline. And, it also has a connotation of being somewhat counter-intuitive, i.e., outside of what we typically and commonsensically would expect. As such, for a text or stretch of talk to count as counter-narrative it must relate to other texts, inviting an analytic perspective that draws on intertextual knowledge. To reiterate, we view the speaker/author of the narrative as intentionally drawing on and positioning themselves vis-à-vis another storyline; or, we as readers or recipients, may bring this perspective to a text as part of our interpretive intertextual repertoire (Kristeva, 1980), i.e., our collective personal knowledge of storylines through which we make sense.

It is these two strands of what intuitively seems to define counter-narratives, (a) in terms of their counter-relationship to other narratives, and (b) in their potential break-away from expectations, that we will further explore, with the aim of explicating the worthiness of counter-narratives as strategic devices in the business of grappling with frame-breaking, diverging from established assumptions, and their potential for facilitating change. To do so, we also may need to consider in more detail how counter-narratives differ from (and overlap with) often called alternative, or contesting narratives. However, before settling deeper into these matters, we see the need to clarify why and how the insistence on analyzing counter-narratives as *narratives* still carries with it certain benefits – in contrast to dealing with the kind of illocutionary force of *countering* as *claims* or *arguments*, or simply as 'contrasting rhetorical strategies'. In a second step, we would like to clarify how positioning counter-narratives vis-à-vis master or dominant narratives can be usefully built into the overarching aim of giving counter-narratives and their analysis a special and relevant place in social theorizing about change and innovation. After having worked through these two aspects of the function of counter-narratives, we will discuss how competing terms such as alternative and contesting narratives differ from counter-narratives and underscore the potential of the latter for the study of power relations and social change.

Frames, metaphor, claims-making, stance-taking, positioning, and membership categorization vis-à-vis narrative practices

There is no space here to launch into an elaborate differentiation between narrative and other discourse modes and rhetorical devices that are being employed in analytic approaches to cultural critique and change. However, a few of them deserve mention – even if only to see how they differ from narrative: first, *claims-making* (cf. Spector & Kitsuse, 1977) and *frame analysis* (going back to Goffman, 1974; elaborated by Reese, Gandy & Grant, 2001) as two quite influential traditions that have successfully grappled with the identification and analysis of social problems and political protest. *Metaphor analysis*, following the groundbreaking book by Lakoff and Johnson (1980) and *stance-taking* (cf. Englebretson, 2007) similarly have evolved as valuable analytic tools to investigate how speakers evaluate and navigate their take on what to consider factual as well as the social relationships that apparently are 'in-the-works'. A rich and diverse body of work under the header of *argumentation theory* also fits the ticket under consideration. This discourse mode differs from narrative in that arguments are uniquely constituted by constellations of propositions (Eemeren, Grootendorst, & Snoeck, 1996, p. 4), typically with a personal intent to justify or refute a statement, fact, or desire (for a more detailed comparison of narrative and argumentation, see Parret, 1987). Over the last decades *membership categorization* (Baker, 1997; Sacks, 1972) as well as *positioning theory* and *positioning analysis* (Bamberg, 2003; Davies & Harré, 1990) have made considerable advances in how to approach discursive sense-making in personal, institutional, and organizational settings. However, *narrative* as a rhetorical discourse mode – in contrast to argumentation, – and also in contrast to the aforementioned rhetorical devices such as framing, metaphor, stance-taking, and positioning differs as a sense-making mode due to its unique and inbuilt characteristic of temporality. Let us sketch out how narrative analysis has advanced over the last two decades and moved into a place from where it can more pointedly illuminate what counter-narratives are and how they function.

A number of reviewers (cf. Herman, 2007; Hyvärinen, 2007; Klapproth, 2006; Laverge, 2007) of previous discussions on counter-narratives (Bamberg & Andrews, 2004), have pointed out a common thread that addressed the under-determination of what was meant by the term 'narrative'. As put by David Herman, the distinction between "TELLING a story" and "LIVING a story", i.e., instances of actual stories told (and analyzed) and an appeal to a more or less hyperextended sense of the term narrative to any instance of sense-making, had been inadvertently blurred (Herman, 2007, p. 279). Since the distinction between 'living stories' and 'telling stories' over the last decade has been discussed and debated extensively, especially under the header of 'Big' versus 'Small Stories', we will confine ourselves to a brief summary of the repercussions of this debate for why and how acts of storytelling ('narrative practices') are a constructive move for the analysis of counter-narratives and how positioning analysis has been fruitfully incorporated into this theoretical approach.

As argued elsewhere (Bamberg, 2006, 2020), an aspiration that inspired a good deal of original narrative research – also called Big Story research – was based on (a) an analogy of life and narrative (both as having a beginning, middle, and ending), and (b) the assumption that a life lived – or at least striven for – can be captured in the form of a (biographical) life story. This short-circuit between people (or institutions) as *having* a story (their <autobiographical> memory) and *living* this story, i.e., the equation of life and narrative, has become widely criticized (cf. Bamberg & Demuth, 2016; Eakin, 2006; Sartwell, 2000; Strawson, 2004 – to name a few). The more radical form of criticism (e.g. Sartwell, 2000; Strawson, 2004) questions the general argument that life is structured like and following a narrative. A weaker criticism is open to the analogy between pre-existing and socially-shared storylines and their impact on lives lived (cf. Bamberg, 2020), but disagrees with the equation of *one* life as having or resulting in *one* story – and vice versa. It is this second line of argument that we will follow up below and further unpack. At this point, however, it should be recalled that approaching narratives empirically as *narrative practices*, i.e., as stories being told in everyday practices, and in addition, not privileging stories about the biographic self, does not start from the premise of an assumed contiguity between life and narrative, but approaches identity and sense-of-self from a radically different angle.

Positioning vis-à-vis: the interactional grounding of narrative practices

To start with, narrating a story requires a great deal of interactive business: shifting into narrating is typically accompanied by a discursive bid to hold the floor for an extended turn; and toward the end of telling the story, cuing the interlocutors that it is their turn to respond. Approaching narrative/story from this kind of narrative practice angle prioritizes the interactive relational business that narratives accomplish. The assumption here is that participants in communities of practice share a cultural understanding of narrating and stories – though not necessarily in the form of technical or theoretical second order concepts, but due to continuous bodily and verbal practices in their social interactions – in mundane and everyday activities (Georgkopoulou, 2007; Heath, 1983). Thus, while the discursive functions of storytelling may be manifold, such as to entertain, showing regret, or to embellish an argument, the relational identity work of storytelling may best be condensed around the concept of positioning, and here in terms of three related positioning strategies.

Although the notion of positioning had originally not been designed as a tool for the analysis of narrating as an interactive activity, it nevertheless was meant to strategically employ the notion of plots and story lines. Davies and Harré (1990) had defined positioning as discursive practice "whereby selves are located in conversations as observably and intersubjectively coherent participants in jointly produced story lines" (Davies & Harré, 1990, p. 48). Thus, in conversations, in line with the intrinsic interactional forces of conversing, people position themselves in relation to one another in ways that traditionally had been defined as roles. More importantly, in doing so, people 'produce' one another (and themselves) situationally as 'social beings'. Although this approach explicitly addresses the analysis of language under the header of how people attend to one another in interactional settings, and although traditional narrative analysis suggests to address what stories are referentially 'about', i.e., the sequential order of events and their evaluations (cf. Labov & Waletzky, 1997), we suggested to apply the notion of positioning more productively to the analysis of storytelling to link and merge these two approaches. For this purpose, we considered the process of positioning to take place at three different levels that are formulated as three kinds of '*positioning-vis-à-vis*'.

First, in our daily practices, we mark ourselves off as different, similar or the same with respect to others. Integrating and differentiating a sense of who we are vis-à-vis others takes place in moment-by-moment navigations; and stories about self and others are good candidates to practice this from childhood onwards. A second identity component can be called 'agency'. And although it seems as if agency is something that exists a priori in the form of a human capacity, i.e., as if selves or organizations "*HAVE* an identity", we suggested to better theorize agency as a space in which we navigate two opposing directions of fit: one going from world-to-person, the other from person-to-world. While it is possible to view oneself as a passive recipient of external forces (typically natural/biological or social – such as earthquakes or climate on the one hand, and parents, teachers, or culture on the other), it also is possible to view the world as a product of the self. In this case selves or institutions position themselves as impacting forces and as actively changing or even producing a world. The navigation between agency and passivity becomes particularly relevant in presentations of selves and organizations as involved and responsible – as for claims to success and aggrandizement – versus denials of culpability in mishaps or wrongdoings. Again, storytelling about (past or future) actions are good candidates to borrow and practice navigations of this sort. Third, when relating past (or future) to present, we can either highlight our constancy, i.e., declare that we are the same person or organization we used to be; or we can present a sense of self as having undergone some gradual (continuous) or radical (discontinuous) change – resulting in a different, new persona or entity. The space for how to navigate the connection of our past (or future) selves with our sense of who we are for the here-and-now, is often seen as closely coupled to acquiring or developing (more) self-worth, or as deteriorating and becoming useless (Bamberg, 2011). While identity navigations between sameness and difference and between the two directions of fit of the person-to-world orientation do not require diachronic temporality as an essential prerequisite, navigations of constancy and change do require the correlation of two events in time – which some narrative inquirers take to be the minimal definition of story (cf. Labov & Waletzky, 1997). Thus, it appears that navigations of constancy and change make a good argument for the privileging of storytelling as an opportune space for identity practices.

Second, we attempt to address the question of how characters are positioned in relation to one another within unfolding stories. At this level, we attempt to analyze how characters within the (typically textual) story world are constructed as, for example, protagonists or antagonists, as perpetrators or victims, and the like. More concretely, this type of analytic lens aims at the linguistic and paralinguistic means that do the job of marking one of the textual characters as, for example, agent who is in control; while the action is inflicted upon other characters; or as an alternative, characterizing the central character as helplessly at the mercy of outside (quasi 'natural') forces – or as being rewarded by luck, fate, or personal qualities (such as bravery, nobility, or simply '*character*'). Simultaneously, we pay close attention to how characters are positioned in alignment or dis-alignment vis-à-vis others; and, last but not least, how characters are constructed as same or as changing over time. The analytic stance that governs this level of doing empirical analysis resembles and takes off from the work of literary interpretation or discursive text analysis along the lines originally suggested by Labov and Waletzky for narratives (1997).

In our final step, after having followed through on the question of how narrators position themselves vis-à-vis their audiences, and consequentially, how narrators position story characters vis-à-vis one another, we turn to the seemingly more interesting and relevant question, namely whether and how narrators actually may position themselves in relation to themselves (cf. De Fina, 2013). More succinctly, we address whether there is anything in narrative practices that we as analysts can interrogate in the form of claims or stances that go beyond the local conversational situation. In other words, we interrogate whether and how the linguistic devices and bodily maneuvers employed in narrative practices actually point to more than the contents of character positioning (i.e., what the narrative is 'about') and directives vis-à-vis the interlocutor in their interactional business. For level three positioning, we posit that in constructing the content *and* one's audience in terms of *role* participants, narrators transcend the question of: "How do I want to be understood by you, the audience?" and are offering a (local) answer to the question: "Who am I?" (cf. Bamberg, 2011). Simultaneously, however, we must caution that any attempted answer to this question is not one that necessarily holds across contexts, but rather is 'a project of limited range'. Nevertheless, we assume that these repeated and refined navigation projects rub off – producing and transmitting a sense of how to engage efficiently and productively in sense-making processes that endure and my turn into habits – and as such may contribute to a sense of self as perpetual.

Master-narratives, dominant discourses, '*the background*' – specifying how '*counter-narratives*' fit into them

In this section we'd like to follow up on our discussion of the positioning concept that was introduced earlier; and here especially on how narrators draw on master and dominant narratives – and thereby bring off a sense of self that may have enduring repercussions. This interactive navigation of positioning work has been characterized as feeding the analytic work at positioning levels one and two, and fusing it into the interpretive layer number three, where we analyze how speakers/narrators can be argued to draw on existing master or dominant narratives, and making them relevant to the here-and-now of their storytelling activities. De Fina (2013) has effectively given more body to this claim by showing in detail how this type of analysis can proceed. Here, we will only elaborate on her insights as far as we can extrapolate considerations that help us better understand the relationship between master and counter-narratives.

In a general sense, the use of the term master narrative, also called dominant or capital-D discourses, goes back to the assumption of the necessity for a horizon or background against which human sense-making becomes possible. While this horizon or background has been theorized as based on a *collective consciousness* (and a 'social mind' or 'intersubjectivity'), Searle (1995, 2010) uses the term *Background* to refer to something that is '*deeper*' and more general, such as the human ability to walk (upright), being equipped with a front (from where we visualize the world) and a back, and using our hands for *manual* labor. Searle juxtaposes this *deep* background with a collective/cultural background providing for what is assumed to be implicit to cultural routines and practices, and allowing for the subtleties of particular kinds of language games. We have tried to put the term master narrative to use by crediting this background, for lack of a better term, with providing 'agency constellations' for individual as well as institutional sense-making strategies (Bamberg, 2005, p. 287), thereby alluding to an affinity to what we also called *story lines* or *narrative threads* with an intrinsic temporality. We would like to add to Searle's two backgrounds a third set of assumptions that springs from interlocutors' bodily engagement in local, situated contexts through which meaning microgenetically is worked up and comes into existence. Relevant for the discussion here is that storytellers in narrative practices always are assumed to find themselves in vis-à-vis positions with regard to preexisting assumptions – where some of these assumptions may come in the form of storylines – providing temporal contours.

Now, we would like to suggest that the span from deep-seated assumptions that are deeply woven into our language habits to assumptions that are more easily reflective and changeable, forms a continuum. For instance, critical considerations of language habits that reflect gender or racial biases may lead to a change in language practices with more ease than assumptions that are much harder to reflect and reconsider – such as how our understanding of spatial dimensions is based off of our human up-right posture and forward-movement with a forward-oriented visual field, or how our understanding of temporal dimensions is based on our understanding of spatial relations.[2] It is against this backdrop that we now can more firmly argue that in small story, narrative practices, narrators by necessity are forced to navigate continuously their vis-à-vis positions in terms of what of 'the background' continues to go without saying, and what is standing out, special and unique to the circumstances of the here-and-now of the storytelling act. And although this can be said to hold for all speech, in storytelling activities this necessity of taking position promptly meets the additional necessity to take position and navigate the three identity dilemmas (agency/passivity, sameness/difference, constancy/change), and do this at three levels of positioning (level-of-interaction/level-of-character-construction/level-of-self-construction). Thus, engagement in narrative practices requires storytellers to engage in a continuous navigation between having faith and maintaining existing background assumptions on one hand, and testing or re-scripting – up to the possibility of challenging and openly countering – them on the other. Both being complicit and countering are at work in narrative practices simultaneously and in concert. And our analysis of them is able to lay open how they are at work and interact in micro-analytic discursive analyses we have published elsewhere (cf. Bamberg, 2011, 2020; Bamberg & Georgakopoulou, 2008; De Fina, 2013; Deppermann, 2013; Georgkopoulou, 2007).

Having clarified that storytellers inevitably position their alignments and divergence vis-à-vis assumptions that can be taken to filter into their narrative (and non-narrative) local and situated practices, and having shown that these positions are analytically accessible, we finally can turn and take issue with a particular interpretation and application of the term master narrative. Changing the focus from master-narratives as enabling individual local storytelling practices to their constraining and limiting powers, especially where they are said to be experienced as hegemonic and subjugating, i.e., as ruling out potential other (counter-) discourses, gives the term counter a special and more concerted force. It is this particular contrast that we originally dwelled on when arguing "that countering dominant and hegemonic narratives is the flip-side of being complicit" (Bamberg, 2004, p. 351). However, in the same breath, we put forth that neither master nor counter-narratives exist as uniform, monolithic or pure, but rather both are plagued by inconsistencies and contradictions, and both also require to be interrogated by the same methodical means as when the lens is not on the master-counter dichotomy. In particular, the above mentioned concluding chapter of the original volume (Bamberg, 2004), from where this chapter is an offspring, attempts to refute two common misconceptions, both seemingly permeating some of the volume's chapters back in 2004, namely first, that personal storytelling is the prime discourse type for countering hegemonic discourses (in the sense of subverting and undermining them); and second, that counter-narratives have a close to unconditioned tendency to be progressive. Admittedly, some first attempts to tackle and work with the master-counter dichotomy (Talbot, Bibace, Bokhour & Bamberg, 1996) may have given rise to these interpretations; and in this respect, Rasmussen's (2017) critique may have been on target. In addition, it is in this context that counter-narratives gain their special meaning as being relatable to other story-products, and also as presentations of unfolding temporal events and constructions of agency relationships that on occasion contrast with routinely practiced and expected ways of unfolding events.[3] And it is also in this context that the analysis of counter-narratives gains its attraction for opening potentially diverging gates into the analysis of power relationships and social change. Notwithstanding this incredible potential, our main bid for analyzing narratives as narrative practices, and thus as processes, and not solely as the product of narrative practices, remains central to our approach.

Returning to the preliminary definition of counter-narratives earlier in this chapter, we now feel better positioned to specify counter-narratives as uniquely distinguished by the aim to transform background assumptions, which typically support a master narrative. In other words, master and counter-narratives are identifiable through the foundational illocutionary criterion of distinction. Which narratives 'master' and which 'counter' remains situationally and contextually dependent, relative to the organization of social and political power in a given context. However, a variety of subcategories of narrative beyond master and counter can be delineated and may prove useful for analytic work with both master and counter-narratives. Unlike master and counter-narratives, parallel, alternative, and intersecting narratives are not identified through illocutionary intent and social context, but rather through content. To illustrate the differences between and utility of these constructs, we shall briefly touch on the alternative narratives of falling-in-love and arranged marriages and see how they differ from counter-narratives.

Marriage functions as a central organizing institution within societies globally (Penn, 2011). Despite this widespread commonality, differing cultures perform narrative practices like romance, marriage, and 'falling in love' according to distinct cultural storylines. In what have been traditionally termed modern societies ('Western' industrialized cultures), love is scripted as a dynamic, spontaneous, mysterious agency. Common phrases like 'falling in love' or being struck by 'love at first sight' imply that the undergoer does not act as a stoic, rational, in-control agent, but rather is deprived of agency by the affective potency of their romantic attraction. Illouz (2015) describes this narrational practice of love as an urgent moment, an overwhelming "epiphany" which consumes the thoughts and feelings of the undergoer. If there is any rational explanation as to how and why the mysterious potency of love strikes, it is typically attributed to static forms within the individual's conscious or unconscious psyche, including parental oedipal schema and cultural familiarity (Illouz, 2015).

The 'falling in love' storyline differs significantly from the prototypical storyline of arranged marriages. While the former describes the love experience as an unexpected, unpredictable, instantaneous cohesive force, the latter characterize it as a controllable, planned, and gradual process, which is intentionally fostered. Arranged marriages differ from 'falling in love' in that parents or matchmakers, rather than prospective partners themselves, take agency to select a spouse for them (Penn & Lambert, 2009). As of 2011, this practice forms the cultural background expectations for approximately half the world's population, particularly in nation states like China, India, Pakistan, Bangladesh, and Indonesia (Penn, 2011). However, what is more interesting, is the fact that here we seem to have the option to choose between two strategic forces giving way to each other: either, we can make the argument that 'falling in love' exists as a (master) storyline that 'informs' the day-to-day narrative practices about love and marriage between interlocutors – all the way down to 'feeling rules' that seemingly govern and regulate what happens emotionally between couples (cf. Hochschild, 1983). Or, and in contrast, it can be reasoned that those daily narrative practices have evolved into routinized embodied ways of feeling practices which may 'call-for' feeling rules and rationalizations of love and marriage – that then, subsequently, are communicated in the form of the particular culturally sequential script of 'falling in love'. Of course, the same arguments could be made for how we arrive at what is called 'arranged marriages' and how they are invested with affect and emotion.

While these diverse accounts of how love functions may in some ways appear as counter-narratives, as diametrically opposed, inimical accounts of the social world, we argue that they are not necessarily mutually antagonistic; and therefore are not typically weaponized as counter-narratives, but rather alternative (master) storylines. We anticipate that most readers will permit that many diverse formulations of love and marriage are ethically permissible, and that human beings are not somehow deficient or less legitimate for practicing one way of "doing love" versus another. The narratives of falling in love and arranged marriages, however, are only interpreted as 'counter' to one another to the extent that the interpreter(s), be it an individual, a collective, or a culture, insist there is only one singular, monolithic way of experiencing love and romance as a human being. Again, while we do not expect this as a common view among our readership, it is admittedly a viable position. Therefore, we posit that alternative narratives *can* be mobilized as counter-narratives, but only if they are taken up with the illocutionary force of undermining an intertextually related, contrary narrative.

Counter-narratives and the narrative practice approach: a complementary methodology

Having reviewed recent developments within fields of narrative inquiry, we advocate for the narrative practice approach (cf. Bamberg 2020; Georgakopoulou, 2015) as a particularly integrative methodology for empirical work with narratives, applicable to individuals as well as institutions, big stories, small stories, and even when no story is told at all (cf. Bamberg, 2011). Central to this approach is a shift in the unit of analysis from speakers' subjective interiorities, to the ethnographic interactive context through which stories emerge and are exchanged for social, relational purposes. In contrast to traditional approaches to narrative analysis, which utilize elicitation techniques attempting to 'uncover' speakers' personal narratives, the narrative practice approach considers the situated, mutual positioning of self and other as the analytic ground for work with narratives. Moreover, narrative form and content are highly contingent upon the particular space and time in which a story is told, which plays a significant role in forming narratives vis-à-vis contextual expectations and local dominant discourses (Bamberg & Georgakopoulou, 2008; De Fina, 2013). Therefore, as narratives vary according to circumstance, it is better to say that people *tell* stories, not *have* them, and certainly not *are* them – or in other words, people can never be reduced simply to narrative. Additionally, as narratives are often in a continual process of shifting, testing, and re-scripting, the narrative practice approach privileges narratives as dynamic, open-ended processes rather than textual products (Bamberg, De Fina & Schiffrin, 2011).

Similarly, the position of a narrative as 'master' or 'counter' is contingent upon the organization of social, cultural, and political power of an interactive location. Speakers must draw on background assumptions in order to make sense in storytelling activities (Searle, 1995, 2010). Counter-narratives are uniquely distinguished by an illocutionary force intended to counter background assumptions that support another alternative narrative. Additionally, considering counter-narratives as narratives distinguished by a characteristic temporal contour carries with it the benefit of revealing the temporally embedded process of how meaning is interactively negotiated in and through storytelling contexts.

Bearing in mind that local environments exert a significant formative force over speakers' storytelling activities, that master and counter-narratives are identified through situationally dependent illocutionary criteria, and that the narrative practice approach emphasizes speakers' situated embeddedness in the interactive storytelling context as the starting point for critical analysis, we argue that the narrative practice approach may occupy a privileged position for empirical investigations of master and counter-narratives. By investigating how storytellers mutually position and co-constitute one another by drawing on master-narratives and supporting background assumptions, we hope that this approach may illuminate the social process of how power is interactively negotiated, maintained, and countered as a practice catalyzing social change.

Notes

1 It is remarkable that the elicitation techniques are attempting to suspend everyday, mundane conversational conditions and generate a state of mind that enables participants to 'deep-reflect' – as in 'getting in touch with their authentic interiority'. Illouz (2008) has criticized these assumptions as upshots of 'the therapeutic ethos' that successfully penetrated and infested our modern discourse about self and identity ever since Freud and Jung gave their Clark University lectures in 1909.

2 For instance, in spite of *knowing* that the Earth rotates around the Sun, we still seem to *believe* that the sun *rises* in the morning and *sets* at night.

3 Hyvärinen (2017) pushes this point of 'running against audience expectations' one step further, and making it more central to storytelling activities. However, we wonder about its relevance for counter-narratives, because the mere fact of 'being counter' may suffice as the tellability criterion; no need to thematize additional plan-breaks.

References

Baker, C. D. (1997). Ticketing rules: Categorization and moral ordering in a school staff meeting. In: S. Hester, & P. Eglin (Eds.), *Culture in Action: Studies in Membership Categorization Analysis* (pp.77–98). Washington, DC: University Press of America.

Bamberg, M. (2003). Positioning with Davie Hogan - Stories, tellings, and identities. In C. Daiute & C. Lightfoot (Eds.), *Narrative Analysis: Studying the Development of Individuals in Society* (pp. 135–157). London: Sage.

Bamberg, M. (2004). Considering counter narratives. In: M. Bamberg & M. Andrews (Eds.), *Considering counter narratives: Narrating, resisting, making sense* (pp. 351-371). Amsterdam: John Benjamins.

Bamberg, M. (2005). Master narrative. In D. Herman, M. Jahn, & M.-L. Ryan (Eds.), *Routledge Encyclopedia of Narrative Theory* (pp. 287f.). London: Routledge.

Bamberg, M. (2006). Biography-narrative research, quo vadis? A critical review of 'big stories from the perspective of 'small stories.' In K. Milnes, C. Horrocks, N. Kelly, B. Roberts, and D. Robinson (Eds.), *Narrative, Memory and Knowledge: Representations, Aesthetics and Contexts.* Huddersfield: University of Huddersfield Press.

Bamberg, M. (2011). Narrative practice and identity navigation. In J. A. Holstein & J. F. Gubrium (Eds.), *Varieties of Narrative Analysis* (pp. 99–124). London: Sage Publications.

Bamberg, M. (2020). "Narrative analysis" an integrative approach – Small stories and narrative practices. In: M. Järvinen & N. Mik-Meyer (Eds.), *Qualitative Analysis – Eight Traditions.* London, Delhi, New York: Sage.

Bamberg, M., & Andrews, M. (Eds.) (2004). *Considering Counter-Narratives: Narrating, Resisting, Making Sense.* Amsterdam, Netherlands: John Benjamins.

Bamberg, M., De Fina, A., & Schiffrin, D. (2011). Discourse and identity construction. In S.J. Schwartz, K. Luyckx, & V.L. Vignoles (Eds.), *Handbook of Identity Theory and Research* (p. 177–199). Springer Science + Business Media.

Bamberg, M., & Demuth, C. (2016). Narrative inquiry: An interview with Michael Bamberg. *Europe's Journal of Psychology, 12*:1, 14–28. doi:10.5964/ejop.v12i1.1128

Bamberg, M., & Georgakopoulou, A. (2008). Small stories as a new perspective in narrative and identity analysis. *Text & Talk, 28*(3), 377–396.

Bamberg, M., & Wipff, Z. (in press). Counter narratives of crime and punishment. In M. Althoff, B. Dollinger & H. Schmidt (Eds.), *Conflicting Narratives of Crime and Punishment*. Palgrave MacMillan.

Bruner, J. (1991). The narrative construction of reality. *Critical Inquiry, 18*(1), 1–21.

Bruner, J. (2004). Life as narrative. *Social Research, 71*(3), 691–710.

Davies, B., & Harré, R. (1990). Positioning: The discursive production of selves. *Journal for the Theory of Social Behaviour, 20*, 1, 43–63.

De Fina, A. (2013). Positioning level 3: Connecting local identity display to macro social process. *Narrative Inquiry, 23*(1), 40–61.

Deppermann, A. (2013). Editorial: Positioning in narrative interaction. *Narrative Inquiry, 23*(1), 1–15.

Eakin, P. J. (2006). Narrative identity and narrative imperialism: A response to Galen Strawson and James Phelan. *Narrative, 14*(2), 180–187.

Eemeren, F.H., Grootendorst, R., & Snoeck, H.A.F. (1996). *Fundamentals of Argumentation Theory: A Handbook of Historical Backgrounds and Contemporary Developments*. Mahwah, NJ: L. Erlbaum.

Englebretson, R. (Ed.) (2007). *Stancetaking in Discourse: Subjectivity, Evaluation, Interaction*. Amsterdam: John Benjamins.

Frandsen, S., Kuhn, T., & Lundholt, M. W. (2017). *Counter Narratives and Organization*. New York, NY: Routledge.

Frandsen, S., Lundholt, M. W., & Kuhn, T. (2017). Introduction. In S. Frandsen, T. Kuhn & M. W. Lundholt (Eds.), *Counter Narratives and Organization* (pp. 1–13). New York, NY: Routledge.

Franzosi, R. (2010). *Quantitative Narrative Analysis*. Thousand Oaks, CA: Sage.

Georgkopoulou, A. (2007) *Small Stories, Interaction and Identities*. Amsterdam: John Benjamins.

Georgakopoulou, A. (2013). Breaking news as a travelling narrative genre. In M. Hatavcara, L-C. Hydén & M.Hyvärinen (Eds.). *The Travelling Concepts of Narrative* (pp. 201–224). Amsterdam: John Benjamins.

Georgakopoulou, A. (2015). Small stories research: Issues, methods, applications. In A. De Fina & A. Georgakopoulou (Eds.) *Handbook of Narrative Analysis* (pp. 255–271). Malden, MA: Wiley-Blackwell.

Goffman, E. (1974). *Frame Analysis: An Essay on the Organization of Experience*. Boston: Northeastern University Press.

Gumperz, J. J. (1982). *Discourse Strategies*. Cambridge, UK: Cambridge University Press.

Heath, S. B. (1983). *Ways with Words: Language, Life, and Work in Communities and Classrooms*. Cambridge: Cambridge University Press.

Herman, D. (2007). Review of: *Considering counter-narratives: Narrating, resisting, making sense. Language in Society*, 36, 2, 278–284.

Hochschild, A. R. (1983). *The Managed Heart. Commercialization of Human Feeling*. Berkeley: University of California Press.

Hyvärinen, M. (2007). Narrative contestations. Review essay of: Michael Bamberg & Molly Andrews (Eds.) (2004). Considering counter-narratives: Narrating, resisting, making sense. *Forum Qualitative Sozialforschung/Forum: Qualitative Social Research, 8*(3), Art. 34.

Hyvärinen, M. (2017). Expectations and experientiality: Jerome Bruner's 'canonicity and breach'. *Storyworlds, 9*, 1.

Illouz, E. (2008). *Saving the Modern Soul. Therapy, Emotions, and the Culture of Self-Help*. Berkeley: University of California Press, 2008. 294 pp. ISBN 978–0–52025373–5.

Illouz, E. (2015). *Why Love Hurts: A Sociological Explanation*. Cambridge: Polity Press.

Kristeva, J. (1980). *Desire in Language: A Semiotic Approach to Language and Art*. Trans. T. Gora, A. Jardine and L. S. Roudiez, ed. L. S. Roudiez. New York: Columbia University Press.

Kuhn, T. (2017). Communicatively constituting organizational unfolding through counter-narrative. In S. Frandsen, T. Kuhn & M. W. Lundholt (Eds.), *Counter Narratives and Organization* (pp. 17–41). New York, NY: Routledge.

Lakoff, G., & Johnson, M. (1980). *Metaphors We Live By*. Chicago: University of Chicago Press.

Laverge, Y. (2007). Review of: Considering counter-narratives: Narrating, resisting, making sense. *Language, 83*(4), 908–909.

Klapproth, D. (2006). Review of: Considering counter-narratives: Narrating, resisting, making sense. *Discourse & Society, 17*, 684–686.

Labov, W., & Waletzky, J. (1997). Narrative analysis: Oral versions of personal experience. *Journal of Narrative and Life History*, 7(1–4), 3–38.

McCraw, D. (2019). Think like a libel lawyer. *New York Times*, NY edition, March 10, p. SR1.

National Academies of Sciences, Medicine and Engineering (2018). Understanding narratives for national security purposes: A workshop. *Social and Behavioral Sciences for National Security*. A Decadel Survey. https://sites.nationalacademies.org/DBASSE/BBCSS/DBASSE_183503

Parret, H. (1987). Arfgumewntation and narrativity. In: F. van Eemeren, R. Grootendorst, A. Blair & C. Willard (Eds.), Argumentation: Across the lines of discipline (pp. 165–175). Providence, RI: Foris Publications.

Penn, R. (2011). Arranged marriages in Western Europe: Media representations and social reality. *Journal of Comparative Family Studies, 42*(5), 637–650.

Penn, R., & Lambert, P. (2009). *Children of International Migrants in Europe*. London: Palgrave.

Pennebaker, J. (2011). *The Secret Life of Pronouns. What Our Words Say About Us*. New York: Bloomsbury Publishing.

Rasmussen, R.K. (2017). Rethinking counter-narratives in studies of organizational texts and practices. S. Frandsen, T. Kuhn & M.W. Lundholt (Eds.). *Counter-narratives and Organization* (pp. 293–332). New York: Routledge.

Reese, S., Gandy, O., & Grant, A. (Eds.) (2001). *Framing Public Life*. Mahwah, NJ: Erlbaum.

Sacks, H. (1972). On the analyzability of stories by children. In J.J. Gumperz, & D. Hymes (Eds.), *Directions in Sociolinguistics: The Ethnography of Communication* (pp. 325–345). New York: Holt, Rinehart, and Winston.

Sartwell, C. (2000). *End of Story*. Albany, NY: State University of New York.

Searle, J. R. (1995). *The Construction of Social Reality*. London: Allen Lane.

Searle, J. R. (2010). *Making the Social World. The Structure of Human Civilization*. Oxford: Oxford University Press.

Smorti, A. (2011). Autobiographical memory and autobiographical narrative: What is the relationship? *Narrative Inquiry, 21*(2), 303–310. Doi: https://doi.org/10.1075/ni.21.2.08smo

Spector, M., & Kitsuse, J.I. (1977). *Constructing Social Problems*. Menlo Park: Cummings.

Strawson, G. (2004). Against narrativity. *Ratio, 17*, 428–452.

Talbot, J., Bibace, R., Bokhour, B., & Bamberg, M. (1996). Affirmation and resistance of dominant discourses: The rhetorical construction of pregnancy. *Journal of Narrative and Life History, 6*, 225–251.

Part II

Methodological considerations

6

Applying Foucault's tool-box to the analysis of counter-narratives

Antoinette Fage-Butler

Introduction

In this chapter, I present analytical approaches that derive from Foucauldian theory that can be used to analyze counter-narratives within the poststructuralist narrative tradition (Squire et al., 2013). My aim is to demonstrate the analytical power of a Foucauldian approach in relation to counter-narratives. I will also show how a Foucauldian approach to narratives and counter-narratives addresses a core division in the field of narrative research (Squire et al., 2013), namely, narrative as expressive of individual agency, on the one hand, and as influenced by and reflective of sociocultural contexts, on the other hand.

I start by characterizing the poststructuralist narrative tradition. I then embark on the main business of this chapter: in line with Foucault's exhortation that his theories be used as a "tool-box" (Foucault, 1994[1974 p. 1391]) and the fact that he welcomed further elaboration of his ideas in new settings (Foucault, 2001[1971]), I present a range of Foucauldian theories and show how two in particular are valuable for the analysis of counter-narratives. I do so by exemplifying their use on health narratives from online forums that relate to the potential advantages and disadvantages of hospital birth vs. homebirth settings. The online setting is relevant, as it can create spaces that support the expression of alternative perspectives, or "more uninhibited expression of marginalised views" (Fage-Butler, 2017, p. 135). I conclude by appraising the strengths and limitations of using a Foucauldian approach to analyze counter-narratives. With this chapter, my objective is to present in a lucid way a set of analytical strategies that contribute to the poststructuralist narrative tradition, thereby addressing criticism associated with narrative research more generally, that "[c]lear accounts of how to analyze the data [...] are rare" (Squire et al., 2013, p. 1).

The poststructuralist approach to narrative and counter-narrative

There are many different understandings of what is meant by "narrative", often with different attendant ontologies. Reflective of this diversity, the field of narrative research is also characterized by an abundance of methods.

The stream of narrative research to which this chapter contributes is the poststructuralist tradition. Poststructuralist conceptualizations of narrative and corresponding analytical approaches are "now relatively frequent" (Squire et al., 2013, p. 10), suggesting the growing significance of this approach. One way of characterizing the poststructuralist approach to narrative is to draw out its differences from the structuralist approach to narrative. Narrative research has been characterized as having a faultline with respect to the importance attached to the stability or fluidity of narratives (Squire et al., 2013), and this can be glossed as the tension between structuralist and poststructuralist approaches to narrative, respectively (Czarniawska, 2004).

In broad terms, structuralist narrative research is concerned with identifying enduring structures in narratives. An exponent of this approach is Propp (1973) who catalogued narratives in terms of archetypal characters (such as beautiful princesses) and storylines (for example, successful completion of a difficult task). By contrast, the poststructuralist approach to narrative as exemplified by the Foucauldian approach outlined in this chapter defines itself in relation to more mutable aspects of discourse. It is primarily concerned with "narratives' social positioning as discourses and [...] the problematics of subjectivity, representation and power" (Squire et al., 2013, p. 10).

"Narrative" as it is employed in this chapter refers to any account of an event or experience that draws on discourses that have cultural currency. Proponents of this approach to narrative include Tamboukou (2013) who presents a Foucauldian approach to (auto)biographical narratives, and Harwood (2001) who employs a Foucauldian approach to individuals' subjugated knowledges. Narratives can also be institutional or organizational in origin (Vaara, Sonenshein, & Boje, 2016). The definition provided by Vaara et al. (2016) of organizational narratives as "temporal, discursive constructions that provide a means for individual, social, and organizational sensemaking and sensegiving" (p. 496) is useful as is their characterization of the concerns of poststructuralist narrative research as hinging upon "uncovering the complexity, fragmentation and fluidity of narrative representations" (pp. 505–506). Summing up the above, of paramount importance in Foucauldian/poststructuralist narrative research is its concern with meaning ("representations"). Given this emphasis, poststructuralist narrative research is heavily reliant on the notion of discourse.

"Discourses", which will be defined in more detail later in this chapter, can be understood as shared, normative and evolving meanings that indicate as well as shape the cultural contours of a society or section of society. As Barker (2004) states, discourses are "regulated maps of meaning or ways of speaking through which objects acquire significance [...]. Discourse is not a neutral medium for the formation and transfer of values, meanings and knowledge [...], rather, it is constitutive of them" (pp. 54–55). Put another way, discourses indicate the cultural DNA of times and places; they provide the meanings that circulate in any society and furnish semantic content for the narratives we are told, the narratives we tell, and the narratives that tell us. Examples of two discourses are environmentalism and climate change denial: either or both can underpin the narratives we tell about the environment. With poststructuralist narrative analysis, meaning is emphasized at the expense of structure, and structure is typically fragmented and non-linear (Johansen, 2014; Vaara et al., 2016).

Clarification of the terminology employed in this chapter can be useful at this point. I use the term "master-narrative" and "counter-narrative" consistently to reflect the thematic focus of the anthology. When I use the word "narrative" by itself, I do so in relation to the field of narratology, as in "poststructuralist narrative research" or in relation to an individual's "story". I use the term "counter-discourse" to refer to discourses that oppose powerful societal "discourses".

Foucault was not a theorist of narrative *per se*, so it is necessary to explore his broader *oeuvre* to identify theories that are valuable for poststructuralist narrative analysis. In doing so, I found it valuable to view Foucauldian theories with respect to Vaara et al.'s (2016) three-way characterization of poststructuralist narrative research. First, Vaara et al. (2016) describe poststructuralist approaches to narrative as being concerned with deconstructing powerful narratives. The poststructuralist approach to narrative thus engages in a critical deconstruction of powerful discourses that set the agenda for individual and collective identities and practices, and legitimize action. In line with this, the poststructuralist approach to discourse in organizational research has been characterized by "radical social constructionism" (Vaara et al., 2016, p. 501) – a critical, reflexive form of social constructionism.

Second, poststructuralist narrative research is preoccupied with counter-narratives that indicate counter-discourses (Vaara et al., 2016). Master-narratives and counter-narratives are interlinked; a counter-narrative assumes the existence of a master-narrative, as it responds to it. Leontini (2010), for example, characterizes counter-narratives' intrinsic, even derivative relationship with master-narratives as follows:

> Counter narratives [...] bear the vestiges of dominant values, complicating their role as manifestations of resistance, for they raise the question of whether people can truly speak outside the systematized productions of knowledge that are formative of their social realities.
>
> *(p. 16)*

The entanglement of discourses and counter-discourses in counter-narratives is reflected in discourse analyses of resistance that reveal that the same discourses can serve diametrically opposing purposes of promoting prevailing practices as well as undermining them (Fage-Butler, 2017). Just as master-narratives draw on powerful discourses with governing effects (Foucault, 1991), counter-narratives too can be equally political (Harris & Fine, 2001). They reflect the concerns of the non-mainstream, the under-represented, the subaltern (Milner & Howard, 2013; Simmons & Goldberg, 2011), performing the important function of validating an alternative "counter-reality" (Delgado, 1995, p. 64).

Third, Vaara et al. (2016) state that poststructuralist narrative research is concerned with examining "what dominant or monological narratives imply for the individuals involved" (p. 506). Indeed, one of the hallmarks of poststructuralist narrative research is its focus on narratives as expressions of resistance by individuals and groups (Squire et al., 2013, p. 4). The *raison d'être* of counter-narratives can thus be considered to be individual and collective resistance. As Leontini (2010) states:

> human beings are never passive recipients of disciplinary discourses, or unquestioning performers in a world bound by rules and prescriptive codes of practice. They feel and recognize the pressure points that are embedded within normalizing discourses and in the very practices of self-discipline and surveillance they engage in.
>
> *(p. 10)*

Counter-narratives thus draw on the cultural resources of counter-discourses to provide speakers with leverage to challenge master-narratives, making space for alternative forms of personal and organisational "emergence and becoming" (Vaara et al., 2016, p. 501). They can empower weaker groups who may feel misrepresented in master-narratives, giving them a form of agency and helping them break the silence on perceived discriminatory practices and representations (Bonilla, 2014; Broderick & Ne'eman, 2008; Harper, 2009; Okigbo & Ezumah, 2017).

Foucauldian theories: exploring the tool-box

Relinquishing any claims to be exhaustive, I now present Foucauldian theories that I consider pertinent to the exploration of the three aspects of poststructuralist narrative research highlighted

Table 6.1 Foucauldian theories relating to the three aspects of master-narrative, counter-narrative and identity identified as pertaining to the poststructuralist narrative research in Vaara et al. (2006)

Master-narrative	*Counter-narrative*	*Identity*
Episteme	Counter-discourse	Subjectification
Dispositif	Subjugated knowledge	Objectification
Discourse	Genealogy	Practices of the self
Power/knowledge	Resistance	

by Vaara et al. (2006) – master-narrative, counter-narrative and identity – and outlined in the previous section (see Table 6.1).

It is relevant to mention at this point that other discourse analytical approaches that are indebted to Foucauldian theory (Jørgensen & Phillips, 2002) have also analyzed counter-narratives – e.g. discourse psychology (Bamberg, 2004; Jones, 2004) which adopts an interactive and contextual approach to narrative, and critical discourse analysis (Souto-Manning, 2014) which focuses on potentially oppressive aspects of discourse/narratives. However, both of these discourse analytical approaches represent inflections of Foucauldian discourse theory with respect to the field of psychology and social theories including Marxist theory, respectively. In this chapter, by contrast, I rely solely on Foucauldian theories, as I believe them to be sufficient for analyzing master-narratives, counter-narratives and identities made possible by counter-narratives.

Master-narrative

Analysing master-narratives in Foucauldian narrative research involves analyzing narratives for powerful discourses that may be underpinning master-narratives. Certain Foucauldian concepts are relevant to outline here.

As described in *The Order of Knowledge* (Foucault, 1970), the *episteme* is understood as "the conditions of possibility" of knowledge (p. xxiii); the episteme is the background that permits certain discourses (and thereby narratives) to prevail. As Bevir (1999) explains, the episteme provides "historical *a prioris*" (p. 347), the taken-for-granted, inherited meanings that shape the meanings that emerge in a society. Given their pervasive influence, we are rarely aware of epistemes and it is difficult to scrutinize them; they saturate the thoughts and practices of an age. Epistemes are supported by the *dispositif* – the institutional, physical and knowledge structures that make power possible. A dispositif includes "discourses, institutions, architectural forms, regulatory decisions, laws, administrative measures, scientific statements, philosophical, moral and philanthropic propositions – in short, the said as much as the unsaid" (Foucault, 1980a, p. 194). As argued by Tamboukou (2013, p. 96), narratives play a role in sustaining and constructing the dispositif.

Discourse is highly relevant to the analysis of master-narratives, as master-narratives draw their power from discourses. As Hall (1996) explains:

> A discourse is a group of statements which provide a language for talking about – i.e. a way of representing – a particular kind of knowledge about a topic. When statements about a topic are made within a particular discourse, the discourse makes it possible to construct the topic in a certain way. It also limits the other ways in which the topic can be constructed [...] Discourse is about the production of knowledge through language. [...] Since all social practices entail meaning, all practices have a discursive aspect.
>
> (*p. 201*)

In this conceptualization and in relation to the present focus on narrative in this chapter, all social practices, including narratives which are language-based, necessarily have a discursive element. Discourses infuse our narrative practices with meaning – importantly, enabling as well as constraining what can be said. Moreover, *power/knowledge* (Foucault, 1980c) is produced through discourse; certain discourses are rendered powerful through their association with what are generally considered to be unassailable truths (power is one of the "effects" of truth (Foucault, 1980e, p. 94)), while other discourses are associated with what are perceived to be less valid forms of truth and are therefore less powerful. An example of a powerful discourse is biomedicine with its superior claims to truth, compared to alternative medicine, which is less powerful as its truth claims are widely considered to be less valid. However, the perceived truth value of a discourse gives discourses economic and political potency (Broderick & Ne'eman, 2008). As Foucault explains:

> 'Truth' is linked in a circular relation with systems of power which produce and sustain it, and to effects of power which it induces and which extend it. A 'regime' of truth.
>
> *(Foucault, 1980d, p. 133)*

What is of central concern, then, is the performativity of discourses – what they make possible, economically and politically. Discourses, critically, harness knowledge in ways that regulate (facilitate as well as limit) people's behavior. More concretely in relation to the data that are explored in this chapter, an example of a discourse is that giving birth in hospital is the best, most moral thing to do for health and safety reasons (Armstrong, 2010; Davis-Floyd, 2004; Snowden et al., 2015). This discourse is embedded in biomedical institutional practices, structuring women's expectations and experiences of pregnancy and birth. And because master-narratives draw on discourses, they too are part of the "mechanics of power" (Foucault, 1980d, p. 116).

Counter-narrative

A *counter-discourse* to the discourse about hospital birth setting just mentioned also exists, namely that *home*births are (also) safe, good for mother and baby, and morally defensible (Broderick, 2016; Fage-Butler, 2017; Radzikowski et al., 2016). This counter-discourse, which underpins counter-narratives about homebirth settings provides legitimation in the form of a set of arguments for women who choose another option than the mainstream one of hospital births.

According to Foucault (1980e), counter-discourses indicate "*subjugated knowledges*" (p. 82) beyond official, approved knowledges. These subjugated knowledges tend to have low epistemic status: they "have been disqualified as inadequate to their task or insufficiently elaborated: naïve knowledges, located low down on the hierarchy, beneath the required level of cognition or scientificity" (p. 82). However, it is through these "local, popular knowledges that criticism performs its work" (p. 82). Counter-discourses thus perform the important task of challenging "the tyranny of globalizing discourses with their hierarchy and all their privileges of a theoretical avant-garde" (p. 83). Foucault (1980e) is interested in "the insurrection of knowledges that are opposed primarily [...] to the effects of the centralizing powers which are linked to the institution and functioning of an organized scientific discourse within a society such as ours" (p. 84). Foucault (1980e) calls the study of the combination of powerful discourses and counter-discourses *genealogy* as it "allows us to establish a historical knowledge of struggles and to make use of this knowledge tactically today" (p. 83). It is therefore important to take counter-discourses and counter-narrative into consideration when exploring the development of ideas over time in genealogical research.

Just as discourses are part of the "mechanics of power" (Foucault, 1980d, p. 116), counter-discourses and associated counter-narratives also serve as a means of counter-power. As Foucault (1978) famously stated, "Where there is power, there is resistance" (p. 95). *Resistance* is clearly very relevant to discussions of counter-discourses. Foucault's conceptualization of "resistance" has been summarized by Kelly (2009) as meaning people opposing power by "going off in a different direction to power's strategies" (p. 109). Kelly (2009) notes that, for Foucault, resistance to power at the personal level, also called "micro-resistance", is inevitable, but as micro-resistance represents isolated moments of resistance, the practices that are legitimized by dominant discourses remain intact. However, "macro-resistance", which is generated by groups, creates "counter-power" and is therefore more organized and strategic. In relation to the empirical data explored in this chapter, the cumulative effects of many different counter-narratives about birth setting in online forum settings means that macro-resistance is possible, and with that a much greater likelihood that powerful discourses are challenged (Fage-Butler, 2017). Foucault (1980b) points out that resistance evolves over time as it involves an ongoing progression between offense and counter-offense, so it needs to be analyzed in relation to contextual developments: "resistances [...] will have to be analyzed in tactical and strategic terms, positing that each offensive from the one side serves as leverage for a counter-offensive from the other" (p. 163). Moreover, with respect to exploring counter-discourses, Gordon (1980), drawing on the Foucauldian perspective, points out that finding "pure" instances of resistance and conformity in discourses can be challenging as they may be difficult to disentangle in practice.

Identity

In a later article where Foucault retrospectively surveyed his output, he identified that the primary concern throughout his work over the years had been the effects of discourse and power on identity (Foucault, 1982); more specifically, he said he had been preoccupied with creating "a history of the different modes by which, in our culture, human beings are made subjects" (p. 777). With respect to this chapter's concern with counter-discourses and counter-narratives, theories of *objectification* and *subjectification* (also called "subjectivation" (Foucault, 2017[1984]; Kelly, 2009, p. 87)) are highly relevant, as they relate to imposed identities (objectification) and claimed identities (subjectification). Objectification involves the "imposition of images and identities" (Martín Rojo, 2008, p. 33) on others – the kinds of identities that might be rejected in counter-narratives. Subjectification, on the other hand, is the "process through which the subject constitutes itself" (Martín Rojo & Gabilondo Pujol, 2011, p. 87), and this can include choosing alternative identities associated with counter-discourses (Andersen, 2003; Foucault, 1987; Leontini, 2010). Identity is constituted through "practices of the self" (*pratiques de soi*) (Foucault, 1984, p. 355), which address the question of "how not to be governed like that, by that, in the name of those principles, with such and such an objective in mind and by means of such procedures, not like that, not for that, not by them" (Foucault, 2007, p. 44).

Resisting the identities and practices supported by discourses and claiming alternative ones can be challenging, as powerful discourses are influential. Discourses have mainstreaming effects, and projections of 'normality' are likely to affect how individuals perceive themselves (Martín Rojo, 1995, p. 51). However, due to reflexivity, the culturally normative identities associated with discourses are not fully predictive of individuals' uptake or acceptance of them. We can still "refuse what we are" (Foucault, 1982, p. 785), expressing this, amongst other things, in our counter-narratives.

Drawing analytical strategies from Foucault's tool-box

The theories presented in the previous section described the broader Foucauldian framework relevant to the analysis of counter-narratives. In this section, I now present two of Foucault's theories to demonstrate how they very usefully support poststructuralist narrative research.

The analytical tools that are presented in this section relate to the three columns of Table 6.1. The first relates to how to analyze the *discourses* (Column 1) and *counter-discourses* (Column 2) that underpin master-narratives and counter-narratives respectively, and the second one indicates how to analyze *identity* as expressed in speakers' counter-narratives (Column 3).

Analyzing discourses and counter-discourses in master-narratives and counter-narratives

Using Foucauldian theory to analyze the discursive basis for master-narratives and counter-narratives involves the approach to discourse that was originally presented in *The Archaeology of Knowledge* (Foucault, 1972). Foucault's theories of discourse have been converted into more operational analytical tools in the hands of a number of scholars (Andersen, 2003; Fage-Butler, 2011; Graham, 2005; Willig, 2013). Before presenting the steps to analyzing discourses and counter-discourses, one Foucauldian concept requires clarification – the "statement" which is the "atom of discourse" (Foucault, 1972, p. 51). It is a stretch of text that usually ranges between a sentence and a few sentences long that constructs (represents) an object such as birth setting in a particular way.

In relation to the topic of optimal birth setting, Foucauldian discourse analysis essentially involves:

1. identifying all the statements in a text or texts that relate to the optimal birth setting – e.g. at home or in the hospital;
2. identifying how the various statements converge around various discourses that relate to the topic (e.g. homebirths as safe or dangerous);
3. discussing what the constructions present in the data are doing – what do they achieve? What "economic advantages or political utility" (Foucault, 1980e, p. 101) may derive from their inclusion? Whose interests do they serve?

I illustrate the Foucauldian approach to analyzing discourses and counter-discourses using examples of online forum data that I compiled for a previous article (Fage-Butler, 2017), which included pro-hospital birth and pro-homebirth narratives. This involved the following steps. After copying all relevant posts into a data file, I used NVivo (2015) to support an inductive analysis of the posts to identify constructions relating to homebirth and hospital birth. These coded extracts were then used to identify discourses that were evident in posters' narratives and counter-narratives using the three-staged approach to Foucauldian discourse analysis outlined above.

Danish legislation does not require ethical approval for this type of study because it does not include any biological material or influence the usual treatment of the participants. The online forum is open and the data were freely available without password protection. However, to avoid traceability of the data with search engines to safeguard the participants' anonymity and confidentiality, I followed the British Psychological Association's (2017) ethical guidance on anonymizing online data. This involved lightly editing the posts by directly correcting typographical errors or grammatical mistakes; directly replacing characteristic phrases; directly replacing abbreviations with full words; directly replacing shorter, less relevant words with [...]; and replacing certain words or phrases with a close synonym in [].A manual check verified the non-traceability of the quotations.

The following statement from a mother's online narrative about her birthing experiences indicates the powerful pro-hospital birth discourse:

> After the shock of giving birth to my perfect baby following a perfect pregnancy and with it being second time round so kind of already knowing about birth and newborns [...], only to find out he needed to be whisked into an Intensive Care Unit and have a six-hour operation to live, nothing would make me even consider a home birth.You just never know what is coming.

This next statement from an online narrative indicates the counter-discourse, where homebirth is constructed as a safer and better choice than hospital birth:

> I was on the floor unconscious after having little one in a hospital, bleeding everywhere and nobody knew.At least if it had happened at home, someone would have been there [...].

This narrative emphasizes the risk of inattention in hospitals, reversing the discourse that hospital births are safest.

In both of these examples of narrative and counter-narrative, then, a discourse of responsible risk avoidance is evident, reflecting the cultural imperative that women should adopt moral and responsible attitudes to birthing (Hallgrimsdottir & Benner, 2014; Lupton, 1999).The same discourse is used to legitimize two very different choices.

Analyzing new subjectivities made possible in counter-narratives

In order to analyze the alternative subjectivities made possible in counter-narratives, Foucault's (1972) theory of subject position can be used.

In *The Archaeology of Knowledge*, Foucault (1972) explains that statements, which are the units of discourse, have associated subject positions. Subject positions can be considered allotted positions for the speakers of a discourse. As Mahon (1993) states, subject positions tie the subject (individual) in to a particular relationship with the statement: "A statement's subject is not equivalent to the author of its formulation; rather a space, the position of the subject determines the relation between statement and subject" (p. 137). Andersen (2003) describes the embeddedness of subject positions within statements as follows: "the statement articulates the space and possibility of subjects" (p. 11).

Just as the starting point for the Foucauldian analysis of discourses is the statement, so too is the statement the starting point for the analysis of subject positions. Foucault (1972) explains that identifying the subject position of a statement involves "determining what position can and must be occupied by any individual if he is to be the subject of it" (p. 96), bearing in mind that there can be more than one subject position associated with a single statement (Foucault, 1972, p. 108). Foucault (1972, pp. 52–53) states that identifying the subject position of a statement involves considering what position it is possible for the subject to occupy in relation to the domain or the object of the discourse. A subject position can thus be considered to be an anonymized "placeholder": a subject position is a "particular, vacant place that may in fact be filled by different individuals" (Foucault, 1972, p. 95). A subject position mobilizes the idea of legitimacy and investigates the key issue of the positioning of the subject in relation to the objects and domain of a discourse. A subject position is adopted by the speaker of a discourse, so subject position analysis enables the analysis of *self-selected* identities. This is very different to objectification, which involves constructing identities for groups and individuals. In a previous study, I explored the tension between identities given (objectification) and identities taken (subjectification) (Fage-Butler & Anesa, 2016), indicating how Foucauldian analysis is perfectly situated to identify negotiations in identity construction. In other words, Foucauldian discourse analysis is very valuable when exploring how counter-discourses and the counter-narratives that draw on them facilitate the adoption of alternative identities. Indeed, because narratives often recount personal experience, it is particularly relevant to look at how identities are constructed in counter-narratives using subject position analysis.

I will now exemplify the analytical strategy of subject position analysis with respect to the same data I used to exemplify statement function analysis. The following statement involves a mother narrating her experience of homebirth:

> I did exactly what I wanted. I was not forced into any position: in fact, my midwife left me alone for most of it, assisted when needed and just followed my lead. [...] [It was] a fantastic experience for me.

The subject position associated with this statement is the empowered mother. This subject position indicates the discourse of patient empowerment, which is generally seen as a desirable, ethical medical practice (Aujoulat, d'Hoore, & Deccache, 2007; Funnell, 2016). As homebirth is discursively constructed as promoting empowerment, this counter-narrative strategically draws on a discourse that has broad sociocultural acceptance and validity. In that way, the legitimizing effect of discourse is used not only to support the usual, recommended institutional practices and discourses, but also counter-practices and counter-discourses.

Other statements indicate a different approach to taking on master-narratives and discourses. There is a widespread discursive construction of birth as hard work, traumatic, extremely painful; women's bodies are often constructed as hardly being up to the task (Hallgrimsdottir & Benner, 2014). By contrast, the mother in the following example describes homebirth as a very positive experience:

> It was so fantastic! I had my other half, my mother and midwife, and [I] labored in my bedroom with [...] music playing [quietly] in the corner. 4 hours of labor and [a few] minutes of pushing and [the baby] was out.

The subject position in this narrative is that of the competent mother who takes care of herself and in doing so, her baby. In her familiar home setting and surrounded by her closest family members, the narrator/subject describes her body as being capable of giving birth with minimal intervention. In focusing on the positives, this counter-narrative confronts the discourse of hospitals as the best birth setting, helping to normalize homebirth as a possible option for other women. In directly opposing powerful discourses and in the context of Web 2.0, which facilitates the promulgation of messages, counter-narratives such as this have political import.

Discussion and conclusion

The present chapter outlines a set of methods derived from Foucault's theoretical tool-box that facilitate analysis of counter-narratives within the poststructuralist narrative tradition. In reflecting how Foucault provides a theoretical apparatus that facilitates the analysis of counter-narratives and resistance, it also redresses the notion of discursive determinism that has unfortunately and erroneously been associated with Foucault (Philp, 1983). Foucault, particularly in his later work, underlines time and again the idea that individuals challenge powerful discourses, finding new subject positions, new spaces for identity: discourses are *inevitably* negotiated at the individual level. Counter-narratives are therefore commonplace, serving the important function of helping to generate subject positions that oppose powerful discourses, practices and identities. In showing the outcome of personal negotiations of discourses, narratives are both highly individual at the same time as they indicate broad sociocultural norms, meanings and values.

The Foucauldian backdrop for this chapter also results in an emphasis on the potential political power of counter-narratives that take on discourses that are used to prop up certain values, practices and institutions. Discourses and counter-discourses as well as master-narratives and counter-narratives can be explored in relation to power as discourses support institutions and reproduce or challenge power relations. In that sense, the very uttering of counter-narratives can be seen as potentially political. Also, as noted in the analysis, counter-narratives often rely on the same discourses as master-narratives for their legitimizing potential, suggesting a limited number of legitimizing discourses in any field.

The data used to exemplify the Foucauldian analysis of counter-narratives were drawn from an online forum. It is likely that the internet, particularly Web 2.0 which facilitates user-generated content, helps to promote the proliferation of counter-narratives, and new quantitative methods have evolved to support the analysis of online digital narratives and counter-narratives (e.g. Tangherlini et al., 2016). Particularly with respect to health-related topics, counter-narratives tend to emphasize the importance of experiential knowledge and alternative epistemologies (Borkman, 1976; Caron-Flinterman, Broerse, & Bunders, 2005). As counter-narratives can proliferate in this new digital environment, a well-known potential drawback has to do with individuals producing counter-narratives that run counter to scientific knowledge, as in the case of online immunization debates, where the public health pro-immunization discourse is confronted with counter-narratives about side-effects. Such counter-narratives, however, are also, in turn, met with counter-counter-narratives that provide counter-accounts to those of the counter-narratives. Further investigation of the counter-narratives that are evident in the online context would certainly be advantageous particularly where topics that have so many moral and practical implications, such as immunization, are concerned.

A word on the potential limitations of a Foucauldian approach to counter-narrative. Not all strands within poststructuralist approaches to counter-narrative are well-served by a Foucauldian approach. For example, psychoanalytical (Lacanian) approaches to narrative are interested in aspects of experience and subjectivity that elude narrative (Squire et al., 2013, p. 10). By contrast, the Foucauldian approach adopted here relies on the surface of discourse (i.e. spoken/written narrative). Indeed, Foucault slightly provocatively called himself a "positivist" (Foucault, 1972, p. 125) in his work on discourse, as he was only interested in exploring the import of actual utterances. Similarly, visual elements such as gesticulation or eye contact, or paralinguistic aspects such as pace and pause are less well-served by the methods presented in this chapter. That said, "[n]arrative is always defined first of all as a kind of language" (Squire et al., 2013, p. 9), so many poststructuralist inquiries into narrative and counter-narrative are likely to fall within its scope, and Foucauldian theory provides an excellent vantage point for such analyses.

In conclusion, Foucault's theoretical tool-box includes many theories that can contribute to better understanding and analysis of counter-narratives. Two in particular, statement function and subject position, are particularly well-suited for analyzing counter-narratives that challenge powerful discourses and master-narratives. Counter-narratives, in the Foucauldian understanding, have particular potential to challenge existing practices, making them highly deserving of our attention. As Gordon (1980) intimates:

> what Foucault may have to offer is a set of possible tools, tools for the identification of the conditions of possibility which operate through the obviousness and enigmas of our present, tools perhaps also for the eventual modification of those conditions.
>
> *(p. 258)*

References

Andersen, N. Å. (2003). *Discursive analytical strategies: Understanding Foucault, Koselleck, Laclau, Luhmann.* Bristol: The Policy Press.

Armstrong, E. M. (2010). Home birth matters—For all women. *The Journal of Perinatal Education, 19*(1), 8–11. doi:10.1624/105812410X482329

Aujoulat, I., d'Hoore, W., & Deccache, A. (2007). Patient empowerment in theory and practice: Polysemy or cacophany? *Patient Education and Counseling, 66*, 13–20. doi:10.1016/j.pec.2006.09.008

Bamberg, M. (2004). Considering counter narratives. In M. Bamberg & M. Andrews (Eds.), *Considering counter-narratives: Narrating, resisting, making sense* (pp. 351–371). Amsterdam: John Benjamins Publishing Company.

Barker, C. (2004). *The Sage dictionary of cultural studies.* London: Sage.

Bevir, M. (1999). Foucault, power, and institutions. *Political Studies, 57*, 345–359.

Bonilla, C. M. (2014). Racial counternarratives and Latina epistemologies in relational organizing. *Anthropology & Education Quarterly, 45*(4), 391–408. doi:10.1111/aeq.12077

Borkman, T. (1976). Experiential knowledge: A new concept for the analysis of self-help groups. *Social Service Review, 50*(3), 445–456. doi:10.1086/643401

British Psychological Society (2017). Ethics guidelines for internet-mediated research. Retrieved from www.bps.org.uk/sites/bps.org.uk/files/Policy/Policy%20-%20Files/Ethics%20Guidelines%20for%20Internet-mediated%20Research%20%282017%29.pdf

Broderick, A. A., & Ne'eman, A. (2008). Autism as metaphor: Narrative and counter-narrative. *International Journal of Inclusive Education, 12*(5–6), 459–476. doi:10.1080/13603110802377490

Broderick, M. L. (2016). Home birth: The wholeness of absence. *Health Communication, 31*(3), 379–381. doi:10.1080/10410236.2014.950928

Caron-Flinterman, J. F., Broerse, J. E. W., & Bunders, J. F. G. (2005). The experiential knowledge of patients: A new resource for biomedical research? *Social Science & Medicine, 60*, 2575–2584. doi:10.1016/j.socscimed.2004.11.023

Czarniawska, B. (2004). *Narratives in social science research.* London: Sage.

Davis-Floyd, R. E. (2004). *Birth as an American rite of passage* (2nd ed.). Berkeley, CA: University of California Press.

Delgado, R. (1995). Storytelling for oppositionists and others: A plea for narrative. In R. Delgado (Ed.), *Critical race theory: The cutting edge* (pp. 64–74). Philadelphia: Temple University Press.

Fage-Butler, A. M. (2011). The discursive construction of risk and trust in patient information leaflets. *Hermes, 46*, 61–73. doi:10.7146/hjlcb.v24i46.97368

Fage-Butler, A. (2017). Risk resistance: Constructing home birth as morally responsible on an online discussion group. *Health, Risk & Society, 19*(3–4), 130–144. doi:10.1080/13698575.2017.1327038

Fage-Butler, A. M., & Anesa, P. (2016). Discursive construction and negotiation of laity on an online health forum. *Pragmatics and Society*, 7(2), 196–216. doi:10.1075/ps.7.2.02fag

Foucault, M. (1970). *The order of things: An archaeology of the human sciences.* London: Routledge.

Foucault, M. (1972). *The archaeology of knowledge.* New York: Pantheon.

Foucault, M. (1978). *The will to knowledge. The history of sexuality, Vol. 1* (R. Hurley, Trans.). London: Penguin.

Foucault, M. (1980a). The confession of the flesh. In C. Gordon (Ed.), *Power/knowledge: Selected interviews & other writings, 1972–1977* (pp. 194–228). New York: Pantheon.

Foucault, M. (1980b). The eye of power. In C. Gordon (Ed.), *Power/knowledge: Selected interviews & other writings, 1972–1977* (pp. 146–165). New York: Pantheon.

Foucault, M. (1980c). *Power/knowledge: Selected interviews and other writings, 1972–1977.* New York: Pantheon.

Foucault, M. (1980d). Truth and power. In C. Gordon (Ed.), *Power/knowledge: Selected interviews and other writings, 1972–1977* (pp. 109–133). New York: Pantheon.

Foucault, M. (1980e). Two lectures. In C. Gordon (Ed.), *Power/knowledge: Selected interviews and other writings, 1972–1977* (pp. 78–108). New York: Pantheon.

Foucault, M. (1982). The subject and power. *Critical Inquiry*, *8*(4), 777–795. doi:10.1086/448181

Foucault, M. (1984). On the genealogy of ethics: An overview of work in progress. In P. Rabinow (Ed.), *The Foucault reader* (pp. 340–372). New York: Pantheon.

Foucault, M. (1987). *The use of pleasure: The history of sexuality, Vol. 2.* Harmondsworth: Penguin.

Foucault, M. (1991). Governmentality. In G. Burchell, C. Gordon, & P. Miller (Eds.), *The Foucault effect: Studies in governmentality* (Vol. 6, pp. 87–104). Chicago: University of Chicago Press.

Foucault, M. (1994[1974]). Prisons et asiles dans le mécanisme du pouvoir [Prisons and asylums in the mechanism of power]. In *Dits et écrits, Vol. 1* (pp. 1389–1393). Paris: Gallimard.

Foucault, M. (2001[1971]). Entretien avec Michel Foucault [Interview with Michel Foucault]. In D. Defert, F. Ewald, & J. Lagrange (Eds.), *Dits et écrits 1, 1954–1975* (pp. 1025–1042). Paris: Gallimard.

Foucault, M. (2007). What is critique? (L. Hochroth & C. Porter, Trans.). In S. Lotringer (Ed.), *The politics of truth* (pp. 41–81). Los Angeles: Semiotext(e).

Foucault, M. (2017[1984]). Le retour de la morale [The return of morality]. In D. Defert, F. Ewald, & J. Lagrange (Eds.), *Dits et écrits 2, 1976–1988* (pp. 1515–1526). Paris: Gallimard.

Funnell, M. M. (2016). Patient empowerment: What does it really mean? *Patient Education and Counseling*, *99*(12), 1921–1922. doi:10.1016/j.pec.2016.10.010

Gordon, C. (1980). Afterword. In C. Gordon (Ed.), *Power/knowledge: Selected interviews & other writings 1972–1977* (pp. 229–260). New York: Pantheon.

Graham, L. J. (2005). Schooling and 'disorderly' objects: Doing discourse analysis using Foucault. Retrieved from http://www.aare.edu.au/05pap/gra05072.pdf.

Hall, S. (1996). The West and the rest: Discourse and power. In S. Hall, D. Held, D. Hubert, & K. Thompson (Eds.), *Modernity: An introduction to modern societies* (pp. 182–227). Malden: Blackwell.

Hallgrimsdottir, H. K., & Benner, B. E. (2014). 'Knowledge is power': Risk and the moral responsibilities of the expectant mother at the turn of the twentieth century. *Health, Risk & Society*, *16*(1), 7–21. doi:10.1080/13698575.2013.866216

Harper, S. R. (2009). Niggers no more: A critical race counternarrative on Black male student achievement at predominantly White colleges and universities. *International Journal of Qualitative Studies in Education*, *22*(6), 697–712. doi:10.1080/09518390903333889

Harris, A., & Fine, M. (2001). *Under the covers: Theorising the politics of counter stories.* London: Lawrence & Wishart.

Harwood, V. (2001). Foucault, narrative and the subjugated subject: Doing research with a grid of sensibility. *The Australian Educational Researcher*, *28*(3), 141–166. doi:10.1007/BF03219764

Johansen, T. S. (2014). Researching collective identity through stories and antestories. *Qualitative Research in Organizations and Management: An International Journal*, *9*(4), 332–350. doi:10.1108/qrom-08-2012-1092

Jones, R. L. (2004). "That's very rude, I shouldn't be telling you that": Older women talking about sex. In M. Bamberg & M. Andrews (Eds.), *Considering counter-narratives: Narrating, resisting, making sense* (pp. 169–189). Amsterdam: John Benjamins Publishing.

Jørgensen, M., & Phillips, L. (2002). *Discourse analysis as theory and method.* London: Sage.

Kelly, M. G. E. (2009). *The political philosophy of Michel Foucault.* Abingdon: Routledge.

Leontini, R. (2010). Genetic risk and reproductive decisions: Meta and counter narratives. *Health, Risk & Society*, *12*(1), 7–20. doi:10.1080/13698570903508705

Lupton, D. (1999). Risk and the ontology of pregnant embodiment. In D. Lupton (Ed.), *Risk and sociocultural theory: New directions and perspectives* (pp. 59–85). Cambridge: Cambridge University Press.

Mahon, M. (1993). Michel Foucault's archaeology, enlightenment, and critique. *Human Studies*, *16*, 129–141. doi:10.1007/BF01318575

Martín Rojo, L. (1995). Division and rejection: From the personification of the Gulf Conflict to the demonization of Saddam Hussein. *Discourse & Society*, *6*(1), 49–80. doi:10.1177/0957926595006001004

Martín Rojo, L. (2008). Imposing and resisting ethnic categorization in multicultural classrooms. In R. Dolón & J. Todolí (Eds.), *Analysing identities in discourse* (pp. 31–56). Amsterdam: John Benjamins.

Martín Rojo, L., & Gabilondo Pujol, A. (2011). Michel Foucault. In M. Sbisà, J.-O. Östman, & J. Verscheuren (Eds.), *Philosophical perspectives for pragmatics* (pp. 85–103). Amsterdam: John Benjamins Publishing Company.

Milner, H. R., & Howard, T. C. (2013). Counter-narrative as method: Race, policy and research for teacher education. *Race Ethnicity and Education*, *16*(4), 536–561. doi:10.1080/13613324.2013.817772

NVivo. (2015). QSR International Pty Ltd (Version 11.1.0).

Okigbo, A. C., & Ezumah, B. A. (2017). Media health images of Africa and the politics of representation: A South African AIDS choir counter-narrative. *Journal of Asian and African Studies*, *52*(5), 705–721. doi:10.1177/0021909615608208

Philp, M. (1983). Foucault on power: A problem in radical translation? *Political Theory*, *11*(1), 29–52. doi:10.1177/0090591783011001003

Propp, V. (1973). *Morphology of the folktale* (2. ed. / rev. and ed. with a preface by L. A. Wagner). Austin: University of Texas Press.

Radzikowski, J., Stefanidis, A., Jacobsen, K. H., Croitoru, A., Crooks, A., & Delamater, P. L. (2016). The measles vaccination narrative in Twitter: A quantitative analysis. *JMIR Public Health and Surveillance*, *2*(1), e1. doi:10.2196/publichealth.5059

Simmons, H. A., & Goldberg, L. S. (2011). 'High-risk' pregnancy after perinatal loss: Understanding the label. *Midwifery*, *27*(4), 452–457. doi:10.1016/j.midw.2010.02.013

Snowden, J. M., Tilden, E. L., Snyder, J., Quigley, B., Caughey, A. B., & Cheng, Y. W. (2015). Planned out-of-hospital birth and birth outcomes. *The New England Journal of Medicine*, *373*(27), 2642–2653. doi:10.1056/NEJMsa1501738

Souto-Manning, M. (2014). Critical narrative analysis: The interplay of critical discourse and narrative analyses. *International Journal of Qualitative Studies in Education*, *27*(2), 159–180. doi:10.1080/09518398.2012.737046

Squire, C., Andrews, M., & Tamboukou, M. (2013). Introduction: What is narrative research? In M. Andrews, C. Squire, & M. Tamboukou (Eds.), *Doing narrative research* (pp. 1–26). London: Sage.

Tamboukou, M. (2013). A Foucauldian approach to narratives. In C. Squire, M. Andrews, & M. Tamboukou (Eds.), *Doing narrative research* (pp. 88–107). London: Sage.

Tangherlini, T. R., Roychowdhury, V., Glenn, B., Crespi, C. M., Bandari, R., Wadia, A., … Bastani, R. (2016). "Mommy blogs" and the vaccination exemption narrative: Results from a machine-learning approach for story aggregation on parenting social media sites. *JMIR Public Health and Surveillance*, *2*(2). doi:10.2196/publichealth.6586

Vaara, E., Sonenshein, S., & Boje, D. (2016). Narratives as sources of stability and change in organizations: Approaches and directions for future research. *The Academy of Management Annals*, *10*(1), 495–560. doi:10.1080/19416520.2016.1120963

Willig, C. (2013). *Introducing qualitative research in psychology* (3rd ed.). Maidenhead: Open University Press.

7

Narrative, discourse, and sociology of knowledge

Applying the Sociology of Knowledge Approach to Discourse (SKAD) for analyzing (counter-)narratives

Reiner Keller

Introduction

The present contribution introduces the sociology of knowledge approach to discourse (SKAD) as a perspective for analyzing competing narratives (including counter-narratives) in and across highly diverse social arenas. The (intended) benefits of such a discursive perspective on narratives and counter-narratives to (counter-)narrative analysis have to be presented in empirical work. They might be the outcome of a shift towards discursive contexts and structuration, different conceptual heuristics, and a general interest in the role of power/knowledge in social meaning-making. The chapter begins with a short account of narrative inquiry in German sociology. It then turns to a consideration of sociology of knowledge and the interpretive paradigm. It finally discusses basic tenets of SKAD analysis, that is the theory, concepts and methodology of an approach to discursive meaning-making interested in social relations of knowledge and knowing, and in the occurring politics of knowledge and knowing. It argues for a perspective following Foucault's footsteps of analyzing power/knowledge regimes, but informed by and grounded in the interpretive paradigm of sociology. In this, "discourse" provides a general contextualization for the analysis of narratives and counter-narratives.

Beyond the linguistic turn

The terms "narrative", "narrative inquiry", "narrative analysis" and so on cover heterogeneous research fields in the social sciences and humanities. A common focus is the reference to different kinds of texts as research data, and to textual analysis as procedure. Such texts could be the outcome of semi-structured or "narrative" interviewing, group discussion and other procedures for generating "story-telling". Or they might be "documents of the field", produced by individuals in their personal life, around a given concern in mass media and social media, for organizational purposes, law-making, campaigning of social movements and similar sources (Prior, 2003).

For quite a while now, "narrative inquiry" has been on the agenda (e.g. Ewick & Silbey, 1995; Hyvärinen, 2017; Reed, 1989). Arguments for a "narrative perspective" sometimes refer to the Chicago School tradition (Maines, 1993). Other authors point towards semiotics and linguistic approaches (Franzosi, 1998), social psychology and identity building (Bamberg, 2012), or theories of communication and cognitive linguistics (Kuhn, 2017).

In German-speaking contexts, "narrative" or its translation "Erzählung" is not a widespread concept in social analysis. Of course, there is a well-established scene of qualitative or interpretive research, (re-)starting after World War II, with group discussion and loosely structured interviewing as data, and developing a broad range of analytical procedures (Keller & Poferl, 2020). An influential concept of the "narrative interview" was established in the early 1980s by the sociologist Fritz Schütze (1983) and was soon directed towards generating autobiographical narratives in order to come "as close as possible" to the individual subject's lived experiences and to questions of identity work (Lucius-Hoene & Deppermann, 2004; Köster, 2009). Following such arguments, narrative approaches have found their place in the German field of qualitative research. But biographical research questioned the "authentic records of individual experience" and started to examine relations between public discourses and personal narratives. Today narrative interview data is widely used without paying, as it seems, particular attention to narrative (or counter-narrative) as a concept. Rather, different perspectives of sequential analysis of fixed oral and visual data or collected texts prevail. We might attribute such a situation to the hermeneutic traditions of German "Geisteswissenschaften" (Wilhelm Dilthey). They lead to a particular focus on interpretation and meaning-making as a basic human condition, and to different procedures used by social scientists, the "interpreters of interpretations", in order to account for their work as analytically valuable "social sciences hermeneutics" (Hitzler & Honer, 1997). This bias partially accounts for the small impact of structuralist linguistics and semiotics in German sociology.

A similar transformation occurred for the linguistic turn, which was influential in German sociology in the 1970s and 1980s. It stimulated inquiry into concrete language usage as an effect of social structure, conversational analysis of the micro-structures of verbal interaction, a general interest in the relations between linguistics and sociology (Luckmann, 1979; Schütze, 1975), and Jürgen Habermas's (1984) comprehensive theory of communicative action. Hubert Knoblauch (2000) then observed "the end of the linguistic turn" in German sociology and a general move from language and interests in language and society towards the sociology of knowledge.

Sociology of knowledge, the interpretive paradigm, and discourse

SKAD is about the discursive construction of reality. It does not use a linguistic concept of discourse, but rather defines discourses as regulated patterns of statement production, as stakes in power/knowledge regimes and the politics of knowledge – as particular forms and processes in the historically ongoing social construction of reality. It reads Foucault as a historical sociologist of knowledge (Keller, 2018), and it refers to the sociology of knowledge and the pragmatist school of sociology (Chicago School and beyond) to establish a theoretical and methodological background for a sociological approach to discourse (Keller, 2005, 2011, 2012a, 2013; Keller, Hornidge & Schünemann, 2018).

In German-speaking contexts, "sociology of knowledge" refers mainly to the work of Peter L. Berger and Thomas Luckmann (Berger & Luckmann, 1971). This is compatible with much of symbolic interactionist work and "old Chicago School" sociology. Anglo-American perspectives in the sociology of knowledge are most often interested only in scientific knowledge. A rapid overview therefore will indicate the range of sociology of knowledge and the interpretive paradigm as perspectives on "cultural reality" (Znaniecki, 1919).

French philosopher and sociologist Auguste Comte started his analysis of social transformations with a comprehensive diagnosis of three historical stages of power/knowledge regimes. Karl Marx and Friedrich Engels argued that the prevailing worldview, ideology, religion, law, and other ideas, are produced by the dominant social class of capitalists and serve its interest in domination. They presented a comprehensive and consequential historical counter-narrative to such dominance. Emile Durkheim and Marcel Mauss were interested in classifications as social phenomena, in the historical genealogy of what they called "collective representations" and "collective consciousness", and in the multiple ways in which social structure shapes "socio-cognitive" structures (symbolic systems or universes). Max Scheler and Karl Mannheim then laid the grounds for a more explicit sociology of knowledge framework. Mannheim, for instance, was interested in competing and conflicting ideologies and utopias, and their anchorage in particular social milieus, or in the emergence of situated, standpoint-related experiences and worldviews in particular positions in social structure – ideas which later became influential in feminist standpoint theories. Ludwik Fleck demonstrated the intersection between culture and the production of scientific knowledge in and between competing thought-styles and collectivities. Max Weber's historical analysis of the Protestant Ethic delivers an almost discourse-analytical approach to a historical counter-discourse, which became, according to his analysis, a main catalyst for the unfolding of European capitalism (Weber, 1992).

Weber's analysis provides a case in point for a most famous conceptual statement in classic pragmatist sociology. William I. Thomas and Dorothy S. Thomas (1928, pp. 571–572) wrote: "If men define situations as real, they are real in their consequences". This was and still is an important account of the core role of human meaning attribution to experiential chaos – about ordering, establishing and organizing situations, the work culture does. It is about the basic condition of the human "animal symbolicum" (Ernst Cassirer). What does such a statement imply? First, there is no "real" or "pure real situation" for action and interaction. The situations we confront and act upon are a result of an interpretive process of sense-making. Second, if multiple actors are involved in a situation, their definitions of "what the situation is", or "what is going on", might vary considerably. Social groups and larger collectivities invest a lot in disciplining humans towards corresponding, related, if not similar definitions, by establishing behavioral norms and cognitive consensus. Third, all "real elements" present in a situation, that is other people, animals, plants, objects, physical materiality, ghosts and spirits, or whatever, the relations they are engaged in, and the interactions they perform, are accessible only via such definitions. This is not to ignore the agency, resistances or obstacles, such elements present for the wiggle room of human actors' meaning-making. You might believe you can fly, but open the window and try it. So fourth, from the point of view of others (and from the actor), given the "proper" conditions of a situation, such an act of defining can be "wrong", that is fail, and lead to fatal consequences. This argument does not affect Thomas & Thomas's statement, for here too a definition proves to be highly consequential.

William I. Thomas had introduced the concept "definition of the situation" before. In the Chicago School of Sociology context, he stated that sociologists should leave aside official norms and moral regimes, and inquire into common people's definitions of situations, in order to understand their action and interaction: institutional powers never have full thought control. A case in point was his research about "The unadjusted girl" (Thomas, 1923). Here he used, analyzed and commented on narrative interview data in order to account for women's perception of their situation, conditions and possibilities of action in daily life and struggle for survival in Chicago. These women presented many "counter-narratives" to the official puritan moral regimes and their established role for women in society, as stated by public authorities.

Thomas was well aware that most often a multiplicity of actors is involved in defining a situation. The means or resources for establishing a then predominant and consequential definition are unequally distributed, for example, in a court trial, or by public authorities, law and police. Some resources are available by (and for) established institutional powers (like the threats of legal physical violence, or prisons), others by socially established "vocabularies of motives". A "satisfactory or adequate motive" accounts, in the eyes of the "members of a situation", in an acceptable way for an involved actor's conduct in that situation (Mills, 1940, pp. 906–907).

"Communication" is the basic social process, which allows the establishing of common realities and symbolic universes. It implies a relation between at least two entities (the one addressed by an act of communication does not have to be present in the situation, and might even be "imagined"), the usage of a sign system, and a reference to a content or (whatever) "object". Communication is a permanent and ongoing performance, which "realizes" worlds. According to John Dewey, "Society not only continues to exist by transmission, by communication, but it may fairly be said to exist in transmission, in communication". Communication establishes the commonality of things and worlds, "aims, beliefs, aspirations, knowledge [...], 'like-mindedness' as the sociologists say" (Dewey, 1916, pp. 7–8). Robert Park and Ernest Burgess commented on Dewey:

> This gesture, sign, symbol, concept or representation in which a common object is not merely indicated, but in a sense created, Durkheim calls a "collective representation". Dewey's description of what takes place in communication may be taken as a description of the process by which these collective representations come into existence.
>
> *(Park and Burgess, 1924, pp. 37–38)*

George Herbert Mead and other pragmatists added ideas about the life of signs and symbols, and the trajectories which transform newborn babies into competent symbol users and members of society (or newcomers in an organization into effective fellow members). They introduced the concept of the "universe of discourse" as a precondition for such processes. A "universe of discourse" is a set of shared social meanings, produced, reproduced and transformed by the ensemble of collective practices called "communication". It is both the precondition and result of such communication (Mead, 1963, pp. 89–90). Charles W. Morris (1946) described how particular "types of discourse" have come into existence, such as poetry, religion or economics – social "sub-worlds" organized around some ongoing concern. Symbolic interactionism (Blumer, 1991) presented an elaborated version of such a perspective. This includes institutions, organizations and social processes, all considered as the situated outcome or crystallization of "continual permutations of action" (Strauss, 1993) in social worlds. The interest in competing and maybe conflictual definitions of situations and their communication via narratives about "what is going on", – counter-narratives being only one possibility amongst others –, the powers and resources implied, the socio-material effects or consequences of such competitions, became and has remained a core interest of associated work ever since (Keller, 2012a). Cases in point are studies on moral entrepreneurship, the careers of social problems, social movement research, or inquiry into public discourses and the "culture of public problems" (Gusfield, 1981).

In 1966, Berger and Luckmann established a systematic account of the dialectics between an historically established and objectified common social reality, and the "subjective realities", experiences, worldviews and practices of individuals. The authors never conceived of it as a "constructivist statement", but as "pure realism" (Pfadenhauer & Knoblauch, 2019). Their main ambition was to bring the sociology of knowledge down to earth, that is no-longer to direct its attention to the history of ideas, scientific knowledge or the *Weltanschauung* of large social groups, but to "concern itself with everything that passes for 'knowledge' in society" (Berger & Luckmann, 1971, p. 26). This is about "what people 'know' as 'reality' in their everyday, non- or pre-theoretical lives. [...] It is precisely this 'knowledge' that constitutes the fabric of meanings without which no society could exist" (ibid., p. 27). German sociologist Stephan Wolff stated that the book offers the most comprehensive and important theory of society as an effect of communication (Wolff, 1997, p. 50). Recently, it was re-interpreted as "communicative construction of reality" (e.g. Keller, Knoblauch & Reichertz, 2013; Knoblauch, 2019).

Berger and Luckmann accounted for the socio-historical processes of institutionalization of "objective reality" in social collectivities. They discussed modes of legitimation, such as "proverbs, moral maxims and wise sayings [...] [or] symbolic universes" (ibid., pp. 112–113). And they pointed to the social-structural base for competition and conflict, including the resources of physical power to impose a particular definition of reality (ibid., p. 127), or the position of the "intellectual" as "the counter-expert in the business of defining reality" (ibid., p. 143). They then discussed how newcomers internalize "objective reality" via socialization and identity building and transform it into their personal "subjective reality". They insist on the dialectics between those two faces of reality. Internalization is important in order to reproduce the "objective order of reality" by permanent action and interaction, including communication:

> The most important vehicle of reality-maintenance is conversation. [...] Thus an exchange such as. "Well, it's time for me to get to the station", and "Fine, darling, have a good day at the office", implies an entire world *within which* these apparently simple propositions make sense. By virtue of this implication the exchange confirms the subjective reality of this world. [...] At the same time, that the conversational apparatus ongoingly maintains reality, it ongoingly modifies it. Items are dropped and added, weakening some sectors of what is still being taken for granted and reinforcing others. [...] We have seen how language objectifies the world, transforming the *panta rhei* of experience into a cohesive order. In the establishment of this order language *realizes* a world, in the double sense of apprehending and producing it. Conversation is the actualizing of this realizing efficacy of language in the face-to-face situations of individual existence.
>
> *(ibid., pp. 172–173)*

Please note that "language" refers to signs and symbols, that is to shared meaning in a universe of discourse. Berger and Luckmann added an important argument to the Chicago tradition by referring to the social phenomenologist Alfred Schütz. He was interested in the transformation of embodied sensual experimentation into reflected, actual experience in the embodied consciousness. How come that you identify these black and white contrasts you are reading first as distinct from the chair you sit on, the tea cup next to you, then as black and white, as signs on paper or electronic devices, as signs of a language, this language as US-English, the meaning of words and sentences and so on. Mead explained how a newborn baby becomes a competent symbol user. But how is this competence at work in the present situation, here and now? Schütz called this capacity and process the "constitution of meaning" in the individual's consciousness. It is not an arbitrary creation *ex nihilo*. He suggests that embodied minds use typified schemes of interpretation, to create order out of the chaos of sensual experience. Here he meets Mead: the individual embodied consciousness and human agency is a social given or effect of social structuration. Such schemes are available via social stocks of knowledge, which provide "objective realities". They are situated historical crystallizations of problem-oriented interaction and interpretation. Individuals might add to the stock of knowledge by creating words and schemes, ways of doing, procedures and techniques, in order to name as yet uncommon experiences, new things like a machine, a discovery, or new solutions to a problem they confront and so on. History, power, communication and other interactions will decide if they, or a group of actors, will be able to establish a new element, a new norm, a new interpretive scheme, a new motive for action, a new object, a new institutional device, a new narrative in the social stocks of knowledge. Occasions for competition between and conflict of interpretations abound. Unexpected problems of action, material or social objects that become obstacles, social norms that are "disregarded", clashes of interest, uneasiness with attributed roles and social identities, confrontation with unfamiliar conditions or social worlds – all such "events" can become anchors and catalysts for interpretive struggle.

"Social construction" is about forms, processes and content of world making, which all imply large registers of regulation and instruction. Schütz and Luckmann pointed to the *economies of communication* of a historically situated social structuration, e.g. "a particular language structure and stratification", or "the social regulation of" the "actual present use of the means of communication" in concrete situations (Schütz & Luckmann, 1989, pp. 155–156). Schütz even used the concept of "universe of discourse" in order to point, in an almost "Foucauldian" way, to such regulations for a newcomer in the field of mathematics:

> [T]he scientist enters a pre-constituted world of scientific contemplation handed down to him by the historical tradition of his science. [...] Any problem emerging within the scientific field has to partake of the universal style of this field and has to be compatible with the pre-constituted problems and their solution by either accepting or refuting them. [...]
>
> *(Schütz, 1973a, pp. 250–256)*

Luckmann later showed a strong interest in communicative genres as elements of economies of communication. Communicative genres provide instructions for issues of communication. One example is the well-explored genre of narratives about religious conversion (Ulmer, 1988); another one is so-called conspiracy theory (Anton & Schetsche, 2014), a main genre for popular counter-narratives ("Armstrong never landed on the moon"; "Germany never became a republic"; "The elites and experts are the enemies of the good people", etc.). There are structural features of populist narratives (right to left) as well as of narratives of emancipation and acknowledgement, of historical and national decline and so on. There are rhetorical forms like irony or drama and tragedy, there are the master-narratives of modernity identified by Jean-Francois Lyotard (1984), and a multiplicity of "minor" patterns for stories and scripts. These are all part of the social stocks of knowledge.

Andrew Abbott (1991) stated that "discourse" had replaced "social construction" as a key concept in the social sciences and humanities. This is mostly due to the influential contributions of Michel Foucault (Keller, 2019). In his book on methodology, *Archaeology of Knowledge* (Foucault, 2010), he defined scientific discourses as regulated practices of statement production, which constitute their objects as particular epistemic phenomena (cf. Foucault, 2001). *L'ordre du discours* ("The order of discourse", translated into English under the inaccurate title "The discourse on language"; Foucault, 2010) presented elements of external and internal discourse regulation. The *Rivière Case* (Foucault, 1982) pointed to discourses as weapons or stakes in discursive struggles for the definition of situations, and thereby joins core interests of pragmatist sociology. Rivière, a young man, had lengthily confessed to killing his mother, sister and brother. A trial took place, involving different experts. Given his confession, was he "really" responsible for what he had done? Should he be considered sane, or insane? This question became the major concern between competing expert definitions of the situation. Rivière himself, and most medical, psychological and police experts confirmed his sanity. Yet one psychologist stated in his report that there were obvious signs of insanity in Rivière's behavior. His expertise determined the outcome and proved to be highly consequential: Rivière was declared insane, and then sent to an asylum.

This case is not just about individual actors. Rather it is about performed expert systems, their established ways of knowing, rules of proof and evidence, that is *discourses*, realized in the confrontation by discursive performances. According to Foucault, even Rivière himself referred to a common public vocabulary of motives about (ruined) honor and its consequences.

Both symbolic interactionism as well as (critical) linguistics added to concepts and interests in such "meso-level" empirical discourse research. This is very different from the particular paradigm of "discourse analysis" rooted in pragmatist linguistics and conversation analysis, interested in the analysis of verbal interaction or talk in a given situation. Instead, such discourse research, which in itself is very multi-paradigmatic, is concerned with broader socio-historical contexts and struggles for definition in and between diverse social arenas (see Keller, 2013). Whatever theoretical and conceptual apparatus is used, whatever research questions are at stake, all such approaches are somehow interested in discursive struggles, the trajectories, competition and interplay between discourses (and counter-discourses), the means and the social effects of such constellations. A few approaches, inspired by the structural semiotics of Alexandre J. Greimas, argue for an elaborated approach of narrative (Viehöver, 2010, 2011; Arnold, Dressel & Viehöver, 2012). Others use a looser idea of "story lines" in order to point to storytelling and narrative in discourses (cf. Hajer, 1997; Keller, 1998). SKAD elaborates an observation by Stuart Hall (1997, p. 224) about the "affinities and continuities" between "Weber's classical interpretative 'sociology of meaning' and Foucault's emphasis on the role of the 'discursive'".

The sociology of knowledge approach to discourse (SKAD)

SKAD's theoretical ground, concepts, methodology and methods build upon the pragmatist, interpretive and sociology of knowledge (including Foucault) traditions discussed above. Its main arguments have been presented in more detail in several books and articles (cf. the work of Keller and co-authors in the reference list). Only a few basic features can be elaborated in what follows. SKAD research is interested in relations of knowledge and knowing, and the politics of knowledge and knowing – that is in the ways "reality is made real", how the reality of reality is questioned and contested, and how new realities come into existence. It uses "knowledge" in the broad sense discussed above, and not only for the realm of science and technology studies. SKAD conceives of discourses as particular forms, levels and sets of processes of the social construction of reality. Discursive construction is performed by communicating social actors and their "serious" signifying acts, which they apply in emerging and ongoing concerns. This includes scientific, religious and political discourses in special arenas of society, as well as hybrid mixtures in public discourses in the media sphere, the patterns of discursive structuration being quite different.

Societies, organizations and social worlds discursively establish asymmetrical hierarchies of truth and (un-)certainty, belief systems, ideologies, religions, technical norms, moral orders and institutionalized claims defining reality "as it is", and what has to be done (next). Discursive construction happens in and in between religious, economic, scientific, political, special interest and public spheres. "Knowledge" here is the general term indicating that discursive meaning-making combines statements about the factuality of the world and the concrete issues, events and action problems at hand, with modes of knowing this by proof, evidence or belief, with legitimation, evaluation, moral and esthetic judgments, material effects and concrete devices to ground such claims. "Discursive" construction, or "discourse", refers to the idea that, despite the need for concrete actors to define a situation and to perform communication, such activities are not to be attributed to individual capacities and agency, but rather to discursive structuration and discursive situational contexts. In the same way as langue is pre-existent to parole, but is performed, reproduced and transformed by parole, discourses are "pre-existent" to concrete speakers, their concerns and situations. But without them, they would not emerge, becoming established, real and consequential, or enter into competition and conflict.

A (particular) discourse then is a regulated, relational and serial practice of statement production, which constitutes its referential phenomena in particular ways and with particular means. A single (textual) document, even a speech, is not a discourse here. It is just a discursive event or set of singular utterances. Such a document establishes fragments of a discourse or a small arena of discursive competition in itself, like in media talk shows. Discourse research therefore is an art of deconstruction and reconstruction – *interpretive analytics*. Empirically, discourses are manifest in series of concrete utterances, ongoing communicative interventions such as speeches, lectures, leaflets, reports, TV shows, newspaper articles, blogs, all bound together by a particular set of instructions. Each discursive structuration has a proper historical, spatial and social trajectory. A single narrative account of "what is wrong here and now", might well be its starting point. But only if it is picked up, performed in similar ways again and again (with variation and elaboration), does it become a manifest discursive form. Much like institutions, discourses come into the world as effects of social actors' interactions, and the permutations of such interactions, by processes of institutionalization of particular modes of defining situations. SKAD grounds discourse theory and research in human performances of sign usage and discursive practice. Competent, skilled actors are seriously needed to perform discursive practices and thereby to make discourses real and manifest. They have to define a particular situation as an occasion for the performance of a particular discursive practice. They are not discursive marionettes, but actively engage in adapting and updating discursive instructions for statement production to the situation here and now. Consider discourses and counter-discourses about climate change and climate skepticism and the (non-) need for action, or the above-mentioned Rivière case. The basic condition is always the presence of performing actors, that is speakers of discourses. Such ongoing discursive meaning-making nourishes the collective stocks of knowledge, the interpretive schemes, values and grounds for action that people use in their everyday life, identity work and sense-making. It may successfully establish institutional resources or devices, a proper infrastructure or "dispositive" of statement production (as in scientific disciplines or religions). It may identify some urgencies, problems for action and (moral) concern, and then establish devices for intervention, such as taxes, objects, tests, actors and practices – a dispositive of world intervention. SKAD research interested in such dispositive structures uses ethnography.

The levels of discursive structuration might be less formal too. A small group of actors with a common concern can successfully establish a particular discourse or counter-discourse, by intervention into informal settings and local public spheres, by organizing bigger events (like manifestations) and creating public awareness, and by using social media. Social movements are cases in point here.

SKAD discourse research starts with an informed interest in a case, and with questions about a concrete discursive struggle, process, a conflictual event and so on (see Keller, Hornidge & Schünemann, 2018, for examples). How many discourses can then be identified, how and by what means they perform, how they relate (in ignorance, indifference, competition, coalition by effect or intent, or confrontation) and with what effects? These are empirical/analytical questions (and issues of the sociological imagination). There might be only one (hegemonic) discourse or several competing discourses, some marginalized, excluded or silenced ones, and some that are, for better or worse, in a relation of conflict as counter-discourses. They draw upon different resources for meaning-making, and generate different outcomes or "power effects".

SKAD research (like other research) performs a discourse about discourses, a second order observation of "discursive reality" which in itself has to be understood by the very basic acts of defining a situation (for inquiry), by making use of available interpretive tools. Discourse research is interpretation – there is no way out. Such interpretation is guided by methodological reflection and transparency, especially by sequential analysis, a device designed to inform data analysis in particular ways. SKAD then uses further methods of interpretive research, such as theoretical sampling in corpus building, document analysis and category building. It thereby fills the methodological black box in Foucault's work.

SKAD proposes a set of heuristic tools for concrete research. First, the human factor: individual or organized (collective) *social actors* can be involved in a discursive conflict or structuration as *speakers* and performers of particular statement practices. Around a discursive arena, there might also be *potential speakers* or *excluded and silent actors* who do not show up despite their having stakes in an ongoing concern. Discourses often imply different *subject positions*. They may include processes of *othering* (who are the others) and "*selfing*" (who are we), templates for *model subjects* (the good environmental citizen) and *implied subjects* ("in the name of women"), which, following a discursive articulation, may organize and become real speakers. *Subjectification* refers to the particular forms and ways social actors interpret the model subjects in question. We should not confuse discursive articulation with concrete effects in a field of concern.

Discourses then are material, performed in concrete *discursive practices* of statement production, with a little help from *non-discursive practices* and other resources related to them (like collecting waste). And they might articulate some *model practices* or *templates for action* (e.g., how to govern a company in heavy waters).

Forms or modes of knowledge and *justification* are further elements: How is a speaker authorized? What kind of knowledge comes into play? How do different forms of evaluation and judgment (by "factual" data, moral values, esthetic reflection, religious beliefs) intervene and combine? Several *mappings* or *cartographies* of *actors, arenas, discourse coalitions, and discourse trajectories* account for the discursive structuration analyzed.

Utterances are the concrete singular data "givens" of discourse. SKAD's interpretive analytics uses concepts from sociology of knowledge in order to analyze the "*statement*" or "*pattern*" part in such data, which allows us to identify different utterances (single data) as being performances of the very same discursive structuration, despite their obvious different and singular concrete Gestalt. One such concept is the *interpretive scheme*, which organizes meaning, norms and action in a typical way (e.g. "technological risk", usable for very different technologies and situations). *Classifications* are consequential devices, which constitute and order experiences into categories. *Phenomenal structure(s)* refers to the way in which a discourse constitutes its core phenomenon, its dimensions and the articulation of these dimensions at a given moment, including, for example, references to causes, responsibility, model subjects, values, othering. According to SKAD, *narratives* (story lines) organize the different means of interpretation into a story to be told: of what happened or what is to come, of responsibility and irresponsibility, of urgency and need for action, of common concern or unacceptable particular interest, and so on. Interpretive schemes, classifications and phenomenal structures are not just loosely assembled elements of discursive structuration. They are composed into comprehensive, competing stories to be told, into competing narratives (and maybe counter-narratives) accounting for what is at stake. This implies that narrative and story-telling is part of discursive construction. Addressing this narrative dimension via "discourse" relates to power/knowledge, to repetition and structuration of such "*mises en intrigue*" (Paul Ricoeur), to the field of actors and symbolic-material resources involved, to the disciplining mechanisms of discursive structuration, to the complexities and trajectories of a given discursive-situational process and constellation.

A particular study will use only some elements of SKAD heuristics, according to its concrete research design and interests. SKAD has to be articulated towards concrete concerns for the research cases at hand. It encourages researchers to consider what a given process of discursive meaning-making "is a case of". Analysis does not stop with a descriptive account of "what happened", but should offer a more general, theoretical reflection on the implications, mechanisms and dynamics observed.

SKAD and narrative

SKAD has been applied across disciplines and to a broad range of topics (see Keller, Hornidge & Schünemann, 2018; Bosančić & Keller, 2016; Keller & Truschkat, 2012). Studies most often use textual data, sometimes audiovisual or visual data, or ethnography (Keller, 2016). Recent work addresses issues of critique (Keller, 2017) or the challenges created by new materialism (Keller, 2019). Questions of narrative and counter-narrative have been analyzed in SKAD research under the terms of discourses and counter-discourses. The main SKAD theory book (Keller, 2005, Chapter 5.2) discusses at length the role of competing narrations of control and danger in risk society. Further examples can be found in the literature referred to. My own comparative work on waste discourses, for example, identified a situation of hegemonic public discursive structuration in France, including a marginalized counter-discourse, and a highly equal public presence of two opposing discourses in Germany, each of them telling a particular story about the present situation of waste, and about what has to be done or not done, in order to save the future (Keller, 2018). For Germany, I established a distinction between a "structural-conservative" discourse, insisting on the established capitalist market economy as a core principle, and a counter-discourse of "cultural critique", struggling for new social structuration on the basis of a different cultural setting of needs and consumption. Whilst German discourses focused on the pros and cons of an announced catastrophic collapse, the hegemonic French discourse performed the ritual of regularly repeating the state's civilizational mastery over nature, waste and risk. Then, Wolf Schünemann and I discussed narrative nationalism from a SKAD perspective (Keller & Schünemann, 2016). Linda Tuhiwai Smith (2012, p. XII) strongly emphasized the role of relations of knowledge for social transformation in post- and de-colonial times. Inquiry into discourses and the politics of knowledge and meaning-making is a good point of entry in such a claim, and one way of addressing questions of "narrative" and "counter-narrative" on local and global levels.

References

Abbott, A. (2001). *The chaos of disciplines.* Chicago: University of Chicago Press.

Anton, A., Schetsche, M., & Walter, M.K. (Eds.). (2014). *Konspiration: Soziologie des Verschwörungsdenkens.* Wiesbaden: Springer VS.

Arnold, M., Dressel, G., & Viehöver, W. (Eds.). (2012). *Erzählungen im Öffentlichen.* Wiesbaden: VS.

Bamberg, M. (2012). Why narrative? *Narrative Inquiry,* 22 (1), 202–210.

Berger, P.L., & Luckmann, Th. (1966). *The social construction of reality.* Garden City, New York: Anchor Books.

Blumer, H. (1991 [1969]). *Symbolic interactionism.* Berkeley, CA: University of California Press.

Bosančić, S., & Keller, R. (Eds.) (2016). *Perspektiven wissenssoziologischer Diskursforschung.* Wiesbaden: Springer VS.

Dewey, J. (1916). *Democracy and education.* New York: Columbia University Press.

Ewick, P., & Silbey, S.S. (1995). Subversive stories and hegemonic tales: Toward a sociology of narrative. *Law & Society Review,* 29 (2), 197–226.

Foucault, M. (1982). *I, Pierre Rivière, Having slaughtered my mother, my sister, and my brother.* Lincoln: University of Nebraska Press.

Foucault, M. (2001 [1966]). *The order of things* (2nd ed.). London: Routledge.

Foucault, M. (2010 [1969]). *The archaeology of knowledge & The discourse on language*. New York: Vintage Books.
Frandsen, S., Kuhn, T., & Wolff, L.M. (2017). Introduction. In S. Frandsen, T. Kuhn, & L.M. Wolff (Eds.), *Counter-narratives and organizations* (pp. 1–14). New York: Routledge.
Franzosi, R. (1998). Narrative analysis – Or why (and how) sociologists should be interested in narrative. *Annual Review of Sociology,* 24, 517–554.
Gusfield, J. (1981). *The culture of public problems*. Chicago: University of Chicago Press.
Habermas, J. (1984). *Theory of communicative action, Vol. 1 & 2*. Boston, Mass.: Beacon Press.
Hajer, M. (1997). *The politics of environmental discourse*. Oxford: Oxford University Press.
Hall, S. (1997). The centrality of culture. In K. Thompson (Ed.), *Media and cultural regulation* (pp. 207–238). London: Sage/The Open University Press.
Hitzler, R., & Honer, A. (Eds.). (1997). *Sozialwissenschaftliche Hermeneutik*. Opladen: Leske & Budrich.
Hyvärinen, M. (2017). Narrative and sociology. *Narrative Works,* 6 (1), 38–62.
Keller, R. (1998). *Müll - Die gesellschaftliche Konstruktion des Wertvollen*. Opladen: Westdeutscher Verlag.
Keller, R. (2005). *Wissenssoziologische Diskursanalyse*. Wiesbaden: Springer VS.
Keller, R. (2011). The sociology of knowledge approach to discourse (SKAD). *Human Studies,* 34 (1), 43–65.
Keller, R. (2012a). *Das Interpretative Paradigma*. Wiesbaden: Springer VS.
Keller, R. (2012b). Entering discourses. *Qualitative Sociology Review,* Vol. VIII (2), 46–55.
Keller, R. (2013). *Doing discourse research*. London: Sage.
Keller, R. (2016). Die komplexe Diskursivität der Visualisierungen. In S. Bosančić, & R. Keller (Eds.), *Perspektiven wissenssoziologischer Diskursforschung* (pp. 75–94). Wiesbaden: Springer VS.
Keller, R. (2017). Has critique run out of steam? *Qualitative Inquiry*, 23 (1), 58–68.
Keller, R. (2018a). Michel Foucault: Discourse, power/knowledge and the modern subject. In: R. Wodak, & B. Forchtner (Eds.), *The Routledge handbook of language and politics* (pp. 67–81). London: Routledge.
Keller, R. (2018b). The social construction of value. In R. Keller, A.-K. Hornidge, & W. Schünemann (Eds.), *The sociology of knowledge approach to discourse*. (pp. 73–90). London: Routledge.
Keller, R. (2019a). New materialism? A view from sociology of knowledge. In U.T. Kissmann, & J.v. Loon (Eds.), *Discussing new materialism*. (pp. 151–172). Wiesbaden: Springer VS.
Keller, R. (2019b). The discursive construction of realities. In M. Pfadenhauer, & H. Knoblauch (Eds.), *Social constructivism as paradigm?* (pp. 310–324). London: Routledge.
Keller, R., & Poferl, A. (2020). (2020). Epistemic Cultures in Sociology Between Individual Inspiration and Legitimization by Procedure: Developments of Qualitative and Interpretive Research in German and French Sociology Since the 1960s [97 paragraphs]. *Forum Qualitative Sozialforschung / Forum: Qualitative Social Research,* 17(1), Art. 14, http://dx.doi.org/10.17169/fqs-17.1.2419.
Keller, R., & Truschkat, I. (Eds.). (2012). *Methodologie und Praxis der Wissenssoziologischen Diskursanalyse*. Wiesbaden: Springer VS.
Keller, R., Hornidge, A.-K., & Schünemann, W. (Eds.). (2018). *The sociology of knowledge approach to discourse*. London: Routledge.
Keller, R., Knoblauch, H., & Reichertz, J. (Eds.). (2013). *Kommunikativer Konstruktivismus*. Wiesbaden: Springer VS.
Knoblauch, H. (2000). Das Ende der linguistischen Wende. *Soziologie*, 2, 16–28.
Knoblauch, H. (2019). The communicative construction of reality. London: Routledge.
Kuhn, T. (2017). Commuicatively constituting organizational unfolding through counter-narrative. In S. Frandsen, T. Kuhn, & L.M. Wolff (Eds.), *Counter-narratives and organizations* (pp. 17–42). New York: Routledge.
Küsters, Y. (2009). *Narrative Interviews*. Wiesbaden: Springer VS.
Lucius-Hoene, G., & Deppermann, A. (2004). *Rekonstruktion narrativer Identität*. Wiesbaden: Springer VS.
Luckmann, T. (1979). Soziologie der Sprache. In R. König (Ed.), *Handbuch der empirischen Sozialforschung. Band 13* (pp. 1–116). Stuttgart: Enke.
Luckmann, T. (1989). Kultur und Kommunikation. In M. Haller, H.-J. Hoffmann-Nowotny, & W. Zapf (Eds.), *Kultur und Gesellschaft* (pp. 33–45). Frankfurt am Main: Campus.
Luckmann, T. (2006). Die kommunikative Konstruktion der Wirklichkeit. In D. Tänzler, H. Knoblauch, & H.-G. Soeffner (Eds.), *Neue Perspektiven der Wissenssoziologie* (pp. 15–26). Konstanz: UVK.
Luckmann, T. (2010). Handlung und Text, Verstehen und Interpretation. In M. Staudigl (Ed.), *Alfred Schütz und die Hermeneutik* (pp. 123–139). Konstanz: UVK.
Lyotard, J.-F. (1984). *The postmodern condition*. Manchester: Manchester University Press.
Maines, D.R. (1993). Narrative's moment and sociology's phenomena: Toward a narrative sociology. *The Sociological Quaterly,* 34 (1), 17–38.

Mead, G.H. (1963 [1934]). *Mind, self and society*. Chicago: University of Chicago Press.

Mills, C.W. (1940). Situated actions and vocabularies of motive. *American Sociological Review*, V (December), 904–913.

Morris, C.W. (1946). *Signs, language, and behavior*. New York: Prentice Hall.

Park, R.E., & Burgess, E.W. (1924). *Introduction to the science of sociology*. Chicago: University of Chicago Press.

Pfadenhauer, M., & Knoblauch, H. (Eds.). (2019). *Social constructivism as paradigm?* London: Routledge.

Prior, L. (2003). *Using documents in social research*. London: Sage.

Rasmussen, R.K. (2017). Rethinking counter-narratives in studies of organizational texts and practices. In S. Frandsen, T. Kuhn, & L.M. Wolff (Eds.), *Counter-narratives and organizations* (pp. 171–192). New York: Routledge.

Reed, J.S. (1989). On narrative and sociology. *Social Forces*, 68 (1), 1–14.

Schünemann, W., & Keller, R. (2016). Narrativer Nationalismus. In W. Hofmann, & R. Martinsen (Eds.), *Die andere Seite der Politik*. (pp. 55–84). Wiesbaden: Springer VS.

Schütz, A., & Luckmann, T. (1989). *Structures of the lifeworld. (Vol. II)* Evanston: Northwestern University Press.

Schütze, F. (1975). Sprache soziologisch gesehen. Vol. 1 & 2. München: Wilhelm Fink Verlag.

Schütze, F. (1983). Biographieforschung und narratives Interview. *Neue Praxis*, 13 (3), 283–293.

Smith, L.T. (2012). *Decolonizing methodologies: Research and indigenous peoples*. 2nd ed. New York: Zed Books.

Strauss, A.L. (1993). *Continual permutations of action*. New York: Aldine de Gruyter.

Thomas, W.I. (1923). *The unadjusted girl*. Boston: Little Brown and Company.

Thomas, W.I., & Thomas, D.S. (1928). *The child in America*. New York: A. A. Knopf.

Ulmer, B. (1988). Konversionserzählungen als rekonstruktive Gattung. *Zeitschrift für Soziologie*, 17 (1), 19–33.

Viehöver, V. (2010). Governing the planetary greenhouse in spite of scientific uncertainty. *Science, Technology & Innovation Studies*, 6 (2), 127–154.

Viehöver, W. (2011). Diskurse als Narrationen. In R. Keller, A. Hirseland, W. Schneider, & W. Viehöver (Eds.), *Handbuch, Sozialwissenschaftliche Diskursanalyse. Vol. 1*. (pp. 193–224). Wiesbaden: Springer VS.

Weber, M. (1992 [1904–1908]). *The protestant ethic and the spirit of capitalism*. London: Routledge.

Znaniecki, F. (1919). *Cultural reality*. Chicago: University of Chicago Press.

8

Counter-narratives as analytical strategies

Methodological implications

Monika Müller and Sanne Frandsen

Introduction

Focusing on a quite rough football game in 1951 between two Ivy League universities, Dartmouth College and Princeton University, Hastorf and Cantril (1954) show how one and the same game was interpreted in totally different ways by audiences tied to these universities. In a questionnaire for students of both universities, the authors of the paper found diverging accounts of what had happened in this complex social event. Of the potentially available matrix of events during the game, some incidents were reactivated by an individual as being significant (through connecting them to past experiences), whereas other incidents were not reactivated and thus had gone unnoticed. The authors conclude: "It seems clear that the 'game' actually was many different games and that each version of the events that transpired was just as 'real' to a particular person as other versions were to other people" (Hastorf & Cantril, 1954, p. 132).

This study centering on the football game provides a great example of conflicting interpretations of events and situations that researchers often encounter in qualitative research. While it might be difficult to establish 'what really happened' (Tracy, 2013, p. 40), we as researchers in organization studies are nonetheless (just like Hastorf and Cantril were) faced with a variety of different narratives that arise around organizational events (Buchanan & Dawson, 2007; Collins & Rainwater, 2005). Narratives, according to Vaara, Sonenshein and Boje (2016), are temporal and discursive constructions that provide a means for individual, collective, and organizational sensemaking and sensegiving. When we analyze these narratives and accounts of organizational events, however, we face critical questions: which accounts, standpoints, and voices can or should we include, and how can we include them to create research contributions in a truthful and trustworthy way? Frandsen, Lundholt and Kuhn (2016) argue for a counter-narrative lens to study organizations, as it enables us to see struggles over meaning, values, and identities in the "complexity and controversy" in organizational life (p. 8). In this chapter, we unfold the theoretical and methodological implications of a counter-narrative lens and illustrate how it may enable us to analyze empirical data in more nuanced ways. To do so, we first review common approaches to qualitative inquiry – typically based on traditional 'laws of thought' – and their limitations to then explain how and why a counter-narrative lens can be a useful addition or alternative.

The most prevalent definition of counter-narratives is based on Bamberg and Andrews (2004), who write that "[c]ounter-narratives only make sense in relation to something else, that which they are countering. The very name identifies it as an oppositional category, in tension with another category" (p. x). Establishing this dual positioning, nonetheless, is complicated: "what is dominant and what is resistant are not, of course, static questions, but rather are forever shifting placements" (Bamberg & Andrews, 2004, p. x). Based on this definition, we as qualitative researchers might find it hard to take these shifting placements into account while trying to include polyphonic voices of people in different organizational roles and their varying interpretations of their social reality. When it comes to social, and more specifically organizational, research, we often find a variety of accounts and interpretations of specific events or people in particular organizations. While some of these accounts appear to confirm one another and start to form a narrative, other statements can be a bit more 'off': either opposing the emerging narrative or overlapping with it while pointing to a different interpretation, or being on the sidelines of the more dominant emerging narrative.

When analyzing empirical material, various narratives or fragments of narratives emerge on two levels. First, we encounter these narratives in the form of diverse accounts or stories of our respondents including conflicting or contradictory statements about certain events or situations in interviews, informal conversations, etc. The concepts of 'narratives' and 'stories' are related to different traditions of usage; in this chapter we use the terminology that our sources use. We see stories as part of a micro-level living story web – as described by Svane, Gergerich and Boje (2016) – from which dominant narratives may emerge. Second, we encounter narratives in the form of our theorization of the findings when we bring together different accounts and statements of our respondents to create convincing research outputs (Czarniawska, 2004; Rhodes & Brown, 2005).

While we are analyzing and constructing narratives on these two levels, nevertheless, we often resort to ways of reasoning or sensemaking (Weick, 1995) that follow the influential classic laws of thought (the laws of identity, non-contradiction, and excluded middle, formulated by ancient Greek philosophers), which have become the basis of 'common sense' in our Western world. In our everyday life situations, these traditional laws of thought tell us that one thing cannot be another thing at the same time, that contradictions mean that one part is true while the other is false, and that there is no 'middle' ground in a contradiction. While common sense reasoning can be important and practical in everyday life situations, it becomes highly problematic when trying to evaluate conflicting or contradictory accounts of complex social situations. Commonsensical reasoning in qualitative research – which we refer to as 'common sense coding' – might limit the possibilities to analyze social situations involving various actors, interests, viewpoints, perceptions, and experiences, as the laws of logic do not easily apply. For example, the management can both be helping and exploiting employees at the same time; employees can both be motivated and de-motivated at the same time. In this chapter, we therefore argue for counter-narratives as alternative analytical strategies on both levels of narratives mentioned earlier.

A brief review: The laws of thought and common sense

Typically, in our Western tradition of reasoning, the ways in which we perceive the material and social world around us are guided by the traditional laws of thought (Berto, 2007), famously formulated by Aristotle (2013) in his 'Metaphysics' (Book IV or Gamma). The three axiomatic rules of thought, which we often connect to 'common sense', are – in a simplified version – the following:

1. the *law of identity*: A=A, and cannot be B, which basically means that one thing cannot be another thing at the same time,
2. the *law of non-contradiction*: something cannot be and not be in the same sense and at the same time, and
3. the *law of the excluded middle*: in a contradiction consisting of an affirmation and negation of the same statement, one statement is true and the other must be false, but there is no third or 'middle' possibility.

With regard to the second law, the law of non-contradiction, Aristotle (2013) writes that this "most firm of all first principles" means that ontologically it is not possible for something to be and not be simultaneously: "For the same thing to be present and not be present at the same time in the same subject, and according to the same, is impossible" (p. 69). He continues that it would be folly of the inquirer to believe that something can be and simultaneously not be:

> But [...] if an opinion contrary to an opinion be that of contradiction, it is evident that it is impossible for the same inquirer to suppose that at the same time the same thing should be and not be; for one labouring under deception in regard of this would entertain contrary opinions at the same time.
>
> *(p. 69)*

At this point, Aristotle also criticizes the view of Heraclitan philosophy of becoming (instead of being), as the ever-changing nature of becoming would not hold true for the law of non-contradiction. In several instances throughout the text, Aristotle criticizes Heraclitus' view that things can be 'true' and 'not true' at the same time.

What might complicate the laws of thought, though (and what Aristotle also mentions) is that there might be different meanings of one word or statement (i.e. different definitions) and changing meanings at different times (before, now, after – which are more explicit in Heraclitus' philosophy of becoming). Aristotle's (2013) response to these problems is to provide precise definitions that do not include a multitude of other possibilities or meanings (in this regard, he distinguishes between essential and accidental properties of a thing) and to relate to things as they are instead of what they had been or will be at another time. These shifting meanings and temporal changes, nevertheless, might be worth considering, especially when it comes to complex social interactions. Moreover, Aristotle (2013) also refutes Protagoras' view that things can be true and not true at the same time when it comes to humans and their perceptions, social judgements and evaluations, ideas etc.

According to Berto (2007), the three laws of thought (identity, non-contradiction, and excluded middle) became the most authoritative principles in the history of Western thought. Although Aristotle, in contrast to Protagoras, did not necessarily refer to human perceptions and social situations, the laws of thought nonetheless appear to be a basis for many people to evaluate natural and social phenomena alike with what we often call common sense. The Cambridge Dictionary describes 'common sense' – a term also coined by Aristotle (2015) to refer to perceptions via the common senses – in its more contemporary form as "the basic level of practical knowledge and judgment that we all need to help us live in a reasonable and safe way".[1] In this everyday life logic of common sense, most people would probably agree that things or situations are either one way or another – but not both ways at the same time (e.g. either you are ill or not, either you want x or not, etc.). This assessment typically helps people to make sense of statements and situations. In organizational research, Weick et al. (2010) describes sensemaking, which is often similar to common sense reasoning, as ongoing cognitive and retrospective construction of plausible images that rationalize what people are doing (p. 83).

Making sense of other people's sensemaking of situations, events, and the people entangled in them, is also what qualitative researchers need to accomplish once they return from 'messy' fieldwork. To be able to analyze and theorize their insights, qualitative researchers need to narrate their results, as Czarniawska (2004) points out: writing up and theorizing research findings "assumes the form of showing 'how come?' where laws of nature, human intentions and random events form a hybrid mixture" (p. 123). Researchers, thus, construct sense in form of 'narrative sensemaking' (Rhodes & Brown, 2005), through finding out how things are connected and providing "a structure that makes sense of the events" (Czarniawska, 2004, p. 23). This narrative then should be trustworthy, convincing (for readers and reviewers), not too long but to the point (relative to the value of the contributions), and follow a rather strict structure of writing (in a formulaic form) (see Czarniawska, 2004, p. 124).

A critique: Common sense coding as analytical strategy

When it comes to the social sphere and human beings, the laws of thought and common sense are of limited value as the epistemological basis for analyzing narratives. Through 'coding', i.e. ascribing a specific fixed meaning we consider to be 'true' to an interview statement, and establishing patterns between emerging categories based on these fixed meanings, we might produce a rigorous research narrative but simultaneously limit the potential for discoveries of alternative and valuable insights. Our own experiences, but also those of colleagues, have shown that qualitative fieldwork often provides material that can be interpreted and theorized in many different ways, which might not necessarily follow the laws of logic and, accordingly, common sense. However, in many accounts of how to analyze empirical material, we find hints that point to commonsensical reasoning, or 'common sense coding', in reducing the material as a way to be 'rigorous'. In this section, we provide some examples of these hints in influential descriptions of how to analyze empirical material.

In many cases, Eisenhardt, Graebner, and Sonenshein (2016) write, qualitative research aims to generate theory from data in an inductive grounded-theory approach proposed by Glaser and Strauss (1967). Grounded theory, according to Charmaz (2014), contains (post-)positivist and interpretivist elements, as "it relies on empirical observations and depends on the researcher's constructions of them" (p. 321). In a (post-)positivist perspective, Tracy (2013) writes, qualitative methods aim toward providing a clear answer to the question of 'what is *really* happening' to account for reliability and formal generalizability.

The main processes of such inductive approaches, according to Eisenhardt et al. (2016), are the following: building thick descriptions from empirical data, coding raw data into first-order themes, raising them to a more abstract level in the form of second-order themes, using constant comparison between emergent theory and data, and engaging with literature to sharpen both the constructs and the theoretical logic of the relationships between constructs (p. 1114). While there is not much detail about how exactly researchers engage in coding and thus develop the narrative of the argument, we find some influential guidelines in Gioia, Corley, and Hamilton (2012) or Charmaz (2014) (see also other examples in Rennstam & Wästerfors, 2018). We briefly introduce these ideas and point to ways in which the logic of common sense, based on the laws of thought, come into play.

When it comes to analyzing empirical material, Gioia et al. (2012) and Charmaz (2014) refer to two phases of coding: first-order or initial coding and second-order or focused coding. Gioia et al. (2012) mention that a first-order analysis is about capturing themes or 'categories' around informant terms, which might result in about 50 to 100 categories. The second-order analysis – similar to the notion of axial coding in Glaser and Strauss (1967) – is then about asking whether the emerging themes suggest concepts that help describe and explain the observed phenomena (Gioia et al., 2012). Gioia et al. (2012) suggest "seeking similarities and differences among the many categories" (p. 20) to eventually reduce the germane categories to a more manageable number (25 to 30) to answer the question 'What is going on here?'. However, while reducing the categories according to 'similarities and differences' (typically based on the law of identity), researchers need to decide about what a statement means and what it does not mean (based on the laws of non-contradiction and excluded middle), thereby excluding other potential overlapping or even contradictory meanings. Faced with the requirement to provide a convincing story within a tight word-content-ratio, researchers thus might use commonsensical reasoning and silence those voices (or codes) within their material that provide different or conflicting accounts of 'what is going on here'.

Both Gioia et al. (2012) and Charmaz (2014) emphasize the active construction of codes, as in the second-order analysis it is the researchers that name concepts and connect them in meaningful ways. While initial coding, according to Charmaz (2014), entails that researchers remain open to many possible meanings and theoretical directions, focused coding means that the researcher "uses the most significant or frequent initial codes to sort, synthesize, integrate, and organize large amounts of data" (p. 113) and to "pinpoint and develop the most salient codes" (p. 114). However, this advice to use the most significant, frequent, or salient codes to develop a convincing argument often results in common sense coding through establishing which accounts are 'true' and 'not true' and excluding ambiguity (as a third option or 'middle'). This way of coding thus might lead to leaving out other less 'significant' or less frequent themes. Although we do not question these guidelines for constructing a convincing analytical narrative and theorization, we still want to add to them with alternative analytical strategies. We argue that counter-narratives, which are not part of the dominant narrative around 'what is going on here', could still be theoretically interesting and provide value to the research findings.

Counter-narratives as alternative analytical strategies

According to Alvesson and Kärreman (2007), the ability to find and embrace 'mysteries' in our fieldwork is the first step towards theory building. A mystery arises as we experience something that runs counter to the dominant and commonsensical understanding of the phenomenon of study and that challenges the conventional way of theorizing and explaining the phenomenon. As such, we may argue that counter-narratives in various shapes and forms are vital in our analytical process and inherent in the process of understanding the 'what is going on here' (Gioia et al., 2012).

Yet, interestingly, most of our analytical frameworks (as described) appear to be focused on establishing main narratives that are based on the most salient, significant and frequent codes, while excluding what could be essential to the empirical discovery: counter-narratives. Our position is that counter-narratives are possible to find through immersive inquiry, yet it may be difficult as they are often more fragile, subtle, often silent and only hinted at in organizational life. Frandsen et al. (2016) argue that "often counter-narratives may only be told within specific storytelling communities [...] and thus not shared with others – let alone the curious fieldworker" (p. x). We are not suggesting that counter-narratives are easily accessible, but that the analytical process can be designed in a way that heightens the sensitivity towards counter-narratives. Frandsen et al. (2016) point out that counter-narratives often arise as a result of 'deep hanging out' (Geertz,

1998) – we posit that such deep hanging out is not only a matter of spending time in the field, but also at 'the desk' to explore different aspects of the empirical material.

In this section, we present alternative strategies for exploring empirical material in ways that allow for counter-narratives to be noticed and examined in order to arrive at a richer understanding of the phenomenon of interest. Our three main strategies are developed as counter-points to Aristoteles' axiomatic laws of identity, non-contradiction, and excluded middle. Each of these strategies also represents different ontological and epistemological perspectives on 'what counter-narratives are' and how they might be analyzed.

Alternative to the law of identity: Untold stories and deconstruction

One way to enrich our understanding of counter-narratives is by viewing them as stories silenced by the dominant narrative. Overlooking such counter-narratives in our empirical material might be due to – in Aristotle's terms of the law of identity – recognizing and identifying merely the A, while at the same time shutting out alternative possibilities of Bs. However, counter-narratives could be a way to also identify the Bs within the A. Izak, Hitchin and Anderson (2014), for example, point out the need to consider the stories that are "the neglected, edited out, unintentionally omitted" (p. 2) by dominating narratives. They argue that dominant narratives leave blind spots or counterpoints of silences, and the job of the critical researcher is to deconstruct the dominant narrative to be sensitive to what has been left out. Moreover, they point out that one untold story often renders other stories untold as well. Their point of view is similar to ours in that they highlight that any event can be made sense of in multiple ways and that any topic can be populated with multiple meanings, yet some of these meanings are rejected, ignored, and neglected in the dominant narrative. From their perspective, counter-narratives are often located in the non-telling.

One way to 'hear' the untold counter-narratives is by deconstructing the dominant narratives. By deconstructing, we come to see what meanings are left out, what alternatives are silenced or what aspects are treated as a taboo within the dominant narrative. Deconstructing strategies are mentioned by Czarniawska (2004), Boje (2001), and Martin (1990). The analytical strategies used in deconstruction include identifying and dismantling the main dichotomies of the dominant narratives and exploring the silences around what is not said and who's point of view is not present in the dominant narratives. The deconstruction approach focuses on disruptions and ambiguities to examine the 'limits' of what is conceivable within the dominant narrative. A focus on the most peculiar phrases, metaphors or connotations informants use might enable the researcher to deconstruct the dominant narrative in a way that allows for imagination of counter-narratives what has been left out, silenced or made taboo (for more insight on deconstructing see Martin, 1990 and Czarniawska, 2004). Using such deconstruction techniques enables us as critical organizational scholars to pay attention to power-dynamics and the ways in which counter-narratives are excluded: they 'disappear' from the 'managed' organization and perhaps rather 'live their life' in the unmanaged terrain of the organization (Gabriel, 1995).

Alternative to the law of non-contradiction: Multiple stories and ambiguity

Another way to understand counter-narratives is to see every story as a potential counter-narrative, or, in contrary to Aristotle's standpoint, to acknowledge several multiple narratives as being 'true'. Instead of excluding one side of a contradiction, the focus is on embracing multiple stories. This enables us to understand how things become enacted or performed as stories and explain the situated enacted of the stories, that is, how the stories we find in our empirical data are often dependent on the social context, time and location of the storytelling (Hammersley & Atkinson, 2007). Svane, Gergerich and Boje (2016) argue that narratives and counter-narratives emerge out of fractal developments of patterns in the 'living story web', which they describe as "open ended and dynamically changing all the time. We understand the living story web as ongoing development of simultaneous, polyphonic, fragmented storylines" (p. 133). In doing qualitative research, we often face problems as we try to make sense of the 'living story web', in which some narratives – while they are not completely silenced or excluded –are not yet fully developed, only hinted at or told in glimpses. The focus of the qualitative researcher is then, from this perspective, not so much on deconstructing dominant narratives but rather on weaving a narrative out of different fragmented stories each attempting to 'make sense' (Weick, 1995; Weick et al., 2010) of the "complex soup of ambiguous and half-understood problems, events and experiences" (Collins & Rainwater, 2005, p. 5).

In this respect, Boje (1995) evokes the metaphor of 'Tamara' for understanding how storytelling can be understood in an organizational setting. Tamara is a play that takes place in a house, where various audiences visit different rooms in which different smaller plays are performed. There are simultaneous stories going on and the spectators are never able to capture the full play, as they visit different rooms at different times. Boje (1995) explains: "*Tamara* is open conversation as a multiplicity of minor narratives; small stories collectively and dynamically constitute, transform, and reform the storytelling organization. Instead of one character acting one story line, there is diversity, multiplicity, and difference" (p. 1031). In organizations and organizational research, this could mean that official stories may be told in one 'room', while simultaneous opposing counter-stories are told in other rooms, performed by other organizational members or stakeholders. Reflecting on the metaphor of Tamara opens up to a more complex and nuanced treatment of counter-narratives: the main point is not the counter-narratives in and of themselves, but how the (fragments of) counter-narratives circulate between rooms, across space and time, and are used in different ways by different people, as also pointed out by Hitchin (2014).

This has implications for how we analyze our data as we might not – contrary to endeavors fueled by a (post-)positivist logic – find out 'what *really* happens here' (Charmaz, 2014), but rather investigate how local and alternative understandings and counter-narratives of 'happenings' emerge and are performed. For example, Humphreys and Brown (2002), in their study of organizational and individual identity narratives at the Westville Institute found that there is never just one story to be told. Similarly, Collins and Rainwater's (2005) analysis of change at Sears shows that the stories – in the eyes of the researcher – can be read as different narratives through continuous reviews in terms of, for example, both a comedy or a tragedy. And Pedersen (2009) argues that in analyzing stories it is important to consider not only how certain stories anticipate certain futures (foreshadowing), but that insights may also be found from considering 'sideshadowing' – considering the possibilities that might have been taken, but were not. From this perspective, counter-narratives are thus not necessarily seen as opposition to the dominant narratives, but rather as emerging in the form of alternative narratives.

Alternative to the law of the excluded middle: Tensions, contradictions and paradoxes

According to the third law of thought, there is no middle ground or third position between contradictions of 'true' or 'not true'. However, when looking closely at contradictions and paradoxes, we might find that often a middle exists in the form of an area of constant tensions and the persisting simultaneous presence of 'true/not true'. But before we elaborate on this point, we refer to Putnam et al. (2016) and their definitions of dialectics, contradictions, and paradoxes

(p. 6f): dialectics consist of interdependent opposites of a unity in an ongoing dynamic interplay of tensions and push-and-pull; contradictions are mutually exclusive interdependent opposites that define and potentially negate each other; and paradoxes are contradictions that persist over time and develop into seemingly irrational or absurd situations. Moreover, paradoxes mark the ongoing simultaneous presence of contradicting truths (Fairhurst, Cooren, & Cahill, 2002; Smith & Lewis, 2011). These three positions, and the tensions that arise around them, are often what researchers encounter in their fieldwork. For example, Vaara et al. (2016) point to complexities and contradictions between narratives of organizational stability and narratives of organizational change operating at the same time. Kreiner et al. (2015) coin the term 'organizational identity elasticity' to illustrate tensions relating to organizational identity changes through pulling conceptions of identity apart and, at the same time, holding them together, like a rubber band. And Fairhurst et al. (2002) explain how contradictions within downsizing strategies arise over missions, values, job expectations, and resources.

Research focusing on dialectics, tensions, contractions, and paradoxes demonstrates that narratives often appear in ways that are inherently dialectic as tensions between poles, whose presence also mutually implicates the other's existence (Deye & Fairhurst, 2019; Putnam et al., 2016). Deye and Fairhurst (2019) argue that tensions in organization studies often fall into three overall categories: 'either-or' tensions, in which the ends of the poles are seen as mutually exclusive and where one is often selected over the other; 'both-and' tensions in which opposites are inseparable and therefore focus on integration and balance between the two; and 'more-than' approaches where the focus is on finding new 'third spaces' for the tensions' position (Deye & Fairhurst, 2019). Putnam, in Grant and Cox (2017), argue that tensions, contradictions, and paradoxes in organization seem not to dissolve, but rather evolve and eventually be seen as normal. The idea of studying counter-narratives in forms of tensions is thus not to get rid of tensions, but to focus on how people come to navigate the organizational complexity, contradictions, and paradoxes.

Empirical studies revolving around tensions, contradictions, and paradoxes often use Charmaz' (2014) grounded theory approach, only to discover that there is a 'middle' that the first level open coding could not adequately address; the codes thus need to be re-organized and re-coded to allow for the exploration of contractions in the narratives (Deye & Fairhurst, 2019; Kreiner et al., 2015). For example, Deye and Fairhurst (2019) study the tweets of US President Trump and Pope Francis and examine the ambiguous and contradictory ways tensions between truth and post-truth are negotiated in the narratives. Exploring counter-narratives from this approach requires what Putnam in Grant and Cox (2017) labels dialectic sensibility to explore mixed messages – for example, clashing management philosophies of bureaucracy and commercialization – that may operate simultaneously (Rasmussen, 2016). Dialectic sensibility thus implies embracing pluralism in organizational narratives, being aware of opposition, multiple voices and alternative meanings – and continuously looking for ways in which two poles continuously exist "within each other and concomitantly define each other" (Grant & Cox, 2017, p. 195). We argue that dialectic sensibility can be sharpened through looking for what Sonenshein (2010) calls 'disconfirming evidence' in a continuously loop of re-interpretation of data.

Ongoing tensions and contradictions – to mention a prominent example from critical management studies – can also be found around issues of power and resistance, which are often not binary but emerging in a relationship where power and resistance are mutually constitutive (Collinson, 1994; Thomas & Davies, 2005; Zoller & Fairhurst, 2007). Thomas and Davies (2005), for instance, view resistance, instead of being diametrically opposed to managerial power, as "a multidimensional, fluid and generative understanding of power and agency" (p. 700). As such we may find organizational members who construct, reinforce, contest, and struggle with power – at times simultaneously (Fleming & Spicer, 2007). The mutually constitutive aspects of counter-narratives and dominant narratives have also been pointed out by Gabriel (2016) as he explores the role of counter-narratives in narrative ecologies.

A comment on writing: Exploring different styles

It appears to be inescapable that all qualitative research implies some form of reduction of complexity and of the 'messiness' of the field in our efforts to engage in academic "story work" (Donnelly, Gabriel, & Özkazanç-Pan, 2013). Yet, we think it is important to highlight that while most studies continuously seem to deploy common sense coding often based on grounded theory, such approaches can be enriched with alternative analytical strategies in the form of counter-narratives as pointed out earlier. In addition, we can also resort to other forms of writing that are less sanitized (Donnelly et al., 2013) and formulaic (Czarniawska, 2004) – yet arguably more meaningful (Alvesson, Gabriel, & Paulsen, 2017). In this sense, Grey and Sinclair (2006) argue for the need to reconsider our way of writing in academia to become less pompous, impenetrable, and occupied with posture.

Ellingson (2014), for instance, argues that a truthful account of a complex social situation can rarely be expressed in a single, unequivocal statement, and that scholars therefore should aim for more complex representation of their research. In this regard, Ellingson (2014) suggests using multiple lenses of studying and analyzing and multiple genres (including more artistic forms) of writing to provide thick descriptions (Geertz, 1973). Ellingson (2014) also proposes to use the analytical framework of 'crystallization' to engage in deep and complex interpretation of a phenomenon, opening up for multiple findings, multiple voices, and multiple genres. Other ways of illustrating sameness and simultaneous differences can be found in portrait-based ethnographic narratives (Frandsen, 2015) or in narrative forms of representation that highlight personal experiences of exclusion, marginalization and silencing is a way to give voice to the untold counter-narratives. Especially within the tradition of critical auto-ethnography (Frandsen & Pelly, 2020) the hidden is brought forward in the form of untold stories that are made visible. Jones, Adam and Ellis (2016), citing Tillmann (2009), for example, state that autoethnography "breaks silences around experiences as they unfold within cultures and cultural practices. In privileging subjectivity, personal voice, emotional experience, autoethnographies subvert traditional norms of scholarships that silence the 'complex and fragility' of life" (p. 35). These varied forms of writing allow counter-narratives to be told, voiced, examined, and celebrated in a way that honors complexity, controversy, polyphony, and power dynamics. "Turning a blind eye to counter-narratives leaves us with a rather one-dimensional understanding of organizational phenomena of any kind" (Frandsen et al., 2016, p. 8).

Conclusion

In this chapter we aimed to emphasize the value of counter-narratives (Bamberg & Andrews, 2004) in qualitative research analysis and in so doing we have advanced our theoretical and methodological understanding of counter-narratives in three different ways.

First, we have pointed to what we call 'common sense coding' based on Aristotle's classic laws of thought (the laws of identity, non-contradiction, and the excluded middle). Common sense coding is typically concerned with finding out "what *really* happened" (Tracy, 2013, p. 40) based on various accounts of informants and often with a (post-)positivist agenda in mind. This common sense approach is often preoccupied with finding the most frequent codes that point to a theme, selecting the most salient codes for developing a theme, or picking the most convincing codes in terms of a pre-formulated research idea. We argue that attempts to find out 'what really happened' are often guided by commonsensical reasoning that limits theoretical insights if not enriched with alternative analytical strategies. Researchers using common sense coding might end up producing a convincing, coherent, and 'smooth' research narrative, while excluding counter-narratives that would have the (creative) potential to interfere with this smoothness of the main narrative through challenging it. We argue that in the construction of a convincing and coherent research narrative through common sense coding, other less frequent nearly silent or merely whispered accounts of counter-narratives might often be overlooked or brushed aside. Through common sense coding, thus, potentially interesting and meaningful aspects of the empirical material might be overlooked and left out.

Second, we have pointed to different ways of understanding and using counter-narratives, which are typically defined as relating to a more 'dominant' narrative in an oppositional manner (Bamberg & Andrews, 2004). We propose three different perspectives on counter-narratives that highlight counter-narratives as a) untold stories or stories silenced by the dominant narrative, b) stories that represent alternative versions of what is 'true', and c) stories emerging as (middle) part of tensions, contradictions and paradoxes in organizational life. As such, we argue for the need to engage in a more nuanced understanding of counter-narratives that can better account for the messiness of organizational life and still embrace critical inquiry into the power dynamics that dominate.

Third, we want to bring together three different alternative analytical strategies, which embrace these more diverse forms of counter-narratives to achieve a richer and more nuanced understanding when working with ambiguous, messy, and potentially 'mystery-bearing' empirical data. These alternative analytical strategies challenge the three classic laws of thought: 1) challenging the law of identity through 'finding B's within the A' in untold stories and the deconstructing of dominant narratives, 2) challenging the law of non-contradiction through embracing multiple and ambiguous stories emerging at the same time, and 3) challenging the law of the excluded middle through accounting for the 'middle' in the form of ongoing tensions, contradictions, and paradoxes. We suggest that various different voices – even though they might lead to commonsensical confusion in the form of untold stories, hints, tensions, ambiguities, and paradoxes – can provide important theoretical insights. Each of the three alternative analytical strategies can serve as guidelines for 'hanging out' with the data at the desk in a way that allows the researcher to review and rediscover counter-narrative in future studies of organizations.

Note

1 https://dictionary.cambridge.org/dictionary/english/common-sense

References

Alvesson, M., Gabriel, Y., & Paulsen, R. (2017). *Return to meaning: A social science with something to say.* Oxford: Oxford University Press.

Alvesson, M., & Kärreman, D. (2007). Constructing mystery: Empirical matters in theory development. *Academy of Management Review, 32*(4), 1265–1281. doi:10.5465/amr.2007.26586822

Aristotle. (2013). *The metaphysics* (J. H. McMahon, Trans.). Mineola: Dover Publications.

Aristotle. (2015). *De Anima* (R. D. Hicks, Trans.). Cambridge: Cambridge University Press.

Bamberg, M., & Andrews, M. (Eds.). (2004). *Considering counter-narratives. Narrating, resisting, making sense.* Amsterdam: John Benjamins.

Berto, F. (2007). *How to sell a contradiction: The logic and metaphysics of inconsistency* London: College Publications.

Boje, D. M. (1995). Stories of the storytelling organization: A postmodern analysis of Disney as "Tamara-Land". *Academy of Management Journal, 38*(4), 997–1035.

Boje, D. M. (2001). *Narrative methods for organizational & communication research*. London: SAGE Publications.

Buchanan, D., & Dawson, P. (2007). Discourse and audience: organizational change as multi-story process. *Journal of Management Studies*, *44*(5), 669–686. doi:10.1111/j.1467-6486.2006.00669.x

Charmaz, K. (2014). *Constructing grounded theory*. London: Sage.

Collins, D., & Rainwater, K. (2005). Managing change at Sears: a sideways look at a tale of corporate transformation. *Journal of Organizational Change Management*, *18*(1), 16–30.

Collinson, D. L. (1994). Strategies of resistance: Power, knowledge and subjectivity in the workplace. In J. M. Jermier, D. Knights, & W. R. Nord (Eds.), *Resistance and power in organizations* (pp. 25–68). London: Routledge.

Czarniawska, B. (2004). *Narratives in social science research*. London: Sage.

Deye, J. M., & Fairhurst, G. T. (2019). Dialectical tensions in the narrative discourse of Donald J. Trump and Pope Francis. *Leadership*, *15*(2), 152–178.

Donnelly, P. F., Gabriel, Y., & Özkazanç-Pan, B. (2013). Untold stories of the field and beyond: narrating the chaos. *Qualitative Research in Organizations and Management: An International Journal*, *8*(1), 4–15.

Eisenhardt, K. M., Graebner, M. E., & Sonenshein, S. (2016). Grand challenges and inductive methods: Rigor without rigor mortis. Article in: Academy of Management Journal, 59(4), (pp. 1113–1123), NY.

Ellingson, L. L. (2014). "The truth must dazzle gradually" Enriching relationship research using a crystallization framework. *Journal of Social and Personal Relationships*, *31*(4), 442–450.

Fairhurst, G. T., Cooren, F., & Cahill, D. J. (2002). Discursiveness, contradiction, and unintended consequences in successive downsizings. *Management Communication Quarterly*, *15*(4), 501–540.

Fleming, P., & Spicer, A. (2007). *Contesting the corporation: Struggle, power and resistance in organizations*. Cambridge: Cambridge University Press.

Frandsen, S. (2015). Portraits of call centre employees: understanding control and identity work. *Tamara Journal for Critical Organization Inquiry*, *13*(3).

Frandsen, S., Lundholt, M. W., & Kuhn, T. (2016). Introduction. In S. Frandsen, T. Kuhn, & M. W. Lundholt (Eds.), *Counter-narratives and organization* (pp. 1–14). London: Routledge.

Frandsen, S., & Pelly, D. (2020). Organizational Resistance and autoethnography. In Herrmann, A. (Ed.), *The Routledge International Handbook of Organizational Autoethography*, (pp. 252–268) London: Routledge.

Gabriel, Y. (1995). The unmanaged organization: stories, fantasies and subjectivity. *Organization Studies*, *16*(3), 477–501.

Gabriel, Y. (2016). Narrative ecologies and the role of counter-narratives. In S. Frandsen, T. Kuhn, & M. W. Lundholt (Eds.), *Counter-narratives and organization* (pp. 208–226). London: Routledge.

Geertz, C. (1973). The Interpretation of cultures: Selected essays, New York: Basic Books.

Geertz, C. (1998). Deep hanging out. *The New York Review of Books*, *45*(16), 69–72.

Gioia, D. A., Corley, K. G., & Hamilton, A. L. (2012). Seeking qualitative rigor in inductive research: Notes on the Gioia methodology. *Organizational Research Methods*, *16*(1), 15–31. doi:10.1177/1094428112452151

Glaser, B. G., & Strauss, A. L. (1967). The discovery of grounded theory: Strategies for qualitative research. Chicago: Aldire.

Grant, D., & Wolfram Cox, J. (2017). Using a discourse lens to explore tensions and contradictions in organizational theory and change: A conversation with Linda Putnam. *Journal of Change Management*, *17*(3), 189–202.

Grey, C., & Sinclair, A. (2006). Writing differently. *Organization*, *13*(3), 443–453.

Hammersley, M., & Atkinson, P. (2007). *Ethnography: Principles in practice*. London: Routledge.

Hastorf, A. H., & Cantril, H. (1954). They saw a game; a case study. *The Journal of Abnormal and Social Psychology*, *49*(1), 129.

Hitchin, L. (2014). Method and story fragments: Working through untold method. In M. Izak, L. Hitchin, & D. Anderson (Eds.), *Untold stories in organizations* (pp. 213–238). London: Routledge.

Humphreys, M., & Brown, A. D. (2002). Narratives of organizational identity and identification: A case study of hegemony and resistance. *Organization Studies*, *23*(3), 421–447.

Izak, M., Hitchin, L., & Anderson, D. (2014). Introduction. In M. Izak, L. Hitchin, & D. Anderson (Eds.), *Untold stories in organizations* (pp. 1–12). London: Routledge.

Jones, S. H., Adams, T., & Ellis, C. (2016). Introduction: Coming to know autoethnography as more than a method. In S. H. Jones, T. Adams, & C. Ellis (Eds.), *Handbook of autoethnography* (pp. 17–48). Walnut Creek, CA: Left Coast Press.

Kreiner, G. E., Hollensbe, E., Sheep, M. L., Smith, B. R., & Kataria, N. (2015). Elasticity and the dialectic tensions of organizational identity: How can we hold together while we are pulling apart? *Academy of Management Journal, 58*(4), 981–1011.
Martin, J. (1990). Deconstructing organizational taboos: The suppression of gender conflict in organizations. *Organization Science, 1*(4), 339–359.
Pedersen, A. R. (2009). Moving away from chronological time: Introducing the shadows of time and chronotopes as new understandings of narrative time. *Organization, 16*(3), 389–406.
Putnam, L. L., Fairhurst, G. T., & Banghart, S. (2016). Contradictions, dialectics, and paradoxes in organizations: A constitutive approach. *The Academy of Management Annals, 10*(1), 65–171.
Rasmussen, R. K. (2016). Rethinking counter-narratives in studies of organizational texts and practices. In S. Frandsen, T. Kuhn, & M. W. Lundholt (Eds.), *Counter-narratives and organization* (pp. 171–192). London: Routledge.
Rennstam, J., & Wästerfors, D. (2018). *Analyze! Crafting your data in qualitative research.* Lund University: Studentlitteratur.
Rhodes, C., & Brown, A. D. (2005). Narrative, organizations and research. *International Journal of Management Reviews*, 7(3), 167–188. doi:10.1111/j.1468-2370.2005.00112.x
Smith, W. K., & Lewis, M. W. (2011). Toward a theory of paradox: A dynamic equilibrium model of organizing. *Academy of Management Review, 36*(2), 381–403.
Sonenshein, S. (2010). We're changing—Or are we? Untangling the role of progressive, regressive, and stability narratives during strategic change implementation. *Academy of Management Journal, 53*(3), 477–512.
Svane, M., Gergerich, E., & Boje, D. M. (2016). Fractal change management and counter-narrative in cross-cultural change. In S. Frandsen, T. Kuhn, & M. W. Lundholt (Eds.), *Counter-narrative and organization* (pp. 129–154). London: Routledge.
Thomas, R., & Davies, A. (2005). Theorizing the micro-politics of resistance: New Public Management and managerial identities in the UK Public Services. *Organization Studies, 26*, 683–706.
Tillmann, L. M. (2009). Speaking into silences: Autoethnography, communication, and applied research. *Journal of Applied Communication Research, 37*(1), 94–97.
Tracy, S. J. (2013). *Qualitative research methods: Collecting evidence, crafting analysis, communicating impact.* Chichester: Wiley.
Vaara, E., Sonenshein, S., & Boje, D. (2016). Narratives as sources of stability and change in organizations: approaches and directions for future research. *Academy of Management Annals, 10*(1), 495–560.
Weick, K. E. (1995). *Sensemaking in organizations.* Thousand Oaks: Sage.
Weick, K. E., Sutcliffe, K. M., & Obstfeld, D. (2010). Organizing and the process of sensemaking. In P. C. Nutt & D. C. Wilson (Eds.), *Handbook of decision making* (Vol. 16, pp. 83). Chichester: Wiley.
Zoller, H. M., & Fairhurst, G. T. (2007). Resistance leadership: The overlooked potential in critical organization and leadership studies. *Human Relations, 60*(9), 1331–1360.

9

Counter-narratives in accounting research

A methodological perspective

Matias Laine and Eija Vinnari

Introduction

In this chapter, we approach the theme of counter-narratives from the perspective of accounting. More specifically, we discuss a phenomenon known in the accounting literature as counter-accounts (Vinnari & Laine, 2017; Denedo et al., 2017), which can be seen as a subtype of counter-narratives (Bamberg & Andrews, 2004; Frandsen, Kuhn & Lundholt, 2017). Often defined as "accounting for the other, by the other" (Dey, Russell & Thomson, 2011, p. 64), counter-accounts refer to accounts, reports and other information produced by actors outside a given organization or industry. Our purpose is to consider counter-accounts from a dual methodological perspective. First, we illustrate how counter-accounts can be compiled by researchers seeking to advance a social cause. Second, we consider counter-accounts as an activist methodology, which can then be studied by researchers with the aid of various theories and methodological approaches. It is noteworthy that the empirical examples we have chosen to include in this chapter constitute only a narrow selection of the broad variety of forms under which counter-accounts can appear.

As with any scholarly work, we maintain that it is essential for the reader to have some understanding of the context from which a paper and the arguments presented therein derive. Further, we acknowledge that the presumed audience of this chapter is likely to reside outside the accounting discipline, or even outside the broader field of management and organization studies. Therefore, we consider it necessary to begin our discussion with a primer on accounting and the key concept of "account". It is useful for the reader to know that organizations produce a variety of accounts, some mandatory, others voluntary, some standardized, others entirely free of form. We do not intend to provide an exhaustive explanation, nor to claim that counter-accounts and the associated literature could not be understood and drawn on by non-accountants, but that such knowledge is useful in seeking to make sense of the argumentation, logics and research settings that appear within the accounting literature on counter-accounts.

The chapter proceeds as follows. We begin with a brief discussion of accounting and the associated academic literature. Next, we delve into counter-accounts, providing an overview of the concept and the ways in which it has been studied. Our subsequent discussion of counter-accounts from a methodological perspective provides illustrative examples of the two ways in which counter-accounts have been respectively produced and studied by scholars. Discussion and conclusions end the chapter.

Accounting and accounts: a brief introduction

Accounting refers to a range of organizational activities that focus on measuring, assessing, processing and communicating financial and non-financial information (e.g. Hopwood & Miller, 1994). While both the traditional emphasis and the current core of accounting have to do with financial information, the relevance of various types of non-financial information for accounting and accountants is steadily increasing, not least because of the growing significance of social and environmental issues for both societies and individual organizations (Unerman & Chapman, 2014). Below we elaborate how organizations can produce not only mandatory accounts but also voluntary ones, the best examples of the latter being sustainability reports.

Accounting is oftentimes divided into two main areas, known as management accounting and financial accounting. The former focuses on calculative activities taking place inside an organization, such as budgeting, cost accounting and investment appraisals. While many management accounting practices are institutionalized, widely spread and shared across global organizations, they are in principle not regulated. This is in contrast to the second area, financial accounting, which concerns the information processed and reported to an organization's external audiences. Financial statements and the bookkeeping practices underlying them are highly regulated; with the intention of having organizations produce and communicate comparable information to those interested in using it. The most prevalent user group is investors, but the information is also relevant for various other groups, such as regulators, other organizations and the organizations' own management.

While there have been considerable efforts to harmonize accounting standards on the international level, particularly through the development of International Financial Accounting Standards (IASB), there are still substantial differences between jurisdictions such as the US, European Union, China and India (Camfferman & Zeff, 2018). It is also relevant to acknowledge that financial accounting requirements vary according to the type of organization, with small businesses differing from large listed entities, and public sector organizations from private ones and NGOs. At the same time, it is worth noting the other end of the spectrum, the various secrecy jurisdictions, which not only impose very few regulatory requirements for resident organizations, but also stipulate that those organizations do not need to disclose any information to external parties (Shaxson, 2011). Such opportunities enable the creation of complex organizational structures, for instance the establishment of holding companies in jurisdictions with appropriate legislation to avoid taxes in other places, to limit the possibilities of interested parties to obtain information about the activities or ownership of a particular organization, or all of these simultaneously. We will return to this theme in more detail below, as this phenomenon relates closely to counter-accounts.

In addition to the mandatory financial disclosures, many organizations, especially multinational corporations and large locally listed companies, publish other types of reports on a voluntary basis. A prominent example is sustainability reports, which have developed into a standard feature of organizational landscape during the last decades. Despite some minor regulatory requirements set in recent years, such as the European Union directive on non-financial disclosures (Johansen, 2016), sustainability reporting remains a predominantly voluntary activity. This implies that organizations have major control over what they decide to disclose, how they do it, which issues they emphasize, as well as which aspects they decide to remain silent on. This continues to engender scepticism as organizations have continuously been noted to use their sustainability disclosures for impression management by, for instance, avoiding controversial topics, bolstering the significance of minor improvements, or seeking to construct new narratives of themselves as green organizations or pioneering trailblazers (Cho et al., 2015). Even though many organizations seek to increase the credibility of their sustainability disclosures by having an independent third party provide assurance on the information, this might not produce the intended effect as sustainability assurance is also a voluntary and unregulated activity, and the assurance providers operate largely under the discretion of the organization's management. As such, many NGOs and civil society actors do not find organizational sustainability reports very informative or credible, and have over the years produced competing interpretations of organizational activities, namely counter-accounts.[1]

Counter-accounts

Counter-accounts can be seen as a subset of counter-narratives, although the two concepts have not, at least to our knowledge, appeared together in prior studies. In the accounting literature, scholars have defined counter-accounts as "accounting for the other, by the other" (Dey et al. 2011, p. 64).[2] Most often, counter-accounts have been discussed in the context of (adverse) social and environmental impacts of organizational activities: as organizations' own sustainability disclosures have been noted to be largely self-serving and biased, counter-accounts produced and published by groups beyond organizational control have been considered as a possible alternative source of information, which could help societal groups make more informed evaluations and decisions of the organization (Tregidga, 2017).

As highlighted by Bamberg and Andrews (2004, p. x), "counter narratives only make sense in relation to something else, that they are countering". Within the broader social science discussion, counter-narratives are understood as alternative storylines used by actors to position themselves, the context they are in, or a wider phenomenon to present a narrative that counters a dominant cultural narrative, or masterplot. Andrews (2004) notes that counter-narratives make visible how a dominant narrative could be told in a different way, that the masterplot might not be the only way the story could be told. In this sense, individuals or groups can use counter-narratives, for instance, to make sense of their own lives or experiences, which seemingly do not fit the dominant normative storyline (see Andrews, 2004, p. 3).

While counter-narratives feature in all spheres of life, the discussion regarding how they can appear in the context of organizations is more closely related to counter accounts. Lundholt et al. (2018), referring to Boje (2001) and Kuhn (2008), describe counter-narratives as those "narrative processes and stories which offer differing interpretations of organizational realities than those constituted by dominant (Boje, 2001) or authoritative (Kuhn, 2008) narratives". Here, Lundholt and colleagues (2018, pp. 4–5) highlight how in organizational contexts counter-narratives can have a variety of relations to the dominant storylines and emphasize that while counter-narratives can at times be oppositional and in conflict with the masterplot, they can also assume a more dialogic and parallel position in relation to the main narrative. Moreover, in an organizational context one can identify several different narratives, in which the dominant and counter-narratives weave into one another through intertextuality.

Within the literature on counter-accounts, the focus is most often on an alternative account of organizational activities produced by an actor outside the range of organizational control. Instead of a broader narrative, the storyline being countered is an organizational account. Now, what an account consists of is obviously a debated question (Arrington & Francis, 1993). For some, accounts include only the formal disclosures published by an organization, such as annual reports, sustainability reports, press releases and corporate websites. For others, an account is a wider concept, including also anything communicated via an organization's social media account, or uttered by their CEO in a press interview. In each case, accounts can be seen to consist of different types of qualitative or quantitative information released by an organization about its activities in general or in regard to some particular event, policy, or issue. Counter-accounts, then, are most of the time alternative narratives, which counter such an official organizational account. A counter-account can be directly opposed to one specific organizational report, such as a CSR report or an initiative regarding a particular social or environmental issue, or it can assume a broader scope by providing an alternative account of the organization's activities, possibly juxtaposing it with the organization's reports from a longer period of time (Thomson, Dey & Russell, 2015).

Counter-accounts have also been defined with reference to the core concepts of traditional accounting, namely information, users and decisions. While the purpose of conventional accounting is to provide investors and creditors with quantitative, predominantly financial, information about economic entities for the purposes of decision-making and assessing management's accountability (Accounting Principles Board, 1970; International Accounting Standards Board, 2010), counter-accounts may contain also qualitative and non-financial information concerning entire industries or governance regimes, for a broad range of constituencies[3] who can utilize this information for making not only economic decisions but also moral and political ones (Vinnari & Laine, 2017).

Counter-accounts appear in various forms, such as one-off written reports, video material, or a longer-term campaign including a range of materials. Often cited examples from the early 2000s include the "Other Shell Report", published by the Friends of the Earth as a response to Shell's report "People, Planet and Profit", and the "British American Tobacco: The Other Report to Society", published by the Action on Smoking and Health as an alternative perspective on BAT's social auditing initiative and associated disclosures. While similar types of accounts have been published also considerably earlier (e.g. the work of Social Audit Ltd., see Gray et al., 1996; Medawar, 1976), it seems that counter-accounts have gained more prominence in the past two decades, possibly in part due to improved access to information and easier communication available through the internet and more recently the social media. Overall, various types of counter-accounts are now clearly a part of social movements' toolkits throughout the world.

An early paper on such alternative accounts is Dey (2003), which distinguished between silent accounts, i.e. accounts created from the information produced and disclosed by the organization itself, and shadow accounts, those produced by using information collected from sources outside and beyond the control of the organization (see Gray, 1997). While silent accounts allow presenting the organization in a different light without needing to collect any competing information, shadow accounts provide the opportunity to shed light on possible gaps as well as misrepresentations in the organization's disclosures. Sometimes creating a silent account by using only the information provided by the focal organization can aid those willing to challenge the entity in creating a more convincing case, as the organization under scrutiny cannot simply attempt to dismiss the source material as unreliable and biased. Continuing on this theme, Dey, Russell and Thomson (2011) examined the potential of shadow accounts in problematizing the institutional conduct of organizations or broader social institutions. Using examples from the accounting literature (e.g. Harte & Owen, 1987; Adams, 2004; Cooper et al., 2005), Dey et al. (2011, p. 71) argue that in order to "promote emancipatory social change" and enhance organizational accountabilities, shadow accounts need to facilitate dialogue and debate, identify alternative courses of action, and also create space and opportunities for change. While neither Dey (2003) nor Dey et al. (2011) use the term counter-account, the phenomena of silent and shadow accounts clearly fall under the broader umbrella of counter-accounts.

We will next turn to a more detailed discussion of counter-accounts as a methodology, dividing our argument in two parts. First, we will discuss the counter-accounts produced by scholars. We claim that this is a particularly relevant theme for accounting scholarship, given the complexity of the accounting practice and the expertise it requires to master the intricacy of the accounting craft. Accounting scholars can use their expertise not only in choosing their research topics, but also in producing and presenting alternative accounts of some perceived problematic organizational or institutional practices. Second, we highlight how the question of counter-accounts' methodology is in fact double-layered, as not only the various NGOs and social movements use counter-accounts in their campaigning work, but also the scholars investigating such counter-accounting will resort to particular theoretical and methodological approaches in their research. As emphasized earlier, our illustrative examples are only a narrow selection of the broad variety of forms that counter-accounts can take.

Counter-accounts as a research methodology

One of the areas requiring specific expertise within the domain of accounting is taxation. A recurring storyline in the 2000s has been the various types of tax avoidance schemes employed by major multinational companies. While journalists have done a commendable job in trying to explain the complexities of the phenomenon and the details of particular cases to the public (e.g. Obermayer & Obermaier, 2016; Barstow, Craig & Buettner, 2018), the relationships between taxation, accounting and international regulation require considerable expertise from anyone willing to understand the details. Combined with most multinationals' pledges of corporate social responsibility and profiling themselves as good corporate citizens, the field of corporate tax avoidance offers those possessing sufficient expertise ample opportunities to engage in counter-accounting.

Even though any larger corporation is usually perceived to be a single entity, virtually all such companies are in fact corporate groups consisting of a parent company and a vast number of subsidiaries, in other words separate organizations varying in size, form and purpose. Given that a substantial portion of the world trade currently takes place between these parent companies and subsidiaries (Ylönen & Teivainen, 2018), and that such intra-firm trade has a significant role in various tax planning and avoidance mechanisms organizations use, it is oftentimes relevant to unpack an organization's financial situation by getting deeper into its accounts. A corporate group's consolidated financial statements, which are included in the annual report, present the group's aggregate financial figures. Despite the plentiful information provided in such consolidated accounts, the aggregation by definition also implies that many details are lost in the process. Therefore, to understand the setting and financial transactions between parent company and subsidiaries, the researcher often needs to gain access to the financial statements of the various subsidiaries. Producing such accounts on an annual basis is mandatory, and in a number of jurisdictions anyone can gain access to these via the local trade registry. Likewise, further information on companies' and their subsidiaries' activities and financial transactions can be obtained through other public registers, such as trade statistics on imports and exports, and customs statistics. Using a combination of various types of records from a long period of time makes it possible for the researcher to produce an alternative account of a tax-avoiding organization and its activities.

A recent example of this is the study by Finér and Ylönen (2017), who conduct a multiple case study of the tax avoidance schemes used by two Canadian mining companies in three of their mines located in Finland. Given that the authors' investigation is based on publicly available data, they can use their knowledge of taxation to publicly problematize the conduct of particular organizations, to make visible elements of current arrangements not otherwise brought to public attention, and also to challenge the existing public governance system, which allows organizations to use legislative loopholes for private gains. Methodologically, Finér and Ylönen (2017) emphasize that the discussion of such complicated organizational structures is only possible via in-depth case studies requiring considerable expertise, as the nuances of the arrangements get lost in the aggregated databases. Finér and Ylönen (2017) also point out that such an investigation is made considerably more challenging and is at times limited altogether by companies' use of secrecy jurisdictions, in which the financial records published by companies resident to the jurisdiction are not made publicly available.

Another somewhat similar analysis is undertaken by Ylönen and Laine (2015), who present a case study of transfer pricing arrangements used by a major Finnish pulp and paper company in its internal pulp trade. Like Finér and Ylönen (2017) above, Ylönen and Laine (2015) base their analysis on a wide range of publicly available data sources, such as subsidiaries' financial statements accessed via trade registers, corporate annual reports, interim reports and press releases, as well as data on imports and exports accessed through customs databases. These are then utilized to present a counter-account of how the organization utilized a small Dutch subsidiary in its internal pulp trade to gain considerable tax benefits, and to discuss how the company had remained silent of the arrangement for years, simultaneously emphasizing its commitment to accurate and transparent communication, to the highest ethical principles, and to being a role model willing to engage in an open dialogue with its stakeholders. It is nonetheless worth noting that in neither of the cases mentioned above do the authors claim that the conduct of the organizations in question would be illegal. Instead, the authors argue that it is important to display such alternative accounts in the public domain to make previously invisible structures visible and to democratize information by making intricate financial accounts more accessible also to those not possessing expertise in accounting and taxation (see also Sikka & Willmott, 2010; Ting, 2014).

These examples of researchers' counter-accounts on corporate taxation also relate to a broader discussion on the role of academics in societies. With the ever-escalating sustainability challenges facing contemporary societies, we remain adamant that scholars should use their position to engage in societal debates as public intellectuals, taking an active role in critically assessing and, if needed, challenging hegemonic political logics and taken-for-granted truths (see Tregidga, Milne & Kearins, 2018; Golsorkhi et al., 2009). The contemporary business world is a fruitful setting for such critique, as currently virtually all multinational corporations and industrial lobby groups advocate responsible business practices and claim to be at the forefront of sustainability. While we are sympathetic to such efforts and encourage corporations to take swift action, in general we remain sceptical of much of the discourses of business sustainability, social good and shared value creation, as despite the beautiful talk and overflowing commitments the major global sustainability trends show no substantial sign of change (see Steffen et al., 2015; IPCC, 2018). As such, we maintain that scholars with accounting expertise are needed to explicate the prevailing business logic and corporate communication to individuals and groups lacking such knowledge but possessing other characteristics and resources needed to take societal action. Moreover, while our examples relate to taxation, we are by no means saying that the role of scholars should be limited to this particular theme; similar counter-accounts are needed across the realm of sustainability.

Counter-accounts as a research topic

In addition to producing their own counter-accounts, researchers have also studied the counter-accounts compiled by social movement activists or NGOs on behalf of some oppressed group or the natural environment. Scholars have sought to add knowledge on counter-accounts with investigations from a range of theoretical perspectives, with varying datasets and methodological approaches. Counter-accounts have often been conducted as single-case studies by contrasting the information provided in an organization's or industry's formal accounts with the counter-account produced by an external actor (see Adams, 2004). Such a setting has then been used in attempts to tease out nuances of organizational activities, the characteristics of counter-accounts and the identities of the groups producing them, the role and relevance of counter-accounts in contemporary societies, as well as the possibilities of counter-accounts to facilitate a transition towards a more democratic society (e.g. Apostol, 2015; Laine & Vinnari, 2017; O'Sullivan & O'Dwyer, 2009; Tregidga, 2017; Vinnari & Laine, 2017).

Here we will present two examples of research on counter-accounts, deliberately chosen to be as different as possible. The first example focuses on Finnish animal rights activists' use of counter-accounts in their campaign against the meat and dairy industry. Our second example concerns international NGOs' use of counter-accounts in campaigning against major oil companies in the Niger Delta.

Vinnari and Laine (2017; see also Laine & Vinnari, 2017) analyze the counter-accounts produced by Finnish animal rights activists on behalf of farmed animals. In practice, these accounts consist of secretly filmed video clips from animal farms that have been uploaded on dedicated websites and occasionally shown on national television. Vinnari and Laine (2017) employ the analytics of mediation (Chouliaraki, 2006), a form of critical discourse analysis, in their examination of the activist videos as displayed on the website and a television news programme. The aim of their study is to shed light on the ways in which the visual counter-accounts might evoke the spectators' sympathy towards the suffering animals and encourage them to take practical action. The authors find that counter-accounts can give rise to different ethical discourses and practical engagement options depending on how they are visually and verbally framed, and whether they are displayed on the activist website or embedded in the news programme. Laine and Vinnari (2017) in turn apply the concepts of discourse theory (Laclau & Mouffe, 1985; Laclau, 1996, 2001, 2005) in their analysis of interview data and documentary material related to the release of the activist videos. Focusing on the potential effects generated by the counter-accounts, the authors note how the dominant social groups attempted to divert attention from the atrocities of animal production by representing the activists as irresponsible, militant and negligent. Making a methodological point that is also of broader relevance, Laine and Vinnari (2017) highlight the difficulty of trying to identify the societal effects of a particular counter-account and thus establish whether it can be deemed effective.

Our second example is set in an oil-rich developing nation with glaring power differentials between marginalized communities and corporations. Denedo et al. (2017, 2019) undertake a single-case study of how international advocacy NGOs have used counter-accounts to combat corruption, environmental degradation, poverty and human rights violations associated with oil production in the Niger Delta. Having begun already in the 1990s, the conflict has assumed diverse forms from peaceful protests to violent struggles with several lives lost, and involved numerous advocacy NGOs, transnational actors, oil companies and the Nigerian government. In their analysis, the authors apply the conflict arena framework (Thomson et al., 2015) to examine interview data and a wide range of counter-accounts, including tangible reports, legal actions, documentaries, petitions, YouTube videos, protests and blog entries. They find that the NGOs employed different types of counter-accounts at different stages of the protracted conflict, depending on the context. The NGO representatives interviewed found the counter-accounts useful for giving visibility and voice to underprivileged indigenous groups; helping those communities build capacity to more effectively defend their rights; and for delegitimizing and reforming problematic governance and accountability mechanisms. However, making a point similar to Laine and Vinnari (2017), the authors note that a snapshot view of NGOs' current satisfaction does not guarantee that counter-accounts have succeeded in permanently improving the situation in the Niger Delta due to the dynamic nature of the conflict.

Conclusions

In this chapter, we have discussed counter-accounts as one sub-type of counter-narratives. We began with a short introduction to the basic notion of "account" and the principles of accounting as a practice. We then provided a definition of counter-accounts and explained how they have been studied in the accounting literature. Finally, we discussed counter-accounts from two different methodological perspectives, counter-accounts as a research method and counter-accounts as a research topic. Based on this discussion, we can draw two main conclusions. First, in a field as technical and specialized as accounting, academics are in a position to undertake social science that matters (Flyvbjerg, 2001) by compiling counter-accounts either by themselves or in collaboration with social movements or NGOs. Second, counter-accounts produced by activists provide fertile ground for academic analyses from multiple theoretical and methodological perspectives. Such examinations also enable scholars with an emancipatory intent to flag questionable or downright despicable corporate practices, although more indirectly. As the sustainability challenges societies are facing loom ever larger, we argue that it is highly relevant for scholars to understand and engage with the various types of counter-accounts, which challenge the hegemonic narratives and vested interests defending the status quo as well as promoting inaction over issues such as climate change, biodiversity loss, human rights breaches and the undermining of democracy.

Notes

1 Like many other disciplines, accounting has competing schools of thought. The adherents of the dominant paradigm draw mostly on economics, subscribe to a post-positivist epistemology and apply quantitative methods to large datasets of capital market information. In contrast, a smaller school of interpretive and critical scholars sees accounting as a social and institutional practice, and draws on a variety of social scientific theories to study the role and implications of accounting and accounting practices in societies. The concept counter-account originates from a subset of this interpretive/critical research, namely social and environmental accounting (SEA) research. SEA scholars examine how accounting, accounting practices and the associated disclosures are related to the social and environmental impacts of organizations, as well as the implications these practices have for the broader sustainability issues in society.

2 While the term counter-account was introduced rather recently, it is worth noting that similar phenomena have also been examined earlier (see Medawar, 1976; Harte & Owen, 1987; Gray, 1997; Cooper et al., 2005).

3 E.g. suppliers, customers, employees, governments, non-governmental organizations and the public at large.

References

Accounting Principles Board. (1970). Statement No. 4, basic concepts and accounting principles underlying financial statements or business enterprises. New York: American Institute of Certified Public Accountants. paragraph 40.

Adams, C. (2004). The ethical, social and environmental reporting-performance portrayal gap. *Accounting, Auditing and Accountability Journal*, 17(5), 731–757.

Andrews, M. (2004). Counter-narratives and the power to oppose. In Bamberg, M. & Andrews, M. (Eds.), *Considering counter-narratives: Narrating, resisting, making sense*. Amsterdam, The Netherlands: John Benjamins, pp. 1–6.

Apostol, O.M. (2015), A project for Romania? The role of the civil society's counter accounts in facilitating democratic change in society. *Accounting, Auditing & Accountability Journal*, 28(2), 210–241.

Arrington, C.E. & Francis, J.R. (1993). Giving economic accounts: Accounting as a cultural practice. *Accounting, Organizations and Society*, 18(2/3), 107–124.

Bamberg, M., & Andrews, M. (Eds.). (2004). *Considering counter-narratives. Narrating, resisting, making sense.* Amsterdam: John Benjamins.

Barstow, D., Craig, S., & Buettner, R. (2018). Trump engaged in suspect tax schemes as he reaped riches from his father. *The New York Times*, October 2, 2018.

Boje, D. (2001). *Narrative methods for organizational and communication research.* London, UK: Sage.

Camfferman, K. and Zeff, S.A. (2018). The challenge of setting standards for a worldwide constituency: Research implications from the IASB's early history. *European Accounting Review*, 27(2), 289–312.

Cho, C.H., Laine, M., Roberts, R.W., & Rodrigue, M. (2015). Organized hypocrisy, organizational façades, and sustainability reporting. *Accounting, Organizations and Society*, 40(1), 78–94.

Chouliaraki, L. (2006). Towards an analytics of mediation. *Critical Discourse Studies*, 3(2), 153–178.

Cooper, C., Taylor, P., Smith, N., & Catchpowle, L. (2005). A discussion of the political potential of social accounting. *Critical Perspectives on Accounting*, 16(7), 951–974.

Denedo, M., Thomson, I., & Yonekura, A. (2017) International advocacy NGOs, counter accounting, accountability and engagement. *Accounting, Auditing & Accountability Journal*, 30(6), 1309–1343.

Denedo, M., Thomson, I., & Yonekura, A. (2019) Ecological damage, human rights and oil: Local advocacy NGOs dialogic action and alternative accounting practices. *Accounting Forum. In press.*

Dey, C. (2003). Corporate 'silent' and 'shadow' social accounts. *Social and Environmental Accountability Journal*, 23(2), 6–9.

Dey, C., Russell, S., & Thomson, I. (2011). Exploring the potential of shadow accounts in problematising institutional conduct. In Osbourne, S. and Ball, A. (Eds.), *Social accounting and public management: Accountability for the common good*, Routledge, Abingdon, pp. 64–75.

Finér, L. & Ylönen, M. (2017). Tax-driven wealth chains: A multiple case study of tax avoidance in the finnish mining sector. *Critical Perspectives on Accounting*, 48, 53–81.

Flyvbjerg, B. (2001). *Making social science matter.* Cambridge: Cambridge University Press.

Frandsen, S., Kuhn, T. & Lundholt, M.W. (Eds.) (2017). *Counter-narratives and organizations.* Abingdon, UK: Routledge.

Golsorkhi, D., B. Leca, M. Lounsbury, & C. Ramirez (2009). Analysing, accounting for and unmasking domination: On our role as scholars of practice, practitioners of social science and public intellectuals. *Organization* 16(6), 779–797.

Gray, R. (1997). The practice of silent accounting. In Zadek, S., Evans, R. & Pruzan, P. (Eds.), *Building corporate accountability: Emerging practices in social and ethical accounting*, Auditing and Reporting, Earthscan, London, pp. 201–217.

Gray, R., Owen, D., & Adams, C. (1996). *Accounting and Accountability: Changes and challenges in corporate social and environmental reporting.* Hemel Hempsted: Prentice Hall.

Harte, G. & Owen, D. (1987). Fighting de-industrialisation: the role of local government social audits. *Accounting, Organizations and Society*, 12(2), 123–141.

Hopwood, A.G. & Miller, P. (Eds.) (1994). *Accounting as social and institutional practice.* Cambridge: Cambridge University Press.

International Accounting Standards Board. (2010). *The conceptual framework for financial reporting.* London: IFRS Publications Department.

IPCC (2018). Summary for Policymakers. In: Global Warming of 1.5°C. An IPCC Special Report on the impacts of global warming of 1.5°C above pre-industrial levels and related global greenhouse gas emission pathways, in the context of strengthening the global response to the threat of climate change, sustainable development, and efforts to eradicate poverty [Masson-Delmotte, V., P. Zhai, H.-O. Pörtner, D. Roberts, J. Skea, P.R. Shukla, A. Pirani, Moufouma-Okia, C. Péan, R. Pidcock, S. Connors, J.B.R. Matthews, Y. Chen, X. Zhou, M.I. Gomis, E. Lonnoy, Maycock, M. Tignor, & T. Waterfield (Eds.)]. World Meteorological Organization, Geneva, Switzerland, 32 pp.

Johansen, T.R. (2016). EU regulation of corporate social and environmental reporting. *Social and Environmental Accountability Journal*, 36(1), 1–9.

Kuhn, T. (2008). A communicative theory of the firm: Developing an alternative perspective on intra-organizational power and stakeholder relationships. *Organization Studies*, 29(8–9), 1227–1254.

Laclau, E. (1996). *Emancipation(s).* London: Verso.

Laclau, E. (2001). Democracy and the question of power. *Constellations*, 8(1), 3–14.

Laclau, E. (2005). *On populist reason.* London: Verso.

Laclau, E. & Mouffe, C. (1985/2001). *Hegemony and socialist strategy: Towards a radical democratic politics*, 2nd ed. London: Verso.

Laine, M. & Vinnari, E. (2017) The transformative potential of counter accounts: a case study of animal rights activism. *Accounting, Auditing & Accountability Journal*, 30(7), 1481–1510.
Lundholt, M.W., Maagaard, C.A., & Piekut, A. (2018). Counternarratives. In Heath, R.L. and Johansen, W. (Eds.), *The international encyclopedia of strategic communication*. New York: John Wiley, 1–11.
Medawar, C. (1976). The social audit: A political view. *Accounting, Organizations and Society*, 1(4), 389–394.
Obermayer, B. & Obermaier, F. (2016). *Panama Papers. Die Geschichte einer weltweiten Enthüllung*. Köln, Verlag Kiepenheuer & Witsch.
O'Sullivan, N. & O'Dwyer, B. (2009). Stakeholder perspectives on a financial sector legitimation process: the case of NGOs and the equator principles. *Accounting, Auditing & Accountability Journal*, 22(4), 553–587.
Shaxson, N. (2011). *Treasure islands: Tax havens and the men who stole the world*, London: The Bodley Head.
Sikka, P. & Willmott, H. (2010). The dark side of transfer pricing: Its role in tax avoidance and wealth retentiveness. *Critical Perspectives on Accounting*, 21, 342–356.
Steffen, W., Richardson, K., Rockstr€om, J., Cornell, S.E., Fetzer, I., Bennett, E.M., et al. (2015). Planetary boundaries: Guiding human development on a changing plane. 13 February 2015 *Science*, 347(6223).
Thomson, I., Dey, C., & Russell, S. (2015). Activism, arenas and accounts in conflicts over tobacco control. *Accounting, Auditing & Accountability Journal*, 28(5), 809–845.
Ting, A. (2014). iTax - Apple's international tax structure and the double non-taxation issue. *British Tax Review 2014*, No. 1.
Tregidga, H. (2017). "Speaking truth to power": Analysing shadow reporting as a form of shadow accounting. *Accounting, Auditing & Accountability Journal*, 30(3), 510–533.
Tregidga, H., Milne, M., & Kearins, K. (2018). Ramping up resistance: Corporate Sustainable Development and Academic Research. *Business & Society*, 57(2), 292–334.
Unerman, J. & Chapman, C. (2014). Academic contributions to enhancing accounting for sustainable development. *Accounting, Organizations and Society*, 39(6), 385–394.
Vinnari, E. & Laine, M. (2017). The moral mechanism of counter accounts: The case of industrial animal production. *Accounting, Organizations and Society*, 57, 1–17.
Ylönen, M. & Laine, M. (2015). For logistical reasons only? A case study of tax planning and corporate social responsibility reporting. *Critical Perspectives on Accounting*, 33, 5–23.
Ylönen, M. & Teivainen, T. (2018). Politics of intra-firm trade: Corporate price planning and the double role of the arm's length principle. *New Political Economy*, 23(4), 441–457.

10

Board games as a new method for studying troubled family narratives

Framing counter-narratives in social design research

Thomas Markussen and Eva Knutz

Introduction

Social design research is essentially concerned with how the practice of designing can be used to foster change and well-being for vulnerable groups in society. Insofar as it aims at bringing about social value by empowering underserved people, social design is related to social innovation and social entrepreneurship, but there are significant differences. Unlike social innovation and social entrepreneurship, social design is not defined by its ability to achieve large-scale systemic changes that can be imitated and transferred to various contexts (Martin & Osberg, 2007). Social design is typically aiming at making social change happen in a confined local context for a limited group of people (Markussen, 2017). Moreover, design – the process of making artifacts, services or systems – is taken to be the central means by which change is achieved. Hence, design must be understood as involving both a *process* and an *artifact* (E. Knutz et al., 2019; Eva Knutz & Markussen, 2019). Importantly, here the process is thought of in participatory terms meaning that the people who are being designed for should have a say in the design process by genuinely participating in researching, generating and realizing new social design solutions (see e.g. Armstrong et al., 2014).

In this chapter, we demonstrate how counter narratives can be applied in social design research as a way of studying narratives and identity making in troubled families. More specifically, we present a study of a board game called *Captivated* that has been designed with and for children and incarcerated fathers in Danish maximum-security prisons. *Captivated* is the result of a three-year research project aimed at investigating if games have the potential to help children (age 11–18) cope better with the negative collateral effects of paternal incarceration (Markussen & Knutz, forthcoming). The design of the game relies on the assumption that the game can act as a facilitating prompt for re-storying troubled family narratives. By allowing inmates and their children to tell family narratives during in-visits it is further hypothesized, based on studies in criminology and psychology that the bonds between them can be strengthened to the benefit of the children's well-being (see e.g. Fivush et al., 2011). However, the question of whether the game actually lead to the well-being of children, who play it with incarcerated fathers requires a longitudinal study beyond the scope of the three-year project, which is focusing primarily on the family narratives that the board game elicits.

Much research has been done already on narratives and their role in family contexts (see e.g. Gordon, 2015). By drawing on this existing work, in the following section we make a theoretical distinction between *master, family* and *personal* narratives. This three-fold distinction is valuable for conducting a subtle inquiry into the narrative acts of countering that may take place in processes of family storytelling. Moreover, we shall point out some methodological pitfalls and explain how we try to avoid them by founding our method of inquiry upon the so-called *small stories* approach.

However, the aim of the chapter is not only to demonstrate how counter narratives can be applied to social design, but also – vice versa – how social design can contribute with innovative methods for studying counter narratives in family contexts. Thus, in the second section, we show how our study diverges methodologically from previous studies insofar as it uses a material artifact – the board game – as a central prompt for the interview setting and recording of family storytelling. In so doing, we get access to study how positioning in family narratives may be expressed multi-modally through verbal language, bodily gestures and visual drawings. Finally, in the third section, we delve deeper into our interviews with Oskar and his incarcerated father John.

Narratives in family contexts

In the seminal book *Considering Counter-Narratives*, Kölbl (2004) critically pointed out a need to work out empirical strategies for studying the origin of master-narratives and how individuals' telling of family stories may counter or challenge master-narratives. Kölbl's concern was primarily motivated by his commentary on Molly Andrews' study of four elderly men and women, whom she interviewed about "the role of their mothers in relation to the children they were and the adults they became" (Andrews, 2004a, p. 7). Despite the fact that all of them had experienced troubled relations with their mother, none of the interviewees indulged in a "deterministic mother-blaming" master narrative as Andrews originally assumed. Rather, in their personal accounts they countered this master narrative by showing empathic understanding of the difficult circumstances, which their mothers had gone through. On the basis of this, Andrews concludes that, while the family stories people tell at some level mirror master-narratives, at the same time they counter them (ibid., p. 23).

However, Kölbl criticizes Andrews' interpretation for at least three reasons. First, Andrews argues that the deterministic mother-blaming should be considered a cultural master narrative having its origin in developmental psychology's idea of "early maternal influence and its long-term effects" (Kölbl, 2004: 29). In so doing, says Kölbl, Andrews incorrectly homogenizes developmental psychology as if it existed as a monolithic discipline. But more importantly, he raises the epistemological question of what exactly is the relationship between scientific theories and master-narratives dominant in society. To answer this question, precise definitions are needed of what we mean by master-narratives (ibid., p. 28).

Second, Kölbl points out a methodological pitfall insofar as Andrews seems to conflate her own theoretical assumptions with the master narrative she presumably uncovers through her analysis of the interview data. Hence, the self-fulfilling risk of "producing findings based on one's own conceptual framework" (Andrews, 2004b: 10).

Third, says Kölbl, the conclusion that personal family stories mirror and at the same time counter dominant master-narratives should hardly come as a surprise. As he rhetorically asks: "Do we not always tell stories which, on the one hand, take up acknowledged common cultural ends

[...] and on the other hand, challenge these ends?" (Kölbl, 2004: 31) What for Kölbl is more interesting is to use family stories as an entry point for studying how "people organize their personal domain of sense-making" (ibid. 28).

Disregarding whether you agree with Kölbl's critique of Andrews or not (for Andrews' reply, see e.g. Andrews, 2004b), his call for working out precise theoretical definitions and consistent methodologies is of general relevance for studying narratives in family contexts. In this and the next section, we focus on how narrative practice research has largely addressed the theoretical and methodological issues, while eschewing the epistemological question of the difference between scientific theories and cultural master-narratives.

Theoretically, McLean (2017) has suggested that a useful analytical distinction can be made between *master*, *family* and *personal* narratives. Master-narratives are taken in the most common use of the term to denote "culturally shared stories that communicate what the standards and expectations are for being a part of a community" (K. C. McLean, 2017, p. 31). Master-narratives become dominant, because they are told often, group consensus makes them seem naturally given and they provide broader cultural frames, values, and beliefs that members of a community can relate and interpret their experiences according to (cf. Bamberg, 2004; Hammack, 2008; Thorne & McLean, 2003). In a family context, for instance, cultural expectations exist about what constitutes a good family, parenting and childhood (Gordon, 2015). Typically, such expectations can be derived from interview data collected from family storytelling. Thus, in their well-known comparative study of Norwegian and American family talk recorded during dinnertime, Aukrust and Snow (1998) found that while Norwegian families tend to value collectivism, their American counterparts favored individualism. But it is important to notice, as pointed out by Mclean (2017) and Gordon (2015, p. 313), that these dominant master-narratives are not identical with family narratives.

Family narratives certainly share some characteristic with master-narratives: they are told often, provide a consensual frame for family members' positioning of their experiences and identity, and so on. However, their difference consists in their influence being confined primarily to the family itself and their lighter nature. Consider, for example, McLean's interview with a family of six, who spent most of the conversation telling stories of "prior injuries and mishaps". In so doing, the family co-authored a small family story emphasizing a few values: "Take risks, stay positive, move forward" (K. C. McLean, 2017, p. 47).

The personal narratives of individual family members may be more or less consistent with the overall family narrative. However, it is usually the case that personal narratives at the same time resist family narratives as both Andrews and Kölbl noticed. This resistance may manifest itself in at least two forms: either personal narratives can be positioned in direct contrast or opposition to the family narratives; or they may be juxtaposed to family narratives without necessarily being in contradictory terms. Mclean (2017) uses the term "alternative narratives" to denote instances of the latter, while we propose using 'counter narratives' in a more restricted sense to designate the former. This differentiation is important as it allows for a better understanding of identity development in context (cf. Kate C. McLean & Syed, 2015), which will become evident in our case analysis below. Moreover, alternative and counter narratives are not reducible to the relationship between personal and family narratives, but may be extended to a more comprehensive analysis of how personal, family and master narrative amalgamate in interview data.

Methodological approach

The central methodological questions Kölbl raised are: How do we avoid only finding in interview data what our conceptual frameworks allow us to see? How do we methodologically approach the inconsistencies of family narratives without reducing them in advance to an oversimplified opposition between master-narratives and the personal domain of sense making? These questions have to a large extent spurred the founding of the small stories approach that has been developed in parallel with the increasing interest in counter narratives (see e.g. Bamberg, 2006; Bamberg & Georgakopoulou, 2008; Georgakopoulou, 2007, 2015). With the small stories approach the idea is given up that speakers' talk can be looked upon as countering or subverting some coherently structured narrative that somehow lurks in the background of the conversation. We can only deal with master-narratives in the piecemeal way in which they are pulled into and articulated through conversations (Bamberg, 2006). This means foregrounding, as the primary unit of analysis, the process of talk-in-interaction as it unfolds through local contexts and social practices (De Fina, 2008; De Fina & Georgakopoulou, 2008). However, it is not only to signal this analytical shift of attention that the approach has been dubbed 'small stories' in contrast to 'big stories'. Small stories also refer to the specific form and content of the stories that are being investigated.

In a family context, big stories refer to past memories that people tell about their childhood, parents or significant so-called *reportable* events in their life. Such stories are typically collected through autobiographical interviews, where a person in a reflective and more or less well-structured manner tells a researcher about her or his life story. Small stories, on the other hand, are about everyday events that are often told among family members during dinnertime or other mundane activities. They tend to be ill-structured, fragmented, about the here-and-now or near projected future (Bamberg & Georgakopoulou, 2008). To collect them researchers often use audio- and video recordings of conversations taking place among family members, while they talk over the phone, at the dinner table, and so on.

The small stories approach has resulted in a significant change in the conception of how family stories can be an entry point for studying how family members use narratives to position themselves and who they are. While big stories can easily lead one to believe that people's self-representation is relatively stable, it becomes clear from studying small stories that identity construction happens through multilevel acts of positioning (Bamberg & Georgakopoulou, 2008). Personal identity is a fluid and changing phenomenon formed through situated narrative processes and the interview setting itself must be regarded as having an influence on how family stories are told.

Constructive design research: social games as research artifacts

While our present study is informed by the theoretical distinctions made above and the small stories approach, we need to make explicit how our approach is different from existing research on narratives. Notably, this difference has to do with i) "mixing" the small stories approach with constructive design research and ii) incarcerated fathers and their children's family storytelling being rather unexplored within the field.

Typically, small stories in family contexts are either audio- or video recorded in people's home with a researcher facilitating a conversation with members of a family. Transcriptions of these recordings are then made the object of coding, analysis and interpretation. In our case, however, we have designed and used a board game as the central material prompt in our audio recording of five interviews with inmates and their children about playing the game during in-visits. Now, it is well known from anthropology that the presence of the researcher and the tools she may use for recording participatory observations must be accounted for as influencing research outcomes. However, we argue that our use of the game goes one step further, because we do not merely observe or talk. As the content and flow of the recorded small story talk was to a large extent generated by the game, it becomes the centerpiece of what we shall call a "constructive design research approach" (Koskinen et al., 2011).

By constructive design research we refer to the idea that processes of making artifacts can serve as a legitimate method of inquiring into certain areas and thereby be a vehicle for knowledge production (Koskinen et al., 2011; Vaughan, 2017). We also consider these design processes as potentially leading to a change of the existing into a presumably "preferred state" (Simon, 1969). This means that constructive design research at its core must be considered a normative or even political practice. Because what is regarded as 'preferred' obviously depends on interests, ideologies and values that need to be made explicit. For the present study, for instance, a game was designed to help children and incarcerated father to re-story family narratives in order to foster a qualitatively better relation between them. Underlying this intervention is a certain ideology implying that family talk is good and that it can increase children's well-being.

In this sense, our constructive design research approach is closely related to how narratives have been brought into action-oriented social work. Here a narrative approach has been taken, as Riessman and Quinney show (2005, p. 396), by practitioners, who help individuals to "restory their situation, emphasizing positive effects of deconstruction and reconstruction of life stories". This is a "therapeutic use of storytelling" aiming at "facilitating discoveries of competences and resilience" (ibid.). However, in their extensive survey of the field, the authors did only find scarce practical work that was theoretically well informed with precise definitions of narrative concepts and at the same time carried out according to a consistent and transparent methodological gathering of data.

Recently, McKenzie-Mohr and Lafrance (2017) have made a promising attempt at developing a theory of master and counter narratives for social practice work and they also show how counter narratives can be used to understand how individuals try to cope with traumatic incidents such as HIV infection and rape. In an effort to extend this prior work, we have introduced the distinction above between master, family and personal narratives and described how they can either counter or be alternative to each other. Yet again, the difference is that we bring a design artifact into people's life that is intended to change their family relation by helping them to create new stories. Additionally, we argue that this artifact is a research artifact insofar as it can be used in a methodological consistent way to study this relationship through the process of family storytelling.

Research context

In Denmark, at any point in time 4,500 children experience having a parent in prison. The majority of these parents are men, and empirical studies have documented that paternal imprisonment is detrimental to most children's well-being and development. For instance, it has been found that prisoners' children show antisocial behavior, they suffer from having mental health problems, difficulties learning in school, eating disorders and troubles building friendships (see e.g. McKay et al., 2018; Murray et al., 2012). At the same time, it has been documented that children can be helped to cope better with these negative effects if visiting facilities in prison are made more family friendly and enduring interactions between father and child is possible (Jones et al., 2013).

Building partially on this knowledge, the Danish Prison and Probation Service established the Child-responsible program in 2013. As part of this program, 80 prison officers with special responsibilities for inmates' families have been appointed; visiting rooms and apartments are constructed as family friendly environments with playgrounds, toys and children books, and so on. Yet, even though much has been done, initiatives are lacking for adolescents as pointed out in a recent report made by The Danish National Centre for Social Research. The report shows, among other things, that the well-being of children from the age of 11–17, who experience parental incarceration, is lower as compared to smaller children. If they lose contact with their

Figure 10.1 The board game designed as a prison. Photo credit Eva Knutz.

fathers in prison, it is assumed that they have a higher risk of ending up in psychiatric treatment, placement with a foster family or that it will significantly reduce their educational performance (Oldrup et al., 2016, pp. 5–14).

The board game *Captivated* is designed to help children in this age group and their incarcerated fathers in maximum-security Danish prisons to maintain a relationship through frequent and meaningful in-visits. 'Meaningful' here refers to the game being designed for three specific game goals. Ideally, it should i) remove the insecurity that these children experience due to ignorance of what a Danish prison is like; ii) increase intimacy through physical interaction between children and their fathers; and iii) build up trust through deeper personal communication.

Captivated is similar to *Monopoly*, but instead of driving around in a city, the players walk into a prison (see Figure 10.1). To start, the players choose a group in the prison that they would like to collect. The groupings consist of The Fraudsters, The Ghetto, The Bikers, The Eastern Bloc, Small Offenders and The Prison Officers. Each member of the group is represented on a character card and inhabits a location in the prison. As the players move around they learn about these places and the people who live there. At the backside of each character card, a story is written about them. For the criminals, the first sentence states what they are convicted of, the next paragraph says something about their family relations and finally there is a humorous line or two providing an impression of their personality (see Figure 10.2). All of the criminals have done something offensive, but they are also fathers.

As the players move around the prison they land on characters or squares that allow them to pick a question card from the pile in the center of the board. The question cards have been

Figure 10.2 Front and back of the character card Jimmy. © 2018 Social Design Unit.

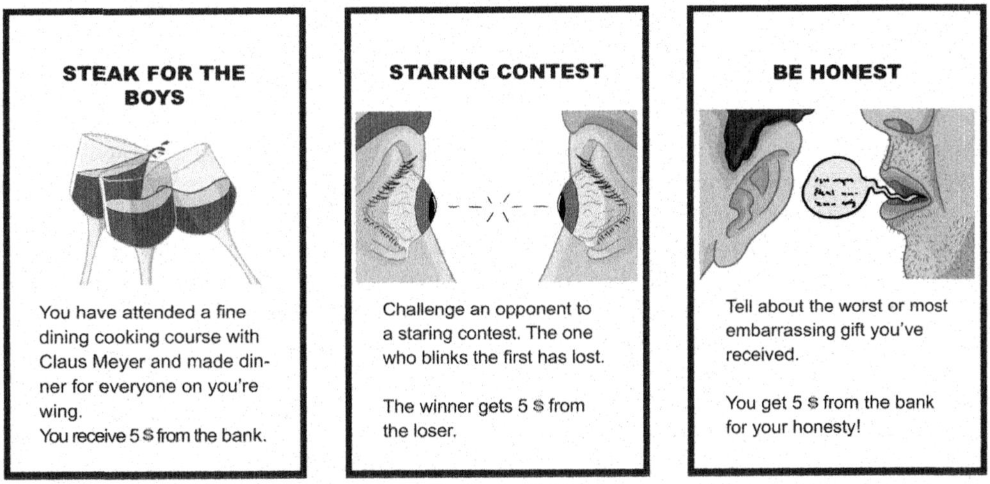

Figure 10.3 Story card, action card and be honest card. © 2018 Social Design Unit.

carefully designed according to three categories that are closely aligned with the game goals: story cards, action cards and be-honest cards.

Story cards (see Figure 10.3) offer stories about everyday prison life that we collected through field studies, co-design workshops and interviews with inmates and prison officers. When playing the game children learn about daily prison activities, and it is assumed that it may help them be less anxious about their father's life. Hence, the story cards are aligned with the first game goal: removing insecurity.

Action cards encourage physical interaction, for instance, through starring competitions or tattooing on each other's arms by using the permanent marker in the game. Many of the inmates and children who were involved in our design process told us that often they had difficulties finding stuff to talk about. Being separated from each other for a while they value physical touch, hugs and wrestling as ways of bonding together again. The action cards are aligned to the second game goal: increasing intimacy. But they also serve as playful starters of conversation and laughing together.

The be-honest cards have been designed in close dialogue with family therapists. These cards invite the players to respond to open instructions such as "Tell about the worst or most embarrassing gift you've received". The be-honest cards are designed to enable deeper personal communication and are aligned with the third game goal: to build up trust. The need for deeper personal communication was identified, as interviews with children and inmates revealed that they wished they could be better at expressing emotions, loss and hope for the future.

Evaluation study design

After approvals were gained from the Danish Data Protection Agency and Ethics Committee the evaluation study of the game was conducted in three maximum-security prisons. Participants were inmates who didn't take part in the design of the game and who were in regular contact with their children. Written consent from prisoners and the primary caregiver of their children was obtained before the game was handed out in prison.

Due to institutional regulations in Danish maximum-security prisons we were not allowed to make observations and interviews in the private visiting room, while inmates and children played the game (Situation A). Instead, interviews were made later with the inmate in prison (Situation B) and his child being at home usually attended by the mother (Situation C) (see Figure 10.4).

This research study design was not intended to somehow try to reconstruct the authentic play situation (A) from the interview situation B and C. Rather, we conceive of interview situation B and C as two separate settings for family storytelling, where fathers and children were asked about what had happened during the game play. In this way, we wanted to study how a game-based intervention can be used to tell, share and scaffold family narratives. What kinds of family narratives are told during the two separate interviews? How do children and their incarcerated fathers use family storytelling to position family identity when troubled by imprisonment? What is the role of alternative and counter narratives in their individual processes of identity making? Are the stories of the child complicit with or countering that of the father?

The interview setting itself acted as a discursive environment. Typically, in the interview with the father a prison officer would be present – sometimes merely as an observer, while on some occasions interfering by taking an active part in the conversation. In the home of the child, the mother would be there and the degree to which she involved herself would vary. An awareness of these local contexts and social practices will be important for understanding how master, family and personal narratives interweave in our interview with John and Oskar.

Analysis

John is a high-ranking member of a criminal biker gang. The maximum-security prison where he is currently serving time is located a couple of hours drive from where his 11-year-old son Oskar lives. John is divorced from Oskar's mother Lea, and he has actually never lived together with Oskar. For Oskar's entire life, John has been in prison as he is serving a long life sentence for murder. Due to his young age Oskar is not allowed to visit John alone. And because Oskar's parents are divorced, he is therefore relying on his father's girlfriend to take him to see John.

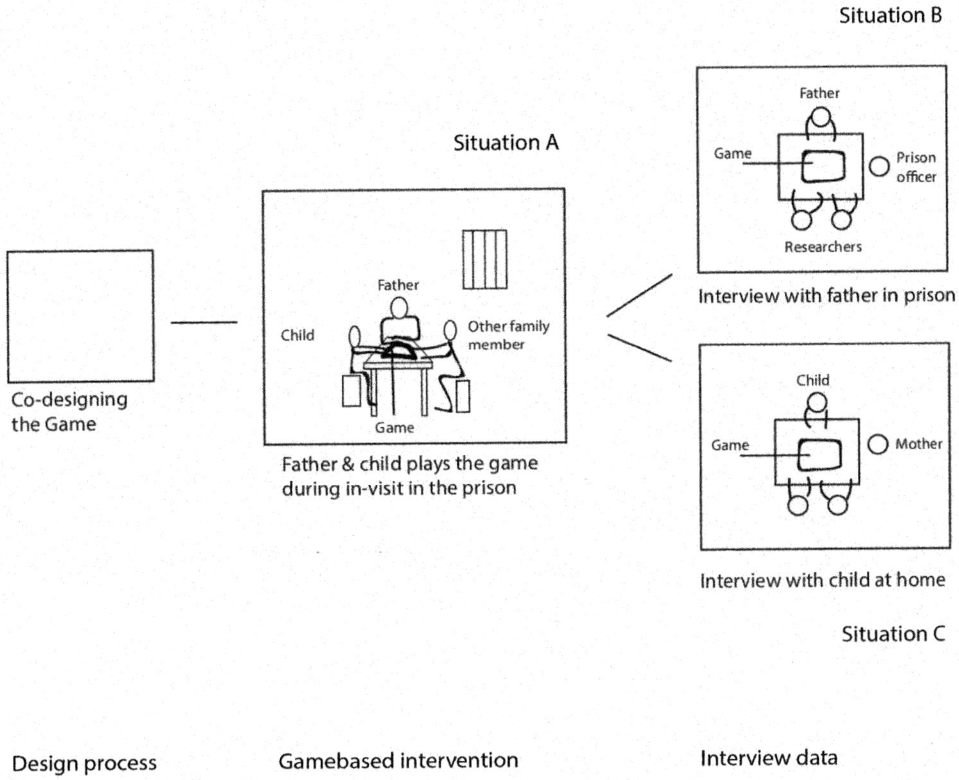

Figure 10.4 Model of the research study design. © 2018 Social Design Unit.

Oskar, John and John's girlfriend have played the game a number of times during visiting hours. Hereafter two researchers (R1 and R2) have interviewed Oskar at home in the presence of Oskar's mother, while interviewing John in the prison with a prison officer attending.

The aim of our analysis is to examine the small stories talk as it takes place in the two research interviews with John and Oskar about their past game events. In so doing, we get the opportunity to study the two family members' retelling of their experiences in relation to the prompting game elements. More specifically, in the Oskar–John case we have identified three small stories that under closer scrutiny show how game elements may elicit complex interactions between personal, family and master-narratives. These stories were either prompted by the story cards, action cards or the be-honest cards.

The tattoo of dad's best friend

During the interview with Oskar, he pulls out the action card Tattoo and tells the story shown in Figure 10.5.

By drawing an anchor on his son's arm John is pulling in a master narrative of tough sailors living adventurous lives at sea. In so doing, John positions Oskar in their family narrative as masculine, heterosexual and virile. This is not unlike how Oskar thinks about his father. Through the interview, we learn that his father has had many alternating girlfriends, whom Oskar is not

TATTOO

Use the black marker pen and give one of your opponents a tattoo on the leg or arm.
You get 10 $ from the bank for your creativity!

Figure 10.5 Tattoo card. © 2018 Social Design Unit.

particularly fond of, which is why he has not come as often as he would have liked. But he likes John's current girlfriend and the three of them playing the game.

However, there is much more at stake in Oskar's personal narrative of how he tattooed his dad. By drawing a heart on John's arm around the name of his dad's best friend, Swing, Oskar's tattoo could be read as if the ties between the gang members are as strong and committing as the emotional ties and relationship between couples. It would point towards Swing being the closest significant other for John; or that the gang in Oskar's opinion is as important for John as his own family and loved ones. Within a tattooed heart on a biker's arm one would typically expect to find the name of a woman, because tattoos are often used as symbolic means for expressing heterosexual hyper-masculinity. But this is not what Oskar seems to have in mind. Through gesturing and laughter he makes the researchers understand that John's tattoos are deliberately placed on his arm to stay visible for everyone on John's ward after the visit. It is Oskar's way of teasing his dad by indicating homosexuality between the two gang members. In this instance Oskar's personal narrative becomes a counter narrative that is oppositional and challenging John's gender identity.

The Fun Family narrative

Teasing each other, making jokes and having fun together is a recurring topic in the interviews with Oskar and John. Apart from the tattoo episode, in the interview with the researchers John tells them about drawing the character card "Mick" (see Figure 10.6). This character is crafted according to insights from our fieldwork, where we learned that bikers in Danish prisons are known for buying expensive beauty products. In the conversation the similarity between Mick and real bikers surfaces in the following way:

> J: That was actually a part of having fun, it was that thing about reading what was on the back [of the character cards].

Figure 10.6 Character card "Mick". © 2018 Social Design Unit.

R1: Mmn.
R2: Yes. And how does that fit with? You know, about the humor and so, did it catch?
J: Yes, it caught pretty well.
R2: Yes.
J: It fits great. I think there was somehting, yes, this guy [Mick], I think, spent a lot of time on expensive creams and face masks. And bikers do that incredibly often... So he [Oskar] laughed a lot about that. Soo he laughed a lot about that.
R2: Yes. (Laughter)
J: So I get made fun of. I have to say that. So we laughed a lot about that.

We cannot tell from these lines whether John actually, in the situation, found it amusing or not. The point we want to make is rather that his personal narrative is constructing what we shall call the Fun Family narrative. With this narrative John positions himself as a father who tolerates being made fun of. Moreover, John emphasizes that teasing each other is a way for him to care for his son, when asked about whom usually wins the game:

> J: Well I think, I lost anyway, I think ...They [Oskar and his girlfriend] cheat like fuck. But it really brings great joy to my ... to my. Yes to my kid. To my son, right? It brings great, great joy.

By and large, Oskar's personal narrative supports this family narrative. When asked the same question, he responds: "Me and my dad's girlfriend. We cheat all the time". In this sense, we argue that Oskar and John are co-authoring the Fun Family narrative. As pointed out by Blum-Kulka (1997) such a narrative can serve two purposes. First, it can be a means for John and Oskar to enact 'sociability', using their family narrative to reconnect and form group identity. Second, the Fun Family narrative can serve the purpose of 'socialization', meaning that it may acculturate the family members into certain shared family norms and values; in this case, making fun of each other and accepting cheating is a way of caring for one another. However, this process of

Figure 10.7 Be-honest card. © 2018 Social Design Unit.

acculturation can be complicated, which is evidenced by a story told by both John and Oskar. The story is prompted in the two interviews by the be-honest card (see Figure 10.7) that asks the players to tell about the most embarrassing gift they have received. John mentions that he once bought a silly birthday present for Oskar:

J: No, I think, I've given him some presents, where he didn't think, it was fun-ny, right? Yes, here. He just had his birthday, where he got a eh … it was just a silly present, where he got a bear costume, he had to wear, right? With ears and stuff like that. He thought that was embarrassing.
R1: (Laughter)
J: He also got a real present, right?
R2: Yes. (Laughter) Okay. That was a bit …
J: And he actually had it a week, before he got his real present. On his birthday.
R2: Yes. (Laughter)
J: He probably won't forget that.
R2: (Laughter)
J: You should ask him about that some day.
R2: I'll remember that.

When the researchers interviewed Oskar some weeks after the interview with John, he gave this account:

O: Well, that was probably a costume I got from my father.
R2: You got a costume?
R1: He also told us about that one.
O: Yes. That might be the most embarrassing and worst one.
R1: Was it something like … a bear costume, I think I remember? Or something like that.

O: Dog costume. And I have NEVER worn it.
R1: (*Laughter*)
O: It was so embarrassing.
R1: So, it was not something that you had wished for.
O: No, it was not.
R2: Where did you get it? Did you get it while you were visiting him, or did you get it as a present out here?
O: As a birthday present.
R2: Okay.
O: I really don't hope, that was my real birthday present.

Interestingly, when comparing John and Oskar's account of the same episode, we realize a slight, yet important difference. According to John it was just meant to be a hoax – "a silly present" – which Oskar received a week before he got a "real present". However, Oskar's statement – "I really don't hope that was my real birthday present" – leaves the impression that he didn't receive the real present, and for that reason he is still uncertain about whether or not this was intended to make fun of him. It is an example of what we have referred to above as an alternative personal narrative. While not being oppositional to the family narrative (as would be the case of counter narratives), Oskar's personal narrative is dissonant to John's account. Oskar thus draws into question the Fun Family narrative as a consensual frame for interpretation.

Counter narratives of good parenting

Throughout the interview with John, he is continuously moving between two opposing father roles. On the one hand, he explains, that he usually avoids talking about feelings and puts up a happy face during visiting hours, "because it shouldn't be associated with something bad to come here [in the prison]". By silencing emotions he strives to protect and keep together his family. On the other hand, John reflects on a therapeutic style of parenting by wanting to embrace confiding and talk about difficult matters with Oskar. In the following excerpt John tells about Oskar drawing the question card that encourage him to tell about what he thinks about before going to sleep:

J: And then it comes: 'I think about my dad every night before I go to sleep.' And then he sometimes has … a hard time holding back … the tears, right? But I also get the chance to tell him how much I miss him and how much I love him, right? But it's something that can suddenly put a stop to the game.
R2: Yes. How did you experience that? Was there like a pause in the game?
J: Yes, there was a pause, because he … And then I RUSHED on so that he wouldn't … that he wouldn't get too sad, right?
R2: Yes. Did you worry about him getting too sad?
J: I was a bit nervous that it got too close, right? But then again: … It's also nice for me to know that …I know that I will value not doing anything stupid, right? So that I can get out to him.
Prison Officer: But it's also brave of him to tell you that he misses you.
J: Yes, that really is brave, right?
Prison Officer: Yes, that's brave.
J: But you know, you get a bit … you get a bit upset, right? When he is talking like that.

In his personal narrative, John positions himself as the caring father who values the opportunity of Oskar and him sharing their emotions and loss. Yet, he is ambivalent about this role. Or to use the concepts introduced above: he is countering the therapeutic father role. Hence, when Oskar is having difficulties keeping back his tears and the game is paused, he acts as a protecting father who rushes onwards and silences his son's feelings. Interestingly, he then points out how important Oskar's emotions are for his own desire to change. John's talk of rehabilitation immediately elicits a reaction from the prison officer who interrupts by appraising Oskar's talk as "brave". In so doing, the prison officer seems to motivate John to accept the therapeutic style of parenting, confiding and talking.

Here one needs to pay attention to the larger discursive environment. In the Danish Prison and Probation Service the task of the prison is often conceived of as a matter of balancing a strict and soft approach: to "exert control and security on the one hand and support and motivate on the other" (The Danish Prison and Probation Service, 2017). The dichotomous relationship between these approaches is articulated as an institutional master narrative that manifests itself in the interview with John. Seated in his uniform, the prison officer is monitoring the interview for security reasons, while at the same time taking part as a discussant that positively motivates emotional family talk. In this sense, disciplining paradoxically becomes a way of enforcing certain parenting styles over others.

Discussion

Returning to Kölbl's critical remarks pointed out earlier in this chapter, it is reasonable to ask if we have avoided reproducing findings based on our own conceptual framework? And, in addition, is the use of the board game a valid empirical strategy for studying processes of family storytelling and identity making in troubled families? Let's us address these questions by discussing what we see as the advantages and weaknesses of the approach.

Using the game instead of semi-structured or open interviews can be a way to avoid cuing family members into making generalized self-reflections of how they see themselves as a family. With changing game elements placed in front of them, children and prisoner fathers were asked to tell about what they did together during visits rather than how they conceive of each other and family life. Such an interview technique allows for studying people organizing their "personal domain of sense making" (Kölbl, 2004, p. 28) by amalgamating master, family and personal narratives; and themes occur along the way depending on what kind of small stories talk game elements elicit.

By using this empirical strategy we strived to snatch family narratives as they emerge in the interview data trying to avoid using, as an interpretative frame, theoretical pre-assumptions of what the child–parent relationship may look like when influenced by imprisonment. Many interviews have been conducted in criminology with inmates and children about their family relations. But much of this work tends to confine the topic of the interview to what it means for inmates to be away from their family and how children live with parental incarceration. Such interviews can easily lead one to believe that two family narratives are dominant: one is the Lamenting Family narrative according to which the criminal father deeply regrets and his children lament his absence; the other is the Relief Family narrative in which the inmate regrets, but his children are relieved, because his absence means that family life is quiet and calm (see e.g. Lanskey et al., 2016). Using game elements can be a way of not taking such family narratives for granted and allows for alternative positions and narratives to occur such as the caring father and the Fun Family narrative.

By interviewing prisoner fathers and children separately we also prevent familial hierarchies and hegemonic narratives to dominate the interview. Often in family narrative research, asymmetrical relationships exist between parents and children, which makes it difficult for children to resist and disagree with what parents tell. In our interview we see counter and alternative narratives occurring, for instance, when Oskar tells about his tattoo on John or his birthday present.

However, we also see some weaknesses. Is the Fun Family narrative actually one that John and Oskar co-author or it is the game that turns the visit into an entertaining situation, which then influences their account? The game is a constructive element, which certainly has an impact on what gets told, and it can be difficult, in the analysis, to separate game and family talk.

Second, as the game is part of the prison's visiting program it inevitably becomes instrumental to the rehabilitative work of the institution, its systems of power and authorities. This raises the question of whether alternative parenting roles such as the caring father is in fact one that John assumes or whether it is a product of the game backed up by the interruption of the prison officer? Moreover, drawing broadly on our research findings we can see that talking about emotions and being honest is sometimes to the dislike of prisoners and their children. Hence, the game can be intimidating and require players buying into certain expectations of what it means to be a 'good family'.

Third, as researchers who have designed the game with inmates and children we actively play a role in the process of making social change happen. This confronts us with an ethical dilemma. Despite inmates, social workers and prison officers saying that children's anxiety is caused by their ignorance of their fathers' prison life, one can rightly ask: Is it really appropriate that children should know more about life in prison? Is it prudent that the game encourages them to collect prisoners and do physical activities like push-ups and arm wrestling? And so forth. Ethical concerns like these must be taken into account and addressed by consulting empirical research to clarify what are the ethically responsible decisions.

Concluding remarks

Empirically, to our knowledge, narrative practice research into family narratives co-authored by inmates and their children are rare. True, in narrative criminology, there is a tradition of studying inmates' narratives of their life story or criminal deeds (Presser & Sandberg, 2015). But these studies tend to focus on inmates' stories of themselves as offenders, not as fathers.

Our interview data offers an opportunity for studying how children and incarcerated fathers engage in identity making through family narratives. Through the three examples taken from the interviews with Oskar and his father, we have demonstrated that family talk can engage issues of gender identity, family identity and parenting roles. Identity making here is conceived of as a process that involves the intertwining of personal, family and master narrative activities, which can either stand counter or be alternative to each other. Oskar's story of how he drew a tattoo on John is a personal counter narrative that challenges John's masculinity; his doubt about his real birthday present is an alternative personal narrative to John's account; and John is caught up in the countering between a protecting father role and an institutionally approved therapeutic style of parenting.

Existing theories of narratives in family contexts have delivered precise concepts for our analysis. However, the aim of the present study was not only to prove the explanatory power of these concepts. Rather we want to demonstrate how social design can contribute with innovative methods for studying counter narratives in troubled families. More specifically, we have argued that a social game can be designed and used in a legitimate way to collect family storytelling that we have recorded and analyzed following the small stories approach. In so doing, we make a plea for merging a descriptive-analytical and constructive research approach.

Acknowledgments

We would like to thank the fathers and children who tested the board game and shared their stories with us; Tau Lenskjold and Nanna Koch Hansen for their work on the interviews and TrygFonden for funding the research project (ID 110492).

References

Andrews, M. (2004a). Memories of mother: Counter-narratives of early maternal influence. In M. Bamberg & M. Andrews (Eds.), *Considering counter-narratives: Narrating, resisting, making sense* (pp. 7–26). John Benjamins Publishing.

Andrews, M. (2004b). Response to commentaries on 'Memories of Mother: Counter-Narratives of early maternal influence'. In M. Bamberg & M. Andrews (Eds.), *Considering counter-narratives: Narrating, resisting, making sense* (pp. 51–59). John Benjamins Publishing.

Armstrong, L., Bailey, J., Julier, G., & Kimbell, L. (2014). *Social design futures: HEI research and the AHRC.* Brighton: University of Brighton.

Aukrust, V. G., & Snow, C. E. (1998). Narratives and explanations during mealtime conversations in Norway and the US. *Language in Society, 27*(2), 221–246.

Bamberg, M. (2004). Form and functions of 'slut bashing'in male identity constructions in 15-year-olds. *Human Development, 47*(6), 331–353.

Bamberg, M. (2006). Stories: Big or small: Why do we care? *Narrative Inquiry, 16*(1), 139–147.

Bamberg, M., & Georgakopoulou, A. (2008). Small stories as a new perspective in narrative and identity analysis. *Text & Talk, 28*(3), 377–396.

Blum-Kulka, S. (1997). Dinner talk: Cultural patterns of sociability and socialization in family discourse. Routledge.

De Fina, A. (2008). Who tells which story and why? Micro and macro contexts in narrative. *Text & Talk, 28*(3), 421–442.

De Fina, A., & Georgakopoulou, A. (2008). Introduction: Narrative analysis in the shift from texts to practices. *Text & Talk, 28*(3), 275–281.

Fivush, R., Bohanek, J. G., & Zaman, W. (2011). Personal and intergenerational narratives in relation to adolescents' well-being. *New Directions for Child and Adolescent Development, 2011*(131), 45–57.

Georgakopoulou, A. (2007). *Small stories, interaction and identities* (Vol. 8). John Benjamins Publishing.

Georgakopoulou, A. (2015). Small stories research. In A. D. Fina & A. Georgakopoulou (Eds.), *The handbook of narrative analysis* (pp. 255–272). Wiley Blackwell.

Gordon, C. (2015). Narratives in family contexts 16. In A. D. Fina & A. Georgakopoulou (Eds.), *The handbook of narrative analysis* (pp. 311–328). Wiley Blackwell.

Hammack, P. L. (2008). Narrative and the cultural psychology of identity. *Personality and Social Psychology Review, 12*(3), 222–247.

Jones, A., Gallagher, B., Manby, M., Robertson, O., Schützwohl, M., Berman, A. H., Hirschfield, A., Ayre, L., Urban, M., & Sharratt, K. (2013). *Children of prisoners: Interventions and mitigations to strengthen mental health.* University of Huddersfield.

Knutz, E., Markussen, T., & Lenskjold, T. (2019). Navigating care in social design: A provisional model. *8th Biannual Nordic Design Research Society Conference.*

Knutz, E., & Markussen, T. (2019). The ripple effects of social design: A model to support new cultures of evaluation in design research. In P. Rodgers (Ed.), *Design research for change symposium* (pp. 223–240). Lancaster University.

Kölbl, C. (2004). Blame it on psychology!? In M. Bamberg & M. Andrews (Eds.), *Considering counter narratives: Narrating, resisting, making sense* (pp. 27–31). John Benjamins Publishing.

Koskinen, I., Zimmerman, J., Binder, T., Redström, J., & Wensveen, S. (2011). *Design research through practice.* Morgan Kaufmann.

Lanskey, C., Lösel, F., Markson, L., & Souza, K. (2016). Children's contact with their imprisoned fathers and the father–child relationship following release. *Families, Relationships and Societies, 5*(1), 43–58.

Markussen, T. (2017). Disentangling 'the social' in social design's engagement with the public realm. *CoDesign*, *13*(3), 160–174.

Markussen, T., & Knutz, E. (forthcoming). Playing games to re-story troubled family narratives in Danish maximum-security prisons. *Punishment & Society*.

Martin, R. L., & Osberg, S. (2007). Social entrepreneurship: The case for definition. *Stanford Social Innovation Review*, *5*(2), 28–39.

McKay, T., Comfort, M., Grove, L., Bir, A., & Lindquist, C. (2018). Whose punishment, whose crime? Understanding parenting and partnership in a time of mass incarceration. *Journal of Offender Rehabilitation*, *57*(2), 1–14.

McKenzie-Mohr, S., & Lafrance, M. N. (2017). Narrative resistance in social work research and practice: Counter-storying in the pursuit of social justice. *Qualitative Social Work*, *16*(2), 189–205.

McLean, K. C. (2017). *The co-authored self—family stories and the construction of personal identity*. Oxford University Press.

McLean, K. C., & Syed, M. (2015). Personal, master, and alternative narratives: An integrative framework for understanding identity development in context. *Human Development*, *58*(6), 318–349.

Murray, J., Farrington, D. P., & Sekol, I. (2012). Children's antisocial behavior, mental health, drug use, and educational performance after parental incarceration: A systematic review and meta-analysis. *Psychological Bulletin*, *138*(2), 175–210.

Oldrup, H., Frederiksen, S., Henze-Pedersen, S., & Olsen, R. F. (2016). *Indsat far udsat barn*. SFI - Det nationale forskningscenter for velfærd.

Presser, L., & Sandberg, S. (2015). *Narrative criminology: Understanding stories of crime*. NYU Press.

Riessman, C. K., & Quinney, L. (2005). Narrative in social work: A critical review. *Qualitative Social Work*, *4*(4), 391–412.

Simon, H. A. (1969). *The sciences of the artificial*. The MIT Press.

The Danish Prison and Probation Service (2017). Goals and Strategy. Ministry of Justice.

Thorne, A., & McLean, K. C. (2003). Telling traumatic events in adolescence: A study of master narrative positioning. In R. Fivush & C. A. Haden (Eds.), Autobiographical memory and the construction of a narrative self (pp. 169–185). Lawrence Erlbaum Associates.

Vaughan, L. (2017). *Practice-based design research*. Bloomsbury Publishing.

Part III

Counter-narratives, organizations and professions

11

The story of us

Counter-narrativizing craft brewery identity

Trine Susanne Johansen

Introduction

This study explores the interplay between the autobiographical texts of craft breweries, i.e. their stories of self, and the collective counter-narrative identity of the craft brewing movement, i.e. their story of us. The brewing industry has changed significantly over an extended time period due to the simultaneous consolidation of multinational, industrial breweries and upsurge of local, craft breweries (McLaughlin et al., 2014; Murray & O'Neill, 2012). The rise in craft breweries, referred to as "the beer revolution" (e.g. Garavaglia & Swinnen, 2017), has been explored through resource partitioning theory (Baginski & Bell, 2011; Carroll & Swaminathan, 2000) and neo-localism (Eberts, 2014; Schnell & Reese, 2003; Flack, 1997). Where the former sees craft breweries as an almost natural supplement to the multinational, industrial breweries, the latter views them as a socially-driven counter-movement against the beer industry's continued corporatization and standardization. Recent work on the collective identity of craft breweries similarly points to conflicting identities of craft and industrial brewers (Lamertz et al., 2016; Mathias et al., 2018).

The oppositional articulation of craft breweries suggests counter-narrative as a potential complementary perspective worth considering in shedding light on the beer revolution by expanding understandings of craft breweries given that counter-narrative is defined as "a positional category, in tension with another category" (Bamberg & Andrews, 2004, p. X). Counter-narrative has already been assigned a triple role in organizational studies as a theoretical concept, an empirical object and a methodological approach (Frandsen et al., 2017). As a theoretical concept counter-narrative can be used to explore craft breweries in light of their shared, oppositional identity. Such exploration can equally provide insights into conceptual understandings and uses of counter-narrative.

In order to shed additional light on counter-narrative as a theoretical concept, this study explores the reciprocal relationship between counter-narrative and identity at the organizational level in the context of the craft brewing industry in Denmark; a country said to have one of the largest number of breweries per capita in the world. The dual purpose is to employ counter-narrative as a conceptual lens for understanding the construction of the collective and organizational identities of the industry; and to consider how such construction may nuance and develop understandings of counter-narrative as a theoretical optic. The craft brewing movement is an interesting backdrop for this discussion exactly because it was born in opposition. However, as the movement is growing, developing, and maturing, its continued oppositional claim may seem less obvious and legitimate. As the counter-movement itself is becoming mainstream, do the craft breweries still tap into the counter-narrative that framed their genesis? Or does the counter-narrative inevitably transform into a master-narrative that supports and sustains the collective identity of craft brewing while opening up for new counter-narrative positions to be inhabited by the individual breweries? In short: how do Danish craft breweries establish, maintain, draw on and alter the counter-narrative of their collective identity as it intersects with their organizational identities?

The chapter begins by sketching out the notion of collective identity in the context of the craft brewing movement. Second, the birth and development of the Danish craft brewing industry is presented as a counter-narrative process to explicate its oppositional nature. Third, this articulation acts as a backdrop for exploring how individual craft breweries accomplish this collective counter-narrative in their online autobiographies. Finally, outcomes related to counter-narrative are discussed before concluding on the implications for its potential as a theoretical concept.

Collective identity in the craft brewing movement

This section introduces the notion of collective identity at the organizational level and contextualizes it within the craft brewing movement. However, first a definition of craft brewery is in order. Craft breweries are referenced in multiple ways; besides 'craft', existing labels include e.g. 'micro', 'artisanal', 'independent', 'specialty' and 'local' (Garvaglia & Swinnen, 2017). Whereas some suggest these labels to refer to different types of breweries, others use them interchangeably. In addition to the different labels, definitions differ greatly, but frequently include size, ownership and production methods. With reference to Gatrell et al. (2018, p. 361), this chapter uses the term 'craft brewery' as a recognized "short hand for smaller and independent firms that deploy traditional production processes (...); emphasize quality, flavour, and diversity; and produce limited quantities". These characteristics – small, independent, traditional, diverse etc. – not only form the identity markers that help narrate the individual craft breweries, but also the collective identity of the craft brewery movement.

Collective identity refers to shared characteristics or similarities among a group of organizations, i.e. "identities that characterise types of organisations rather than individual organisations" (Lamertz et al., 2016). Whereas organizational identity focuses on the meaningful, ongoing construction of the organization as an entity, collective identity is a question of what unites organizations. When constructing collective identity, organizations tend to draw upon remnants from their industry's past. In exploring the craft brewing industry in Ontario, Lamertz et al. (2016, p. 797) explicate how different identity elements have been "mutated, were discarded, or became adopted" over more than two centuries. Their study shows how the (re)emergence of craft breweries marks a return to the idea of locally anchored businesses with strong community ties. Thus, when referring to craft breweries as 'traditional' it is not just a question of brewing methods and ingredients, but also an identity claim that ties in with local belonging as explicated in the notion of neo-localism, i.e. a craving for a sense of place and community (Flack, 1997; Schnell & Reese, 2003).

Collective organizational identities are sometimes oppositional identities. As a case in point, the neo-local sentiment of the craft brewing movement is explained as "a rejection of national, or even regional, culture in favour of something more local" (Flack, 1997, p. 49), and seen as a counter-move to the homogenization of communities, markets and societies brought on by globalizing corporatization (Schnell & Reese, 2003). According to Mathias et al. (2018, p. 3089), oppositional collective identity

> is commonly rooted in notions of authenticity (i.e. being true to "who we are"), and offers differentiation from and protection against dominant "generalist" market categories (McKendrick & Hannan, 2014). [...] it reflects an identity shared among category members who are ideologically opposed to the dominant market logic of existing firms (Vehaal, Khessina, & Dobrev, 2015).

The oppositional aspect is visible among craft breweries who position themselves against the standardization of industrial brewers by emphasizing e.g. craftmanship, tradition and local origins. Identified as an oppositional, or counter-cultural, movement, craft brewing aligns with the idea of counter-narrative "which offer resistance, either implicitly or explicitly, to dominant cultural narratives" (Andrews, 2004, p.1).

Whereas oppositional identity is considered important in nascent industries as a means to building awareness and securing legitimacy, the importance diminishes as the market matures (Mathias et al., 2018). In maturing markets, the individual organization may experience a growing need to construct an identity that allows it to tell a unique story and to stand out from the collective. As Lamertz et al. (2005, p. 819) point out, the beer revolution "has given rise to a large number of small organizations that have collectively differentiated themselves from the large national breweries but are now competing among each other". In a study on coopetition, i.e. the balancing of cooperation and competition, in the American craft beer industry, Mathias et al. (2018, p. 3094) show how the breweries came together in the shared belief that "a rising tide lifts all boats", which lead to a collective focus on quality and mutual support. However, they also posit that the emphasis on collaboration may be moving towards competition over time. Whereas an oppositional collective identity can be articulated as counter-narrative, the need for developing a differentiated organizational identity for the individual craft breweries potentially changes and challenges the counter-narrative that unifies the collective. Thus, inspired by Bakhtin (1981), the shared counter-narrative of the craft brewing movement becomes a centripetal force that pulls the individual breweries towards similar stories of self, whereas the centrifugal pull of the differentiation stories has the potential to dismantle or disperse the counter-narrative.

The Danish craft brewing movement as counter-narrative

Having outlined the notion of collective identity in the context of the craft brewing movement, and linked its oppositional nature to counter-narrative, the focus turns to explicating the birth and maturation of Danish craft brewing. This explication serves a dual purpose by providing background information for the study, and illuminating how the movement has been articulated as inherently counter-narrative.

According to the Danish Brewers' Association, there are close to 200 small-scale breweries in Denmark. However, that was not the case 20 years ago when industry consolidation and large-scale production had severely reduced the number of breweries to 18 (Bentzen & Smith, 2017). Based on news reporting in national newspapers and magazines (located through a search in the Infomedia database), the development of the industry – starting in the year 2000 – is outlined in Figure 11.1 illustrated by a few central terms and ideas expressed in the media.

The craft beer movement takes off around the millennia with increased consumer interest in novel, specialty beer. The interest leads to the establishment of a growing number of craft breweries, and in 2005 the term "beer revolution" appears for the first time (Hvelplund, 2005). In addition, the so-called 'wineification' becomes visible in news stories featuring a vocabulary of beer allowing connoisseurs to classify and describe beer types, appearance, smell and taste in the same fashion as wine. The news coverage also reflects a continued discussion on the economic

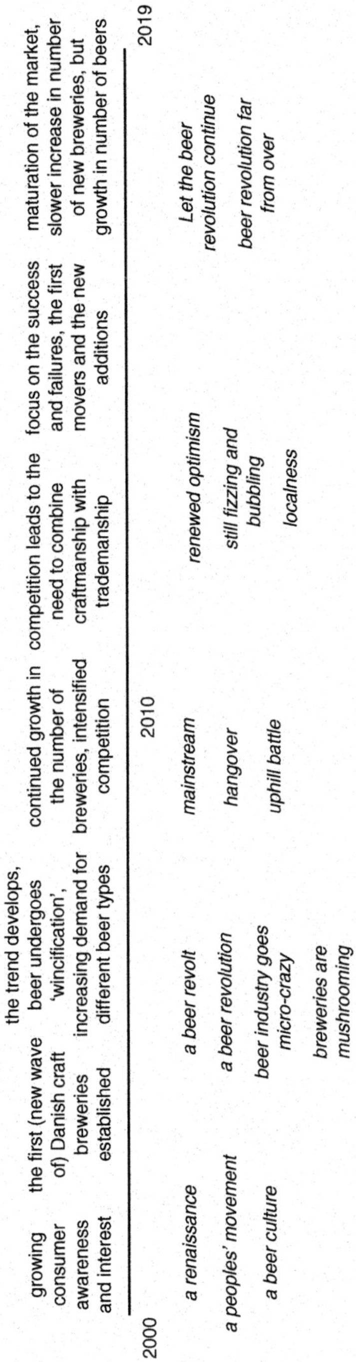

Figure 11.1 The development of the Danish craft brewing industry.

viability of the breweries with stories depicting hardship, bankruptcy, intensified competition and, as a result, an increased focus on quality and innovation. However, the stories also reveal that each year the number of new breweries who join the market surpass the number of breweries exiting it. Throughout the 20-year period, the media portray new, upcoming breweries, success stories frequently stressing local affiliation and personal histories and accomplishments of the brewers.

In terms of the interplay, or conflict, between craft and industrial breweries, media reporting supports the idea of a rebellious counter-movement; 'underdogs' taking on the 'big guns'. The head of communication for the Danish Brewers' Association suggests in an interview that the growing number of small-scale breweries can be seen as "an anti-industrialization move in a time when the beer markets have been consolidated by very large breweries" (Lai, 2006). The Goliath of the beer industry in Denmark was, and is, Carlsberg. In a newspaper article, one microbrewer is quoted as saying: "it is Carlsberg's own fault. They have squeezed the turnip so much with their monopoly that a counter-reaction has manifested" (Juhler, 2004).

The craft brewing counter-movement is also articulated with reference to beer types:

> the wild growing supply of good and challenging beers from the micro-breweries is a demonstrative reaction against the blind ally of flavor uniformity, the poor beer culture, and monopolization which became more and more pronounced in Denmark during the 90s.
>
> *(Andersen, 2007)*

The traditional lager, produced by the industrial breweries, becomes challenged by a variety of beers, e.g. India pale ale, stout and Lambic, establishing a stark contrast between the bland, boring lager and the exciting, experimental brews. As one microbrewer puts it: "we brew out of love for beer. There are so many boring beers from the large breweries. Their beer is often like plain chicken: a cheap, industrial product" (Juhler, 2004). As such, the Danish beer revolution is inscribed in the anti-industrialization and anti-homogenization counter-narrative identity that frames small-scale brewers as heroes in a quest for better brews.

Exploring the identity of Danish craft breweries

Against the backdrop of reading the Danish beer revolution as counter-narrative, the analysis explores how the craft breweries narrate their collective identity vis-à-vis their organizational identities. The analysis rests on archival documents in the form of online autobiographical webpage texts as routine, explicit and deliberate expressions of organizational identity (see e.g. Lamertz et al., 2005). The craft breweries were identified based on their inclusion on a list published by the Danish Brewers' Association of the estimated 200 Danish breweries (accessed in October 2018). Not all breweries are included in the analysis: some do not have webpages, a few have gone out of business and some are industrial brewers (e.g. Carlsberg and Unibrew). Consequently, the final list includes 91 craft breweries who all inscribe themselves in the craft brewing movement. While a few of the breweries have longer histories, most are born out of the beer revolution. They span from one-man, part-time enterprises to larger, professionally operated breweries. The corpus consists of texts retrieved in November 2018 from webpages that explicitly contain autobiographical references, e.g. 'about us' and 'our history'.

The autobiographical texts are analyzed with inspiration from Davies and Harré's (1990) notion of subject positioning as the ongoing process through which identity is located and accomplished in narrative discourse. Subject positioning takes its point of departure in the existence of multiple, dynamic identities, actively constructed in different discursive contexts. As narratives unfold, individuals can be constituted in one position or another, stand in multiple positions and seek to negotiate new positions by refusing those that have already been articulated. Originally developed in the context of individual identity, subject positioning is here applied to organizational identity claims. Attention is given to both reflexive positioning, i.e. how the craft breweries position themselves, and interactive positioning, i.e. how they position other breweries, the craft brewing movement, and the brewing industry per se (including industrial breweries).

In addition to subject positioning, the analysis draws terminological inspiration from organizational identification literature. Organizational identification addresses the interplay between organizational identity and the individual identity of employees (e.g. Larson & Pepper, 2003; Kreiner & Ashforth, 2004; Humphreys & Brown, 2002). However, the vocabulary can be transferred to the interplay between collective identity and organizational identity similarly to the way in which the concept of identity itself has migrated from individuals to organizations and collectives. Beside identification, the vocabulary consists of dis-identification, ambivalent identification, and neutral identification (e.g. Kreiner & Ashforth, 2004). Where identification is a question of defining oneself with what the collective is believed to represent, dis-identification suggests defining oneself through different characteristics or principles than those assigned to the collective. The simultaneous presence of identification and dis-identification is called ambivalent identification (Kreiner & Ashforth, 2004), whereas an absence of identification and disidentification is labelled neutral identification. In the analysis, the first three concepts are used to generate insights into how constructions of collective and organizational identity intersect. Neutral identification does not address the intersection, and, moreover, it is difficult to apply analytically. The identification vocabulary invites the exploration of variations and contradictions of organizational selves suggested by the notion of subject positioning, i.e. identification relates to how the breweries story themselves with reference to the positions created by the centripetal counter-narrative of the craft brewing movement's collective identity; dis-identification allows focus on the possibility for refusing positions made available by the counter-narrative; and ambivalent identification highlights options for inhabiting multiple positions at once and telling complex stories of organizational self that draw on, constitute and challenge the shared counter-narrative potentially subjecting it to a centrifugal pull.

The analytic aim is to illustrate the interplay between collective and organizational identity in relation to counter-narrative. The analysis begins by addressing how the craft breweries construct collective identity before turning attention to how they identify with it. Finally, counter-narrative is discussed as a lens for addressing the analytic insights related to collective and organizational identity. Main points are exemplified by selected extracts. Most of the examples are translated from Danish (a few were originally in English), as are the names of some of the breweries (again: some have English names).

Collective identity

At first glance, collective identity is constructed by the craft breweries' shared reference to identity markers such as craftmanship, tradition and local belonging. Craftmanship and tradition are key e.g. when Bie's Brewhouse talk of "respect for the old craft" or when Skands Brewery refer to their vision of "giving the old brewing craftmanship pride of place again". Local belonging is pronounced in the many breweries who name themselves after their cities or regions of origin as well as in articulations of community, e.g. when Halsnaes Brewhouse "emphasize playing a positive role in our lovely local community – as a gathering point, as an employer, and as a producer of the local beer".

The collective identity similarly emerges as the breweries mention the beer revolution as a nexus of their own genesis, e.g. Croocked Moon Brewing (deliberately misspelling their name) who suggest: "with the beer revolution in Denmark, we have opened our eyes and ears to what this amazing world has to offer", and Grauballe Brewhouse who lay claim to being "one of the very first microbreweries in what later became the Danish beer revolution". In addition, many breweries refer to growing consumer interest in and demand for specialty beer, and thereby construct a shared story of the craft brewing movement as a consumer cultural phenomenon rooted in a longing for local community, e.g. Jellinge Brewhouse, taking its name from the city of Jellinge: "with the blossoming in demand for specialty beer, Jellinge also began to long for a local brewery". There are also tentative elements in the autobiographical texts that point towards the movement's maturation. Alefarme Brewing, who opened in 2015 and thus is a fairly late addition to the market, state that their plan "is not to revolutionize the craft beer world, but to put out a consistent, high-quality and passionately crafted product with high drinkability that will leave a huge impact in the current craft beer scene". A few years ago, "the craft beer world" was considered to be the revolution, but here it seemingly is open to a revolution itself pointing to its potential maturation; and new centrifugal forces that potentially disrupt the centripetal pull of the movement's collective narrative.

A third element of the collective identity lies in how the breweries, in part at least, view themselves as collaborators rather than competitors. This is pronounced in how they reference each other, e.g. The Brewery Devil's Brew which state:

> the success of the many, new Danish breweries suggests that a large segment of the Danish consumers is adventurous and interested in local products. We don't wish to – how hypothetical it may seem at the present time – to dominate the market in any way. Our vision and passion send us in a different direction. That is why we view the other (micro)breweries as colleagues with whom we can easily co-exist.

In addition, to referencing consumer culture and local belonging as central to the movement, the brewery takes a collaborative stance by referring to other breweries as "colleagues", and not competitors. Equal to Alefarm Brewing, Devil's Brew denounce any intention of market domination. The collaborative aspect is also stressed as the breweries mention collaborations, e.g. Refsvindinge Brewery who praise their collaborative effort claiming that it allows for a wider distribution of their beer, "and frees up time to find new beer types". Along the same lines, Skands Brewery claim to be "known for collaborating with people, who have interesting ideas", and suggest that it "makes our working day different and varied. And it also ensures that the beer connoisseur always is able to taste our loving and uncompromising approach in every sip". As such, the collective identity is based on a sense of cooperation and shared purpose (Mathias et al., 2018). However, as indicated by the notion of revolutionizing the craft beer movement, there are slight shifts suggesting a potential move towards increased competition as well, as exemplified by e.g. Oerbaek Brewery who describe a market "where a growing number of microbreweries heighten the competition and the interest for Danish quality brew". As suggested in the notion of coopetition (Mathias et al., 2018), craft brewery growth helps build and sustain consumer awareness and stimulates demand, but also means that the consumer has greater choice.

Collective identity can be oppositional (Mathias et al., 2018) as also seen by the news media's portrayal of the craft breweries which talk of "anti-industrialization" and position the craft brewers as an exciting, revitalizing counter-move to the bland, uniform and boring beers from industrial brewers; i.e. a shared counter-narrative identity. However, while the oppositional element also is visible in the autobiographical texts, it emerges in subtle, implicit ways. Aarhus Brewhouse, for instance, describe their relationship to the industrial breweries as follows:

> we produce handcrafted specialty beers, which can supplement the assortment from the large breweries. These handcrafted specialty beers are niche products which are not feasible for the large breweries to produce because they are geared towards large batches. Aarhus Brewhouse is better equipped for working with the small batches and special ingredients or processes, which the large breweries cannot handle.

Initially, Aarhus Brewhouse framed the industrial breweries as non-competitors in the sense that they are geared towards different kind of beers, i.e. "large batches". But implicitly, the extract also articulates an oppositional identity that distinguishes craft brewing from industrial brewing, i.e. "handcrafted specialty beers", "niche products" and "special ingredients or processes" versus "large batches" and "cannot handle". This dichotomy between craft and industry is also implicitly articulated in Skands Brewery's vision of "giving the old brewery craftmanship pride of place again" (suggesting that craftmanship has vanished from the industry), and by Trolden Brewhouse who claim to "take craftmanship seriously", and add: "unlike other, more modern breweries, we still take pride in producing the best possible beer, on its own terms. Trolden beer is handmade, without computers, by living people ...". Moreover, Boegedal Brewhouse refer to how the increased "rationalization of production processes and economy of scale have outweighed quality". And continue:

> the industry with all its innovations is not only good, it is excellent and even necessary if you are to produce advanced telecommunications – try to imagine a unique, handmade mobile phone – but when it comes to food, industry seldom benefitted quality.

This opposition to industrially produced beer is equally present in WinterCoat Brewery's description of how the brewer got started in the first place by realizing "(as many hand brewers do) that he could brew much better and interesting beer than he could buy". This extract implicitly makes a distinction between hand brewed beer (as being good and interesting) and industrial beer (as being poor and bland), thereby also indirectly referencing the homogeneity of industrial production while reproducing the quest of craft breweries for better beers that construct and support the movement's counter-narrative.

Other breweries articulate peaceful co-existence when it comes to the industrial brewers celebrating the plentitude of the brewing industry as such. Devil's Brew in continuation of their emphasis on industry collaboration write:

> we have great respect for the many years of "trial and error" which have made brewing what it is today. There is everything from super high-tech larger-industries to small and "dirty" gueuze breweries in the brewing world; and that is a beautiful thing! They all make beer, and they each play a part.

Here, it is not as much a question of oppositional identities but of multiple identities, i.e. constructing a diversified collective identity for the brewing industry embracing all brewers potentially inscribing the craft brewing movement in the existing industry master-narrative.

In short, the Danish craft breweries articulate their collective identity in different ways, i.e. referencing shared identity markers, the beer revolution, collaboration and opposition to industry. However, for the most part, these counter-narrative articulations are implicitly embedded in the autobiographical texts, rather than explicit statements often intertwining collective and organizational identities, which is explored further below.

Organizational identity in the context of the collective

The reflexive positioning of the breweries points to complex processes of identification, dis-identification, and ambivalent identification intertwined with the interactive positioning of the movement. There are distinct examples of how identification with the movement is used as an organizational identity marker, e.g. Croocked Moon Brewery and Grauballe Brewhouse who associate their breweries with the beer revolution. As such, positioning the individual breweries reflexively is frequently connected to positioning the collective interactively. Another example is Aarhus Brewhouse positioning themselves as producers of traditional, specialty beer implicitly articulating a dichotomy between craft and industrial brewers. In addition, it is visible in how the breweries associate themselves with the movement, as when Noerrebro Brewhouse state they "were established in 2003 and were from the beginning somewhat of a shining light in the young and future oriented beer culture, which started to grow together with the young brewery". Here, the development of the movement and the brewery are closely intertwined; almost articulated as being one and the same pointing to the simultaneously reflexive positioning of the brewery ("a shining light") and interactive position of the movement (or "beer culture").

While the breweries share an emphasis on the defining features of their interactive collective identity position, e.g. craftmanship and local embeddedness, they simultaneously construct reflexive positions distancing themselves from other craft breweries. One example is the distinction between owning a brewing facility and having to borrow facilities, i.e. being a so-called contract – phantom, nomad, or gypsy – brewer, as Birkeroed Brewhouse state: "the brewhouse is a phantom brewery – my beer in others' vats". Contract brewers highlight flexibility as a key aspect, as do Hop Bottle Brewery who refer to "the safe and solid gypsy-brewing model", and comment that the model "leads us clear of having to deal with investors or banks" and "gives us the ability to focus 150% on creating honest and delicious beers". Moreover, they frequently address the issue with a sense of playfulness, e.g. The Syndicate: "with a sparkle in our eye, we refer to ourselves as gangster brewers as a self-invented synonym for contract/gypsy/nomad brewers". At the other end of the spectrum, are the breweries who emphasize that they produce their own beer, e.g. Ribe Brewhouse: "you can be a 100% sure that the beer is brewed by us – using our own recipes, and not imported or brewed by license a completely different place on the globe". And Moen Brewhouse:

> the entire process from grain to finished product takes place at the brewery. We do not have agreements with other breweries to aid in brewing or bottling, and you can count on that beer from Moen Brewhouse is brewed and bottled locally with the help of good, local employees.

Here, the breweries dis-identify with those breweries who operate as contract brewers, insisting that in order to have legitimacy as a 'real' brewery, you need your own facilities.

Another mark of distinction for the breweries is how they navigate their own genesis within the context of the beer revolution, i.e. how they associate their own birth with the movement. One example is, the previously referenced, Noerrebro Brewhouse's linking of their brewery and the movement, i.e. as "a shining light in the young and future oriented beer culture". It is a shared feature among many breweries that they were born out of the beer revolution, established by beer enthusiasts who, to put it in the words of WinterCoat's founder, "could brew much better and interesting beer than he could buy". Being among the first of the new generation of craft breweries is highlighted by several breweries besides Noerrebro Brewhouse, e.g. "Andrik

Brewhouse were established in 2003 as one of the first ten microbreweries in this country" and "Fur Brewhouse were opened in 2004 – as one of the first microbreweries in Denmark".

However, some breweries have histories dating back more than a century, e.g. Hancook who can trace their history back to 1876, Thisted Brewhouse established in 1902 and Oerbaek Brewery established in 1906. Others are revivals, i.e. breweries that have gone out of business as a result of increasing competition and consolidation, but have been brought back to life. One revived brewery is Bie's Brewhouse. The first brewhouse dates back to 1841, it had to close in 1980, but was reborn with the craft beer movement: "in 2006 the idea of reestablishing one of Denmark's oldest breweries was born. With the reopening of a brewery in these buildings, the place is filled with life and atmosphere as in the good old days". Here, they simultaneously identify and dis-identify themselves with the new generation of craft brewers by using both heritage and rebirth in their positioning. The extract also illustrates how the heritage of the brewery and its local, historical anchoring are evoked as a potential expression of neo-localism (e.g. Flack, 1997) as is also the case with Halsnaes Brewery's claim to "playing a positive role" in the local community. In contrast, some of the new generation of craft brewers dis-associate themselves with the heritage claims of the old generation, e.g. Two Beers [To Øl]:

> when To Øl was founded, we were sick of hundred years of old breweries claiming territory only due to old age – old age withers; it does not necessarily improve the recipe. Instead we wanted to *give beer some youth!*

Here, tradition, which is frequently articulated as a marker of collective identity, is denounced, and replaced with an emphasis on innovation and renewal by contrasting "old age" with "youth" similar to Noerrebro Brewhouse's reference to the "young and future oriented beer culture". Potentially, such articulations dis-identify with tradition, but also suggest a possible decoupling of tradition and craftmanship, pointing to a centrifugal pull that reorganizes and destabilizes part of the shared counter-narrative.

A third mark of distinction is associated with the industry-craft opposition that is suggested to exist, albeit implicitly. In constructing collective identity, a dichotomy emerges between beers brewed by modern, industrialized techniques and "traditional", "handcrafted" beer brewed "without computers, by living people". However, not all breweries inscribe themselves into a narrative where craft means 'brewed by hand'. Whereas some explicitly reference traditional brewing methods and position themselves as anti-industrial, e.g. Trolden Brewhouse, others seek to dissolve the constructed opposition between being a craft brewery and using modern techniques. The Art Brewery Father & Son describe their methods as based on a "revival of the farm beer production methods of past times" and claim to be "inspired by the way in which the brew was made before the industrialization and large-scale production". In contrast, The Brewery Devil's Brew address the "romantic notions of how a brewery *should* be" positioning themselves "closer to high-tech" and claiming it to be "a crucial point that the opportunity for experimentation and giving flavor to the beer in no way suffers from this. In our opinion, on the contrary!" In that sense, not all breweries subscribe to traditional, non-industrial, brewing techniques, and thus dis-identify with the suggestion that craft brewed means hand brewed; challenging part of the dichotomy that shapes the counter-narrative and acting as a centrifugal force.

The examples connected to the three markers mentioned here illustrate how individual and collective identities intersect through processes of identification, dis-identification and ambivalent as exemplified in Figure 11.2.

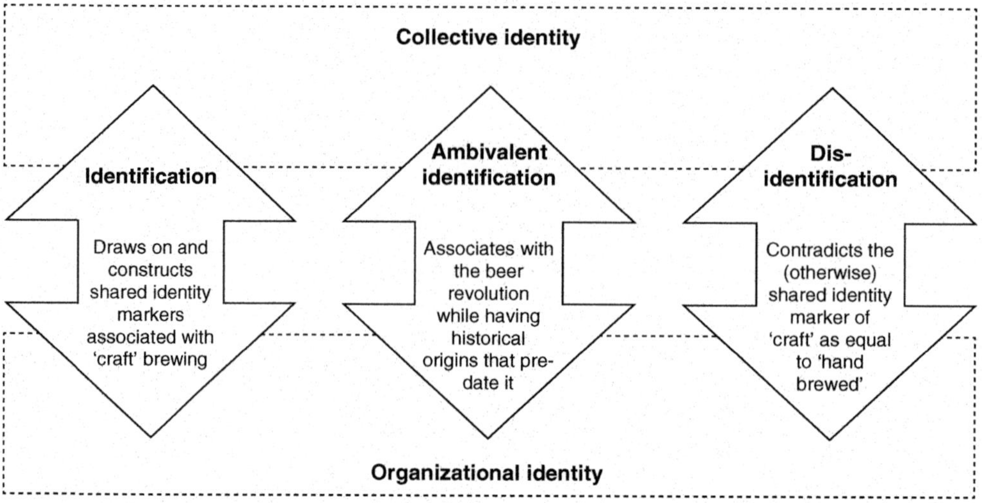

Figure 11.2 Examples of the intersection of collective and organizational identity.

The craft breweries make use of complex patterns of identification as they simultaneously inscribe themselves into and construct the collective counter-narrative identity of the craft brewing movement. However, while they build associations with the shared characteristic and the beer revolution per se, there are also attempts to dis-identify with (parts) of movement. This potentially points to ambivalent identification as the individual breweries tap into certain elements of the collective identity while distancing themselves from others, or seek to re-construct certain elements of the collective identity.

Counter-narrativizing collective and organizational identity

Drawing on subject positioning and identification, the analysis illustrates how complex patterns of relatedness construct both collective and organizational identities. Viewing the complex interplay in a counter-narrative perspective suggests it to be plural processes of counter-narrativizations, rather than a single, uniformizing and unifying counter-narrative. The multiplicity of the dynamics involved suggests that speaking of *a* counter-narrative is potentially futile if the goal is to shed light on the complexity of the collective and organizational identities continuously constructed in the craft breweries' autobiographical texts. Instead, the analysis suggests the presence of evolving counter-narrativizations that each construct their own embedded, implicit master-narrative. The craft breweries implicitly create a partly shared counter-narrative position for themselves as revolutionaries in a marketplace previously characterized by industrialized homogenization and bland beers. However, the shared position is not a static entity or *narrative*, but rather gets told, or *narrativized*, in different ways, with different emphases and from different perspectives. In other words, counter-narrative is not something that is, it is something that is becoming through narrativizing, i.e. "the activity of engaging in narratives" (Bamberg, 2004, p. 359). Moreover, other narrativizations emerge that simultaneously oppose the collectivized narrativization, e.g. being a real brewery with its own facilities instead of being a contact brewery – a narrativization which is then opposed by contract brewers who do not buy into the claim of the so-called 'real' breweries and narrativize the craft brewing movement as being about a certain style and approach

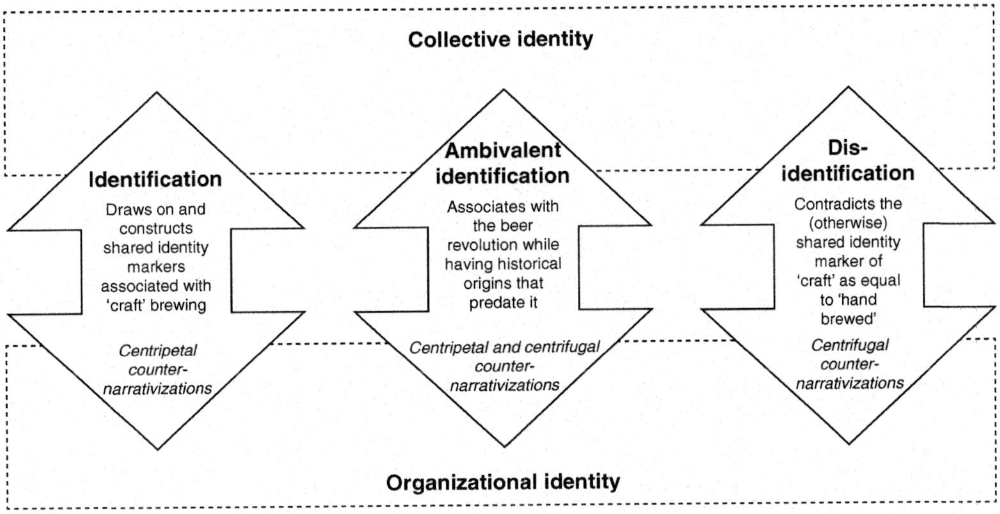

Figure 11.3 Counter-narrativizations in the intersection of collective and organizational identity.

to brewing (not a question of facilities). These centripetal and centrifugal forces as illustrated in Figure 11.3.

In addition to shifting focus from counter-narrative to counter-narrativizations, the analysis potentially opens up for a discussion on the labelling of the craft brewing movement as counter-narrative. Speaking of the movement as counter-narrative, or rather as constituted in counter-narrativizing, is meaningful in a number of ways. It ties in with its contradictory, conflicting and revolutionary collective identity, and thereby it can be seen as a category in tension with another category (cf. Andrews, 2004, p. 1). In constructing the movement as counter-narrativized, the multinational breweries' focus on consolidation, standardization and industrialization becomes the master-narrative countered; which perhaps also can be understood as master-narrativizations constantly produced and re-produced through counter-narrativizations. Bamberg (2004, p. 360) argues that master-narratives have the potential to "normalize" and "naturalize" phenomena, suggesting that counter-narratives in some ways legitimize the master-narrative. However, in exploring the counter-narrativizations of the craft breweries' collective identity, it seems that the narrativization itself has similar normalizing and naturalizing capabilities as centripetal forces generate unifying characteristics, e.g. craft, tradition and localness. In other words, the collective identity is the 'new normal' as also made visible in the way in which some of the craft breweries are ambivalent in their identification with the shared storying of their collective identity, i.e. seeking different ways of 'being and doing' a craft brewery by e.g. highlighting innovation instead of or in cohesion with tradition. The question becomes whether or not the narrativizations of the craft brewing movement, itself, can be considered a dominant cultural narrative (Andrews, 2004) subject to countering or centrifugal mechanisms that seek to reshape and reconfigure it. Consequently, as suggested by Johansen (2017), it is possibly an open question which narratives are seen respectively as dominating and resisting, and whether or not these categories are stable or dynamic.

As discussed by Rasmussen (2017), the implied ontological dichotomy of master and counter is potentially problematic as it implies counter-narrative to be a causal outcome of a master-narrative. Instead, not all competing narratives necessarily fit the dichotomy, but can be seen as a struggle between two master-narratives. An alternative perspective could therefore be to approach the narrativizations of industrial and craft breweries as co-existing, or perhaps even as narrativizations that hold both. As suggested by The Brewery Devil's Brew: the industry entails large and small breweries, "and that is a beautiful thing!". Perhaps the master-narrativizations of brewing have been reconfigured to accommodate the changing composition of the industry; not as a hegemonic narrative but as narrativizations constituted in centripetal and centrifugal forces. Or perhaps it speaks to previous claims by Kuhn (2017, p. 38) who suggests that counter-narratives "need not be starkly or diametrically oppositional". Viewing counter-narratives as alternative accounts, rather than oppositional accounts, perhaps better embraces the subtle, indirect ways in which the craft breweries contrast themselves with the industrial breweries and narrativize their collective identity. This potentially aligns with resource-partitioning theory's central claim that mature markets typically consist of a few large, generalized producers and a number of small, specialist producers (Baginski & Belle, 2011). The chapter concludes by reflecting on the implications for understanding and utilizing counter-narrative as a theoretical concept.

Conclusions

This chapter set out to shed light on the reciprocal relationship between counter-narrative and identity at the organizational and collective levels by exploring how they intersect through an analysis of the online autobiographical accounts of Danish craft breweries. The analysis illustrates the complex, interdependent nature of collective and organizational identity. It shows collective identity not as a static, single counter-narrative, which craft breweries construct and re-construct by repeatedly drawing on their shared cultural (counter)position as a resource for identification, but as dynamic and evolving processes of counter-narrativizations. These counter-narrativizations are both centripetal and centrifugal: centripetal in that they create a unifying, shared understanding of craft brewing as something to do with craft, tradition and local belonging and centrifugal in that the craft breweries develop unique, diverging understandings when addressing the significance of tradition (versus innovation) or when gypsy breweries challenge localness by creating license brews that are brewed nationally or even internationally. Moreover, the analysis shows how applying counter-narrative as a conceptual lens opens up for discussions on how to understand the otherwise seemingly inherent oppositional collective identity of craft breweries associated with the beer revolution. Thus, the concept can be said to open up for new, relevant insights that allow for reflections on 'what' counter-narrative has to offer, but also informs debates on 'how' counter-narrative is meaningful as a theoretical optic. As such, it opens up for discussion existing conceptualizations of counter-narrative and points to new avenues of exploration.

The avenues of exploration, or implications, relate to both identity studies and counter-narrative. The analysis could be seen as an indication that the many levels of identity, or rather identities, in the craft brewing movement mark a fruitful terrain for counter-narrative explorations. An additional focus could be to direct attention to the identity of the individual brewers as well. There is a potential complex dynamic that plays itself out between different identities, e.g. the brewing industry, the craft brewing movement, the individual craft breweries, and the individual brewers. These complex interplays where multiple identities are co-constructed and re-constructed could add to understandings of where and how counter-narratives are formed and develop, i.e. their narrativizing, and potentially contribute with insights into what constitutes counter-narrativizations. Along these lines, there is further potential for exploring the ontology of what 'counter', and 'master', imply, nuancing and broadening existing understandings. Such explorations could also entail the implications of incorporating dynamic and processual dimensions that are highlighted with the conceptual shift from counter-narrative to counter-narrativization. In order to develop the notion of counter-narrativizations as a theoretical lens, attention could be given to exploring the counter-acting centripetal and centrifugal forces that seem to simultaneously create unification and diversification.

References

Andersen, C. (2007, January 14). Nybryggerne. *Morgenavisen Jyllands-Posten*. Retrieved from Infomedia.

Andrews, M. (2004). Opening the original contributions: Counter-narratives and the power to oppose. In M.G.M. Bamberg & M. Andrews (Eds.), *Considering counter-narratives: Narrating, resisting, making sense* (pp. 1–6). Philadelphia, PA, The United States: John Benjamin.

Baginski, J. & Bell, T.L. (2011). Under-tapped? An analysis of craft brewing in the Southern United States. *Southeastern Geographer, 51*(1), 165–185.

Bakhtin, M.M. (1981). *The dialogue imagination: Four essays by M.M. Bakhtin* (Ed. M. Holquist). Austin, TX, The United States: University of Texas Press.

Bamberg, M. (2004). Considering counter narratives. In M.G.M. Bamberg & M. Andrews (Eds.), *Considering counter-narratives: Narrating, resisting, making sense* (pp. 351–371). Philadelphia, PA, The United States: John Benjamin.

Bamberg, M. & Andrews, M. (2004). Introduction to the book. In M.G.M. Bamberg & M. Andrews (Eds.), *Considering counter-narratives: Narrating, resisting, making sense* (pp. ix-x). Philadelphia, PA, The United States: John Benjamin.

Bentzen, J. & Smith, V. (2017). Entry, survival, and profits: The emergence of microbreweries in Denmark. In C. Garavaglia & J. Swinnen (Eds.), *Economic perspectives on craft beer: A revolution in the global beer industry* (pp. 161–182). London, UK: Palgrave Macmillan.

Blum-Kulka, S. (1997). Dinner talk: Cultural patterns of sociability and socialization in family discourse. Routledge.

Carroll, G.R. & Swaminathan, A. (2000). Why the micro brewery movement? Organizational dynamics of resource partitioning in the U.S. brewing industry. *American Journal of Sociology, 106*(3), 715–762.

Davies, B. & Harré, R. (1990). Positioning: The discursive production of selves. *Journal for the Theory of Social Behaviour, 20*(1), 43–63.

Eberts, D. (2014). Neolocalism and the branding and marketing of place by Canadian microbreweries. In M. Patterson & N. Hoalst-Pullen (Eds.), *The geography of beer. Regions, environment, and societies* (pp. 189–199). New York, NY, The United States: Springer.

Flack, W. (1997). American microbreweries and neolocalism: "Ale-ing for a sense of place". *Journal of Cultural Geography, 16*(2), 37–53.

Frandsen, S., Lundholt, M.W., & Kuhn, T. (2017). Introduction. In S. Frandsen, T. Kuhn & M.W. Lundholt (Eds.), *Counter-narratives and organization* (pp. 1–13). New York, NY, The United States: Routledge.

Garavaglia, C. & Swinnen, J. (2017). Economic perspectives on craft beer: A revolution in the global beer industry. In C. Garavaglia & J. Swinnen (Eds.), *Economic perspectives on craft beer: A revolution in the global beer industry* (pp. 3–51). London, UK: Palgrave Macmillan.

Gatrell, J., Reid, N., & Steiger, T.L. (2018). Branding spaces: Place, region, sustainability and the American craft beer industry, *Applied Geography, 90*, 630–670.

Humphreys, M., & Brown, A.D. (2002). Narrative of organizational identity and identification: A case study of hegemony and resistance, *Organization Studies, 23*(3), 421–447.

Hvelplund, F. (2005). Ølrevolutionen. *ErhvervsBladet*. Retrieved from Infomedia.

Johansen, T.S. (2017). Countering the 'natural' organizational self on social media. In S. Frandsen, T. Kuhn & M.W. Lundholt (Eds.), *Counter-narratives and organization* (pp. 64–82). New York, NY, The United States: Routledge.

Juhler, S. (2004, June 19). Vores helt egen øl. *Ekstra-bladet*. Retrieved from Infomedia.

Kreiner, G.E., & Ashforth, B.E. (2004). Experience toward an expanded model of organizational identification, *Journal of Organizational Behavior, 25*(1), 1–27.

Kuhn, T. (2017). Communicatively constituting organizational unfolding through counter-narrative. In S. Frandsen, T. Kuhn & M.W. Lundholt (Eds.), *Counter-narratives and organization* (pp. 17–42). New York, NY, The United States: Routledge.

Lai, A. (2006, August 7). Branchekompasset: Det flasker sig for øllet. *Morgenavisen Jyllands-Posten*. Retrieved from Infomedia.

Lamertz, K., Foster, W.M., Coraiola, D.M., & Kroezen, J. (2016). New identities from remnants of the past: An examination of the history of beer brewing in Ontario and the recent emergence of craft breweries. *Business History*, *58*(5), 796–828.

Lamertz, K., Heugens, P.P., & Calmet, L. (2005). The configuration of organizational images among firms in the Canadian beer brewing industry. *Journal of Management Studies*, *42*(4), 817–843.

Larson, G.S., & Pepper, G.L. (2003). Strategies for managing multiple organizational identifications: a case of competing identities. *Management Communication Quarterly*, *16*(4), 258-257.

Mathias, B.D., Huyghe, A., Frid, C.J. & Galloway, T.L. (2018). An identity perspective on coopetition in the craft beer industry. *Strategic Management Journal*, *39*, 3086–3115.

McLaughlin, R.B., Reid, N., & Moore, M.S. (2014). The ubiquity of good taste: A spatial analysis of the craft brewing industry in the United States. In M. Patterson & N. Hoalst-Pullen (Eds.), *The geography of beer. Regions, environment, and societies* (pp. 131–154). Dordrecht, The Netherlands: Springer.

Murray, D.W. & O'Neill, M.A. (2012). Craft beer: Penetrating a niche market. *British Food Journal*, *114*(7), 899–909.

Rasmussen, K.R. (2017). Rethinking counter-narratives in studies of organizational texts and practices. In S. Frandsen, T. Kuhn & M.W. Lundholt (Eds.), *Counter-narratives and organization* (pp. 171–192). New York, NY, The United States: Routledge.

Schnell, S.M. & Reese, J.F. (2003). Microbreweries as tools of local identity. *Journal of Cultural Geography*, *21*(1), 45–69.

12

Organizational storymaking as narrative-small-story dynamics

A combination of organizational storytelling theory and small story analysis

Ann Starbæk Bager and Marianne Wolff Lundholt

Introduction

There is a growing body of organizational research that engages the concept of *counter-narratives* as a means to reflect, analyze, and challenge power relations (Frandsen, Lundholt, & Kuhn, 2017; Lundholt & Boje, 2018; Svane, Gergerich, & Boje, 2017). Organizational counter-narratives are perceived as stories that people enact, which are in opposition to more hegemonic and culturally created narratives (Bamberg & Andrews, 2004; Boje, 2001; Frandsen, Lundholt, & Kuhn, 2017; Jørgensen & Boje, 2009; Lundholt & Boje, 2018). Narratives can in this sense be understood as crystallized knowledge forms that are recurrently enacted in organizational writings or sayings often appropriated and strengthened by the management group. A basic assumption is that the study of organizational counter-narratives that oppose the more solidified master-narratives provides important insights into organizational struggles of meaning and polyphony of voices together with resistive forces (Bamberg & Andrews, 2004; Frandsen, Lundholt, & Kuhn, 2017; Jørgensen & Boje, 2009).

We propose a methodological framework that binds together two diverse approaches to storytelling, namely, *storytelling organization theory* (SOT) and *small story analysis* (SSA). SSA is also referred to as the narrative practice approach (See Bamberg & Wipff, in this handbook). The former has evolved mainly within organizational studies in the works of Boje (2011) that invite us to grasp organizations as (re)constituted through intense, chaotic, and ambiguous storytelling practices, thereby offering a strong and ontological view of organizational narratives (Rantakari & Vaara, 2017). The latter has mainly emerged in the writings of Bamberg (1997, 2004b) within the field of cultural, narrative, and discursive psychology. SSA offers a *micro-generic* approach to the study of how storytellers work up stories in situ to juggle claims about who they are. These stories can be hearable as both countering and supporting narratives and discursive formations. It gives directions on how to study issues such as social relationship formation, personal identity, professional identity, identity dilemmas, and a sense of self with an emphasis on how these phenomena are under construction in processes of social interaction (Bager, 2015b, 2019; Bamberg, 2004b, 2016). SSA is not directed at organizational practices but focuses on how subjects co-construct and co-create identity in everyday settings (Bager, 2019). We bring the approach to the study of situated organizational identity work.

We suggest that a combination of the two approaches provides a methodological frame through which we can reflect and study storytelling and its role in organizational transformations spanning from more abstract and philosophical dimensions to the concreteness of everyday interaction. SOT provides a potent frame and solid experience with reflecting organizations as storytelling ensembles made up through intense, chaotic, and ambiguous storytelling practices. SSA offers a potent discourse analytical lens that captures the small, "messy", and interactional aspects of storytelling practices and identity work that can benefit our perception of organizational storytelling practices and narrative-small-story dynamics. An important part of the chapter's discussion is that an inquiry into organizational storytelling practices is a complex, analytical task. One of our main arguments is that we can design more egalitarian and ethical change processes from studying how resistance and complicity are made up in organizational interaction.

The chapter is structured into five parts: in section one, we posit a short description of a case study conducted on counseling practices in a Danish bank that we will reflect throughout the chapter to anchor the methodological discussion in relation to an organizational change process.

In section two, we present an overview of SOT and position it within dialogic organizational studies and Bakhtinian thinking. The overview concentrates on selected literature on the concept, *living stories*, together with the framing of the *narrative-counter-narrative dynamics*. Here we explain how the Danish bank is reflected through the SOT perspective. The section reveals how analyses in SOT often overlook close-up interactional aspects of storytelling practices.

In section three, we zoom in on SSA and discuss how the discourse analytical lens in the form of a positioning model can assist the analysis of organizational storytelling practices by taking a closer look at situated interaction and identity work. Part of this section comprises a close-up analysis of interview data from the Danish bank, which offers important nuances to the narrative-small-story dynamics.

Section four reflects a summary where we posit an overview chart that sums up central elements in SOT and SSA and spotlights similarities and differences.

As part of the concluding remarks in section five, we discuss what we can learn from the analyses. We further elaborate on new tendencies in and avenues for research on organizational storytelling. Additionally, it is highlighted how scholars can benefit from considering multimodal features, including how diverse material and technological aspects affect organizational meaning-making to reflect the complexities inherent in everyday work lives.

A case study in a Danish bank

We will ground the methodological discussion in a case study conducted in a Danish bank as we continually elaborate how we can perceive of it through the framework. The bank has recently been through a change process where four departments were merged into one. As part of the process they moved to a new location and implemented a new material discursive design for their counseling practices. This entails a rather strict and streamlined concept spanning décor in an open office landscape (in new Nordic style), digital templates for preparing and holding counseling meetings along with physical arrangements in the counseling rooms – such as full-grain leather chairs, wooden interior, organic and locally produced chocolates, high quality mineral water, and Danish designed coffee cups. The interview data that we analyzed was gathered as part of a larger Danish research project on communication counseling that counts 100 qualitative interviews with counselors across disciplines.

Storytelling organization theory: understanding of organizations as assemblages of storytelling practices

Boje (1995) wrote about the polyphonic nature of organizations through the metaphor of a *Tamara-play*. Thereby, he invites us to regard organizations such as the Danish bank as a meta-theatre, that is, an arena in which a multiplicity of simultaneous and discontinuous dramas occurred. In a Tamara-play, the game is performed in various rooms and settings in which the audience members choose to follow specific characters and story lines (which come close to the plots in interactive movies). Therefore, each participant is co-creating a certain story according to his or her own choices in interplay with the affordances of the theater setting, which most likely differs from the other participants' story lines and stories. Boje adopted the Tamara-metaphor in his perception of organizational meaning making: through this we can perceive of organizations and the Danish bank as constituted by a diversity of circulating voices and stories, which often run counter to the more official organizational narrative (cf., Bakhtin's dialogue philosophy; Boje, 2001). Hence, SOT represents a postmodern reading of organizations, in which the coherent and complete organizational course of events and plots are nonexistent as organizational members continually follow, retell, and reconfigure the stories they engage with. SOT thereby dismisses the idea of a shared collective organizational memory or subculture and replaces it with the idea of organizations as a form of fragmented hotchpotches of situational stories and clashes between them.

Dialogic organizational studies

In Boje's conflictual perception of organizational meaning making practices as ensembles of storytelling activities, there is a clear link to a Bakhtinian philosophy of the language of life. This invites a perception of the creation of meaning making, knowledge, and identity as continually (re)configured through intense and conflictual culture creating processes. In such processes, features such as ambiguity, otherness, and clashes between often opposing voices and discourses from within and without subjects are premises (Bager, 2013, 2015a, 2015b; Bakhtin, 1993).

The inspiration from Bakhtinian thinking has made an entry into organizational studies, particularly within the last two decades (see Bager, 2015b; Barge & Little, 2002; Clegg, Kornberger, Carter, & Rhodes, 2006; Iedema, 2003; Kornberger, Clegg, & Carter, 2006; Rennison, 2014; Shotter, 2011). This body of organizational research calls the imagination of organizational stability and consensus into question and replaces it with a dissensus oriented perception of organizations as shaped by conflicts, opposing voices/discourses /stories, and otherness. These are all intrinsic organizational features that we need to consider to perceive of and orchestrate organizational reality and support egalitarian change processes. Within organizational studies, such dissensus orientation is termed *dialogic studies* by Deetz (2001), which is in opposition to consensus-oriented perspectives, such as *interpretative* and *functionalistic studies.* The latter two perceive of organizational change processes, culture, and reality as rather linear, coherent, and smooth entities where conflicts and polyphony should be fixed and overcome to reestablish organizational consensus and a common ground. The polyphonic perspectives change the traditional organizational thinking from ideals of stability, consensus, linearity, and coherency together with rather fixed and neat structures to foreground aspects as instability, chaos, polyphony, ambiguity, and fragmentation. In such framings, organizational polyphony is always present even though it may be silenced by a dominant discourse or narrative. In the Bakhtinian sense, meaning making, identity, and culture are worked up in heteroglossic battles between diversifying (centrifugal) and monologizing (centripetal) forces of interaction. A main point is that the monologizing forces that close down complexity tend to overpower the diversifying forces over time, so that knowledge forms crystallize into monologic authoritative narratives and discourses that we tend to take for granted and that direct us in our everyday (organizational) conduct (Bager, 2013; Bakhtin, 1986, 1993; Deetz, 2001).

Narrative versus (living) story

Arriving from the Bakhtinian line of thought, Boje has played an important role in making the distinction between narratives and storytelling and what he has termed *living stories*. According to Boje, narrative is something that is narrated in retrospective sensemaking (backward-looking). Boje (2001) referred to narrative sensemaking stemming from Weick (1995) or narrative as emplotment with a beginning, middle, and end (BME), following Aristotle's work. He sees living stories as accounts of incidents or events and relationships to people in other living stories, all unfolding in-the-moment-of-beingness with clear references to Bakhtin (1993). The concept of a living story emphasizes that organizational interpretations and experiences are always open, polyphonic, equivocal, dialogical, unfinished, and unresolved. Thus, retro-narrative comes after and adds more "plot" and "tighter coherence", thereby reducing living variety to a line. Living stories are what Bakhtin (1973, p. 60) called a "polylogic manner of the story". In this framing, the Bakhtinian centripetal and monologizing force sort of crystallizes (organizational) living stories into narratives that are more linear, coherent, retrospective, and less chaotic – coming close to a plot. Jørgensen (2010, p. 109) stressed the difference between narrative and storytelling following Boje's and their shared work (Jørgensen & Boje, 2009). Here, narrative is framed as monologic, linear, closed, retrospective, rational, and clear-cut, whereas storytelling is dialogic, polyphonic, fragmented, open, emergent, irrational, and ambiguous.

This distinction between narrative and storytelling enables a reflection of organizational reality as co-created and emerging in tension between narrative work on the one hand and situated organizational storytelling practices on the other. The former organizational monologic narrative mode reduces complexity in its contestation for coherence and unity through retrospective sense making and the latter story mode reflects the ambiguous and complex dynamics of everyday organizational life. An organizational narrative mode and its representations strive to make order out of and direct everyday storytelling chaos, so to speak. Another important reflection is that living stories and their manifestations in organizational narrative modes and representations – such as strategy work (Boje, 2008) and organizational texts (Jørgensen, 2011) – are seen as the monologized results of such complex chains of interactions, negotiations, and struggles between many different actors, groups, organizations, and institutions. According to Boje (2008), most organizational strategy work is narrative, and he thereby sees organizational strategy as directly linked to narrative. When studying storytelling and living stories, focus shifts from neat narrative structures to ways in which stories spontaneously emerge between participants in situated organizational settings (Jørgensen & Boje, 2009).

In the case of the Danish bank, part of their narrative strategy work was crystallized into a mission statement and set of values that prompted the employees to have certain actions and attitudes (cp., value-based leadership). Their mission statement is to be "the personal bank in a digital world. [Xx] is a bank that seeks to combine attentive personal counseling and service with contemporary and innovative digital offers". This mission statement is supported by the four values: "competent, ambitious, decency and presence", which are the guiding principles that all employees have to navigate. These are also part of the organizational dialogue in department meetings and employee development conversations played out continually between the department head and the employees and counselors, from which their actions and performance are evaluated and guided. These narrative representations are quite easy to detect and study, whereas the complex network of living stories that make up everyday organizational life – and in which the values are enacted, countered, and/or supported – are more complex affairs to study.

Counter-narrative and narrative-counter-narrative dynamics

Recently, Boje has adopted the term *counter-narrative*; nevertheless his extensive body of work has provided important contributions and a strong theoretical platform for future work. With concepts such as *hegemony* (i.e., privileged voices taken-for-granted or too subtle to be acknowledged (Boje, 2001, p. 35) and *story coercion* (i.e., the [un]conscious efforts to create universal meaning; Boje, Luhman, & Baack, 1999), he has studied ways in which dominant groups control others as well as ways in which local stories (what Boje refers to as *microstoria*; Boje, 2001, p. 55) or a living story web (Svane et al., 2017)) resist narratives.

When introducing the concept of counter-narrative, Boje and his co-authors define counter-narrative as "those narratives that are arising in opposition to the narrative by taking a conflicting position. Both the fragmented narratives and the counter-narratives together form a fragmented cluster of narratives" (Svane et al., 2017, pp. 132–133). In that sense, the main narrative may give rise to a series of counter-narratives rather than just a single counter-narrative (Svane et al., 2017. p. 133). In Svane, Gergerich, and Boje, (2017) the narrative-counter-narrative dynamic is explained through fractal management theory in combination with the triad storytelling model to which we will return. The authors talk about the relation between narrative-counter-narrative with the term *counter-narrative fractal*. They point to the evolvement of counter-narratives splitting into more and more counter-narratives like a tree growing in various directions though still in accordance with its root. The ubiquitous nature of the counter-narrative is encapsulated in the mathematical term, *fractal*, as it encompasses a detailed, recursive, and almost identical appearance. According to Boje (Svane et al., 2017, p. 133), a fractal narrative is a narrative that finds its best accomplished form in the web of communicative praxis in discourse and in ritual relationships. Within an organizational context, *fractal control narratives* refer to the narratives narrated by managers. Along with the attempt to tell one story only, the narrative turns into a fractal control narrative exercising social control (Boje, 2011). With their aim to achieve generality and universality and thereby "neglecting, silencing, and erasing its living stories and to collapse them into legitimate, institutionalized story" (Boje, 2011, p. 3), the fractal control narrative provides safe grounds for passive or active polarized resistance emerging as fractal (counter-)narrative (Svane & Boje, 2015). A fractal living story is thus different from the fractal narrative. Whereas the fractal (counter-) narrative is characterized by coherency, order, and consensus, the fractal story is characterized by disorder and dissensus. The fractal story is an unfinalized and unfinished patterning, a living patterning that emerges, scatters, and transforms through the polyphonic dialogue in the living story web (Svane & Boje, 2015). In Svane et al. (2017, p. 136), the authors explain how the living story web emerges on the micro practice level of organization through the *Deleuzian Rhizome* metaphor. Here fractal stories are overlapping and even conflicting with each other in the web of fluid living story.

Antenarrative and antenarratology

Another central concept in SOT that we will only touch upon is the antenarrative, that is, "a bet on the future" (Boje, 2011). The antenarrative is proposed as being the bridge that brings story (present) and narrative (past) into stories on possible futures. These three storytelling elements comprise a storytelling triad that is the center of SOT's antenarratology and reflection/study of organizational storytelling (Boje, 2001; Svane et al., 2017).

When studying antenarrative methods of deconstruction of for instance interview data is called upon. In his early work, Boje (1991) offered suggestions on how participatory observation could be used to study organizational antenarratives. In Jørgensen and Boje (2009), a genealogic approach based on Foucauldian studies is presented. Here a diversity of data types – such as a variety of organizational documents (e.g., minutes and code of conduct) – together with interview data are part of the analysis of organizational life (Jørgensen, 2011). In recent texts, the triad storytelling model together with the narrative-counter-narrative dynamics are nuanced through rather abstract and philosophical discussions with little empirical orientation (e.g., Svane et al., 2017).

Jørgensen (2010) points out that a focus on storytelling and living stories implies perceiving research practice as a complex storytelling practice in which the major challenge is to understand and represent multiple possibilities. We question whether living stories are best inquired into and represented by deconstructing people's accounts of events or through abstract retrospective and highly interpretative movements. As an alternative, we find that the discourse analytical purview in SSA is a potent way of turning the analytical gaze more toward situated storytelling contexts.

Small story analysis

The concept of *small stories* has close affinities to the term, living stories (Bager, 2015b). The concept of small stories that has emerged in Bamberg's work offers an interesting analytical gaze that brings us closer to the reflection and study of storytelling efforts in organizational interaction. The underlying assumptions here are how interlocutors create and construct identity and a sense of self through everyday interaction (Bamberg, 1997; Bamberg & Georgakopoulou, 2008). According to Bamberg and Georgakopoulou (2008), small story analysis offers a window "… into the micro-genetic processes of identities as 'in-the-making' or 'coming-into-being'" (Bamberg & Georgakopoulou, 2008, p. 3). Reading a strip of interaction "… as 'small story' reveals aspects of identity construction that would have otherwise remained unnoticed" (Bamberg & Georgakopoulou, 2008, p. 393). Thus, when studying small stories, focus is in sync with SOT's ideas on the rhizomatic living story web, on fragmented and fleeting subjects that co-create identity in interactions with others. On the same note as Boje's antenarratology, Bamberg and Georgakopoulou propose small story analysis as an alternative that opposes the traditional way of looking at big stories in which more coherent and linear narratives are pursued with a BME. (Bamberg, 1997; Bamberg & Georgakopoulou, 2008). In this quest, Bamberg (1997) seeks to link two approaches for doing narrative analysis, namely, what he terms a traditional, structural approach with a more performance-based approach. The first tends to start the analysis from what is said (and the way it is said) and works toward answering why it is said and its meaning. The latter focuses more on how it was performed "as a main index for what the narrative as an act of instantiation means to the performer" (Bamberg, 1997, p. 335). This coupling is reflected in the three levels of positioning analysis that we present later.

In SSA, the relation between the master-narratives and small stories is less abstract and philosophical/theoretically oriented than in SOT and becomes more a matter of what appears in (organizational) interaction. The inspiration from ethnomethodology and conversation analysis draws attention to how small stories are worked up in interaction (Bamberg 1997, 2016; Bamberg & Georgakopoulou, 2008). In an ethnomethodological perspective, participants are constantly making interpretations of others' actions: they continuously select, pay attention to, pick up, and elicit – that is, they make sense of others who are inevitably and continually bound to the in situ creative events and practical circumstances. The heritage from ethnomethodology demands that canonical descriptions of practices are not enough. Instead of relying on theories about social life, it insists on a close-up analysis of situated encounters (Bager, 2015a).

Sense making and positioning strategies

In SSA, narratives are one discourse genre among many others, such as argumentations and explanations. These are used by subjects as an "attempt to make sense and signal this 'sense' to others" (Bamberg, 2004b, p. 354). Opposed to analyses of narrative structures, SSA studies small storying as intrinsic to how we co-perform identity in interaction.

SSA shows sensitivity toward how participants position themselves through talk to enact positions that are complicit to or counter to dominant discourses (signified by D in Table 12.1) and narratives. This brings the possibility to the study of how interlocutors and storytellers position themselves in relation to a multiplicity and often-contradictory set of discourses and narratives (cp., heteroglossia), by which they are positioned through small story efforts. Bamberg regarded the construction of counter claims as the flip sides of master-narratives that go hand-in-hand in interaction with complicit ones that cannot always be clearly distinguished (Bamberg, 2004a). Through intense, entangled interactive struggles between positions and discourses, identity work is co-accomplished. Counter narratives are not something we "have" that pop up in certain situations, such as research or therapeutic settings, which can be taken as reflective of people's authentic selves. They become real and are co-created in interactive situations. Identities emerge in the data as a part of "doing" complicity and resistance as interactive co-accomplishments (Bamberg, 2004a). Bamberg finds that youngsters narrate the same story differently in different contexts addressed to different audiences. This resembles what Boje (2011) has identified in organizations: that employees narrate themselves differently across contexts with different audiences. Based on these findings, they further challenge the traditional BME approaches to narrative analysis and claim that they tend to foreground linearity and overlook important, situated, and messy features of storytelling practices.

Stories as both countering and being complicit to master-narratives

Bamberg stressed that SSA's focus of analysis represented a slightly different orientation that changes the more traditional question of whether the speaker is complicit with or countering dominant discourses or narratives or whether the speakers engage in countering those. Instead, focus is shifted to "how speakers employ narratives to juggle claims as to who they are that are hearable both as complicit with and as countering" (Bamberg, 2004a, p. 363). The question is how they create a sense of self and identity that maneuvers simultaneously between counter and complicit established narratives that give guidance to people's actions and constrain and delineate agency (Bamberg, 2004a). It further provides insight into identity dilemmas (Bamberg & Georgakopoulou, 2008) that we will tap into as part of the close-up analysis.

Analysis: positioning model and questioning methodology

SSA involves a *positioning model* and questioning methodology consisting of three levels of analysis composed of questions (Bamberg, 1997, 2004b, 2011; Bamberg & Georgakopoulou, 2008). We will now exemplify the positioning model through an analysis of three data excerpts from an interview conducted in a Danish bank. The purpose of the analysis is to give an example of how a bank counselor is constructing his professional identity in the interview situation in a mix of countering and complicit forces and stories toward the bank's master narrative.

Level one: who are the characters, and how are they relationally positioned?

Level one pays attention to how characters in the story are positioned in relation to each other and in space and time (Bager, 2019). The aim of the interview was to study counselor's identity work in their accounts of their counseling practices and gain knowledge about the counselor position from a counselor perspective. The interview was conducted in Danish and translated into English and counted three participants: John (Bank Counselor) and two researchers, Ann (one of the authors) and Amy. The names, except for the author's, are pseudonyms used because of confidentiality issues. The interview took place in one of the counseling rooms in the bank. The first excerpt is approximately 15 minutes into the interview. The first part of the interview concerns John's background experiences after which he accounts for the competencies that he finds important for being a competent counselor. John has just accounted for how he sees trust as crucial to the good customer/counselor relation and how the bank management more strongly encourages sales as part of the recently introduced counselor concept.

On level one of the analysis, John answers the interviewer's question with an account in which he positions himself in an agentic position. For instance, this is detectable in his utterances, "I still feel that we are directors at our own desk … . I decide how to manage my bank, my portfolio … But I decide how to reach … that I set the agenda" (l. 2). Furthermore, he rejects with strong modality that the increased emphasis of sales measurements affects his room for agency, as seen in "I do not think that I've experienced that at all" (l. 2) and "so I do not think so" (l. 2).

Before we move on to level two of the positioning analysis, two additional excerpts will be displayed. The first occurs approximately four minutes later where John is telling about a newly implemented agenda template woven together with an argument on how he sees "sincerity" as one of the most crucial counselor competencies.

John's response to the question triggers a rather lengthy story line in which he explains the agenda template and its implications on his agency as a counselor. On the one hand, he positions himself as a counselor who benefits from the template structure-wise ("so it helps create structure" [l. 2]), and he positions himself as having the agency to modify the use of it in correlation with his demands. As part of the same story line, he positions the template as a feature that does not merely fit his personal preferences of being a personal and sincere counselor, as for instance, detectable in " the other is frosting on the top" (l. 2) and "… so the agenda can just help to make it beautiful, but they laugh when they come to me because they know it's not like me" (l. 4). Here something interesting occurs, where John is positioning himself positively as well as negatively toward the agenda template as it also seems to be at odds with his personal preferences.

1	Ann	Have you experienced conflicts between what, well what is sort of your ideals for how to be together and make relations with the customer as I interpret your earlier sayings and what the bank actually wants sales wise. Well, can you sometimes feel like that?
2	John	Clearly, it sounds wrong to say that, but no, I do not think so.... I do not think that I've experienced that at all, I still feel that we are directors at our own desk. I decide how to manage my bank, my portfolio. Of course, there is focus on selling some products and we need some sales figures, we have to show some results. That's how the bank is organized, but I decide how to reach the goal and what funds I spend and how I do things and that's what at least for me 100 percent is the most important thing that I set the agenda for how I create ... so I do not think so.....

Figure 12.1 Excerpt 1: Transcription (15.59–16.02).

1 Amy	Which agenda is that?
2 John	Well we make such a… we have this good customer meeting we are initiating, then we send an agenda in advance to the customer, so they kind of know a little about what we are talking about. Many times, I have changed a little in it before they come, but we sort of have a template for it, and then they also know a little about what I thought before they came in. We use it and then we take it as a starting point. Then I may have also found two things more, which I also want us to go through or something from last meeting or this or that, but then we write again when the meeting is over, we write a summary. What was it we agreed on. So, it helps create structure for me, but I think again as already said. I think 9/10 customers in the bank even if I was the world's most structured counsellor, where they came in and there were flags and it was so well structured and you got materials with home and one and the other, so I still think that it is the one who sits on the chair that is important to them. The other is frosting on top, what they are happy about it is the one sitting there. Because you have all their trust, they expect you to get them the very best and if you can get there with your customers, that this is what they believe. Because I really want them the very best, honestly and I think they get the feeling that it will.
3 Ann	So, sincerity?
4 John	Well, sincerity is the key to all my customers, it concerns that I say things as they are, and it concerns the fact that, I think that there's something they do not have to have or something I think they should have, so therefore I think they listen carefully to what one says because that's the fact, and so the agenda can just help to make it beautiful, but they laugh when they come to me because they know that It's not like me.
5 Ann	Do you say that to them?
6 John	Yes, yes, but I have to make fun of it, because otherwise I cannot be part of it because they know that's not what I invented. You know, it's clearly something that comes from the outside, so they laugh at it when I get in that situation because I'm not like that at all and they know it, right.

Figure 12.2 Excerpt 2: Transcription (20.01–21.02).

Throughout the interview he positions himself as a less structured counselor who prefers personal and sincere relations at the expense of structure and professional distance. He further expresses how he uses humor as a distancing strategy in relation to how he handles the agenda template in interaction with the customers. A positioning strategy that is proceeded in data excerpt three, approximately 18 minutes later. John has just accounted for how he sometimes sees his customers outside working hours and terms them as friends.

John's answer to the question reveals a story line in which he positions himself in friendly relationships with some of his customers. Through the excerpt, he further positions himself as a counselor who balances dimensions of being sincere, personal, and friendly on the one hand and professional and structured on the other. He uses the word "sacrifice" (l. 2), which connotes that he finds that something is at stake identity wise in this balancing act. When asked further about this, he utters that "… but some things you may feel are prostitution at the workplace because that's where you say: now I do something solely because it's my job …" (l. 4). Prostitution is a rather strong word and metaphor that clearly indicates that he has something at stake identity wise when enacting the material discursive design for his counseling practices. He further positions himself as a counselor who avoids some aspects of the bank's code of conduct because he finds them in conflict with his preferences of how to make personal relations to his customers: "then they know what I'm doing, because now I'm the bank and not John" (l. 6); "It seems false, it gets strange and I do not do it" (l. 10). His story line reveals how he sees a mismatch between the two diverse aspects of the counselor position. He further positions himself as a counselor who treasures being himself, which is sometimes in conflict with the bank's master-narratives.

1	Ann	Do you see your customers as friends?
2	John	It is again give and take I will say because some of them you get a relationships with and also do something together with outside the bank because you have come to where it fits in and then you might have this or another... but it is also because my network is very wide so it is something I may say that you... but therefore, one can well separate things, it is not so that they become a friend in the portfolio, but it is about saying I want to sacrifice it, in order to maintain the confidence.
3	Ann	What is that you sacrifice?
4	John	Well it's probably about separating things. These are some of the things I do... now I just use that expression, I do not know if I get quoted for it, but some things you may feel are prostitution at the workplace because that's where you say: Now I do something solely because it's my job, and now I have a social arrangement with these guys, and I do not really feel like attending.... sometimes where I do something outside the bank, that's because I want to. That's because I think that guy he means something to me.... I actually think he was a nice guy too.... Then we can go out and see football or something, so you get there where you can say that, but it's far from everyone. It's very few you have such a relationship with, but all the customers I know I do stop and talk to if I meet them.
5	Amy	Yes.
6	John	So, what I say is that sometimes you can feel that you are there to do something and the worst thing you can do to me is to make calls at evening time. If I got a little call-out night. No, I simply do not because they can hear and sense it when I call out. I could never dream of doing that. Then they know what I'm doing, because now I'm the bank and not John.
7	Ann	So, it's important for you, that you are John in this?
8	John	Yes 100 percent.
9	Ann	Does it collide? This being the bank and being John? Can it in some situations clash?
10	John	Yes that may be, that is if you have chosen this... where I say it just doesn't match. It does not get well, it seems false, it gets strange and I do not do it... it can be these situations where the bank has a campaign, it has done some studies. Now we do this, then you have been sitting there in the bank and then you have made some nice concept and then it just seems strange.
11	Ann	It seems foisted?
12	John	Yes... then we will not succeed... Many times I separate what comes out it and I say... fine if you just use the standard... then I do like that and I get the same out of it.

Figure 12.3 Excerpt 3: Transcription (39.02–40.06).

Level two: how does the narrator position self (and how is the narrator positioned) in the interactive situation? How is the relation between the participants managed?

Level two of the analysis deals with the sequential aspects and the interactive accomplishments of the situation. Here, analytical moves are derived from conversation analysis where interactional aspects, such as turn taking patterns, are investigated to see how the tellers link up to previous accounts/turns and what happens next in interaction (Bamberg & Georgakopoulou, 2008). The turn taking pattern in all three excerpts is characterized by pairs of questions and answers, where the researchers ask rather short questions, sometimes by paraphrasing John's choices of words, and afterward, John takes rather lengthy turns. This turn taking pattern is characteristic of the interview as a whole. So, the participation hierarchy or interaction order is obvious. John is positioned and is positioning himself as the "good" research participant who answers the questions asked by the researchers, thereby aligning himself with the topic of the interview and the research situation in general. The research situation is obvious through the interaction order in sync with typical interview setups together with the tape recorder on the table.

Level three: how do narrators position themselves to themselves? Who am I in all this?

As part of level three, we investigate how John establishes a particular kind of person or identity toward the wider social world (Bamberg, 1997, 2011; Bamberg & Georgakopoulou, 2008). John's story efforts provide interesting insights into how he positions himself according to the new counseling design as part of the overall organizational cultural change process that is a part of the bank's new grand narrative. Throughout the interview, John continually aligns positively to the change process and his room for agency within the rather strict material discursive design. Nevertheless, as the interview progresses, we see identity dilemmas coming alive concerning how parts of the design do not suit his personal preferences and thereby also restrain and delineate his agency.

We find it quite interesting that he at one and the same time accounts for these aspects in both a complicit and countering manner, as they also seem to challenge him identity wise. In other parts of the interview, he mentions the décor and the overall material design in the bank in a positive as well as a negative manner. For instance, the full design of the bank makes him feel proud toward the customers as it expresses "professionalism" contrary to the earlier interior which he addresses as more "provincial" and "hotchpotch-like". As part of the same story efforts, he simultaneously positions himself as a certain kind of person and counselor who does not altogether applaud these aspects, as he finds them "superficial" and "false" and in conflict with his sense of self and preferred actions. In several incidents he seems to use humoristic distancing as a coping strategy toward the customers when he experiences that part of the design and practices that do not match his preferences.

Following the positioning model creates the opportunity to see how the small story efforts and local identity work draw trajectories to broader and more manifest narratives (discourses). We saw how John's stories draw lines to organizational narratives such as the values of the bank. He continually talks about the values of "decency", "sincerity", and "presence" that are important to him and direct his actions and preferences of how to be around his customers. Nevertheless, some of the newer material design and technological aspects (e.g., the digital agenda platform) in the bank also clearly prompts identity dilemmas on how to put these values into play. The affordances of the technology and material design seem to create a professional and structural distance to the customers that puts his usual casual ways of being around his customers at stake. Thereby these multimodal features can be said to delineate his agency as a counselor, and they might also paradoxically threaten actualization of the bank's values and ideals of being present around their customers (cp., the personal bank in a digital world). Similar identity dilemmas are present in interviews conducted with other counselors in the bank. It is an obvious next step to bring such analytical insights on identity dilemmas and how to handle them into reflexive and change oriented dialogue in the bank.

So, here is an example of how an organizational subject, John, simultaneously enacts stories that are both complicit to and countering organizational grand narratives as part of the same story efforts/lines. This reveals how identity dilemmas are integral parts of an organizational implementation and change process. We claim that paying attention to such small aspects of organizational story efforts can provide important insights into organizational identity work and subjectification processes. This counts issues of identity dilemmas and mechanisms of agency versus control within implementation and change processes. Such analyses give insights into organizational struggles of meaning and polyphony of voices together with resistive forces that change the orientation in the more traditional narrative-counter-narrative dynamics. Focus is shifted from questions of how organizational members' stories are either countering or supporting grand narratives and toward questions of how they simultaneously can be both, thereby representing a subtle view of organizational subjects and change processes as fragmented, conflictual, and ambivalent.

Storytelling organization theory versus small story analysis

The table below sums up central aspects of the chapter's discussions and highlights similarities and differences between SOT and SSA (see Table 12.1).

Table 12.1 The similarities and differences between important aspects of SOT and SSA

	Storytelling organization theory	*Small story analysis*
Main focus	Conceptualization of organizational storytelling practices often through rather abstract and philosophical discussions. Studying and managing organizing processes and cultural dynamics.	Reflection and analysis of discourse, meaning making. and identify work/formations in everyday interactional settings. Adolescent and post-adolescent identify formation, particularly the emergence of professional identities.
Sources of inspiration	Bakhtinian thinking together with a range of philosophical/theoretical sources employed over time, such as Foucault, Deleuze, Derrida, Hegel, Heidegger and others. Fractal change management studies, Quantum storytelling, etc.	Bakhtinian thinking together with inspiration from discourse psychology, symbolic interactionism, ethnomethoddogy, and Conversation analysis (CA).
Main concepts	living stories, antenarrative, fractal narrative, control fractal narrative, counter-narrative.	Small stories, position, positioning, identity, sense of self, counter and complicit stories/discourses.
Critique of traditional narrative approaches	Critique of traditional BME and Big story approaches. Critical toward linear approaches seeking for fixed structures and categories.	Critique of traditional BME and Big story approaches. Critical toward linear approaches seeking for fixed structures and categories. Positioning in between a structural and performance-based approach.
Understanding of organizations	Organizations as ensembles of storytelling practices. Organizations as Tamara plays. Organizations as a Rhizome (Deleuze).	No specific reflection of the organizational context.
Understanding of (organizational) meaning making and identity	Organizational meaning making as polyphonic, unstable, chaotic, and power infused processes. Organizational members co-create identity in interaction with others in everyday socio-material settings. Anti-essentialist, anti-cognitive view.	Everyday meaning making as polyphonic, ambivalent and paradoxical. We continuously co-create meaning, positions, stories, knowledge, and identify in interaction. We co-create identity in interaction with others. Anti-essentialist, anti-cognitive view.
The role of storytelling	An ontological and strong view on the role of storytelling in the creation of organizational reality and identity.	Storytelling as one discourse type among others: nevertheless, he talks of small storying as intrinsic to how we co-perform meaning and identify in everyday life.

(*continued*)

Table 12.1 Cont.

	Storytelling organization theory	*Small story analysis*
Understanding of narrative vs. story	Narratives as retrospective and crystallized sense making. Living stories as here-and-now sense making. Counter-narratives arise in opposition to narrative by taking a conflicting position. Narratives give rise for a series of counter-narratives.	Narratives as retrospective and crystallized sense making. A critical stance toward the term counter-narrative. Small story efforts as hearable as simultaneously countering and supporting more hegemonic narratives that cannot be separated clearly in interaction. Storytellers construction cf of counter claims is viewed as the flipside of master narratives, that goes hand in hand.
Analysis strategies and typical data	Observation studies. Genealogical strategy (organizational documents). Deconstruction (interview data). Counter-narratives are in recent texts reflected through retrospective interpretations with little empirical orientation. No close-up analyses that focus on interactional and multimodal aspects of org. meaning making.	Moving identity research more into empirical studies. Micro-generic study of storytellers sensemaking strategies and identify work in interaction. Positioning model and questioning methodology: a way of asking questions to data (3 levels, 5 steps). Interview data involving interactional aspects and some multimodal features (audio and some gestures).
Aim of the analysis	Insights into the polyphonic, fragmented and chaotic aspects of organizational change processes.	How storytellers/narrators co-produce stories and discourses in situ (d) which are often complicit to and countering dominant discourses (D).

We have discussed how SOT provides a thorough platform for the reflection of organizations as storytelling ensembles from a dissensus perspective. We have argued how there is a range of similarities between the two approaches, for instance, their shared basis in Bakhtinian thinking that frames dialogue and situated storytelling practices as fundamentally fragmented and conflictual. These messy features are embraced in the similar concepts, living stories and small stories. SOT provides pivotal dimensions to the understanding of the narrative-counter-narrative dynamics that are increasingly pursued within organizational storytelling studies as a means to inquire into organizational power dynamics, such as struggles of meaning and agency versus control mechanisms. What is of particular interest in this chapter is the approaches' different reflections on the narrative-counter-narrative dynamics together with their analysis strategies. In recent texts, SOT focuses on explaining the relation between narrative and counter-narrative in rather philosophical, retrospective, and interpretative movements with little empirical attention. SSA is critical toward focusing on a dichotomic relationship between narrative and counter-narrative, which changes the orientation of the analyses and questions that are often asked. As an alternative, SSA turns our gaze toward how small stories and identity work are co-accomplished in interaction and changes the analytical orientation toward the narrative-small-story dynamics. From here we can investigate how subjects' stories can be hearable as both countering and supporting narratives simultaneously. Therefore, we do not freeze our analysis dichotomically on whether stories are either countering or complicit to more manifest narratives and thereby most likely overlook important nuances of situated storytelling efforts. Following the small story questioning methodology, we nuance the analytical outlook to capture how identity dilemmas emerge in organizational everyday life, as for instance, in the Danish bank's implementation of the new material design for their counseling practices.

Discussion and concluding remarks

The chapter has provided a substantial reason for an integration of SOT and SSA in a combined organizational storytelling methodology. This methodological outlook gives us a lens through which we can perceive of and analyze organizational storytelling practices ranging from abstract and philosophical dimensions to the concreteness of everyday interaction. SSA further orients our analytical gaze toward the sequential aspects of organizational meaning making, which we have also touched upon in level two of the analysis. It is worth mentioning that the analysis of the interactive engagement between participants can be investigated more thoroughly through the positioning model in order to scrutinize the co-construction of identities in further detail (see Bager 2015b, 2019; Bamberg & Georgakopoulou, 2008).

We detect this tendency within narrative studies in general. Here, attention is increasingly placed on the situated together with the multimodal dimensions of organizational storytelling as several scholars have pointed to the need of taking such an aspect into account in analyses (Boje, 2008; Rantakari & Vaara, 2017). This is opposed to more traditional narrative analyses of texts, documents, and organizational members' accounts and retrospective sayings of practices often acquired through interview techniques (Bamberg, 2004a; Boje, 2008: Lundholt & Boje, 2018; Rantakari & Vaara, 2017). Bamberg also invites more multimodal features to be involved in analyses. Thus, multimodality plays an important role when we co-create meaning and identity in messy every day (organizational) interaction.

Nevertheless, neither SOT nor SSA has provided careful empirically oriented strategies of how to deal with such multimodal aspects. In Bager's studies (2015a, 2015b), small story analyses were conducted with video data from leadership educational settings. Here, the small story analysis methodology is supplemented with inspiration from interaction analysis (Jordan & Henderson, 1995) together with Kendon's (1994) gesture studies and Goodwin's (2000) contextual configurations that allow analytical focus on multimodality. These analyses show that the scenic incumbency, together with the affordances of the technological and material (multimodal) scene, has a crucial influence on the identity work and knowledge production that take place in situated organizational encounters. The interviews from the bank further reveal interesting stories on how the increased digitalization of banking practices fundamentally gives rise to new practices that change how employees make relations internally and externally. Hence, digitalization effects radically change how the employees create knowledge and identity in everyday organizational life. In these digitalization times, we believe that a multimodal storytelling methodology is called upon as we cannot grasp organizational practices and identity work without it. Such aspects provide a good reason for further research on organizational storytelling efforts that include the multimodal features of the organizational scenes and phenomena that we wish to understand and possibly change.

We further propose that this turn to multimodality and embodiment within organizational narrative studies invites the term *storymaking* rather than storytelling, thereby emphasizing that the study of organizational storymaking counts much more than merely what organizational members verbally enact.

The study of narrative-small-story dynamics enables a designing of organizational processes that challenges more hegemonic narratives and discourses to create more egalitarian organizational practices. We align with the Bakhtinian normativity (Bager, 2013, 2015a, 2015b) to foster the diversifying (cp., centrifugal) forces of interaction to overcome monologizing (organizational) tendencies that close down complexity, suppress voices, and delineate agency. In line with Bamberg's and Boje's thinking, our interest in counter and complicit stories is closely tied to power and hegemony. By paying attention to organizational narrative-small-story dynamics, we sharpen our ears for the small aspects of identity work, such as how identity dilemmas arise in organizational (change) processes. It gives us a lens to study how power/control versus agency mechanisms come alive in a mix of resistive and complicit forces. From there we can create organizational reflexivity and change.

References

Andrews, M. (2004). Counter-narratives and the power to oppose. In M. Bamberg & M. Andrews (Eds.), *Considering counter-narratives: Narrating, resisting, making sense* (Studies in narrative, 4; 1–6). New York, NY: John Benjamins Publishing.

Bager, A.S. (2013). Dialogue on dialogues: Multivoiced dialogues (dialogism) as means for the co-production of knowledge in and on leadership communicative practices. *Academic Quarter, 6*, 146–169.

Bager, A.S. (2015a). Theorizing and analyzing plurivocality and dialogue in leadership development practices: Discussion and discourse analysis of dialogic practices in a leadership development forum (Doctoral dissertation). Retrieved from https://vbn.aau.dk/ws/files/215976661/Ann_Starb_k_Bager_EPUB.pdf

Bager, A.S. (2015b). Organizational (auto)-ethnography: An interaction analysis of identity work through the study of other-orientation and storytelling practices in a leadership development forum. *Tamara Special Issue on Organizational Ethnographies, 13*(3), 35- 56.

Bager, A.S. (2019). A multimodal discourse analysis of positioning and identity work in a leadership development practice. *Communication & Language at Work, 6*(1), 40–62.

Bakhtin, M. (1973). Problems of Dostoevsky's poetics (R.W. Rotsel, Trans.). Ann Arbor, MI: Ardis.

Bakhtin, M.M. (1986). *Speech genres & other late essays.* Austin, TX: University of Texas Press.

Bakhtin, M.M. (1993). *Toward a philosophy of the act.* Austin, TX: University of Texas Press.

Bamberg, M. (1997). Positioning between structure and performance. *Journal of Narrative and Life History*, 7(1–4), 335–342.

Bamberg, M. (2004a). Considering counter-narratives. In M. Bamberg & M. Andrews (Eds.), *Considering counter-narratives: Narrating, resisting, making sense* (Studies in narrative, 4; 351–371). Philadelphia, PA: John Benjamins Publishing.

Bamberg, M. (2004b). Talk, small stories, and adolescent identities. *Human Development, 47*, 366–369.

Bamberg, M. (2011). Who am I? Narration and its contribution to self and identity. *Theory & Psychology, 21*(1), 3–24.

Bamberg, M. (2016). Language, interaction, and culture. In H. Miller (Ed.), *The Sage encyclopedia of theory in psychology* (pp. 497–470). Thousand Oaks, CA: Sage Publications.

Bamberg, M., & Andrews, M. (Eds.). (2004). *Considering counter-narratives: Narrating, resisting, making sense* (Studies in narrative, 4). Philadelphia, PA: John Benjamins Publishing.

Bamberg, M., & Georgakopoulou, A. (2008). Small stories as a new perspective in narrative and identity analysis. *Text & Talk, 28*(3), 377–396.

Barge, J.K., & Little, M. (2002). Dialogical wisdom, communicative practice, and organizational life. *Communication Theory, 12(*4), 375–397.

Boje, D.M. (1991). The storytelling organization: A study of story performance in an office-supply firm. *Administrative Science Quarterly*, 106–126.

Boje, D.M. (1995). Stories of the storytelling organization: A Postmodern analysis of Disney as "Tamaraland". *Academy of Management Journal, 4*, 997–1035.

Boje, D.M. (2001). *Narrative methods for organizational & communication research.* London, UK: Sage Publications.

Boje, D.M. (2008). *Storytelling organizations.* Los Angeles, CA: Sage Publications.

Boje, D.M. (2011). Introduction to agential antenarratives that shape the future of organizations. In D.M. Boje (Ed.), *Storytelling and the future of organizations: An antenarrative handbook* (pp. 19–38). New York, NY: Routledge.

Boje, D.M., Luhman, J.T., & Baack, D.E. (1999). Stories and encounters between storytelling organizations. *Journal of Management Inquiry*, *8*(4), 340–360.

Clegg, S.R., Kornberger, M., Carter, C., & Rhodes, C. (2006). For management? *Management Learning*, 37(1), 7–27.

Deetz, S. (2001). Conceptual foundations. In F.M. Jablin & L.L. Putnam (Eds.), *The new handbook of organizational communication*. Los Angeles, CA: Sage Publications.

Frandsen, S., Lundholt, M.W., & Kuhn, T. (2017). *Counter-narratives and organization*. Routledge

Goodwin, C. (2000). Action and embodiment within situated human interaction. *Journal of Pragmatics*, *32*(10), 1489–1522.

Iedema, R. (2003). *Discourses of post-bureaucratic organization*. Amsterdam, Netherlands: John Benjamins Publishing.

Jordan, B., & Henderson, A. (1995). Interaction analysis: Foundations and practice. *The Journal of the Learning Sciences*, *4*(1), 39–103.

Jørgensen, K.M. (2010). Narrativ og storytelling i organisatorisk coaching. In E. Laursen, J. Nørlem, & U. Thøgersen (Eds.), *Coaching og organisationer: Ledelse, læring og magt* (pp. 101–129). Copenhagen, Denmark: Hans Reitzels Forlag.

Jørgensen, K.M. (2011). Antenarrative writing: Tracing and representing living stories. In D.M. Boje, *Storytelling and the future of organizations: An antenarrative handbook* (pp. 284–297). New York, NY: Routledge.

Jørgensen, K., & Boje, D. (2009). Genealogies of becoming: Antenarrative inquiry in organizations. *Tamara Journal for Critical Organization Inquiry*, *8*(1).

Kendon, A. (1994). Do gestures communicate? A review. *Research on Language and Social Interaction*, *27*(3), 175–200.

Kornberger, M., Clegg, S.R., & Carter, C. (2006). Rethinking the polyphonic organization: Managing as discursive practice. *Scandinavian Journal of Management*, *22*(1), 3–30.

Lundholt, M.W., & Boje, D. (2018). Understanding organizational narrative-counter-narratives dynamics: An overview of Communication Constitutes Organization (CCO) and Storytelling Organization Theory (SOT) approaches. *Communication and Language at Work*, *5*(1), 18–29.

Rantakari, A., & Vaara, E. (2017). Narratives and processuality. In A. Langley & H. Tsoukas (Eds.), *The SAGE handbook of process organizational studies* (pp. 271–285). Los Angeles, CA: Sage Publications.

Rennison, B.W. (2014). Polyfont lederskab-fra monofiens kontrol til polyfoniens coping. In K. Majgaard (Eds.) *Sprækker for Fornyelse* (pp. 145–170). Copenhagen, Denmark Djøf/Jurist-og Økonomforbundet.

Shotter, J. (2011). Reflections on sociomateriality and dialogicality in organization studies: From 'inter-'to 'intra-thinking'. In *Performing practices – how matter matters* (pp. 32–57). Oxford: Oxford University Press.

Svane, M.S., & Boje, D.M. (2015, April). Tamara land fractal change management: In between managerialist narrative and polyphonic living stories. Standing Conference for Management and Organizational Inquiry (Sc'Moi). Las Vegas, NV.

Svane, M., Gergerich, E., & Boje, D.M. (2017). Fractal change management and counter-narrative in cross-cultural change. In S. Frandsen, T. Kuhn, & M.W. Lundholt (Eds.) *Counter-narrative and organization*. London, UK: Routledge.

Weick, K.E. (1995). *Sensemaking in organizations* (Vol. 3). Sage.

13

Narratives of recruitment

Constructions of policy, practice and organizational identity in a Danish bank

Lise-Lotte Holmgreen and Jeanne Strunck

Introduction

What makes an organization? According to recent contributions to organizational research (e.g. Alvesson & Willmott, 2002; Brown, 2006; Humle & Frandsen, 2017; Svenningsson & Larsson, 2006), a salient aspect of organizational formation is the continuous negotiation for a shared organizational identity. Scholars have approached this negotiation process from various theoretical viewpoints, including dialogue and conversation (Ford, 1999; Hatch & Schultz, 2002), discourse (Fairclough, 2003, 2010, 2012) and narrative (e.g. Boje, 1995; Brown, 2006; Humphreys & Brown, 2002; Linde, 2009), each contributing different perspectives to the field. However, these approaches also share a number of common traits that emerge from a social-constructionist approach to identity, in which notions of the self, human interaction and the relationship between language and identity are central (De Fina, 2011). In an organizational context, this means the constitution of identity becomes a matter of negotiation (Humphreys & Brown, 2002) between influences within and outside the organization, with insiders such as management and employees constituting core actors (Humle & Frandsen, 2017). In the following, our perspective on organizational identity will derive from insights in (counter) narrative and discourse research, which will be further developed below.

In this chapter, we will explore the construction of organizational identity through the analysis of middle managers' narratives on the recruitment processes that led to their current position in a Danish bank and building society. Recruitment constitutes an important process for the promotion of an organizational identity through its embedding of organizational culture into the social and discursive practices of the process, e.g. by the very construction and enactment of the process itself as well as the profiling of the organization and desired candidates. This is typically the result of management's strategic considerations in the area, but it is equally influenced by the individual experiences of successful candidates and the stories they choose to tell, underscoring that organizations are pluralistic and polyphonic (Humphreys & Brown, 2002).

Of particular interest to this study is the individual manager's construction of organizational identity in relation to what he/she considers to be normal recruitment procedures in the bank, contributing to a number of alternative, and yet apparently complementary, versions of reality. Thus, the chapter sets out to answer the following question:

How do individual narratives of recruitment construct organizational identity?

Additionally, whereas narrative inquiry is generally little interested in the linguistic and discursive elements contributing to the unfolding of a story, in this chapter we will be concerned with the close analysis of the language and discourse used by respondents for making identity claims and for substantiating the validity of their stories. The reason for this focus is that it is, among other things, in the details of discourse we can identify the subtle and often inconspicuous differences that lead to the dominant status of one story over another and thus of one identity construction or narrative over another (cf. Boje, 1995). For this part of the analysis, we will be inspired by the work of notable critical discourse analysts (e.g. Fairclough, 2003, 2010, 2012; Fairclough & Wodak, 1997; Wodak, 2011), who engage in situated linguistic analysis.

The construction of organization identity

In organization research, recent decades have seen a turn away from essentialist and monolithic approaches to the organization towards views that recognize its pluralistic and polyphonic nature. One of these views has come to be known as the Communication as Constitutive of Organization (CCO) approach, according to which communication is not just one of many activities in the organization, but *is* the organization (Cooren, 2015; Cooren, Kuhn, Cornelissen, & Clark, 2011; Kuhn, 2017). This view builds on a social-constructionist approach, according to which language constitutes the social world instead of merely representing it (Jørgensen & Phillips, 1999). Thus, organizations emerge as the result of "ongoing and interconnected communication processes" (Kuhn, 2017, p. 19), which unfold in various communicative events, involving a broad understanding of communicative practices that go beyond the text and verbal message (e.g. to include contextual factors), as well as the acknowledgement of the co-constructed nature of communication in which many forces interact to produce meaning. Similarly, communication, and thus the constitution of the organization, will be seen as an ongoing struggle over meaning, with some interests being promoted over others (Fairclough, 2003; Kuhn, 2017; Humphreys & Brown, 2002).

The understanding of the organization as communication resonates with recent research into organization identity (Bamberg & Andrews, 2004; Boje, 1995; Frandsen, Kuhn, & Wolff Lundholt, 2017; Humphreys & Brown, 2002). Following this view, it is through language (as the primary symbolic mode) we construct our personal and social identities, i.e. who we are, what we do, where we belong and what we believe in, but it is also the means to constructing and identifying others (Alvesson, Ashcraft, & Thomas, 2008; Ashcraft, 2007; De Fina, 2011). This understanding implies that identities are not fixed, but will continuously be constituted, negotiated and reproduced, making them fragmented and even conflicting at times (Alvesson & Willmott, 2002; Svenningsson & Larsson, 2006).

The fact that identities are fragmented also impinges on the way we can understand organization identity. Whereas mainstream organization research would assume that a common organization identity could be established and controlled through the implementation of organizational structures and designs, the regulation of identity through discursive processes is an equally important means to making organizational members identify with (dominant) constructions of organization identity (Alvesson & Willmott, 2002; Alvesson et al., 2008). Thus, organizational identity will continuously be constituted and negotiated, with some discursive constructions invariably dominating others, in part as the result of contextual factors such as the power relations between social actors and the social and cultural conventions of organizational settings that govern discursive practices, allowing for the hegemonic status of particular discourses (Brown, 2006; Boje, 2006; Fairclough, 2003, 2010, 2012; Humphreys & Brown, 2002). This means the ability of various organizational actors to influence the construction of organizational identity is considerable, opening up to multiple constructions that exist in tension and yet variously contribute to the creation of a collective identity (Alvesson & Willmott, 2002; Boje, 1995; Brown, 2006; Humle & Frandsen, 2017; Humphreys & Brown, 2002).

The ability to exert influence is closely connected to legitimacy. Thus, the achievement of a dominant status is in part contingent on the attribution of trustworthiness and attractiveness to the actor(s) who seek to dominate the discursive space. On the one hand, senior management will seek to "reduce identity plurality" (Humphreys & Brown, 2002, p. 423) through legitimation strategies in order to present a coherent image to various stakeholders, and on the other, there may be ongoing individual identity work within the organization involving other legitimation strategies. This also appears to be the case among the middle managers in our study who seek to establish individual legitimacy through the construction of narratives that present their recruitment processes as special incidents, feeding into the construction of a common organizational identity.

Besides being a matter of trustworthiness and attractiveness, the attribution of legitimacy depends on the (organizational) context in which it is invoked (Pedersen, 2014). Therefore, organizational members' legitimation strategies are often closely tied to their relation to the organization they work for, based on assumed congruence between their own notions of right and wrong and the identity and image of the organization (Brown, 1997).

The question is, however, how the complex process of organizational identity construction may be studied. Two approaches appear particularly promising, i.e. (counter)narrative and critical discourse analysis, and so, in the following we will discuss how they can be meaningfully employed to analyze middle managers' construction of recruitment processes and organizational identity.

(Counter)narratives and critical discourse analysis

Narrative studies and critical discourse analysis share the social-constructionist premise that our access to social reality takes place through language and other symbolic modes. Thus, when we talk about the construction of organizational identity, we also talk about the way discourse, context and subject positions interact to construct this identity (Ashcraft, 2007; Brown, 2006, Humle & Frandsen, 2017).

In organizational identity research, narrative studies have become increasingly frequent, as in organizations narratives (or stories)[1] form an important part of the ongoing processes of identifying who we are and what we do, i.e. they are concerned with the ways through which we "make sense of our experience and evaluate our actions and intentions" (Cunliffe & Coupland, 2012, p. 66). In the case of the middle managers who were encouraged to tell about their experiences with being recruited to their present positions, sense-making and evaluation are important processes to study as they will provide insight into how these managers understand the organization they are part of as well as how their individual stories contribute to (or not) a collective organizational identity.

A story is here defined as "an oral or written performance involving two or more people interpreting past or anticipated experience", requiring no beginning, middle or end (Boje, 1995, p. 1000). It is considered an open-ended and ongoing process, a conversation, and a creative redescription of the world, in which actors construct stories of self, others and their organization and constantly negotiate these with other actors and stories (Humle & Frandsen, 2017; Rhodes & Brown, 2005). Consequently, it is a process that cannot be understood outside the context in which it takes place, nor without recognition of its connection to other stories within or outside the organization (Brown, 2006). Thus, while an organization's identity may appear coherent, this may, in fact, be constituted by multiple narratives that coalesce to form a whole. These narratives may be of many different types and concern different events and people, but importantly they will be shaped by the continuous negotiation and dialogue in the organization that ensure the emergence of "many shared storylines and themes" (Brown, 2006, p. 734). In this chapter, we follow Brown's (2006, p. 735) definition of organizational identity, according to which it is "constituted by the totality of collective identity-relevant narratives authored by participants".

Talking about organizational identity as the collection of multiple identity-relevant narratives makes the introduction of the concept of counter-narrative relevant. According to Bamberg & Andrews (2004, p. x), counter-narratives "make sense in relation to something else, that which they are countering". This may imply the dominance of a narrative, a master narrative, in opposition to which other narratives unfold. However, the relation between narratives is more complex than this may suggest, and often what is considered the dominant and oppositional may vary according to context, so that counter-narratives may, in fact, be countering other counter-narratives and may even become master-narratives themselves. Therefore, we may think of the relation between the various kinds of narratives as one of fluidity in which the relation between narratives and matters of dominance are constantly negotiated.

In narrative studies, there is, with few exceptions (e.g. Lundholt, 2008; Norlyk, 2017), little attention paid to the linguistic realization of narratives. However, in this chapter we argue that in order to assess the constitutive 'strength' of a (counter-)narrative, we must study the linguistic choices made to represent social reality. This is a line of thought prevalent in various strands of critical discourse analysis, CDA, which argues that it is, among other things, in language that power resides (cf. Fairclough, 2010, 2012; Wodak, 2011). This echoes the claims in narrative studies; however, with the one important exception that in CDA the attention to linguistic detail is seen as critical for revealing the often inconspicuous and apparently innocuous ways in which particular constructions are naturalized and rendered common sense. Thus, if we want to study and assess the relative power or struggles going on between various narratives of identity and recruitment in the case organization, we must study the lexical and syntactic choices respondents make to present their stories as legitimate within the larger framework of the organization. In the following, we will introduce the combined model of narrative and critical discourse analysis that will form the basis of the analysis of interview data.

Data and methodology

The background of the analysis presented in this chapter is a four-year research project conducted with a large Danish bank and building society between 2010 and 2014 with the aim of studying organizational discourses on leadership and identity. The combined organization employs 3,600 staff across the country, and the departments involved in the project are placed in more regions and cities in Denmark. For some years, the bank and building society has been dedicated to the work for diversity and equality, especially at management levels, and so, in order to attract a variety of applicants from different sexes and backgrounds to positions in the organization, transparency in recruitment processes has become corporate policy. The policy has partly been realized by making it compulsory to advertise every vacant position on the company intranet as well as in relevant public media for interested stakeholders outside the organization.[2]

Semi-structured interviews with middle managers were chosen as data collection method to generate qualitative data; however, as narratives originate in specific contexts, it was important to obtain more general knowledge about recruitment policies and processes in the case organization before designing and starting the interview rounds with managers. To this end, we gathered information from different written sources, which gave us insight into the structure and strategic goals of the organization and its management.

The interview data consist of selected parts from two semi-structured interviews conducted with a male and female middle manager.[3] These two respondents were chosen for their ability to unfold relevant and detailed narratives, which at the same time reflect tendencies identified in the remaining eight interviews with middle managers. Initially, possible respondents were identified by the HR department of the organization and were then contacted by the researchers via email. Here, we presented the details of the project as well as the extent to which each respondent was expected to participate, before asking for their consent.

Before starting an interview, the first minutes are important to motivate the respondent to reveal her self-narrative (Kvale & Brinkmann, 2009). Therefore, to create a positive relationship between interviewers and respondent, we used the first minutes to brief the respondent about our backgrounds, the purpose of the investigation, the focal themes of the interview and the timeframe. To ensure a comfortable situation and tone, we carried out the interviews at the workplace of the respondents, just as we made it clear at the beginning of each interview that we were not sent by top-management, but conducted the interviews as part of a large research project at the university.

However, even when paying respectful attention to the respondents' perspectives, the presence of the researchers and the interview process play an important role for the quality of data (Creswell & Miller, 2000). Therefore, when analyzing data, it is necessary to take into account the co- and context to ensure the validity of the interpretation of data (Silvermann, 2014). Another important factor is that interviewers possess the role of guides of the session, but they are also co-constructors of meaning when participating in the dialogue. Thus, interview data are "reflecting a reality jointly constructed by the interviewee and interviewer" (Rapley, 2001, p. 304).

Analytical frame

When approaching narrative analysis from a critical discourse perspective, this involves, on the one hand, studying linguistic features that realize the traits of the narrative. This means studying the linguistic realization of the respondents' sense-making and evaluation of their recruitment processes. On the other hand, it also means studying linguistic features in the context of both the interview and the organization, critically assessing how this promotes preferred (counter-) narratives of organizational identity.

As mentioned, a core feature of respondents' narratives appears to be the legitimation of organizational identities. As the attribution of legitimacy is dependent on something or someone appearing trustworthy, desirable, appropriate and correct (cf. Pedersen, 2014), this is also reflected in the discursive constructions in respondents' narratives. Thus, they use language, first, to make sense of and evaluate the process, and second, as a result of the sense-making and evaluation process, to make identity claims that appear trustworthy and desirable, and which may or may not challenge the dominant narrative in the organization.

In order to be trustworthy and desirable, authors or speakers have to "commit themselves to values" (Fairclough, 2003, p. 171). In Fairclough's terms, authors and speakers identify themselves in texts when committing to values such as what is true (epistemic modality) or what is necessary (deontic modality), and what is desirable or undesirable (evaluative statements, value assumptions, affective mental process verbs) (Fairclough, 2003, p. 164).

Furthermore, to legitimize their narratives about recruitment processes respondents may refer to different categories of legitimation. Van Leeuwen (2008) describes four main categories that authors or speakers may refer to: 1) 'authorities' such as tradition, custom and law or regulations, or they may use 2) 'moral evaluation' by referring to value systems. Respondents may also choose to use 3) 'rationalization' as a legitimation strategy by referring to institutionalized social action or knowledge and finally, they may use 4) 'mythopoesis' – "legitimation conveyed through narratives whose outcomes reward legitimate actions and punish nonlegitimate actions" (Van Leeuwen, 2008, pp. 105–106).

On the basis of the theoretical approaches advanced by Fairclough and Van Leeuwen, analysis is carried out to study how managers construct identity and how they legitimize their narratives about recruitment processes performed in the Danish bank and building society. Where relevant, the linguistic realization of the above categories will be analyzed in excerpts from the two interviews with the aim of identifying a number of prototypical (counter-)narratives.

Analysis of middle managers' narratives: Richard and Betty

Richard

Richard is a middle manager who has been with the organization since 1994. When we met him, he had been in his current position for one and a half years following major organizational changes. However, since his first employment with the organization he had been in different managerial positions, all with a significant number of staff under his command. At the time of the interview, he was the manager of seven employees.

As with all respondents, we start the interview by asking how Richard was recruited for his present position. This triggers the following narrative,

> (1) Richard:
>
> My current management position? I'm inclined to say that perhaps it happened more or less automatically, that is, there were these organizational changes about, let's see, one and a half years ago, when I was the manager of a larger share of the staff than I am today, and then they decided to split it up. And with my background and professional competence, it was completely natural that I continued with the business team I'm responsible for today. So there was no process here.

Richard presents the way to his current position as middle manager as a sequence of events that eventually led to his recruitment. He describes this as an almost automatic process in light of organizational changes as well as his background and professional competence (ll. 2–5). As a consequence, a transparent process of advertising the job (cf. Data and methodology), with Richard then applying for it and being interviewed along with other candidates was made irrelevant. In other words, he is firmly convinced he was the right man for the job, using lexis revolving around professionalism, levels of management and structural reform plans.

Fairclough (2003) argues that what we commit ourselves to as well as the way we represent the world is all part of who we are, i.e. part of our identities. This commitment may e.g. be expressed through evaluation and modality, in turn serving the purpose of legitimation.

First, by using the adjective 'natural' (l. 4), Richard implicitly states that he was the right choice. In terms of evaluation, 'natural' may be used to signal that his hiring was inevitable and desirable, as this is the type of evaluative expression where desirability is assumed, i.e. this is generally taken as being a self-evident part of its meaning (cf. Fairclough, 2003, p. 172). Richard's commitment to this is further strengthened by his choice of the pre-modifier 'completely', a modal adverbial which leaves little room for discussing the truth of his statement due to its high level of commitment. "Naturalization" is, in fact, a kind of moral evaluation that replaces the moral and cultural order with the "natural order" (Van Leeuwen, 2008, p. 111), making it difficult to challenge the value of the statement.

Another way to present processes as legitimate is to construct them as conforming to standards (Van Leeuwen, 2008). Richard does so by referring to the process as automatic (l. 1), forestalling any critical comments that may follow. Thus, when a process is constructed as automatic, it is seen as following the normal recruitment procedures of the organization, implying the unproblematic and generally accepted side to it. However, this is also where he talks about the process in less categorical terms, using modifiers such as 'inclined' and 'more or less' (l. 1) perhaps to initially signal a less confident attitude.

Finally, Richard also foregrounds his expertise to present himself as the obvious choice, i.e. he focuses on his background and professional competences to argue his case. This strategy is known as legitimation through expert authority, by means of which the speaker can assert his right to engage in a particular action (Van Leeuwen, 2008). In Richard's case, this reference is yet another way to avoid any critical comments or questions to the fairness of the entire recruitment process and its opaqueness.

A little later in the interview, after a minor excursion into his previous experiences as a manager with the bank, we return to the recruitment to his present position,

> (2) Interviewer:
>
> *Well, do you think it's a normal procedure, the way you, well, is this the typical way to do it in the organization?*
>
> Richard:
>
> I think you need to see this from two contexts, i.e. the one situation where they made the major organizational change, and I think if they had established committees and made it all open, then they would still be working on it today. So, when big changes and change processes like these take place, then at the top management level they have to make a decision and say, this is the way it looks ... So the process was actually okay, where we as managers were involved in the process of finding out where we would be placed, this was more or less given ...

When asked whether his recruitment process may be considered normal procedure, Richard becomes aware of its potential problems, and so he presents it as one of two possible processes, where both, according to him, would be acceptable in the organization. The first one is the one he followed and which is connected to the organizational changes that took place one and a half years before the interview. This constitutes the key point of his argument: the change process would not have been effective, had top management not decided to involve key managers in the process. Thus, Richard makes sense of and evaluates the situation in terms of a process that would quickly lead to the desired outcome, e.g. ll. 4–5 ´I think if they had established committees and made it all open, then they would still be working on it today'. This strategy is known as instrumental rationalization (Fairclough, 2003).

However, it is not all purposeful actions that may serve as legitimation; only those which have a moral element to them will count as such, e.g. in the form of teleological action, which refers to whether something works or not (Van Leeuwen, 2008). In Richard's narrative, this takes the form of goal orientation, where the moralized (positive) value derives from the implied and assumed negative outcome, i.e. the lack of results, if top management had decided not to involve key managers. The ascription of positive values is further strengthened by the authority that top management represents, cf. ll. 5–6 'then at the top management level they have to make a decision and say, this is the way it looks', and their obligation to take action, cf. the deontic modal expression 'have to'. From this follows that placing Richard and other middle managers in key positions was a perfectly legitimate process, involving the management of an organizational identity, which he fully endorses (cf. ll. 6–7 'we' and 'so the process was actually okay').

However, despite the positioning of managers as legitimate agents, Richard talks about the process as a special case vis-à-vis other recruitment processes in the organization,

> (3) Richard:
>
> … where it is clearly my, both as a feeling and what I've experienced myself, it is, we take pride in, err, when we have vacancies, making them visible for in-house recruitment and mobility. There is no doubt about that, so what is dug into right here, it is a special situation to do with organizational changes in XX. So I think there are two sides to it, that what we'll do in the future and also have done previously – it [a vacancy] will be advertised, in collaboration with HR and consultants, and if we advertise vacancies externally, well, then we get assistance, etc., to make career opportunities and mobility visible …

This part of the interview is where Richard emphasizes that the process he went through was a special case, which had to do with organizational changes. In the narrative, he goes to great lengths to explain how recruitment is normally handled, involving many details of the process both when advertising vacancies inhouse and to outside candidates. This is, among other things, based on his own experience and on talks he would have had with colleagues. Thus, he uses the pronoun 'we' extensively to demonstrate his own commitment to an organizational policy of transparency, underscoring the tradition this represents by the use of deontic modality in ll. 2–3 'There is no doubt about that'.

Across the three excerpts we see that Richard's identity as a manager with a strong personal and professional record as well as with a firm position in the group of managers makes it possible for him to defend the officially proclaimed and transparent recruitment process as well as the less official and opaque process. These findings will be dealt with in more detail in the discussion further below.

Betty

Like Richard, Betty has been with the organization for many years, since the late 1990s. Most of the time she has been a middle manager for parts of the IT and system administration of the organization. She was recruited for the present position in connection with major strategic changes in the organization three years before we met her, moving her from operations into development. At the time of the interview, she was the manager of 15 employees and acted as a liaison for 13 external consultants.

When asked about her recruitment for the current position, she unfolds the following narrative,

> (4) Betty
>
> I received a phone call while I was on maternity leave. Well, I've been with XX many, many, many years, as it is. I've been here about 14–15 years and I've been a manager the vast majority of the years. And my present position, I switched into it when I was on my last maternity leave. Before this, I was in a position which was more in operations, and today I'm in development and project management, and we had a major strategic change in 2009 when I was asked to take care of the control side of it. And this is what I did. So you may say, it was a phone call when I was on maternity leave.

Interviewer:

So what was the motivation in the organization to ask you if it [the shift] was between two different business fields?

Betty:

Originally, I was a project manager. And then I switched from being a project manager to being part of operations and now back to development, so I actually just moved across the two, and I don't have problems with being in one or the other. The primary reason they asked me is because it is my professional competence. What they wanted to do back in 2010 was something I, as one of the few, could do in XX. So this was the reason.

In her introductory narrative (ll. 3–6), Betty describes the transition from her previous management job to the present as a consequence of organizational changes, which took place before the one forming part of Richard's narrative. While this was the point in time when the transition took effect and is seen as the direct cause, she also explains her shift in terms of other factors, both implicitly and explicitly. Thus, in ll. 11–13 she very explicitly states that she was one of the few who could do the job due to her professional competence. This appears not only to be the result of her background as a project manager, but also her many years in the organization and the ease with which she has moved back and forth between business fields and positions (ll. 9–11). All these factors support her claim to being special and make up her argument for being appointed.

Betty uses a number of legitimation strategies that are quite similar to Richard's. Thus, her coming to the conclusion that she was the right woman for the job is matter-of-fact and action oriented, foregrounding herself, 'I', and using a material process verb, 'do' (Halliday, 1994), to underline her commitment, cf. l. 12 'What they wanted to do back in 2010 was something I, as one of the few, could do'. In addition, she makes claims about her professionalism (ll. 10-11), which among other things comes from numerous unproblematic job changes over the 15 years (ll. 9-10), promoting an expert authority (Van Leeuwen, 2008) that leaves little doubt about her capabilities in relation to the job and her value to the organization. The ease with which she has changed positions and departments (cf. l. 9 'switched' and l. 10 'just moved') underscores this feature as well as her dynamic character.

This part of the interview is followed by a minor digression about organizational structures and where her department is placed, until we once again return to the dialogue about recruitment. At this point, we ask Betty whether her recruitment process would be considered normal, which makes her continue her narrative:

(5) Betty:

Well, it's not unusual. These two paths exist. Either it's the path where you see someone with potential, and you work with this, and then you contact this person. Or, alternatively, there is the path where I indicate in my staff development interview that this is something I'd like to pursue, and if management agrees, well, then this is the path you follow. And then we make a plan for this. These are the two existing paths. And I've actually tried both.

Interviewer:

So this means that it isn't normal that this type of position is advertised inhouse, for instance?

Betty:

No! Precisely what I'm doing, no, it probably wouldn't be, because it required my competences. But normally we advertise these branch manager positions. So, it would go

> like "Well, this is the position that must be filled, and we want someone with a project management profile, or we want someone with a professional profile", or whatever we need. It'll be advertised inhouse, and if we can't recruit inhouse, we advertise the position externally. Incidentally, my positions were not advertised.

Like Richard, Betty argues for the existence of two paths of recruitment. But whereas Richard's narrative revolves around what is special and what is normal, in Betty's narrative both paths are constructed as normal, depending on the requirements of the organization at any given time and the competences of the individual. In other words, she is not buying into the interviewer's frame that her own recruitment was unusual, except for the way she was approached, i.e. by means of a phone call (cf. extract 4).

This has consequences for the discursive construction of the narrative and the two possible recruitment processes it unfolds. In this part of the interview, Betty is quite confident about the contents of the narrative, which is exemplified by her factual statement that 'these two paths exist' (l. 1), followed by a fairly detailed account of how the two work, and then a reiteration of the fact that the two paths exist (ll. 4-5). There is no use of modality to signal weak commitment to this state of affairs; instead, she presents the two paths as a sequence of events in which the employee ('I') and management ('you' and 'we') (cf. ll. 1–5 + 7–11) play active parts, and where each step contributes to the initiation of the next. The choice of personal pronouns suggests that here Betty identifies both with being an employee and a manager, depending on the path represented, but more importantly, it does not weaken her belief that she is in control of the situation, and that she (or anyone else in the organization) may actively choose her career moves (cf. Fairclough, 2003).

These discursive choices reflect legitimation through reference to custom or tradition instead of established procedures, cf. the advertising of positions (Van Leeuwen, 2008). In making fairly firm statements about the two recruitment processes, Betty represents these as being habitual and unquestionable – something which is further underlined by the double negation 'not unusual' in l. 1. Referring to something as habitual may be a way to make implicit moral evaluations, which serve the purpose of ensuring acceptance of certain policies or practices (cf. Van Leeuwen, 2008, p. 110). In Betty's case, this implicit moral evaluation clearly functions as a way to legitimize her own recruitment, which followed the path of being asked to consider the job, cf. l. 7.

As with Richard, we see Betty's construction of herself as an expert in certain critical fields combined with a long track record in management makes her eligible for management positions outside the official procedure of advertising. Again, this is clearly sanctioned by top management.

Discussion

The narrative and linguistic analysis of the two interviews reveals a number of interesting things: first, despite the official narrative of openly advertising all vacant positions in the organization (cf. 'Data and methodology'), a counter-narrative on recruitment seems to exist. Second, from the respondents' point of view the organizational status of the two narratives is almost identical, i.e. they appear both to be in line with and represent company policy. This suggests two narratives which struggle to claim hegemonic status, but which are both talked into being as naturalized narratives that construct organizational identity.

In the interviews, recruitment by means of selection is constructed as a process used in connection with organizational changes; however, at two different points of time. This suggests that while the official narrative is that positions are advertised at any given time to allow for transparency and equal access, the short-term need for effectively reconstructing (parts of) the organization may overrule this practice, making recruitment by selection an accepted counter-narrative, which is part of organizational identity. This interpretation is supported by the more or less implicit role of (top) management in the narratives (referred to either as 'they' or as an implicit agent in the two interviews), which ensures the acceptance of processes that are not formally documented. However, it also appears that an important component in the counter-narratives is the respondents' individual capabilities and expertise. Thus, in the unfolding of the narratives, they construct their selection for positions as being dependent on their long-term experience in the organization as well as on the match of their qualifications and competences to the position in question.

Altogether, the analysis of the two interviews suggests that while there is an officially proclaimed policy in the area of recruitment, which first and foremost contributes to the image of a transparent, open and sympathetic organization, there is an opaque layer of alternative 'inhouse' counter-narratives that serves the purpose of keeping the organization agile when facing various challenges. This suggests that in terms of identity, the bank and building society has more than one string to its bow: in line with an egalitarian and non-hierarchic approach to organizational management and development, it proclaims an identity of transparency and openness, which is keenly promoted to the outside world, but when it comes to acting in a highly competitive market, the efficiency of organizational processes is given precedence, encouraging alternative policies and identities within the organization.

These findings may, of course, be extracted from a cursory study of the interview data. However, as demonstrated by the analysis, the assessment of how the two narratives are legitimized and given a dominant status requires a closer study of their linguistic realization and contextualization. Thus, combining narrative inquiry with discourse analysis makes it possible to uncover the linguistic details that may be inconspicuous, but nonetheless decisive for the strength and direction of the narrative. This is an insight that is relevant for the analyst, but also for actors who intend to engage with organizational identity narratives, e.g. by agreeing with or challenging them.

Conclusion

How do individual narratives of recruitment construct organizational identity? In the literature, there is widespread consensus that organizational identity is continuously constructed on the basis of the many identity formations within the organization. Thus, hegemonic struggles are likely to occur between what may be considered dominant narratives and counter-narratives before organizational identity is temporarily established. Nonetheless, the analysis in this chapter suggests that this struggle may, in fact, be quite unproblematic, when counter-narratives are endorsed by top-management and are constructed as part of an ongoing strategic effort to keep the organization nimble. Thus, besides the presence of a dominant actor in the counter-narratives (i.e. top-management), it appears that legitimation through reference to standards, tradition, goal orientation and expert authority is contributory to upholding the impression of an organization in sync despite the existence of conflicting narratives. Furthermore, it may be argued that the narratives serve different purposes, with one being primarily constructed for the sake of promoting a certain organizational image, i.e. a policy, whereas the other is the outcome of daily intra-organizational practices.

Notes

1 In line with much of the literature in the field, 'narrative' and 'story' will be used interchangeably (see e.g. Rhodes & Brown 2005: 170)

2 It will be against this policy that the narrative analysis of interview data will be conducted.

3 Altogether, we interviewed ten middle managers and seven lower-level managers across the organization. The duration of each interview was approx. one hour. The interviews were recorded and transcribed verbatim.

References

Alvesson, M., Ashcraft, K.L., & Thomas, R. (2008). Identity matters: Reflections on the construction of identity scholarship in organization studies. *Organization*, 15(1), 5–28.

Alvesson, M., & Willmott, H. (2002). Identity regulation as organizational control: Producing the appropriate individual. *Journal of Management Studies*, 39, 619–644.

Ashcraft, K. (2007). Appreciating the 'work' of discourse: Occupational identity and difference as organizing mechanisms in the case of commercial airline pilots. *Discourse & Communication*, 1(1), 9–36.

Bamberg, M., & Andrews, M. (2004). *Considering counter-narratives: narrating, resisting, making sense*. Amsterdam/Philadelphia: John Benjamins.

Boje, D. (1995). Stories of the storytelling organization: A postmodern analysis of Disney as "Tamara-land. *Academy of Management Journal*, 38(4), 997–1035.

Boje, D. (2006). Breaking out of narrative's prison: Improper story in storytelling organization. *Story, Self, Society: An Interdisciplinary Journal of Storytelling Studies*, 2(2), 28–49.

Brown, A. (1997). Narcissism, identity and legitimacy. *Academy of Management Review*, 22, 643–686.

Brown, A. (2006). A narrative approach to collective identities. *Journal of Management Studies*, 43(4), 731–753.

Cooren, F. (2015). *Organizational discourse*. Cambridge, UK: Polity Press.

Cooren, F., Kuhn, T., Cornelissen, J.P., & Clark, T. (2011). Communication, organization, and organizing: An overview and introduction to the special issue. *Organization Studies*, 32(9), 1149–1170.

Creswell, J.W, & Miller, D. (2000). Determining validity in qualitative inquiry. *Theory Into Practice*, 39(3), 124–130.

Cunliffe, A.L., & Coupland, C. (2012). Narrative sensemaking: From hero to villain to hero: Making experience sensible through embodied narrative. *Human Relations*, 65(1), 63–88.

De Fina, A. (2011). Discourse and identity. In T.A.V. Dijk (Ed.), *Discourse studies* (pp. 263–282). London: Sage.

Fairclough, N. (2003). *Analysing discourse: Textual analysis for social research*. London and New York: Routledge.

Fairclough, N. (2010). *Critical discourse analysis. The critical study of language*. Harlow: Pearson Education.

Fairclough, N. (2012). Critical discourse analysis. In J.P. Gee, & H., Michael (Eds.), *The Routledge handbook of discourse analysis* (pp. 9–20). London and New York: Routledge.

Fairclough, N., & Wodak, R. (1997). Critical discourse analysis. In T.A.V. Dijk (Ed.), *Discourse as social interaction* (pp. 258–284). London: Sage.

Ford, J.D. (1999). Organizational change as shifting conversations. *Journal of Organizational Management*, 12, 480–500.

Frandsen, S., Kuhn, T., & Wolff Lundholt, M. (2017). *Counter-narratives and organization*. New York: Routledge.

Halliday, M. A. K. (1994). An introduction to functional grammar, 2nd ed. London: Edward Arnold.

Hatch, M.J., & Schultz, M. (2002). The dynamics of organizational identity. *Human Relations*, 55(8), 989–1018.

Holmgreen, L. (2020). Leadership identities: Whose construction? *Text & Talk*, 40(1), 5–28.

Humle, D.M., & Frandsen, S. (2017). Organizational identity negotiations through dominant and counter-narratives. In S. Frandsen, K., Timothy, & W.L., Marianne (Eds.), *Counter-narratives and organization* (pp. 105–128). New York: Routledge.

Humphreys, M., & Brown, A.D. (2002). Narratives of organizational identity and identification: A case of hegemony and resistance. *Organization Studies*, 23(3), 421–447.

Jørgensen, M.W., & Phillips, L. (1999). *Diskursanalyse som teori og metode [Discourse analysis as theory and method]*. Roskilde: Roskilde Universitetsforlag.

Kvale, S., & Brinkmann, S. (2009). *Interviews. Learning the craft of qualitative research interviewing*. Los Angeles/London: Sage.

Kuhn, T. (2017). Communicatively constituting organizational unfolding through counter-narrative. In S. Frandsen, K., Timothy, & W.L., Marianne (Eds.) *Counter-narratives and organization* (pp. 17–42). New York: Routledge.

Linde, C. (2009). *Working the past, narrative and institutional memory*. Oxford: Oxford University Press.

Lundholt, M.W. (2008). *Telling without tellers: The linguistic manifestation of literary communication in narrative fiction*. Copenhagen: Medusa.

Norlyk, B. (2017). Designer or entrepreneur? Counter-narratives in the professions. In S. Frandsen, W.L., Marianne, & K., Timothy (Eds.) *Counter narratives and organization* (pp. 155–170). New York/ London: Routledge.

Pedersen, J.S. (2014). Institutionel teori. In Signe V., & Kjær, P. (Eds.) *Klassisk og moderne organizationsteori [Classic and modern organizational theory]* (pp. 233–256). Copenhagen: Hans Reitzels Forlag.

Rapley, T. (2001). The art(fulness) of open-ended interviewing: some considerations on analysing interviews. *Qualitative Research*, 1(3), 303 – 323. London: Sage.

Rhodes, C., & Brown, A. (2005). Narrative, organizations and research. *International Journal of Management Review*, 7(3), 167–188.

Silvermann, D. (1998). The quality of qualitative health research: The open-ended interview and its alternatives. *Social Sciences in Health*, 4(2), 104–118.

Silvermann, D. (2014). *Interpreting qualitative data*. Los Angeles: Sage.

Suchman, M.C. (1995). Managing legitimacy: Strategic and institutional practices. *Academy of Management Review*, 20(3), 571–610.

Svenningsson, S., & Larsson, M. (2006). Fantasies of leadership: Identity work. *Leadership*, 2(2), 203–224.

Van Leeuwen, T. (2008). *Discourse and practice. New tools for critical discourse analysis*. Oxford: Oxford University Press.

Wodak, R. (2011). Critical discourse analysis. In K. Hyland, & P., Brian. (Eds.), *The Continuum companion to discourse analysis* (pp. 38–53). London: Continuum.

14

Temporal aspects of counter-narratives and professional identity formation in the establishment of a new hospital department

Astrid Jensen and Jette Ernst

Introduction

The aim of this chapter is to explore counter-narratives as a theoretical and analytical concept, by linking the narrative micro analytical level of everyday practices with the macro analytical level of the wider field, through Bourdieu's (1985, 1990) field, habitus and capital concepts. In this, we aim to achieve a multilevel theorization of the establishment of a new hospital department, involving a merger between two departments, as we pay attention to the temporal aspect of the narratives constructed. We suggest this as a valuable framework for understanding how, and why the establishment of the department was interwoven with competing and contrasting stories affecting nursing legitimacy and identity, and we suggest that Bourdieu's concepts enable a deep and contextualized understanding of counter-narratives and why they may emerge.

We see the merger as part of a new forceful master-narrative in the wider field that concerns hospital efficiency and quality through the re-organization, coordination and integration of care that materializes in the national concept of united acute admission (FAM), locally adapted as a new organizational concept. FAM stands for the Danish 'Fælles Akutmodtagelse', where the term 'fælles' (united) embeds intentions of care integration across sectors and medical specialties. The aim of care re-organization is to improve care pathways through improved collaboration between medical specialties and nursing de-specialization and thus increased care flexibility (Ernst & Jensen, 2018). However, nursing de-specialization is potentially problematic, since clinical specialization is historically anchored and institutionalized in the field as the core of professional competence, legitimacy and status (Abbott, 1988). In this chapter, we will show how care re-organization is approached differently by the two groups of merging nurses, as the members of one group made a deliberate choice to become part of the FAM concept, whereas the other group was forced into the new organizational concept. This led to multiple competing narratives, where the nurses struggled for new professional legitimacy and identity in the merged department. In this, narrative positioning and nursing identity were closely connected to the temporal aspect of care as it relates to departmental specialization, but also to the temporal aspect of the establishment of the department. We therefore focus on time and space as important elements in the construction of narratives in the local adaption of the FAM concept, where multiple and competing stories emerging as side shadows in 'what might have been' aggregate into a forceful counter-narrative invoking and challenging the dominant master-narrative of the FAM concept of seamless care.

Theorizing counter-narratives in organizational change

Narratives and counter-narratives

In our exploration of the concept of counter-narratives, we draw on Andrew's (2004) definition of counter-narratives as 'stories which people tell and live, which offer resistance to, either implicitly or explicitly, dominant cultural narratives' (Andrews, 2004, p. 1), identifying it as an 'oppositional category in tension with another category' (ibid.). Though counter-narratives exist in relation to master-narratives, they are not necessarily used as dichotomous entities, which Bamberg and Andrews (2004) demonstrate in their book *Considering Counter Narratives*, where various contributions show that the potential for opposition presented by a counter-narrative is achieved through multiple stories (Lundholt, Maagaard, & Piekut, 2017, p. 2) or antenarratives (Boje, 2001) expressing diverse perspectives. Gabriel (2017) further emphasizes that narratives are relationally constituted, in that counter-narratives invoke the master-narrative by drawing it into awareness.

Recent studies have attempted to bring the concept of counter-narratives into an organizational context (Kuhn, Lundholt, & Frandsen, 2016). However, still more knowledge about (counter)-narratives as a theoretical and dynamic concept is needed, and in particular, we believe that a temporal aspect of (counter)-narratives is vital for understanding their complex and dynamic role in organizational change. We therefore complement these studies with a dynamic notion, where narratives can be understood as a way of linking objective and subjective perspectives of time (Cunliffe, Luhman, & Boje, 2004). Accordingly, stories and narratives are not just retrospective reflections of past events, but situated, responsive performances, where the past is interpreted through the present, and where the past and the future exist in our experience of the present. Narratives are then a way of thematizing the past and the future (Atkinson, 2018), where multiple stories grounded in actors' sense of position and temporality in the field allow them to discursively construct a rationalizing link between the past, present and future (Bourdieu, 1987). The theoretical framework we use in this chapter enables us to understand how counter-narratives are shaped by the past, produced by frustrations in the present, and represent hopes for the future.

We understand narratives in terms of fragmented antenarratives, (counter) stories, or as full blown (counter)-narratives with a beginning, middle and end (Boje, 2001).

Narrative time and organizational change

Pedersen (2009, p. 309) highlights 'narrative time' as a viable concept in creating new understandings to theories of organizational change, where time can be understood as 'open time' reflecting different understandings of (change) events, and where 'narrative time' can be defined as historical time, living time, as foreshadows of time or as time bound to space.

In a similar vein, Vaara and Pedersen (2014) connect 'narrative time' to organizational strategizing, arguing that strategic sensemaking cannot be fully comprehended without understanding temporality and how it is construed:

> The very idea of a strategy is to create images of the future that can serve as compelling objectives, while constructing the future, one also explicitly or implicitly defines the present and the past by focusing attention on specific ideas and thus creating particular meanings.
>
> *(Vaara and Pedersen, 2014, p. 7)*

From this perspective, stories of organizational change are understood as representing different stories of time, drawing attention to two concepts of narrative time, Bakhtin's concept of chronotope (1981) and Morson's concept of the shadows of time, 'foreshadowing' and 'sideshadowing' (1994). Bakhtin (1981) points to the need for multiple concepts of time, or multiple 'chronotopes' for diverse purposes and circumstances, and he introduced the term to analyze the spatio-temporal basis of narratives and other linguistic acts. Borum and Pedersen (2008) see chronotopes as a way of visualizing how space affects time, and how events in time do not take place in a void, but in a particular location. The concept of chronotopes is often found in connection to 'foreshadowing' and 'sideshadowing' (Borum & Pedersen, 2008; Jørgensen, 2011; Morson, 1994; Pedersen, 2009), where time is defined as asymmetric and reflects the relation of past, present and future (Pedersen, 2009). In foreshadowing, the sequence of events is already given as a specific outcome of a linear sequence of events, which in the context of organizational change may be in the form of a dominant managerial master-narrative, where the future is foretold, and the present is experienced in the form of a shadow from the future. Foreshadowing foretells a hypothetical future in which the present evolves around preparation (Pedersen, 2009). Sideshadowing, on the other hand, can be combined with Boje's (2001) antenarrative approach, where antenarratives are seen as bets on future potentialities and imply working with open time through a process of sideshadowing (Jørgensen, 2011). Sideshadowing is defined as a 'plurality of possibilities' (Morson, 1994, p. 118) and conveys the possibility that actual events might not have happened because casting the shadow from the side creates a sense that something else could have happened. Pedersen (2009) illustrates how the concept of 'narrative time' opens up a 'dynamic view of the shadows of time' (p. 394), and how shadows of time describe time as a relational phenomenon:

> In organizational settings, change can occur as a foreshadowing of time if change events are already predictable in the future of organizational plans. Sideshadows reflect the way in which employees understand the present in relation to change events that might have occurred, but never did.
>
> *(Pedersen, 2009, p. 394)*

Also, Borum and Pedersen (2008) focus on 'narrative time' when they argue that a narrative understanding of a merger can be in a foreshadowed future. In this chapter, we build on this literature of 'narrative time', and we use a conceptualization of the shadows of time, where foreshadowing conveys that which is foreseeable in future plans, and by some perceived as necessary or inevitable, and where sideshadowing conveys alternative readings of 'the space of the social possibles' (Bourdieu, 1990, p. 162), carrying with it the material of counter-narratives. We propose that combining 'narrative time' with a Bourdieusian perspective, enables us to see how nurses' and managers' temporal consciousness, and their understanding of the merger, is constituted by wider field level forces and their position in the field. We explain this perspective in the following.

Bourdieu's concepts and field temporalization

For Bourdieu, the field is a space of relations between individuals and groups, who have an interest in something at stake in the field. It is a space of necessity and belief for the agents belonging to it, with potential symbolic and material gains. Something is strived for in fields, which renders them spaces of struggle and competition (Bourdieu, 1985; Bourdieu & Wacquant, 1992). In the present case, we analyze the organization of care as that which is at stake in the field, which we term the hospital field. The hospital field envelops all who have a stake in hospital services and it is structured by health care policy and professional interests, among others. It consists of multiple analytically interlaced layers where hospital work happens in a continuous dialectic between the practitioner and the forces that structure professional conduct (Bourdieu, 1990). In the particular case, it means that the macro level structuring forces of the hospital field, discursively represented by a master-narrative of good, efficient and seamless care, set the conditions for identity constructions on the hospital floor while simultaneously they are also influenced by the actions of hospital staff and management, for example, in their interpretation, adaption and responses to the master-narrative.

Agents position themselves in the field in relation to each other based on the kind and amount of capital they possess. Capital is that which has particular value in a field and is used by the members of a field in symbolic and material forms to construct positive differences in relation to other agents (Bourdieu, 1986). Hence, agents who are differently positioned in the field are actively performing ongoing acts of positioning, as they strive to uphold their present position or to improve it, based on their possession and continuous acquisition of capital.

Positioning and the overall being in fields is temporally constituted (Bourdieu, 1998). Here Bourdieu is inspired by Husserl's concept of foresight, also termed protention, as the sense for what can be expected from the future grounded in one's experience of the past. The experience of the present is a horizon of anticipation (Zahavi, 2003), a relation to a future that is almost present founded on experiences of the past and, thus, the past, present and future are intertwined (Bourdieu, 1998). Protention is interlaced with Bourdieu's habitus concept, which is socialization, life experience, and the knowing of one's place in the world stored in a body. Habitus forms dispositions for perceiving the world and acting in it (Bourdieu, 1990). All fields exert a socializing function on their agents, which means that the structuring principles of the hospital field are present as socialized dispositions in the bodies of nurses through the training they have received, which furnishes them with an ability to navigate what Bourdieu (1990) often terms 'the game'. Thus, navigating the hospital field amounts to knowing its spoken and unspoken rules and handling them competently to build capital. In this way, the concept links with Morson's sideshadowing, since sideshadowing focuses on agents' understanding of the field's possibilities. Yet, where protention emphasizes the deep but unconscious knowing of how to navigate the field, sideshadowing emphasizes the reflexive practice of imagining and wishing for other states of the field and thus to understand any moment by grasping its 'space of social possibles' (Bourdieu, 1990), i.e. change events that might have occurred. In relation to foreshadowing, as we use the concept here, there is also an important element of reflexive choice, yet in this case, choice is connected to the predictable or to that which seems unavoidable and necessary – an already told future, as we will elaborate in the presentation of our data. We suggest that the ability and chances one has of grasping the possibilities of the field is nothing random but will depend on the amount and type of capital one possesses, one's position in the field, the socialization one has received, and the wider field level forces that shape the conditions for change.

In summary, Bourdieu's field, habitus and capital concepts situate stories in a larger structuring context, enabling analyses of temporal and social aspects of organizational identity formation in a multi-level and dialectic perspective between macro level political action and micro level hospital floor activities. The narrative constructions of nurses and managers are thus the products of a temporal horizon of consciousness (Atkinson, 2018), which is conditioned by their position in the field, but also by the specific rhythm of the hospital field. Atkinson (2018) suggests that we look at the field's sequence of revolutions to understand its inner workings and present state, which we will do in the following.

A new master-narrative of seamless care in the Danish hospital field

The Danish hospital field has not experienced many revolutions. It possesses a large degree of autonomy and stability, primarily because the medical professions, as the dominant agents in the field, have been able to resist change (Borum, 2003; Kirkpatrick, Dent, & Jespersen, 2011). However, resulting from healthcare reform, the field is under pressure and it seems that the forces aiming at transformation are stronger than the forces aiming at preserving the status quo.

Through the 1990s and 2000s, the reports and ranking lists by agents such as The Organization for Economic Co-operation and Development and The World Health Organization unmistakably pointed out that the Danish healthcare system was affected by problems related to expenditure level and the quality of services (Knudsen, Christensen, & Hansen, 2008). Politically, it produced the perception that stricter regulation of the health sector was urgent and unavoidable, and the overarching argument for healthcare reform was the need to improve hospital services in terms of quality, safety and efficiency (Christiansen, 2012).

The following restructuring and reorganization of the hospital sector resulted in a new acute care structure to deal with problems of care coordination and integration. New large acute care hospitals were constructed to house the new acute care departments (Christiansen, 2012) that were declared as the cornerstone of a hospital structure leading towards 'the hospital of tomorrow' by the health authorities (Aslaksen, Brismar, Kirk, Møller Pedersen, & Juhl, 2008). The new departments were established to achieve better organization of care to be realized as seamless and efficient care pathways that should be obtained by breaking with medical specializations as the main principle for care organization. Medical specializations are often seen as 'medical silos' hindering effective collaboration across specialities, which is a core idea of these departments (Ernst, 2017; Ernst & Jensen, 2018; Hajek, 2013). For the nurses in the departments, breaking with the medical silos meant that de-specialization and professional flexibility was emphasized as a way of improving care (Ernst & Jensen, 2018). In this way, we see the merger as part of a forceful dominant master-narrative of seamless care in the wider hospital field, which in a local adaption foreshadows hospital effeciency and quality through care re-organization, where the merger investigated in this chapter represents preparation for a 'given' future of effective care coordination and integration, leading to seamless care.

Methods

We draw on an ethnographic study of the establishment of the new department, involving participant observations of nurses and doctors for 13 months, as well as one-to-one and group interviews with nurses, doctors and managers, conducted according to a semi-structured interview guide, inspired by Kvale and Brinkmann (2009). The study also included meeting observations and the study of internal documents such as strategy papers. Further, we include secondary data in the shape of a large body of textual material, such as white papers, white books, policy agendas for action, national and regional strategy papers, research papers from peer reviewed journals, articles from professional journals, and newsletters. All participants as well as the department are referred to by pseudonyms and all years mentioned in the following are fictional for anonymization purposes.

Analysis of the ethnographic data

Creating the new department in time and space

The merger concerns two previously separate and specialized acute care departments and completes the establishment of department FAM – one of the 21 new acute care departments across the country that all rest on a common acute care concept that was adapted by the five Danish regions to fit their needs and aspirations and re-adapted by their local acute care hospitals.

Chronologically, the formation of the new department took place in two main phases. The initial phase was when the acute admission department (AAD) was established in 2010, when the medical visitation unit was closed down (see Table 14.1). The hospital, which we term Pinevale, had successfully competed against a neighboring hospital to become an acute care hospital. This was a prestigious nomination, as it provided the hospital with a central role as one of the 21 Danish acute care hospitals. The process of establishing the AAD was led by the former management, and staff were recruited through job postings.

The second phase began in 2013, when the AAD merged with the accident and emergency department, and the new acute care department (A&E) was established to form a single and united acute care admission to the hospital. After the merger, the new department, FAM, consisted of an admission unit, a bed unit and an accident and emergency unit that functioned as differentiated work zones in the daily operations. The three units were based on the organizing structures of the two former, now merged, admission departments: 1) AAD, which accommodates the bed and admission units (B&A), and 2) A&E[1], accommodating the accident and emergency unit. Moreover, the management of the merged department had chosen to maintain the original employment structures, which means that the B&A units made up one occupational zone (the B&A zone) headed by one ward nurse, and the A&E made up another occupational zone (the A&E zone) headed by a second ward nurse. In this way, the nurses preserved their departmental affiliations, which reinforced the feeling of belonging to two distinct groups (see Ernst & Jensen, 2018).

The choice to divide the merger into two phases with a three-year interval and upholding the previous physical divisions between departments had consequences for the post-merger positioning and identity construction possibilities of the two groups of nurses. The fact that the AAD nurses had initiated the department gave them a symbolic lead in these struggles. These nurses had already established themselves as acute care nurses in the hospital organization when the A&E nurses joined the department. Although this position was met with resistance

Table 14.1 Occupational zones and management of the merged department

FAM	*Occupational Zone 1*	*Occupational Zone 2*
Care units	The space of the bed and the admission units (the B&A zone)	The space of the accident and emergency unit (A&E zone)
Head of wards	Ward nurse 'one'	Ward nurse 'two'
Department management	A head senior doctor and a nursing unit manager	

Source: Adapted from Ernst & Jensen, 2018.

Table 14.2 The shadow of time

The FAM creation process	*Department timeline*	*Primary battleground*
First phase (2010)	The AAD established. (B&A nurses)	Hospital field competition and positioning. Nurses and managers in the AAD aspire to become the first and best. - The merger is foreshadowed as a part of a master-narrative (FAM)
Second phase (2013)	The AAD (B&A nurses) merges with the accident and emergency department (A&E nurses). FAM is established.	FAM becomes the primary ground where the groups of nurses struggle to establish an attractive space for themselves as groups. - The merger is sideshadowed by the A&E nurses in antenarratives of alternative possibilities

Source: Adapted from Ernst & Jensen, 2018.

by the rest of the hospital organization, it defined the 'space of the possible' (Bourdieu, 1990) for the newcomers whose habitus struggled to adapt to the new circumstances. These two different aspects of identity and positioning struggles materialized in the nurses' narratives, five years after the establishment of the department:

Phase one: 'frontrunners' winning new capital in the field, the story of the B&A nurses

The nurses were recruited to the new department through job postings, and had thus actively applied to become part of the local adaption of the new acute care concept and thereby the establishment of the new hospital department. It was also a reflexive choice to become involved in de-specialized care organization and thus to work as nursing generalists rather than specialists within a given clinical area. A new and recently qualified nurse in the department, Amelia, explained:

> Since we meet all kinds of patients here, the new department is the perfect place for me to learn the medical specializations.
>
> *(Fieldnotes)*

According to a nurse, June, de-specialization as an organizing principle of care works as a democratizing principle creating equality and community in the staff group:

> I enjoyed being a part of this. We had to build the department from scratch and the good thing was that no specialty owned it already, no one had more right than others to decide what was going to happen. We were in it together.
>
> *(Interview)*

Aspiring to be the best

Although establishing a new department from the ground was hard work, the staff was energized by the ambition of being the leading acute care department in the country, and managers and nurses cast themselves as victorious conquerors of the new acute care field:

> The best acute care department in Denmark, well the best of all specialist departments, is nominated each year by Dagens Medicin (a medical professional journal) [...] and we were in the top every year [...]. You can ask the nurses who were here back then about that feeling of wanting to be the best and I'm sure they will tell you that they recognize it.
>
> *(Interview, head specialist doctor)*

This story conveys how the local adaption of the dominant master-narrative allowed the department to earn new capital as a symbolic gain when they became frontrunners of the FAM concept in competition with the other FAM departments in the country. Moreover, the management of the department interpreted and constructed new acute care capital as not only related to being frontrunners, but also to innovativeness and ambition in ways that benefitted the patient. The Head Specialist Doctor told how the nurses were involved in care optimization following the LEAN system:

> We worked with patient progress descriptions in groups of mixed actors, who described 3–4 major patient cases [...]. Everyone sat around the table and clarified good LEAN style [...]. Then, we developed alternative models, removing everything unnecessary.
>
> *(Interview)*

Being the best and first to define the practices of an acute care department was thus essential to the competitive energy that drove the staff of the AAD forward in the early establishment phase and it was a core ingredient in their construction of new field level capital. A nurse, Bella, explained that the department was the first to receive patients according to a new system termed triage that was considered to improve patient admittance by postponing diagnosis and instead, initially, considered symptoms only to avoid premature allocation of a medical specialty to the patient.

> We looked at the patients' symptoms. Previously, we would just measure the patient's temperature and use our clinical judgement and sometimes it was the patients who shouted the loudest who would be admitted first.
>
> *(Fieldnotes)*

The new acute care concept embedded new professional roles for the nurses, who not only hugely outnumbered the doctors in the department, but were also central nodes in new, efficient care organization and the overall materialization of the new concept (Ernst, 2017). Since medical staffing in the department was almost exclusively covered by junior doctors, who were replaced every six months, the nurses often had superior experience in care, and doctors drew on this experience, as illustrated by the following excerpt:

> We know so much and they (the doctors) have to listen to us. They often come and ask us things – especially the junior doctors.
>
> *(Fieldnotes)*

New professional opportunities

The department thus offered new opportunities for the nurses who participated in many clinical decisions. Moreover, care pathways were often interrupted when patients waited for a doctor to perform a certain task. Therefore, to render the care pathways more efficient (seamless), it was decided that nurses should take over minor and uncomplicated tasks from the doctors. The new role as Acute Care Nurse Practitioner is part of an international development promoting new nursing roles in care (Ernst, 2017; Norris & Melby, 2006). Alice explained how some of the nurses saw this as an opportunity for professional development:

> Some of us wanted to take over tasks from the doctors which we believed we could handle, and which would create a better care pathway flow where the patient wouldn't have to wait for a doctor.
>
> *(Fieldnotes)*

For many of the nurses in the department, additional training and new roles in practice were important elements in career development and for claiming new capital that could position them in the hospital field in relation to other acute departments, as well as internally, in the organization, in relation to the other departments. Like management, these nurses saw the new department as a space for necessary improvements to care and as promoting the inevitable future of care organization. They believed in 'the stakes of the game' (Bourdieu, 1990) and were actively constructing new capital related to being the 'first' and 'best' among acute care departments. They therefore engaged in a co-construction of the local adaption of the master-narrative of seamless care, a local narrative that foreshadows their understanding of the present as acute care nurses, providing them with an agentic identity of promoting progressive change. This gave them a feeling of being together in a specific chronotope (time/space), where a new acute-care identity was defined by efficiency and the short duration of patient hospitalization that characterizes an acute care department (up to 48 hours).

Phase two: the history of the A&E nurses

The A&E department was part of the orthopaedic department and was formerly under its jurisdictional authority, yet in reality, the A&E department had been run by the nurses for many years, many of whom had acquired the title of 'practice nurse' through supplementary education. This allowed them to treat minor injuries independently from doctors. According to the Head Nurse, this history of the A&E department had furnished these nurses with a distinct identity and considerable self-confidence:

> They have their own culture and identity that resembles the anaesthetist nurse's. It is characterized by a stand-by approach to things, a state of readiness. They like that things move fast, that patients move rapidly in and out, and urgency in care. They are skilled nurses.
>
> *(Interview)*

In this narrative, the head nurse defined the A&E department as a specific space, with a specific conceptualization of time, where things move fast, and where readiness and unpredictability are key components in what differentiates these nurses from the other nurses in the hospital, i.e. an 'alertness gene', which is a central component of their professional habitus, and their nursing specialization. These nurses are positioned high in the organizational nursing hierarchy because they are seen as autonomous and skilled nurses and thus as holders of professional craft and nursing autonomy, which are striven for capitals. In the following narratives, we see how the FAM concept and its local adaption challenged this core capital.

The merger and capital erosion: poor management

The merger in 2013 initiated the second phase of the establishment of FAM. Naturally, it involved major changes in the nurses' working conditions. Moreover, the A&E nurses had not been part of the initiation of FAM and had not been invited to discuss the concept and provide their points of view on the new department. The A&E nurses felt that they had not received clear announcements from management about what the merger would entail for them since neither new tasks nor a division of labor were defined, and physically they had been kept in two separate occupational zones (Table 14.1).

> T: We were not told much.
> P: We knew that we should merge, but we were told nothing about our new roles.
> *(Group interview, A&E nurses)*

The A&E nurses, as late-arrivers, were left with a feeling of being less important in the new organizational set-up, which was a feeling of capital erosion, where the special value associated with being A&E nurses was crumbling (Ernst & Jensen, 2018).

This led to two different temporal understandings of the merger process. Whereas the B&A nurses experienced the merger in terms of an already told or inevitable future of seamless progressive care, the A&E nurses saw the merger in terms of past events and lost future opportunities, where management had robbed them of the opportunity to convert their long-earned capital into new capital that could be converted to an attractive professional identity in accordance with the master-narrative. This frustration emerged in the form of multiple antenarratives working as "hidden processes of change" (Svane, Gergerich, & Boje, 2017, p. 143) sideshadowing (Morson, 1994) alternative futures in tension to the already told future of the master-narrative.

> I think this is poor management. We could not maintain our professionalism and what we were proud of. I mean, I was proud of working in the A&E department and I was insecure about my position and my tasks in the new setting. Would I be some kind of 'nebengeschäft' [on the side] to the acute care department, which I found we had no relation to?
> *(Group Interview, A&E nurses)*

Narrative sideshadowing as a return to the past

While nursing de-specialization and medical collaboration across specializations are important ingredients of seamless care and the FAM master-narrative, the identity of the A&E nurses hinges on their capital as autonomous practice nurses and thus specialized nurses. In the new department, all nurses would in principle take part in all tasks, which drew the A&E nurses out of their professional comfort zone as they would have to participate in lower ranked (unspecialized) tasks associated with less capital. The fear of having to share job functions with the bed unit of the B&A zone that performs what is often termed basic nursing (Apesoa-Varano, 2007) became a significant part of their fight to maintain their professional identity and thus hold on to their capital. Basic nursing lacks capital, since capital in the field tends to be associated with knowledge and specialized competence and thus the form of capital which Bourdieu (1986) terms cultural capital:

> We are emergency nurses, and we are good at what we do. Many of us envision that we now have to take shifts in the bed zone, give bedpans, and wash the patients - all of which we, I would not say we have fled from, but we want to distance ourselves from.

> This is probably our reason for choosing to work in an emergency department. We want to move away from the bed department mentality - from the predictable to the unpredictable.
>
> *(Group interview, A&E nurses)*

These antenarratives are anchored in the professional habitus of the nurses, and are defined by a specific chronotope (time/space) of the emergency department, which is based on a constrast between a bed department, the 'predictable', and an emergency department, the 'unpredictable', and a temporal constitution of care, where risk is high, thus necessitating a habitus dispositioned with a taste for 'alertness'.

The A&E nurses had not chosen to become part of new care organization and generalist nursing, and they had not been given a role in the local adaption of the grand master-narrative of future seamless care pathways. Therefore, they experience the new organizational set-up as having been forced upon them – 'it was get on the bus or get off' (group interview, A&E nurses) – and they were left in a narrative space of opaque 'social possibles' (Bourdieu, 1990) with multiple or competing interpretations of the future work space, where they made sense of the change by sideshadowing stories of alternative futures. In anticipating the future, the protention by the A&E zone nurses revealed a temporal lag between their aspirations, which are the products of habitus as dispositions of the past, and the imposition of 'new rules to the game' (Bourdieu, 1990) as products of the FAM master-narrative and its local adaption. This gave rise to an antenarrative, sideshadowing a future return to the past, about how things would be better if the merger was abolished:

> A: We will probably end up with the previous set up.
> L: I think so. But that'll cost a horrible lot of money, won't it?'
>
> *(Group interview, A&E nurses)*

Sideshadowing the future as a joint space

Keeping the B&A zone and the A&E zone as two separate occupational zones (Table 14.1), evoked contrasting time/space understanding of being emergency nurses and bed department nurses. This was particularly clear in the narratives of the emergency nurses, as the physical division of the departments into two occupational zones emphasized the different temporal aspects of care, i.e. acute care nursing vs. bed department nursing. This generated an antenarrative that sideshadowed an alternative future of being together as a 'joint' unit in a shared physical space/time:

> We all had the same wish that we should be a joint unit over here, and that all reported for work in the same place.
>
> [...] we would like to have a common attendance profile and a common room where all report for duty. Then we would be a large department with around 15 (nurses) for the day shift, and resources could be distributed from that point (to the three zones of the department).
>
> *(Group interview)*

In this narrative, there is acceptance of the new and merged department as a future frame for work, which is narratively sideshadowing a future where tolerable and fair working conditions apply, and the two groups of nurses are treated equally. This entails a conditioned concession to the dominant master-narrative of seamless care (the FAM concept), but at the same time countering its local adaption, where physically integrating the two departments in time and space was never completed.

In the analysis, we see how the nurses' narratives reflect an asymmetric understanding of time, where the two nursing groups moved in two different temporalities, the future and the past, defined by the capital they possess. Hence, the B&A nurses and their managers invested in the master-narrative, understood its 'rules' and actively entered the game of capital construction, the other group related their stories to past nursing specialization and their experience of capital erosion. The A&E nurses were unable to construct capital in the new 'game', as they were left with a feeling of inferiority without a defined role in the locally foreshadowed master-narrative of the FAM concept, and without physical integration in a joint space. This created multiple competing antenarratives, where acute/emergency nurses and bed department nurses were anchored in different temporalities of patient care and in the perceived capital levels of these different forms of nursing.

Nursing de-specialization and professional flexibility therefore became a less attractive position in the merged work space where multiple antenarratives sideshadowing alternative futures formed a counter-narrative that contested the local adaption of the master-narrative at Pinevale Hospital, as well as the principle of de-specialization in the dominant master-narrative.

Conclusion

The chapter aimed at exploring counter-narrative as a theoretical and analytical concept to analyze identity struggles and capital construction during the establishment of a new hospital department and a subsequent merger. To this end, we combined Bourdieu's theoretical triad of habitus, capital and field with a temporal perspective on counter-narratives. We build on the literature of 'narrative time' (Pedersen, 2009), where we used the concept of foreshadowing regarding that which is foreseeable or seems unavoidable in policies and future plans, as well as the concept of sideshadowing, which conveys alternative readings of 'the space of the social possibles', which depends on the agents' position in the field and thus by the capital they possess (Bourdieu, 1990).

Bourdieu's concepts allowed us to understand the importance of the context and historical background of the identified narratives and the nurses' very different understandings of the new department and thus to achieve a multi-level theorization of the nurses' experiences of the new department. The different points of departure of the two groups of nurses led to conflicting approaches to the master-narrative. The B&A nurses felt empowered as nurses who promoted a better organization of care and whose department was the leading acute care department in the country. The A&E nurses, on the other hand, felt that their previous capital was eroding, and they struggled to obtain new professional legitimacy and identity in the merged department. We see how antenarratives, sideshadowing alternatives to a future that was inscribed in the master-narrative, emerged as reflexive responses to a habitus out of synch with the new 'rules of the game' (Bourdieu, 1990) and thus as a state of disrupted navigation in the field. We have termed this 'protention' after Bourdieu (1998), where effortless protention happens as a sense of what can be expected from the future based on socialized and competent understandings of the past. The A&E nurses were unable to carve out an attractive position for themselves in the merged work space and struggled to convert previous capital of specialization into new effective capital. Sideshadowing is their imagination of how things could have been, reflecting their socialized understandings of work.

In the analysis, we focused on time and space as important elements in the construction of narratives in the local adaption of the FAM concept. For both groups of nurses, their narrative positioning and nursing identity were closely connected to the temporal aspect of care and occupational work zones, and we see how their narratives reflected an asymmetric understanding of time that produced a tension between the two nursing groups as they moved in two different temporalities. We saw this as a consequence of management's local adaption of the master-narrative of 'FAM', as well as the built-in tension between two competing forces in the hospital field, i.e. the institutionalized connection between medical specialization and the organization of care and the belief in professional flexibility and seamless care, as represented by the FAM master-narrative. This tension produced a counter-narrative invoking and challenging the FAM master-narrative in its local implementation in Pinevale.

In this chapter, we conceptualized counter-narratives as evolving from multiple antenarratives, sideshadowing alternative futures, informed by a habitus that is unable to navigate in a field that is dominated by an imposed master-narrative. The counter-narrative resulted from the unsettled protention of the A&E nurses, i.e. when their socialized understanding of the past does not correspond with the current conditions of the field and their ability to foresee what is expected in the future. As our data showed, this is a condition associated with a sense of capital inadequacy and lack of agency, where the possibility of attractive positioning is limited. Our theoretical framework thus demonstrates the importance of understanding counter-narratives in their local and wider field level contexts, where institutionalized understandings may compete with new ideologies.

Note

1 The difference between the two departments pertained to the types of patients they admitted. In the AAD, patients were referred for admission from General Practitioners, whereas in the A&E department, patients were either self-referrals or arrived by ambulance.

References

Abbott, A. (1988). *The system of professions: An essay on the division of expert labor.* Chicago: The University of Chicago Press.

Andrews, M. (2004). Opening to the original contributions. In M. Bamberg, & M Andrews (Eds.), Narrating, resisting, making sense, 1–6. Philadelphia: John Benjamins.

Apesoa-Varano, E. C. (2007). Educated caring: The emergence of professional identity among nurses. *Qualitative Sociology, 30*(3), 249–274. doi:http://dx.doi.org/10.1007/s11133-007-9069-6

Aslaksen, R., Brismar, B., Kirk, H., Møller Pedersen, K., & Juhl, E. (2008). *Regionernes investerings- og sygehusplaner: screening og vurdering. Afgivet af regeringens ekspertpanel november 2008.* København: Ministeriet for Sundhed og Forebyggelse.

Atkinson, W. (2018). Time for Bourdieu: Insights and oversights. *Time & Society, 28*(3), 951–970. 0961463X17752280. doi:10.1177/0961463x17752280

Bakhtin, M. M. (1981). *The dialogic imagination: Four essays by mm bakhtin (m. holquist, ed.; c. emerson & m. holquist, trans.).* Austin: University of Texas Press.

Bamberg, M. G. W., & Andrews, M. (2004). *Considering counter narratives: Narrating, resisting, making sense.* Amsterdam: John Benjamins Publishing Company.

Boje, D. M. (2001). *Narrative methods for organizational and communication research.* London: SAGE Publications Ltd.

Borum, F. (2003). Sygehusledelse under forandring. In Borum, (Ed.), *Ledelse i sygehusvæsenet.* København: Handelshøjskolens forlag.

Borum, F., & Pedersen, A. R. (2008). *Fusioner, ledelse og fortællinger: integration og polyfoni i det danske sundhedsvæsen.* Copenhagen Business School Press.

Bourdieu, P. (1985). The genesis of the concept of habitus and field. *Sociocriticism, 2*(2), 11–27.

Bourdieu, P. (1986). The forms of capital. In J. G. Richardson (Ed.), *Handbook of theory and research for the sociology of education* (pp. 241–255). New York: Greenwood Press.

Bourdieu, P. (1987). The biographical illusion (Y. Winkin & W. Leeds-Hurwitz, Trans.). In (2000), P. Du Gay, J. Evans, & P. Redman (Eds.), *Identity: A reader* (pp. 297–303). London: Sage Publication.

Bourdieu, P. (1990). *The logic of practice*. Cambridge: Polity.

Bourdieu, P. (1998). *Practical reason: On the theory of action*. Cambridge: Polity Press.

Bourdieu, P., & Wacquant, L. J. D. (1992). *An invitation to reflexive sociology*. Cambridge: Polity Press.

Christiansen, T. (2012). Ten years of structural reforms in Danish healthcare. *Health Policy, 106*(2), 114–119. doi:http://dx.doi.org/10.1016/j.healthpol.2012.03.019

Cunliffe, A. L., Luhman, J. T., & Boje, D. M. (2004). Narrative temporality: implications for organizational research. *Organization Studies, 25*(2), 261–286. doi:10.1177/0170840604040038

Ernst, J. (2017). Between change and reproduction: Profession, practice and organizational space in a hospital department. *Journal of Organizational Ethnography, 6*(3), 177–189. doi:10.1108/JOE-02-2017-0007

Ernst, J., & Jensen, A. (2018). Merger as field transformation: Nurses' positioning and metaphoric journeys. *Culture and Organization, Published online first: 15 Feb. 2018*. doi:10.1080/14759551.2018.1435656

Gabriel, Y. (2017). Narrative ecologies and the role of counter-narratives: The case of nostalgic stories and conspiracy theories. In S. Frandsen, T. Kuhn, & M. W. Lundholt (Eds.), *Counter-narratives and organization* (pp. 208–226). New York: Routledge.

Hajek, A. M. (2013). Breaking down clinical silos in healthcare. *Frontiers of Health Services Management, 29*(4), 45–50. doi:10.1097/01974520-201304000-00006

Jørgensen, K.M. (2011). Antenarrative writing-Tracing and representing living stories. In D. Boje (Ed.) *Storytelling and the Future of Organizations: An Antenarrative Handbook*, (pp. 284–297). New York: Routledge.

Kirkpatrick, I., Dent, M., & Jespersen, P. K. (2011). The contested terrain of hospital management: Professional projects and healthcare reforms in Denmark. *Current Sociology, 59*(4), 489–506. doi:http://dx.doi.org/10.1177/0011392111402718

Knudsen, J. L., Christensen, M. E., & Hansen, B. (2008). *Regulering af kvalitet i det danske sundhedsvæsen*. København: Nyt Nordisk Forlag.

Kuhn, T., Lundholt, M. W., & Frandsen, S. (2016). *Counter-narratives and organization*. New York: Routledge.

Kvale, S., & Brinkmann, S. (2009). *Interviews: Learning the craft of qualitative research interviewing* (2 ed.). London: Sage Publications Ltd.

Lundholt, M. W., Maagaard, C. A., & Piekut, A. (2017). *Counter-narratives: International encyclopedia of strategic communication*. Wiley-Blackwell.

Morson, G. (1994). *Narrative and freedom: the shadows of time*. New Haven, CT: Yale University Press.

Norris, T., & Melby, V. (2006). The acute care nurse practitioner: challenging existing boundaries of emergency nurses in the United Kingdom. *Journal of Clinical Nursing, 15*(3), 253–263 211p. doi:10.1111/j.1365-2702.2006.01306.x

Pedersen, A. R. (2009). Moving away from chronological time: Introducing the shadows of time and chronotopes as new understandings of narrative time. *Organization, 16*(3), 389–406.

Svane, M., Gergerich, E., & Boje, D. M. (2017). Fractal change management and counter-narrative in cross-cultural change. In S. Frandsen, T. Kuhn, & M. W. Lundholt (Eds.), *Counter-narrative and organization* (pp. 129–155). New York: Routledge.

Vaara, E., & Pedersen, A. (2014). Strategy and chronotopes: A Bakhtinian perspective on the construction of strategy narratives. *M@n@gement, 16*(5), 593–604.

Zahavi, D. (2003). *Husserl's Phenomenology*. Stanford, CA: Stanford University Press.

15

Using counter-narrative to defend a master narrative

Discursive struggles reorganizing the media landscape

Hanna Sofia Rehnberg and Maria Grafström

Introduction

What is considered journalism is under negotiation. In a digitalized world – where an increasing number of actors fight for attention and legacy media struggle to create sustainable business models – the functions of the media are changing; the media's established role as a safety valve and an indisputable part of a democratic society is being disputed. Part of the ongoing change is new actors challenging the traditional narrative of journalism – a narrative which we here understand as a master narrative.

This master narrative of journalism, as described in research, portrays an institution that is necessary in a democratic society. It developed in states with a democratic form of government and was consolidated in the twentieth century. When journalism became more professional, "independent scrutiny" and being "a free forum for debate" emerged as two of its most vital functions (Wiik, 2010, p. 45). Nonetheless, journalism will never be able to achieve full professional status, simply for ideological reasons – insisting on professional certification would be an attack on freedom of expression – and so its status is often described as semi-professional. This, according to Wiik (2010), creates a particularly acute need for constant negotiation with regards to the status and autonomy of journalism.

In this chapter we use a narrative lens to understand and interpret ongoing changes in the media landscape. We examine the creation of meaning that is guiding the emergence of a new type of news production in Sweden, namely news produced and disseminated by public organizations. Our analysis concerns the debate that arose when one Swedish county council – Region Västra Götaland (VGR) – started a digital communication channel with journalistic overtones in the fall of 2017. Our analysis comprises a text published by the county council in conjunction with the launch of the communication channel and subsequent articles published in legacy media.

Our purpose is to develop the concept of *counter-narrative* through using it in an analysis of a discursive struggle taking place in a transforming media landscape. Theoretically we are interested in how counter-narratives emerge and how different narratives are positioned in and through discursive struggles. We use and explore the concept of *counter-narrative* to analyze the ongoing debate of what is understood as journalism and who can claim to be doing journalistic work. Who creates the counter-narrative and with what objective? How does the counter-narrative relate to, and how is it dependent on, the master narrative? And – on a more general level – how are various narratives affected when the advocates of different perspectives meet in a discursive struggle?

The concept of counter-narrative in our study

To shed light on and create a deeper understanding of what journalism is, or could be, in a time of radical change, we turn to literature on the role of narratives as "powerful sense-making and order-producing devices" (Frandsen, Wolff Lundholt & Kuhn, 2017, p. 1; see also Ricœur, 1991), which offers a fruitful analytical framework. In particular we draw on recent studies suggesting that narratives are interdependent and that meaning is created in processes where different types of narratives 'meet' or contradict one another.

The concept of *counter-narrative* has been applied in research on individuals or groups who deviate from the dominating cultural norms (Bamberg & Andrews, 2004; Nelson, 2001). These studies have shown how counter-narratives are used by individuals to position themselves in relation to societal master-narratives. More recently, the concept has also been applied in studies of organizations as well as professions. The distinction between master narrative and counter-narrative has then been used, for example, to distinguish between a preferred organizational story and alternative visions (Frandsen et al., 2017, p. 2) or to construct and express professional identities (Norlyk, 2017). Accordingly, one reason to focus on counter-narratives is their ability to capture political and social tensions and complexities in organizing activities. Furthermore, the concept of counter-narrative could be used to illuminate struggles over values and identities (Mumby, 1987).

Counter-narratives are usually constructed as being in opposition to other narratives, more specifically master-narratives, which dominate in some way. While the master narrative is widely told and cherished in society, not least by powerful groups, the counter-narrative leads a more moderate life, only cherished by a few and in need of explicit supporters. However, as shown by Norlyk (2017) in a study on professional designers, counter-narratives can challenge established powers and societal norms, specifically in times of turbulence and disturbance. Norlyk (2017, p. 156) finds that "[i]n a professional context, counter-narratives appear when professional values and norms are being questioned or threatened by powers outside of the professional community".

In our analysis we strive to go beyond a static normative dichotomy and examine how a more complex tissue of narratives develops, and how these narratives relate to and position themselves in relation to each other. We align with Rasmussen (2017, p. 171; see also Humle & Frandsen, 2017) who criticizes the presumption of an "*a priori* existence of a fixed dichotomy between a master and a counter-narrative", partly for its normative bias with an implicit assumption of negative hegemonic power and positive oppositional emancipation. Rasmussen (2017, p. 174) ascribes this normative dichotomy to "the origin of the concept of counter-narrative in a critical tradition within humanities concerned with societal and discursive phenomena as part of an emancipating agenda". Within this tradition, counter-narratives are often examined from a minority viewpoint. This dichotomy, he states, "tends to exclude complex power struggles in and around organizations, which may exhibit more messy empirical configurations than the dichotomy allows for" (Rasmussen, 2017, p. 171).

Gabriel (2017, p. 220) has coined the term *narrative ecologies* for "spaces where, by analogy to natural ecologies, different elements and populations of narrative emerge, interact, compete, adapt, develop and die". We suggest the media landscape to be one such ecology, and we study a delimited part of this narrative landscape: the region where the discursive struggle between journalism, civic information and strategic communication takes place. Gabriel (2017, p. 222) further suggests that [master] narratives and counter-narratives "can be thought of as co-constructing elements of narrative ecologies", and proposes that "different types of narrative ecologies can be viewed as fostering different configurations of narrative patterns".

In our analysis, we examine how advocates of journalism and organizational communication respectively define each of these activities – based on a shared interest in the journalistic processes and methods of operation – and how they position their activities in relation to each other, a discursive struggle which we here interpret as an expression of a shift in the balance of power between journalists and communicators. We thereby investigate an aspect of narratives which earlier tended to be obscured in many analyses, which is "how narratives intersect, relate to, challenge and reinforce each other" (Frandsen et al., 2017, p. 2).

Previous research: the master narrative of journalism

What we understand as the master narrative of journalism is expressed – created and recreated – in the daily professional practice, in journalistic products and in political debates in legacy media. It is also told by researchers. We do not understand this as a static narrative established once and for all but rather as a hegemonic narrative which is constantly negotiated.

In scholarly work the professionalization of journalism has been described as a process through which common ideas develop about who can be said to be a "real" journalist and what "real" journalism is (e.g. Deuze, 2005). In concert with this development, a professional identity built upon particular working ideals has been constructed. This means that a consensus of what constitutes the practice of professional journalism has been established. We therefore understand the master narrative of journalism as being closely intertwined with the professional identity of journalists – with their shared perceptions and evaluations of their work and assignments.

Deuze (2005), and also others, have identified a number of ideals that can be said to constitute the core of the journalistic profession. Five ideals in particular recur in studies of what unites journalists in their work and, according to Deuze (2005, p. 447), make up an "occupational ideology". Journalists:

1. provide a public service – they provide citizens with useful information;
2. are objective, neutral, fair and (thus) credible;
3. must be autonomous, free and independent;
4. have a sense of immediacy, actuality and speed;
5. have a sense of ethics, validity and legitimacy.

These widely cherished ideals manifest themselves in and form the journalistic work, create meaning, and act as a justification in the event of external criticism (cf. Wiik, 2010). They are recurrent in journalism in elective democracies all over the world, although they are applied in different, context-specific ways depending on culture and country (see Deuze, 2005, p. 445); for instance, a characteristic trait for Nordic journalists seems to be that they, to a remarkably high degree, see themselves as detached watchdogs, thereby stressing scrutiny as an essential journalistic task (Ahva et al., 2017).

In our analysis we use the master narrative of journalism presented above as a reference point. However, as stated earlier – and as suggested by our analysis – this master narrative is under attack. It is challenged by representatives of different narratives partaking in discursive struggles shaping the media landscape of tomorrow.

How to capture and analyze a discursive struggle

In order to investigate the discursive struggle concerning journalism, we conduct an analysis departing from a linguistic, social constructivist perspective, where language and narratives are seen as not simply mirroring a pre-existing reality but also expressing, shaping and actively constituting social realities (see Bruner, 1991). The narratological concepts *master narrative* and *counter-narrative* guide us in our analysis. To us, *narrative* is both a way to experience, structure and express reality, and an analytical concept which can be used to grasp and understand ongoing interactions. Essentially, a narrative can be defined as (a story about) a protagonist with a project, i.e. a protagonist striving to achieve a certain goal (Israel, 2010). A narrative has also – by uncountable researchers – been defined as a chain of events bound together by causality and intentionality, a definition implying that causes and reasons play a central role in narratives (e.g. Rossholm, 2004). A distinctive feature of narratives is values, which are expressed in and through the narrative, as well as in the act of telling (Rehnberg, 2014). Another constituent of narratives is problems; narratives tend to be built around conflicts that call for a solution (cf. Labov & Waletzky, 1967).

In order to understand the web of narratives, and specifically how the narratives relate to each other, we use three interrelated concepts: *intertextuality* and *recontextualization* (which have been used earlier in analysis of counter-narratives, see e.g. Johansen, 2017; Wolff Lundholt, 2017) as well as *provenance*. We understand *intertextuality* as "a relationship of co-presence between two texts or among several texts for example in quotes and allusions" (Wolff Lundholt, 2017, p. 49). Obviously, master-narratives and counter-narratives are intertextual by nature. In our analysis, we focus on the textual devices realizing this intertextuality in order to deconstrue the tissue of narratives. *Recontextualization* refers to the transferring of something from one (con)text to another (con)text (Linell, 1998). This something which is transferred might be a word, a concept, an element of a narrative or a narrative. The concept implies that the transferred object is given a somewhat different meaning in the new context, even if the object itself remains intact. The term *provenance* is used to highlight the fact that a transferred object carries meanings from its original context (Kress & van Leeuwen, 2001). This too implies that creation of meaning is tied to specific contexts, but while *rexontextualization* emphasizes the transfer and the new meaning arising from it, *provenance* foregrounds the meaning that can be tied to the source of the object transferred.

In our analysis, these three interrelated concepts have been used as interpretative tools on a macro level. In order to examine on a micro level how different narratives are constructed and positioned in relation to each other we have focused on a number of discursive resources which play a central role in the construction and argumentation of the texts analyzed. These resources, which we have distinguished inductively by making a close reading of the texts, are negations (e.g. *not*, *never*), adversative conjunctions (e.g. *but*), distance markers (e.g. quotation marks), emphasis markers (e.g. stressing of a word in oral communication), and specific wordings (e.g. a journalistic vocabulary). In the material of analyses these discursive resources are used to construe narrative elements, i.e. content elements essential for the narratives, such as key concepts (e.g. *democracy*) definitions and characterizations (of journalism and of VGRfokus), problem formulations, and reasons.

The launching of VGRfokus

The communication channel VGRfokus covers Västra Götaland, a geographical area and an administrative unity consisting of 49 municipalities in southwest Sweden. VGR is answerable to healthcare services and public transport as well as some cultural, environmental and educational issues in the region. Another of VGR's assignments is to contribute to growth and development in the area. VGR is governed by democratically elected politicians, and with more than 50,000 employees, it is one of Sweden's biggest employers.

At the time for our data collection, the editorial team of VGRfokus consisted of three communicators and was headed by an editor. Two of the team members were recruited from the leading regional newspaper. Above the editorial staff in the organizational structure was first the head of public relations, brand and media, and on the next level the director of communications and public affairs (more about the case of VGRfokus, see Grafström & Rehnberg, 2019).

In conjunction with the launching of VGRfokus on November 12, 2017 an article written by the communications director was published. When collecting material for the analysis, we used this article, hereinafter referred to as *the launching text*, as our point of departure. The launch attracted attention in legacy media; it functioned as a catalyst generating both news articles and critical opinion pieces. In several of these texts the communications director was interviewed, thereby given the opportunity to respond to the criticism. Further, a reply written by the communications director was published in legacy media. These articles, which we collected from the Nordic media database Retriever Research, using the search word *VGRfokus*, are included in our analysis material, in addition to the launching text. Altogether our analysis builds on 20 unique articles and 1 radio news report published in November 2017, whereof 10 are quoted and referred to specifically in our analysis (see Table 15.1).

The media landscape as a narrative jungle

Below we analyze the gradual emergence of a narrative jungle in three steps. First, we analyze the VGRfokus narrative as it is told by VGR in the launching text, and thereafter we focus on the reactions expressed by the opinion journalists. In the last section, we analyze the response of VGR's communications director as it is expressed in legacy media.

Table 15.1 Cited material of analysis – nine articles and one radio news report

Publication date	*Category*	*Title of outlet*	*Type of outlet*
November 12, 2017	opinion article	VGRfokus	county council communication channel
November 13, 2017	news article	Resumé	trade magazine
November 14, 2017	news article	Dagens Medicin	trade magazine
November 15, 2017	news report	Sveriges Radio P4 Skaraborg	regional radio channel
November 17, 2017	opinion article	Bohusläningen	local newspaper
November 18, 2017	opinion article	GT	regional tabloid
November 20, 2017	opinion article	Smålänningen*	local newspaper
November 21, 2017	opinion article**	Medievärlden	trade magazine
November 23, 2017	news article	Dagens Samhälle	trade magazine
November 25, 2017	opinion article	Östersunds-Posten	local newspaper

* One of the articles included in the material was published first on the news site Altinget and then in 10 local newspapers, starting with *Smålänningen*.

** Reply by VGR.

VGRfokus: a parallel narrative to the master narrative of journalism

The launching text, entitled "Editorial: Why VGR is starting its own news site", is manifesto-like and presented the initiative to start a new type of communication channel. It was published under the heading Editorials on VGRfokus' website, whose appearance and structure resemble a legacy news site, with content classified as Care, Politics, Traffic, Business, and Culture & Entertainment.

The launching text gives a number of reasons for why the site is being launched. One is that VGR is a large organization with a broad scope of activities which affect many people: "the nature and breadth of our business deserves to be made visible". It is stated to be a problem that journalists do not write about the county council often enough:

> If the journalists do not write about the county council, how will residents have an insight into our activities? How can our elected politicians tell their voters what they have achieved?
>
> *(VGRfokus; our underlining)*

The use of the negation *not* in the quotation above indicates that journalists should indeed write about the county council. One of the implied tasks of journalism, according to the quotation, is to give residents an insight into the activities of public authorities and to let voters know what the elected politicians have achieved, in other words to fill a core function in upholding a democratic society. But, according to the director, the editorial staff of the local newspapers do not have the time, knowledge or commitment to write about VGR on a regular basis.

A further (implicit) reason to launch VGRfokus is that the region wants VGR to be highlighted in more and other ways than is done in legacy media. This can be seen in the assertion that while it is true that scandals in the care services are reported almost every week, "VGR is a large actor that can be highlighted in many different ways". More or less explicitly today's journalism is here accused of not giving a full and broad image of reality. An additional alleged reason for launching VGRfokus is that "utter falsehoods" are sometimes spread online. VGRfokus is seen by the region as a means to counter this disinformation, and democracy is thus explicitly used as an argument to justify the existence of VGRfokus:

> It is not unusual to see utter falsehoods being spread online, which also shows clearly that we need our own news site where we can guarantee that the information is correct. As one of the institutions in a Swedish democracy, that is our responsibility.
>
> *(VGRfokus)*

Given that the core of a narrative is a protagonist with a project, VGR could in the launching text be discerned as a hero striving to reach out with correct, straightforward and interesting information about the county council in order to give a fuller and more balanced image than legacy media do today. But the reasons for launching VGRfokus could also be interpreted as a way to (more or less explicitly) delegitimize the achievements of today's journalism, i.e. to criticize journalists for not fulfilling their professional task properly. VGRfokus is thereby challenging journalists in their role as rightful representatives of the master narrative of journalism, while presenting itself as an appropriate candidate to shoulder at least part of the journalistic mantle.

In the launching text VGRfokus is described both as a "result of the modern media development" and as a partaker in the ongoing transformation of the media landscape. It is consistently termed a *news site* and said to be run by an "autonomous editorial staff of public servants". The director insists that he, in the role of publisher, only makes editorial decisions when the editor asks him to do so. He further points out that what is published on the site must be credible and have news value, and that both difficult questions and causes for celebration will be reported.

The launching text echoes all the values, which, according to Deuze (2005), are shared by the majority of the world's journalists and which are also reflected in journalistic publishing regulations all over the world: public service, objectivity, autonomy, immediacy, and ethics. Further, transparency, credibility, responsibility, correctness and democracy are here presented as essential values and elements of the VGRfokus narrative. Obviously, the resemblance to the cornerstones of the master narrative of journalism is striking.

At the same time as VGR lays claim to several of journalism's characteristics – the production form, the way of working, the organization form (with a publisher), the vocabulary (*editorial, news value, editorial staff, publisher*) and the professional ideals – the director takes precautions not to present VGRfokus as a threat to legacy media. The rhetorical question "Will VGRfokus be competing with traditional news media?" is followed by a denial:

> No, but we will be a complement and a place where the media can find – and our residents be given – clear, credible and easy-to-read information. But a public service cannot scrutinize itself, that is the job of the journalist. We will, however, not be afraid to address issues which may lead to conflict.
>
> *(VGRfokus; our underlining)*

The initial negation (*No*) makes it clear that VGRfokus will not compete with legacy media. However, it is followed by an adversative conjunction (*but*) modifiying the assurance; the statement that VGRfokus will not compete with journalism would have been more convincing had the conjunction not been there. A second adversative conjunction (*But*) is used to chisel out the difference between journalism and VGRfokus, namely that scrutinizing is an exclusively journalistic task. In the last sentence of the quotation the same discursive resources are used not only to modify the preceding statement but also to characterize VGRfokus: here one function of the adversative conjunction (*however*) and the negation (*not*) is to distance VGRfokus from the traditional image of public relations and to instead align it with a recurrent ideal typical description of journalism.

The launching text even implies that the ambition of VGRfokus to some extent is to do a better journalistic job than today's editorial offices; the negation in the following quotation fills the function to establish a contrast between VGRfokus and legacy media, promoting VGRfokus as the more journalistic publication in terms of (implied) traditional journalistic values:

> We will give a voice to all those involved and provide a context that today's editorial staffs are not able to do to the extent desired.
>
> *(VGRfokus; our underlining)*

So, what actually distinguishes VGRfokus from journalism? The only difference mentioned in the launching text is that a public authority cannot scrutinize itself; scrutiny of the public sector is presented as an exclusive task for journalists. At the same time the analysis above shows how negations and adversative conjunctions are used in an intrinsic way to grind down this allegedly sharp difference between journalism and communication and to carve out a yellow brick road for VGRfokus through the narrative jungle of today's media landscape.

It is usually claimed that narratives are based on an underlying problem (e.g. Labov & Waletzky, 1967). How the problem is perceived and portrayed is crucial for the narrative being construed. In the VGRfokus narrative, the problem is the prevailing media situation, which is characterized by the weakened position of legacy media and not least the inability of journalists to cover the county council. VGRfokus is presented as a solution. The result is that certain tendencies towards its positioning as a counter-narrative can be. This is in line with Fine and Harris (2001, p. 13), who state that counter-narratives "expose the construction of the dominant story by suggesting how else it could be told". At the same time – and this may seem contradictory – since so many of its characteristics have been appropriated from journalism, VGRfokus can be interpreted as an attempt by VGR to include part of their public relations in the journalistic master narrative. Another way to interpret this tendency (or strategy) of VGRfokus to lend (or take or steal, depending on perspective) credibility from journalism through appropriating journalistic features is in terms of *provenance* (Kress & van Leeuwen, 2001).

Positioning VGRfokus strategic as a counter-narrative to defend the master narrative of journalism

Even though some tendencies could be discerned already in the launching text, the real transformation of VGRfokus from an aspiring parallel narrative to a counter-narrative is made in and through the opinion pieces, where a number of discursive resources are used to position VGRfokus as a narrative that does not ring true with the master narrative of journalism. The opinion journalists position themselves not only as representatives but also as defenders of the master narrative of journalism. The project of the opinion writers thus becomes to defend the master narrative of journalism by revealing the true nature of VGRfokus that is by convincing the readers that VGRfokus is not a parallel narrative to the master narrative of journalism but rather a counter-narrative.

The following quotation, containing a characterization of VGRfokus, is a clear example of a definition used in order to reposition the VGRfokus narrative:

> I would say that it [VGRfokus] is, rather, an example of how authorities have misunderstood the concept of credible news flow. It's an attempt to dress communication and information up as journalism.
>
> *(Östersunds-Posten)*

As in the launching text, today's media situation, with declining resources for legacy media, is seen as a dilemma; yet in the opinion articles it is still VGRfokus that is construed as the main problem. Firstly, there are insinuations that VGRfokus consists of promotion material, treacherously dressed up as journalism. To take an example, it is claimed in one of the articles that VGRfokus' mission is to "cement the picture of the region's activities" (Smålänningen). Secondly, there are fears that the readers/residents might not understand that VGRfokus is not journalism. Thirdly, there are concerns that the new communication channel will not only further blur the already vague border between journalism and strategic communication but also, in a worst-case-scenario, lead to a reinforced contempt for journalism. Fourthly, the fear is raised that VGRfokus and similar publications might in the long term replace journalism. In one article it is even claimed that VGRfokus is nothing less than an example of "public sector-financed media criticism" (GT).

Problem representations constitute both intertextual links and matters of recontextualization in the text chain consisting of the launching text and the ensuing opinion articles. The fact that today's media landscape has serious problems is a fundamental narrative element appearing not only in the VGRfokus narrative as it is presented in the launching text, but also in the opinion articles. However, the most disturbing problem as presented in the opinion articles is VGRfokus – meaning that VGRfokus is recontextualized from being a solution in the launching text to being the main problem in the opinion articles.

The opinion articles contain many quotations from the launching text, some literal and others paraphrased or distorted (depending on whose perspective is adopted). These quotations represent a kind of easily identifiable intertextual links. Another obvious intertextual relation is summaries of the content. But the opinion articles also contain many allusions to the launching text, echoes which can be discerned for example in the form of contradictions, expressed with the help of negations and adversative conjunctions. Also, distance markers are used as tools when the opinion journalists formulate their criticism of VGRfokus:

> Västra Götalandsregionen [VGR] has started what they call a news site. But it is not independent journalism.
>
> *(Bohusläningen; our underlinings)*

Negations and adversative conjunctions are used repeatedly in the opinion articles, to draw a clear line between journalism on the one hand and information and (strategic) communication on the other hand – and to make it clear to the readers that VGRfokus is not (pure) journalism, as in the quotation above. That the word *news* is something which is (at least according to the writer behind the quotation) normally associated with journalism is made clear both by the phrase *what they call*, which marks distance, and the conjunction *But*. The quotation also contains a formulation worth some extra attention, since it says something essential about the concept of journalism. The phrase *independent journalism* indicates that the concept of journalism today does not naturally imply independence, since this is a characteristic that needs to be explicitly stated. Further, that the attribute *independent* needs to be stated also indicates that in the current situation it might not be safe to establish that VGRfokus has nothing at all to do with journalism.

The fact that the opinion articles so insistently claim that VGRfokus is not journalism can be seen in part as a reaction against the fact that the launching text is unclear on that point; the launching text never explicitly states that VGRfokus is not journalism. It can also be seen as a reaction to the fact that VGRfokus has borrowed – or appropriated – many features from journalism. In and through expressing this clarification, the opinion articles reinforce the impression that VGRfokus is a counter-narrative to the master narrative of journalism.

The use of distance markers indicates that the advocates of VGRfokus use, unreasonably, a journalistic vocabulary which the opinion journalists do not want to use in relation to VGRfokus; adopting this vocabulary would mean they were taking part in construing VGR's version of the VGRfokus narrative. In the opinion articles, distance is marked not only by the use of phrases but also by placing quotation marks around words such as *editorial*, *news media* and *autonomous*. The distance markers imply not only dissociation, but also disqualification of certain central elements in the VGRfokus narrative, and thereby disqualification of the narrative's very foundations. The distance markers also contribute to greater polarization: writing "what they call a news site" implies not only that it is not in reality a news site but also that there are two parties with differing views – *they*, who unreasonably use a certain vocabulary and – by implication – *we*, who have every right to use it.

Not only wording is targeted by the opinion writers, but also appearance and structural arrangements behind VGRfokus, as in the following quotation:

> Lagersten is clear here that this is a question of communication, not independent journalism. Yet VGRfokus looks like a news site and they have also applied for authorization to publish from the Swedish Post and Telecom Authority. But readers must be aware that it is actually the region's officers who have repackaged the message they want to send so that it looks like a piece of journalism.
>
> *(Bohusläningen)*

In sum, the main problem, as it is formulated in the opinion pieces, is the fact the VGRfokus makes allegedly unrightful journalistic claims. The opinion journalists view (the launching of) VGRfokus as a means to undermine trust in journalism and, even more, as a treacherous way of unreasonably borrowing credibility from journalism. This in turn poses a threat to the master narrative of journalism. What the opinion journalists are doing is arguing that the master narrative of journalism cannot be told in the way that it is being done in and by VGRfokus.

At the same time as the opinion journalists position VGRfokus as a counter-narrative, they (re)formulate and defend the master narrative of journalism. They now include VGRfokus as an element of this master narrative, more specifically as an opponent, which means that yet another recontextualization has taken place.

Retelling the narratives in a discursive struggle

The communications director – in answering the criticism leveled against VGRfokus – retells and partially reformulates both the VGRfokus narrative and the master narrative of journalism. In and through comments reported or published in legacy media, the director defends VGRfokus. He develops and chisels out the original VGRfokus narrative and he even goes to attack. Like the opinion journalists, he asserts that VGRfokus is not journalism:

> This is communication, not journalism

(GT; our underlining). The fact that the director makes such a clear statement, using a negation to maintain a distinction between communication and journalism, is one difference compared to his original statements in the launching text. The narrative of VGRfokus as told by the director thus changes when it meets other narratives – in the discursive struggle, certain aspects become clearer while at the same time being ascribed new meaning.

In the next example, first a negation is used to clarify what VGR cannot do, and then an adversative conjunction is used to make clear what the organization is expected to live up to:

> An authority cannot scrutinize itself. […] However, we do have a duty of information.
>
> *(Sveriges Radio P4 Skaraborg; our underlinings)*

As in the launching text, scrutiny is presented as an essential difference between journalism and communication, but in the quotation above the director makes the distinction even clearer by highlighting VGR's duty of *information*. In the next quotation the distinction is sharpened, since the director puts forward a further distinguishing factor, namely that the task of VGRfokus is to support political goals:

> There are political goals which I am expected to support, but I do this by means of a credible, transparent and well-thought-out product.
>
> *(Dagens Samhälle; our underlining)*

The use of *but* in the quotation above indicates that it is unexpected, unusual, or in some other way remarkable that political goals are supported via a "credible, transparent, and well-thought-out product". VGRfokus is thereby implicitly presented as a pioneer. This example thus shows how an adversative conjunction is used to chisel out a clearer identity for VGRfokus.

Unlike the opinion journalists, who state that the political goals put VGRfokus' credibility as a news channel at risk, the director claims that the political goals imply that VGRfokus' editorial staff must not be afraid to tackle "difficult questions":

> My duty as a communications director is to support the political goals. VGRfokus is one way to do this and a prerequisite is that we also dare to tackle difficult questions.
>
> *(Resumé)*

This reinterpretation of political goals can be seen as a recontextualization of a narrative element. The recontextualization of specific terms and elements of content, as illustrated above, contributes to an increased polarization: VGRfokus and the master narrative of journalism are portrayed in and through this transformation of meanings as more apart than in the launching text, something which could be seen as a consequence of the director being forced to step in and make distinctions that were not originally his business.

Although the director is about clear that VGRfokus is not journalism, a number of the launching text's journalistic connotations are also found in his replies. Among other things, he says that the staff of VGRfokus will take an "editorial approach" to news (Resumé) and that they will work with "news evaluation, angles and other such things" (Dagens Medicin).

The director maintains that the problem is the declining resources of legacy media. He even sharpens this problem formulation while at the same time rejecting the problem formulation put forward by the opinon journalists, as can be seen in the following quotation, taken from a radio news report in which the director was interviewed:

> it is a problem for society that the resources media houses and journalism have today for scrutiny are declining, and I think that's a genuine problem for society
>
> *(Sveriges Radio P4 Skaraborg)*

The word *genuine* is pronounced with emphasis, which implies that the problem discussed earlier in the interview (namely a potential risk of a shift in power between legacy media and communication departments) is not genuine – perhaps an imaginary, contrived or make-believe problem?

In a written debate between the director and the president of the Swedish Union of Journalists, the director points out the president's numerous failings. According to the director, the president does not communicate the whole picture, he does not quote in a correct way, and he does not take the trouble to check available sources. These accusations, which are aimed at not just anyone but at the president of the Union of Journalists, can be interpreted as a criticism of journalism itself. The impression that the main problem is not VGRfokus but the malpractices of journalism is reinforced by the following statement made by the communications director and targeting the president:

> VGRfokus is not in competition with traditional media. The problem facing the Union of Journalists is not that large authorities are developing forms for their own communication, but the way the media industry is developing. It might be good to have straw men but they won't help [NN's] difficult and important task of upholding Swedish journalism.
>
> *(Medievärlden)*

In this way the director continues to build the VGRfokus narrative as a parallel narrative to the master narrative of journalism. At the same time, he positions the narrative as more of a contrast to the master narrative of journalism, thereby contributing to a polarization. VGRfokus is still described as a complement to journalism, but the picture that emerges is in fact the picture of a playing field with two teams – communicators (who uphold and defend democracy) and journalists (who have inadequate resources and who fail to carry out their duties in a proper way). Yet at the same time as this polarization becomes more apparent, the boundary between both teams remains blurred, since the director continues to talk about VGRfokus in journalistic terms while at the same time claiming that VGRfokus is not journalism.

Concluding discussion

In this chapter we have shown a dynamic that is more complex than the development of a counter-narrative in opposition to a master narrative. Rather, in our study the narratives develop and are chiseled out in an interplay where the narrators do not always have the power over their own narratives. The counter-narrative in focus does not develop in opposition to the master narrative but becomes a counter-narrative first when it is positioned as such by actors defending the master narrative.

Our analysis demonstrates that in some contexts it is necessary to take a step back from the normative view which is inherent in the pair of concepts *master narrative* and *counter-narrative*, where the master narrative is implicitly seen as "evil" and the counter-narrative as "good", formulated and lived by the weaker, even oppressed, party (cf. Rasmussen, 2017). The narrations that we examine, and the context in which they are played out, encourage a less normative – and less dualistic – approach. The narratives emerge and are transformed throughout the discursive struggle, and it is not a question of a simple dichotomy but rather of a *narrative jungle* (Gabriel, 2017, p. 220).

Further, our analysis suggests that the tissue of narratives surrounding a professional institution becomes even more complex when there is no strong master narrative. The struggle itself tends to make the narratives more polemic. We therefore suggest that it might be a fruitful analytical perspective to focus on *how* different actors retell and position specific narratives, rather than to assume that the narratives themselves *are*, for example, counter-narratives.

We also illustrate how the concepts of *master narrative* and *counter-narrative* can be used to understand ongoing societal change. While focusing on the reorganization of the media landscape, we have shown how recontextualizations are a distinctive feature of the discursive struggle. It is not only specific narrative elements and concepts that are recontextualized in the fabric of narratives, but also journalism as such – its rhetoric as well as its methods and forms are recontextualized in the VGRfokus narrative. And this, we argue, can be seen as the epicenter of the discursive struggle. Journalism is not only about rhetoric, methods and forms, but also very much about values such as credibility, public welfare, and 'standing with the individual against the powerful'. When authorities dress up their information as journalism - an act whose logic is captured by and made visible with the help of the term *provenance* - representatives and advocates of journalism may therefore feel that fundamental journalistic and democratic values are threatened.

Journalistic norms and ideals are suggested to be reinforced when under threat. Wiik (2010, p. 196) shows that along with the weakened position of journalism, Swedish journalists have become increasingly protective of traditional values, and she argues that "professional ideals are being used as symbolic capital in the struggle to maintain professional boundaries". Our analysis of the discursive struggle supports her results. A different picture might, however, emerge from an analysis of enacted narratives. A next step would therefore be to examine how and to what extent references are made to VGRfokus in everyday news coverage (see Rehnberg & Grafström, 2020), as well as how and to what extent content from VGRfokus is recontextualized in legacy media channels. Another way would be to focus on what is communicated in and through VGRfokus and to what extent this corresponds with the stated ambitions. The addition of such analyses would allow us to gain a deeper understanding of the dynamics behind the emergence of narratives – not least counter-narratives – in transforming "narrative jungles".

References

Ahva, L., van Dalen, A., Hovden, J.F., Kolbeins, G.H., Löfgren Nilsson, M., Morten, S., & Väliverronen, J. (2017). A welfare state of mind?: Nordic journalists' conception of their role and autonomy in international context. *Journalism Studies, 18*(5), 595–613.

Bamberg, M.G.W., & Andrews, M. (Eds.). (2004). *Considering counter-narratives: Narrating, resisting, making sense.* Amsterdam: John Benjamins.

Bruner, J. (1991). *Acts of meaning.* Cambridge, MA: Harvard University Press.

Deuze, M. (2005). What is journalism?: Professional identity and ideology of journalists reconsidered. *Journalism, 6*(4), 442–464.

Fine, M., & Harris, A. (2001). *Under the covers: Theorizing the politics of counter stories.* London: Lawrence & Wishart.

Frandsen, S., Wolff Lundholt, M., & Kuhn, T. (2017). Introduction. In S. Frandsen, T. Kuhn, & M. Wolff Lundholt (Eds.), *Counter-narratives and organization* (pp. 1–13). New York, NY: Routledge.

Gabriel, Y. (2017). Narrative ecologies and the role of counter-narratives: The case of nostalgic stories and conspiracy theories. In S. Frandsen, T. Kuhn, & M. Wolff Lundholt (Eds.), *Counter-narratives and organization* (pp. 208–225). New York, NY: Routledge.

Grafström, M., & Rehnberg, H.S. (2019). Public organizations as news producers – an odd species in the local media landscape. *Nordicom Review, 40*(2).

Humle, D.M., & Frandsen, S. (2017). Organizational identity negotiations through dominant and counter-narratives. In S. Frandsen, T. Kuhn, & M. Wolff Lundholt (Eds.), *Counter-narratives and organization* (pp. 105–128). New York, NY: Routledge.

Israel, S.B. (2010). Inter-action movies: Multi-protagonist films and relationism. In M. Grishakova, & M.-L. Ryan (Eds.), *Intermediality and storytelling* (pp. 122–146). New York, NY: De Gruyter.

Johansen, S.T. (2017). Countering the "natural" organization self on social media. In S. Frandsen, T. Kuhn, & M. Wolff Lundholt (Eds.), *Counter-narratives and organization* (pp. 64–82). New York, NY: Routledge.

Kress, G., & Van Leeuwen, T. (2001). *Multimodal discourse: The modes and media of contemporary communication.* London: Arnold.

Labov, W., & Waletzky, J. (1967). Narrative analysis: Oral versions of personal experience. In J. Helm (Ed.), *Essays on the verbal and visual arts: Proceedings of the 1966 annual spring meeting of the American ethnological society* (pp. 219–247). Seattle, WA: The Inst.

Linell, P. (1998). Discourse across boundaries: On recontextualizations and the blending of voices in professional discourse. *Text, 18*(2), 143–157.

Nelson, H.L. (2001). *Damaged identities, narrative repair.* Cornell, NY: Cornell University Press.

Mumby, D.K. (1987). The political function of narrative in organizations. *Communication Monographs, 54*(2), 113–127.

Norlyk, B. (2017). Designer or Entrepreneur?: Counter-narrative in cross-cultural change. In S. Frandsen, T. Kuhn, & M. Wolff Lundholt (Eds.), *Counter-narratives and organization* (pp. 155–170). New York, NY: Routledge.

Rasmussen, R.K. (2017). Rethinking counter-narratives in studies of organizational texts and practices. In S. Frandsen, T. Kuhn, & M. Wolff Lundholt (Eds.), *Counter-narratives and organization* (pp. 171–192). New York, NY: Routledge.

Rehnberg, H.S. (2014). *Organisationer berättar: Narrativitet som resurs i strategisk kommunikation.* [When organizations tell stories: Narrativity as a resource in strategic communication.] Doctoral Dissertation. Uppsala University, Uppsala, Sweden.

Rehnberg, H.S. & Grafström, M. (2020). Uppluckrade gränser-kommunikatören som journalist? [Blurred boundaries - the communicator as a journalist?] In E. Gardeström & H.S. Rehnberg (Eds.), *Vad är journalistik?* [What is journalism?] (pp. 27–39). Huddinge: University of Södertörn.

Ricœur, P. (1991). *Narrative and interpretation.* New York, NY: Routledge.

Rossholm, G. (2004). Koherens och direkthet. [Coherens and directness]. *Tidskrift för litteraturvetenskap, 2004*(3–4), 22–37.

Wiik, J. (2010). *Journalism in transition: The professional identity of Swedish journalists.* Doctoral Dissertation. Gothenburg University, Gothenburg, Sweden.

Wolff Lundholt, M. (2017). Counter-narratives and organizational crisis: How LEGO bricks became a slippery business. In S. Frandsen, T. Kuhn, & M. Wolff Lundholt (Eds.), *Counter-narratives and organization* (pp. 43–63). New York, NY: Routledge.

Part IV

Counter-narratives and education

16

Countering the master-narrative of "good parenting"?

Non-academic parents' stories about choosing a secondary school for their child

Denise Klinge, Sören Carlson and Lena Kahle

Introduction

In recent decades, various societal developments have changed perceptions of and expectations towards parenting in many societies. These changes have given rise to a new kind of master-narrative about parenting, focused on the need for "good" parenting, that is, on a parental approach that seeks to make the "right" choices for one's child and to ensure her or his constant (educational) cultivation. Taking into consideration that families' endowment with different forms of economic, cultural and social capital differs due to their class position (Bourdieu, 1984, 1986), we argue that some parents, especially those from the upper and middle classes, should find it easier to relate to the master-narrative of constant educational cultivation than parents from other classes. In so doing, we do not claim that class differences cause parents to differ in their general narrative abilities. Rather, we contend that class affects how well people can identify and conform with certain (master-) narratives.

One central playing field in which the master-narrative of "good" parenting unfolds its full power is the issue of school choice, which in many countries is crucial for children's further education and life trajectory (Montt, 2011). In this context, we ask to what extent parents with a non-academic or working-class background develop counter-narratives (cf. Bamberg, 2004a) to this dominant master-narrative of "good" parenting. To address this question, we analyze narratives of secondary-school choice among non-academic parents by drawing on ideas in narrative theory, developed by Bamberg (2004a) and Schütze (1983, 1987).

In the pages below, we first give an overview of the state of research on what we regard as the master-narrative of "good" parenting, based on research on parenting and on images of what constitutes a "good" childhood. Focusing more specifically on the issue of school choice as one arena of "good" parenting, we move on to explain our methodical and methodological approach, arguing that the analysis of counter-narratives may be enriched by drawing on Schütze's idea of text structure analysis. We then present our analysis and conclude by offering some insight into how such an approach allows for a more detailed understanding of how actors position themselves vis-à-vis specific master- and counter-narratives.

The master-narrative of "good parenting" in education

A specific and widely reinforced expectation about parents' role in and responsibility for their children's care and education has emerged over the last decades. This is the result of various political, societal and scientific developments, *inter alia*, changed understandings of the societal role of education (now increasingly seen as a means to generate human capital, serving labor market needs), the rise of so-called evidence-based research, and a new understanding of children as being competent and eager to learn, thus necessitating stimulation for learning from an early age (Gillies, 2012; Lange & Thiessen, 2018).

As a result of these developments, the role of families in rearing and educating children has taken center stage and shifted from being a predominantly private concern to a public one (Gillies, 2012, p. 15). Today more than ever, education is often perceived as a parental responsibility, which means that parents are expected to ensure a purposeful, education-oriented cultivation of their children (Lange & Thiessen, 2018). Given this specific shift in perceptions of and expectations towards parents' role, one can also speak here of a master-narrative of "good parenting" in the area of education, one that frames parental self-perceptions and identities and – to some extent – prescribes specific kinds of behaviors (cf. Bamberg, 2004a).

While generally directed towards *all* parents, this master-narrative tends to obscure the fact that parents' ability to relate to this normative construction of "good parenting" differs by social class background (Bischoff & Betz, 2015, p. 264). Following Bourdieu (1986), one can say that these differences stem from families' unequal economic, cultural and social capital, that is, their possession (or lack) of wealth and income, their incorporated knowledge, preferences and dispositions (*habitus*) and their social relations. Thus, parents not only differ with respect to the resources they can draw on, but also in terms of their education-related habits, practices and perceptions (cf. also Betz, 2012, p. 117).[1]

According to Lareau (2002), middle-class families display a child-rearing approach that can be characterized as "concerted cultivation". Such parents, she suggests, create a stimulating learning environment for their children by organizing age-specific leisure activities for them and actively fostering each child's specific talents and skills (cf. also Carlson, Gerhards, & Hans, 2017; Lange & Thiessen, 2018; Vincent & Ball, 2007). They also tend to raise criticisms with and to intervene on their children's behalf vis-à-vis institutions such as schools, if they perceive this as necessary (Lareau, 2002).

By contrast, working-class families follow a child-rearing approach based on the idea of "natural growth", which means that while they care for their children, they "believe that as long as they provide love, food, and safety, their children will grow and thrive. They do not focus on developing their children's special talents" (Lareau, 2002, pp. 748–749). As a result, such families "are far less likely to involve their children in enrichment activities [..., and] to see their children as a project for development. Instead, the children just *are*, with characteristics, skills and talent being understood as more fixed and static" (Vincent & Ball, 2007, p. 1068, emphasis in original). Thus, Gillies (2008) concludes that working-class parents basically have a different understanding of their role and duties towards their children that does not easily align itself with official constructions of "good parenting". Furthermore, working-class parents tend to feel more dependent on educational institutions and to experience powerlessness and frustration more easily than do their middle-class peers (Lareau, 2002). Unsurprisingly, Lange and Thiessen (2018, p. 286) thus note that middle-class parents are more likely to embrace this specific master-narrative than lower-class parents do, who are more prone to experience overload, resignation and self-inefficacy when subjected in equal measure to such education-related demands.

Despite this solid research confirming class-related differences in education, which in turn highlights parents' unequal possibilities to live up to the master-narrative of "good parenting", we do not know much about the extent to which parents – especially from a non-academic or working-class background – actually subscribe to this master-narrative, or whether there are also signs of resistance (Gillies, 2012, p. 25). In other words: how far do such parents develop counter-narratives (cf. Bamberg, 2004a; Lundholt, Maagaard, & Piekut, 2018) to this dominant imagination of "good parenting" that would allow them to position themselves differently from the otherwise therewith associated expectations?

Parental school choice as a matter of "good parenting"

One important issue through which the master-narrative of "good parenting" plays out in practice is school choice. Especially in countries with highly tracked secondary school systems, where different school types offer either vocationally or academically oriented degrees and rarely enable students to switch from one type of schooling to another, deciding for a specific type of school is generally seen as having far-reaching consequences for the child's further educational and occupational trajectory (cf. Allmendinger, 1989; Kerckhoff, 2001). Thus, from the perspective of the master-narrative of "good parenting", parents are deemed responsible for making "good", i.e. "informed" and "appropriate" decisions about their child's schooling.

Similar to child-rearing at the preschool level, parents' choice of schools is closely linked to their social class and inequality. Research has repeatedly and consistently shown that such decisions depend greatly on the social background of parents (for example, Blossfeld & Shavit, 1993). Even for students who present equal levels of academic achievement, parents with higher social status are more likely to send their children to more academically demanding school types than parents with lower social status (Dumont, Klinge, & Maaz, 2019). Furthermore, parents' differing educational orientations not only affect their school choices for their children; their orientations also affect the specific knowledge, talents and abilities that those children bring with them into the school system (Busse, 2010). Research that uses social status as an indicator of social background shows that parents with a high socioeconomic status tend to support their children more in the areas of homework and learning than do parents whose socioeconomic status is relatively low (Baker & Stevenson, 1986). Parents of higher status also establish a home learning culture for their children that fits well with the demands of more academically stringent school types, and they also tend to know more about the school system itself (Hatcher, 1998; Schümer, Tillmann, & Weiß, 2004). Other research that employs a Bourdieusian, milieu-specific perspective highlights that parents choose school types that are highly consistent with their own cultural practices, knowledge and expectations (Klinge, 2016).

This short overview of the research on school choice and social inequality thus shows that while all parents are subjected to the master-narrative of "good parenting" and the associated expectations, they nevertheless start out from very different positions, depending on their social class background. Parents from higher versus lower classes differ not only in terms of their capital endowment (Bourdieu, 1986), but also in their general expectations and orientations in relation to education and schooling (Klinge, 2016). The findings raise questions as to how parents from a non-academic background are able to negotiate this master-narrative when recounting their choice of school for their children, and whether they can develop a counter-narrative that conveys their own expectations and ideas in this context.

Methodology: reconstructing counter-narratives via text structure analysis

Before we turn to a description of our interview data and the methods we chose for their analysis, some methodological comments on how we approach the issue of counter-narratives are in order. Bamberg (2004a) frames narratives in a context of social expectations about how knowable, tellable and doable certain courses of action are. But countering these expectations is not easy to accomplish because "master-narratives are setting up sequences of actions and events as routines and as such have a tendency to 'normalize' and 'naturalize'" (Bamberg, 2004a, p. 360). It is thus easier, we would argue, for parents with an academic background to adapt to and interpret this master-narrative in relation to their own practices, experiences and resources than for parents from other backgrounds.

To the act of constructing story content, Bamberg (2004b, p. 135) adds "the concept of positioning [...], identities to the speaking (storytelling) subject". Positioning as the negotiation of one's position in society is an important empirical and theoretical point of reference in migration research (e.g. Anthias, 2009), but it can also be applied to the field of educational inequalities. Anthias (2009, p. 243) differentiates between social position "as a set of effectivities: as outcome" and social positioning "as a set of practices, actions and meanings: as process" (emphasis in original). Thus, "position" is an effective social ascription, whereas "positioning" is a participatory act in which social positions are interpreted, for example through biography and self-representation. Analyzing narrative interviews with parents who recount the secondary school choices they made for their children thus allows us to trace such positioning. The concept of counter-narrative goes along with positioning. During the interview's narrative process, individual positioning is negotiated and subjected to processes of transformation against socio-structural positions that may arise during the course of the narration (cf. Kahle, 2017, p. 16). The questions posed are "[h]ow are the characters positioned in relation to one another [...]? How does the speaker position him- or herself to the audience? [...] How do narrators position themselves to themselves?" (Bamberg, 1997, p. 337; quote originally in italics). In analyzing parental narratives of school choice, we thus focus on this conflicting field between position and positioning in relation to the described master-narrative and possible counter-narratives.

This leads to the question of how to analyze these different acts of positioning, and how to identify instances of counter-narrative vis-à-vis the identified master-narrative. For this, Bamberg (2004a, pp. 366–367) suggests reconstructing two levels of positioning, which refer to the content of the story and its represented characters, respectively. Based on that, one can then reconstruct the ideological master-narratives the interviewees work up a position within (ibid., p. 367). Other than that, Bamberg's remarks on the analysis of counter-narratives remain rather general, however. For this reason, we also draw on Schütze's (1983) narration theory when analyzing how non-academic parents refer to the process of school choice and how they position themselves within the master-narrative, with its expectation of making "good" educational decisions.

Schütze (1987, p. 14) assumes that spontaneous – that is, unprepared – narrations are most likely to reproduce the past experience if the speaker uses a narrative format to convey that experience, because then the so-called "constraints of narration" are most likely to set in, which "force" the narrator to be as detailed, explicit and comprehensive as possible (Kallmeyer & Schütze, 1977). However, present-day narrations about the past are always entangled with evaluation and argumentation, since experiences in a story arrangement are selected, organized and evaluated (Riessman, 2006, p. 186). As a result, not only narrative but also descriptive, argumentative and evaluative communication schemes are used.[2] In contrast to narrative forms, argumentation and evaluation are most likely related to the present (Schütze, 1987, p. 149). According to Schütze

(2016, pp. 67–68), there are good reasons for using argumentation in overall narrations. Non-narrative texts serve not only to explain complex contexts to the listener, but also to illustrate basic principles and problems of life and to defend one's narrative presentation (for a further analysis of why argumentation and evaluation may predominate in narrative interviews, cf. Carlson, Kahle, & Klinge, 2017). Furthermore, argumentations express biographical issues that have not yet been processed, and do not essentially serve to represent the dominant, thematically focused chain of events and experiences (Schütze, 1984, p. 98). Instead, they bring to light elements of the narrator's orientation, explanation and/or biography or identity theory that serve to justify the narrative (ibid., p. 92).

For these reasons, we would expect argumentation and evaluation to appear more often in overall narrations of an experience or event if there is a habitual distance towards a specific master-narrative. One may also say: the more closely one's own experiences align with a specific master-narrative, the easier it should be to render those experiences in narrative form, that is, narrative schemes of communication should prevail over argumentative or evaluative ones. In view of our previous discussion of the master-narrative of "good parenting", its relationship to school choice and its inherent interlinkage with social class and inequality, we would thus expect non-academic parents to rely quite strongly on argumentation and evaluation in their overall narratives about how and why they chose a specific type of secondary school for their children. If true, this could be interpreted as an attempt to conform to the underlying master-narrative of "good parenting" or – conversely – an effort to lay forth the parent's own conceptions vis-à-vis a master- narrative that they may view as not quite "fitting". Drawing on Bamberg (2004a) and Schütze (1983, 1987, 2016), we thus propose to reconstruct counter-narratives by examining how this "struggle" between master-narrative and counter-narrative(s), between position and positioning, plays out on the level of the actual text structure, that is, through the use of different communication schemes.

Context, data and methods

For the analysis, we draw on interview material from a study on parental decision-making related to secondary schooling in Germany (Klinge, 2016), which was based on 25 narrative interviews with parents of different social backgrounds. In order to allow for a better understanding of our analysis, it needs to be highlighted in advance that in Germany the transition into secondary school is organized via a comparatively rigid and early tracking system (Shavit & Müller, 2000). Once children are 10 to 12 years old, parents must decide whether they should attend the "Gymnasium" (a higher, academically-oriented track leading directly to the "Abitur" certificate, which in turn provides access to university studies) or other forms of secondary schooling (lower or intermediate tracks, traditionally more vocationally oriented; cf. Becker, Neumann, & Dumont, 2016).

Because we are interested in the narrations of non-academic parents, we chose to base our analysis on three cases from Klinge's study. These three cases represent families (for anonymization purposes we call them *Oak*, *Pine* and *Maple*) whose class background in terms of educational level and occupational position conforms most closely to this category: all of these parents finished the lower or intermediate school track and thus have neither the *Abitur* nor a university (academic) degree:

- The father *Oak* has not finished vocational training or an apprenticeship and is unemployed. His wife works in housekeeping. They have three children: a son and two daughters. The father's narration focuses mainly on how he and his wife made up their mind about the eldest daughter's vocational secondary schooling, but he also refers to experiences made when choosing a primary school for their younger daughter.

- The interviewed mother *Pine* and her husband work in trade and have vocational training. They have four children of school age and thus a variety of experiences with schooling; however, the narration mainly deals with their secondary school decision regarding one of their daughters. A good student, she had been recommended for the Gymnasium by her teachers. Even so, her mother initially thought about placing her in a middle-track school, but then decided for the Gymnasium in the end.
- The third interviewees, mother *Maple* and her husband, have both finished vocational training and work in administration and in the healthcare sector, respectively. The interview was conducted with both parents. Their son had good grades and could have gone on to the Gymnasium, but his parents found him "too lazy" and thus decided for a vocational secondary school. Their older daughter finished the Gymnasium, but she was also more studious than her brother, according to the parents.

Our analysis proceeded as follows. Based on the interview transcripts, we first selected interview passages that offered the greatest amount of detail regarding the parents' struggle to make a "good" educational decision with regard to their child's secondary schooling. Our assumption here was that we might also find indications that would clue us in to counter-narratives. One passage that we always included is the interviewees' starting sequence, since this part of the interview is particularly important in narrative theory: as a result of the first, narrative-inducing question, interviewees are supposed to generate a consistent story of their life or of a specific experience (Schütze, 1983, pp. 285–286). Ideally, this spontaneous narration creates a continuous text that reproduces the social process that shapes identity (Schütze, 1983, p. 286), thus marking the first positioning. Second, we used Schütze's distinction between narrative, descriptive, argumentative and evaluative text types to analyze the textual structure of the chosen interview passages, including the starting sequences. Finally, we applied a sequential in-depth analysis to reconstruct how the text-type patterns in each interview relate to parents' framing of the master-narrative in question and their counter-positioning(s). This approach allowed us to work out how non-academic parents relate to the master-narrative of "good parenting" and its implications for educational decision-making, and how they simultaneously attempt to position themselves by conveying their own ideas in this context, thus potentially giving rise to counter-narratives.

Analysis

We present our analysis in two steps: first, we take a closer look at the starting sequences of parents' narrations about their secondary schooling choices for their children. To make our analysis of the textual structure as transparent and comprehensible as possible, we start with one longer interview excerpt, highlighting it with different color shades to indicate the different text types. Second, we show how interviewees position themselves vis-à-vis more general school-related issues, such as the perceived function of schooling, recent school reforms and issues of child development and performance requirements at school.

The starting sequence of the school choice narrative

For a detailed analysis and interpretation of the starting sequence, we draw on the interview with *Oak* (including, for illustrative purposes, the interview stimulus). The different text types are marked as follows: argumentation, evaluation, description and narrations (without color shade):

> *Interviewer:* "And you had to decide now for your child for a school uh, can you tell us how the process was what happened there?"

Oak: "So with us it comes to the fact that the older one, the older one has ADHD and there are already some schools out of the range. the older one is also schoolwise not so: it's not quite easy for her so she is simply a little worse, and also had a learning therapy and everything, in the end she came through in any case they had worse fears but it went somewhat okay (.) yes and there weren't really many schools that came into question for us, so to speak; so we had a look at the K-School again, but because it was my school back in the days, it was no option for me; because um it has become quite strange I find this school principle there at this school, I mean they already have higher requirements than on a pure Gymnasium and that's not a piece of cake, and now she ends up on the X-secondary school which has been specialized in former times for children like that now unfortunately it is no more because the schools have all now become secondary schools afterwards; but they are eventually still for these children because the teachers are simply (.) yes they know more about these children than in the normal case and yes this school I find also had a very good offer (.) so they also have a climbing wall inside and somehow they have a telescope there somehow and so it's real: craftsmanship and practical and also a good offer it will be fun for her and so we actually decided quite quickly for this school [...]".

Thus, right after the narrative-inducing stimulus, *Oak* starts with an argumentation, referring to his daughter's ADHD, followed by some short descriptive additions and some argumentative and evaluative passages about why the range of different schools on offer for his daughter is limited. He then closes by describing the perceived advantages of the chosen secondary school.

Besides the fact that he renders these experiences without in any way drawing on the narrative text type, his choice of words at the very end of the first argumentative passage is also very revealing. To sum up his daughter's school achievement at the end of primary school, he says: "in the end she came through in any case they had worse fears but it went somewhat okay". Thus, underlying *Oak*'s argumentation is a theory about individual achievement as something that "naturally" comes from the child. In other words, school achievement is seen here as a process whose outcome is predetermined by "nature", rather than something that parents can substantially influence or for which they can be responsible. This fits with Lareau's finding that "natural growth" is a prominent parenting style in working-class families. *Oak*'s way of starting the overall narration can, therefore, be interpreted as a first (albeit relatively implicit) sign of counter-positioning. In fact, we would argue, *Oak* is almost obliged to draw on argumentation here rather than on the narrative text genre, since his underlying ideas do not fit well with the master-narrative in question, thus triggering a need to argue rather than narrate.

As stated before, he does not use narrative forms of communication in the remaining part of the starting sequence either, but rather continues to tell his story through argumentation, evaluation and description. During this part of his account, *Oak* refers to the structural school reform that took place in some German states, in which lower- and middle-track schools were merged. Objecting to this structural change on the grounds that the new system is foreign to his own experiences, he mentions the role of teachers and their special knowledge and expertise. In this way – by highlighting the role of teachers in schooling, rather than that of parents – *Oak* can argumentatively justify his and his wife's choice of secondary schooling for their daughter. This can also be seen as another attempt to counter-position himself vis-à-vis a master-narrative that predominantly stresses parents' responsibility for their children's education.

From this illustrative analysis of the textual structure, we find a clear prevalence of description, argumentation and evaluation in the narration as a whole, leading to the tentative conclusion that (for the case of *Oak*) no *habitual* positioning within a "naturally" occurring (master-) narrative is possible. Instead, it appears that this parent needs to argue and evaluate his school choice, and he does so by referring to the special needs of his daughter and to his implicit theories about school achievement and the "need" to achieve a "match" with school requirements, even if these are personally deemed "strange".

Turning to the two other cases – *Pine* and *Maple* – but without such a detailed analysis of their starting sequences, we get a similar overall finding. After some meta-communication, *Pine* starts her narration with an argumentatively-based theorization about school type choices. She then goes on to evaluate the (new) school system, which she sees as rather opaque, referring argumentatively to her daughter's ability and motivation (pointing out that she is a high achiever and personally motivated to do well in school, and that her grades do not fluctuate). Thus, instead of rendering her experiences in narrative form, *Pine* produces a rather long sequence of argumentation and evaluation in order to justify why she finally decided for the Gymnasium. As a result, it rather seems as if *Pine* is defending the choice of the Gymnasium (a type of school she herself has no practical knowledge of). Here again, a lack of habitual experience is thus expressed through a lack of narration.

Looking at the *Maple* parents' account, we find the following text structure pattern. After the narrative-inducing stimulus, the mother begins with a non-detailed narration (which is supplemented by argumentative statements from the father) about how their son was actually enrolled one year too early in primary school so that they (not the teachers) decided to let him repeat one class. She then continues with her narration, but increasingly falls into the argumentative text type, citing several reasons why in the end they decided not to send their son to the Gymnasium, despite the teacher's recommendation. Interestingly, one of the reasons they mention is that they perceive him as being "not so diligent". Similar to *Oak* and *Pine*, "motivation" or "diligence" are thus perceived as personal, "fixed" characteristics of the child, rather than as something parents might somehow influence (cf. Lareau, 2002). By conceiving such traits as givens and using these as a basis for their decision-making, non-academic parents thus frame the issue of their child's school performance as a question of "nature" rather than one of parental influence. Here again, we can speak of an implicit form of counter-positioning. Overall, talking about school choice in narrative form does not seem to "come naturally" for these parents; instead, their experiences in this context are predominantly rendered in an argumentative and evaluative form since they start out from rather different positions and basic perceptions.[3]

General school-related issues: non-academic parents' ideas about the function of schools, their perception of child development, and the segregated school system

Apart from the starting sequence, we also find in the further course of the interviewees' accounts a frequent and recurrent use of argumentation and evaluation. A closer look at these text passages reveals that the interviewees often grapple with specific issues towards which they then seek to position themselves. This, in turn, makes them likely to draw on non-narrative communication schemes when recounting their experiences.

One of these issues concerns the parents' general perception of the raison d'être or function of (secondary) schools. *Oak*, for example, first shortly describes a visit to the chosen secondary school, noting its program and equipment (see quote above), but then veers off into a longer narration (not shown here) about choosing a primary school for the younger daughter and how they had to wait quite some time for the school to confirm that choice. He then evaluates this experience as a "stupid process" and contrasts it argumentatively to his own experience when he went to school. *Oak*'s comparison of past and present continues and leads eventually to the following descriptive-evaluative statement about the teachers at the chosen secondary school:

> "Their goal is to provide the children with any certificate when they leave school and I think that is the most reasonable principle a school can have. And they also offer a vocational internship twice, which I think is a really good thing."

Here, secondary schools' foremost function is seen as that of providing certificates, whereas questions of teaching and learning culture are dismissed. Neither is schooling perceived as being related to progress and success, or to encouraging and challenging students intellectually. Instead, a certificate is already deemed to be a good achievement. Furthermore, *Oak* stresses the importance of a vocational (rather than academic) school orientation, which he positively evaluates.

A similar kind of positioning can be found in the interview with *Maple*. Here, the father compares his current experiences with schooling to his own experiences in the German Democratic Republic, where he was born, arguing that it is quite important to try out different (vocational) subjects in order to be prepared for different kinds of vocational or office jobs. This is followed by his evaluation that his son should "do something that makes sense and so [they] thought vocational training makes sense". However, as Bourdieu (1984) has argued, the question of what makes sense to actors is strongly class-related. Thus, by framing schools' general function as a matter of providing certificates and vocational orientation, to some extent these non-academic parents are assuming a counter-position against narratives that stress the idea of children's self-realization, and the processual and non-instrumental nature of learning in school. They do so, however, by predominantly drawing on argumentation and evaluation, which makes their accounts appear to be justifications rather than something that could be told in narrative form.

Another issue with which interviewees grapple, drawing on argumentation and evaluation in the interview process, is the question of children's abilities and development. Like *Oak*, *Pine* refers to this issue using an argumentation in which she contrasts the different school types and the associated certificate options (especially the *Abitur*) with the question of children's abilities and the extent to which all of these fit together. Weighing all the possible risks, she then argues in favor of the less challenging school track. She justifies her reasoning by pointing out that one cannot estimate how children might develop in the future, which makes deciding for the Gymnasium rather risky. "[...] you have to be pretty sure that your child can make it", as *Pine* says in this context. Thus, making "good" educational decisions means here to take into account the development of one's child and to avoid riskier schooling options, if these seem to run against the child's development so far. Just as with *Oak*, we again see here how children's abilities and possibilities for development are conceived as relatively "fixed" and "naturally" determined, that is, as qualities that are hard to estimate or influence by parents. This kind of perception also shows up in the following argumentation by *Maple*:

> "[...] we said immediately this pressure and stress [at the higher school track] arguing with him all the time and then also him going through puberty; we don't do that to him and to us, because I freak out every time he comes home with wrong – so bad marks, because he is just too lazy, yes."

Finally, we should mention one last issue, linked to how the interviewees position themselves towards the segregated school system. *Oak*, for example, states that he finds the performance requirements of some secondary schools to be "quite extreme", and develops a counter-position by resorting to his own biographical knowledge:

> "In my opinion they should have merged all school types, because this social separation between the bad and the good students doesn't work out and back in the days at the school for all it *had* to work, even if there were some frictions. But yeah in my opinion this other; it is too separated between too good and too bad."

Similarly, both *Maple* parents evaluate as "sad" the high performance requirements of secondary schools and raise the question of what "normal people should do", referring to those "normal" people as "partly not less clever, just lazier". Thus, in contrast to the foregoing rather implicit forms of counter-positioning, the interviewees are quite explicit here. They start to express their own convictions about class differences, based on felt injustices and the perception of unequal chances, and set out their own theorizations and normative stances, thereby engaging in counter-positioning.

Conclusion

Our analysis started from the observation that there is a specific master-narrative in the realm of education – often referred to as "good parenting" – that assigns parents a central role and responsibility for the upbringing of their children, which includes the important issue of school choice. We argued that, due to class-based differences, this master-narrative is more closely aligned with the experiences, resources and practices of parents with an academic background than of non-academic parents. This prompted us to ask how non-academic parents relate to this master-narrative when recounting their decision-making processes with regard to their child's secondary schooling, and whether they also develop forms of counter-narrative in this context. Supplementing Bamberg's (2004a) work on counter-narratives with Schütze's (1983) idea of text structure analysis, we can draw several conclusions.

First of all, our analysis confirmed our starting assumption that non-academic parents would find it more difficult to render their experiences of school choice in a predominantly narrative form (as compared to middle-class or academic parents). Instead, in all three cases we analyzed longer narrations were clearly absent, with argumentation, evaluation and description predominating at the level of the actual text structure. This can be ascribed to the different set of assumptions and beliefs about education apparently held by non-academic parents in comparison with academic parents, pointing to the former group's habitual distance towards the master-narrative of "good parenting" and its implications. Thus, as our analysis has shown, our interviewees see their children's abilities and motivations with regard to schooling as "naturally given" rather than as a principal matter of parental responsibility and effort. They also stress the teachers' responsibility for their child's educational development, perceiving them as the experts on this matter. And, finally, non-academic parents apparently tend to emphasize the need for a "useful" – that is, a vocationally-oriented – education, which shapes their general perception of a school's function. These findings mirror closely what Lareau (2002) has described as a parenting style of "natural growth" among working-class families, and they also fit well to Gillies' observation (2008) that working-class parents find it difficult to align themselves with the master-narrative of "good parenting", because their understanding of their parental role differs from that of middle- and upper-class parents. This means that, even in narrative-inducing interview formats, non-academic parents cannot simply recount their experiences of school choice in an overall narrative form. Rather, they are obliged to draw on non-narrative schemes of communication, which becomes apparent when one looks closely at the actual text structure of interviewees' accounts.

Second, we interpret these diversions from other, more distinctly narrative ways of recounting school choice as signs of counter-positioning, which usually take a more implicit, but occasionally also quite an explicit form (for example, when touching upon the issue of recent school reforms). By predominantly drawing on argumentation and evaluation, our respondents are able to set out their own theoretical conceptions in relation to education and schooling. Thus, counter-positioning through the elaboration of such (argumentatively-based) theories can be seen as one strategy to cope with the master-narrative in question. Of course, this begs the question as to whether and to what extent we can also speak here of a distinct counter-narrative. While difficult to assess, we would argue that overall no clear counter-narrative is discernable, despite the aforementioned instances of counter-positioning. Such instances are only occasionally brought into their accounts by respondents, without solidifying into a narrative of its own. By mainly using non-narrative communication schemes, the respondents still relate to the master-narrative (albeit in a negative way), thus partially confirming it even as they try to demarcate their own position. As a consequence, their accounts still miss the normalizing and naturalizing quality of narrative forms of representation. Whether those counter-positionings may actually develop into a clear counter-narrative at some point must therefore remain an open question. But analyzing the actual text structure and determining the type of text genres used, as we tried to do, may help us to achieve a deeper understanding of how people position themselves between different master- and counter-narratives.

Notes

1 In this chapter, we only focus on issues of social class and inequality. As intersectionality has stressed, however, one would ideally have to take other analytical categories into account as well – such as gender, immigrant status, race or single parenthood – as these refer to dimensions that might also be crucial to the resources parents can or cannot mobilize in relation to the education of their children.

2 This differentiation draws on insights by Labov (1972) and other sociolinguists and rests on specific linguistic characteristics (cf. Kallmeyer & Schütze, 1977).

3 This is in noticeable contrast to the academic parents in the original sample of the primary study (Klinge, 2016), who generally present their school choices in a much more narrative form. Among our non-academic respondents, however, there is one remarkable exception to the dominant use of non-narrative forms of communication: namely, when they recount their conflictual interactions with teachers. These experiences are clearly conveyed in narrative form, probably due to the fact that the interviewees refer in this instance to a concrete and personally felt issue that also affects their sense of justice.

References

Allmendinger, J. (1989). Educational Systems and Labor Market Outcomes. *European Sociological Review, 5*(3), 231–250.

Anthias, F. (2009). Intersectionality, Belonging and Translocational Positionality: Thinking about Transnational Identities. In A. Bogner & G. Rosenthal (Eds.), *Ethnicity, Belonging and Biography. Ethnographical and Biographical Perspectives* (pp. 229–250). Berlin: LIT.

Baker, D.P., & Stevenson, D.L. (1986). Mothers' Strategies for Children's School Achievement: Managing the Transition to High School. *Sociology of Education, 59*(3), 156–166.

Bamberg, M.G.W. (1997). Positioning between Structure and Performance. *Journal of Narrative and Life Story, 7*(1–4), 335–342.

Bamberg, M.G.W. (2004a). Considering Counter-narratives. In M.G.W. Bamberg & M. Andrews (Eds.), *Studies in Narrative: Vol. 4. Considering Counter-narratives. Narrating, Resisting, Making Sense* (pp. 351–371). Amsterdam: John Benjamins.

Bamberg, M.G.W. (2004b). Positioning with Davie Hogan. Stories, Tellings, and Identities. In C. Daiute & C. Lightfoot (Eds.), *Narrative Analysis. Studying the Development of Individuals in Society* (pp. 135–157). Thousand Oaks: Sage.

Becker, M., Neumann, M., & Dumont, H. (2016). Recent Developments in School Tracking Practices in Germany: An Overview and Outlook on Future Trends. *Orbis Scholae, 10*(3), 9–25.

Betz, T. (2012). Early Childhood Education and Social Inequality: Parental Models of a "Good" Childhood. In M. Richter & S. Andresen (Eds.), *The Politization of Parenthood. Shifting Private and Public Responsibilities in Education and Child Rearing* (pp. 113–126). Dordrecht: Springer.

Bischoff, S., & Betz, T. (2015). "Denn Bildung und Erziehung der Kinder sind in erster Linie auf die Unterstützung der Eltern angewiesen." Eine diskursanalytische Rekonstruktion legitimer Vorstellungen 'guter Elternschaft' in politischen Dokumenten. In S. Fegter, F. Kessl, A. Langer, M. Ott, D. Rothe & D. Wrana (Eds.), *Erziehungswissenschaftliche Diskursforschung. Empirische Analysen zu Bildungs- und Erziehungsverhältnissen* (pp. 263–282). Wiesbaden: Springer VS.

Blossfeld, H.-P., & Shavit, Y. (1993). Dauerhafte Ungleichheiten: Zur Veränderung des Einflusses der sozialen Herkunft auf die Bildungschancen in dreizehn industrialisierten Ländern. *Zeitschrift für Pädagogik, 39*(1), 25–52.

Bourdieu, P. (1984). *Distinction. A Social Critique of the Judgement of Taste.* Abingdon: Routledge.

Bourdieu, P. (1986). The Forms of Capital. In J. Richardson (Ed.), *Handbook of Theory and Research for the Sociology of Education* (pp. 241–258). Westport, CT: Greenwood.

Busse, S. (2010). *Bildungsorientierungen Jugendlicher in Familie und Schule: Die Bedeutung der Sekundarschule als Bildungsort.* Wiesbaden: VS Verlag für Sozialwissenschaften.

Carlson, S., Gerhards, J., & Hans, S. (2017). Educating Children in Times of Globalisation: Class-specific Child-rearing Practices and the Acquisition of Transnational Cultural Capital. *Sociology, 51*(4), 749–765.

Carlson, S., Kahle, L., & Klinge, D. (2017). Wenn Narrationen nicht zustande kommen... Wie hochreflexive Berufsfelder dazu beitragen, dass argumentativ-evaluative Darstellungsweisen im narrativen Interview dominant werden. *Zeitschrift für Qualitative Forschung, 18*(2), 239–262.

Dumont, H., Klinge, D., & Maaz, K. (2019). The Many (Subtle) Ways Parents Game the System: Mixed-method Evidence on the Transition into Secondary-school Tracks in Germany. *Sociology of Education, 92*(2), 199–228.

Gillies, V. (2008). Perspectives on Parenting Responsibility. Contextualizing Values and Practices. *Journal of Law and Society, 35*(1), 95–112.

Gillies, V. (2012). Family Policy and the Politics of Parenting: from Function to Competence. In M. Richter & S. Andresen (Eds.), *The Politization of Parenthood. Shifting Private and Public Responsibilities in Education and Child Rearing* (pp. 13–26). Dordrecht: Springer.

Hatcher, R. (1998). Class Differentiation in Education: Rational Choices? *British Journal of Sociology of Education, 19*(1), 5–24.

Kahle, L. (2017). *Zugehörigkeit und Agency in polarisierten Gesellschaften: eine biographieanalytische Studie in Israel.* Opladen: Barbara Budrich.

Kallmeyer, W., & Schütze, F. (1977). Zur Konstitution von Kommunikationsschemata der Sachverhaltsdarstellung. In D. Wegener (Ed.), *Gesprächsanalysen. Vorträge gehalten anläßlich des 5. Kolloquiums des Instituts für Kommunikationsforschung und Phonetik, Bonn, 14.–16. Oktober 1976* (pp. 159–274). Hamburg: Helmut Buske.

Kerckhoff, A.C. (2001). Education and Social Stratification Processes in Comparative Perspective. *Sociology of Education, 74*(extra issue), 3–18.

Klinge, D. (2016). *Die elterliche Übergangsentscheidung nach der Grundschule – Werte, Erwartungen und Orientierungen.* Wiesbaden: Springer VS.

Labov, W. (1972). *Sociolinguistic Patterns.* Philadelphia: University of Pennsylvania Press.

Lange, A., & Thiessen, B. (2018). Eltern als Bildungscoaches? Kritische Anmerkungen aus intersektionalen Perspektiven. In K. Jergus, J.O. Krüger & A. Roch (Eds.), *Elternschaft zwischen Projekt und Projektion. Aktuelle Perspektiven der Elternforschung* (pp. 273–293). Wiesbaden: Springer VS.

Lareau, A. (2002). Invisible Inequality: Social Class and Childrearing in Black and White Families. *American Sociological Review, 67*(5), 747–776.

Lundholt, M.W., Maagaard, C.A., & Piekut, A. (2018). Counternarratives. In R.L. Heath, W. Johansen, J. Falkheimer, K. Hallahan, J.J.C. Raupp & B. Steyn (Eds.), *The International Encyclopedia of Strategic Communication.* Hoboken: Wiley.

Montt, G. (2011). Cross-national Differences in Educational Achievement Inequality. *Sociology of Education, 84*(1), 49–68.

Riessman, C.K. (2006). Narrative Analysis. In V. Jupp (Ed.), *The Sage Dictionary of Social Research Methods* (pp. 186–189). Thousand Oaks: Sage.

Schümer, G., Tillmann, K.-J., & Weiß, M. (Eds.). (2004). *Die Institution Schule und die Lebenswelt der Schüler. Vertiefende Analysen der PISA-2000-Daten zum Kontext von Schulleistungen.* Wiesbaden: VS Verlag für Sozialwissenschaften.

Schütze, F. (1983). Biographieforschung und narratives Interview. *Neue Praxis, 13*(3), 283–293.
Schütze, F. (1984). Kognitive Figuren des autobiografischen Stegreiferzählens. In M. Kohli & R. Günther (Eds.), *Biographie und soziale Wirklichkeit. Neue Beiträge und Forschungsperspektiven* (pp. 78–117). Stuttgart: J.B. Metzler.
Schütze, F. (1987). *Das narrative Interview in Interaktionsfeldstudien: erzähltheoretische Grundlagen. Teil I.* Hagen: Fernuniversität Gesamthochschule Hagen.
Schütze, F. (2016). Biographieforschung und narratives Interview. In F. Schütze (Ed.), *Sozialwissenschaftliche Prozessanalyse. Grundlagen der qualitativen Sozialforschung* (pp. 55-73). Opladen: Barbara Budrich.
Shavit, Y., & Müller, W. (2000). Vocational Secondary Education, Tracking, and Social Stratification. In M. Hallinan (Ed.), *Handbook of the Sociology of Eduation* (pp. 437–452). New York: Springer.
Vincent, C., & Ball, S.J. (2007). "Making Up" the Middle-Class Child: Families, Activities and Class Dispositions. *Sociology, 41*(6), 1061–1077.

17

Countering the paradox of twice exceptional students

Counter-narratives of parenting children with both high ability and disability

Michelle Ronksley-Pavia and Donna Pendergast

Introduction

Students who are twice-exceptional exhibit traits of both exceptionalities: giftedness – the potential for advanced achievement; and, disability – possessing one or more disabilities which impact on their learning, behavior and attention (Foley-Nicpon, Assouline, & Colangelo, 2013; Ronksley-Pavia, 2015). Despite the rise of research in the area of twice-exceptionality over the last 20 years, there is limited exploration of parents' perspectives and the intricacies of parenting children with both high potential and disability (Besnoy et al., 2015). Indeed, there is limited evidence to suggest that educators understand the existence of the apparent paradoxical nature of twice-exceptional students (Besnoy et al., 2015; Neumeister, Yssel, & Burney, 2013; Ronksley-Pavia, 2016).

The prevailing narrative of conceptions of twice-exceptionality is that high-ability implies high achievements, and disability implies a lack of ability (Neumeister et al., 2013; Ronksley-Pavia, 2015; Ronksley-Pavia, Grootenboer, & Pendergast, 2019b). These disparate stereotypes reinforce the misunderstandings that educators and others frequently hold; that children cannot possess both exceptionalities (Besnoy et al., 2015), reinforcing stereotyped narratives of what constitutes giftedness and ability/disability. In this study we use the theory of counter-narratives to add to the developing body of knowledge about the lived experiences of parents of twice-exceptional children. Through privileging parents' voices that are frequently silenced and marginalized in schools, we present counter-narratives of parental experiences in raising and educating their twice-exceptional children.

Twice-exceptionality

To frame an understanding of twice-exceptionality it is necessary to explore the dual exceptionalities that constitute this phenomenon: giftedness and disability. The concept of giftedness is complex and there is no universally agreed upon definition (Ronksley-Pavia, 2015). According to Gagné's model (2009), giftedness is said to occur in the top 10 per cent of age-peers where it is deemed to be natural abilities occurring in one or more domains of intellectual, sensorimotor, creative and/or socioaffective (Gagné, 2009).

The concept of disability is also complex; the World Health Organization defines disability as persons "who have long-term physical, mental, intellectual or sensory impairments which in interaction with various barriers may hinder their full and effective participation in society on an equal basis with others" (UN General Assembly, 2006, p. 3). Hence, disability is multifaceted "reflecting an interaction between features of a person's body and features of the society in which he or she lives" (World Health Organization, 2017, para. 2).

With the complexities and problematic definitions of both giftedness and disability, conceptualizing twice-exceptionality is also complex (Ronksley-Pavia, 2015). Twice exceptional children may possess one or more disabilities coalesced with giftedness, for example: mental health issues (e.g., anxiety, depression); autism spectrum disorders (ASD); dyslexia; cerebral palsy; motor skill impairment; Attention Deficit Hyperactivity Disorder (ADHD); dysgraphia (writing disability); Developmental Coordination Disorder (DCD) or dyspraxia (motor skills disorder); fundamentally, any disability that impacts on a child's ability to learn in a regular classroom environment (Assouline, Foley Nicpon, & Whiteman, 2010; Foley-Nicpon et al., 2013; Ronksley-Pavia, 2015). It is estimated that between 7–9 per cent of children may be twice-exceptional (Barnard-Brak, Johnsen, Pond Hannig, & Wei, 2015), however, due to the challenges of identifying both exceptionalities the exact prevalence rates remain unknown (Ronksley-Pavia, 2014). What is known however, are the uneven academic achievements and often negative experiences that these children experience in their years of formal schooling (Barber & Mueller, 2011; Ronksley-Pavia, Grootenboer, & Pendergast, 2019a).

The amalgam of giftedness and disability typically impacts on learning, interpersonal relationships and emotional coping (Silverman, 2005). While there is no homogenous twice-exceptional child, there are common characteristics such as: possessing high-levels of intelligence characterized by extensive vocabularies; being highly creative, skillful problem solvers; and having extensive yet focused interests (Assouline et al., 2010; Ronksley-Pavia, 2016). However, these traits are often impeded in skills needed for processing information, working memory and producing work that reflects their intelligence due to the impact of their disabilities (Ronksley-Pavia, 2016; Silverman, 2005). Thus, there is a discrepancy between their perceptible abilities, or potential, and their actual achievement and performance and this is often obvious in their schoolwork.

Dominant narratives in twice-exceptional discourse

In exploring the uniqueness of giftedness and disability the literature reveals the overarching narrative of stigma (Ronksley-Pavia et al., 2019b) – both of giftedness (Cross, Coleman, & Terhaar-Yonkers, 2014) and of disability (Quinn, 2006). This is a double stigma dominating twice-exceptional children and their education, and by association, their parents as these children do not fit into either *category* (Ronksley-Pavia et al., 2019b). The stigma of disability points to educational narratives of un-intelligence and dis-ability (being unable), while the stigma of giftedness intimates narratives of high achievement and child *genius*. Both narratives stem from the field of eugenics (Priestley, 2003) and from the concept of the bell curve of *normality*, where those on either end of the scale are discernably *different* from the *norm* (Gould, 1996; Murdoch, 2007) and essentially at opposing ends of a telelogical narrative from disability to giftedness. We argue that the parents of these eight twice-exceptional children challenged the dominant teleological diagnosis and cure narrative with a non-linear narrative that enabled them to move through an initial process of teleological narratives; involving a complexity of despair, seeking expert support, despondency and then into non-linear future-orientated narratives involving self-education and advocacy for their child; all the while set against dominant education narratives of high ability equating to giftedness and high performance, and disability equated to low ability and performance. We sought a nuanced understanding of the parents' lifeworlds, which challenged these linear dominant narratives through a future-orientated narrative of optimism and encouragement for their child's strengths. We contend that this process led to parents confronting and defying the dominant narratives and identities assigned to them and their children by an educational system often caught in the medicalized model of disability and the mythical narratives of giftedness, thus, finding a space for narratives of parental resilience and agency.

Method

Methodology

In order to explore the counter-narratives in the lifeworlds of parents of twice-exceptional children, we selected narrative inquiry as our methodology, which is a way of understanding the lifeworlds of people that "begins and ends with respect for ordinary lived experience" (Clandinin, 2013, p. 18). Narrative inquiry not only focuses on recognizing and acknowledging individual experiences but is also an "exploration of the social, cultural, familial, linguistic and institutional narratives within which individuals' experiences were, and are, constituted, shaped, expressed, and enacted" (Clandinin, 2013, p. 18).

Context and participants

Parents of eight twice-exceptional children participated in our study. Their children had confirmed disability diagnoses from specialists and were also identified as gifted by independent specialists separate from this study. Eleven parents agreed to be interviewed comprising five mothers and six mother/father couples (see Table 17.1). All parents were married, and from middle-class backgrounds living in south-east Queensland and northern New South Wales, Australia. The children attended a range of schools including government (n=4), private Catholic (n=2) and private independent (n=2). The table below provides details about the participants and their children.

Data collection

Data were collected through free-form interviews with each of the parents, either individually or as couples. The interviews took place in participants' homes where a rapport had been developed over the previous four months with both the children and parents as part of a wider study exploring the children's lived-experiences (Ronksley-Pavia, 2016). Parents were first invited to give retrospective accounts of their experiences of raising their twice-exceptional children, including their school and out-of-school experiences. The purpose was for parents to direct their own interview and discuss experiences they felt were important in terms of raising a child with dual exceptionalities. We invited parents to give both descriptive accounts of their experiences, and to give some interpretation to those experiences; often this was contrasted against prevailing narratives of misunderstandings and ignorance about twice-exceptionality, which the parents encountered.

Table 17.1 Participant details

Parents#	*Occupation*	*Child#*	*Child's diagnoses*	*Child's giftedness*
Blondie (mother)	Stay-at-home parent	Turbo (male, 13 years)	Anxiety; dysgraphia; dyspraxia; ADHD; sensory; dyslexia	Aged 9 years 8 months – FSIQ^ 113, GAI* 129 (WISC-IV**)
Purple (mother)	Stay-at-home parent	Cat51 (male, 9 years)	CAPD; anxiety; ASD	Aged 7 years 9 months, FSIQ - Not reported, GAI 121 (WISC-IV); achievements
Susanna (mother) Lesley (father)	Stay-at-home parent Stay-at-home parent	Ashley (female, 16 years)	Anxiety; ASD	Aged 4 years 1 month, FSIQ 103, PRI^^ 122 (WPPSI-R); Sayler's; achievements
Linda (mother)	Stay-at-home parent	Boomstick (male, 10 years)	Anxiety, ADHD; dyslexia	Aged 8 years 3 months, FSIQ – not reported, GAI 132 (WISC-IV)
Skye (mother) Jon (father)	Teacher Teacher	Harry (male, 15 years)	Anxiety; ASD	Aged 6 years 1 month, FSIQ 135 (WISC-III***)
Julie (mother)	Teacher	Anny (female, 12 years)	CAPD; anxiety; ADHD	Aged 6 years, 5 months, FSIQ 138 (SB-5)
Kate (mother) Trevor (father)	Teacher Small business manager	Buster (male, 13 years)	CAPD; anxiety; ASD; dysgraphia; ADHD; dyslexia	Aged 9 years FSIQ 120, GAI 130 (WISC-IV)
Godmother (mother)	Stay-at-home parent	Bob (female, 11 years)	Anxiety; dyspraxia; ADHD; dyslexia	Aged 7years - FSIQ 126, GAI 136 (WISC-IV)

Notes: ADHD – Attention deficit hyperactivity disorder; CAPD – Central auditory processing disorder; ASD – Autism spectrum disorder; ^FSIQ – Full-scale intelligence quotient; *GAI – General Abilities Index; **WISC-IV – Wechsler Intelligence Scale for Children (4th edition); ***WISC-III – Wechsler Intelligence Scale for Children (3rd edition); ^^PRI – Perceptual Reasoning Index (sub-test of WISC-IV)
Pseudonyms selected by participants are used in this study

Data analysis

We employed Polkinghorne's (1995) analysis of narrative as a starting point to organize different experiences into categories. Looking across the parents' narratives we sought to "identify common themes or conceptual manifestations discovered in the data" (Kim, 2016, p. 196). In this way we used the data to uncover themes representing counter-narratives from the stories the parents told and lived, which offered resistance to dominant narratives of dis-ability and ability. These themes emerged inductively from the data and were relational within each participant's experiences and across the participants' narratives. Analysis of narrative enabled us to speak to the commonalities that were present across the multiple experiences of the participants (Kim, 2016) and to fit individual experiences into larger patterns that emerged from the data.

The inductive analysis of narrative approach began by reading each interview transcript in full in order to gain an understanding of each as a whole; discussing emerging categories of particular themes and summarizing the data. Coding for the themes were configured from inductive reading and re-reading of the transcripts, recording statements, segments of text and language/words that suggested resistance to normative interpretations of both disability and giftedness (e.g., advocacy, support, "educate yourself", "people don't see what you see"). From this inductive analysis and coding we developed a framework of thematic categories, which illustrates the emerging counter-narratives. Three counter-narratives evolved from this process, each with a unique focus: the first around diagnosis and identification; the second featuring resiliency and advocacy; and, the third shaped around enabled parental agency.

Findings

Conceptualizing counter-narratives

The three counter-narratives that emerged from the interviews with parents were: 1) Diagnosis and identification counter-narrative; 2) Resiliency counter-narrative; and, 3) Parental agency counter-narrative.

Diagnosis and identification counter-narrative

In order to understand the diagnosis and identification counter-narrative we first explore the related dominant narrative; that is a teleological narrative of diagnosis and *cure*. This narrative of diagnosing disability and of identifying giftedness generally consists of: finding the disability – ***the problem*** (e.g., medical specialists – undertaking diagnostic assessments); intervention (e.g., medication); *cure* (as a *positive* outcome) – that is implementing the recommendations and thus *curing* the individual of their dis-ability. This dominant teleological narrative emerges from the expectation that interventions will *fix* or *cure* disabilities, or at least negate their impact. This dominant narrative is embedded in the medicalization of disability so that disability is seen as residing in the individual and can be *cured* by medical and educational interventions (Figure 17.1). But what if the disability cannot be *cured*?

The parents' diagnosis and identification counter-narratives followed some features of the dominant diagnosis-cure narrative. Each parent sought to find out *why* their child was having difficulties at school (e.g., learning to read and write, and fitting-in at school), and/or *why* their child seemed to have some advanced abilities, countered with the aforementioned significant difficulties—essentially seeking to answer what it was that made their child *different* and what they could do to support them. The figure below (Figure 17.1) details the sub-narratives that form the diagnosis-identification counter-narrative.

The initial discerning of differentness of their child from peers, or friends' children was common to all of the parents, what varied was which exceptionality was identified first. For some children the disabilities came to the forefront, thus, began a cycle of diagnoses as one disability was identified, interventions performed but with mixed success, then further rounds of assessments identified additional disabilities. All of the parents had children with multiple, or co-morbid (co-occurring) disabilities.

Giftedness was often underdiagnosed. For five of the eight children their giftedness was identified first, then their disabilities. For three children an initial diagnosis was made of one or more disabilities, with the giftedness exceptionality identified later. All parents reported a rollercoaster

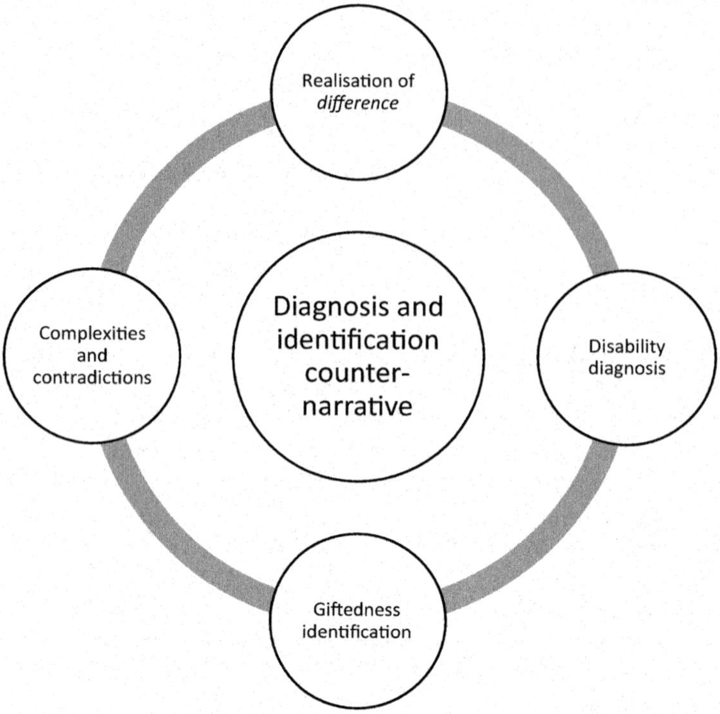

Figure 17.1 Sub-narratives evident in the diagnosis-identification counter-narrative.

of ongoing multiple specialist visits for a range of assessments over months and even years, seeking initially to find an elusive *cure* or intervention that promised to *fix* their child's disabilities.

For the parents, diagnosis and identification were not linear processes, as Godmother exemplified when she spoke of it taking "five specialists of 80 years combined experience" to even begin to understand her daughter's complexities (WISC-IV GAI 136, disabilities of anxiety, dyspraxia, ADHD and dyslexia). Purple (Cat51's mother), explained the initial process of identifying her son as being gifted, but the paradox of this identification with the difficulties he was having:

> I went to see a psychologist and she said, "Okay he's probably gifted". But then there were all the other sensory things I've found, but what is that? Is that gifted or is there something wrong with him? We were lost for quite a while... By the time he was six we were on track of gifted ASD, but we had no idea what to do about it!

Likewise, Linda's expectation and relief about finally getting a confirmed diagnosis for her son's reading and attention difficulties, which were subsequently quashed by the school:

> I'd gotten the Guidance Officer's report, I'd gotten the paed [pediatrician] report, and I was all ready to go with the educational psychologist, she confirmed that it was ADHD and phonological dyslexia, and I felt really relieved, I didn't really know where I was going to go with it but I just thought *all the cavalry was going come.* It's not recognized as a learning disability in the school system and all it gets him is like an extra half an hour in reading groups a week basically, that's it!

The contradictions between abilities and disabilities were difficult for parents to understand and deal with, as evident in Susanna's comment:

> It was a bit difficult for me to tell what was really wrong with Ashley… I always thought that Ashley was pretty good. But generally, her speech wasn't brilliant. But she was a very inquisitive child…she was sort of a busy kid . . . she was really good at music [at a young age] yet, she wasn't very good at language.

Kate and Trevor also discussed their journey on the identification-diagnosis rollercoaster:

> We took him for his first assessment to see what was going on when he was in year 1. I didn't think he was gifted, because I'd heard if kids were gifted they were reading, they were doing all these things that he wasn't. His handwriting was terrible, he could hardly write his own name, but he could draw a circuit diagram! I thought he's bright because I could see, compared to what other kids were doing, he was doing totally different, more advanced things… Where other kids, if they were interested in dinosaurs like him, they knew a few dinosaur names, but he knew everything! All the dinosaur names, where their fossils came from, scientific names, pictures, *everything*!

Identifying giftedness, and the complexities and paradox of twice-exceptionality required skilled and experienced specialists. Again, a non-linear process that began with parents often recognizing their child's giftedness, or difference to age-peers, which they often observed at an early age. Jon recalled Harry's exceptional memory:

> We already knew that he was different at an early age. I remember when he was eighteen months old, and we were walking to the hospital to visit his mum, only for the second time, I didn't know where I was going, he just grabbed my hand and said, "Come on, it's room number 29". He's pointing at the numbers at the top of each room, he knew!

Similarly, Julie shared her initial realization that Anny was *different*:

> There's been something very different about her…she'd sit for hours looking at pictures in picture books, she'd sit there for three to four hours without moving, just looking, it was a bit unusual.

All parents saw multiple clinicians, and consequently their children had multiple assessments as they tried to find something that worked for their child in terms of supporting them, both at school and outside school, with their difficulties. Some parents detailed feelings and experiences of being "taken advantage of" by some clinicians, where specialists frequently recommended costly interventions and treatments. For example, Buster's parents Kate and Trevor detailed the expense of "a working memory training program" that their pediatrician used in his clinic:

> We looked at the supporting [research] studies he showed us, and there were a lot, it all looked good to us, so we paid the $1,000 plus to put Buster through the program, only to find out months later that independent research had shown that this program improved a kid's ability to play those types of games but actually didn't improve those areas of concentration in real life at all!

In other words, the program's skills were not transferable to the classroom and real-life situations where Buster had difficulty concentrating. Kate elaborated, "[W]e felt duped, taken for a ride, we'd paid all that money and it didn't work!" Similarly, Linda spoke of feeling she had been taken advantage of with pseudo-interventions:

> I just started to feel like I was getting a bit conned and he wanted to sell me these goggles that flashed flashing lights in his eyes to try and promote brain something or others, and that was $500, and then he wanted to do some other program with him, and that was $500 through another process . . . So, I just started feeling really frustrated with that whole thing because I just felt like I was throwing good money after bad!

What became evident to all of the parents was not just finding a specialist who could *diagnose* disabilities and identify giftedness and twice-exceptionally, but specialists who could work with parents and their child by providing a suite of recommendations for interventions and school-based support. The parents' experiences suggested this was particularly challenging. The difficulty of finding reputable and experienced clinicians able to provide the necessary support was often exacerbated by parents' circuitousness from one clinician to another in their pursuit of answers. Blondie summed this up when she stated, "[I]t was always the case of the chicken and the egg—what do you deal with first, and what do you leave alone?"

Resiliency counter-narrative

The resiliency counter-narrative challenges the dominant narrative that school personnel know what to do to educate individual students (Figure 17.2). Parents described how they contested the separation between specialist knowledge of professionals and educators from that of parents. Parents are the first educators of their children and also the ones who most often know their child the best (Goodall & Montgomery, 2014). This counter-narrative describes the evolution of strong parental advocacy for their children, set against a background of increased mental, emotional and financial stress. Through this resiliency perspective parents moved from the uncertainties of initial diagnoses and identification towards efforts to work with teachers and schools to find ways to support their child in their learning. Parents initially anticipated that schools would know what to do as professional educators, but parents reported this was frequently not the case and many educators embraced dominant narratives of giftedness equaling high ability, and disability equaling low ability. This counter-narrative explores the gradual realization for parents that many educators were ill-equipped and frequently lacking in motivation to challenge counter-narratives in supporting their children. The figure below (Figure 17.2) illustrates the sub-narratives evident in the resiliency counter-narrative.

Parents discovered there was little understanding of twice-exceptionality in schools. For example, what began as "expecting the cavalry to come" (Linda) when parents provided the specialist reports to schools, soon turned to consternation at most schools' deficient knowledge and understanding. Godmother summed up this frustration when she commented that she

> just got tired of them [teachers] telling me that Bob's fine. She's not fine! And telling me that she wasn't gifted, and she doesn't have any disabilities and that they know what a disability is, and she doesn't have it!

Likewise, Julie revealed how Anny's school experiences were:

> [P]retty dismal . . . the school claimed to do certain things for her, but it's a lot of talk and not much action. It's frustrating at times, and very sad as well and when teachers don't see what

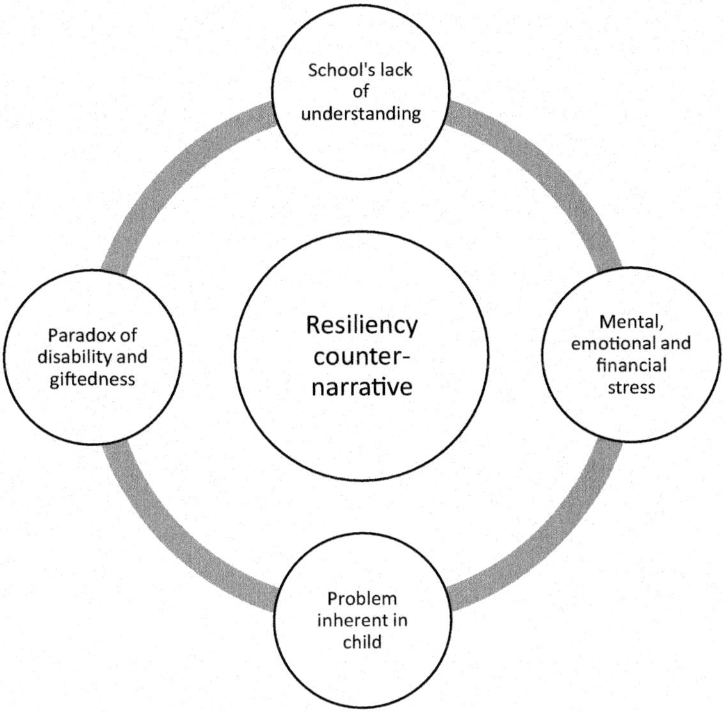

Figure 17.2 Sub-narratives evident the resiliency counter-narrative.

> you see, and when schools don't understand what you know is going on, and when you like say something a gazillion times and it's still not getting done!

Godmother expressed her exasperation at the lack of assistance from the school, "[N]ot the school, not the teacher, nobody helped, no support. I just get tired of fighting, because we just fought for two years to get one thing instituted at the school". Similarly, Kate shared her frustration at the school's inaction "[M]eeting after meeting again with the school, they kept saying they were going to do all these things that the specialists' had recommended in their reports. Nothing ever happened!" Kate detailed her experiences of attempting to get support for her son at school:

> [T]he psychologist recommended that Buster needed to start to use a keyboard at school because of his dyslexia and dysgraphia. We battled for about 18 months to get him allowed to use a laptop in class; he was ten when he was finally allowed. Silly obstacles were brought up by teachers at the meetings, like, "Other students might trip over the power cord!" Really? And other kids might say it's not fair that he gets to use a laptop and they don't!

Linda explained how Boomstick's teacher dismissed specialists' reports she shared at one of many school meetings stating that '[T]hese aren't done by the Education Department and they aren't valid.' And that was it! That was the end of the discussion on his reports!"

In some instances, the diagnosis of giftedness and disabilities were called into question, and sometimes it became incumbent on the children to *prove* their giftedness, for example, Julie detailed her experiences of teacher skepticism:

> [T]he teachers say things like, "Well you're supposed to be gifted why can't you do this?!" And that's probably why she doesn't believe she's gifted, but she didn't know she was gifted then, and they shouldn't have told her because I didn't want her to know, didn't want her to be aware of any labels around her. I can't imagine the damage this has done to her.

Many parents took the disability perspective because that was frequently resourced for support at school rather than giftedness, which received little in terms of support from schools. This suggests a dominant narrative of deficit perspectives of disability by educators. Parents found that their child's exceptionalities were either not acknowledged, or one was supported but not the other.

When giftedness was acknowledged by schools, teachers found the paradox of combined disabilities difficult to comprehend, as Purple explained,

> [I] think they don't understand it [disabilities] because he's gifted, they can see that in his math, but not in English, not with his writing. But they think because he's smart he should be able to do everything well, they don't always understand the other things [disabilities].

Often because the children were performing at an average level academically schools were reluctant to acknowledge anything needed to be undertaken. As Trevor (Buster's father) explained:

> [T]hey said, "Okay he's not doing so well with spelling but he's alright, he's getting by". But to us it was like, "What can we do to support him better, so he can really show what he can do?" Rather than just getting by, provide him with the accommodations that his specialists have asked for and let's see what he can do when he's got a level playing field.

Parents were frequently dismissed by schools as being *pushy* when they sought support from schools. Godmother declared, "[I] know they saw me as a pushy parent". Likewise, Kate described how she was positioned as problematic:

> I know they were fed up with me asking for meetings and asking for things to be done but they just wouldn't help, I don't know why. There's the problem, there's the accommodations that can address those problems, but the mentality of "You're the problem!" Me, my child, was awful! I used to get ignored by many teachers when they saw me at school, they'd look the other way; pretend they hadn't seen me!

In some cases, children were blamed by teachers for their difficulties, the issues seen as inherent to that particular child; evident in being told they were lazy. Blondie illustrated this when she recounted Turbo's experiences:

> [H]e was told he was being lazy because he couldn't read very well. The word lazy, really, really upsets Turbo because school has used it so much to describe him. And that's what the teacher would do a lot; call him lazy in front of the other kids.

Linda pointed to the laziness label adding other problems:

> [H]e [Boomstick] used to get in trouble a lot because he was just seen as the distracted, larrikin, naughty boy and he used to spend a lot of lunch times outside the office finishing work

> off. They just thought he was being lazy... it's just he really can't stay on a task for very long without a lot of help.

The financial cost of repeated assessments, interventions with specialists (e.g., occupational therapy), was burdensome for many of the participants. Julie explained how costly the clinical visits and interventions were, "[I]t's been very costly, financially and emotionally". Blondie talked of wasting money on interventions, "[W]e've wasted thousands and thousands of dollars, nothing has worked significantly where I can say you go do this program as that will help!" Financial problems were also exacerbated for some of the parents as they could no longer work, as Purple explained:

> Cat51 was five when I tried to go back to work, and it just didn't work because the school would always be calling me to go in and collect him ... his eyes were hurting, he can't breathe very well, he's got headache, he feels sick, stress and avoidance I think it was!

Turbo would frequently run away from school so Blondie could not work and had to remain at home during the day,

> [H]e wasn't coping with the noise at all in the classroom were quite small, and he kept running away, he kept bolting from classes . . . I couldn't do anything, I couldn't work, I was stuck at home, because we were worried that he may turn up.

The complexities of these experiences took their toll on both the children and their parents. All parents spoke of the stress felt by their families. Recurring emotions throughout the parents' narratives were terms such as *stress*, *worry*, *frustration* and *anger*. The emotional toll of seeking support for their children was immense. Godmother told how she developed a mental illness as a result of her attempts at advocacy,

> [E]ventually I ended up with a high anxiety disorder and depression last year because it was so incredibly stressful trying to work with the school. And I just never knew what was going to happen to Bob when she went to school.

This was frequently coupled with anger at the lack of support, "I'm just really angry that so many teachers say bad things to Bob on purpose".

As a result of their initial advocacy experiences the parents developed a sense of resilience, despite the many negative interactions and experiences; they began to construct their own paths through the confusion of seeking interventions, funding support and ultimately educational support for their children. The parents developed agency by navigating the various systems.

Parental agency counter-narrative

The parental agency counter-narrative is about the *outcomes* of parental *growth* – self-education, increased confidence, support from schools, teachers and others; ultimately the results brought about through improved and targeted advocacy for their child; working against the dominant narratives around giftedness and disability (Figure 17.3). Parental agency refers to the capacity to advocate for their child's learning needs. This was established by negotiating with schools

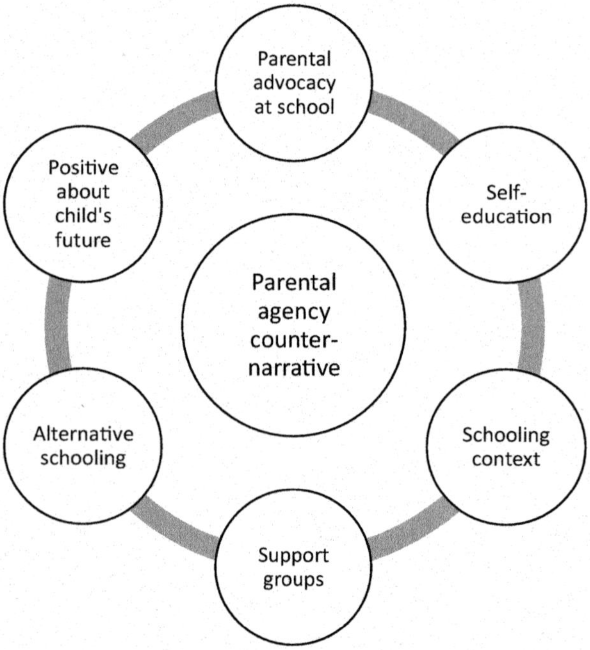

Figure 17.3 Sub-narratives evident in the parental agency counter-narrative.

sometimes involving changing schools or homeschooling for limited periods. The figure above (Figure 17.3) details the sub-narratives evident in the parental agency counter-narrative.

Skye typified the role of parental agency when she explained how you "... have to fight for every moment because Harry's so different and the teachers don't understand him, there's not going to be many advocates for him. So, us advocating for him is really important". Jon explained the process in gaining support for his son:

> [Y]ou go through these stages of how you perceive your child's education, especially so when you've got some disability and giftedness there. You go from the, "I want support—where's the support?" stage, to the angry stage, then again support and the school's just telling you stuff they think you want to hear, but not actually doing anything, and then you go to a third stage, "I've heard it all, don't need to hear it anymore, just deal with it!" ... Let's just get him through [school].

Many of the parents explained how their choices and decisions were met with consternation by others,

> [W]hen I decided to home school Turbo I lost friendships. I was told that I must be the cruelest mother in the world. As far as I'm concerned I'm meant to protect him from the system and it's the only way I could think of to do it.
>
> *(Blondie)*

The lack of support from others was evident in the parents' narratives, as Purple summed up,

> [T]hat's another thing that we did find, it was harder to keep up friendships with friends because they didn't understand your kid and they'd think, "Ah, they need a smack", or you weren't parenting them right, it was your fault how they were.

As a result of the lack of support from schools and others, parents sought support elsewhere, and thus began a gradual process of parental learning which further supported their advocacy efforts. Not only did parents seek experienced and understanding clinicians, they also sought support from disability groups and giftedness associations. Purple explained how these groups helped her,

> [I]'ve joined a couple of support groups for ASD and for gifted and that's been probably more helpful because then you're speaking to people who've got kids that are similar, they know what you're going through, and you can learn and share with each other.

Linda also felt she had more understanding from some of these groups:

> [E]ven within the disability community groups the kids may not be technically gifted, but the parents have an understanding because the kid has a disability; they're able to understand how a kid could have a disability and an ability. The dyslexia group they have been wonderful, I've learnt so much and so much support.

The development of parental advocacy was founded in parents educating themselves. All spoke of how learning and arming themselves with knowledge increased their self-confidence to advocate for their children. One instance where parental self-confidence was evident related to homework, which often took children a long time to complete and was an added burden on top of other interventions. Many parents explained how they regulated their child's homework by rejecting excessive assignments and crossing out unessential tasks that were sent home. Linda recounted, "[W]ith his homework I'd just cross out things on the sheet, it just gave me a lot more confidence instead of doing everything, because homework for him, what they [teachers] think is 10 minutes, would take him 45 minutes".

One of the parents, Godmother, made a formal complaint of discrimination against her school through the Australian Human Rights Commission, citing the schools lack of implementation of the clinicians' recommendations. She believed it not only gave her more confidence in endeavoring to work with the school, but meant they had to implement the recommendations, "[M]aking that complaint and getting the ruling meant they had to act. Now she has this lovely teacher that I love, and he works with me on everything, because I'm sure he's terrified of me".

Having the self-confidence to develop strategic relationships with school personnel also formed a pivotal part of the approaches parents developed, with many finding supportive guidance officers, teachers, and special education teachers. Parents either worked with schools to gain support for their child or alternatively moved to a more accommodating school. Three parents moved their child to different schools, endeavoring to find the right educational *fit* and support for their child. Kate's son Turbo attended six schools in eight years and was homeschooled for a period. Others, like Skye and John, did part-time homeschooling and part-time schooling when Harry was in Year 3. Accommodations for their children gradually began to occur as the parents either found supportive teachers at their child's current school or moved to different schools and/or undertook homeschooling.

All the parents believed strongly that the development of advocacy strategies and finding supportive schools and teachers contributed directly to their children being happy at school and worked against the dominant narratives held by educators of giftedness equating to high ability, and disability equating to low achievement and low potential. Parents felt that the happiness of their child was of utmost importance, in some instances this meant compromises, accepting that to some extent disability would be catered for over giftedness. Purple summed up this sentiment,

> I always feel like we're doing a focus on disability, we can never do the two [disability and giftedness] together in school, and mostly they don't get giftedness, but disability attracts attention and is usually funded but anything to do with giftedness gets nothing.

The results of improved and targeted parental advocacy were evident across all of the parents' narratives. Linda typified this when she stated,

> Cat51's now got this amazing grade 4 teacher; she's very accommodating to everything. The schools' been really supportive with developing and implementing an IEP [Individual Education Plan], it's got all of his accommodations in there. We've worked with the school and the psychologist as a team to develop it.

The parents all placed considerable emphasis on just getting their child through school relatively unscathed by their experiences as a twice-exceptional child. They felt that once through school their children would come "into their own" [Susanna]; be recognized as independent and capable. Nearly all of the parents expressed a strong impression their child would do well post-school. Blondie typified this:

> I know that he [Turbo] will be a contributing member of society, if school doesn't crush him. I always say to the school at the beginning of the year, "Your job is to keep that child's self-esteem intact, that's your only job!" We really don't care what he learns and what he doesn't learn because his self-esteem is the number one priority!

Discussion

The three counter-narratives uncovered in this study indicate how parents of eight twice-exceptional children resisted the dominant narratives that embraced pre-determined and frequently misunderstood notions of both disability and giftedness within education systems. The progression, although not linear, through these resistant counter-narratives suggests that parents of twice-exceptional children labor through complex processes of: diagnosis and identification of both exceptionalities; lack of understanding from schools and others; through to self-education and the development of parental agency in advocating for their children. This process of developing advocacy is fraught with considerable obstacles – identifying and assessing both exceptionalities; lack of understanding from clinicians, schools, teachers and others; and, schools seeing the issues as inherent to the child. This is not uncommon (Assouline, Megan Foley, & Huber, 2006; Besnoy et al., 2015; Neumeister et al., 2013), and thus, suggests an immense need for more societal understanding of twice-exceptionality.

Our study reveals that the parents recognized, from a very early age, their child to be different from age-peers, yet, they presented with paradoxical complexities that became evident in most cases, when the children started formal schooling. This finding concurs with Assouline et al. (2006) and Neumeister et al., (2013) and also supports previous research, which showed schools generally blamed the child for their difficulties (Assouline et al., 2006). The difficulties parents encountered in obtaining disability diagnoses and gaining identification of co-occurring giftedness has parallels in literature with Besnoy et al. (2015) and others also elaborating these difficulties. Other studies (e.g., Foley-Nicpon & Assouline, 2015) have touched on the stress felt by twice-exceptional children of the impact of their exceptionalities. However, our finding about the mental and emotional impact of twice-exceptionality on parents and their families appears to be a new finding in relation to twice-exceptional parenting experiences. Difficulties in identifying twice-exceptionality compound this stress and have parallels in previous research (e.g., Buic-Belciu & Popovici, 2014; Pfeiffer, 2015). However, the tenacious pursuit of identification and parent advocacy evident in our study speaks to the agency and resilience of these parents despite obvious adversities.

Findings from this study support previous research that emphasized the importance of parental advocacy in supporting the education of twice-exceptional children (Neumeister et al., 2013). The development of parental confidence and educating themselves about the systems and processes confirms previous research by Besnoy et al. (2015) who also asserted that parents need to be conversive in procedures and educational jargon in order to successfully advocate for their children. Moreover, support and resources for parents of these children in schools are ad-hoc at best, and non-existent in the experiences of many of these parents. This finding suggests an under-identified need for schools to develop, or at least be able to direct parents to support groups and resources. This echoes calls from other recent studies for the development of a centralized collection of resources and online and face-to-face support networks for parents of twice-exceptional children (Neumeister et al., 2013; Park, Foley-Nicpon, Choate, & Bolenbaugh, 2018). Parents in our study had to independently source information and support to arm themselves with the necessary resources to educate school personnel as well.

Conclusion

Findings from this study point to strong parental advocacy to ensure twice-exceptional children receive an equitable education and this was often met with opposition by schools and educators who tended to embrace stereotyped dominant narratives about how children with giftedness and disability should be. The parental counter-narratives suggest that many of their children's teachers embraced dominant narratives; considering giftedness as high achievement and disability as low achievement, and frequently possessed very limited understanding of both exceptionalities co-existing in an individual student and how to cater for these students in their classrooms. The implications for policy and practice are that failure to recognize and cater for the unique needs of twice-exceptional students can lead to considerable parental and child stress, conceivably "leading to a loss of potential for both the individual and society as a whole" (Morawska & Sanders, 2009, p. 163). Thus, the need for parental advocacy speaks to a disparity in educators' understandings and knowledge about catering for these students in their classrooms.

References

Assouline, S. G., Foley Nicpon, M., & Whiteman, C. (2010). Cognitive and Psychosocial Characteristics of Gifted Students With Written Language Disability. *Gifted Child Quarterly*, *54*(2), 102–115. https://doi.org/10.1177/0016986209355974

Assouline, S. G., Megan Foley, N., & Huber, D. H. (2006). The Impact of Vulnerabilities and Strengths on the Academic Experiences of Twice-Exceptional Students: A Message to School Counselors. *Professional School Counseling*, *10*(1), 14–24. https://doi.org/10.5330/prsc.10.1.y0677616t5j15511

Assouline, S. G., & Whiteman, C. S. (2011). Twice-Exceptionality: Implications for School Psychologists in the Post-IDEA 2004 Era. *Journal of Applied School Psychology*, *27*(4), 380–402. https://doi.org/10.1080/15377903.2011.616576

Barber, C., & Mueller, C. T. (2011). Social and Self-Perceptions of Adolescents Identified as Gifted, Learning Disabled, and Twice-Exc. *Roeper Review, 33*(2), 109–120. https://doi.org/10.1080/02783193.2011.554158
Barnard-Brak, L., Johnsen, S. K., Pond Hannig, A., & Wei, T. (2015). Roeper Review The Incidence of Potentially Gifted Students Within a Special Education Population. *Roeper Review, 37*(2), 74–83. https://doi.org/10.1080/02783193.2015.1008661
Besnoy, K. D., Swoszowski, N. C., Newman, J. L., Floyd, A., Jones, P., & Byrne, C. (2015). The Advocacy Experiences of Parents of Elementary Age, Twice-Exceptional Children. *Gifted Child Quarterly, 59*(2), 108–123. https://doi.org/10.1177/0016986215569275
Buic-Belciu, C., & Popovici, D. (2014). Being Twice Exceptional: Gifted Students with Learning Disabilities Selection and Peer-Review Under Responsibility of PSI WORLD 2013 and their Guest Editors: Dr Mihaela Chraif, Dr Cristian. *Procedia - Social and Behavioral Sciences, 127*(2014), 519–523. https://doi.org/10.1016/j.sbspro.2014.03.302
Clandinin, D. J. (2013). *Engaging in narrative inquiry.* Walnut Creek, CA: Left Coast Press.
Cross, T. L., Coleman, I. J., & Terhaar-Yonkers, M. (2014). The Social Cognition of Gifted Adolescents in Schools: Managing the Stigma of Giftedness. *Journal for the Education of the Gifted, 37*(1), 30–39. https://doi.org/10.1177/0162353214521492
Dare, L., & Nowicki, E. A. (2015). Twice-Exceptionality: Parents' Perspectives on 2e Identification. *Roeper Review, 37*(4), 208–218. https://doi.org/10.1080/02783193.2015.1077911
Foley-Nicpon, M., & Assouline, S. G. (2015). Counseling Considerations for the Twice-Exceptional Client. *Journal of Counseling and Development, 93*(2), 202–211. https://doi.org/10.1002/j.1556-6676.2015.00196.x
Foley-Nicpon, M., Assouline, S. G., & Colangelo, N. (2013). Twice-Exceptional Learners. *Gifted Child Quarterly, 57*(3), 169–180. https://doi.org/10.1177/0016986213490021
Gagné, F. (2009). Building Gifts into Talents: Detailed Overview of the DMGT 2.0. In B. MacFarlane & T. Stambaugh (Eds.), *Leading change in gifted education: The festschrift of Dr. Joyce VanTassel-Baska.* pp. 61–80 Waco, TX: Prufrock Press.
Goodall, J., & Montgomery, C. (2014). Parental Involvement to Parental Engagement: A Continuum. *Educational Review, 66*(4), 399–410. https://doi.org/10.1080/00131911.2013.781576
Gould, S. J. (1996). *The mismeasure of man.* New York, NY: W. W. Norton.
Kim, J. H. (2016). *Understanding narrative inquiry: The crafting and analysis of stories as research.* Thousand Oaks, CA: SAGE Publications.
Morawska, A., & Sanders, M. R. (2009). Parenting Gifted and Talented Children: Conceptual and Empirical Foundations. *Gifted Child Quarterly, 53*(3), 163–173. https://doi.org/10.1177/0016986209334962
Murdoch, S. (2007). *IQ: A smart history of a failed idea.* Hoboken, NJ: Wiley.
Neumeister, K. S., Yssel, N., & Burney, V. H. (2013). The Influence of Primary Caregivers in Fostering Success in Twice-Exceptional Children. *Gifted Child Quarterly, 57*(4), 263–274. https://doi.org/10.1177/0016986213500068
Park, S., Foley-Nicpon, M., Choate, A., & Bolenbaugh, M. (2018). "Nothing Fits Exactly": Experiences of Asian American Parents of Twice-Exceptional Children. *Gifted Child Quarterly, 62*(3), 306–319. https://doi.org/10.1177/0016986218758442
Pfeiffer, S. I. (2015). *Essential of gifted assessment* (1st ed.). Hoboken, NJ: Wiley & Sons.
Polkinghorne, D. E. (1995). Narrative Configuration in Qualitative Analysis. *International Journal of Qualitative Studies in Education, 8*(1), 5–23. https://doi.org/10.1080/0951839950080103
Priestley, M. (2003). *Disability: A life course approach.* Malden, MA: Polity Press.
Quinn, D. M. (2006). Concealable Versus Conspicious Stigmatized Identities. In S. Levi & C. Van Laar (Eds.), *Stigma and group inequality: Social psychology perspectives* (pp. 83–104). Mahwah, NJ: Lawrence Erlbaum Associates.
Ronksley-Pavia, M. (2014). *An empirical investigation of twice-exceptional research in Australia: Prevalence estimates for gifted children with disability · Australian Association for Research in Education.* Brisbane, Australia: Australian Association for Research in Education. Retrieved from www.aare.edu.au/publications-database.php/8885/an-empirical-investigation-of-twice-exceptional-research-in-australia-prevalence-estimates-for-gifted
Ronksley-Pavia, M. (2015). A Model of Twice-Exceptionality. *Journal for the Education of the Gifted.* https://doi.org/10.1177/0162353215592499
Ronksley-Pavia, M. (2016). *The lived experiences of twice exceptional children: Narratives of disability and giftedness.* Griffith University.
Ronksley-Pavia, M., Grootenboer, P., & Pendergast, D. (2019a). Bullying and the Unique Experiences of Twice Exceptional Learners: Student Perspective Narratives. Gifted Child Today, 42(1), 19–35, doi.org/10.1177/1076217518804856.

Ronksley-Pavia, M., Grootenboer, P., & Pendergast, D. (2019b). Privileging the Voices of Twice-Exceptional Children: An Exploration of Lived Experiences and Stigma Narratives. *Journal for the Education of the Gifted*, *42*(1), 4–34. doi 10.1177/0162353218816384

Silverman, L. K. (2005). *The Two-Edged Sword of Compensation: How the Gifted Cope With Learning Disabilities.* Retrieved from http://citeseerx.ist.psu.edu/viewdoc/download?doi=10.1.1.511.5584&rep=rep1&type=pdf

UN General Assembly. (2006). *United Nations Convention on the Rights of Persons with Disabilities.* Retrieved from www.un.org/esa/socdev/enable/rights/convtexte.htm

World Health Organization. (2017). *WHO | Disabilities.* Retrieved November 1, 2018, from www.who.int/topics/disabilities/en/

18

The use of counter-narratives in a social work course from a critical race theory perspective

Maria Avila, Adriana Aldana and Michelle Zaragoza

Introduction

This chapter aims to share insights gained from teaching and learning about social justice via the use of counter-narrative in a master of social work program, supported by the department's theoretical foundation of Critical Race Theory (CRT). The class is titled Critical Race Studies in Social Work Practice, which is taught to all students during their first semester in the program. Exploring the connection between our narratives and our experiences teaching and learning CRS is the central reason why we are interested in writing this chapter. We write about our respective experiences teaching the class (Maria Avila and Adriana Aldana), and as a student enrolled in the class (Michelle Zaragoza). We concluded all three of us could learn a great deal by reflecting on the ways in which studying and teaching in our MSW program, particularly through the CRS class might have enhanced our own understanding of our narratives and how we have created counter-narratives in the classroom.

Thus, we engaged in conversation about the ways in which our personal narratives inform experience teaching and learning about CRT, as a form of narrative inquiry. Our conversations were rich, emotional, and enlightening. We offer more details on our narrative inquiry later in the chapter. First, we begin with a brief overview of the theoretical connection between CRT, Social Work, and Counter-narrative. Next, we provide background information about the educational and course context for our work. Our narrative reflections, which were informed by our conversation, are organized around three areas of discussion related to the narrative self, creating space for counter-narratives, and transformational learning.

Critical Race Theory and counter-narratives in social work

Critical Social Work challenges the status quo, and in doing this, it runs counter to the service oriented approach predominant in the profession in the United States. Campbell and Baikie (2012) underscore the importance of context in the practice of critical social work that moves beyond service. In a similar fashion, a CRT perspective urges social work practitioners to move beyond service, particularly in attending to racism as a contextual factor that shapes the lives of our clients.

In the United States, the relevance of CRT to social work has been an area of study in recent years (Abrams & Moio, 2009; Constance-Huggins, 2012; Ortiz & Jani, 2010). CRT is a dynamic theoretical framework surfaced in the late 1970s as a critical response to the color-blind justice occurring in schools of law (Delgado & Stefancic, 2001; Razack & Jeffery, 2002). Through its core tenets, CRT provides a guide for analyzing the dynamic nature of racism and addressing intersecting systems of oppression in social work practice and policy. Yet, in the United States, attention to racism embedded in our cultural, economic, and political institutions has been relatively absent from social work pedagogy and scholarship. Instead, the anti-oppression framework common in social work education has inadvertently minimized the significance of racism (Graham & Schiele, 2010).

Specifically, the CRT tenet often referred to as counter-storytelling or voices of color interchangeably, speaks of the power of counter-narratives. This tenet suggests that people of color are holders and creators of knowledge (Delgado-Bernal, 2002; Yosso, 2005). This CRT perspective counters dominant epistemology centered on the contributions of Eurocentric ideology, along with middle and upper class social capital. CRT also argues that narratives have been socially and hegemonically constructed. These narratives are part of what we call the master-narrative, a narrative that favors those in power and privilege. As an oppositional strategy, counter-narratives enable us to expose dominant narratives that perpetuate the justification for subordination, and offers alternative stories that challenges taken for granted dominant narratives (Delgado, 2013).

The use of personal narrative is an action oriented tool to change the status quo by challenging narratives of ourselves, our communities, societies, and of the world. Avila (2017) writes about the connection between reflecting on our narratives, finding our purpose in life, and creating change through community organizing. She states that, community organizing requires for us to be in touch with our purpose in life. Similarly, the late Brazilian, adult educator Paulo Freire (1995) talks about the importance of reflecting on our historical reality as a way to develop our power to understand the way we exist, in order to transform ourselves and our world.

Narrative inquiry

There is a wide range and historical legacy of social science research based on personal writings. Social science scholarship based on personal narrative inquiry include autobiographies, autoethnographies, introspections, self-study, and testimonio (Albert & Couture, 2014). Of these types of narrative research, testimonio more specifically speaks to the type of inquiry used for this chapter. Testimonio is a written account about life experiences typically spoken by a person from a marginalized group in society to shed light on sociopolitical realities (Prieto & Villenas, 2012). Testimonios originated from an oral tradition in Latin American, but has been further developed by educational researchers, predominantly Chicanas and Latinas, in the United States as a methodological, pedagogical, and reflexive approach to social justice education (Delgado-Bernal, Burciaga & Flores, 2012). Testimonios aim to promote social change through consciousness raising.

Testimonio, as a methodological approach to narrative inquiry aligns with CRT, through its tenet of counter-storytelling. More specifically, the use of testimonio – as counter-narrative work – in academic writing emerged from LatCrit scholarship, a theoretical branch extending from CRT with a specific focus on the experiences unique to people of Latin American descent in the United States (Huber, 2009). Pedagogically, testimonios serve to engage learners in transformational and dialogic reflection to build counter-narratives and oppositional knowledge. Coleman (as cited in Albert & Couture, 2014) assert that: "Experiential learning consists essentially in transforming one's own lived experience into personal knowledge. Instead of trying to understand information, learners must be able to make sense of their experiences and build useful knowledge" (p. 794).

Building on insights into the transformational potential of experiential testimonios, we make a connection with Freire and Horton's (1990) book *We Make the Road by Walking.* In this book, the authors speak and reflect on their experience as social justice educators. Freire says to Horton that a spoken book "should give us a duality in the conversation, a certain relaxation, a result of losing seriousness in thinking while talking" (p. 5). Thus, in our conversation for this chapter, we found ourselves making sense of, and transforming our personal experiences into useful knowledge. To this effect, we organized the second half of the chapter in narrative form to demonstrate our individual and collective reflections on counter-narrative work in social work education.

Educational context and course background

Before we present our narratives we present a brief description of the educational context and background information about the CRS course as the historical context of the university is relevant to our discussion of counter-narratives. The California State University, Dominguez Hills (CSUDH) is located in Carson, in the South Bay region of Los Angeles County, near Watts, Compton, and South Los Angeles. All of these communities are mostly inhabited by working class African American and Latino residents. The institution first opened its doors in 1965 in affluent Palos Verdes, however, following the 1965 Watts Rebellion, (CSUDH, 2018e):

> Governor Pat Brown determined there was a community in crisis and turned to higher education, a proven path to upward mobility, as a way of bringing greater opportunity and hope to individuals and the community at large. The governor made the historic decision to relocate our university from Palos Verdes to its present location in Carson, providing increased access to a college education to our surrounding communities.
>
> *(Hagan, 2015, p.2)*

The Watts rebellion (better known as the Watts Riot) is the largest racially motivated event during the US Civil Rights era. It began with the arrest of a young African American man by a white, California Highway Patrolman for suspicion of drunk-driving. In six days, August 11–17th, 1965, 34 people lost their lives, more than 1000 were injured, and an estimated 4000 were arrested. A gubernatorial investigation concluded that the riot was caused by the long-term injustices that included unemployment, along with inadequate housing and education (The Digital Library of Georgia, 2013).

The university's historical origin and the sociopolitical context of the surrounding community give special relevance to CRT as the underpinning theory to CSUDH's Department of Social Work. Founded in 2006, our department houses the newest Master of Social Work (MSW) program in the CSU system. This theoretical framework was intentionally chosen by the founders of our department, as a way to offer a more contextually relevant political education than is common for most social work programs in the United States. It is in this context that the Critical Race Studies (CRS) course that we will discuss was created (find more details at csuDHTVlive, 2015).

The CRS course is offered during the first semester of the MSW program. The title of the course was chosen to underscore the use of transdisciplinary scholarship from social science disciplines and other professional fields (e.g., public health, law, and public policy) that include content relevant to various types of oppression such as ablelism, heterosexism, religion persecution, classism and sexism, in addition to racism. Yet, CRT and its tenets underpin the course, as a theoretical framework that explores how race and its intersections with other social identity markers are socially constructed to set the groundwork for the systemic oppression of marginalized groups (Delgado & Stefancic, 2001). This official, brief description of the course summarizes its purpose:

> In-depth overview of Critical Race Studies (CRS) in social work fields. Examination of the causes and symptoms of structural racism and social/racial hierarchies in underserved communities. Analysis of the history and development of CRS' application to practice issues.
>
> *(CSUDH, 2018c)*

At the time of writing this chapter, Maria had taught CRS three times and Adriana four times. Michelle took the class in the fall of 2016. She graduated in May 2018.

Narratives reflections: experience with counter-narrative work

This section is the spoken part of this chapter, reflecting the conversation we had about our experiences teaching and learning CRS. The conversation lasted approximately four hours. We created these narratives in an iterative process of dialogue, reflection, and writing. First, we engaged in a conversation about our life story, our experiences in the Critical Race Studies Course, and counter-narrative work. Each of us then listened to audio recording to draft a personal narrative that synthesized our contributions to the conversation. We present our narrative self first because in the beginning of our recorded conversation we established that our personal stories are directly related to our experience teaching CRS (Adriana and Maria), and learning as a student in a CRS class (Michelle). We continue with excerpts from our conversations on our experiences with the CRS course, focusing on two assignments that are designed to guide students in narrative and counter-narrative work.

Personal stories and the narrative self

Writing this chapter, we came to an agreement that storytelling can be a starting point for creating new, oppositional knowledge. Through testimonios, Latina academics bare witness to their collective experiences as racialized, gendered, and classed women in the United States (Prieto & Villenas, 2012). Thus, in the tradition of Latina feminist scholarship, our first set of excerpts presents each of our narrative self introductions, or the personal story we have constructed about family, identity, and experiences in United States (U.S.) society.

Michelle. My narrative begins with my family's history. The city of Los Angeles became home to my parents after they immigrated from Michoacan, Mexico in the early 1970's. My mother had a relatively safe passage crossing the border because of her light complexion, while my father endured a more difficult journey laced with fear and uncertainty. Both of my parents left their home lands and family in pursuit of a dream for a better life, believing that their hard work would be rewarded. They came to Los Angeles with their culture, history, and unwavering hope. They slowly started acclimating to a new land, going to school, learning English, and obtaining employment. My brother and I grew up in a relatively low-income, predominantly latinx1 neighborhood with my mother, grandparents, and two uncles. My mother, who was separated from my father for most of my childhood, was tirelessly working to make ends meet. She felt like her dream of a better life for herself and now, for her children, had not yet been realized and so she pushed my brother and I to work hard and focus on education.

My mother's dream fueled my own pursuit towards higher education and success. For a long time that pursuit was often intertwined with negotiating aspects of my identity including, who

I am, what I am, who I should love, and how I dress, talk, and act. From the insights I gathered sharing my experiences with my classmates and discussing the Cycle of Socialization (Harro, 2000), I feel like I was trying to be someone else all those years rather than discover who I really was. I was socialized to act in certain ways and my identity became dependent on these early childhood messages. Through the process of engaging with my narrative, I found myself beginning to challenge the idea of "who I should be" and began my journey of unravelling "who I am".

Adriana. My story also begins with my parents' immigration to the U.S. My mother and father had very different arrival stories. For instance, my mother's border crossings were relatively easy. At the age of 9, in the early 70's, she came to the U.S. riding in a family car with her older sister and two American born cousins. At the border, she "passed" as one of my aunt's children without any questioning. My grandparents sent her to the U.S. to obtain a better education. My mother returned to Mexico a few years later. In the early 80's she returned to the U.S., again crossing the border without documentation and passing as an American citizen given her fair skin and ability to speak fluent English.

My father, in his mid-twenties, also crossed the border in the early 80's. Unlike my mother, my father--who is a darker shade of brown and didn't speak English--attempted to cross the border several times by walking through the desert unsuccessfully. Border patrol caught him and sent back to Mexico many times before he was finally able to make it into the U.S. Fortunately, both of my parents applied for and were granted amnesty in the late 1980's.

As a child, I moved several times from one racial-ethnic enclave to another. By the time I was 15 years old, my parents had moved our family between various cities in Southern California, and even across the U.S. border into Mexico. We lived in Pacoima and Lakeview Terrace close to African Americans. We also moved to Palm Springs, which at the time was a mostly White community. During 5th grade, I moved to Baja California to live with my maternal grandparents while my parents worked multiple jobs and saved money to buy a house. These relocations taught me two things. First, I learned that educational texts are sociopolitical artifacts that hold national narratives (e.g., Mexican history textbooks had a different interpretation of the Mexican-American war); and second, that segregation was linked to social inequities across communities.

Having attended multiple elementary and high schools, I could see the difference in schooling. I observed how schools with more Black and Latinx kids were highly policed and underfunded than the schools that I attended with more affluent White and Asian students. I grew up making observations and making connections between the demographics of the context I was in and the resources available. While I made these observations growing up, I didn't have the language to articulate them until college exposed me to Chicana/o Studies. As an undergrad student, I spent time thinking critically about gender dynamics and sexism. Although my family moved across multiple racial communities, I was raised in predominantly Mexican neighborhood blocks. Consequently, I didn't give race and ethnicity much thought growing up, instead gender was the most salient social identity for me. I noticed and critiqued gender norms and expectations held by my immediate and extended family.

When I moved to Michigan for graduate school, I became focused more on race, ethnicity, and racism. As a graduate student my work in Detroit--a highly segregated Metropolitan City--reconnecting me to my early ideas about the role of segregation in shaping people's lives and shapes how people see themselves. My graduate training also introduced me to the use of narrative work in my teaching and youth organizing work. My work taught me the power of narrative as a tool to move people from self-reflection to collective consciousness.

Maria. Let me first mention that I became interested in understanding my story as a community organizer with the Industrial Areas Foundation (IAF), the network that Saul Alinksy started in 1940 in Chicago (Industrial Areas Foundation, 2018). I organized with the IAF from 1990 to 2000, in Albuquerque NM, in Los Angeles, and in Northern California. As an organizers, we learned that in order for us to be effective in finding others to join, and to sustain our work for the long-term, understanding our story, particularly related to why we became organizers was a must. I remember feeling that I did not have the clarity others had about why they organized, that there were no role models in my family I could point to who were politically involved, or who fought for justice. I realized then that I was not in touch with my story. This realization led me to visit my family in Mexico, and ask my mother and older siblings for help. I traveled to the states of Chihuahua and Durango in Northern Mexico, where my family comes from. I heard many stories. Thus, for the first time I heard that my maternal grandmother had been part of the Mexican Revolution, which lasted roughly from 1910 to 1917. Growing up I had heard stories about the women who followed the revolution, some as fighters and some washing clothes and cooking for the soldiers, some did both. This triggered things I did remember about her as a young girl, such as that she was a curandera (a healer), and that people came from near and far seeking her healing powers.

In conversation with my siblings I also remembered that when I was three or four I used to see men coming in the house to visit my father, but I did not know why and had not thought about it until then. It turns out that these men and my father were meeting to organize about ways to get land that they could own and work, instead of working someone else's land. I don't know if these efforts succeeded, but I know my father did not obtain land.

There were other stories I learned about in this trip to Mexico, but most of all, stories like these about my grandmother and my father helped me realize that there have been leaders in my family who had fought for justice, and that I have their blood and genes in me. I had thus begun the life-time journey of understanding my narrative so that I could add to the collective of the many stories that have been buried or denied by the master narrative.

I began my social work education in the 1970s, motivated by the experience of injustice at my first job at a factory in Ciudad Juarez, in the state of Chihuahua. I started this job just before I turned 17. I had an opportunity to work as a community organizer in the rural areas of Ciudad Juarez through my field assignment, and felt I had found my calling. When I came to the US in the early 1980s I learned that community organizing was not a popular social work practice. After several years of trying to figure out how I could continue working as a community organizer, I finally left mainstream social work. Thus, in 1990 joined the IAF network2, where I worked from 1990 to 2000. During these ten years I did not see myself as a social worker. This changed when I became a full-time professor in our MSW program. I took the job because of the department's theoretical foundation of Critical Race Theory. I wanted to explore whether the field of social work had changed, specifically in its full acceptance of community organizing, and thought CRT could offer the political context for this to be the case.

Our personal narratives shared some cross-cutting themes. First, we all trace our ethnic roots back to Mexico; Maria as an immigrant, and Michelle and Adriana as descendants of immigrants. These ethnic roots informed how we have constructed our narrative self, but also how we have come to understand our position in the sociopolitical context of the United States. We all used our conversation to reflect about our journeys of self discovery and in a sense, finding our political identities.

Creating space for counter-narratives

The CRS course aims to make students aware of the historical institutionalized injustice that is at the root of the conditions of poverty and disenfranchisement that they, and many of the communities with whom they will be working as professionals experience. Students engage in readings and assignments relevant to this aim. For instance, students complete a narrative assignment that requires them to write about their lived experiences in the context of their various social positionalities such as race, gender, sexual orientation, faith, and nationality. A separate assignment, asks students to critically revise their narrative by analyzing the ways their experiences can be understood through intersection of social systems structure power, privilege, and oppression. This revision is also an opportunity for students to make explicit the connections between the course readings and their lived experiences. As a final assignment students present a CRT informed critique of a contemporary social issue in the form of a creative exhibit (e.g., spoken word, theater, art instillation) and a critical essay.

These assignments highlight the CRT tenets voices of color and intersectionality. Voices of color, as mentioned earlier, suggests that those who are marginalized in society – via storytelling and counter narrative analysis – have the power to expand our understanding of society, build community, and subvert oppressive dominant ideology. Intersectionality, on the other hand, brings awareness that all of us have multiple identities such as those related to gender, race, faith, sexual orientation, faith, and ethnicity (Delgado, 2013). Our narrative excerpts describe each of our thoughts and engagement with these elements of the course.

Michelle. In this class, I was in a space where I was challenged to navigate conversations about isms and oppression, conversations that I never thought I would have in a higher education setting. I took an undergraduate class in multicultural education that was heavily influenced by Critical Race Theory. It was also in this class when I first became aware about systems of oppression and about what it meant to be oppressed, but we didn't share stories or our experiences to demonstrate its relevance to and impact on our lives. The Critical Race Studies class provided that link by challenging us to reflect on our experiences and focusing on conversations with our classmates with whom we would share those stories.

Coming into a classroom where you could share your experiences in a space where your stories were valuable, it was hard to get used to that and was initially completely unfamiliar to me. CRS class disrupted the notion of the banking model of education, posed by Paulo Freire (1995), and provided a safe space to explore with others the applications and relevance of CRS concepts.

The process of writing the assignments were so difficult. Not that writing about yourself is, but reflecting on "well what is my story?", especially after spending most of your life never really being prompted to think about yourself on that level of understanding. So, the task seemed daunting and unfamiliar to me. I dreaded starting the writing process for a while because, honestly, I didn't know where to begin. It wasn't until one day, when I forced myself to sit down and do some free-writing responding to the guided questions that were provided with the assignment. The assignment asked questions such as "How do you define your own ethnic-racial identity along with any other social identities that have shaped your life experiences? How did you come to learn about your social group memberships?"

I think that is what helped guide what I should reflect on and what to think more deeply about. It helped organize my story so that I could make better sense of it. Writing my narrative and engaging with my story brought up intense, yet conflicting emotions. I ended up writing so much about myself and my experiences with the social categories I identify with. Then, it was a matter of acknowledging the way they interweave with each other and throughout my life. This was aided by everything that was happening in our classroom. We were learning different ways of thinking and seeing the world, hearing different stories in class and having conversations with my classmates; it all shifted my perspective; creating a different lens through which I could articulate my experiences.

Through these conversations, I listened to the truths and lived experiences of others and spoke my own truth. The "Danger of a Single Story" (Adichie, 2009) became apparent to me as I grew more conscious of different stories that challenged what I thought I knew and what I have always believed. My understanding of society and social problems operated from single stories I learned through the media, in books, and from others.

Through the articles we read, I learned the language and concepts to describe, connect, and validate what I have experienced and it made me realize that our individual problems are collective, our oppression connected. Many of us in class realized oppression comes in different forms.

Adriana. My exposure to difference--having different contextual experiences growing up--and interactions with different types of people fostered my consciousness and awareness of oppression. Consequently, in the classroom, I try to simulate that exposure to difference in various ways. I like to give students as many opportunities to tell their personal stories, to be self-reflective, and to hear the stories of others. Another way I like to help students engage with narrative work is by modeling. I use self-disclosure to share aspects of my story relevant to class discussions. I also provide examples of the ways in which I benefit from membership in privileged social groups.

While the narrative assignments are meaningful on their own, I am intentional about the activities that happen in the classroom before the narrative assignments are due. In the CRS class, my aim is to prime students to think about their story as a racialized person. How students come to define racialization is an open ended task. To this end, I ask students to consider if their life has been racialized, and to explain why or why not that is the case. For example, if a White student is having a difficult time with this assignment, I might recommend that the student to describe why it may be that they had never thought about race because of their whiteness.

In class, I also encourage students to share their unique experiences to facilitate the understanding of abstract theoretical concepts. For instance, in preparation for the first narrative I assignment, I teach about the cycle of socialization (Harro, 2000) by having students break up into small groups and discuss the different messages we receive about who we are and how we are supposed to act. I let students know that messages can be intersectional, and encourage them to think of any early socialization messages. Often, this activity results in a broader discussion about gender, and heteronormativity. Another narrative-related classroom activity is the racial timeline in which students outline what they have learned about themselves as a member of a racial-ethnic group. Students shared their personal experiences in class and discussed the commonalities and differences across individual experiences. Thus, the role of storytelling is to identify the dominant narrative that have touched our lives and surface multiple counter-narratives.

I use the grading of narrative papers to help students further reflect and think critically about the concepts discussed in class. As Michelle mentioned, in my grading remarks to her narrative I posed questions (e.g., how did you first learn that heterosexuality was the norm?) to help her identify the dominant narrative. In this way, the grading of narrative assignments allows me to guide students through the process of identifying dominant narratives without giving them the answers.

Maria. I taught CRS for the first time in my second semester in the department, in the spring of 2015. While CRT and specifically this class do create a context that intentionally aims to deepen students' understanding of the political dynamics that underpin the field of social work, community organizing is still not a central social work practice. That is, social work practices tend to focus on mental health related practices, with policy, administration, and community organizing occupying a lesser role. In the three semesters I have taught CRS I have observed that most students come in the program with not a very deep level of awareness about their political, social, and economic positionality and how this all connects with a master-narrative that dehumanizes and disempowers marginalized communities; including those they come from. Often at about a third of the semester, students experience reactions of anger, pain, frustration, and disbelief at what they were not aware of for most of their lives, and a lot of which they had internalized as truths.

They then understand that a Master narrative exists, and that through working on their narratives individually and as a collective, the process of creating a counter-narrative and liberation begins.

In our conversation about the assignments above, we found ourselves delving into further reflections. Maria shared that she wonders whether, to some extent, assignments such as the two narratives listed above, may not at some point lend themselves to students using intimate, narrative stories against each other. Adriana suggested that facilitation of storytelling also includes creating a space that allows students to share narrative in an equitable manner. Historically, the sharing of counter-narratives in classroom settings has often involved tokenizing students with marginalized identities. Therefore, it is necessary for instructors to continually assess the power dynamics at play as students share their stories. Moreover, unraveling complicated layers of identity and sharing narratives requires courage, vulnerability, and risk taking. She adds that it is important to be transparent about the need for vulnerability and invite students to envision class as a "brave space" that will require engagement with conflict and accountability across group differences (Arao & Clemens, 2013).

We see the role of the instructor not as imparting information to students, but rather as a facilitator of experiential learning that surfaces student's implicit knowledge. This practice is in line with a CRT approach to education that centers the experience and cultural wealth of students of color (Delgado-Bernal, 2002; Yosso, 2005). It also reflects the power of testimonio as a pedagogical tool for transformational and experiential learning (Albert & Couture, 2014). As Michelle astutely pointed out, the CRS course, by using storytelling and centering the narrative of students disrupts the banking model of education (Freire, 1995).

Storytelling for transformational learning

The process of surfacing counter-narratives in the classroom can be a transformational learning experience. The last sections of our conversation below, give insights into the transformational aspect brought by CRS.

Michelle. Through exposure and awareness of other stories, and reflection of my own experiences, I was challenged to question how I came to think a certain way and why I believed certain things were normal. For example, in the revision of my narrative, [Adriana] asked me to expand on the time I first became aware that heterosexuality was normal. I remember having to think deeply about this question and ask myself well when did I? I went my whole life knowing things a certain way, believing, assuming, and accepting things as the way things have always been, instead of questioning, exploring, and being curious.

Adriana. One of my goals is also to help our students, many of which are students of color, to reflect on their privilege. In doing so, I ask them to consider how racism is not a black and white binary, that it is not an "us" versus "them" situation because we are all complicit in systems of oppression. I have witnessed students' transformation in that students often indicate that learning about their privileges was one of the significant things they learned from that class. I also know that transformational learning is not always easy. For white students, or students learning about another privileged identity, I try to normalize feelings of guilt and anxiety by letting them know that the affective response to learning about privilege and oppression is typical. Personally, teaching and using narratives in the CRS course has helped me refine my skills and understanding of privilege. I try to teach to the group, as a result of my experience teaching this course shifts from year to year.

Maria. Teaching this class and being in conversations with my colleagues in the department have contributed to my professional and personal growth, and to my political development and transformation. Teaching this class requires a great deal of mental and intellectual preparation, self-awareness, as well as openness and receptivity for the various, often unexpected dynamics that students bring to every class. Most of all, teaching this class requires a significant amount of humility, patience, and compassion toward ourselves as instructors and toward students in the class. Working on our narratives is an ongoing process. Sharing our narratives with others can be uncomfortable, and sometimes painful. Yet, all this and more is necessary if we are to challenge the Master-narrative individually and as a collective, and in this process, heal ourselves.

During our conversation we also found opportunities to interrogate ourselves and each other, in a reflexive fashion. This way of engaging with one another, and our testimonios, provided a way for us to theorize and to create new knowledge about counter-narrative work in our classrooms (Delgado-Bernal, Burciaga & Flores, 2012). For instance, in addition to discovering ways in which the master-narrative has often affected our sense of self and social positionality, Adriana helped us realize that the narrative assignment may also help students examine one's complicity in the dominant narrative through membership in privileged groups.

Maria, on the other hand, reflected about whether and to what extent in our aims to uncover the damage of institutionalized racism and its intersections with other oppressions students may not reach a point of numbness, with a backfiring-type-of-result. To this effect, Michelle commented that she has witnessed students often feeling overly saturated with too much discussion on race, but she also pondered if this was the case with her cohort because they were taking CRS while the 2016 US presidential elections were going on, and which led to the election of Donald Trump. Adriana, on the other hand, offered that aversion to having continued and meaningful discussions about racism and other forms of oppression is part of the learning process.

Conclusion

Reflecting on and sharing our narratives and experiences with the CRS class with each other was illuminating and at times emotionally moving. Adriana and Maria, for instance, found themselves sharing ways in which the dynamics with their partners in some ways influence their teaching of CRS. Adriana shared, for instance, that she and her partner talk about race every day. Their experience as people of color, the current political climate, and their scholarship on race makes racism a common topic of discussion. Maria shared that sharing her life with her African American husband who was born and raised in the US, has made her aware of the ongoing challenges he has faced all his life. Adriana shared that in conversation with her partner, an academic in political science who studies the political participation of African Americans, they believe that to politically mobilize people of color racial justice and political issues should be framed in a way that inspires hope and motivate for change. Thus, one of the purposes of the course and the narrative assignments is both to motivate students to work toward social change, but also to inspire them and give them hope.

Often in sharing our narrative and talking about how they are similar or different, we can identify the patterns of oppression and of the dominant narrative present across communities or social groups. This happens through the act of thinking, the act of writing, the act of sharing, and the act of listening. The act of thinking and writing gives space for reflection, critical awareness, and making connections. The act of sharing one's story can be more emotional and at times healing. For the storyteller, telling one's story can help release certain emotion or embodied trauma. The act of listening also offers many benefits. In listening to others, we may be able to broaden our perspective, build empathy for others, or connect our disparate experiences with those of others.

Writing this chapter has given us the opportunity to reflect together about our experiences as a student and two instructors teaching and learning Critical Race Studies, in a department whose theoretical foundation is Critical Race Theory. The class is taught to all students (part-time and full-time) during their first semester in the program. We engaged in conversation about these experiences, contextualized by the way in which our narratives have influenced the way we approach our teaching and learning in this class. In writing this chapter, we were curious about the extent to which this class, the CRT materials students read and discuss, and in particular three assignments in which they write about their personal narratives may lead students to creating narratives that are counter to the master, predominant narratives as marginalized people they have internalized. From our shared experiences we concluded that the class, and the department's CRT theoretical foundation has had an effect on our approaches to teaching the class, our understanding of the students' interests and needs, and in some instances, the evolving of our own narratives and counter-narratives.

Our engagement with narrative inquiry is framed by theories of narrative and counter-narratives in the context of critical social work. We conclude by affirming our commitment to the value of narrative as a way to create a new, collective counter-narrative through a critical social work lens.

Notes

1 *Latinx is a gender-neutral alternative to the term Latino. It is used to identify people of Latin American descent beyond gender binaries.*
2 www.industrialareasfoundation.org/

References

Abrams, L.S., & Moio, J.A. (2009). Critical race theory and the cultural competence dilemma in social work education. *Journal of Social Work Education*, 45(2), 245–261.
Adichie, C.N. (2009). The danger of a single story [Video file]. Retrieved from www.ted.com/talks/chimamanda_adichie_the_danger_of_a_single_story?language=en
Albert, M.-N. and Couture, M.-M. (2014). *Management Decision* 52(4), 794–812.
Arao, B., & Clemens, K. (2013). From safe spaces to brave spaces. In L. Landreman (Ed.), *The art of effective facilitation: Reflections from social justice educators* (pp. 135–150). Sterling, VA: Stylus.
Avila, M. (2017). *Transformative civic engagement through community organizing*. Sterling, VA: Stylus Publishing.
Bell, B., Gaventa, J., & Peters, J. M. (1990). We make the road by walking: Conversations on education and social change. Philadelphia: Temple University Press.
Beverley, J. (2003). Testimonio, subalternity, and narrative authority. In Denzin, N. K. and Lincoln, Y. S. (Eds.), *Strategies of qualitative inquiry* (pp. 319–335). Thousand Oaks, CA: Sage.
California State University Dominguez Hills. (2018a). Campus history. Retrieved from www.csudh.edu/campus-history/
California State University Dominguez Hills. (2018b). CSUDH points of distinction. Retrieved from www.csudh.edu/about/points-distinction/
California State University Dominguez Hills. (2018c). Master of social work: Course description. Retrieved from www.csudh.edu/social-work/course/
California State University Dominguez Hills. (2018d). History, mission & vision. Retrieved from www.csudh.edu/about/history-mission-vision/
California State University Dominguez Hills. (2018e). The 1965 Watts rebellion. Retrieved from www.csudh.edu/watts/history/about/
Campbell, C., & Baikie, G. (2012). Beginning at the beginning: An exploration of critical social work. *Critical Social Work: An Interdisciplinary Journal Dedicated to Social Justice*, 13(1), 67–81.

Coleman, J. S. (1976). Differences between experiential and classroom learning. In Keeton, M. T. (Ed.), *Experiential learning* (pp. 49–61). San Francisco, CA: Jossey-Bass.
Constance-Huggins, M. (2012). Critical race theory in social work education: A framework for addressing racial disparities. *Critical Social Work*, 13(2), 1–16.
csuDHTVlive. (2015, December 21). CSUDH: Master of social work: Critical race theory [Video file]. Retrieved from https://youtu.be/KM1k5Tr4Xsw
Delgado-Bernal, D. (2002). Critical race theory, Latino critical theory, and critical raced-gendered epistemologies: Recognizing students of color as holders and creators of knowledge. *Qualitative Inquiry*, 8(1), 105–126.
Delgado-Bernal, D., Burciaga, R., & Flores Carmona, J. (2012). Chicana/Latina testimonios: Mapping the methodological, pedagogical, and political. *Equity & Excellence in Education*, 45(3), 363–372.
Delgado, R., & Stefancic, J. (2001). *Critical race theory: An introduction*. New York, NY: University Press.
Delgado, R. (2013). Storytelling for oppositionists and others: A plea for narrative. In R. Delgado & J. Stefancic (Eds.), *Critical race theory: The cutting edge* (3rd ed.) (pp. 71–80). Philadelphia, PA: Temple University Press.
Freire, P. (1995). *Pedagogy of the oppressed*. New York, NY: Continuum.
Graham, M., & Schiele, J.H. (2010). Equality-of-oppressions and anti-discriminatory models in social work: Reflections from the USA and UK. *European Journal of Social Work*, 13(2), 231–244.
Hagan, W.J. (2015, November 30). Honoring history. *Dominguez Today*, 2. Retrieved from https://issuu.com/csudh/docs/domingueztodayfall2015
Harro, B. (2000). The cycle of socialization. In M. Adams, W.J. Blumenfeld, R. Casteneda, H.W. Hackman, M.L. Peters, & X. Zuniga (Eds.), *Readings for diversity and social justice: An anthology on racism, anti-Semitism, sexism, heterosexism, ableism, and classism* (pp. 15–21). New York, NY: Routledge.
Huber, L.P. (2009). Beautifully powerful: A LatCrit reflection on coming to an epistemological consciousness and the power of testimonio. *American University Journal of Gender, Social Policy & the Law 18*, 839.
Industrial Areas Foundation. (2018). History. Retrieved from www.industrialareasfoundation.org/content/history
Ortiz, L., & Jani, J. (2010). Critical race theory: A transformational model for teaching diversity. *Journal of Social Work Education*, 46(2), 175–193.
Prieto, L., & Villenas, S.A. (2012). Pedagogies from Nepantla: Testimonio, Chicana/Latina feminisms and teacher education classrooms. *Equity & Excellence in Education*, *45*(3), 411–429.
Razack, N. & Jeffery, D. (2002). Critical race discourse and tenets of social work. *Canadian Social Work Review*, 19(2), 257–270.
Ryan, A.B. (2001). *Feminist ways of knowing: towards theorizing the person for radical adult education*. Leicester, Ireland: National Institute of Adult Continuing Education.
The Digital Library of Georgia (2013). Civil Rights Digital Library: Watts Riots. http://crdl.usg.edu/events/watts_riots/?Welcome Viewed April 28, 2019.
Yosso, T.J. (2005). Whose culture has capital? A critical race theory discussion of community cultural wealth. *Race Ethnicity and Education*, 8(1), 69–91.

19

Hegemonic university tales

Discussing narrative positioning within the academic field between Humboldtian and managerial governance

Klarissa Lueg, Angela Graf and Justin J.W. Powell

Introduction: an on-going field transformation in higher education

In recent decades, we observe fundamental changes in many Higher Education (HE) systems in Europe and beyond, often labeled as "academic capitalism" (Münch, 2014; Slaughter & Leslie, 1997; Slaughter & Rhoades, 2004) or "academic neoliberalism" (Bottrell & Manathunga, 2019; Frickel & Hess, 2014). Universities face increasing national and international competitiveness for status and financial resources and respond to this with different policy measures and strategic organizational development. These changes go along with the idea that the production of internationally visible top-level research and teaching is best stimulated by market-based competition and is to be professionally managed. This notion of research and higher education being manageable "products" is no longer new. In fact, universities worldwide have established governance systems responding to this powerful discourse since early in the 1970s (Antonsen & Jørgensen, 2000; Kristensen, Nørreklit, & Raffnsøe-Møller, 2001; Mendiola, 2012). However, albeit an established form of university governance in many countries, the discourse on HE still treats this managerialist development as novel, obviously standing in contrast to an "older" model and established systems. We argue that this is rooted in the perception of scholars that the notion of the managerial university stands in contrast to a perceived "righteous" idea of the university. Such a moral stance and perspective corresponds with the "Humboldtian ideal" of university construction,[1] conduct, and governance that maximizes professorial autonomy and self-administration.

The construction of these two opposing narrative positions comes with major implications for current and future academic practice: first, clinging to the narrative of the Humboldtian university model might be idolizing and idealizing, ignoring critical insights as to social classism, asymmetries in within-faculty-power, and male hegemony that impacted and still impact the university experience (Bagilhole, 2010; Graf, 2015; Graf, Keil, & Ullrich, 2020; Hartmann, 2002). As much as the managerial university deserves criticism, it would be wrong to construct the Humboldtian university model as some sort of better, golden age of university development. Especially given the myriad tenets that have been ascribed to it over the decades, it remains a myth-laden narrative (see

Ash, 2006). Second, we argue that criticism of the managerial governance system rooted in idolization of the Humboldtian university model is in fact naïve. Because it clings to a utopian ideal, discursively redlining improvements the managerial university – or other form of university governance – might bring about, the Humboldtian idolized model does not foster a constructive dialogue of options in contemporary organizational governance, especially as HE has indeed massified to serve the majority of each cohort in many countries and thus is no longer the province of a small elite. The myth-rooted opposition gives way to the managerial university becoming an ante-narrative: a bet on the future, placed by university management, relying and hoping that the managerial university will make retrospective sense as the hegemonic tale of the future (Boje, 2001a, 2001b). Deriving from this assumption, our chapter is structured as follows: first, we motivate our narratological stance on the issue of university governance. Here, we also elaborate on the different narratological concepts we employ in order to approach the two selected stances towards righteous university governance: hegemonial narrative, counter-narrative, and ante-narrative. Second, we apply these concepts to the Humboldtian and the managerial narratives. We emphasize characteristics of the Humboldtian tale as hegemonic, and we draw attention to the, initially, counter-narrative character of the managerial narrative. Then, we discuss the transition from counter- to ante- to hegemonic narrative of the managerial perspective. We call special attention to tellers (authors) of the Humboldtian narrative and how the perseverance of traditional power structures may have facilitated the rise of managerialism. Finally, we point out implications of our considerations for both academic practice and conceptual development.

Why a narrative perspective on this struggle for authority in the university?

Here, we show how promising it is to explore the on-going discourse among multiple university stakeholders from a social interactional narrative perspective. In doing so, we see the conflicting perspectives on university governance as narrative units and make these the subjects of our sociological observations. Narratives, consequently, are considered social practices (Georgakopoulou, 2010). We concur that narratives, in their social context, have the potential to reproduce or challenge "existing relations of power and inequity" (Ewick & Silbey, 1995, p. 197) as they are interwoven with and constitutive of social relations, interactions, and the institutionalized organization of those (as represented by the university). Narratives hinge upon, but also constitute, social life. They are deeply entangled with the social rules for "when, what, how, and why stories are told" (Ewick & Silbey, 1995), and, most importantly, they determine, by whom they may be told, and whose view and perspectives they represent. In this setting, paying attention to the power (im)balance for groups and individuals involved in the university field, is vital to interpreting Humboldtian and managerial tales. Whilst the managerial narrative has been brought forward by external agents, to professors and faculty at universities, the Humboldtian narrative is being told and reproduced by these faculties themselves.

In general, understanding patterns of consistent social interpretations and representations of certain events as narratives is highly useful for the sociological endeavor of critiquing existing and shifting power relations. Understanding a narrative means being able to answer the question how social groups inter-subjectively account for social life. With a view to the interrelation between narratives and organizations (here: the university), scholars have long relied on narratives to learn about organizational practices. One established perspective is that of "communication as constitutive of organizations" that proposes to think of organizations as "talked into being" (Heritage, 1984, p. 290). Related to the concept of narrative, we aim to specify those inter-relations, the transactions, and the positionings of and around different narratives that create the organization in the first place (Frandsen, Lundholt, & Kuhn, 2017). In the following, we present and distinguish from one another various notions of narrative that are employed in our observations and that may usefully serve generally in social science applications.

What is a narrative?

A narrative in its most general sense can be described as "sequences of statements connected by both a temporal and a moral ordering" (Ewick & Silbey, 1995, p. 198, citing Ricoeur, 1984, 1985, 1988). The eminent position of the term narrative in social science, outside of literature studies, is based on the assumption that all identities and social action, all positionings (Bamberg, 1997), are brought forward as stories. In consequence, non-literary narratives are social interactions in themselves, and they represent and reproduce (sometimes defy) larger social structures. These social interactions can be represented in manifold different forms: mostly, scholars have referred to language (Ewick & Silbey, 1995, p. 198) as mediating a narrative. However, an increasing number of studies does consider embodied narratives, material narratives (Strand, 2014), sociomaterial narratives (Flora, Boje, Rosile, & Hacker, 2016; Lueg, Boje, Lundholt, & Graf, 2019), multimodal narratives in business (Bager, 2019), or art and design (Pantaleo, 2019). Being observant, as a scholar, of the narratives represented in the social world, can contribute to the gathering of insights on marginalized views. A narrative is often described as "having" three features: the first feature is the feature of temporal order. The understanding of narrative as a sequence of statements connected by temporality is anchored, mostly, in the field of literary studies. Increasingly, social scientists have challenged the notion of the one clearly identifiable narrative structure, including Bamberg (2011, p. 15) and Boje (2014), who argue for the eminence of surfacing and testing "small stories" (Bamberg, 2011, p. 15) and for the fragmented and living character of narratives (Boje, 2014), respectively. The second feature of a narrative would be a "selective appropriation of past events and characters" (Ewick & Silbey, 1995, p. 200) by a teller. Third, there is the feature of emplotment, or recently "emplacement" (Jackson, 2013), meaning that sequences, statements, and characters are, or will be, interrelated by patterns of belonging. As a fourth feature, narrative structure leads to cohesion, causality and, most prominent in fairy tales, closure. Closure here means the provision of a moral principle in light of which the sequence can be evaluated (White, 1990). Again, moral interpretations of ideal social behavior are densely interrelated with social power structures. Narratives, thus, are instruments, consciously or unconsciously to produce a normatively laden social order (Frandsen, Lundholt et al., 2017; Giddens, 1991; Ricoeur, 1991).

What is a *hegemonic* narrative?

In line with the approach of this handbook, our focus is on narratives as fostering, and as being representative of, social power relations. In this vein, many observations focus on conflicts between agents bringing forward a narrative in favor of dominant power structures, and those agents pushing a marginalized and/or opposing perspective (a *counter*-narrative). First, when trying to disentangle the many notions that come with narrative social interpretation, we depart from that notion serving as foil of comparison, the "hegemonic narrative". Common other, similar terms that express a concentration and representation of power are "master-narrative" or "dominant narrative". "Hegemonic narrative" applies to those "stories that reproduce existing relations of power and inequity" (Ewick & Silbey, 1995: 198). Whilst "dominant narrative" is mostly being used as a synonym to this, a "master-narrative" is often used to describe such types of dominant narratives that occur in and around organizations (Frandsen, Kuhn, & Lundholt, 2017; Lueg, 2018).[2] The notions overlap, and do not exclude, but rather specify each other. We draw on the notion "hegemonic narrative" since it emphasizes the rather subtle, sometimes veiled, socio-structural aspect in charge of reproducing contemporary power structures between agents, organizations, and larger social structures. As a synthesis from numerous definitions, we propose:

> Socially hegemonic narratives are stories
>
> *told in favor of* those holding power over social matters relevant to that story,
>
> *told by* those agents who actually are in power or benefit from this power structure, and
>
> *outlining moral rules* (if subtly) that prevent and *oppose* the imagining of *any other power structure.*

Consequently, hegemonic narratives are tough to challenge successfully. Perhaps the most effective maneuver of hegemonic storytellers is their being in charge of deciding who holds what position. Hegemonic storytellers legitimate, by means of their actual power positions, how stories are told, and by whom. Social norms specify rules of participation. Rules assign roles of storyteller and audience, but also the roles of those who may not interfere, inquire, or challenge. Storytelling, in consequence, can serve to preserve, to challenge, to weaken dominant structures, and might even propose and provide pathways to new structures. It is a strategic expression; "strategic" meaning serving the purposes of certain social groups of agents, despite not being an explicitly planned and rationally chosen behavior. In this, storytelling is as inherently strategic as is taste, liking, and lifestyle, in Bourdieusian sociology (Bourdieu, 1984): it does, in fact, express how its bearer perceives of the world and themselves, but it also expresses how they wish the world and themselves to be (see also the concept of symbolic violence; e.g. Bourdieu, 1991; Bourdieu, Passeron, Nice, & Bottomore, 1977; Bourdieu & Wacquant, 1992; Krais, 1993). Again, with a view to our comparing the Humboldtian and managerial tales, this matters, since we emphasize that *both* narratives certainly do display characteristics of hegemonic claims benefitting one social group only.

What is a *counter*-narrative?

A "counter-narrative", in its core, is a simple, but much needed concept: in relation to organizations it has been described as an account that somehow resists another, more dominant narrative (Bamberg & Andrews, 2004, p. 1), and, we might add, sometimes only a narrative *perceived* as being more dominant. This does not automatically make "the other" account a master-narrative or a hegemonic narrative. It simply indicates that there are (at least) two narratives that stand in tension with each other. All those interrelated narratives then are embedded in other types of narratives that may again disaggregate into several counter-narratives. In relation to organizations, this has been called "polyphony" (Frandsen, Lundholt et al., 2017, p. 4). This notion of "counter-narrative" is quite modest and not meant to be as absolute or dichotomy-inducing as one may think. In contrast, the term "subversive" narrative has been used in a rather less encompassing way. Kuhn (2017, p. 2) has brought forward the useful metaphor of the "authoritative text". This notion, going beyond taking text for an entity in its most simple form (e.g., written protocols, policies, statements) describes the fight over power and sense-making by the involved agents.

> The textual metaphor suggests that its production is the ongoing result of a process of authorship—and that authorship is where a multiplicity of actors vie to inscribe their visions of the whole into the conception of "we" while simultaneously contesting the writing efforts of others. Counter-narratives are those that contend for authorship by reinterpreting or challenging a plot line; they disrupt canonical stories, dominant identities and master-narratives.
>
> *(Kuhn, 2017, p. 22)*

Here, it is worth adding, that counter-narratives can entail different levels of social advocacy: some counter-narratives may argue against persisting structures with a goal of liberating manifold, diverse social groups by unveiling how these groups are affected (Ewick & Silbey, 1995, p. 197). Other counter-narratives advocate strategic self-interest, with authors focusing narrowly on their very own interests.

What is an *ante*-narrative?

We employ Boje's concept of "ante-narrative processes" as a canvas for our analysis. Ante-narrative is the one moment of story development where "living story webs" unfold (Henderson & Boje, 2016). These living stories are told and unfolded by agents in the present, in our case: professors and other proponents of the Humboldtian narrative, and management and other proponents of the managerial narrative. They serve to bridge a grand narrative of the past and a story to be, an image of how the future could look (Boje, 2001b; Henderson & Boje, 2016). At the stage of ante-narrative, stories told contribute to or contest an emerging story. An ante-narrative is a bet, by one social group of tellers, that a fragmented polyphonic story will make retrospective sense in the future (Boje, 2007). This process hinges upon faith, rationality, and obviously on the actual resources tellers have to push "their" ante-narrative. As Boje points out, the strategic employment of ante-narratives is of importance to strategy, and to leader visioning, inter alia, as it is the "before" of a story (Boje & Rosile, 2010). Ante-narrative allows the focus on the collective story-making of different actors, together, who will manage to bring forward a successful story, and those who will end up with a counter-narrative position. In our case, we think it is important to bring in ante-narrative to illuminate the contributions of the Humboldtian and the managerial narratives to the rise of the managerial narrative.

The Humboldtian university model – a hegemonic narrative?

What we call the Humboldtian narrative is, in fact, a second-order observation (Luhmann, 2013): actually, we observe the *narrative of the narrative* by Wilhelm von Humboldt, the influential Prussian scholar and education minister. He, Humboldt, delineated the internal and external structure a university should possess in his 1810 memorandum on the occasion of the foundation of the University of Berlin (today: Humboldt Universität zu Berlin). Employing a liberal political stance, he elaborated on suggestions, i.e., as to the so called "unity of research and teaching", on the organization of research, and on the various responsibilities of university and state. Even though Humboldt's ideas have not been implemented in an accurate sense,[3] they massively influenced the development of the organizational structure of universities, in Germany, throughout Europe, to North America and East Asia (cf. Powell et al., 2017). Those ideas pertaining to governance and agency of scholars being ascribed to Humboldt, serve as "a powerful rhetoric appeal and formative influence on policy debates by shaping corporate and professional identities" (Jessop, 2008, p. 4; cited in Lüde, 2012, p. 151). Most important, here, is the observation that despite Humboldt never having described the one legitimate form of university governance, his name is continuously used to defend the idea of the primacy of scientific autonomy, professorial authority, and self-governance. It is this interpretation of the Humboldtian perspective that we call "Humboldtian narrative". By way of example, Mitchell Ash argues that "'Humboldt' is a symbol of the autonomy and predominance of the faculty in university affairs" (2006, p. 249).

This mental model implies that scientific advancement results from scholars' individual efforts within a community of equal scholars, protected by extensive autonomy against state interventions. This "autonomy-claim" of academia responds to Humboldt's idea of solitude and freedom ("*Einsamkeit und Freiheit*"; own translation from original German) as core principles of scholarship. The scientific community should be free from state interventions to devote their energy to "pure science" in order to, over the long run, benefit society. Consequently, the professoriate should have the decision-making power over research and teaching issues without any external interference. These visions have left their mark on both the organizational structure of many universities, and on scholarly identity. Ideas of the "Humboldt model" have morphed as they moved globally (Cowen, 2009). This brought about an administrative structure mainly based on academic self-governance and notable professorial power (Hüther, 2010; Rüegg, 2004), while university leaders (presidents and deans) were gazed upon as serving as "*primus inter pares*". Decisions were made by professors themselves or committees of professors. In this sense, universities have been characterized as "organized anarchies" (Cohen, March, & Olsen, 1972) or "professional bureaucracies" (Mintzberg, 1979) within "loosely coupled systems" (Weick, 1976). Notably, again, these descriptions center on professors as agents and main benefactors of this anarchy; not considering further stakeholders.

Much doubt can be raised as to whether administrative staff and subordinated faculty below the professorial position shared (and share) this perception. Since professors, in the Humboldtian narrative, are not only "chairholders" but also award relevant degrees for academic careers and control access to scholarly positions, non-tenured faculty and staff are highly dependent on their personal support and decision-making (Graf, Keil, & Ullrich, 2020; Kreckel, 2008). These highly self-referential power structures (Bourdieu, 1988) also result in socially exclusive personnel structures and intersectional inequalities, bordering on "institutional discrimination" (Gomolla & Radtke, 2002). In most HE systems, women are still significantly underrepresented (e.g. UNESCO Institute for Statistics, 2018; Zippel, 2017), and moreover, the proportion of female scholars decreases the higher the position, often described as the "law of increasing disproportionality" (Putnam, 1976, 33 ff.) or glass ceiling (e.g. Cech & Blair-Loy, 2010; Rosser, 2004). Furthermore, there is some empirical evidence that there are analogue processes regarding social background (Blome, Möller, & Böning, 2019; Bourdieu, 1988; Graf, 2015; Hartmann, 2013; Möller, 2015), ethnicity or race (e.g. Bernal & Villalpando, 2010; Coleman, 2005; Gabriel, 2017; Gutiérrez y Muhs, Harris, González, & Niemann, 2012), disability (Dolmage, 2017; Kerschbaum, Eisenman, & Jones, 2017), and further categories of belonging.

The managerial university: a counter-narrative?

Since the 1970s, professorial self-governance has been increasingly questioned. For manifold reasons, "there is a considerable loss of confidence in the capacities for self-governance of the academic community" (Krücken & Meier, 2006, p. 244). Decreasing trust and lower financial resources available raised political and public claims for more transparency and audit as well as for more efficiency and effectiveness in academic governance (Engwall & Scott, 2013; Enders, 2013; Weingart, 2013; Weingart & Maasen, 2007).[4] Hence, politically initiated, structural transformations at universities ensued.

New Public Management (NPM) quickly became a field-wide notion to describe the improved ("new") way of dethroning old authorities allegedly responsible for slow organizational decision-making ("management") at state financed organizations ("public"). This idea, of dethroning old authorities, qualifies the managerial narrative as being, initially, a counter-narrative. Universities were to be turned "into organizational actors, which are able to act strategically and position themselves with regard to their competitors" (Krücken & Meier, 2006, p. 242). Such organizational agency, reflecting heightened competition, extends to disciplinary groups and organizational subunits (Marques & Powell, 2020). The transformation toward NPM is often (critically) discussed under terms such as the "entrepreneurial (enterprise) university" (Clark, 1998, 2001; Davies, 2001; Weingart & Maasen, 2007) or the "neoliberal university" (Bottrell & Manathunga, 2019; Rustin, 2016; Valero Duenas, Jørgensen, & Brunila, 2019) or, more generally, "academic managerialism" (Krücken, Blümel, & Kloke, 2013; Meier, 2010). Along with these structural changes, a "new" paradigm has emerged of how science and academia should be organized to efficiently achieve scientific progress.

In contrast to the Humboldtian idea of individual freedom, and scholarly autonomy, now, market-like competition is deemed to be key to scientific progress. Though the production of scientific knowledge has always been driven by competition on an individual level, what is "new" is the idea that professional managerialization of university governance and harsh (international) competition between scientific organizations should stimulate scientific knowledge production and thus promote top-level research. Yet, over the past several decades, with on-going HE expansion and the globe-spanning communication advances facilitated by the information technology revolution, widespread competition has been matched by vastly increasing collaboration across borders, be they cultural, disciplinary or academic status – with implications for how universities are to be managed (cf. Powell, 2018). Universities are considered an "organizational problem" demanding solutions (Wissel, 2007).

Just as the previous Humboldtian narrative, this "managerial narrative" also entails specific structural frame conditions. Hence, since the late 1970s, we observe a distinct shift towards organizational economization and a transformation of universities into "entrepreneurial universities", mimicking private for-profit organizations. In the course of these structural changes, there are fundamental changes of the inner-university power relations, too. Especially university management decision-making power has been distinctly extended. However, these power shifts do not proceed conflict-free, but evoke struggles for power and dominance between professors and university leadership. In view of this, the amplification of centralized management power does pose a threat to the status of the individual scholar as "*primus inter pares*", this representing the traditional construction of scholarly preoccupation and conduct (Hüther, 2010). Due to this struggle for power, it is not surprising that critical voices arise among the professoriate defending the "old system" and the managers of the "new system". In particular, it is emphasized that now decisions on scientific issues are influenced by "external" stakeholders who follow their own interests instead of following the greater interest of science.

Many of the scientific articles criticizing the shift in university government refer, explicitly or implicitly, to Humboldt's ideas as they argue against the new paradigm. By way of example, Schimank describes this process as the "threat of de-professionalization" ("*drohende Entprofessionalisierung*", own translation from the original German) (Schimank, 2005). By referring to Humboldt to defend their own position of power and privileges, this narrative turns into a nearly uncritical, hegemonic tale of a better past. Titles like, "Matthew defeats Humboldt" ("*Matthäus schlägt Humboldt*", own translation from original German) (Meier & Schimank, 2009) or "The University in Ruins" (Readings, 1996) obviously reflect this verdict.

Discussion and conclusion: transitioning from counter- to ante- to hegemonic narrative?

In both cases, the master-narrative and the counter-account stipulate the ideal organizational structure and power distribution. Consequently, the further the university's transformation progresses, the more the "managerial" becomes common and turns from a "counter-narrative" to the new "hegemonic-narrative" as it becomes the legitimate "blueprint" for "framing self-perceptions and identity as well as behavior" (Lundholt, Maagaaed, & Piekut, 2018, p. 3). Indeed, what is "counter" and what is "hegemonic" narrative hinges upon the social stakes involved: Bamberg and Andrews emphasize "[w]hat is dominant and what is resistant are not, of course, static questions, but rather are forever shifting placements" (Bamberg & Andrews, 2004, p. X). Humboldtian and managerial narratives are interdependent as they serve one another as a reference. Due to the changed structural political conditions and requirements in many countries, university management as well as individual scholars have to respond; they have to position themselves – for better or worse. Aiming at favorable positions on the university market (Berman, 2012), universities implement performance measurement systems and business-like management tools as well as undertake efforts to foster a university's specific corporate identity (Graf & Lueg, 2019). Strategic organizational development and branding processes become important factors of success in global competition and contribute to institutional narratives (Drori, Delmestri, & Oberg, 2016). Hence, it is obvious that the NPM model, the executive strength of the managerial narrative, is on a winning streak.

In view of the deep disapproval by numerous and still legally powerful professors, and from a narrative perspective, we ask: how could the managerial narrative diffuse so successfully through virtually all levels of the contemporary university? In order to explain the transition from counter-narrative to hegemonic narrative, we turn to the concept of ante-narrative. Ante-narrative, again, is that moment within a discourse where the story is not yet told, however agents do take their bets on what morale will prevail in an uncertain future (Jørgensen & Boje, 2009). The ante-narrative, here interpreted as a managerial politically induced bet on the future (see above), could also be connected to the Bourdieusian notion of field struggle (Bourdieu, 1988, 1998). In the crucial moment of powerful forces introducing their counter-narrative, proponents of the Humboldtian narrative missed out on the opportunity to create a rational opposition that criticized the deliberating effects of managerialism for all agents involved. Instead, moments of ante-narratives were (and are) being used to secure professorial group privileges; an eminently conservative approach in an era characterized by transformative change. Becoming a discursive fight over privileges and ownership, the narrative clash was prone to be won by strong, external forces.

The role of the proponents of the Humboldtian tale was, and is, more often than not, the one defending privileges and old benefits for the professorial elite insofar as inherent problems are ignored. Many other stances against and critiques of the managerial narrative could have been conceived: in answering the efficiency-demand of the managerial narrative, a restructuring of the university system could have been possible. This restructuring could have been used to liberate subordinated researchers from hitherto career-impeding structures, to foster inclusion, to change an authoritarian discourse (e.g. Bowen & Tobin, 2015; Blome, Möller & Böning, 2019; van Dyk & Reitz, 2017). However, the lack of advocacy of the traditional symbolic elite is telling. Likewise, the new academic elite in economics and business has been exceedingly effective in expanding their authority, in particular due to the on-going educational expansion and globalization (cf. Maeße, 2015). By way of example, eloquent silence meets activism initiated by non-tenured faculty in Germany (e.g. Netzwerk für Gute Arbeit in der Wissenschaft; N^2 - Network of Networks, 2019; cf. also Gallas, 2018; Graf, Keil, & Ullrich, 2020). Professors, in fact, do little to extend their privileges of tenure and social security to their immediate coworkers. Those favorable structures that are to support research freedom and unbiased service to society are cherry-picked for those (still) in power: professors. Yet this strategy did not promote success vis-à-vis an equally hegemonic, new, and politically supported managerial narrative. In this vein, tellers of the (selectively told) Humboldtian narrative have played their part in facilitating the rise of new public management. Now, as exemplified by our own question "how could this happen?", the managerial narrative has turned into a narrative offering closure, a story that also describes the besieged and defeated noble Humboldtianism.

However, none of these narratives is suited to function as a subversive, a counter-narrative inasmuch as it would allow "the silenced to speak" (Ewick & Silbey, 1995, p. 199). Persisting inequalities and power imbalances are scarcely addressed. In the rare case these dimensions are addressed, the actual arguments are often dispelled and reinterpreted in light of the managerial paradigm. For example, gender equality and diversity are addressed as important issues in the context of the German excellence initiative ("*Exzellenz Inititative*"), a competitive funding program initiated by the Federal Government, as a prime example for NPM measures. However, gender equality is not framed as a central moment of equity but as a factor of success in the international competition for excellence (Engels, Beaufaÿs, Kegen, & Zuber, 2015).

In this sense, both university tales can be regarded as hegemonic narratives, as "stories that reproduce existing relations of power and inequity" (Ewick & Silbey, 1995, p. 189). Which narrative is dominant depends on nationally-specific traditions and the varying institutionalization of Humboldtian or managerial principles. The struggle for primacy between two fractions of the dominant academic class – the professors and university management – continues. In order to address and challenge problematic issues inherent to both of these narratives, a narrative beyond the existing opposition would have to emerge.

Notes

1 The notion "Humboldtian" refers to a ideal-type of university construction and governance, going back to Wilhelm von Humboldts suggestions for structuring a university.
2 In discourse analysis, the term "master-narrative" is sometimes applied to substitute the notion of "Discourse". Discourses, often also described as "capital D-discourses" are socially created identities or images of groups of people that agents refer to in their sense-making processes (Gee, 2015; Georgakopoulou, 2010).
3 For a historical subsumption, see, for example, Lüde (2012); Schelsky (1960); Ashby (1967).
4 These developments have been embedded in a wider societal claim for responsible use of public finances not only concerning the HE sector, but also other public organizations, such as hospitals, in which New Public Management was widely implemented.

References

Antonsen, M., & Jørgensen, B. (Eds.). (2000). *Forandringer i teori og praksis: Skiftende billeder fra den offentlige sektor. demokrati projektet*. København, DK: Jurist- og Økonomiforbundet.

Ash, M. G. (2006). Bachelor of What, Master of Whom? The Humboldt Myth and Historical Transformations of Higher Education in German-Speaking Europe and the US. *European Journal of Education, 41*(2), 245–267.

Ashby, E. (1967). The Future of the Nineteenth Century Idea of a University. *Minerva, 6*(1), 3–17.

Bager, A. S. (2019). A Multimodal Discourse Analysis of Positioning and Identity Work in a Leadership Development Practice. *Communication & Language at Work, 6*(1), 40–62.

Bagilhole, B. (2010). Challenging Equal Opportunities: Changing and Adapting Male Hegemony in Academia. *British Journal of Sociology of Education, 23*(1), 19–33.

Bamberg, M. (1997). Positioning between Structure and Performance. *Journal of Narrative and Life History, 7*(1–4), 335–342.

Bamberg, M. (2011). Who am I? Narration and its Contribution to Self and Identity. *Theory & Psychology, 21*(1), 3–24.

Bamberg, M. G. W., & Andrews, M. (Eds.). (2004). *Considering Counter-Narratives: Narrating, Resisting, Making Sense* (4th ed.). Amsterdam: Benjamins.

Berman, E. P. (2012). *Creating the Market University: How Academic Science became an Economic Engine*. Princeton, NJ: Princeton University Press.

Bernal, D. D., & Villalpando, O. (2010). An Apartheid of Knowledge in Academia: The Struggle over the "Legitimate" Knowledge of Faculty of Color. *Equity & Excellence in Education, 35*(2), 169–180.

Blome, F., Möller, C., & Böning, A. (2019). Open House? Class-Specific Career Opportunities within German Universities. *Social Inclusion*, 7(1), 101–110.
Boje, D. M. (2001a). *Narrative Methods for Organizational and Communication Research*. London: Sage Publications.
Boje, D. M. (2001b). What is Antenarrative? Retrieved from https://business.nmsu.edu/~dboje/papers/what_is_antenarrative.htm#what_is_ante
Boje, D. M. (2007). From Wilda to Disney: Living Stories in Family and Organization Research. In D. Clandinin (Ed.), *Handbook of Narrative Inquiry: Mapping a Methodology* (pp. 330–354). Thousand Oaks: Sage Publications.
Boje, D. M. (2014). *Storytelling Organizational Practices: Managing in the Quantum Age*. London: Routledge.
Boje, D. M., & Rosile, G. (2010). Storytelling. In A. Mills, G. Durepos, & E. Wiebe (Eds.), *Encyclopedia of Case Study Research* (pp. 899–901). Thousand Oaks: Sage Publications.
Bottrell, D., & Manathunga, C. (Eds.). (2019). *Resisting Neoliberalism in Higher Education Volume I: Seeing Through the Cracks. Palgrave Critical University Studies*. Cham: Springer International Publishing.
Bourdieu, P. (1984). *Distinction: A Social Critique of the Judgement of Taste*. Cambridge: Harvard University Press.
Bourdieu, P. (1988). *Homo Academicus*. Stanford: Stanford University Press.
Bourdieu, P. (1991). *Language and Symbolic Power*. Oxford: Polity Press.
Bourdieu, P. (1998). *The State Nobility: Elite Schools in the Field of Power*. Stanford: Stanford University Press.
Bourdieu, P., Passeron, J.-C., Nice, R., & Bottomore, T. (1977). *Reproduction in Education, Society and Culture* (2nd ed.). London: Sage.
Bourdieu, P., & Wacquant, L. (1992). *An Invitation to Reflexive Sociology*. Chicago: University of Chicago Press.
Bowen, W. G., & Tobin, E. M. (2015). *Locus of Authority: The Evolution of Faculty Roles in the Governance of Higher Education*. Princeton: Princeton University Press.
Cech, E. A., & Blair-Loy, M. (2010). Perceiving Glass Ceilings? Meritocratic versus Structural Explanations of Gender Inequality among Women in Science and Technology. *Social Problems*, *57*(3), 371–397.
Clark, B. R. (1998). *Creating Entrepreneurial Universities: Organizational Pathways of Transformation*. Oxford: Press Pergamon; Emerald.
Clark, B. R. (2001). The Entrepreneurial University: New Foundations for Collegiality, Autonomy, and Achievement. *Higher Education Management*, *13*(2), 9–24.
Cohen, M. D., March, J. G., & Olsen, J. P. (1972). A Garbage Can Model of Organizational Choice. *Administrative Science Quarterly*, *17*(1), 1–25.
Coleman, M. G. (2005). Racism in Academia: The White Superiority Supposition in the "Unbiased" Search for Knowledge. *European Journal of Political Economy*, *21*(3), 762–774.
Cowen, R. (2009). The Transfer, Translation and Transformation of Educational Processes: and Their Shape-Shifting? *Comparative Education*, *45*(3), 315–327.
Davies, J. L. (2001). The Emergence of Entrepreneurial Cultures in European Universities. *Journal of the Programme on Institutional Management in Higher Education*, *13*(2), 25–44.
Dolmage, J. T. (2017). *Academic Ableism: Disability and Higher Education*. Ann Arbor: Michigan University Press.
Drori, G. S., Delmestri, G., & Oberg, A. (2016). The Iconography of Universities as Institutional Narratives. *Higher Education*, *71*(2), 163–180.
Enders, J. (2013). The University in the Audit Society: On Accountability, Trust and Markets. In L. Engwall & P. Scott (Eds.), *Trust in Universities: Proceedings from a Symposium held in Stockholm, 26–28 May 2011* (pp. 53–68). London: Portland Press Limited.
Engels, A., Beaufaÿs, S., Kegen, N. V., & Zuber, S. (2015). *Bestenauswahl und Ungleichheit: Eine soziologische Studie zu Wissenschaftlerinnen und Wissenschaftlern in der Exzellenzinitiative. Hochschule und Beruf*. Frankfurt am Main: Campus.
Engwall, L., & Scott, P. (Eds.). (2013). *Trust in Universities: Proceedings from a Symposium held in Stockholm, 26–28 May 2011*. London: Portland Press Limited.
Ewick, P., & Silbey, S. S. (1995). Subversive Stories and Hegemonic Tales: Toward a Sociology of Narrative. *Law & Society Review*, *29*(2), 197–226.
Flora, J., Boje, D., Rosile, G. A., & Hacker, K. (2016). A Theoretical and Applied Review of Embodied Restorying for Post-Deployment Family Reintegration. *Journal of Veterans Studies*, *1*(1), 129–162.
Frandsen, S., Kuhn, T., & Lundholt, M. W. (Eds.). (2017). *Counter-Narratives and Organization. Routledge Studies in Management, Organization and Society: Vol. 39*. New York: Routledge.
Frandsen, S., Lundholt, M. W., & Kuhn, T. (2017). Introduction. In S. Frandsen, T. Kuhn, & M. W. Lundholt (Eds.), *Routledge Studies in Management, Organization and Society: Vol. 39. Counter-Narratives and Organization* (pp. 1–13). New York: Routledge.

Frickel, S., & Hess, D. J. (Eds.). (2014). *Fields of Knowledge: Science, Politics and Publics in the Neoliberal Age*. Bingley: Emerald.

Gabriel, D. (2017). Race, Racism and Resistance in British Academia. In K. Fereidooni & M. El (Eds.), *Research. Rassismuskritik und Widerstandsformen* (pp. 493–505). Wiesbaden: Springer VS.

Gallas, A. (2018). Precarious Academic Labour in Germany: Termed Contracts and a New Berufsverbot. *Global Labour Journal, 9*(1).

Gee, J. P. (2015). Discourse, Small d, Big D. In K. Tracy, T. Sandel, & C. Ilie (Eds.), *The International Encyclopedia of Language and Social Interaction* (pp. 1–5). Chichester: Wiley-Blackwell.

Georgakopoulou, A. (2010). Narrative Analysis. In R. Wodak, B. Johnstone, & P. E. Kerswill (Eds.), *The SAGE Handbook of Sociolinguistics* (pp. 396–411). London: Sage Publications.

Giddens, A. (1991). *Modernity and Self-Identity: Self and Society in the Late Modern Age*. Cambridge: Polity Press.

Gomolla, M., & Radtke, F.-O. (2002). *Institutionelle Diskriminierung: Die Herstellung ethnischer Differenz in der Schule*. Wiesbaden: VS Verlag für Sozialwissenschaften.

Graf, A. (2015). *Die Wissenschaftselite Deutschlands: Sozialprofil und Werdegänge zwischen 1945 und 2013*. Frankfurt am Main: Campus.

Graf, A., Keil, M., & Ullrich, P. (2020). Exit, Voice und Loyalty: (Un)Möglichkeiten kollektiven Widerspruchs im akademischen Mittelbau in Deutschland. *Leviathan*, 48(2), 293–317.

Graf, A., & Lueg, K. (2019). Designing the Organizational Future: How German Universities communicate Governance Changes by means of Corporate Design. *Communication & Language at Work, 6*(2), 42–54.

Gutiérrez y Muhs, G., Harris, A. P., González, C. G., & Niemann, Y. F. (2012). *Presumed Incompetent: The Intersections of Race and Class for Women in Academia*. Logan: Utah State University Press.

Hartmann, M. (2002). *Der Mythos von den Leistungseliten: Spitzenkarrieren und soziale Herkunft in Wirtschaft, Politik, Justiz und Wissenschaft*. Frankfurt am Main: Campus.

Hartmann, M. (2013). *Soziale Ungleichheit - kein Thema für die Eliten?* Frankfurt am Main: Campus.

Henderson, T. L., & Boje, D. M. (2016). *Organizational Development and Change Theory: Managing Fractal Organizing Processes*. London: Routledge.

Heritage, J. (1984). *Garfinkel and Ethnomethodology. Social and Political Theory from Polity Press*. Cambridge: Polity Press.

Hüther, O. (2010). *Von der Kollegialität zur Hierarchie? Eine Analyse des New Managerialism in den Landeshochschulgesetzen*. Wiesbaden: VS Verlag für Sozialwissenschaften.

Jackson, M. (2013). *The Politics of Storytelling: Variations on a Theme by Hannah Arendt*. Copenhagen: Museum Tusculanum Press.

Jørgensen, K., & Boje, D. (2009). Genealogies of Becoming: Antenarrative Inquiry in Organizations. *Tamara Journal for Critical Organization Inquiry, 8*(1), 32–47.

Kerschbaum, S., Eisenman, L., & Jones, J. (Eds.). (2017). *Negotiating Disability: Disclosure and Higher Education*. Ann Arbor: University of Michigan Press.

Krais, B. (1993). Gender and Symbolic Violence: Female Oppression in the Light of Pierre Bourdieu's Theory of Social Practice. In C. J. Calhoun, E. LiPuma, & M. Postone (Eds.), *Bourdieu: Critical Perspectives* (pp. 156–177). Cambridge: Polity Press.

Kreckel, R. (Ed.). (2008). *Zwischen Promotion und Professur: Das wissenschaftliche Personal in Deutschland im Vergleich mit Frankreich, Großbritannien, USA, Schweden, den Niederlanden, Österreich und der Schweiz*. Leipzig: Akademische Verlagsanstalt.

Kristensen, J. E., Nørreklit, H., & Raffnsøe-Møller, M. (2011). Introduction: University Performance Measurement at Danish Universities. In J. E. Kristensen, H. Nørreklit, & M. Raffnsøe-Møller (Eds.), *University Performance Management: The Silent Managerial Revolution in Danish Universities* (pp. 7–17). Copenhagen: DJØF Pub.

Krücken, G., Blümel, A., & Kloke, K. (2013). The Managerial Turn in Higher Education? On the Interplay of Organizational and Occupational Change in German Academia. *Minerva, 51*(4), 417–442.

Krücken, G., & Meier, F. (2006). Turning the University into an Organizational Actor. In G. S. Drori, H. Hwang, & J. W. Meyer (Eds.), *Globalization and Organization: World Society and Organizational Change* (pp. 241–257). Oxford: Oxford University Press.

Kuhn, T. (2017). Communicatively Constituting Organizational Unfolding Through Counter-Narrative. In S. Frandsen, T. Kuhn, & M. W. Lundholt (Eds.), *Routledge Studies in Management, Organization and Society: Vol. 39. Counter-Narratives and Organization* (pp. 17–42). New York: Routledge.

Lüde, R. von. (2012). From Humboldt to Market: Competition and Excellence as New Governance Principles in the German University System. In H. G. Schuetze, G. Á. Mendiola, & D. Conrad (Eds.), *Comparative and International Education, A Diversity of Voices: Vol. 13. State and Market in Higher Education Reforms: Trends, Policies and Experiences in Comparative Perspective* (pp. 149–164). Rotterdam: Sense Publishers.

Lueg, K. (2018). Organizational Changes towards a European Academic Field: A Case Study of Frictions in the Narratives of Europeanization at a German University from an Institutional Perspective. *Innovation: The European Journal of Social Science Research, 31*(4), 484–503.

Lueg, K., Boje, D. M., Lundholt, M. W., & Graf, A. (2019). *How an Organizational Narrative Creates a New Doxa in Higher Education: A Case Study of Sociomaterial Construction of Educational Value in a Danish University.* 35th EGOS Colloquium, Edinburgh, United Kingdom.

Luhmann, N. (2013). *Theory of Society: Volume 2. Cultural Memory in the Present.* Stanford: Stanford University Press.

Lundholt, M. W., Maagaaed, C. A., & Piekut, A. (2018). Counternarratives. In R. L. Heath, W. Johansen, & J. Falkheimer (Eds.), *The International Encyclopedia of Strategic Communication.* New York: Wiley.

Maeße, J. (2015). *Eliteökonomen: Wissenschaft im Wandel der Gesellschaft.* Wiesbaden: Springer VS.

Marques, M., & Powell, J. J. W. (2020). Ratings, Rankings, Research Evaluation: How do Schools of Education behave Strategically within Stratified UK Higher Education? *Higher Education*, 79, 829–846. doi:10.1007/s10734-019-00440-1.

Meier, F. (2010). *Die managerialisierte Universität – Zum Organisationswandel der Hochschule.* Bremen.

Meier, F., & Schimank, U. (2009). Matthäus schlägt Humboldt? New Public Management und die Einheit von Forschung und Lehre. *Beiträge zur Hochschulforschung, 31*(1), 42–61.

Mendiola, G. Á. (2012). State and Market in Higher Education Reforms. In H. G. Schuetze, G. Á. Mendiola, & D. Conrad (Eds.), *Comparative and International Education, A Diversity of Voices: Vol. 13. State and Market in Higher Education Reforms: Trends, Policies and Experiences in Comparative Perspective* (pp. 7–23). Rotterdam: Sense Publishers.

Mintzberg, H. (1979). *The Structuring of Organizations.* Englewood Cliffs: Prentice Hall.

Möller, C. (2015). *Herkunft zählt (fast) immer: Soziale Ungleichheiten unter Universitätsprofessorinnen und -professoren. Bildungssoziologische Beiträge.* Weinheim: Beltz Juventa.

Münch, R. (2014). *Academic Capitalism: Universities in the Global Struggle for Excellence.* New York: Routledge.

N² - Network of Networks (2019, November 10). Network of Doctoral Researcher. Retrieved from http://n2-network.net/

Netzwerk für Gute Arbeit in der Wissenschaft. Eine Plattform für gute Arbeit in der Wissenschaft. Retrieved from www.mittelbau.net/

Pantaleo, S. (2019). Creativity and Elementary Students' Multimodal Narrative Representations. *Australian Journal of Language and Literacy, 42*(1), 17–27.

Powell, J. J. W. (2018). Higher Education and the Exponential Rise of Science: Competition and Collaboration. In R. A. Scott & M. Buchmann (Eds.), *Emerging Trends in the Social and Behavioral Sciences* (pp. 1–17). New York: Wiley.

Powell, J. J. W., Baker, D. P. & Fernandez, F. (Eds). (2017). *The Century of Science: The Global Triumph of the Research University.* International Perspectives on Education & Society, Vol. 33. Bingley: Emerald Publishing.

Putnam, R. D. (1976). *The Comparative Study of Political Elites.* Englewood Cliffs: Prenctice-Hall.

Readings, B. (1996). *The University in Ruins.* Cambridge: Harvard University Press.

Ricoeur, P. (1984, 1985, 1988). *Time and Narrative.* Chicago: University of Chicago Press.

Ricoeur, P. (1991). Narrative Identity. *Philosophy Today, 35*(1), 73–81.

Rosser, S.V. (2004). *The Science Glass Ceiling: Academic Women Scientists and the Struggle to Succeed.* New York: Routledge.

Rüegg, W. (2004). *Geschichte der Universität in Europa: Band III: Vom 19. Jahrhundert zum zweiten Weltkrieg 1800–1945.* München: C. H. Beck.

Rustin, M. (2016). The Neoliberal University and its Alternatives. *Soundings, 63*, 147–176.

Schelsky, H. (1960). *Einsamkeit und Freiheit: Zur sozialen Idee der deutschen Universität.* Münster: Aschendorff.

Schimank, U. (2005). Die akademische Profession und die Universität: ›New Public Management‹ und eine drohende Entprofessionalisierung. In T. Klatetzki & V. Tacke (Eds.), *Organisation und Profession* (pp. 143–164). Wiesbaden: VS Verlag für Sozialwissenschaften.

Slaughter, S., & Rhoades, G. (2004). *Academic Capitalism and the New Economy: Markets, State, and Higher Education.* Baltimore: Johns Hopkins University Press.

Slaughter, S., & Leslie, L. L. (1997). *Academic Capitalism: Politics, Policies, and the Entrepreneurial University.* Baltimore: Johns Hopkins University Press.

Strand, A. M. (2014). Material Storytelling: Introduction. In D. M. Boje & T. L. Henderson (Eds.), *Being Quantum: Ontological Storytelling in the Age of Antenarrative* (pp. 232–248). Newcastle upon Tyne: Cambridge Scholars Publishing.

UNESCO Institute for Statistics. (2018). *Women in Science* (Fact Sheet No. 51 (FS/2018/SCI/51)).

Valero Duenas, P. X., Jørgensen, K. M., & Brunila, K. (2019). Affective Subjectivation in the Precarious Neoliberal Academia. In D. Bottrell & C. Manathunga (Eds.), *Palgrave Critical University Studies. Resisting Neoliberalism in Higher Education Volume I: Seeing Through the Cracks* (pp. 135–154). Cham: Springer International Publishing.

Van Dyk, S., & Reitz, T. (2017). Projektförmige Polis und akademische Prekarität im universitären Feudalsystem: Zwei Diagnosen und eine Fünf-Jahres-Perspektive. *Soziologie, 46*(1), 62–73.

Weick, K. E. (1976). Educational Organizations as Loosely Coupled Systems. *Administrative Science Quarterly, 21*(1), 1–19.

Weingart, P. (2013). The Loss of Trust and how to Regain it: Performance Measures and Entrepreneurial Universities. In L. Engwall & P. Scott (Eds.), *Trust in Universities: Proceedings from a Symposium held in Stockholm, 26–28 May 2011* (pp. 83–95). London: Portland Press Limited.

Weingart, P., & Maasen, S. (2007). Elite Through Rankings – The Emergence Of the Enterprising University. In P. Weingart, R. Whitley, & J. Gläser (Eds.), *Sociology of the Sciences Yearbook. The Changing Governance of the Sciences* (Vol. 26, pp. 75–99). Dordrecht: Springer Netherlands.

White, H.V. (1990). *The Content of the Form: Narrative Discourse and Historical Representation. A Johns Hopkins paperback.* Baltimore: Johns Hopkins University Press.

Wissel, C. von (2007). *Hochschule als Organisationsproblem: Neue Modi universitärer Selbstbeschreibung in Deutschland.* Bielefeld: transcript Verlag.

Zippel, K. (2017). *Women in Global Science: Advancing Academic Careers through International Collaboration.* Stanford: Stanford University Press.

Part V

Counter-narratives, literature and ideology

20

Amidst narratives and counter-narratives

A traveler's report

Georgii Prokhorov and Sergei Saveliev

Introduction

Travelogue is an umbrella term which embraces a huge number of texts including, but not limited to, naïve descriptions of real journeys, literary journalism, 'armchair travels' and even novels (Saveliev & Savelieva 2018; cf. Bale & Sobecki 2019, pp. 467–476). Still, the core of this multifaceted genre make up the texts, which deal with travelling from point A to point B. Among the travelogues initially written as reports, there are ones, which were later transformed or viewed as having not only factual, but also artistic value. The texts share a common narrative form. Thus, when we use the word 'travelogue' in the article, we mean a text: a) inspired by real voyage or journey; b) focused on impressions and thoughts of the traveler; c) providing information about a country and thus by virtue of being travelogues, are linked with other texts on the country in question. The ambassadors' writings on Russia give us some quite interesting examples – especially from counter-narrative perspective. Ambassadors do not just travel – they are what we might now call proxies, standing between different places, governments, courts, societies, countries, etc. Thus, both their acts and their reports are filled with counter-narratives. To protect the honor of the ambassador's sovereign, to defend the national interest of their realm as well as to show the rulers of the country he visits the benefits of this interaction – all those essential diplomatic goals can only be achieved via either a narrative or counter-narrative, or sometimes both. Moreover, in the ambassadors' writings the counter-narrativeness is not limited by the *story* (what was said and what was the answer). Ambassadors' reports are polemical, as such. Before a voyage began, an ambassador prepares for his mission – he reads texts, analyses the setbacks of predecessor, and questions the existing diplomatic tradition. After their return, ambassadors need to demonstrate the results of their mission. Thus, the travel reports from the very beginning are created inside a highly vibrant rhetoric field where counter-narrativeness is traced on two levels – in a history and in a discourse.

In the seventeenth century Russia was not really a terra incognita. Official relations between Western Europe and Muscovy were established in the mid-sixteenth century when Richard Chancellor reached the Russian White Sea coast and Moscow (1553) and when the Muscovy Company was set up. Since that very moment merchants of the West had been visiting Muscovy on a regular basis. Merchants of the Dutch Republic began to use the same route thus challenged English dominance on this market. However, the mainstream narrative names Peter the Great as the monarch who 'opened' Russia for Europe (Freeze 2009, pp. 117–124). Thus, the seventeenth century is a 'gap' between the first encounter and the reforms of Peter the Great – a period crucially important but somewhat obscure and understudied. That is why Orlando Figes chooses the laying of St. Petersburg's cornerstone as the moment when European Russia was born (Figes 2003, pp. 4–5). If we look at the bibliography of M. Poe or F. Adelung, we will find a wide range of travel reports created in the period. That was the time when the Kukuy Quarter – a Moscow district for foreigners – emerged. That was the time when the first theaters and first university came to Russia. That was the time when Moscovy emerged in European literature: in Shakespeare's *The Winter's Tale*, Lope de Vega's *El Gran Duque de Moscovia y emperador perseguido*, Grimmelshausen's *Simplicius Simplicissimus*, etc. (Draper 1954, pp. 220–221; Alekseev 1937). That was the time when discussions of Westernizers and Russophiles began and Likhuds brothers quarreled with Simeon Polotsky and his cycle. Last but not the least, the seventeenth century was the epoch that formed Peter the Great's mindscope. But, maybe due to linguistic obstacles, the period remains highly obscure.

In the seventeenth century, Muscovy was not a terra incognita but still not a destination for ordinary travelers. Among those welcomed in Russia, were medics, military experts, merchants and ambassadors. From this short list, only the latter wrote texts, which bear some resemblance to literature. In what follows, we turn to two travelogues written in the beginning and in the second half of the seventeenth century. The first is the anonymous *Sir Thomas Smyth's Voiage and Entertainment in Rushia* (1602–1603). The text follows in detail the voyage of Thomas Smith, the ambassador who witnessed the beginning of the Russian Time of Troubles. He described the rise and fall of three Emperors of Muscovy in just one year. What makes the text special in the context of counter-narrativeness is the writer's perception of Russian history via images of English literature – *The Hamlet* by Shakespeare or *The Arcadia* by Philip Sidney. The second text is *The perillous and most unhappy voyages of John Struys: Through Italy, Greece, Lifeland, Muscovia, Tartary, Media, Persia, East-India, Japan, and other places in Europe, Africa and Asia* (1677), which follows voyages of John Struys. The ways of almost all parts of the world as known in the seventeenth century was rich in both funny and gruesome detail that the story of a globetrotter from Wormer in the Netherlands was translated into all major European languages, sometimes more than once. In some cases the translation went beyond the mere rendering of a text into another language. Change of message, its purpose, style and imagery were a typical thing for the English edition. The text also reached Russia where it underwent significant political censorship, in both pre-Soviet and Soviet era. Being a popular reading, these texts were fine-tuned by translators or editors according to the demands of new styles of epochs and political realities. The mechanics of translation – what to select for translation and how to perform this – create another level of counter-narrativeness.

To put it another way, travelogue and counter-narrative are intertwined concepts and the connections between them are manifested on different levels of poetics and for different purposes.

Counter-narratives in non-fiction and travelogues

Historically, travel writing emerged from reports of ambassadors, other officials and merchants. Thus, they are quite serious and pragmatically motivated texts based on real facts about a far-away country's geography and climate, government, politics and military power as well as the customs of the indigenous peoples. Sometimes it might even seem that travelogues equip readers with bare facts more suited for a list than for a narrated story:

> Novgorod the Great, to the West near lake Il'men', is more than 300 miles from Moscow; Pskov is 100 miles beyond Novgorod. Riazan', facing East in the land between the Oka and Don rivers, is 100 miles from Moscow. Kolomna, lying to the southeast, on the road from Moscow to Riazan', is 54 miles from Moscow. Kazan, the former capital of the Tatar Horde conquered by the present Prince, Ivan Vasil'evich, is located to the East on the bank of the river Volga, 180 miles from Moscow.
>
> *(Possevino and Graham 1977)*

But, even scrupulous historic writing is not able to totally obfuscate a sophisticated narrative system with different strategies of voices and acts beyond its surface. That is what Robert Alter had once dissected in the historical books of the Bible:

> it is quite possible that the writer faithfully represents the historical data without addition or substantive embellishment. The organization of the narrative, however, its brief but strategic uses of dialogue, produce an imaginative reenactment of the historical event, conferring upon it a strong attitudinal definition and discovering in it a pattern of meaning. It is [...] a history in which the feeling and the meaning of events are concretely realized through the technical resources of prose fiction.
>
> *(Alter 2011)*

We see the very same model in contemporary Literary Journalism – thousands of years after the Bible was completed.

> Some people criticize nonfiction writers for appropriating the techniques and devices of fiction writing. Those techniques, except for invention of character and detail, never belonged to fiction. They belong to storytelling. In nonfiction, you can create a tone and a point of view. Point of view affects everything that follows.
>
> *(Sims 1995)*

The literary journalist boldly accentuates that they compose their texts in a manner distinct from writers per se because every single detail is quite factual. Yet, they do not invent protagonists and events. In any case, the verisimilitude of every fact is accompanied by fiction-style framing. The history as a single real sequence of events becomes one of many possible options. It acquires a sense, but the sense is intended by the journalist. Is there any alternative? Yes, a slightly different selection of facts, which are viewed and perceived from a different point of view or framed in a different cultural background. The journalist turned real events into a narrative and at the same moment, the journalist opened a possibility of another voice and, hence, another interpretation.

In a narrative, eventivity, point of view and authorship are intrinsically fused. Fact-based stories are filled with a variety of voices and visions not less intensive than creative writings. Travel writings "invite narrative, everyday interactions, and the voice of a guide <...>, [which] serve as a measure of cultural difference, bridging the distance between the subjects' world and the readers'" (Sims 1995). Thus, they contain a special condition for the narrative variety. As for travelogues of diplomats and other officials, this group of people had always acted on the verge of conflict. They tried to juxtapose interests of opposing parties and tried to turn a potential foe or rival into an ally. Thus, in such texts we find four levels of counter-narratives: 1) polemics against predecessors, 2) rivalry against politically other agents, 3) skepticism on aborigines' knowledge as well as, 4) the counter-narrativeness which emerges in translations and adaptations of a piece of travel writing for another culture and/or epoch.

Counter-narratives as a part of the story

Travels across totally uncharted areas are not a typical situation. Very often these travelers have at least some predecessors. Nobody travels just to simply repeat someone else's experience, to get precisely the same impressions. A traveler follows some of their predecessors' path, but then tends to turn the old story into something new, topical, own. In these cases the new travelogue is tailored as an answer to and a replica of the stories, which were read before leaving home for the journey. Thus, the travelogues function as counter-narratives of their ur-texts.

A dangerous and highly hostile country – avers Antonio Possevino, a legate from the Vatican, well known for his influential book on Muscovy:

> Since he tries to find out everything his subjects do, very few of them dare to say anything, and they speak only to curry favor or avoid punishment. His subjects are not allowed to associate with foreigners unless the Prince has been informed and given his personal permission. Traders from other countries frequently visit Muscovy, but Muscovites go to other countries only on official business. They cannot even own ships, for fear that they would use them to escape or to form too close ties with foreigners, which is considered an embarrassment for the Prince. He does not even allow the representatives he occasionally sends to the Christian rulers to talk to the envoys whom these rulers in turn send to him. For example, lstoma Shevrigin was not permitted to talk to us even though on the instructions ofYour Beatitude we conducted him through Italy in a most friendly and honorable manner. Perhaps, however, this is less surprising when one realizes that even most important envoys, who are provided with splendid accommodations in Moscow, are assigned to a building surrounded with very high stakes, from which they cannot see other houses, speak to anyone, or even go out to water their horses, as our drivers found out.
>
> *(Possevino 1977)*

It is not that hostile – answers Thomas Smythe, an ambassador of James I:

> the same house the yong Prince Iohn of Denmarke, Brother to that King, and our now Queene of England did lodge in, who would haue married the young Princes Oucksinia, the Emperors onely Daughter, but that hee vnhappily there died of a surfet <...>. [B]eing brother to our Noble and vertuous Quee. wroght a desire in vs to see his toomb. The kings gentlemen and some others, hauing the Emp. horses and sleads, rode to their Sloboda, as we call it Suberbes, wher in the Chancell of the dutch Church he vvas interred, with a great and Princelie obsequy: the Emp himselfe and Prince, attending the corps to the first gte, but all his Councellors, Nobles, gentlemen, &c, following to the Church where they stayed tyll the Sermon was ended. Hee had a large toombe couered with blacke veluet, many banners and Scutcheons hanging about the body of the Church and chancel, with his Armes and Creast, and considring the countrey, very princely.
>
> *(Smythe 1602)*

Muscovy is a country where nobody even speaks European languages and acts in European style – Possevino maintains:

> The Muscovites owe the very slight knowledge of the Croatian language they possess to the fact that it displays affinities with Polish, Russian, and other similar languages. I sent a Croatian priest to Moscow and he at once acquired a good knowledge of the Muscovite

language, whereas the Muscovites appear to experience considerable difficulty in mastering the Croatian language. Since the only language the Muscovites know is their own, it is useless to give the Prince the Proceedings of the Council of Florence in Greek <...>. The Prince has no one in his service who understands that language, with the exception of a few Greeks who, so we are told, came from Byzantium last year at the Prince's request to train a Muscovite interpreter. I think they taught their student the corrupt jargon the Greeks speak nowadays instead of Ancient Greek or the language in which the Early Fathers wrote their books and the Synods were published. <...>The Muscovites could not even read, much less understand, the translation of the Diploma because, as the associates I had brought with me from the Russia controlled by the Kingdom of Poland and Austria observed, the translation had been made into a mixture of Bosnian and Croatian. <...>The Muscovites possess only a handful of people who know Latin.

(*Possevino 1977*)

The situation has changed and the perception is not the whole truth – that is Thomas Smythe's reply:

My Lorde was met vpon the riuer with one other Prestaue, named Constantine Petrovvich Artishoue, a man of farre much better esteeme then the former. A graue, honest, and peaceable gentleman, a happines to any Ambassadour, and as necessarie in this Countrey as may be, the contrary whereof other Ambassadors and the laste that honourable and renowned Gen. Sir Richard Lea, found his greatest crosse, for pride, opinion, and selfe will.

(*Smythe 1605*)

The counter-narratives emerge from a principle to see and check by own eyes. They are directed against the pre-existing literary and perceptive tradition, which is now deemed 'ingenuine' if not 'incorrect' but still influential amidst their readers. The counter-narratives mark the possibility for a traveler to find their own place in the world, to find and justify the uniqueness of their new experience as well as to accentuate boldly the stand-off from pre-existing stories.

Verbal counter-action of the official level

While we turn to travel prose of ambassadors, we encounter a quite specific sort of counter-narrative, which is essential for the type of literature. The travelers take position in between the two official narratives. They are on a mission aimed at making a trade deal, reaching another agreement or breaking a peace treaty; thus the travelers listen attentively to their vis-a-vis. Official narrative of a foreign country glorifying its might enters the travelogues:

Being thus set ... we beheld the Emperors table serued by two hund. Noblemen, all in coates of cloth of gold. The Princes table serued with one hun. yong Dukes and princes of Cassan, Astrican, Syberia, Tartaria, Chercasses, & Russes, none aboue twenty yeares olde.

(*Smythe 1605*)

On the other hand, the ambassadors have to hold their own face to protect the dignity of their own lord, court and country:

Likewise vnderstanding of the strange Ceremony of first allighting from their horses, <...> as they thinke much honour is loste to dismount first <...> The Ambassador then thinking

> they would be tedious and troublesome with their vsuall Ceremonies; preuented their farther speeche with this (to them a *Spell*) *That it vvas vnfitting for subiects to hold discourse in that kinde of complement, of tvvo such mighty and renowmed Potentates on horsbacke.* They hereby not only put by their ceremonious saddle-sitting, but <...> they allighted sodainly, as men fearing they were halfe vnhorsed, and the Ambassador presently after them.
>
> (*Smythe 1605*)

Speaking is a tool of defense of the high diplomat status. As well as the status grants right and skills to evaluate the official narratives of the visited country and to question it. If not directly to mock:

> Here the *Ambassador* laie some fourteen dayes, or lesse, where in the meane time, there was demanded a particular note of the names of all the *Ambassadors* traine, fyrst of the Kings Gentlemen (which name not onely the Emperor, but the *Great Turke, Persian & Moroco Princes* do highly account of) as indeed soothing their own greatnes therwith.
>
> (*Smythe 1605*)

Thus, the ritualized and routinized diplomatic skirmish develops another sort of counter-narrative in travel writings.

The concept of counter-narrative becomes an important tool for the study of a travel narrative from a colonial and post-colonial perspective. Indeed if we look at the process of colonizing the New World as a form of travelogue, it would be a journey from a cultural, political and economic 'center 'to the wild, savage and barely charted 'periphery'. Indeed, it might look somewhat strange, but in the seventeenth century Russia was not an empire. Yet, its sheer size made it if not a real but at least potential aim for colonization (Dunning 2007, pp. 277–302). In this model, a European traveler is initially intended to be perceived as an embodiment of the 'norm', which is often the case of colonial travel narratives written from the position of authority. However, this is not always the case. Since a travelogue often relies on earlier accounts both factual and fictional, the idea of savagery as a *modus operandi* for indigenous peoples is challenged in a form of counter-narrative in which the European traveler acknowledges that the indigenous people may excel in certain occupations, but are still entrapped in savagery. A good example of this is the remark on Russians being in the permanent state of war and thus having a formidable army:

> ...[we] are to returne the same vvay againe: knovving, that God doth oftentimes vse his creatures (and none oftner then the Sea) to execute his Iudgements: let vs then be hartily hankefull for our deliuerance, and shew our obedience thereafter in our liues, especially in a strange Country, where he is not rightly knowne.
>
> (*Smythe 1605*)

In the case of Jan Struys' *Drie aanmerkelijke en seer rampspoedige Reysen* (*The perilous and most unhappy voyages of John Struys*) we see a more complex structure in which we see the beginnings of a postcolonial vision. In the first voyage to Madagascar Struys tells his reader the story of a native Diembo, a former slave of one of the captains who, thanks to his knowledge of Dutch and European manners became a chief of his tribe and was more than happy to see his former master. Whereas Kees Boterbloem takes this an example of affirming Western superiority over the colonized peoples and affirming the idea of slave trade (Borebloem 2008) we think that at least the English translation of *Reysen* goes slightly further. The case of Diembo is employed as a case example, which confirms the possibility of European cultural project in which a savage can be civilized. A further step in acknowledging the human element in the indigenous people is when the Struys takes in his third voyage to Muscovy. Even though his observations largely confirm those of Olearius, Struys confronts the earlier accounts of Russians being resistant to cold and enjoying cold weather as untrue. Thus, stating that Russians too freeze their ears and noses off like Europeans but still remain somewhat worse than actual Europeans:

> Slaves they are by nature, and born to servitude and Bondage, seldom ever aspiring so high, as to indeavour to make themselves franc, and yet will be excited to nothing by fair means, or use diligence about any affair, save what they are driven to by constraint and blows: and yet so sweet this Slavery seems to be to them, that rather than to become free upon the Decease of their Lords to whom they ow allegiance by nature or o|therwise, that they will immediatly sell themselves durante vitâ to some other Patron.
>
> *(Struys, Butler, and Morrison 1684)*

The same pattern can be traced in the descriptions of streets, daily routines, customs, manners, with passages being framed with refrains "unlike in our country", or "contrary to what other geographers wrote".

Traveling to evaluate and contradict

Thus, a set of counter-narratives emerges, which demonstrates how travelers evaluate folklore, 'folk etymologies', etc. A visitor to another country, especially, of a simpler stock, has, unlike an ambassador or any other high status individual, a unique chance to have a first-hand experience of a foreign culture. These experiences often contribute to the exotic component of the travel narrative, which is so much loved by the reader. In the case of *Reysen* we have fairly large passages on 'curiosities' of Muscovy and its 'strange customs', which pose a challenge to both the writer of the narrative, the initial, or as we may call it, intended audience, and the readers, who were originally not thought of by the author of Reysen, i.e. the readers of Russian translation, made in 1935 in Stalinist Russia. As Kees Boterbloem rightly points out *Reysen* was primarily aimed to entertain, not to educate the reader (Borebloem 2008) At the same time, the curiosity and the narrative limits of the traveler are restrained by the discourse into which the resulting text has to fit. Namely, the writer, or, in case of *Reysen*, the ghostwriter, has to fit new information into a preexisting frame of reference. A case example of adding a folklore element to what we might call a non-fictional narrative is the story of a bear, which is inserted in the chapter on Novgorod and Pskov as a cut-in element. The cut-in story is intended to be perceived as something that the narrator wants to mark as a narrative, which exists 'out there' and over which the narrator has no authority. In order to achieve this the narrator adds a source of this story – a Hamburger – and the story of a she-bear who killed and devoured a peasant family, save for an infant whom it brought to her den and fed like one of its cubs with milk before being shot by the local people. The baby was recovered and returned to the relatives. The cut-in narrative is presented to the reader in a different typeface – italics – to differentiate the narrative voice of Jan Janzoon Struys from that of the Hamburger. This in turn allows us to avoid the fallacy of reading the passage *'brought to* Pletskou, *to be nurs'd up by his VVives Sister, where out of curiosity I went to see it'* (Struys 1684) as something done by Struys.

Another cut-in narrative follows almost immediately and is a retelling of a story of St. Anthony of Rome, who allegedly sailed all the way up from Rome to Pskov and founded a Church there. Here, although this story is in italics too, the role of formatting is slightly different. Struys gives a critical evaluation of the story. Even though Struys does not call it an explicit lie, his lack of checking the claims of the locals against the facts:

VVith the money he built there a Chappel where he lies interred, and (as they tell us) his Body is yet to be seen, fresh and undecay'd, by which many miracles have been done, but none can see him, or them, but such as are of their own Faith.

(*Struys 1684*)

These two instances of folk tales shape the main approaches to the 'field data' – a local curiosity recounted to impress a reader at home or a reevaluation of earlier accounts. The latter rationale can be clearly seen in the Translator's preface to the English version of the *Reysen*, in which the translator clearly puts 'truth' and 'accuracy' above other aspects of travel narrative. That said, we cannot but notice that the translator in fact partially transforms the narrative of the *Reysen* into one of his own, thus creating a counter-narrative within the narrative. By adding marginalia and rewriting passages, which the translator deems contradictory to what his English readers might consider either upsetting, or implausible, or in any other sense not fitting. For example in the description of the first voyage to Madagascar, the translator changes the number of cannons from 6 on *St. John Baptist* and 8 on *St. Bernard* to 26 and 28 respectively. This seemingly minor correction though being textually wrong does give us some idea of the aspirations that the English reading public have. Indeed, could the Dutch, the arch enemy of the English, have the ships so badly equipped? From the translators' perspective – no. A more vivid example of the translator's voice is the description of the mercenaries hired by Genoa. The Dutch original lists them as German landsknechts, whereas the author of the English translation – John Morrison – transforms them into Dutch mercenaries, thus contributing to the image of the Dutch as foul players, ready to fight for money, not for their own country. This framing can be seen in the Russian translation of 1935, which was probably made from the Dutch, rather than English translation. The Russian text, at least the *Third Voyage*, poses a serious challenge for the study from the narrative perspective. If the English translation had to adapt the Dutch vision of the exotic places like Madagascar, Iran or Muscovy to the tastes of the English public, making what we might call minor alterations, the Russian translator had to squeeze the narrative into the limits of ideology. From the soviet perspective Jan Struys is an example of ur-proletarian, who is immune to certain vices of his age. At the same time, his observations of Muscovy, if translated accurately, may cast some negative light on the Soviet Union, which at that time was reestablishing its link with its pre-Bolshevik past and developing a kind of national identity. A case example here is the episode of the Third Voyage in which, according to the Dutch and English versions, Jan Struys sues the captain of the ship that brought him to Riga for not paying him for the repair of sails after the storm. For E. Borodina, the author of the 1935 translation this posed a significant challenge as a turning to bourgeois courts and receiving a just decision from them was something that a simple sailor could obtain, at least in the communist ideological framework. Thus, this scene was removed from the Russian translation altogether, thus turning the story of an adventure and entrepreneurship in an exotic land into a mere travel log. A similar example is seen in the Russian translation of the description of Moscow in which the Russian translation becomes a counter-narrative in the sense that it tells a story which is not a rendering of the observations made by Struys. Rather, it draws a picture, which fitted the communist propaganda. Namely, when describing the burial of Maria Miloslavskaya, the first wife of the Russian tsar Alexey Mikhalovitch, who died in labor in 1669. The Russian narrative lacks the ideologically alien elements. Namely, lamenting of this death by ordinary Russians, her generosity and the giving of alms to the poor. In this respect the seventeenth-century narrative is included in the official discourse not as a literary or historical source, but rather as a tool of political struggle, aimed to negatively frame the rule of the early Romanovs and monarchy in general.

Tall tales and the art of disbelief

Local folklore and customs, as well as etymologies have a twofold function in the travel narrative. They contribute to the 'exotic' atmosphere of the narrative (Huberman 2008) and aid the narrator in charting the yet unknown area by providing the data not likely to be found in official sources. However, the credibility of folklore or its relevance for the purposes of travel becomes something that Early Modern travelers start to question (Hayden 2012). This quite plausible assumption appears to come into contradiction with a case example of a folk tale of 'Baranez plant' mentioned in the *Reysen* when Struys reaches Astrakhan. Baranez is described as a plant with a head, tail and legs which resembles a sheep (*baran* in Russian), hence the name. On top of that, Struys claims that this plant has a very fine and delicate fur, resembling that of a 'lamb', which costs a fortune. What is more, he claims to have possessed such a skin, which he later had to sell, and thus cannot produce it. In this case, we see a great potential for creating a counter-narrative on behalf on the English translator who could have questioned the truthfulness of this tale. On the one hand, the English translator, indeed, contributes to the narrative but strangely enough joins the play by adding a commentary in italics which states that such a plant can indeed exist like the mandrake exists, which resembles a man. On the one hand, it does not make much sense as in an earlier passage on St. Anthony of Rome, who, allegedly, sailed to Pskov on a stone is perceived by the translator with a lot of skepticism which manifests itself in a wry remark on the margins: '*Which is a Lake and has no com/munion with any other Sea*' (Struys 1684). Not making much sense on the surface level, it is an example of a counter-narrative that challenges 'false geographers' so much condemned by the English translator. It becomes especially interesting in the case of the connection between the rivers Don and Volga. If the Dutch text simply states that the rivers were not connected as was believed before, the English translator makes this statement more vivid, turning a mere comment into an attack on previous writers: '*This River was of old supposed to run into the VVolga, as some Geographers have been pleased to write, but later experience has fairly contradicted that opinion*' (Struys 1684). This comment perfectly complements the earlier note on the margin concerning St. Anthony. The reader of the English version is encouraged by the translator to read the story both critically and remove from it the elements that were deemed too entertaining for a travelogue. Thus, the English translation transforms a Dutch text which clearly follows the pattern of the *lust et lering* (entertainment and education) textual tradition of the Netherlands (Michajlova 2015) into a purely 'educational' text, as the translator states in his preface. The lack of the original Foreword from the narrating persona of Jan Struys adds to this, making the whole translation a counter-narrative which either coincides with the translator's vision in which case we have a very accurate rendering of the Dutch text or digresses from it significantly when the translator feels that certain details are not relevant or are incorrect. Forging his counter-narrative, the translator has to eliminate Struys from the text, which he successfully does by eliminating the human touch from the text. For example, the English translation lacks the scene of the marriage between a member of Struys's team and a Tatar girl educated by Herr Van Sweeden, or the episode in which Struys saves one of his compatriots from drowning during a skating exercise.

But if a travelogue receives huge popularity, another kind of counter-narrativeness arises. That sort is inspired not by the author's intention but rather by the acts of interpreters, translators, editors, commentators, etc.

Traveling in the 'grand time'

Russian translation of 1935 is an example of a counter-narrative of another sort. Having chosen Reysen for translation, a task so often attempted in previous decades (Borebloem 2008), Russian publishers had to create a version of the narrative which would be more favorable to Muscovy than earlier published accounts. Having whitewashed certain observations of Struys which resonated with the conditions of everyday life in the early 1930s, Russian translators forged a counter-narrative by inventing a new Struys who sympathized with ordinary working class people, showed moral proletarian character and smeared Russian clergy. Ideological censorship was apparently the least part of the translation process. Indeed, if we look at the commentary of the slave nature of Russians and their happiness with being slaves and thieves, as presented in the English and Dutch version of the *Reysen*, we would see that all the Russian translators had to do was to omit the last part of this observation. A more significant challenge came with the chapters of Stenko Razin. The preface to the Russian edition has to explain that Struys was not exactly a lower class traveler, hence his skeptical opinion of the uprising. However, the need to fit the text into the discourse of class struggle results in the creation of a Struys who clearly understood the rightfulness of Razin's cause. What is more, the observations on Razin's egalitarian behavior towards his comrades and the disobedience of the tsarist troops to their foreign superiors is shown though the eyes of the 'soviet Struys' as an inevitable resolution of a class war crisis, understood even by a foreign national (Morozov & Borodina 1935).

Conclusion

To travel means to communicate with different cultures, perceive them, evaluate and debate them as well as with traveler's predecessors. Thus, travel writing is a discourse where a narrative emerges as a voice, surrounded by other voices, i.e. as a counter-narrative. In the small time, understood in Bakhtinian sense, to underline the uniqueness of a given voyage as contrasted with the previous travels and, consequently earlier travel narratives. Thus, a new narrative challenges earlier ones by taking an aggressive stance towards predecessors, accusing them of lies.

The problem of counter-narrative reemerges when we talk about the Early Modern travel narrative in the Bakhtinian 'great time' when it is read by the audience for which it was not initially intended. Indeed, the observations of Thomas Smythe or Jan Struys have little, if any, practical value for a contemporary reader as a travel narrative proper. One of the most curious examples of travel narratives as counter narratives is the situation of translation, especially in the language of the country that is perceived as the heir of the land that was the destination of the Early Modern traveler. In the case of the Russian translation of Reysen done in the mid-1930s and published in 1935, just on the verge the Purges and the rise of the cult of Stalin, who was achieving the status of the living god. In this context the translated travelogue becomes a counter-narrative of its original self. The translators of the totalitarian regime invent a new past, very much in the Orwellian sense by cutting out the passages not fitting into the new historiography of the mighty Russia ridden by corrupt clergy and aristocracy ready to sell the country to foreign powers. Where the proletariat is oppressed and a nobody, but Razin can challenge the old regime as a proto-socialist and revolutionary. Thus, the travel narrative confronts both the past and serves the current political agenda. Alternatively, its translation can function as a form of text domestication, making it more fit for the home audience. Thus, the English translator of *Reysen* converts Dutch units of length and money into English or uses a more familiar English metaphor for poorly dressed inhabitants of Lifland, or even adds additional edge to the story of a suggestive inscription on the stone and aimless labor with the help of a Shakespearian insult.

References

Adams, P. G. (1983). *Travel literature and the evolution of the novel.* Lexington: University Press of Kentucky.
Alter, R. (2011). *The art of biblical narrative* (Rev. & updated ed.). New York: Basic Books.

Alekseev, M. P. (1937). *Ocherki iz istorii anglo-russkikh literaturnykh otnosheniy (XI-XVII v. v.)*: (Tezisy diss.). Leningrad: [b. i.].

Bakhtin, M. M., Bocharov, S. G., Nikolaev, N. I., Melikhova, L. S., & Popova, I. L. (1996). *880-02 Sobranie sochineniĭ: V semi tomakh / M.M. Bakhtin; [redaktory toma, S.G. Bocharov, N.I. Nikolaev]*. 880-03 Moskva: Russkie slovari.

Bale, A. P., & Sobecki, S. I. (2019). *Medieval English travel: A critical anthology / edited by Anthony Bale and Sebastian Sobecki* (First edition). Oxford: Oxford University Press.

Boterbloem, K. (2008). *The fiction and reality of Jan Struys: A seventeenth-century Dutch globetrotter / Kees Boterbloem*. Basingstoke: Palgrave Macmillan.

Draper, J. (1954). Shakespeare and Muscovy. *The Slavonic and East European Review, 33*(80), 217–221. Retrieved from www.jstor.org/stable/4204621.

Dunning, C. (2007). A "singular affection" for Russia: Why King James offered to intervene in the Time of Troubles. *Russian History, 34*(1/4): 277–302. Retrieved from www.jstor.org/stable/24662955.

Freĭdenberg, O. M. (1998). *Mif i literatura drevnosti* (2. izd. ispr. i dop). *Issledovaniia︡ po folʹkloru i mifologii Vostoka.* Moskva: Vostochnaia︡ literatura RAN.

Freeze, G. L. (2009). *Russia: A history / edited by Gregory L. Freeze* (3rd ed.). Oxford: Oxford University Press.

Hayden, J. A. (2012). *Travel narratives, the new science, and literary discourse, 1569–1750*. Farnham, Surrey, England; Burlington, VT: Ashgate.

Huberman, A. (2008). The lure of the exotic: The travel writings of María De Las Mercedes Santa Cruz Y Montalvo, Countess of Merlin (1792–1852). *Hispanic Journal 29*(1) (2008): 71–89.

Markham, C., (Trans.). (1908). *The Life Of Lazarillo de Tormes His Fortunes & Adversities*, London: Adam and Charles Black.

Michajlova, I. (2015). *Van Reynaert de Vos tot Godenslaap: Geschiedenis van de Nederlandse Literatuur* (III). Sankt-Peterburg: Alexandria.

Morozov, A. (Ed.) & Borodina, E. (Trans.). 1935. *Tri puteshestviia Ia. Ia. Streisa.* , (Moskva).

Possevino, A., & Graham, H. F. (1977). *The Moscovia of Antonio Possevino, S.J. UCIS series in Russian & East European studies: no. 1*. Pittsburgh: University Center for International Studies University of Pittsburgh.

Pushkin, A. (1881), *Eugene Oneguine [Onegin]: A Romance of Russian Life in Verse*, H. Spalding (Trans.). London: Macmillan and Co.

Saveliev, S.V., & Savelieva, I. G. (2018). An outlook on approaches to the theory of travel writing in UK and US academia. *New Philological Bulletin, 2*(45), 247–260.

Sims, N. (1995). The Art of Literary Journalism. Literary Journalism. Ballantine Books.

Smith, T. (1605). *Sir Thomas Smithes voyage and entertainment in Rushia: With the tragicall ends of two emperors, and one empresse, within one moneth during his being there and the miraculous preseruation of the now raigning emperor, esteemed dead for 18. yeares*. Printed at London: [by J. Roberts and W. Jaggard] for Nathanyell Butter.

Struys, J. J., Butler, D., & Morrison, J. (1684). *The Voiages and travels of John Struys through Italy, Greece, Muscovy, Tartary, Media, Persia, East-India, Japan, and other countries in Europe, Africa and Asia: Containing remarks and observations upon the manners, religion, polities, customs and laws of the inhabitants; and a description of their several cities, towns, forts, and places of strength: together with an account of the authors many dangers by shipwreck, robbery, slavery, hunger, torture, and the like. And two narratives of the taking of Astracan by the Cossacks, sent from Captain D. Butler. Illustrated with copper plates, designed and taken from the life by the author himself. Done out of Dutch by John Morrison*. London: Printed for Abel Swalle.

21

Restorying Kenya

The Mau Mau War counter-narratives

Wafula Yenjela

Introduction

The Mau Mau War in Kenya shattered the imagination of Kenya as a settler's paradise. Gicheru (1991, p. 196) best demonstrates this in his novel *The Mixers*: the "blissful life of a successful settler [became] a thing of the past." Historically, the Mau Mau Freedom War has been credited with reformulation of the colonial declaration that Kenya is "a white man's country" (A. Odhiambo, 2002, p. 236). The decree was asserted more forcefully in Huxley's (1935) *White Man's Country* in which she employed her creative talents to claim that white settlers in Kenya, led by their pioneer settler Lord Delamere, were the founders of the country, and that the indigenous Black people in the country were sub-human, with intellectual powers too inferior to claim possession of anything in the land. Achebe (2000, p. 60) flaunts Huxley's works as quintessential of colonial/ settler dispossession stories that "explain or camouflage" the conqueror's acts. On the flipside, Mau Mau stories by the forest fighters and pioneer post-independent novelists such as Ngugi wa Thiong'o, Meja Mwangi, and Charles Mangua in *Kenyatta's Jiggers* (1994) participate in repossession by charting stories that are "reconstitutive annals made up by those who will struggle to reclaim their history" (2000, p. 60).

Reclaiming a tainted humanity after the Mau Mau War appears to have been foremost on the agenda of pioneer post-independent Kenyan novelists. The pro-Mau Mau writers reconfigure and reinforce the moral-political convictions that defined the guerrillas' struggle. To the chagrin of historians like William Ochieng (1992, p. 134), the novelists elevated historical Mau Mau figures like Dedan Kimathi "to the ranks of Mao, Lenin and Guevera." It appears the settler Mau Mau literary enterprise found legitimacy in the horrors the Mau Mau guerrillas unleashed through gruesome ritual killings of their targets. The initiation into Mau Mau was also portrayed as occultic in the way the oath to kill European colonialists and settlers as well as Africans who collaborated with them was administered: initiates tasting raw goat entrails and blood (both claimed to be human flesh and blood) as they solemnly swear before revered oath administers (mostly guerrilla commanders) that if they break the vow the oath should kill them. Thus, to the settlers, Mau Mau exemplified the savagery the British were presumably tasked to eradicate in 'primitive' Africa. But Furley (1972, p. 106) posits that the missionary version of Mau Mau "ignored the political aspect" of the war and focused on portraying it as "anti-Christian, a reversion to tribal atavism, paganism, and cultural barbarism." Those dreadful oaths had their political edge: Green (1990, p. 69) argues that "the oathing rituals are to be understood as part of the ideological apparatus of the movement along with rallies and songs"; that reading African anti-colonial revolutions in "terms of tradition serve effectively to depoliticise actors' motivations and levels of awareness, which, while they may not be expressed in terms of Western revolutionary theory, are nevertheless evident."

The shift from negative to positive portrayals of Mau Mau upon Kenya's independence in 1963 can be read as a way of ushering in a new era, a way of signifying triumph over the protracted colonial bondage. Such a shift is captured in Maughan-Brown's (1985) in-depth reading of the war and its ideological representations in both settler and freedom novels. Ngugi's *A Grain of Wheat* (1966) ideologically emplots colonial atrocities by subverting white supremacism employed to undermine the war: John Thompson, Dr Henry Van Dyke, and Thomas Robson *alias* Tom the Terror are utterly vain and/or brutal.[1] Thompson deludedly believes in the supremacy of "their British heritage and tradition" and that "the growth of the British Empire was the development of a great moral idea," a "moral scheme for rehabilitation" of peasants in Asia and Africa (pp. 51, 52). His mission in his idea of Africa is soiled when he is indicted for the massacre of 11 Mau Mau detainees at Rira camp, a historical reference to the 3 March 1953 Hola Camp massacre. Van Dyke is portrayed as an adulterous brute who swore "he would kill himself if Kenyatta was ever set free from [detention]. His car crashed into the train soon after Kenyatta's return home from Maralal" (p. 32). Robson is described as the "epitome of those dark days in our history [...] when the Emergency raged in unabated fury" and is remembered for arbitrarily rounding up Mau Mau suspects, driving them to the edge of the forest, ordering them to dig their graves before shooting them dead (pp. 177, 178).

In reading similar nationalist Mau Mau novels, Coundouriotis (2014, p. 38) observes that the fiction presents "a conversation among three modes of writing about Mau Mau: the ironic, the sentimental, and the naturalist" with each remembering "the conflict differently." The Mau Mau fiction that would follow half a century after the unfolding of the Mau Mau War, which is key to this chapter, presents entirely different ideologies germane to uses of traumatic memories in relation to the present. Indeed, memory is endowed with "a demystifying effect [and] can be treated as a counter-hegemonic chronicle, in which an imagined 'other' history is narrated, thereby destabilizing dominant histories" (Woods, 2007, p. 21). Narrative demystification needs to be continuous since hegemonies easily evolve from counter-hegemonies. To Huyssen (2003, p. 6), memory provides a precious pedestal from which we can "articulate our political, social, and cultural dissatisfactions with the present state of the world."

This chapter engages with novels that provide counternarratives to Kenya's pioneer post-independent Mau Mau ideology. While the Mau Mau pioneer writers spiritedly counter settler novelists' ideology that constructed Mau Mau as the epitome of savagery, the new millennium Mau Mau fiction counters the nationalist variant of the post-independent ideology that reconfigured Mau Mau into the embodiment of heroism/patriotism in Kenya; a heroic chapter in the history of the colonized people. Ngugi (1972, p. 28) asserts:

> To most Africans, Mau Mau [...] was a heroic and glorious aspect of that mainstream. The basic objectives of Mau Mau revolutionaries were to drive out Europeans, seize the government, and give back to the Kenya peasants their stolen lands and property.

Furthermore, Ngugi (p. 30) sees Mau Mau "as a cultural, political and economic expression of the African peasant masses [...] in its revolutionary context." One of the Mau Mau detainees and historian, Kinyatti (2006, p. xxvi), believes that it was the Mau Mau fighters "who made our country honored in the progressive world through their determination, courage and great sacrifice." But the post-independent state held different views. In Kenyatta's (1968, p. 80) words, "Mau Mau was a disease which had been eradicated, and must never be remembered again." Ironically, as this chapter eventually demonstrates, Kenyatta himself would later seek legitimacy and authority in Mau Mau memory when his grasp to power became increasingly threatened by a radical opposition's quest for ethnic inclusivity.

Unquestionably, the new millennium Mau Mau counter-narratives unearth many gaps created by pro-Mau Mau writers who, with unequalled profundity, rebranded the war and successfully made the fictional version the heritage of post-independent Kenya. Historically, Mau Mau hardly achieved the objectives that Ngugi outlines: "Unlike other liberation movements, such as those in Algeria or Zimbabwe, [Mau Mau] was defeated almost a decade before the formal transfer of power to an African government" (Furedi, 1989, p. 3). Mau Mau appears to have derived its power in the stories written about it; stories that glorified it beyond limits. Granted, the novel charts its own powerful essence. J. M. Coetzee (1987) contends the relegation of the novel to "imaginative investigations of real historical forces and real historical circumstances" (qtd in Gallagher, 1997, p. 397). Gallagher reads Coetzee's contestations as his reference "to the *discourse* of history, a constructed text of what has happened, a myth, a metanarrative, which might be resisted, deconstructed, or even destroyed by a rival discourse of the novel" (p. 378). What happens, then, when the rival discourse of the novel reincarnates into a ruinous narrative? Note, the "teller of a story can become a powerful force in shaping the way people think about their social and political order, and the nature, desirability and direction of change" (Diamond, 1989, p. 435). Stories replenish or desecrate the human ideal. Luwisch (2001, p. 145) writes: "telling our stories is indeed a matter of survival: only by telling and listening, storying and restorying, can we begin the process of constructing a common world."

Despite the factual military defeat of Mau Mau by the British colonial power, Mau Mau memory grew more portent in post-independent Kenya, transmuting into not only a basis for legitimizing ethnic exclusionary entitlement to state resources and power, but also reincarnated in various forms of ethnic and/or state violence. Thus, Mau Mau narratives by various stakeholders in the problematic memory not only expose contestations of national identity through sentimental glorifications of ethnic communities claimed to have sacrificed their lives leading to the birth of the Kenyan nation, but also unmask ironies of the Kenyan state that violently solicits the public's cooperation through methods established by the Mau Mau counter-insurgency regiment. This phenomenon is best articulated in what I refer to as new millennium Mau Mau novels that are skeptical of the war. Here, I read the novels as counter-narratives that "represent non-mainstream stories which represent other truths, and other experiences that directly refute hegemony" (Iv & Howard, 2013, p. 542). For instance, Yvonne Owuor's *Dust* (2013) engages Mau Mau War trauma through deconstructing its heroic myth that has hampered any efforts to atonement of the victims. The novel's unapologetic portrayals of Mau Mau War as, in Odhiambo's (2002, p. 236) reading of the war, "an intra-Gikuyu civil war," seems to locate origins of ethnic and state violence in Kenya in the uncritical perpetuation of Mau Mau memory.

On the other hand, Mwenda Mbatiah's *Wimbo Mpya* (2004), "A New Song" (my translation from Kiswahili, including others below) engages with Mau Mau fighters' plight after independence; and appears to contest exclusive ethnicization of Mau Mau memory mostly attributed to the Kikuyu in literary and public memory. Mbatiah shows that Meru and Embu people actively participated in the war as well as the building of post-independent Kenya. This suggests that most non-Kikuyu ethnic communities' contest for Mau Mau memory is motivated by desires for ethnic inclusivity in the Kenyan state. In rewriting the Mau Mau memory and its affirmation of entitlement, Mbatiah's *Wimbo Mpya* appeals for a new order where citizens' selfless contributions to the country are prized more than the other way around. The earliest Kiswahili novel on Mau

Mau, Kareithi's *Kaburi Bila Msalaba* (1969), "Graves Without Crosses" catalogues a genocide the colonial forces caused to the colonized people. But, like Mau Mau novels of the time, it emphasizes Kenyans' indebtedness to the forest fighters. In a preface to the novel, Kareithi (1969, p. 7) reiterates that "uhuru tulio nao ulipatikana kwa damu na maisha yao,""the freedom we have was realised on the blood they shed, the lives they sacrificed." Mbatiah's new song is the ideal where service to humanity is rendered without mutating into a bondage.

Contesting Mau Mau's ethnic bend: *Wimbo Mpya* (2004)

Wimbo Mpya engages with Mau Mau and its relationship to Kenya four decades after the war. The novel revisits the marginalized Mau Mau contributions of the Meru and Embu as it chastizes state neglect of the freedom fighters. In *A Grain of Wheat*, Ngugi (1966, p. 125) writes in passing that "[m]any of the fighters [in the Thika detention camp] came from Embu, Meru and Mwariga." But it is Mbatiah who gives agency to these forgotten Mau Mau veterans. *Wimbo Mpya* can be read as a response to novels that privilege Kikuyu participation in the quest for Kenya's liberation while excluding the Meru and Embu people who were similarly profiled during the State of Emergency. Yet, while it memorializes the Meru and the Embu veterans of the struggle, it similarly excludes the Kikuyu's participation in the revolution as if every community fought separately. This speaks to Mbatia's disquiet on the Kikuyu novelists' absolute ethnicization of the Mau Mau memory. In a critique of Ngugi's selective historification of the Kenyan nation, Omuteche (2014, p. 108) contends that "hegemonic historical remembering has systematically undermined the multiplicity of Kenya's historical experiences during the colonial displacements and anti-colonial nationalism across the country." Mbatia's counternarrative disrupts the hegemony constructed by Ngugi, Mwangi, Mangua, Kareithi, and other Mau Mau novelists.

Wimbo Mpya enters the terrain of Kenya's literary histories with the author's critical understanding of the contested re-membering of Kenya. Mbatiah's reconfiguration of pertinent memories of the Meru and Embu peoples' anti-colonial campaign can be well grasped in Simatei's (2001, p. 9) view that "African novelists do conceive themselves as their nation's conscience." The novel uses an epic form that borrows from Meru people's mythology. Mbatiah, himself a Meru, invokes a Meru legendary tale of Kamaangura whose extra-ordinary military exploits set him apart in society, especially when he single-handedly rescues the Meru people's thousands of cattle rustled by the Mianzi, a warrior community. This feat is achieved after the Meru community deliberate on the dangers posed by the Mianzi and their recourse to the supernatural gifts of Kamaangura.

Notably, fictional creations of ethnic heroes can be problematic in a country like Kenya where ethnicity has evolved into a flashpoint for exclusion or unspeakable atrocities. In *Echoes of Silence* (1981), the late Ugandan dramatist Ruganda explicitly dissects selective constructions of presumed Kikuyu heroes as basis for excluding other ethnic groups. Ruganda's edgy character Okoth-Okach, or Double O as he is referred to in the play, speaks his mind to Wairi: "I guess I shouldn't be telling all this. But one gets tired of being told, 'You didn't go to the forest, you are not entitled. You are not qualified'" (p. 13). In a tone that reminds one of Langston Hughe's "I, Too, Sing America," Double O reminds Wairi of various communities' anti-colonial struggles: "But let me tell you this: I, too, did fight for this goddam *Uhuru* of yours, you know. [...]. In my own way, of course" (p. 10). Ruganda's criticisms of Mau Mau's heroism which, through Okoth-Okatch he refers to as "forest mentality" (p. 14) seem inspired by the ethnocentric nature of Mau Mau narratives. For instance, Ngugi's construction of the Kikuyu myth of creation with its concomitant claims to natural resources, especially land, in *The River Between* (1965) and *Weep Not, Child* (1964) propagate his sentimental attachment to the imagined precolonial ideal that is juxtaposed with the violence and dispossession occasioned by colonialism. However, his invocation of Kikuyu military legends such as Wachiori who "killed a lion" at a young age; "who had led the whole tribe against Ukabi, Masai"; who left behind "a great name, the idol of many a young warrior" when he was killed by "a straying white man" (1965, p. 2) demonstrates the ethnocentric inclination of such narratives. Wachiori seems a replica of Achebe's Okonkwo whose macho prowess memorably opens *Things Fall Apart* (1958), except that for the latter, Obierika and other characters condemn his excesses and slavish allegiance to cultural institutions that at times are callous and calamitous.

Mbatia's recourse to the Meru community's military legend seems a correspondence to Mau Mau narratives that have, over time, entrenched a cult of Kikuyu heroism through Mau Mau narratives. Through constructions of a non-Kikuyu Mau Mau hero, Meja Marete who traces his lineage to Kamaangura, Mbatiah demonstrates that every community has its own military legends. Meja Marete's genealogy suggests Mau Mau heroes' redemption of the Meru society's stolen treasures – freedom and land. Importantly, Mbatiah's novel is sensitive to Kenya's ethnic sensibilities as it imagines Kamaangura rescuing the Meru people's livestock from Mianzi, an imaginary warrior community.

In narrating forest combat histories, *Wimbo Mpya* underscores the hardships and sacrifices of the Mau Mau fighters more than victories. Most memorable of this is the 1942–1946 season of "Gharika la Damu" (7) "the Flood of Blood." This memorializes the peak of military contact between Mau Mau and the colonial counter-insurgency forces. In one incident, Meja Marete's troops ambush colonial forces on transit, kill hundreds of enemy soldiers and loot weapons, but hours later, fighter jets launch a retaliatory offensive causing major casualties among them. Even though *Wimbo Mpya* shows Mau Mau military offensive in the forests, it also demonstrates that the Mau Mau story is a story of defeat. Above all, the burden of the struggle is not clearly loaded unto the shoulders of the beneficiaries of the freedom. This portrayal is different from other Mau Mau novels in which the writers carve liberation martyrs who should be 'worshipped.' Mwangi's *Carcase for Hounds* excellently portrays guerrilla combat since the Haraka-led army is known for unpredictable swoops against settlers and police posts. Haraka is ready to die for "a worthwhile cause" (1974, p. 68). Gicheru's (1991, p. 208) *The Mixers* shows Ngobia as the saviour of the colonized people as he leads Mau Mau fighters, most of whom are World War II veterans, in night offensives against settlers: "Kuu Valley or 'Cool Valley' had been transformed overnight into Death Valley" (1991, 208). Ngugi's Mau Mau novels mostly focus on colonialists' torture of Mau Mau suspects, including children, for instance, Njoroge in *Weep Not, Child*; torture and murder in detention camps as in the imagined Rira Camp massacre in *A Grain of Wheat* (1966, p. 125). In *A Grain of Wheat*, Kihika is the martyr, the grain that dies for the colonized to acquire freedom. Kareithe's *Kaburi Bila Msalaba* (1969) focuses on torture, victimization, rape, and murder of Mau Mau suspects and collective punishment of communities. These novelists appear to underscore claims that post-independent Kenyans are collectively indebted to the sacrificial deaths of Mau Mau veterans.

Even though *Wimbo Mpya* revisits the freedom fighters' warfare sacrifices and the betrayals they encountered from their community members as well as from the post-independent state which chose to neglect them upon independence, it demonstrates that they were not fighting for themselves. This is seen in the writer's treatment of the colonial loyalists' socioeconomic prosperity in wartime. The loyalist figure represented in Marete's neighbor M'Keambati, his son Nthambori, and daughter Miriamu is not wholesomely condemned: a patriot such as Miriamu who chooses to work for the good of the nation is a daughter of a Mau Mau traitor. Indeed, this is a profound response to pro-Mau Mau novelists who employed a blanket condemnation of the so-called loyalists, together with their descendants. In a preface to *Thunder From the Mountains: Mau Mau*

Patriotic Songs, Kinyatti (1980, p. x) asserts: the songs "point out that both these foreign occupiers and the local traitors should be regarded as Kenya's enemy number one who should be wiped out mercilessly."

In the advocacy for 'a new song' in a manner that mitigates the post-independent states' betrayal of Mau Mau freedom fighters, the narrator reveals the sharp moral dichotomy spearheaded by Mau Mau narratives' creation of 'loyalists': 'Loyalism' is an element of post-independent state-citizen relationship whereby perceived traitors of Mau Mau movement rose to leadership positions and reaped greater economic gains. *Wimbo Mpya* revisits the same through portrayals of Marete's neighbor, M'Keambati, a colonial police officer who actively participates in hunting down, detaining, and even executing Mau Mau suspects. The colonial government rewards him with Marete's as well as other Mau Mau suspects' land. M'Keambati, who represents agents and supporters of the Mau Mau counterinsurgency, also holds expansive coffee plantations and is a progressive urbanite with highly educated children; in sharp contrast to bitter, poor, landless former freedom fighters.

The narrator engages with the 'loyalist' creature further through the words of an embittered Marete during the struggle. Notably, Rogere, not Marete, is the one who embodies the new song in the novel. When the colonial government announces amnesty for Mau Mau fighters who would willingly surrender, Marete scoffs at the logic of amnesty:

> Kusamehewa na nani? [...] Hatutaki msamaha. Hawa mbwa wanaoramba matako ya mkoloni ni watu wa kutusamehe sisi?
>
> *(2004, p. 11)*

> To be forgiven by whom? [...] We don't need amnesty. Are the dogs licking the dirty buttocks of the colonialist worth extending amnesty to us?

Meja Marete's stance elicits memories of the Lari Massacre where Mau Mau fighters targeted the lives and property of loyalists in the jurisdiction of Luka Wakahangare killing over 500 people in a single night, making it "the greatest bloodletting of the entire Mau Mau war" (Anderson, 2005, p. 119).[2] However, the Emergency landscape was too entangled and fluid for such sharp dichotomies: strategic as well as compulsory enlistment in accordance to dynamics of the war (see Branch, 2007, There existed pp. 292–293). In public memory, most of the Kenyan ethnic communities that were not victimized by colonial forces during the Mau Mau War have been labelled homeguards, loyalists, traitors. This inclination partly informs contestations against ethnicization of Mau Mau memory.

Wimbo Mpya invokes Harambee, Kenyatta's rallying call and motto that he proclaimed in a swearing-in ceremony on 1 June 1963, upon attainment of Kenya's internal self-governance: "We must work harder to fight our enemies — ignorance, sickness and poverty. I therefore give you the call: HARAMBEE! Let us all work together for our country, Kenya" (1964, p. 7). To Kenyatta (1964, p. 13), Harambee represented Kenya's solution to the "challenge of the future." *Wimbo Mpya* is a title that implies erasure of an old song saturated with vengeance and acrimony. Furthermore, the old song that entailed demand for land and freedom portended some disaster to Kenyatta's regime. As a pre-condition to independence, the British Empire "required Kenyatta and his followers to compromise on the historic nationalist principle that Europeans had no just claim to the land they were about to try to sell" (Harbeson, 1971, p. 244). Despite Kenyatta's compromise which thwarted peasants' aspirations to landholding, earlier Mau Mau novels still portrayed him as the messiah of the liberation struggle. What mattered in that dispensation was flaunting the victory of Black people to the retreating colonial powers, not the welfare of the newly independent Kenyans.

Land was the colonized people's symbol of socio-economic progress and the major drive for the liberation war. The new post-independent state seemed to counter the old song with its emphasis on "uhuru na kazi," "freedom and work" that was the slogan of the ruling party KANU (Kenya African National Union). But the slogan seemed inappropriate because the impoverished and unemployed majority, especially in the urban centers, could see through the pervasive economic inequalities. They therefore reformulated the slogan to "uhuru na taabu' (freedom and suffering). [...]. Here, then, was a clear statement of the demand for redistributive politics" (Branch, 2012, p. 35). Little was done for the majority public dispossessed by colonialism. It is in this context that Mau Mau veterans represented in *Wimbo Mpya* feel aggrieved: their mission to redeem Kenya from colonialism and restore stolen lands was incomplete.

The represented Mau Mau veterans' rebellion against the new post-independence Kenyan state reveal difficulties in the founding of nations. Experiences with the colonial state, which had its remnants in the post-independent state in the form of structures of power and its clienteles, had taught the colonized subjects to be suspicious of government. In the Tanzanian case, for instance, resistance to post-independent state had its roots in "the colonial state [that] claimed the right and obligation to count and classify its population, to define what constituted social improvement, and to intervene in social affairs in order to achieve it" (Maddox & Giblin, 2005, p. 4). *Wimbo Mpya* explores difficulties encountered in attempts to foster a state-citizen relationship in an environment where the colonial regime had demonstrated to the public that the state exploits, oppresses, and even commits large-scale atrocities such as the ones experienced during the State of Emergency in Kenya (see, for instance, Anderson, 2005).

Wimbo Mpya suggests that individual citizens should aspire to diligently and selflessly develop their country rather than expect the state to improve their socio-economic statuses. This is an allusion to JKF Kennedy's inaugural speech "Ask Not What Your Country Can Do for You" to which the narrator explicitly refers when explaining the meaning of freedom (Mbatiah, 2004, p. 63). However, Malcom X laid bare the hypocrisy embellished in the speech by pointing out JKF Kennedy's inaction when African-Americans were facing racial persecution in Georgia, Alabama, Mississippi, among other states (see PBS, 2013). In the novel, the bearer of this new song is Mariamu who mobilizes the community to build schools and set up development projects in Gaito village, in Meru. On his part, Rogere, a Mau Mau veteran who left the forest upon independence is troubled by the reluctance of his comrades to join and develop the new country: "Ukitaka uhuru na ardhi upate uhuru tu, upokee, mambo mengine uyafuatilie baadaye. [...]. Imba wimbo mpya wa uhuru. [...]. Labda watoto wetu ndio watakaofaidika kutokana na uhuru" (2004, pp. 74–75), "if you fight for freedom and land and achieve freedom alone, embrace it, afterwards you can pursue other things. [...]. Sing the new song of independence. [...]. Maybe it is our children who shall reap the fruits of freedom." Here, the novel optimizes freedom as opposed to the culture of entitlement that characterized the early years of post-independent Kenya; as opposed to the endorsement of violence in Ngugi wa Thiong'o's *Matigari* (1986) in which a Mau Mau veteran single-handedly unleashes an insurrection against a post-independent bourgeois state, other peasants join in the great class revolution. Indangasi (1997, p. 199) writes: *Matigari*

> elevates the armed struggle into some kind of absolute. [...] Power emanates from the barrel of a gun, he seems to say with Mao Tse Tung. "Justice for the oppressed comes from a sharpened spear," he says in *Matigari* (p.131). It is an unblushing endorsement of the cult of violence, misconceived as revolutionary thought.

Through Rogere and Mariamu, Mbatiah redefines heroism in post-independent Kenya's socio-political landscape: selflessness. This is an incisive critique of earlier Mau Mau narratives that highlight sacrifice but still reek with entitlement, with murderous lust. The philanthropic acts of Mwathi, an elderly man in Gaito with expansive land who donates part of it to Mariamu's school project and promises to resettle Marete and his family as an alternative solution to forest fighter's grievances against the state, reinforce the novel's vision of fostering nationhood – a new song. Mwathi's philanthropy speaks to nationhood because it intervenes where the state, due to neglect or economic constraint, fails to provide land to the war veterans. This happens at a time when Mau Mau veterans still in the forest are facing imminent assault by Kenya's post-independent forces for the former's refusal to disband the militant group. By offering land for the building of a pioneer school in his village, Mwathi extends his contribution to the future generation. Through the philanthropic acts, the narrator broadens the understanding of heroism in the aftermath of war.

The kind of heroism underscored in the earlier Mau Mau novels is problematic since a post-war situation is not a conducive environment for searching heroes and persecuting those deemed not to have bled enough for the survival of the country. Ruganda's (2001, p. 75) *Shreds of Tenderness* is a classic example of how to rebuild a nation shattered by war. Indeed, Marete remains a hero for fighting for liberation, but the narrator undercuts his determination to prolong the violence. Yvonne Owuor's *Dust* further presents us with incisive critiques of heroic myths which thrive on atrocities.

Contesting the Mau Mau heroic myth: *Dust* (2013)

As the latest engagement with Mau Mau historiography across post-independent Kenya's four regimes, Yvonne Owuor's *Dust* has the benefit of a longer historical tracking of the shifting fortunes and abuses of the war. Owuor uses the protagonist Nyipir Oganda and his haunted family as the ultimate allegory of both Kenya's and Mau Mau discourse shifts over the years. Despite distinguishing himself as an active agent of colonialism when serving as a counter-insurgency soldier, it is Nyipir who flies the new Kenyan flag the night the Union Jack is lowered. This signifies the betrayal of Mau Mau's liberation mission as well as foreshadowing the continuity of colonial legacy. Nyipir's biography is an encoding of the continuity of histories of state violence: he was an active member of Mau Mau counterinsurgency in the colonial state; he is also an indomitable post-independent state soldier during the Shifta war which I discuss below. When Tom Mboya, Kenya's historical figure who championed nationhood, is assassinated in 1969, Nyipir suffers ethnic victimization and narrowly escapes execution. This prompts him to renounce his allegiance to the Kenyan state as he becomes an active member of cattle rustling in Northern Kenya. Nyipir is a character whose allegiances have shifted according to different forms of political expedience over the years; violence defines Nyipir right from his childhood when the colonial powers conscript his father and brother in World War II.

Owuor's *Dust* heavily borrows from Kenya's troubled histories to the point that a reader unfamiliar with the country's histories may find it difficult to appreciate its depth. Nyipir, his wife Akai-ma, their son Moses Ebewesit Odidi, their daughter Ajany are fictional, but their lives are interweaved with Kenya's histories such as Mau Mau, Independence celebrations, the Shifta war, Kenya's 2007/2008 post-election violence (PEV) among other major events. The PEV coincides with police extra-judicial killing of Odidi. The events shaping the destinies of Oganda's family are juxtaposed with the family of colonial officer Hugh Bolton, his wife Selene, and son Isaiah Bolton. Nyipir and Hugh Bolton's paths crossed during the Mau Mau War when the former was assigned as a native aide to the latter, both working for the colonial forces. Nyipir would later kill his boss and conceal the remains in a cave, marry the boss's mistress Akai-ma, and inhabit Bolton's house in the desert. This occurs after Selene, pregnant, and traumatized by colonial atrocities and Hugh's involvement in it, escapes to England: "*but first I want* … to belong to something real, like truth. Erase unspoken things, like Hola—a work camp where an unnamed man goes berserk and pounds eleven inmates into pulp" (103). To trace his disappeared father, Isaiah Bolton arrives at Nyipir's home when Odidi's body is lying in state. This re-awakens dangerous family ghosts. Significantly, the two families can be read as allegories of Kenya's nationhood transacted in ominous secrets but whose time for truth has come.

The novel situates PEV in the legacies of the Mau Mau War and demonstrates that the atrocities experienced in Kenya thrive on the covenants of silence – ethnic or state-administered oaths of secrecy in the face of atrocities. These ominous covenants are a heritage from the internecine Mau Mau War. Also, while in the pro-Mau Mau novels Jomo Kenyatta is the symbol of freedom from colonial bondage, Tom Mboya is a looming figure of nationhood in *Dust*. The inclusion of Mboya whose profound dream for a better Kenya is well expressed in his memoir *Freedom and After* (1963) and in the education programs he initiated unsettles heroic narratives built around Jomo Kenyatta.

The novel foregrounds Mau Mau's reincarnation in post-independent Kenya as it indicts narratives that uncritically perpetuated the war's version of heroism. For instance, the novel alludes to ethnic murders in which Kikuyu reprisal attackers locked and burnt to death a Luo fisherman's eight children and two wives in Naivasha at the peak of the violence in January 2008. The novel links the atrocity to Mau Mau:

> Nyipir has seen this before. / Touched it. / Hidden it. / His mind tumbles back to a different time, when brother, son, mother, father sealed family members in rooms and huts and set these alight in honor of covenants of terror that guaranteed silence: *If I speak, may the oath kill me*. Much later, the horror was painted over and replaced with myths of triumph, repeated, repeated again, then adorned in all seasons of retelling. Nyipir waited for the inheritors of these silences to call out the names of their undead dead. Not a word. Now, fifty years later, the murdered were shrieking from earth tombs of enforced, timeless stillness, wailing for their forgotten, chopped-up lives. They seemed to accuse every citizen inheritors of their haemorrhaging.
>
> *(Owuor, 2013, pp. 83–84 original emphasis)*

Here, Owuor enables readers a glimpse into Mau Mau atrocities through the eyes of a man who actively participated in the counterinsurgency. The loyalists were not as cowardly as earlier Mau Mau novels would have us believe. Even though Nyipir fought on the side of the colonialist, his memory of the Lari massacre among other guerrilla killings undercuts Mau Mau's heroic myth. *Dust* questions the morality of the oaths by demonstrating that they conceal atrocities and undermine atonement. Hence, postmemory glorifications of the oaths construct conspiracies with perpetrators against victims of Mau Mau atrocities. While the logic of covenants of silence worked to unite an aggrieved colonized group against colonizers, the same is used to mobilize one ethnic group against another, as seen in the annihilation of the Luo fisherman's family. The novel's silence on 2 January 2008 Kiambaa church arson in which 35 Kikuyus had been targeted and killed by Kalenjins in Eldoret before the Naivasha reprisal attacks, is telling.

To understand Nyipir's reflections on the Mau Mau oaths and consequent atrocities, one needs glimpses into earlier Mau Mau novels' portrayals of the same. In *A Grain of Wheat*, General R.'s persistent search for Kihika's traitor seems grounded in the oath: "We must find our traitor, else you and I took the oath for nothing. Traitors and collaborators must not escape revolutionary justice" (1966, p. 26). Kihika himself, the martyred commandant of the anti-colonial war, seemed aware of the oath's limitations (his tragic flaw). In persuading his would-be traitor Mugo to be the underground leader of Mau Mau in New Thabai, Kihika says: "But what is an oath? For some people you need the oath to bind them to the Movement. There are those who'll not keep a secret unless bound by an oath" (p. 184). Similarly, in Peter Kareithi's *Kaburi Bila Msalaba*, the oath is portrayed as the ultimate guarantor of secrecy, as an indispensable unifying factor for 'Black' people's quest for freedom from colonial bondage: "Kuishinda Serikali, siri ndiyo iliyokuwa kifaa cha vita cha kwanza" (1969, p. 44), "To defeat the colonial government, the foremost weapon of war was secrecy." Like Karanja who betrays the cause to pursue his elusive first love in *A Grain of Wheat*, a Mau Mau treasurer who had similarly taken the oath in *Kaburi Bila Msalaba* is driven by greed to become a colonial informant. In Mwangi's (1974, 60) *Carcase for Hounds*, General Haraka turns to the oath to bind the colonized people to the cause for liberation whenever the colonial forces intensify their offensive. Haraka argues that the oath needs to be renewed now and again because "tribal marks grow dimmer" with time (p. 63). As is the case in *Kaburi Bila Msalaba*, the oath is forced upon villagers. Owuor's reading of the oath is strikingly conflictual with the pro-Mau Mau novelists: "*Would they drink human blood to emphasize their separation from our lives?*" (p. 102 original emphasis). Here, Selene's anxieties during the Mau Mau War is a resounding indictment of the Mau Mau oaths – therein lies the foundations of ethno-racial cleansing.

Mau Mau oaths administered by combatants to the civilians is one side of the coin, the other is state administered oaths whereby state agents are sworn to secrecy as they commit atrocities. *Dust* archives the reincarnation of Mau Mau counter-insurgency during the Shifta war in which the "Kenyatta regime launched a repressive campaign to quell [the Pan-Somali secessionists through] heavy military assault [and] propaganda that branded those fighting for the union with Somalia as shifta (or bandits)" (Weitzberg, 2016, p. 66). Nyipir is part of the vicious team of the platoon enforcing 'territorial integrity':

> man hunting man in comradeship. Predatory subtlety; soft, no-fuss walking. Silent gestures — a look could say everything. He was in a platoon fanning out in the northern terrain, tracking scents. Women, children, and elderly equalled prey, equalled game. Blasting hapless homesteaders, AK-47-ing camel herds to encourage cooperation. [...]. The national economy of secrets. One night, a human screams, "Am I now the enemy, *afande*?" Nyipir remembered that despised things also cried. / But. *Thou shalt not kill*? That was for another season. It was simpler to obey commands for the good of the nation. No questions asked.
>
> *(2013, p. 124 original emphasis)*

Like Mau Mau counterinsurgency, the war against the Shiftas targeted not only the militants, but mostly the civilians, their property, and cultural systems. *Dust*'s portrayals of Shifta war here are converse to the Kenyatta regime's Harambee rallying call invoked in *Wimbo Mpya* discussed above. The violence against civilians to enforce 'patriotism' executed by state security agents is founded on oaths and utmost loyalty to the commander, the president. Nyipir later reckons that the oaths illusively conceal atrocities: "Silence's oaths, slow-dripping venom with their seductive promise of memory loss. Erasure of secrets, as long as the oath was fed in intermittent seasons with spilled human blood" (p. 68).

When the Kenyatta regime faced a robust challenge from the Oginga Odinga-led opposition in 1968, a situation that worsened with Tom Mboya's assassination in 1969, it reverted to Mau Mau tactics. Odhiambo (2002, p. 241) writes: "truckloads of Agikuyu voluntarily went or were coerced into going to Gatundu, Kenyatta's country seat, to take oaths to guarantee that the Kenyan flag would never leave the House of Mumbi." Similarly, Ogude (2003, p. 277) asserts:

> Kenyatta was forced to turn to Mau Mau, and duly transformed it into the ultimate bulwark of Kikuyu nationalism, those belonging to the house of Gikuyu and Mumbi, now threatened by other ethnic groups with their eyes on the ultimate seat of authority in the land.

Oathing for ethnic mobilization overseen by state agents would lead to seemingly permanent dangerous polarization of the country, the effects of which exploded during the 2007/2008 PEV. At the same time, Kenyatta's messianic image as portrayed in the Mau Mau novels is undercut by his actions in ethnic exclusion and persecutions.

Indeed, *Dust* invokes the Jomo Kenyatta's 1969 oathings of political supporters in Gatundu, but emplots it in the aftermath of Tom Mboya's assassination that polarized the country. The oaths ushered in a secret massacre of individuals perceived as a threat to the Kenyatta regime:

> A hundred, and then a hundred more, herded into holding houses. Picked up — taken from homes, offloaded from saloon cars, hustled from offices, stopped on their way from somewhere else — prosecuted, and judged at night. Guilty, they were loaded onto the backs of lorries. And afterward, lime-sprinkled corpses were heaped in large holes dug into the grounds of appropriated farms. Washed in acid, covered with soil that became even more crimson, upon which new forests were planted.
>
> *(273)*

Here, the novel reconfigures classified state violence against perceived enemies and shows that this is reminiscent of Mau Mau counterinsurgency, where, in both cases, state security agents summarily executed suspects and secretly buried them in mass graves in forests. These Mau Mau methods that the Kenyatta regime uses to augment its power in the early decades of post-independence Kenya lead to a divided Kenya. After ruining the vision of a united and inclusive nation, Kenyatta's regime actively participated in the construction of the Luo as "the ultimate 'other'" (A. Odhiambo, 2002, p. 242).

In his insightful reflections on Ngugi wa Thiong'o's *Weep Not, Child*, a novel that exposes the crudeness of the Mau Mau counterinsurgency in colonial Kenya, Indangasi bears witness to the ethnic violence meted against the Luo in Nairobi in the aftermath of Tom Mboya's assassination. Indangasi too, like Owuor, links the Kikuyu violence against the Luo in 1969 to Mau Mau, which found its legitimacy in the Kikuyu myth of creation that propagates exceptionalism and entitlement to resources and power as it denounces defilement by the so-called outsiders. Indangasi (2018, p. 28) writes: "What happened in 1969 [...] made me see the myth of Gikuyu and Mumbi in a new light: that people were made to actualize a fabricated creation myth to the detriment of their fellow human beings."

Conclusion

Memory is fluid; its uses and misuses can either be transformative or detrimental. Indeed, novelists tap into memories of violent liberation wars to ascertain the morality of a war, but also to claim entitlement after liberation. However, valorization of violent memories seems to normalize violence in the society hence undermining aspirations for and sustenance of nationhood. The reading of new millennium Mau Mau counternarratives shows novelists' continuous revisionist tasks of problematic memories. While the militant Mau Mau War has been portrayed as primitive in the settler novels; as heroic in the post-independent pro-Mau Mau novels: the conversation on the war comes full circle in the new millennium Mau Mau novels that contest the war's post-memories. In a space where ethnic nationalists and/or state agents enter covenants of silence as they unleash atrocities against dissenting voices, *Dust* calls for a rethinking of problematic ideologies incubated in violent memories. On its part, *Wimbo Mpya* contests for the inclusivity of the liberation struggle memories as it redesigns heroism: selfless people who are ready and committed to develop the nation as opposed to the sense of entitlement to state resources. Perhaps the passage of time is prompting novelists to redefine heroism in spaces where power and violence is at the core of memory projects.

Acknowledgment

This is a revised version of my PhD thesis's section in chapter three pp. 82–92. The thesis is titled "Narrated Histories in Selected Kenyan Novels, 1963–2013." I'm indebted to my supervisors Prof. Grace A. Musila and Dr Godwin Siundu for their instrumental reviews of the earlier draft.

I presented a section of the chapter at the Association of Commonwealth Literature and Language Studies (ACLALS) held at Stellenbosch University, Cape Town, South Africa (10–15 July 2016) under the title "Nation and Human Destiny: Reading Mau Mau Histories in Yvonne Owuor's *Dust* (2013)."

Notes

1 The fictional Thompson seems a historical nod to Willoughby Thompson who was a District Officer in the regions affected by the war in the 1950s Kenya colony. But he is also constructed to carry the role of John Cowan, the Superintendent of Prisons in the colony at the time the Hola camp disaster occurred: Cowan ordered the prison warders to brutalise Mau Mau detainees on a hunger strike resulting to the killing of eleven while sixty suffered critical injuries.

2 The victims of the Lari Massacre vary from 500 to 1500 and it is also claimed that retributive attacks on survivors who were suspected to have harbored the Mau Mau guerrillas was higher than those killed by the guerrillas.

References

Achebe, C. (1958). *Things Fall Apart*. Nairobi: East African Educational Publishers.

Achebe, C. (2000). *Home and Exile*. New York: Anchor Books.

Anderson, D. (2005). *Histories of the Hanged: Britain's Dirty War in Kenya and the End of Empire*. London: Weidenfeld & Nicolson.

Branch, D. (2007). The Enemy within: Loyalists and the War against Mau Mau in Kenya. *The Journal of African History*, *48*(2), 291–315.

Branch, D. (2012). *Kenya: Between Hope and Despair, 1963–2012*. New Haven: Yale University Press.

Coundouriotis, E. (2014). *The People's Right to the Novel: War Fiction in the Postcolony*. New York: Fordham University Press.

Diamond, L. (1989). Review: Fiction as Political Thought. *African Affairs 1*, *88*(352), 435–445.

Furedi, F. (1989). *The Mau Mau War Perspective*. London: James Currey.

Furley, O. (1972). The Historiography of Mau Mau. In B. A. Ogot (Ed.), *Politics and Nationalism in Colonial Kenya* (pp. 105–133). Nairobi: East African Publishing House.

Gallagher, S. (1997). The Backward Glance: History and the Novel in Post-Apartheid South Africa. *Studies in the Novel*, *29*(3), 376–395.

Gicheru, M. (1991). *The Mixers*. Nairobi: Longhorn Publishers (K) Ltd.

Green, M. (1990). Mau Mau Oathing Rituals and Political Ideology in Kenya: A Re-Analysis. *Africa: Journal of the International African Institute*, *60*(1), 69–87.

Harbeson, J. W. (1971). Land Reforms and Poiltics in Kenya, 1954–70. *The Journal of Modern African Studies*, *9*(02), 231–251. https://doi.org/10.1017/S0022278X00024915

Huxley, E. (1935). *White Man's Country*. London: Chatto & Windus.

Huyssen, A. (2003). *Present Pasts: Urban Palimpsets and the Politics of Memory*. Stanford: Stanford University Press.

Indangasi, H. (1997). Ngugi's Ideal Reader and the Postcolonial Reality. *The Yearbook of English Studies, 27*, 193–200.
Indangasi, H. (2018). *Rethinking Literature: My Personal Essays on a Troubled Discipline.* Nairobi: Kenya Literature Bureau.
Iv, H. R. M., & Howard, T. C. (2013). Counter-Narrative as Method: Race, Policy and Research for Teacher Education. *Race Ethnicity and Education, 16*(4), 536–561. https://doi.org/10.1080/13613324.2013.817772
Kanyinga, K. (2009). The Legacy of the White Highlands: Land Rights, Ethnicity and the Post-2007 Election Violence in Kenya. *Journal of Contemporary African Studies, 27*(3), 325–344. https://doi.org/10.1080/02589000903154834
Kareithi, P. M. (1969). *Kaburi Bila Msalaba.* Nairobi: Phoenix Publishers Ltd.
Kenyatta, J. (1964). *Harambee! The Prime Minister of Kenya's Speeches 1963–1964* (A. Cullen, Ed.). Nairobi: Oxford University Press.
Kenyatta, J. (1968). *Suffering Without Bitterness: the Founding of the Kenya Nation.* Nairobi: East African Publishing House.
Luwisch, F. E. (2001). Understanding What Goes on in the Heart and the Mind: Learning about Diversity and Co-Existence Through Storytelling. *Teaching and Teacher Education, 17*, 133–146.
Maddox, G. H., & Giblin, J. L. (2005). Introduction. In G. H. Maddox & J. L. Giblin (Eds.), *In Search of a Nation: Histories of Authority and Dissidence in Tanzania* (pp. 1–12). Oxford: James Currey.
Maughan-Brown, D. (1985). *Land, Freedom & Fiction.* New Jersey: Zed Books.
Mbatiah, M. (2004). *Wimbo Mpya.* Nairobi: Jomo Kenyatta Foundation.
Mboya, T. (1963). *Freedom and After.* Nairobi: East African Educational Publishers.
Mwangi, M. (1974). *Carcase for Hounds.* Nairobi: East African Educational Publishers.
Ochieng, W. R. (1992). Dedan Kimathi: The Real Story. *Maseno Journal of Education, Arts and Science, 1*(1), 132–134.
Odhiambo, A. (2002). Hegemonic Enterprises and Instrumentalities of Survival: Ethnicity and Democracy in Kenya. *African Studies, 61*(2), 223–249. https://doi.org/10.1080/0002018022000032938a
Ogude, J. (2003). The Nation and Narration: "The Truths of the Nation" & the Changing Image of Mau Mau in Kenyan Literature. In A. E. S. Odhiambo & J. Lonsdale (Eds.), *Mau Mau & Nationhood: Arms, Authority & Narration* (pp. 268–298). Oxford: James Currey.
Omuteche, J. (2014). Historification and Kenya's Plural Identities: Re-reading Ngugi's Historiography. *Eastern African Literary and Cultural Studies, 1*(1–2), 107–116. https://doi.org/10.1080/23277408.2014.941753
Owuor, Y. (2013). *Dust.* New York: Alfred A. Knopf.
PBS. (2013). *Malcom X: Make It Plain.* Retrieved from www.youtube.com/watch?v=3zIGNkR62Mo&t=195s Accessed 13/02/2017
Ruganda, J. (1981). *Echoes of Silence.* Nairobi: East African Educational Publishers.
Ruganda, J. (2001). *Shreds of Tenderness.* Nairobi: Oxford University Press.
Simatei, T. P. (2001). *The Novel and the Politics of Nation Building in East Africa.* Bayreuth: Bayreuth African Studies 55.
wa Kinyatti, M. (1980). *Thunder from the Mountains: Mau Mau Patriotic Songs.* London: Zed Press.
wa Kinyatti, M. (2006). *The Pen and the Gun: Selected Essays, Letters and Poems.* New York: Mau Mau Research Center.
wa Thiong'o, N. (1964). *Weep Not, Child.* London: Heinemann.
wa Thiong'o, N. (1965). *The River Between.* London: Heinemann.
wa Thiong'o, N. (1966). *A Grain of Wheat* (Revised 20). Nairobi: East African Educational Publishers.
wa Thiong'o, N. (1972). *Homecoming: Essays on African and Caribbean Literature, Culture and Politics.* London: Heinemann Educational Books.
wa Thiong'o, N. (1986). *Matigari.* London: Heinemann Educational Publishers.
Weitzberg, K. (2016). Rethinking the Shifta War Fifty Years after Independence: Myth, Memory, and Marginalization. In M. M. Kithinji, M. M. Koster, & J. P. Rotich (Eds.), *Kenya After 50: Reconstructing Historical, Political, and Policy Milestones* (pp. 65–81). Basingstoke: Palgrave Macmillan.
Woods, T. (2007). *African Pasts: Memory and History in African Literatures.* Manchester: Manchester University Press.

22

Australian speculative indigenous fiction as counter-narrative

Post-apocalyptic environments and indigenous ancestral knowledge in Alexis Wright's *The Swan Book*

Sonja Mausen and Judith Eckenhoff

Positioning Alexis Wright's *The Swan Book* within a discourse of 'counter-narratives' offers a multitude of options: viewing the novel as part of post-colonial literature, we may read the novel in opposition of the 'colonial' and its 'post', wherein the latter can be interpreted less as the time *after* colonialism, but more as political activism directed at *bringing* a state of post-coloniality *about*. As a Waanyi author, Alexis Wright is also situated within a native minority group in her own country, which offers a perspective of indigenous countering Australian settler literature, or in other terms, the 'periphery' versus the 'center' of the Australian canon. Both terms – the post-colonial and the periphery-center binary – are problematic since they replicate a Eurocentric worldview.[1] Neither fully acknowledges a formation of new centers in their specific localized, historic, and socio-economic context. From an ecocritical perspective, the novel is positioned to counter the Anthropocene, as dystopia counters present day reality, as futuristic fiction counters a localized present and past. And last, but not least, through the protagonist Oblivion "Oblivia" Ehyl(ene) and the European refugee figure Bella Donna, we can read the novel through a feminist lens countering patriarchal power structures. Clearly, a discussion addressing all these aspects would go far beyond the scope of this chapter. We thus decided to focus on an indigenous, ecocritical perspective, though we will refer to other aspects mentioned above where sensible.

One of the essential features of master-narratives, according to Molly Andrews,

> is that they offer people a way of identifying what is assumed to be a normative experience. In this way, such storylines serve as a blueprint for all stories; they become the vehicle through which we comprehend not only the stories of others, but crucially of ourselves as well. For ultimately, the power of master-narratives derives from their internalization.
>
> *(Bamberg and Andrews, 2004, p. 1)*

Resisting the internalized normative story structures, counter-narratives can offer an active strategy of challenging homogenizing master-narratives by articulating experiences that deviate from such blueprints, validating them within a plurality of perspectives. Beyond 'counter' as "contrary" or "opposing", the prefix also carries the meaning of "complementary" as in "corresponding" and "counterpart", or "duplicate" and "substitute" (Merriam-Webster, 2018). The first meaning of 'counter', as in *counter*-narrative, presumes that there is one in power and one that needs to make herself heard – it does not equate equal standing to both. This is an aspect that we take issue with – for it reproduces this imbalance in its analysis. As Alexis Wright states in "Weapons of Poetry":

> Aboriginal people have continued to develop a very sophisticated interest in other cultures. But you cannot have a partner who thinks less than you do about who you are, or who is lazy and places no value in new ideas, and who cannot understand the complexity and richness of Indigenous humanity.
>
> *(Wright, 2008a, p. 22)*

In any discourse, the respect for and willingness to listen to the other must exist on both sides – the burden to 'convince' cannot merely be placed on the marginalized narrative. It is marginalized precisely because of this power imbalance it (often) aims to rectify. Bill Ashcroft refers to Homi Bhabha's *Location of Culture* when he summarizes that

> Bhabha cautions against the (regrettably common) tendency to fall into the trap of installing a "unity" of binary oppositions in the practice of critique, the desire to seek a "resolution" of real or symbolic contradictions by asserting one dogma over another.
>
> *(Ashcroft, 2017, p. 10)*

Therefore, even when we approach counter-narratives as texts intended to deconstruct a master narrative, we must keep in mind that complexity often overrides binary opposition. Wright's novel resists internalized master-narratives of colonization and continued oppression through racism and patriarchy. According to our understanding, counter-narrative articulates indigenous identity not in opposition to or dependence on a master-narrative of Western colonial oppression, thereby asserting its own place at the periphery, but draws on indigenous perspectives, mythology, and narrative mode for mapping its story on its own blueprints, offering a 'multiplicity of options' that move beyond counter-discourse. In the following chapter we will first offer a short theoretical introduction to the field of ecocriticism before we turn towards *The Swan Book* and a close textual analysis.

Ecocritical approaches and speculative indigenous narrative

The inevitable and yet still incalculable consequences of anthropogenic climate change have become an increasingly pressing concern for the humanities regarding the ways in which the environmental fluctuations and risks that await human and non-human inhabitants of the planet are imagined, communicated, and processed. The ecological turn has also addressed more deeply underlying assumptions in the way Western thought has conceptualized 'nature' and our place in it. As the concept of the Anthropocene for delineating a new geological epoch marked by man-made changes on a global scale is gaining momentum, the realization of the lasting impact the human species has had on the surface of the Earth and its atmosphere has seen a broad range of reactions in public discourse. They range from outright denial of a causal connection between industrial carbon emissions and the warming of the planet's atmosphere, over doubt concerning the serious quality of the possible consequences for a majority of currently living species, to activist and political efforts to control the damage by reducing carbon emissions, which is often at odds with continued pursuit of capitalist growth. Comprehension of scientific fact and environmental policy decisions remain deeply entangled with ideology and conflicting interests.

The project of ecocriticism is invested in drawing attention to discursive figurations of our relationship with non-human nature, exposing anthropocentric and exploitative ideology and practices. Similarly, the politics of environmental and indigenous literatures tend to involve the articulation of perspectives that challenge the status quo of people (still) being denied basic human rights or land being drained of resources. Such literature also often implicitly or explicitly challenges the ways in which dominant discourses of 'nature' continue to conceive of the relationship between humans and their non-human environment as a dichotomous opposition instead of an interrelated eco-system of complex interdependencies. The idea which Timothy Morton has introduced as the 'mesh', a metaphor conceptualizing the material interconnectedness of human beings and their environments, is already deeply ingrained in indigenous knowledge systems, where land and people are not regarded as separate, or even adverse, entities to begin with. Indigenous Australian cultures have preserved traditional understandings of the environment as animate entity and manifestation of the Dreamtime:

> The Aboriginal English word "Country" describes conceptions of land and its complex interrelations with human and non-human beings that are central to Australian Indigenous Law. Country contains Aboriginal knowledge systems; it also designates an active living presence, and the reciprocal relations of care between Aboriginal people and their land.
>
> *(Gleeson-White, 2016, p. 29)*

This relationship, while crucial to indigenous identity, is under attack from two opposing directions: the othering that is contingent on a moral idealization of indigenous spirituality as "radical alterity safe-guarding a threatened world against a devastating technological modernity" (Neumeier, 2018, p. 222) ironically reinforces the dichotomy of nature and culture as polar opposites and perpetuates harmful stereotypes of the 'noble savage' by supposedly celebrating indigenous superior understanding of the natural world.

The more direct and violent interference with the relationship between people and country lies in the colonization and genocide that have not only robbed indigenous Australians of the sovereignty over their land but also uprooted and displaced them, thus brutally severing the connection and causing (sometimes irreparable) damage to humans and country. This violence is still on-going in the present day. Australia is the only former British colony – though the ongoing argument is that the colonizers never left – without a treaty with its original inhabitants. Policies such as the White Australia policy that was not completely abolished until 1973, or more recently, the Northern Territory Emergency Response Bill that allowed the military to intervene in Indigenous communities, though none of the claimed cases of children's sexual abuse or neglect used to justify the intervention have been brought to prosecution, continue a politic of discrimination and colonization that excludes the indigenous "other" from the national and societal image of Australia. Australia was one of only four countries to vote against the United Nations Declaration on the Rights of Indigenous Peoples in 2007 and has been criticized by the United Nations Human Rights Council in 2015 for its treatment of Indigenous peoples and refugees.

Another disruption of the relationship manifests itself in the environmental harm that Rob Nixon calls slow violence, meaning "a violence that occurs gradually and out of sight, a violence of delayed destruction that is dispersed across time and space, an attritional violence that is typically not viewed as violence at all" (Nixon, 2011, p. 2). Encompassing the effects of climate change, environmental pollution, and exploitation of material resources, slow violence is inflicted on the poor, marginalized communities of the Earth by the global north and goes largely unnoticed not just because the long-term consequences and suffering it causes are almost impossible to quantify but also because it represents a form of "environmentally embedded violence that is often difficult to source, oppose, and once set in motion, to reverse" (Nixon, 2011, p. 7). Ultimately, this is a continuation of colonialist practices, serving a neoliberal master-narrative of Western entitlement and in a global perspective the actors that determine future consequences of climate change enact a neo-colonial power-play.

Speculative fiction, which we use here as an umbrella term encompassing dystopian, (post-) apocalyptic, and climate change fiction, as well as other futuristic, often non-realist, narratives, opens a literary space for imagining possible future worlds affected by such processes, confronting both the injustices, problems, and anxieties of our present reality and possible developments. As these works often take a pessimistic perspective towards the stability of societies, governments, economies, and environments, the future they evoke makes this slow, environmentally embedded violence explicitly visible by projecting the consequences of current practices onto the screen of an imagined, but possible future.

Eric Otto (2012) observes how in both environmental utopian and dystopian fiction, literary techniques of cognitive estrangement "enable the critical interrogation of the social reality undergirded by dominant ideology" (Otto, 2012, p. 9) because the speculative quality of the storyworld requires the readers' repeated reflection on the current state of affairs in our reality by comparison. While such strategies, employed in ecocritically invested dystopian fiction, can posit environmental counter-narratives, it is important to note that Wright does not write for a white audience but primarily for her own community, so that the very situatedness of approaching a novel like *The Swan Book* from a Western, non-indigenous perspective will necessarily involve a higher degree of aesthetic estrangement in readers who are not immersed in the mythology, language, and tradition in which the narrative is steeped. For indigenous readers, on the other hand, the familiarity with the culture and experiences that inspire and inform the text allows both the recognition of these elements as grounded in the reality of the present as well as the estrangement of the narrative's extrapolation of future social, political, and ecological developments.

The potential of speculative narratives like *The Swan Book* also lies in the immersive and affective qualities of fiction. In combining ecocritical reading strategies and narratological analysis, Erin James analyzes post-colonial texts and discusses "the potential of narratives and their world-creating power to increase understanding among readers of different environmental imaginations" (2015, pp. 3–4). She argues that the evocation of storyworld as the mental and emotional projection of a narrative's environment allows readers to approximate a sense of "what it is like for people in different spaces and times to live in their ecological homes" (p. 23). This approach, as it highlights readers' perspective-taking and imaginative inhabitation of fictional spaces that are grounded in material realities, puts a clear emphasis on the power of literary writing to foster cross-cultural dialogue and ultimately reshape and broaden environmental imaginations. Similarly, Alexa Weik von Mossner (2017) draws attention to the affective dimension of environmental narrative and explores how emotional engagement and empathy in interacting with fiction depend on both embodied cognition and culturally and physically embedded experience. In her discussion of eco-dystopian narrative, she argues that in light of global environmental risk, the desolation and disaster of dystopia depend on balancing counterpoints of positive affect to keep readers engaged, either on a formal level by means of aesthetic foregrounding or engaging narrative strategies like suspense, or by offering a sense of hope (cf. 2017, pp. 161–163).

The Swan Book

Alexis Wright's *The Swan Book* tells the story of Oblivia Ethylene, an indigenous woman from the swamp "Swan Lake", which functions as a detention camp for both indigenous peoples and climate refugees from the Northern hemisphere. Set some 100 to 200 years in the future, climate change has irreversibly changed the world, geologically and politically. The arrival of large numbers of refugees in Australia has allowed one indigenous group – the Brolga Nation – to negotiate a treaty with the state and gain sovereignty over their land and people. Other language groups – such as the Swan Lake people – were forgotten and pushed aside. Oblivia is of the Swan Lake people, but after a group of young boys from the community gang rape her, she crawls into the base of a tree and falls into a deep sleep. She survives an indeterminable amount of time, until Bella Donna of the Champions, a climate change refugee, finds her and returns her to the community. The people there, however, reject her and treat her like a stranger, claiming the lost little girl had died years ago. Traumatized, Oblivia is left without a voice and only manages to communicate with the black swans that live on the lake, and later on with Warren Finch, a young politician from the Brolga Nation to whom she was promised as wife at birth and who later on abducts her and keeps her locked in a tower in the city. The novel narrates Oblivia's life with Bella Donna, her forced travels through Finch's Country on his way to the city, and her life in isolation in the city, before she finally returns to her homeland after her husband's murder.

The virus

The prologue, narrated by Oblivia in the first person retrospectively, introduces the reader to a virus that is living inside her mind: "The virus thinks it is the only pure full-blood virus left in the land. Everything else is just half-caste. Worth nothing!" (Wright, 2015, p. 1) The virus thus becomes a metaphor for what Franz Fanon in his seminal works *Black Skin, White Masks* and *The Wretched of the Earth* discusses as "colonization of the mind". The thought patterns of the imperial Master-narrative have been internalized, and despite Oblivia's awareness, changing the status quo is challenging. The thought-patterns of the colonizer, the British Empire, are made obvious. So called "half-caste" children were often taken from their parents and brought into group homes on missions, or given to white settlers as domestic workers. The rationale behind this was that while "full-blooded" Aboriginals could not be civilized and would eventually die out, "half-castes" had "at least some European blood" in them and could thus be assimilated. This led to thousands of children being taken from their parents and family ties being ruptured, now referred to as the Stolen Generation. That the virus employs this language shows that it thinks in the colonizers' thought patterns. Property ownership in the Western sense was unknown to Aboriginal peoples before contact. Australian aboriginal connection to country is one of *people belonging to country*, in contrast to the Western concept of *country belonging to people*.

The virus is an "assimilated spirit", a spirit that has given up its own identity in favor of white settler identity. Oblivia's insight that this is a virus, an illness, shows a crisis of identity that is struggling to forge a "mind" unpossessed. Wright herself refers to this process as regaining "sovereignty of the mind" (Wright, 2008b). About the Aboriginal activist and poet Oodgeroo, Wright says:

> She used words as a shield to hold back the full effect of colonialism, and the power of those words have lasted through many decades to remind us, as if they were written yesterday, where we come from and who we are and what we stand for. Poems such as Oppression and

> We Are Going are so potent they actually reinvigorate the sovereignty of the mind with new energy and resolve to say no to assimilation.
>
> *(Wright, 2008b)*

Literature, for Wright, is more than a source of strength and motivation. It is active cultural work targeting social change. A land rights activist since even before she became a successful author, her texts are political beyond Althusser's postulation that nothing exists outside ideology:

> in the fight for sovereignty over this land – that if you could succeed in keeping the basic architecture of how you think, then you owned the freedom of your mind, that unimpeded space to store hope and feed your ability to survive.
>
> *(Wright, 2008a, p. 21)*

However, sovereignty over country is not the primary goal in the novel. Instead, Wright's "narrative suggests, with its focus on the protagonist Oblivia, that retaining a sovereignty of the mind may be more important to foster and sustain in the future than a quest for political sovereignty at any cost" (Rodoreda, 2018, p. 193). Rodoreda further highlights that indigenous sovereignty over country stands *counter* to the state's claim of sovereignty over the land. But furthermore, in its epistemology of indigenous peoples being caretakers, it also stands despite and beyond the state's claim of ownership. Oblivia

> *created* illusionary ancient homelands to *encroach on and destroy* the wide-open vista of the virus's real-estate. The prairie house is now surrounded with mountainous foreign countries that dwarf the plains and flatlands in their shadows, and between the mountains, there are deserts where a million thirsty people have travelled, and to the coastlines, seas that are stirred by King Kong *waves that are like monsters roaring at the front door.* Without meeting any resistance whatsoever, I have become a gypsy, addicted to journeys into these distant illusionary homelands, to try to lure the virus hidden somewhere in its own crowded globe to open the door. This is where it begins as far as I am concerned. This is the *quest to regain sovereignty over my own brain.*
>
> *(Wright, 2015, p. 4, our italics)*

The apocalyptic image of the landscape of her mind reconquers sovereignty. This creates an analogy between the effects of climate change as active resistance against human violators and the struggle to upset the (neo-)colonial oppression of indigenous minds. Nature must upset the established order to make space for a new one. This awards the land an agency that Western knowledge systems fail to recognize. As Gleeson-White states, the novel as a whole describes the effect of a

> clash between two cosmologies with different understandings of land. These cosmologies [...] can be distinguished chiefly on the basis of how they conceptualise land and the relation of humans to it. In the former, land is a vital ecological system with its own being and agency to which humans belong; it is "Country". In the other, land is viewed as economic wealth, property to be developed, exploited or otherwise "improved" for profit, with humans raised above it.
>
> *(Gleeson-White, 2016, p. 30)*

At the root of the virus lies a need for the belief in a better future. In Wright's own words:

> Racism is strong in this country, make no mistake about it. And it will remain that way as long as it promotes the notion that there can be only one Australia. This country too, just as did Germany after the war, wants to forget the past, scrub it from the history books.
>
> *(Wright, 2002, p. 15)*

Wright, then, sets out to draw attention to the very past the nation state tries to forget. By elongating past and present injustices into the future in a speculative form that combines them with the continuation of racist policies and – in Warren Finch's case – fulfilment of sovereign fantasies, she exposes the imagined utopia as dystopia. As Heather Taylor Thompson puts it, "[u]ltimately this is a Dreamtime story, teaching us about our past and cautioning us about our future" (Johnson). Imagining the future as a warning is what Wright sees as her duty as a writer. In her inaugural lecture as Boisbouvier Chair at the University of Melbourne, she states:

> we need deep thinking and deep imagination in our literature to shock the daylight out of us, to make us see what is happening in the world, to make us think, and if we teach how to read more deeply, think more, then perhaps, perhaps, we might stop harming ourselves and the planet.
>
> *(Wright, 2018)*

This correlates to Bill Ashcroft's analysis of the utopian in post-colonial fiction in the sense that utopian "does not mean that literary works themselves are always utopian, nor even necessarily hopeful, but rather that the imaging of a different world in literature is the most consistent expression of the anticipatory consciousness that characterizes future thinking" (Ashcroft, 2017, p. 37). In *The Swan Book*, Wright powerfully imagines what a future might look like that connects Australian indigenous *Dreamings* with the realities of global warning. Yet the dystopian storyworld offers no clear path to a better future, and in fact not even one character that could offer true moral guidelines to a "new beginning". Nonetheless, she elucidates that "the predominant dynamic is the belief in the possibility of social change" (Ashcroft, 2017, p. 37), a characteristic that Ashcroft postulates as the underlying criterion for the "utopian".

The Swan Lake swamp and community

The swamp is the one place Oblivia feels truly connected to, since it is the only country whose stories she knows, but it is a perversion of what anyone would imagine a "home" would look like. It bears striking resemblance to the refugee camps we see on Manus Island and Nauru. Rodoreda even suggests that the "swamp can be read as a metaphor for the most *un*-sovereign place imaginable" (Rodoreda, 2018, p. 195), which is epitomized in its material environment as well as the community of the people who live there.

The portrayal of the environment in *The Swan Book* resists anthropocentrism in rendering country as a living entity not just through the focalization of human characters perceiving it as such but also in the way that "non-human language is given expression: the swan talk; the tree song; the swamp's sounds" (Daley, 2016, p. 314). The shifting narrative perspective, employing an omniscience that encompasses thoughts and histories of the people in the text as well as insight into the birds and land, thus offers a multiplicity of viewpoints, which, as Linda Daley argues, "dissolve the distinction between a human subject and a world of non-human objects. They dissolve an external reality to show that each of these viewpoints has its own individual reality" (2016, p. 308). Wright's characterization of the swamp draws together the sensual evocation of the voices of country and people, locally affected by climate change and the resulting drought, expressing their futile protest with images of the apocalyptic wasteland:

> The swamp's natural sounds of protest were often mixed with lamenting ceremonies. Haunting chants rose and fell on the water like a beating drum, and sounds of clap sticks oriented thoughts, while the droning didgeridoos blended all sounds into the surreal experience of a background listening, which had become normal listening. Listen! That's what music sounds like! The woman once explained to the world that the music of epic stories normally sounded like this.
>
> This is the world, disassembling its thoughts.
>
> It was just the new ceremony of the swamp dreaming, the girl thought, for what she called, Nowhere Special. She thought it suited the wind-swept surroundings of the dead swamp, where children played with sovereign minds, just by standing out in the wind to fill their cups with dust given to them by their ancestors.
>
> *(Wright, 2015, p. 54)*

The combined effect of the non-human and human sounds as articulation of stories and manifestation of the swamp dreaming emphasizes the subject position of country, which, as Gleeson-White points out, "interrupt a western narrative which has figured land as lacking in agency, as an inert resource to be 'improved' and 'developed'" (2016, p. 29). Simultaneously highlighting the land degradation that results from that very narrative of objectifying, subjugating, and draining the natural environment, Wright's depiction of the swamp exposes both the immediate and the slow violence of colonization. In this context, the image of the ubiquitous dust epitomizes the apocalyptic destruction and recalls a sense of live burial in also severing of the connection to the world beyond the swamp: "Dust covered the roads and nobody knew where they were anymore, and the old woman claimed that even the bitumen highways were disappearing. Soon, no one would have any idea about how to reach this part of the world" (Wright, 2015, p. 54). The passage also echoes indigenous song lines and the mutual discourse between people and country. Song lines are more than just stories. They are a map to their people that tells of country, origin, and boundaries. As such, song lines have been in direct opposition to Western maps throughout the colonial history. The scripture-oriented Western culture would not accept oral maps as markers of territory and aboriginal peoples have sung their song lines to counter Western claims to their lands for centuries.

The swamp is toxic and covered in waste, illustrating Nixon's concept of slow violence in the way that its inhabitants are impacted. The army is ever present, even though the people like to pretend it is not and community, one of home, belonging and security, is perverted to maintain an illusion of harmony. Instead of protecting Oblivia, or at the very least prosecuting the group of boys who gang raped her, the swamp people prefer to forget she ever existed. However, their behavior is not intrinsic (Harris, 2017, p. 194). On the contrary,

> [t]he West's acquisitive wanderings and trespass across the entire Earth, and its exploitation of the planet's resources in search of cheap natures, have so transformed Country and its creatures that they have lost their ancestral stories connected with specific land forms and locations.
>
> *(Gleeson-White, 2016, p. 31)*

This disconnection is detrimental. Mudrooroo[2] explains that "if a person's country, over which he has custodianship, is injured, then the person becomes sick and dies" (Narogin, 1994, p. 58). A similar thing holds true in the swamp because both land and Swan Lake are certainly anything but well taken care of. This illness of the land has infected the people living there, the supposed custodians, leading to a degeneration of social responsibility.

Geoff Rodoreda reads the swamp people differently (Rodoreda, 2018, p. 205). Approaching the novel through the lens of sovereignty, he argues that in their resistance to the government controller Weisenheimer sent from Canberra to oversee the swamp, they enact what Wright describes as "sovereignty of the mind, even [if they] haven't got sovereignty of the country or the land" (Wright and Zable). But in light of Oblivia's rapists still living undisturbed in the swamp and the Swan Lake people's reluctance to accept her as one of their own, this interpretation is problematic. Wright's depiction of sovereignty is multifaceted. Again, Rodoreda points out that the novel "highlights different understandings of sovereignty among Aboriginal people" (Rodoreda, 2018, p. 206). We argue, however, that the Swan Lake version of sovereignty is not a complete sovereignty of the mind. As Wright says:

> With Oblivia, I wanted a character who, in a way, is unable to grow up. It's a reflection on Aboriginal communities – unable to grow up if we keep on being shackled by policy and by other people's ideas of how we should be.
>
> *(Wright and Zable, 2013)*

The inability to grow up also applies to the people of Swan Lake. They may still be living in their ancient homeland, but their connection to country is polluted – both figuratively and literally – and this affects their "minds". This also becomes apparent when Oblivia criticizes the Harbour Master, who is the only one enacting any form of custodianship over Swan Lake:

> Oblivia watched the Harbour Master who she thought ought to be doing something more about the sand mountain - unblocking the swamp for instance - he was taking long enough, and he should be more involved in fixing and healing like a real healer, instead of swooning about like some stupid cringing dog after Bella Donna. He splattered his soul that was fat with complaints all over the kitchen table for the old woman to see what the world had come to, of how difficult it was to heal anything these days in a place controlled by the Army like the swamp was. He was not superman was he? How could he take the love of Aboriginal children the Army men had stolen from parents and return it to them? And moreso, he thought that instead of Bella Donna wasting her time on the useless girl, she should be consoling him and giving him some excellent full-bodied strength platitudes about how everything would work itself out for the best in the end.
>
> *(Wright, 2015, p. 37)*

The point of view changes mid-paragraph. While the first half focalizes through Oblivia's character, the second half changes to the Harbour Master's excuses. It remains unclear whether this is recounted through Oblivia's memory in free indirect discourse or whether the focalizer changes. In either case, the passage highlights the constant conflict of living under oppression – the idea that it rests upon the individual to forge her own path, and the structural discriminatory policies causing dejection.

The Harbour Master's depiction does not amount to the preservation of dignity in face of oppression that Wright refers to in an interview with Arnold Zable:

> oppression is there, but you can unshackle yourself in the same way, and be able to maintain your own thoughts and dignity and culture, no matter what happens. This is the strength of Aboriginal law – and a lot of people would say that it is this idea of ourselves that is stronger than any other law, because it's unbroken – and you can still see this happening and the strength of belief in our world today.
>
> *(Wright and Zable, 2013)*

The Swan Lake people's treatment of Oblivia shows a similar disregard of dignity and culture, further underlining our interpretation of a polluted sovereignty of the mind in Swan Lake.

For Wright, law of country and the safe-guarding of stories offers a solution. At the same time, she avoids mitigating the effects of the government policies that continue to undermine Aboriginal self-determination. Explicit policies named in the text include the Northern Territory National Emergency Response Bill and Closing the Gap. Both policies are based on the master narrative of the Australian government "parent" looking after its Aboriginal "children" incapable of taking care of themselves. Wright powerfully subverts the national narrative by focusing on the indigenous characters' complexity. She neither vilifies nor glorifies any of her main characters, carefully describing the context of their socialization and reasonings. This does not mean that she excuses their actions, as the narrator clearly interposes, while also criticizing Bella Donna's neo-colonial treatment of the indigenous peoples. However, an indigenous worldview is focalized throughout the novel. White people – mostly men – are no more than minor characters, though the effect of their decisions on indigenous peoples is far from marginal. The Swan Lake people's seemingly passive disinterest in politics is turned on its head and into active rebellion against a government that passes judgment on them without ever truly exchanging a word with them.

Oblivia's silence goes beyond the symptom of her trauma. Her refusal to speak is an act of active resistance, which becomes most clear in two short passages opposing her to Bella Donna on the one hand, and the traditional caretaker of Swan Lake, the Harbour Master, on the other. When Bella Donna tells Oblivia that "*Yes,* [...], *I have used my opportunities for influencing people across the world. You must use the voice*", Oblivia strongly rejects this notion as nothing more than an extension of colonization: "The girl thought that she should be silent if words were just a geographical device to be transplanted anywhere on earth" (Wright, 2015, p. 23). In her silence, Oblivia is acutely aware of the power that words yield. At the same time, she is aware of their limitations:

> [H]er stomach muscles tried to shove a jumble of dog vomit words up her windpipe, although always in the nick of time, any of those screaming words that made it up to her mouth, crashed like rocks landing on enamel at the back of her clenched teeth. So, by remaining silent, saying nothing and stewing with hate and spitefulness in her guts, she reminded herself with a shiver down her spine that she would rather be dead, than waste her breath speaking to an idiot.
>
> *(Wright, 2015, p. 38)*

The idiot referenced is the Harbour Master, and the passage illustrates the violence with which the words try to break free. Silence, for Wright, goes beyond passivity or the inability to integrate trauma into a narrative structure. Instead, it can be an act of resistance that is more powerful and more complex than visible at first. Wright herself declares that the "most interesting voice to [her] is the voice [she has] to search for. The voice that is silent or elusive" (Wright, 2002, p. 20). Oblivia may be silent, but she goes in no way unheard.

As mentioned above, silence is also connected to country. Part of the connection Oblivia forms with the swans lies in her ability to truly listen not only to other people, but especially to country. Her muteness is equated with stupidity by the people surrounding her – a pattern that repeats itself in the treatment of Aboriginal peoples by the government – and her only refuge are the swans. In an analogy to her own relationship to Warren Finch, Oblivia muses:

> Swans mate for life: that was what she thought. And if a swan loved its mate, then what would make one kill its mate as she had seen once in a sudden and vicious attack, alongside the hull? It was a silent death. There was no such thing as the dying swan call. It died without sound. She had no sound either, and knew what it was like to be without sound. This country would never hear her voice, or the language she spoke.
>
> *(Wright, 2015, p. 174)*

The silence of death is analogous to both Finch's abduction of his girl-bride (since he faces no resistance from anyone but the silent Oblivia), and the silent violence of colonization in Australia at large. Seen in its harshest light, it is a continuing, silent genocide of Aboriginal peoples. References to the dead women all over the country both outside Swan Lake and the Brolga Nation (Wright, 2015, pp. 87, 173) draw specific attention to the precarity of indigenous women in this context.

Oblivia's silence extends from simply not having a voice to not having the language she needs to speak to country. All she has are the stories of the white swans she adopted from Bella Donna. She has taken the intertextually referenced Eurocentric canon of white swan stories and transforms them into a new language of belonging with the displaced black swans. Finch, on the other hand, has all the languages of the world, but has lost his true connection to place. He has become so adept at adapting that he is not more than an empty projection of himself. At the same time, this passage can also be read as an analogy for the human treatment of the earth. Despite their dependency, humans decide to kill their environment through negligence and pure violence, causing a silent death that will only be selectively heard in the mourning of the survivors of climate catastrophes.

Reclaiming wilderness

Upon her arrival at the unnamed city, which appears to Oblivia initially as "a world shrouded in fog and darkness" (Wright, 2015, p. 208), the novel juxtaposes the natural environments of the swamp, the Brolga nation, and the outback with a decaying urban space that complements the postapocalyptic wasteland with a ruinous architecture on the brink of becoming materially enmeshed in the natural landscape again, a city that has "cracked … as though the land beneath it had collapsed under its weight" (Wright, 2015, p. 208). Iva Polak, in her analysis of the novel's futuristic worldbuilding, observes that "the cityscape is unequivocally portrayed as a decrepit space lacking cultural historicity, mirroring moral as well as material decay" (pp. 212–213). Meanwhile, however, the images of wilderness invading and re-absorbing neglected human habitats invoke the trope of the postapocalyptic city, albeit this one is not abandoned but continues to house human city dwellers alongside spreading the non-human life:

> The neglected city had thousands of pigeons flying around the rooftops of buildings, and trees sprouting out of the sides of cathedrals, chestnuts growing from the alcoves, fig trees

> roots clung to the walls, and almond and apple trees grew from seeds that flourished in the damp cracks.
>
> *(Wright, 2015, p. 264)*

This slow transformation into a wild garden, while illustrating that "rebirth is possible only when nature grows over and dismantles culture that neglects its past" (Polak, 2017, p. 213), also draws attention to the disconnection and alienation from natural environments associated with industrial cityscapes. Oblivia's detainment at the People's Palace, which stands out from the decrepit city as an architectural symbol of power, is marked by alienation from its decadence and splendor. In contrast, her nightly forays into the city, motivated by the kinship with the swans that increasingly spread out through the urban space, underline her outsider position and solidarity with the displaced animals and liminal spaces of wilderness.

Oblivia's exploration of the city encompasses both the deserted buildings invaded by smaller creatures and the thick wilderness of the old botanical gardens, where the swans take up residence. Polak points out how in the midst of "this decrepit futuristic urban chaos, the narrator inserts several microspaces, whose appearance does not add to the construction of the city as a SF icon, but creates a spatio temporal crevice evoking a distant bygone era" (p. 213). For instance, upon following an owl to the "long-abandoned, boarded and nailed-up" magic shop (p. 259), her first impression upon entering is that the floor "was alive with the city's lizards and skinks that had gathered in the warmth of the room. Perhaps, she thought, they were participating in a historical conference about old homelands when lizards lived in trees" (Wright, 2015, p. 260). The comment concerning old homelands is both ironic and emotionally charged as it projects Oblivia's own sense of displacement. Similarly, she perceives the abandoned botanical gardens as the kind of

> place that serves no purpose to city people who grew nothing, but ate their food from packets. They called this sprawling greenery a *flippen and friggen untidy mess!* And saw no point in having this overgrown park in a city where there were people starving.
>
> *(Wright, 2015, p. 268)*

The ambivalence of disregarding the plants' nurturing potential while distressed at poverty and starvation further exemplifies the city people's alienation and moral decay. Looking back, the narrator recounts the relationship between the city people and nature:

> Whatever was in man's power to save his environment was done for the rare old trees, flowers and shrubs, but in the end the struggle to save greenery seemed meaningless. The long drought killed kindness in hardened hearts. Then, when the drought was replaced by sodding rains, year in year out, the canopy grew into an impenetrable wilderness too dangerous to people, and the precinct was just another place locked up forever.
>
> *(Wright, 2015, p. 269)*

Oblivia, however, whose nightly wanderings have her constantly pursued by street kids and their dogs, fearlessly steps into that liminal wilderness. Although she remains alien in the strange country and dilapidated city, the space of the overgrown, reconquered parts of the urban environment mirrors her envisioned mental landscape, discussed above, over which sovereignty can be regained through thorough environmental transformation of apocalyptic dimensions. Ultimately, although the novel offers little hope in the way of redemption, healing, or justice, both with regard to indigenous experience and environmental disaster, the sense of nature's perseverance is encapsulated in one of the final images of the narrative: Wright evokes a landscape where there are

> stranded swans scattered all over the open bush, among the spinifex, caught on power lines, on the edges of dried up soaks and inland lakes. If you were there you would have seen them everywhere. But the main flock struggled on, continued flying during the night.
>
> *(Wright, 2015, p. 327)*

While the reader is directly invited to create this mental image of death and place herself in that devastated, apocalyptic storyworld, covered in dead birds, the remaining flock of migrating swans – the ones that lead Oblivia back to her home country of Swan Lake – might be read, if not as hope, at least as embodying a continued struggle for survival.

Conclusion

In this chapter, we have explored Alexis Wright's *The Swan Book* as an indigenous, ecocritical counter-narrative and traced some of the ways in which the novel resists Western, colonial and anthropocentric master-narratives. The cultural work that literature performs in articulating experiences and identities counters and, beyond these master-narratives, plays an important part in consolidating these experiences, and also fostering cross-cultural dialogue. We have argued how the narrative problematizes and critiques internalized colonial language, sovereignty of both country and mind, and the detrimental, violent effects of environmental destruction on indigenous communities and of climate change on a global and local scale by building a speculative, dystopian storyworld. The geographical and psychological displacement of the protagonist Oblivia as well as her silence are inextricably linked with her connection to and communication with the black swans, a relationship that emblematized also what Harris calls "the novel's driving force: an Indigenous onto-epistemology or relational philosophy which irreducibly entangles human and non-and-more-than-human" (Harris, 2017, pp. 192–193). While it is deeply embedded in indigenous knowledge systems and clear regarding its politics concerning the specific ongoing injustices it addresses, *The Swan Book* thus additionally asserts a more general perspective on the interconnectedness between people, country, animals and history, politics, and culture.

Notes

1 The authors of this chapter would like to acknowledge that their reading of Alexis Wright's *The Swan Book* is a *possible* interpretation of the text by European researchers. We made every effort to critically reflect on our own Eurocentric position, but we will always remain 'outsiders' looking in.

2 Mudrooroo grew up during the time of the Stolen Generations and for a long time believed himself to be a descendent of the Narogin nation. It later turned out that he was not of Australian Aboriginal, but of African descent. He has since been excluded from the Narogin nation, but continues to argue that his identity, due to his long believe of culturally belonging to this group, is still Aboriginal.

References

Ashcroft, B. (2017). *Utopianism in Postcolonial Literatures*. London, New York: Routledge.

Baehr, E., & Schmidt-Haberkamp, B. (Eds.). (2017). *'And There'll Be No Dancing': Perspectives on Policies Impacting Indigenous Australia since 2007*. Newcastle upon Tyne, UK: Cambridge Scholars Publishing.

Bamberg, M., & Andrews, M. (Eds.). (2004). *Studies in Narrative: Vol. 4. Considering Counter-narratives: Narrating, Resisting, Making Sense*. Amsterdam: John Benjamins Publishing.

Bhabha, H. K. (2012). *The Location of Culture*. Routledge Classics: Routledge.

Butler, J. (2009). *Frames of War: When is Life Grievable?* London: Verso. Retrieved from www.loc.gov/catdir/enhancements/fy1312/2009280684-b.html
Daley, L. (2016). Fabulation: Toward Untimely and Inhuman Life in Alexis Wright's The Swan Book. *Australian Feminist Studies, 21*, 305–318.
Department of the Prime Minister and Cabinet. (2018). Closing the Gap: Prime Minister's Report 2018: Executive Summary. Retrieved from http://closingthegap.pmc.gov.au/executive-summary
Gardiner-Garden, J., & Social Policy Group. (2011). Defining Aboriginality in Australia: Current Issues Brief Index 2002–03. Retrieved from www.aph.gov.au/About_Parliament/Parliamentary_Departments/Parliamentary_Library/Publications_Archive/CIB/cib0203/03Cib10#blood
Gleeson-White, J. (2016/2017). Country and Climate Change in Alexis Wright's *The Swan Book*. *Australasian Journal of Ecocriticism and Cultural Ecology, 6*, 29–38.
Harris, D. (2017). *Contemporary Australian Novels and Crises of Ecologies* (Dissertation). Deakin University.
James, E. (2015). *The Storyworld Accord: Econarratology and Postcolonial Narratives.* Lincoln: University of Nebraska Press.
Knudsen, E. R. (2004). *The Circle and the Spiral: A Study of Australian Aboriginal and New Zealand Māori Literature. Cross Cultures: Vol. 68.* Amsterdam: Rodopi.
Merriam-Webster (Ed.). (2018). *Merriam-Webster.com.* Retrieved from www.merriam-webster.com/dictionary/counter
Morton, T. (2010). *The Ecological Thought.* Cambridge: Harvard University Press.
Mukherjee, A. P. (1990). Whose Post-colonialism and Whose Postmodernism? *World Literature Written in English, 30*, 1–9. https://doi.org/10.1080/17449859008589127
Narogin, M. (1994). *Aboriginal Mythology: An A - Z Spanning the History of Aboriginal Mythology from the Earliest Legends to the Present day.* Hammersmith, London: Aquarian.
Neumeier, B. (2018). Nature and Environment in Performance: Trees, Storms, and Devils. In B. Neumeier, B. Braun, V. Herche, & V. Herche (Eds.), *Konzepte, Orientierungen, Abhandlungen, Lektüren, Australien-Studien (KOALAS): Vol. 14. Nature and Environment in Australia* (Vol. 14, pp. 221–238). Trier: WVT; WVT Wissenschaftlicher Verlag Trier.
Nixon, R. (2011). *Slow Violence and the Environmentalism of the Poor.* Cambridge: Harvard University Press.
Otto, E. (2012). *Green Speculations: Science Fiction and Transformative Environmentalism.* Columbus: The Ohio State University Press.
Polak, I. (2017). *Futuristic Worlds in Australian Aboriginal Fiction. World Science Fiction Studies: Vol. 1.* Oxford, New York: Peter Lang.
Rodoreda, G. (2018). The Mabo Turn in Australian Fiction. *Australian studies - interdisciplinary perspectives.*
Tiffin, H. (1991). Introduction. In I. Adam & H. Tiffin (Eds.), *Past the Last Post: Theorizing Post-Colonialism and Post-Modernism* (pp. vii–xvi). New York: Harvester Wheatsheaf.
United Nations Declaration on the Rights of Indigenous Peoples, United Nations 13 September 2007.
United Nations Human Rights Council. (2015). *Report of the Human Rights Council on its Thirty-First Session.* Retrieved from www.ohchr.org/EN/HRBodies/UPR/Pages/AUIndex.aspx
Weik von Mossner, A. (2017). *Affective Ecologies: Empathy, Emotion, and Environmental Narrative.* Ohio State University Press.
Wright, A. (2002). Politics of Writing. *Southerly, 62*, 10–20.
Wright, A. (2008a). A Weapon of Poetry. *Overland, 193*, 19–24.
Wright, A. (2008b, November 15). Rebel Voice. *The Age*, pp. 12–13.
Wright, A., & Zable, A. (2013). The Future of Swans: A PEN dialogue between Arnold Zable and Alexis Wright. *Overland, 213*, n.pg.
Wright, A. (2015). *The Swan Book.* London: Constable.
Wright, A. (2018). Boisbouvier Oration 2018: The Power and Purpose of Literature. *Meanjin*

23

Countering prescriptive coherence in narratives of illness

Sarah Manguso's *The Two Kinds of Decay* and Maria Gerhardt's *Transfer Window*

Cindie Aaen Maagaard

Introduction

Illness is an aspect of human life that for many people awakens a need for narrative, whether in the attempt to make sense of the experience of it, to communicate it, or to learn from or find comfort in the stories of others. For decades scholars across fields of narrative medicine, the humanities and health sciences have acknowledged and argued persuasively that stories are indispensible for understanding what illness means in the lives of human beings, how illness may be treated, and how patients, relatives and health care professionals may deal with the physical and mental trials of illness, trauma and loss.

Although narratives of illness have been acknowledged as ways for individuals to give structure and meaning to their own unique experiences, stories of illness are, like any narrative, shaped by the generic repertoire available to the teller within a culture. As Behrendt (2017), Conway (2007), Jurecic (2012), Wasson (2018), Woods (2011) and others have shown, there are generic preferences, which reflect and reinforce cultural ones, for stories that achieve coherence and culminate in the patient-protagonist finding a meaning or value in illness. Thus the triumphant patient-storyteller capable of telling a coherent story is at the center of a preferred cultural model, or a prescriptive "masterplot" (Abbott 2003) for patients' stories of illness.

Increasingly, however, scholars within narrative and the medical humanities have questioned these cultural and generic narrative preferences, arguing that they may impose coherence and meaning on events that are in fact chaotic, difficult to manage and painful (Mattingly & Garro 2000; Wasson 2018; Woods 2011). In their critique, they have called for alternative ways of representing illness that do justice to illness' discomfiting complexities, shifting the dynamic away from coherence and chronology, whether through experimentation with narrative form or by abandoning narrative altogether. They call for narratives that offer perspectives counter to the masterplot of the triumphant patient-storyteller.

This chapter examines this call through the conceptual lens of counter-narrative, and it explores examples of how two writers resist generic and cultural preferences. In Andrews's often-cited formulation, counter-narratives are "the stories which people tell and live and which offer resistance, either implicitly or explicitly to dominant cultural narratives" (2004, p. 1). I will discuss how this is achieved in two works which in different ways navigate temporalities of illness and narrative: the memoir *The Two Kinds of Decay* (2008) by the American author Sarah Manguso and the novel *Transfervindue. Fortællinger om de raskes fejl* (2017) by the Danish author Maria Gerhardt, which is translated in this article as *Transfer Window. Stories about the mistakes of the well.* In texts of non-fiction and fiction respectively, the authors counter prescriptive coherence in two ways: 1) they shift the textual dynamic away from a trajectory that strives towards closure to a more segmented, episodic form, and 2) they utilize form to embrace ambiguities and contradictions about what illness is and means, and thus resist the prescriptive narrative of triumph.

The organization of this chapter

The rest of this chapter begins by introducing Manguso's and Gerhardt's works as a frame of reference for the reader. Then I establish a theoretical framework by which to understand what I characterize as a prescriptive masterplot for illness narratives, as well as the recent calls for alternative forms that I place within a counter-narrative perspective. Together, these sections inform a discussion of how Manguso's and Gerhardt's works form answers to those calls. As I suggest, their texts provide counter-narratives that give voice to subjective experiences that are potentially contradictory, and insight into the complexities of time in illness.

Manguso's and Gerhardt's narratives of illness

Admired by readers and critically acclaimed, Manguso's memoir and Gerhardt's novel both concern themselves with what Charon describes as the "divides" that separate the ill and the well (2006, p. 22) and create radically different positions from which they confront contexts, causes and consequences of illness.

Manguso documents the nine-year period in which she suffered from chronic idiopathic demyelinating polyradiculoneuropathy (CIDP), a rare autoimmune disorder. Manguso was 21 and in her third year at Harvard University at the onset of illness, and the memoir recounts the difficulties of diagnosis, the progression of illness and treatment, including blood transfusions and the insertion of a large catheter, as well as debilitating fatigue. In addition to these physical trials, Manguso's narrative depicts psychological and emotional ones: shock and fear, the uncertainty of not knowing what was wrong, and once diagnosed, of whether she would recover and, at times, depression caused by her treatment with steroids. Yet, just as importantly, her memoir conveys the day-to-day experience of being in the care of others. An unflinching observer of herself and the people around her, Manguso explores character, passing judgment, for example, on others' empathy or lack of it, as in the small details – like mint candies remembered by a nurse – that are testimony to seeing patients as whole human beings. As I will discuss in the analysis, Manguso adopts a fragmentary and achronological form that shifts the textual dynamic away from its diachronic progression and enables a focus on the unfolding of individual episodes. The longest chapters consist of three to four pages, while the shortest chapter is a sentence long.

Gerhardt's text is a work of fiction, but in form closely resembles Manguso's memoir. Spare, occasionally aphoristic, chapters shift between past memories and the present of telling and stand alone without explicit connections to help the reader navigate temporalities. The novel, which has been described as "utopian" fiction (Kassebeer 2017), imagines the northern part of the Danish island of Zealand as a large hospice where the dying live together, separated from the well. Place becomes indicative of time, with a temporal "before" situated outside the hospice wall, and a temporal "after" inside its borders, from which Maria, who is terminally ill with cancer, narrates. The hospice is a temporal "transfer window," a passage from life to death.

Transfer Window depicts a world that is both recognizable and defamiliarized, where nuns grow cannabis in greenhouses and the Internet is forbidden, as is music, because it wakes feelings of overwhelming intensity. Residents are cared for by professional staff who give them massages, lead them in exercises, see to it that they eat well and distribute the medicinal oil that residents take to alleviate physical and mental anguish. The text shifts unpredictably among memories of life among the well, and the present, in which the protagonist wanders the coastal area along with her friend Mikkel, reminiscing about their youth in the 1980s and observing the foibles of the well people beyond the wall.

Although the work is fiction, Maria Gerhardt – the widely known Copenhagen DJ Djuna Barnes who was also a writer – was herself suffering from cancer as she wrote the novel and died at the age of 39, shortly after its publication. The novel is thus in reviews and in the eyes of many readers strongly associated with the author and is assumed to be partly an exploration of Gerhardt's own experiences.

Manguso's and Gerhardt's works were selected because their fragmented composition and thematization of contradictory and ambiguous responses to illness make them relevant examples for examining a counter-narrative perspective on cultural and generic prescriptions about narrative coherence.

Theoretical framework

The genre of illness narratives

Manguso's and Gerhardt's works are examples of illness narratives, a genre which is concerned with "how contemporary writers compose illness and how readers receive these accounts" and can include "fiction and blogs, as well as academic and popular commentary" as well as a range of authors that embraces "family members, physicians, caregivers – even novelists" (Jurecic 2012, p. 2). The "composition" of illness refers not only to its rendering through discourse, but to the use of narratives as a resource for working through the past, through ongoing situations and through the new and unfamiliar, including an uncertain future. Narratives of illness thus "shape action just as actions shape stories about them" (Mattingly & Garro 2000, p. 17) and are also means to communicate the lived experiences that can involve radical changes to body and mind.

Illness narratives have been widely recognized across disciplines for their ability to "reclaim patients' voices from the biomedical narratives imposed on them by modern medicine" (Jurecic 2012, p. 3). In her formulation of the tenets that inform the field of narrative medicine, its founder Rita Charon (2006) highlights the ethical imperative of attending closely to, and honouring, the singularity of the individual patient's life and story.

Amid such recognition, however, contesting perspectives have emerged on the usefulness of narrative and the form that stories of illness should take. At the heart of these are cultural assumptions about how individuals should deal with illness and the larger question of the role of narrative in identity. In this section, I sketch two overarching perspectives: one representing normative views towards narrative meaning and wholeness, and one which addresses concerns about the potentially detrimental effects of these and calls for other ways of representing illness. My focus here is on attitudes towards a particular type of narrative that frames the patient as heroic, and towards the value of narrative coherence. It is within these differing perspectives that the counter-narrative potential of Manguso's and Gerhardt's work can be situated, as I will discuss in the analysis further on.

The prescriptive masterplot: coherence and triumph

The first perspective may be summarized through the influential and oft-cited metaphor suggested by sociologist Arthur Frank, that of the "shipwreck" caused by serious illness. This "interruption" in a life story destroys

> the central resource that any storyteller depends on: a sense of temporality. The conventional expectation of any narrative, held alike by listeners and storytellers, is for a past that leads into a present that sets in place a foreseeable future. The illness story is wrecked because its present is not what the past was supposed to lead up to, and the future is scarcely thinkable.
>
> *(1995, p. 55)*

In this view, narrative becomes a privileged mode of understanding that enables human beings to salvage the "wreckage" that remains in the storm's wake and either restore a life story or navigate a new one that can meaningfully integrate temporalities into a coherent trajectory.

This conception of the ill person as storyteller embodies cultural preferences for how human beings should deal with illness. First, these are reflected in a type of narrative, referred to by Conway (2007) as the "narrative of triumph" prevalent in first-person narratives, in which the ill person overcomes adversities and emerges a better, stronger person (p. 4). In such narratives, the character "takes action, battles heroically, and maintains an optimistic attitude" (p. 4). Some self-help narratives and first-person narratives of illness emphasize aspects such as "positive thinking and proper behaviour," "insistence on hope and denial of negative feelings" and a trajectory that may include pain and suffering, but often offers the conclusion that "illness is an opportunity for growth or transformation for which the author is grateful" (2007, p. 7). Similarly, in literature about disability, Garden finds generic conventions that are reinforced by cultural preferences for "'the good patient'" who displays good nature and a "cheerful stoicism" (2010, p. 127).

Related to the narrative of the heroic storyteller are prescriptive views on narrative coherence, which grow out of a tradition of narrative as a privileged mode for the construction of identity represented by theorists such as MacIntyre (1984) and Ricoeur (1991). On this view, the creation of a coherent narrative life story is a prerequisite for selfhood and self-understanding – or, as Ricoeur writes, echoing Socrates, for living an examined life (1991). This normative view has long been a pillar of narrative theory. As Hyvärinen et al. explain in their critical examination of narrative coherence, in the narrative turn issued by Bruner among others, "[c]oherence was assumed as a norm for good and healthy life stories" (2010, p.1), that as a consequence could enable a person to "live better and in a more ethical way" (p. 2). "From the beginning," Hyvärinen et al. write, "the concept of narrative identity was thematized from the perspective of unity and coherence it was able to afford, not in terms of complexities, contradictions and undecided elements it might include" (p. 2).

Even in illness, when such complexities and uncertainties prevail, coherence has been valued as a means to repair its disruptions. As Rimmon-Kenan writes, "the pull toward coherence, continuity, transformation – motivated by a transitory or permanent need on the part of ill subjects to counter the rupture [of illness] – is [...] affected by socially and culturally constructed expectations" (2002, p. 14). These expectations inform preferences for certain kinds of narratives and are anchored in foundational concepts of narrative construction: the relation between temporality and causality, between story and discourse, and the function of narrative in identity.

Together, cultural attitudes about narrative coherence and the heroic patient who finds meaning in illness can be considered to shape a prescriptive masterplot for the "good story": the patient as protagonist who both navigates the trials of illness and can tell a coherent story about it. In Abbott's formulation, masterplots are "recurrent skeletal stories, belonging to cultures and individuals, that play a powerful role in questions of identity, values, and the understanding of life" (Abbott 2003, p. 192). Abbott's term conveys the way that culturally sanctioned storylines provide a blueprint for individuals' fleshing out their own stories, as well as the aspect of cultural power conveyed by "master" and the elements of time and causality that characterize plots.

The culturally value-laden masterplot of the triumphant patient storyteller offers individual storytellers a generic repertoire which is, as Medved and Brockmeier point out, "not just about language but about accumulated human experiences, not least of which are experiences of crisis" (2008, p. 469). Accordingly, narratives may prescribe "instructions and norms of what is to be done and not to be done in life, and of how individual experiences might be integrated into a generalized and culturally established canon" (Medved & Brockmeier 2008, p. 469).

The challenges to the masterplot: critiques and calls for other representations

But what if an individual's experience does not fit into the generic repertoire available? Can, and should, the disruptions and complexities of illness be "repaired" through a coherent story? Are all lives lived and experienced as narrative?

In critical reflections on the role of narrative in illness, scholars address these questions and offer counter perspectives to the prescriptive views contained in the masterplot outlined above. In the following, I sketch aspects of this critique as voiced by Woods (2011) and Wasson (2018) among others. As I will discuss, they propose that a shift away from narrative chronology and coherence toward more experiential and momentary aspects may enable alternative, and potentially truer, insights into how illness is experienced.

In her influential article "The limits of narrative: a provocation for the medical humanities," Woods aims to "stimulate a robust discussion about the limits of narrative" (2011, p. 75) in the field. She argues that we should question claims that identity requires that individuals interpret their lives as stories and that illness necessarily requires stories (p. 77). With reference to another provocative text, Strawson's "Against Narrativity" (2004), Woods takes issue with the notion that identity universally, and across all cultures, is contingent upon the ability to narrate a coherent life story. Not all people live life narratively, she asserts, echoing Strawson; some live more episodically, leaving past behind them, experiencing more segmented presents, without necessarily considering implications for a future. She encourages the medical humanities therefore to consider whether illness always compels human beings to think diachronically, or whether they may not instead find value in the contemplation of the significance of individual moments.

Woods both challenges normative types of narrative and more broadly calls us to question the usefulness of narrative per se. She argues that "promoting a particular form of narrative as *the* mode of human self-expression" should be avoided, because it in turn "promotes a specific model of the self" (p. 74). Accordingly, she offers a critique of the "quest" narrative in Frank's (1995) typology of illness narratives, for although the pattern stresses the *process* of searching for a meaning with illness, it nevertheless forces the patient to perform what may be the insurmountable task of becoming "effectively, the hero of her own story, such that the creation and performance of narrative is a form of testimony which re-claims and re-orients the self" (2011, p. 75).

"If we limit ourselves to specific forms of narrative, and to narrativity per se," Woods asserts, "we run the risk of both isolating and distressing people who see themselves as 'Episodics'" (p. 77). Therefore, she proposes that other forms of expression, such as photography, art, metaphor and poetry may enable tellers and receivers to place less emphasis on diachronicity, the forward push of plot, the work of coherence and resolution, in order to allow space for moments of situated, embodied experience. Citing Kirmayer (1992, p. 155), she suggests that poetic fragments and metaphor may enable us to "articulate our suffering without appeal to elaborate stories of origins, motives, obstacles, and change. Instead, we may create metaphors that lack the larger temporal structure of narrative but are no less persistent and powerful" (in Woods 2011, p. 75).

Like Woods, Wasson (2018) calls for a (re)questioning of narrative within the medical humanities, arguing that there is a need for a richer vocabulary of temporality, as well as an alternative practice of reading stories of illness. Her focus is on the experience of pain, a condition that may place patients in a temporal suspension, an "emergent present that resists a narrative form" (2018, p. 106) as well as marginalize them, as a result of the incommunicability of pain. Wasson's proposal is for an alternative approach to reading that she refers to as "episodic reading." Episodic reading may occur in parallel to reading for plot and entails being "less in search of narrative coherence or self-authorship" and instead directing our interest towards "the value of textual fragments, episodes and moments considered outside a narrative framework" (p. 106). As with Woods, Wasson's proposal is to shift the dynamic away from the overarching arc of a story:

> If reading for narrative is "reading for the direction of its point" and for the degree of narrative coherence or narrative drama, then I suggest that reading episodically is to read looking for a place to pause – to cease looking for the arc of the individual longitudinal journey and instead to consider how a particular scene constructs an emergent *present.*
>
> *(p. 108)*

The benefit of this close attention to moments is that through affect, the reader may become "attuned to the social context for chronic pain suffering and the complex temporality of marginalization" (p. 106). Moreover, episodic reading quiets readers' demand for a forward-directed push for "meaning," which may be impossible for tellers, who, from within situations of illness or pain, may be unwilling or unable "to adapt the proleptic subjectivity attendant on a particular teleogenic narrative" (p. 107).

Episodic reading, then, can perhaps align the reader more closely to the teller. While tellers may "flout the narrative conventions to which illness experience should conform" (p. 107), Wasson urges us as readers to "surrender – even if briefly – to the instant of the textual encounter" and to "let that extract sit with you, remain with you, haunt you, without closing it off within a narrative arc" (p. 111).

Counter-narratives

As I will discuss in the analysis below, Manguso and Gerhardt's works, through their thematization of ambiguities that resist resolution and their experimentations with fragmented form offer the kinds of alternative representations that Woods, Wasson and others call for. In doing so, they function as counter-narratives, offering for readers' contemplation stories about illness and dying that do not fit the narrative model prescribed by the cultural masterplot of narrative coherence and the heroic patient for whom illness is meaningful.

Andrews (2004) writes in her definition of counter-narratives that they can only be understood *as* counter-narratives through a perceived relation to that which they are countering. The relation between master and counter is thus necessarily relational and intertextual, but also more than that: to count as a *counter*-narrative, it must offer a particular stance of critique or resistance towards some dominant cultural narrative or narratives (2004, p. 1). It is this positionality that helps us recognize the "countering" function, while it raises the question of how we understand the meaning of "counter" in the case of a specific narrative. Following from this are the questions that must be addressed concerning who is countering whom, in what context and for what purpose, and, importantly, who is in the position to perceive the master-counter relation: is it the storyteller who deliberately invokes the masterplot, or is it the reader or researcher who discerns the critical relation? I will return to these questions in the discussion of Manguso and Gerhardt.

In Andrews's formulation, the resistance of counter-narratives may be attempted either explicitly or implicitly – that is, announced as such, or not (2004, p. 1). As I will discuss below, these strategies seem to be represented by Manguso and Gerhardt respectively. In the words of Gabriel (2017),

> a counter-narrative articulates and posits a particular narrative as a master narrative, it demonstrates some of the flaws and contradictions of this narrative and it proposes an alternative narrative line with a new plot and metamorphosed characters that ostensibly redefine a particular phenomenon and offer a superior explanation for it.
>
> *(p. 210)*

This is apparent in Manguso's memoir, as she makes explicit, if ironic, reference to the "usual sort of book about illness" (2008, p. 33), which is contrasted by its *un*usual form and contradictory impulses. In Gerhardt's fictional narrative, however, the strategy is more implicit and its function to *counter* depends upon readers' recognition of a different, canonical, masterplot. The story she tells of the exile of the dying counters the masterplot without referencing it, but by defamiliarizing familiar Danish locations in ways that jar the reader and by creating a disjointed, but moving, representation of what life is like among the dying.

Analysis

Giving pause: form and fragmentation

The two writers adopt a fragmented and achronological composition with brief chapters consisting of single episodes, short anecdotes, or, especially in Gerhardt, aphoristic commentary. Each chapter is surrounded by space with no transitional material to explicitly establish narrative continuity or a coherent argument, with the result that events remain isolated from others, standing out as moments worthy of consideration on their own, apart from their meaning within a sequence. The text creates opportunities to pause and guides readers to direct their attention to these episodes and, in accordance with Wasson's proposal, to dwell on what the text conveys about the experience of a moment as it unfolds.

Form in Manguso

Manguso's text mingles all kinds of events, experiences and thoughts, most of them occurring during her period of illness, some having to do specifically with physical symptoms and treatments or with her fear and uncertainty, others describing her encounters with medical personnel or other patients, and still others that occur at other times in her life. Although bookended by chapters entitled "The Beginning" and "The End," the episodes obey no clear chronology, and many appear unrelated. In the middle of the memoir, for example, a chapter entitled "The Neurologist" is followed by "Steroids," which is followed by "The "Sixth Sense," then "Hobbies," and then "A Gift," a chapter that recounts in detail a memory of a cocktail dress she had inherited from her mother and the social significance of the high-school dance at which she would wear it. Within each of the chapters in her episodic composition, Manguso unfolds a specific dimension of the narrator's life and explores its significance.

Although not situated temporally within the period of the narrator's illness, "A Gift" is characteristic of Manguso's technique. The title awakens a set of expectations about the topic and its meaning, yet the chapter seems to veer along other, somewhat unrelated paths that both direct readers' interpretations in certain directions, and thwart them. Much of "A Gift" consists of a description of the dress and the occasion of its use, but the chapter becomes a deeper meditation on inheritance, both material and social. The chapter ends with the narrator's externalization of, and reflection on, her younger self:

> There I am, about to face the receiving line, about to walk across the stage of my life in my town in my velvet dress. About to start learning why I don't belong here, why I don't want to belong here, yet do belong, whether I want to or not, in the torrent of people who walk through history in one direction.
>
> *(Manguso 2008, p. 99)*

The narrator draws the past into the present of narration through the present tense, inflecting the episode with the significance she recognizes retrospectively, that she is a product of her social inheritance and subject to history, even as she seeks to resist these conditions. In this, as throughout the memoir, Manguso uses episodic form to layer temporalities and to represent herself through a piecemeal, multidimensional and reflective portrait.

Form in Gerhardt

Like Manguso's memoir, Gerhardt's short novel is narrated largely without explicit connections between episodes. Each of her chapters comprises one untitled paragraph, some of only a single sentence, so that the ratio of white space to writing often creates more pause than text. Through this sparse, stark style, the significance of the isolated moment is given room to reverberate. For example, the sentence "I remember the list that I revised weekly, of which friends no longer could bear me" (p. 26) punctuates painful episodes about the loosening of bonds with others as illness progresses. Similarly, a single-sentence chapter transmits the bad news from one of Maria's pen pals: "Louise wrote at Easter, directly from the ambulance: 'It's spread to my spine, it went really fast,' followed by a smiley with tear on its ochre-yellow cheek" (p. 46). Positioned at the top of the page, the sentence is mirrored on the facing page by another single sentence, 'This life, thanks for shit', wrote Charlotte, before it [the cancer] was found in her eyes" (p. 47). The two chapters condense the narratives of cancer into sentences voiced by Maria's friends, reflecting each other and surrounded by silence.

Through silences and gaps, Manguso and Gerhardt place the reader in uncertainty about where the illness story is headed, how one event leads to another. Indeed, Manguso's narrator herself points to the illusory nature of narrative coherence as she writes, "Narratives in which one thing follows from the previous thing are usually imaginary" (p. 30). The two texts require the reader to do more of the work of inference, and this enhances, perhaps, the potential for wonder and curiosity.

As they foreground experiential time and downplay the diachronic momentum of plot, Manguso and Gerhardt explore the tension for the ill person between these two ways of being in time. Manguso in fact evokes this tension through metaphors of "the point" and "the ray": time experienced as "a speck of light," a concentrated attention to a singular, present moment, and life imagined as an extension through time, an "arrow of light pointing into the future" (p. 165). Although the narrator is "looking forward to recovering" (p. 165), that is, desiring the return to life-as-ray, the point – made necessary by illness – demands a close attention to brief moments, a being in the present. The ray is a movement towards death or recovery, both of which entail loss. Manguso mourns this loss:

> I tried to find the point after the latest, longest remission began. I thought of the point as a moment in spacetime where I could be free of all memory and desire — a point that existed apart from everything before and after it.
>
> *(p. 165)*

In the structure of Manguso's and Gerhardt's texts, the point and the ray – the episodic and the diachronic – also become opportunities for reading that counter prescriptions of coherence.

Themes: exploring ambiguities, resisting triumph

Because events and experiences are not gathered into clear teleological structures, form facilitates the two narrators' explorations of contradictory and ambiguous responses to situations without striving normatively for resolutions. By rejecting generic conventions, Manguso explicitly, and Gerhardt more implicitly, offer counter-narratives to stories of triumph and improvement, as well as to the claim that narrative is restorative.

Manguso's subversion of the triumph narrative

Manguso meta-narratively questions the premises that illness can be understood, and more specifically, that narrative is a means of achieving this. From the opening Manguso dissociates acts of remembering and understanding: "Now I can try to remember what happened. Not understand. Just remember" (p. 3). The sentiment is reiterated on the final page: "You can't learn from remembering" (p. 184). A few lines before this, Manguso asserts, "This is the usual sort of book about illness. Someone gets sick, someone gets well" (p.183). This becomes a subversive comment on the genre of illness narrative, as it concludes a narrative whose experimental form deviates from "the usual" as well as shows that the narrator does not ever finally "get well," but that illness "may keep on happening to me as long as things can happen to me" (p. 4).

Manguso also explicitly rejects the narrative prescription of improvement, upon which illness brings out the best in a person, with the ill person battling heroically against all odds. Towards the end of her memoir, for example, Manguso invokes the bipartite temporality of illness (Rimmon-Kenan 2002, p. 10) in her chapter "Before and After." There, she examines the proverbial "lessons" of illness within the context of her own life, finding that illness had made her a self-centered person whose only accomplishment was recovery. The illness leaves Manguso anything but heroic:

> [T]he disease made me furious, jealous, resentful, impatient, temperamental, spiteful. My sense of entitlement grew enormous. [...] The hardest thing I had ever done, the hardest thing I'd ever have to do, had made me a worse person! That wasn't how it was supposed to work. Tribulation is supposed to make strong people, people who radiate mercy, leaders of their kind.
>
> *(2008, p. 137)*

While this self-examination is itself a kind of "lesson," it is subverted through Manguso's critique of the cultural narratives of how it is "supposed to work" and her suggestion that, in this model, she is not one to be emulated.

Subversion of the restorative claims about narrative also occurs through a number of tensions in Manguso's chapter "The End." Far from bringing closure, the chapter comprises a series of unconnected, brief paragraphs, the juxtapositions of which lead to contradictions rather than resolutions. Manguso claims enigmatically both that illness is unique to the individual and that it is common; that there are "two kinds of decay" – her own and "everyone else's" – but then again, that "Most people consider their own suffering a widely applicable model, and I am no exception" (p. 183). On the final page, she asserts that "everything that happens is the last time it happens," although she has earlier revealed that illness "keeps happening" (p. 4), continuously felt through a fear of its return. The lesson from this book of remembering is that "You can't learn from remembering" (p. 184), but only, mysteriously, from "moving forward at the rate you are moved, as brightness into brightness" (p. 184). Through her disclaimers, Manguso questions the legitimacy of narrative as a way for her to understand illness. As Behrendt writes, Manguso "does not apparently arrive at an enhanced sense of her own identity; if anything, the practice of narrative serves to reinforce her resistance to narrative's alleged benefits" (2017, p. 59).

In its ambiguities and tensions, its alinear, aphoristic form, its rejection of a clear path towards understanding illness, Manguso's text counters prescriptions not only for narrative coherence but also for lessons and a moral of triumph. Instead, she offers the paradoxes and contradictions of illness, but not a way to resolve them.

Gerhardt's space, time and conundrum of meaning

As a counter-narrative, Gerhardt's novel, unlike Manguso's memoir, does not overtly reference a masterplot; instead, she invokes a setting that would be familiar to Danish readers and defamiliarizes it through elements of the strange and unreal, in order to evoke the disconcertedness and pain of exile. The countering aspect of her work thus depends upon how readers interpret the juxtaposition of real and unreal elements in light of cultural assumptions and preferences concerning the way terminal illness should be narrated. Yet regardless of these prerequisite assumptions, readers encounter a text that mingles temporalities and rejects easy interpretation, not least on the basis of the novel's ambiguous ending.

The northern part of Zealand, in real life a scenic coastal enclave of the wealthy, has in the novel been expropriated and transformed into a huge hospice. There, not wealth, but illness, is the criterion for admission; physical and emotional suffering – as well as staff's efforts to assuage these – are the rule, not the exception. The overarching trope in Gerhardt's novel is thus a spatialization of the existential separations of the ill and the well within chronotopes of "there/ before/ then" and "here/after/now." Through the world of the novel and her achronological organization of episodes, Gerhardt explores how different temporalities are lived by a person who is terminally ill.

Closed off by a double fence, the hospice is a place of transition, of waiting, of limbo. Days flow into one another, marked by the repetitiveness of daily tasks. Like an inmate, Maria scratches marks on the wall beside her mattress to keep track of how long she has been there. Time is kept by daily routines that keep the treadmill of life in motion: exercising, taking medicinal oil, adhering to a proper diet and getting massages.

Gerhardt offsets the fluidity of time through the brevity of chapters, as described in the discussion of form above, with the result that the protagonist and the text navigate among them: the bipartite "before" and "after," the continuous present, episodic experiences within Maria's past and within the present of narration, as well as the permeations of memory that transcend the fence. Memories of "before" with her son and partner intervene constantly in the present "after," of days of crying from morning to afternoon; days at the hospital with seven different doctors who quizzically "looked at me with their heads to one side" (p. 20), a hoodie splattered with blood because it was so difficult to find a good vein (p. 21), days spent lying in the fetal position until fighting her way out of bed in the afternoon to do dishes left from morning or fetch her son.

Memory, Gerhardt shows, situates the ill person across temporalities; this is powerfully evoked through the virtual reality shop: in the here and now, an episode from the past is recreated by the staff, relived by the patient and re-layered with emotions from within the existential and physical position of the present:

> The summer day that we were trapped by a rainstorm in a pavilion at your parents' place on the island of Møn. And we just had to sit and wait until the thunder passed, and we could see the horizon moving [...], and our son had fallen asleep on top of me. I've asked them to lengthen that last part. I'm sitting in a chair here on Strandvejen with big glasses on. I'm sitting in a pavilion on Møn. They've looped our son's snoring. The joy of still being able to keep him safe, being big and strong enough for someone to sleep on.
>
> *(p. 64)*

With its many layers of temporality, past emotions are configured with new meanings, made clear to Maria from her present perspective. Through these mingled emotions Gerhardt's text portrays the impossibility of finding a clear chronology in the experience of illness, as well as in the telling of it.

Gerhardt's narrative confronts head on the fact that there is nowhere for the ill person to go, no time or place that offers comfort. In the hospice, the pain of what is lost from life before, Maria says, "tears at my body and is worse than the pain for which I must take medicine in exceedingly large doses" (p. 83); yet life among the living was *also* too painful to bear. Maria recounts in episodes the gradual realization of where illness was "headed" and having to force herself to loosen the bonds and convince herself that "it was okay that he didn't want me as a parent, now that I was soon going to die" (p. 25). The decision to leave them, Maria relates towards the end, was to spare her family from the pain of her decline and herself from their pain: "I didn't want you to see me bent over, limping, with crutches, with a walker. I didn't want you to have to push my wheelchair. This eternal shame of being the mom on the sofa, the girlfriend from hell" (p. 84).

Ultimately Gerhardt's novel powerfully dramatizes the inescapability of the hospice and of illness itself. Only two outcomes are possible, Maria says – death or a miracle:

> [E]ither you rise from the ashes and run a marathon. The self-healing human. Or you are the tragedy. My mother will lose me again. This time for good. My son will call for me in his sleep.
>
> *(p. 67)*

Accordingly, a final way that Gerhardt resists the masterplot of triumph is through her enigmatic ending, with Maria, resolved, making her own passage through the transfer window. Whether to death, to the living, or in a dream is unclear. Having forced the double fence, she discovers herself in a supermarket, buying bananas and honey, because "We're always out of it" she says – before realizing that she is about to "pay with a miracle" (p. 90), that is, a currency note donned with the picture of those cured by a miracle.

With this unexpected ending, Gerhardt offers the reader not an ending as a "cure," but as a conundrum. The miracle may be a magical rescue; Maria's forcing the fence may be a courageous act of defiance; or the reader may be duped by the implausibility of the ending, moved by the desire to wish it were true, or disappointed *qua* its impossibility. In its ambiguity, the ending joins multiple possibilities, but bets on none of them. Hope, futility, courage and despair are represented as simultaneous aspects of the final moments of this ill protagonist's life.

Conclusion

As seen in the analysis and discussions above, Manguso and Gerhardt foreground ambiguities, contradictory emotions and irresolvable situations as the conditions that characterize severe illness and the prospect of death. Through their fragmented compositions and their rejection of the narrative of "triumph" for the ill person, they provide counter-narratives to the cultural masterplot that models coherence and triumph, and they answer calls for representations that concern themselves less with narrative coherence and chronology and more with the exploration and representation of episodes pregnant with meaning.

While Manguso explicitly references the types of narratives she is writing against, Gerhardt counters generic prescriptions without naming them. Yet, in accordance with Gabriel's definition of counter-narrative, each author "demonstrates some of the flaws and contradictions" of the masterplot, and "proposes an alternative narrative line with a new plot and metamorphosed characters that ostensibly redefine a particular phenomenon and offer a superior explanation for it" (2017, p. 210). While "superior" may arguably depend upon a reader's (culturally informed) evaluation, the narratives can be said to be so in light of scholars' cautions against narratives that prescriptively impose narrative coherence and a foregrounding of the positive effects of illness.

With respect to form, as we have seen, the texts' lack of explanatory material, the use of gaps and white space, allow moments to reverberate, showing, as Wasson puts it, "that the meaning of a scene may not stem only from its sequel but is meaningful in itself" (2018, p. 111). Moreover, because their fragmented forms make an overarching *fabula* difficult to recover, readers, in the attempt to piece one together, are positioned in uncertainty and must navigate the different temporalities of illness that the writers explore. They address fundamental questions about temporal disjunctions of illness, like those articulated by Woods:

> Does illness propel us in the direction of diachronicity, forcing us to mourn a healthy past which cannot be recuperated and a future which feels more fraught, more finite? Or is it the case that illness demands instead that we attend to the right now, either because pain returns us to the immediacy of the body, or because the uncertainty of the future encourages us to invest more intensely in the self-experience of the present?
>
> *(2011, p. 75)*

The answers from Manguso and Gerhardt appear to be "yes" to all these aspects, and all at the same time. Both explore the diachronicity of time; the mourning of the past and the rejection of it; the fraught future, and an attention to the present.

Accordingly, Manguso and Gerhardt offer counter-narrative responses to the paradigm critiqued by Hyvärinen et al. (2010) that equate a coherent story with a "good" story – one that can help the patient integrate illness into the larger narrative arc of the life story and thereby make illness "meaningful." Their singular narratives resist such prescriptions and show instead the unpredictability, uncontrollability and temporal disjunctions of illness. As such, they contribute to an ethic that says experiences of illness must insist on their own form.

Finally, neither of the works follows the path of the triumph narrative, or resolves the quest for meaning. Manguso's contradictory pronouncements about finding meaning in illness – and through stories – as well as both authors' enigmatic endings refuse the clear attribution of meaning to illness and dying. In doing so, they counter prescriptions for lessons of illness to be discovered by the heroic protagonist. As such, we may see their works as calls to attend differently to stories of illness and, in the words of Hyvärinen et al., to "suspend [our] preconceived narrative norms" and "treat these stories as invitations to listening in new and creative ways" (2010, p. 2).

References

Abbott, H.P. (2003). *The Cambridge introduction to narrative.* Reprint. New York: Cambridge University Press.

Andrews, M. (2004). Counter-narratives and the power to oppose. In M. Bamberg & M. Andrews (Eds.), *Considering counter-narratives: Narrating, resisting, making sense* (pp. 1–6). Amsterdam, The Netherlands: John Benjamins.

Behrendt, K. (2017). Narrative aversion: Challenges for the illness narrative advocate. *Journal of Medicine and Philosophy*, 42, 50–69.

Charon, R. (2006). *Narrative medicine. Honoring the stories of illness.* Oxford: Oxford University Press.

Conway, K. (2007). *Beyond words. Illness and the limits of expression.* Albuquerque: University of New Mexico Press.

Frank, A. (1995). *The wounded storyteller: Body, illness, and ethics.* Chicago: University of Chicago Press.

Garden, R. (2010). Telling stories about illness and disability. The limits and lessons of narrative. *Perspectives in Biology and Medicine*, 53(1), 121–135.

Gabriel, Y. (2017). Narrative ecologies and the role of counter-narratives: The case of nostalgic stories and conspiracy theories. In S. Frandsen, T. Kuhn & M. Wolff Lundholt. (Eds.) *Counter-narratives and organization.* New York and London: Routledge, 208–225.

Gerhardt, M. (2017). *Transfervindue.* [Transfer Window.] Copenhagen: Politikens Forlag.

Hyvärinen, M., Hydén, L.C., Saarenheimo, M. & Tamboukou, M. (2010). Beyond narrative coherence. An introduction. In M. Hyvärinen, L.C. Hydén, M. Saarenheimo & M. Tamboukou et al. (Eds.) *Beyond narrative coherence.* Amsterdam and Philadelphia: John Benjamins, 1–15.

Jurecic, A. (2012). *Illness as narrative.* Pittsburgh: University of Pittsburgh Press.

Kassebeer, S. (2017, 13 March). Den er jo så hvid, så udskyldsren. [It is so white, so innocently clean.] Review of Maria Gerhardt's *Transfervindue* [Transfer Window]. *Berlingske* online.

Kirmayer L. J. (1992). The body's insistence on meaning: Metaphor as presentation and representation in illness. *Medical Anthropology Quarterly* 6(4), 323–346.

MacIntyre, A. (1984). *After virtue: A study in moral theory.* 2nd ed. Notre Dame, IN: University of Notre Dame Press.

Manguso, S. (2008). *The two kinds of decay.* London: Granta Press.

Mattingly, C. & Garro, L.C. (2000). Narrative as construct and construction. In Mattingly, C. and Garro, L.C. (Eds.) *Narrative and cultural construction of illness.* Berkeley: University of California Press, 1–49.

Medved, M. & Brockmeier, J. (2008). Continuity amid chaos: Neurotrauma, loss of memory, and sense of self. *Qualitative Health Research*, 18(4), 469–479.

Ricoeur, P. (1991). Life in quest of narrative. In D. Wood (Ed.) *On Paul Ricoeur: Narrative and interpretation.* London: Routledge, 20–33.

Rimmon-Kenan, S. (2002). The story of I: Illness and narrative identity. *Narrative,* 10(1), 9–27.

Strawson, G. (2004). Against narrativity. *Ratio,* 7, 428–452.

Wasson, S. (2018). Before narrative: episodic reading and representations of chronic pain. *Medical Humanities,* 44, 106–112.

Woods, A. (2011). The limits of narrative: provocations for the medical humanities. *Medical Humanities,* 37, 73–78.

Part VI

Counter-narratives, belonging and identities

24

After Charlottesville

Using counter-narrative to protect a white heritage discourse

Katherine Borland and Amy Shuman

The August 14, 2017 white nationalist rally in Charlottesville, Virginia (protesting the removal of a statue of Confederate leader Robert E. Lee) prompted violent clashes between protesters and counter protesters that left one woman dead, run over by a white nationalist from Toledo, Ohio (Astor, Caron, and Victor, 2017). In the wee hours of August 22nd, as part of a national wave of protest against publicly sponsored symbols of the Confederacy, someone snuck into the Camp Chase Confederate cemetery in the Hilltop neighborhood of Columbus, Ohio and toppled a Confederate soldier who had stood since 1902 atop a stone arch inscribed with the word "Americans." Columbus Mayor Ginther quickly condemned the act as vandalism. The Office of Veterans Affairs, which oversees the heritage site, vowed to restore and return the statue (Burger and Ferenchik, 2017; Thompson 2017).[1]

The Hilltop Historical Society (HHS), the organization responsible for an annual memorial ceremony at the cemetery, responded somewhat differently, posting the following statement on their website:

> Our organization abhors racism, bigotry, and violence and condemns it in the strongest possible terms. There is no place for hatred in any discussion, especially one surrounding the history of our great nation. As we reflect on the achievements—and imperfections—of those who came before us, it is important that we consider multiple points of view, including those different from our own, so that we may learn from our past to move toward a brighter future together.
>
> *(Hilltop Historical Society, Nd)*

National and local discourses about Civil War monuments serve as an occasion to consider how a heritage site both deploys and prompts counter-narratives. Our discussion considers not only different accounts of events, but also who controls the narrative. Along those lines, we are particularly interested in the HHS's request for others to "consider multiple points of view, including those different from our own," as if they were defending a counter-narrative, as one perspective among many. A heritage site, in this case one that includes a mural, plaques, a cemetery and ritual events, is not just one voice among many but instead claims special legitimacy to control the narrative. Heritage narratives by their very nature selectively bring into the present aspects of the past that suppress, marginalize, or make invisible other, equally historical realities (Lowenthal 1994, 53). In this chapter, we explore two kinds of positioning: that of a state-sanctioned group who present their narrative as one among many, and that of a minority spokesperson who, in the face of such strategies, must forge a story of neighborhood belonging that navigates continuing exclusions. We conclude that a multicultural approach that recognizes everyone's story as valid does little to foster the kinds of difficult conversations that are necessary to further the Hilltop's stated goal to "move toward a brighter future together" or more broadly, to mediate the controversy surrounding Confederate commemorations today.[2]

In recent years, the concept of counter-narratives has become useful for discussing how narrators understand their experiences in relation to the stories told about them or for them (Andrews, 2002; Bamberg and Andrews, 2004). Counter-narrative refers to a variety of forms, from narratives contesting the factuality of publicly-mediated stories (Horigan, 2018; Lindahl, 2012), to those that reject how an individual's experiences are scripted and conceptualized (Shuman, 2005; Hyvärinen, 2008, 455), to narratives that rescue previously unknown accounts from obscurity (Schiffrin, 1996), to competing accounts of historical events (Portelli, 2003), to the personal as distinct from the more accepted better-known story (Romero, 1999). These categories overlap and are by no means exhaustive. As many scholars have observed, counter-narratives exist in dynamic relationship with master-narratives, dominant narratives, or culturally available narratives (Bamberg and Andrews 2004). However, rather than regard counter-narratives as the opposite of dominant, over-determined narratives, *or individuals as countering social scripts* we are interested in *how groups counter each other.* How do neighbors position their own accounts of belonging in relation to the claims of others? And why, in an ethnically diverse context, does the multicultural framework fail them?

As folklorists, we approach counter-narrative as multi-generic, including not only autobiographical verbal accounts but also monuments, murals, ceremonies, and public discourses. Indeed, counter-narratives reference not only alternative texts but also alternative geographies, spaces, and cognitive landscapes. Much of the literature on dominant and counter-narrative positions individuals against hegemonic social constructions and discourses (Ewick and Silbey, 1995; Bamberg, 2004). As folklorists, we understand individual identities to be formed through affiliations with multiple intersecting groups and society to operate as an arena of contest among those groups. As the example we discuss attests, counter-narratives do not necessarily interrupt dominant narratives. Whether or not a resignification is effective and whether a particular interpretation prevails depends on who controls the dialogue.

Heritage narratives, like those accompanying the Camp Chase monument, are often taken to be dominant, representing the views of those in power or with authority (Lowenthal, 1994; Johnson, 1995). We observe that the Camp Chase heritage narratives pose as counter-narratives, as if they are worthy of respect as a "point of view," even by those who find them to be offensive or repressive. How the Camp Chase heritage narratives are understood depends on how they are situated intertextually, in dialogue with other narratives that either confer or challenge their authority. As heritage narratives, they suppress critique and produce exclusions by promoting a supposedly unproblematic, nostalgic view of the past. Until recently, the Camp Chase narrative has remained uncontested, in part because most residents of the city of Columbus remain unaware of the site's existence and commemorative activities.[3] The Charlottesville events provided an opening for critique, represented thus far by the toppling of the Confederate soldier. However, this act has not sparked a larger conversation.[4] Instead, it was dismissed as vandalism, foreshortening a consideration of what a "brighter future together" might look like.

Our discussion brings the literature on public monuments as expressions of popular history in conversation with narrative oral histories in the constitution of place and belonging to place (Gillis, 1994; Norkunas, 2004; Rosenzweig and Thelen, 1998; Handler, 1994; Savage, 1994; Modan, 2007). Also, and importantly, considering these heritage narratives from the lens of critical race theory illuminates the ways that discourses of tolerance for multiplicity can serve as rationales for retaining exclusionary narratives that continue to forestall interracial understanding (Collins, 1999).

Our study of the heritage narratives accompanying the Camp Chase cemetery derives from a multidimensional study of the Hilltop, a declining neighborhood on the West side of Columbus. Building on our previous research on narrative (Borland, 2017; Shuman, 2005, 2006), we examine the multiple verbal and visual representations that comprise the Camp Chase heritage complex and then turn to the personal accounts of A., an African American Hilltop resident, who offers a perspective on the Camp Chase heritage complex, on historical recuperation and on her own sense of neighborhood belonging. The resulting narratives point to the necessity of rethinking the heritage complex from the standpoint of the excluded.

A large and diverse neighborhood on the West side of Columbus, the Hilltop is cut off from other city neighborhoods by highways and patchy industrial development. Once a vibrant working and middle-class neighborhood, the community began to lose its manufacturing base in the 1970s, and by the early 1990s, was experiencing increased transience and blight. Today, many residential blocks are peppered with empty lots. Drug addiction and the related issues of prostitution and crime are evident, and the area suffers the highest infant mortality rate in the city. In spite of these difficulties, many families have lived in the Hilltop for generations and evince strong attachments to place. Older residents recall a stable, village-like community that was neither city nor true suburb. Largely populated by in-migrating white Appalachians, the Hilltop has included a small Black community since at least the turn of the twentieth century. More recently, newcomers have revitalized aging infrastructure. Sizable communities of African refugees and Latin American immigrants among others are now bringing new life to abandoned strip malls, city parks and places of worship.

The Camp Chase heritage complex

To identify something as heritage is a powerful valorization. Practices and narratives built up over time accrete around a kernel idea, become symbols of a neighborhood identity and are then picked up and repeated in subsequent heritage representations (Palmenfelt, 2010). Understanding how this occurred in the Hilltop can illuminate the ongoing nature of the struggle that dissenting residents face as they try to challenge heritage statements that privilege the white experience.

The HHS has worked diligently to amass and preserve images of Camp Chase, a Civil War era prison and training camp that was once located in the neighborhood. They have produced a 28-page booklet of correspondence from, newspaper reports and statistics about, and photographs and diagrams of Camp Chase with the stated aim of preserving a "balanced" accounting of the northern and southern soldiers who passed through its gates (Clay, Neff, and Ongaro, 2015). This effort toward balance forms a major justification for narratives about the current heritage site. What remains of the camp today is a cemetery where an estimated 2,168 Confederate soldiers are buried. Absent from the HHS records is the reason why these soldiers became stranded in the North: after 1863, the prisoner exchange system between the warring parties broke down, when the Confederacy refused to treat Black Union prisoners of war as of equal value to white southerners (Pickenpaugh, 2007; Zombek, 2011). In 1995, the HHS assumed responsibility from the United Daughters of the Confederacy for organizing a memorial service for the Confederate dead, an event that had occurred annually on the second Sunday of June since 1895. Although such commemorative services abound in the Southern United States and are present in smaller numbers in the formerly Union states (Bump, 2017), the practice on the Hilltop puzzles many of its Black and white residents.

In its booklet, the HHS traces the history of the cemetery to an 1868 chance meeting between a Union and Confederate soldier:

> In 1868, William H. Knauss went to North Carolina and Virginia on business. A friendship was formed between him and an ex-Confederate who was acting as his guide. They soon determined that they both were wounded in the battle of Fredericksburg. The Confederate lost a leg. A friendship was formed, and both agreed to return to their homes determined to assist the comrades of the other, as best they could. Upon coming to Columbus in 1893, Knauss learned of the Confederate cemetery on the west side of the city where over 2000 ex-Confederates had died while imprisoned at Camp Chase, and that the burial place was in very bad condition. The gates were overrun with weeds and all sorts of stray animals. Knauss arranged with Mr. Henry Briggs, owner of a farm opposite of the cemetery to have it cleaned up; in the spring a few friends distributed some flowers about the place.
>
> The following year, a small memorial service was planned by Knauss. The trees were trimmed, the gates and gateposts reset, and the brush once again cleared. Three days before the planned service, all participants backed out, fearing reprisals from friends. However, the following years, 1896 and 1897 saw a more favorable atmosphere prevailed (sic), and almost 1500 persons attended the 1897 service.
>
> *(2015, 28)*

To legitimatize a practice that might seem to appeal exclusively to people who identify with the South, this origin narrative establishes the authorship of the memorial by a Union army veteran, who recognized the common humanity of soldiers fighting on both sides.[5] Indeed, the phrase "a friendship was formed" is repeated twice, underscoring the importance of healing the rift between white northerners and white southerners. The description of a graveyard left to grow wild in the absence of relatives to tend to the dead appeals to human values that transcend partisan loyalties. Additionally, the narrative depicts the group as underdogs who must struggle to prevail. We learn that the first memorial service is inhibited by fears of censure, but two short years later, it is popular. By this point the group appears to have successfully reframed a divisive symbol as one of friendship.

In addition to the sanctioned Knauss narrative, which is reproduced on the US Veterans Affairs website, among other places, another narrative credits a Columbus resident who remained a Confederate sympathizer after the war with assisting in the cemetery's renovation. Nicknamed "the veiled lady of Camp Chase," (see Figure 24.1) Louisiana Ranburgh Briggs, originally from Missouri, was described as having such antipathy for Northerners that she refused to sit next to her classmates at Ohio Wesleyan and was said to have rejoiced when Abraham Lincoln was assassinated. According to legend, she visited the cemetery heavily veiled at night to place flowers on the Confederate graves. Always a larger-than-life rebel, she is reported to have died at age 100 after choking on brandy that she had enjoined a younger relative to sneak into her hospital room (Columbus Dispatch, 2011). Mixing supernatural imagery with an ardent anti-establishment attitude, the story preserves a counter-narrative of Confederate sympathies to the more official reconciliation narrative attributed to Knauss.

In addition to the memorial service, Knauss and friends erected a series of monuments inside the graveyard to advance their message of peace and reconciliation. In 1902, a makeshift wooden arch was replaced by one made of granite with the word *Americans* etched into its southern face. A bronze statue of an anonymous confederate soldier stood atop the arch

Figure 24.1 The "Americans" arch in the Camp Chase Cemetery after the removal of the statue of the Confederate soldier in August 2017. Photo by Katherine Borland.

with hands resting on his rifle until August 2017. Underneath the arch is a boulder with an inscription that reads "2260 Confederate soldiers of the war 1861–65 buried in this enclosure." Framed by a narrative of peace and reconciliation, this war memorial complex was erected at a time when monuments to the Confederacy were proliferating (1900–1920s) and violence against Black people was at its most intense. As Savage reports, "Americans perceived this kind of monument building as part of a healthy process of sectional reconciliation—a process that everyone knew but no one said was for and between whites" (1994: 132). On the other hand, between 1885 and 1910 Ohio, Indiana and Illinois witnessed more than 30 lynchings, attempted lynchings, and race riots (Blocker, 2006). White animosity towards Blacks, then, provided one important context for the "more favorable atmosphere" that allowed the memorial to proceed unopposed. The continued efforts to erect and celebrate the ordinary Confederate soldier, always in a spirit of purported reconciliation between north and south, leaves out the particular local context of anti-Black violence that responded to an influx of people from elsewhere to the lower Midwest (Blocker, 2008).

Once a site is reframed as heritage, it accretes value through a process of official and unofficial citation – new forms and occasions grow up in dialog with the original monument. By the late 1920s, the Hilltop Businessman's Association further elaborated on the Civil War theme by organizing the Hilltop Bean Dinner community festival along the pattern of Union Civil War veterans' events common during the late 1800s across Appalachian Ohio. Over the years the annual cemetery memorial service continued but by the mid-1990s the cemetery was again in poor repair. Between 1989 and 1994 the HHS in partnership with the nearby Mary Magdalene Catholic Church sponsored a Camp Chase Civil War Encampment and Living History Reenactment. In 1995, when the HHS assumed sponsorship of the memorial service, they inserted elements of living history reenactment, encouraging participants to attend in period costume. In 2016,

Figure 24.2 Detail of the "Heroes of Camp Chase" mural in Westgate Park. Photo by Katherine Borland, August 2017.

the 73rd Voluntary Infantry Regimental Band played period music on period instruments at the service. Other activities included planting confederate and American flags at each grave marker and providing a short biographical remembrance for one Union and one Confederate soldier with ties to Camp Chase. Although HHS sponsors presented these activities as neutral, balanced, memorializations of history, they demarcated a white space in an increasingly integrated neighborhood.

In 1999 a State Historical Marker was erected at the site. A second marker was erected on the National Road (Broad Street), which used to border the camp. Then in 2009, the Friends of Westgate Park hired Hilltop artist Curtis Goldstein, to design a mural representing Camp Chase (see Figure 24.2). Drawing on and perhaps limited by existing photographic images, Goldstein, who identifies as a political progressive, was determined not to create a monument to the Confederacy. He therefore worked to "balance" the representation of the neighborhood's heritage site (*Columbus Dispatch* 2009). The mural's background depicts several landscapes from left to right: the officers' headquarters, an aerial view of Camp Chase, the main thoroughfare of the barracks crowded with anonymous figures, and the Union railway station where prisoners would have disembarked. Union soldiers holding an American flag and partially obscured by cannon smoke on the top left are balanced by similarly obscured confederate soldiers on the bottom right. On the bottom left a foregrounded bust painted in blue depicts Colonel George W. Neff, the longest serving commander of the camp. On the bottom right, similarly foregrounded, slightly smaller, and painted in a golden orange hue is Colonel William Stewart Hawkins, who was popularly heralded by Confederate prisoners as their Governor at the camp. Next to Neff and also in blue is a scene of two camp surgeons operating on a patient. Next to Hawkins and strongly foregrounded is the iconic image of the 1902 Confederate cemetery arch, statue and boulder.

Goldstein attempted to rebalance the meaning of that image by introducing a number of changes. In the mural, the figure on top of the arch is a Union soldier, and the inscription on the boulder to reads, "15,000 Union soldiers and 25,000 Confederate prisoners, four future presidents passed through the camp." This approach, however, continues to promote a narrative of north-south white reconciliation that effectively erases the Black experience of the Civil War and Jim Crow. Furthermore, by relocating the iconic figure atop an arch from the walled cemetery to a public park, the mural effectively forced the larger Hilltop community to engage with what some regarded as an affront to their sense of belonging.

A *Columbus Dispatch* reporter contrasted the generally effusive responses to the mural of white residents with the dismissive perspectives of African Americans. Then 70-year-old Earl Potts, for instance, questioned why his neighbors were so fixated on the Civil War. He confided that the leader of the sponsoring organization had accepted his objections during a planning meeting, but the mural went up anyway. (*Columbus Dispatch* 2009) For nonwhite community elders, the central question was not one of balance but of relevance. Indeed, although African Americans were certainly active in the Civil War era, not one figure in the mural is recognizably African American. Moreover, in the current era of border patrols gone wild, placing an armed white soldier on top of an arch that reads "American" in an increasingly immigrant community invites exclusionary readings. The mural was defaced shortly after its unveiling and had to be repaired. Black and white neighbors were unsure about whether to read this act of vandalism as an expression of protest. By 2017, however, after Charlottesville and the toppling of the statue in the Confederate cemetery, Goldstein admitted to a *Columbus Dispatch* reporter, "We may need to revisit the imagery. I don't know" (Burger and Ferenchik, 2017).

The HHS works hard to distinguish between a war memorial to ordinary soldiers and a monument that glorifies Confederate leaders, protecting the former and condemning the latter. The website statement posted after the Charlottesville tragedy rationalizes the yearly ceremony in this way: "The solemn occasion is meant simply to instruct the audience about those who passed through here, of which 2,260 remain buried here. We make no political statements." Probably the most contested "non-political" statement is the inscription "Americans," on the arch. A *Columbus Dispatch* story after the desecration of the statue provides one resident's interpretation: "One of the things you'll notice on the archway, what does it say? 'Americans.' Not Confederates," said Harry Pearson, 70, who lives a few blocks away from the cemetery. "We're all Americans" (Burger and Ferenchik, 2017). However, the *we* in this statement remains simultaneously inclusive and exclusive when seen through the prism of race and national origin.

The African American counter-narrative

In spite of the HHS's success in establishing Camp Chase as the state-sanctioned heritage marker for the neighborhood, the group actively involved in the Confederate memorial service constitutes only a small minority, and the event attracts little attention beyond their small circle. In the interest of elevating suppressed narratives and honoring the standpoint of excluded figures, we turn to the opinions and narratives of African American resident A., who not only experienced life as a minority in this majority white community, but who served for many years on the board of the Greater Hilltop Area Shalom Zone, a multiracial organization dedicated to bringing people together to work cooperatively towards an improved and livable Hilltop.[6] Now in her 70s, A. opines, "I would say if you asked people about the Hilltop, ninety-five percent of people would not mention Camp Chase. Camp who? Where? What?"[7] Although she recalls taking grade school trips to the cemetery, she confesses she didn't really know what a Confederate soldier was until much later. In fact, in a life history interview, A. describes an exceptional childhood in which her younger self avoided the injuries of racism that earlier generations had suffered. She credits her parents with providing her all the accoutrements of a mainstream American childhood – travel for leisure and edification, lessons in citizenship, an ethic of saving, full participation in extracurriculars – despite the fact that they and their Hilltop African American community lacked the economic security of their white middle class neighbors. Demonstrating three generations of loyalty to the neighborhood, she begins her own life story with a quote from her father "I was born on the Hilltop and I'm going to die on the Hilltop." In a subsequent interview focused on the Camp Chase heritage complex, however, A. focused less on her exceptional childhood and more on the challenge of negotiating a white-defined space.

When A. returned to the Hilltop as a new homeowner in 1976 after a 10-year absence, she became more aware of the HHS's memorializing activities at the cemetery:

> Well, I paid dues, but I never went to any [HHS] meetings. But I've known over the years what they were doing. And some of the things they did were good. I've even, um, made presentations to their group. But never, never could agree with them on commemorating the fallen soldiers that are in the Confederate cemetery. And their standpoint is they're Americans. Well so was Timothy McVeigh. Should we celebrate him? My thinking is these people were against the United States of America. Why would you put the stars and stripes on their grave? They would probably turn over if they knew. They'd rise up and snatch it away! They died for the stars and the bars!

Rejecting the peace and reconciliation narrative at the cemetery, A. focuses primarily on the miscategorization of Confederate soldiers as Americans. She even draws on the imagined perspective of the deceased soldiers to support this standpoint. When Borland offers that a Pre-Civil Rights era Act of Congress declared Confederate soldiers to be US Veterans in 1950, she simply raises her eyebrows. Throughout the interview she repeatedly emphasizes her inability to understand how the soldiers could be viewed as anything other than terrorists. And yet, when Borland asked whether she was aware of any public resistance to the memorial service prior to the toppling of the statue, she replied: "There was no concerted effort that I'm aware of. It was just individuals voicing their displeasure. And the organization stands. Note taken. This is what we're going to do." A. describes a climate in which white HHS members acknowledge but do not engage the Black critique, as if everyone had agreed to disagree, and no correction or further action is called for. This stance forces people like A. into a position of silence, because they do not control the dialog. Another anecdote about her first visit to the cemetery as an adult in the company of an HHS docent vividly conveys this silencing:

> Because one year we did a tour of the Hilltop. And of course, if you're going to do a tour of the Hilltop, you have to include it. So we asked him to come and speak about it. That's when I heard, "We view them as Americans." (Keep quiet. Just listen. Yes, they're Americans but not of the United States). Why would we honor someone who is not of the United States and who did all they could to institute our demise? It doesn't make sense to me. I don't understand it.

A.'s self-censorship in this instance aptly demonstrates how those committed to the Camp Chase heritage project succeed in claiming public space for their narrative of north-south white reconciliation by creating conditions that make it difficult for dissenters to openly challenge them. First, a tour of the Hilltop requires a Camp Chase visit, because it has the official markings of a heritage site. Second, the docent offers what appears to be a benevolent counter-narrative to a mixed group who are ostensibly gathered to celebrate pride in their neighborhood. Silently, however, A. qualifies the docent's claim that the Confederates are Americans by arguing that they are not "of the United States." Borland's interview also offers a back-channel for her to voice her opposition,[8] and in this context, she rejects the narrative. Indeed, as a Black citizen of the Post-Civil-Rights era, she must refuse it. Otherwise, she lays her own subjectivity open to the damaging effects of racism, as W.E.B. Dubois' so eloquently described in his early twentieth-century articulation of double consciousness (1903).

A. has participated, however, in other HHS events. She has accepted two invitations to speak, once to trace the history of African Americans on the Hilltop and more recently, in February of 2017, to discuss African American women during the Civil War, a program that she reports was well-attended and well-received. A. laughs and comments, "So maybe that was their attempt to be well-rounded." This kind of inclusion, however, does not diminish the ongoing threat to African American subjectivities posed by the Camp Chase heritage complex, a complex that ignores the ways in which the reconciliation of northern and southern whites 30 years after the Civil War coincided with a new wave of violence against in-migrating Black and immigrant others. It ignores the way that the narrative obscures slavery as a fact of the Civil War. And it ignores the way that the narrative, once established, forms a readily available resource for other neighborhood events and monuments, most notably, the Camp Chase Mural at the much more public venue of Westgate Park. The multicultural stance of embracing all stories fails to adequately address the harm that one group's stories pose for another, historically subordinated group.

As a living history presenter herself, A. has actively recuperated other stories from the historical record. This avocation began in college, when she delivered Sojourner Truth's "Ain't I a Woman" speech at a forensics competition. For many years she served on the Ohio Humanities Council roster, but she explains, "It's different from being a reenactor. Reenactors dress from the skin out. Presenters, well, we try to be authentic, but if [the visual element is] not exact, it's okay." Her research focuses on the personality and accomplishments of historic figures rather than on their costumes. A. sees this work as filling a hole in African Americans' awareness of their own history. Typically, she performs at the State House, schools, colleges, prisons, churches, and historical societies. Much of the focus of this work, however, is on the exceptional Black woman, in contrast to the HHS project of honoring ordinary soldiers. In both forms of historical recovery, the ordinary Black experience poses the challenge of bringing into the present uncomfortable realities of victimization, debasement, dehumanization, and dishonorable violence that trouble popular history's celebratory thrust.

Although A.'s performative presentations of historical Black women leaders might conceivably interrupt the white narrative of reconciliation encoded in the Civil War memorial heritage complex, groups on the Hilltop avoid staging such a challenge, as they must work together to address more pressing problems of deepening poverty and blight in this once stable community. For A., the question becomes where one is going to put one's energy. Avoidance is less taxing than confrontation. In fact, A. remarks that she knows the HHS docent well, but she has never shared her perspective with him. Nevertheless, as she underscores her strategies of indirection when dealing with the heritage narrative, she offers an unprompted comment on a relatively new neighborhood phenomenon:

> And we have a neighbor on this street who has a big picture window on the front of his house and draped across the window, it's a Confederate flag. Right up the street. He has no clue. No clue what that flag stands for. No clue what it means. Just ignorant.

With the spatial shift from the cemetery to right up the street, A. points to a symbol of the Confederacy that is less easily ignored, and she makes the surprising assertion that the owner of the flag "has no clue what that flag stands for … Just ignorant."

The neighbor's "ignorance" points to a fracture in the production of knowledge in the community. The neighbor does not need to know what the flag means for A., but A.'s safety depends on knowing. Charles Mills describes this as an "epistemology of ignorance," a tacit agreement in which white people can ignore the Black interpretation of a given symbol and can willingly promote misinterpretations. Mills argues that the epistemology of ignorance results in a situation in which "whites will in general be unable to understand the world they themselves have made" (1997: 18). In contrast to the Camp Chase docent, whom A. has known most of her life, the symbol wielder up the street is a stranger. In contrast to Camp Chase, which sits at the southern corner of Westgate, an area, originally redlined, that remains largely white, the symbol appears in a part of the neighborhood where Black people now reside.

As A. continues, she connects this current gesture of white exclusion with similar incidents from the neighborhood's past:

> My dad um tells the story, and I think maybe I said this to you, when they were little the Klan would give food baskets to Black people. He said they would come to their house dressed in their white uniforms and give out food baskets. And then they would go, he said, they would go up on Broad Street and burn a cross. This is the story my dad told me. So, he said, people would say, "It's the Klan." They were the Klan. Now, I grew up on Wayne Avenue. The next street over was Eureka. When the Klan began to make a resurge in the late 60s, early 70s, there was a cross burned on Eureka, because Eureka really wasn't a street where Black people lived, but some Black families had moved in. Wayne was the last frontier (laughs) you know, you didn't live [past] Wayne Avenue if you were Black.[9] And we would have to walk through the white communities to get to West High School and back. But we knew not to loiter. You don't loiter. You walk. You come on home.

In A.'s narrative, the idea of the Confederate flag is linked to the idea of Klan terror, but her father's peculiar story provides an image of this terror masquerading as benevolence. From the perspective of the Black family, the actions of white people in white garb are incomprehensible – generous up close but menacing at a distance, so much so that the identity of these strangers as Klansmen has to be confirmed by the community as a whole. Just as white explications of the Camp Chase memorial make terrorists into Americans, here white Klansmen behave as charity workers, momentarily concealing their animosity towards their Black neighbors.

As A. moves from her father's to her own historical memories, she underscores the way that the Klan, as the embodiment of racism, disappears and reemerges with each generation. Her story also emphasizes how the white community policed their borders even during her own youth. Nevertheless, Black integration of formerly white areas progressed with each generation, as her final narrative explains:

> When I was growing up the Black community was on these certain streets from Broad Street to Sullivant! But in [my parents'] day it was just certain blocks. And you'd better be careful about going into other blocks where black people didn't live. And my mother would say, "you couldn't light over on Westgate Park," and to have her grandchildren go to Westgate School! You know, that was something. (laughs) She thought that was good! (laughs) And um in fact, when my children were there, I remember going to the school, and the principal thought--you know, there was bussing. She thought my children were bussed in from outside

the neighborhood, and she said as much to me, "Oh you live so and so--" I said, "No, my children walk to school." So that let her know, "No, we live right here." (Laughs) Those kind of separations.

In each episode of A.'s account, she describes both her complex knowledge of the neighborhood and her white neighbors' and teachers' refusal to recognize her belonging. As this Black family moves progressively westward, something A.'s mother views as an accomplishment, they must forcefully assert their belonging to white people who presume that *their* knowledge of neighborhood and history is authoritative, and that *they* control the meaning of the symbols they deploy.

Conclusion

In late spring 2019, the statue of the Confederate soldier was reinstalled atop the arch in the Camp Chase Cemetery to very little public outcry. Tim Nosal, a spokesman for the VA National Cemetery Administration explained, "It's our responsibility to preserve its historic integrity" (Ferenchik, 2019). The exclusionary narrative introduced in 1902 was thus restored in the present to little fanfare, but, as an NAACP representative pointed out, at significant public expense. (The restoration of the statue cost $40,804. Additionally, the VA has installed surveillance cameras at the cemetery to deter future assaults on the memorial complex.)

The Hilltop Historical Society discourses are intertextual and dialogic, selectively invoking and privileging particular texts (such as Knauss's story), permitting some (such as the "veiled lady"), and excluding others (such as A.'s), to produce partial histories. We have placed A.'s narrative and the Camp Chase heritage discourses in conversation with each other in this chapter, and at the same time, we acknowledge that they are narratives that are otherwise not in conversation. Just as those committed to the Camp Chase memorial ceremony hear but do not engage the critiques of their African American neighbors, they interpret the toppling of the statue fundamentally as a misunderstanding of its meaning, a meaning that proponents insist is balanced and *inclusive*. The society's assertion that critics misunderstand, that they wrongly conflate violent white supremacy with memorials honoring ordinary soldiers, presumes that the society members control the meaning of the symbols they have constructed, preserved, and proliferated.[10] This strategy has so far worked to maintain the site as a neighborhood heritage complex, and to allow the small group involved with the memorial to continue their activities undisturbed. However, it has alienated those who cannot be included, producing segregated cognitive landscapes even as physically, the community becomes more integrated. The white members of the HHS cannot be viewed as malicious; nevertheless, in presuming to know their history, they refuse an African American counter-narrative that forces a recognition of the ways in which the current heritage statement is neither innocent nor "apolitical."

On the other side of the coin, A.'s claim to exceptionality marks the extent of the liberation possible when one deploys a counter-narrative in a space where someone else controls the dialog. She asserts her sense of belonging against a white assumption that she doesn't belong, both with regard to American history, and in her lived experience on the Hilltop. A.'s integrationist stance, however, sometimes requires her to swallow her words or practice indirection when she is confronted with the stories her white neighbors like to tell. In her personal accounts of belonging to her neighborhood, A. defends her own subjectivity. She practices complexity on the ground, claiming belonging in spite of discrimination, in spite of economic hardship, because the Hilltop is where she comes from, who she is, and what she's committed to. With all its problems, it's a good place. Given limited energy, A. would prefer to minimize the impact of the Camp Chase heritage complex and dismiss the memorial. However, the more recent appearance of a Confederate flag on her street forces her to consider the potential menace that white ignorance, or, in other words, the privilege to ignore a Black perspective, poses.

We have argued that one of the ways that a heritage narrative sustains itself even during a mounting national crisis is by posing as a counter-narrative. The substance of the HHS claim, the possibility of "a better future together" supported by "multiple points of view" preserves the dominant narrative and suppresses others. Alternatively, those currently in control of the dialog would have to be willing to subject their own understanding of the events they sponsor to critique, to recognize the interested nature of all public history displays, and in particular, to include African American experiences of the Confederacy, the Civil War, and the Jim Crow era during which these monuments were first erected. However, such critiques threaten to dismantle their project. This case study demonstrates that counter-narratives can be deployed by people in power, especially as heritage discourse. Further, heritage projects that masquerade as counter-narratives by purporting to be one narrative among many, serve crucially to protect an exclusionary white heritage discourse.

Notes

1 According to an anonymous employee of the National Cemetery Administration, this statue was mass-produced in the late nineteenth century and installed in cemeteries throughout the South. (08/2/18)

2 In a related recent case in South Africa and England, Amit Chaudhuri (2016) points to similar failures of multiculturalism to address enduring relations of colonialism that the Rhodes Must Fall protesters have challenged.

3 We thank Sydney Varajon for alerting us to the existence of the heritage complex and for conversations regarding its salience to neighborhood identity.

4 An historian observing the memorial service at the cemetery commented in a 2015 blog that the massacre of nine Black worshippers in Charlotte, North Carolina that year by white supremacist Dylann Roof might spark some rethinking of the event. It did not.

5 In 1906 Knauss published *The Story of Camp Chase* an account of both the camp and his subsequent peace and reconciliation effort that supplies the details for this text (Nashville: Methodist Episcopal Church, South). A keyword search of the text for *slave, Negro, Black, African* yields no citations.

6 See Sandra Harding (2004) and Patricia Hill Collins (1999) for an extended discussion of the epistemological advantages of centering an investigation from the standpoint of the excluded. We do not propose to oppose individual and collective memory (Olick, 2007:10), but instead suggest that A.'s perspective represents the voice excluded by HHS. As Maynes, Pierce, and Laslett observe, "Personal narratives are contextualized by, reflect on, and explore the individual's place in collective events and historical time" (2012: 43).

7 This and all subsequent quotations from A Jefferson are from interviews archived at the Ohio State University Folklore Archive, "Be the Street" collection.

8 See Modan and Shuman, 2011, for a discussion of how interviews can provide opportunities for people to present views not otherwise discussed.

9 When Annette moved back into the neighborhood as an adult she purchased her current residence on Hague Avenue, several blocks west of Wayne.

10 Indeed, the sponsors of the Westgate mural installed an elaborate key to the mural imagery at the site in order to prevent it from being misread, demonstrating a similar anxiety to control its meaning.

References

Andrews, M. (2002). Introduction: counter-narratives and the power to oppose. *Narrative Inquiry 12*, 1–6.

Astor, M., C. Caron and D. Victor (2017). A guide to the Charlottesville aftermath. *New York Times.* August 13, 2017. Retrieved from www.nytimes.com/2017/08/13/us/charlottesville-virginia-overview.html

Bamberg, M., & M. Andrews (Eds.) (2004). *Considering Counter-Narratives: Narrating, Resisting, Making Sense* (Vol. 4). Philadelphia, PA, John Benjamins Publishing.

Burger, B. and M. Ferenchik. (2017).Vandals decapitate Confederate soldier statue at Camp Chase Cemetery. (08/22) www.dispatch.com/news/20170822/vandals-decapitate-confederate-soldier-statue-at-camp-chase-cementery (accessed September 10, 2017).

Blocker, J. S. Jr. (2006). Race, sex and riot: the Springfield, Ohio race riots of 1904 and 1906 and the sources of anti-black violence in the lower midwest. *Ohio Valley History 6*, 27–44.

Blocker, J. S. (2008). *A Little More Freedom: African Americans Enter the Urban Midwest, 1860–1930*. The Ohio State University Press.

Borland, K. (2017). Co-narration, intersubjectivity, and the listener in family storytelling. *Journal of American Folklore* 130, 438–456.

Bump, P. (2017). About one of every 12 confederate memorials in the U.S. is in a Union State. www.washingtonpost.com/news/politics/wp/2017/08/15/about-one-out-of-every-12-confederate-memorials-in-the-u-s-is-in-a-union-state/?utm_term=.442aa06d533f.

Chaudhuri, A. (2016). The real meaning of Rhodes must fall. *The Guardian* www.theguardian.com/uk-news/2016/mar/16/the-real-meaning-of-rhodes-must-fall

Clay, P., L. Neff, and P. Ongaro. (2015). *Men and Women of Camp Chase*. Columbus, OH: Hilltop Historical Society.

Collins, P. H. (1999). *Black Feminist Thought: Knowledge, Consciousness, and the Politics of Empowerment*. New York: Routledge.

Columbus Dispatch. (9/13/2009). Hilltop mural depicting area's Civil War history inspires some and upsets others. Retrieved from www.dispatch.com/content/stories/local/2009/09/13/MURAL.ART_ART_09-13-09_B1_B6F297I.html (accessed 07/04/2018)

Columbus Dispatch. 2011. The Veiled Lady of Camp Chase. Retrieved from www.dispatch.com/content/blogs/a-look-back/2010/08/the_veiled_lady_of_camp_chase_1.html (accessed 07/04/2018)

DuBois, W. E. B. (1903) *The Souls of Black Folk*. Chicago: AC McClurg.

Ewick, P. and S. S. Silbey. (1995). Subversive stories and hegemonic tales: toward a sociology of narrative. *Law and Society Review 29*, 197–226.

Ferenchik, M. (5/2/2019). Statue of Confederate soldier restored at Camp Chase. *Columbus Dispatch*: B4.

Gillis, R. (1994). Memory and identity: the history of a relationship. In R. Gillis (Ed.), *Commemorations: The Politics of National Identity*, Princeton, NJ: Princeton University Press, 3–24.

Handler, R. (1994). Is "identity" a useful cross-cultural concept? in R. Gillis (Ed.), *Commemorations: The Politics of National Identity*, Princeton, NJ: Princeton University Press, 27–40.

Harding, S. G., (Ed.) (2004). *The Feminist Standpoint Theory Reader: Intellectual and Political Controversies*. Psychology Press.

The Hilltop Historical Society. (2015) [1990]. *The Men and Women of Camp Chase*. Columbus, OH: The Hilltop Historical Society (compiled by Paul Clay, Patti Ongaro, Lois Neff).

The Hilltop Historical Society. N.d. Statement. Hilltopusa.tripod.com (Accessed 07/04/2018).

Horigan, K. P. (2018). *Consuming Katrina: Public Disaster and Personal Narrative* Jackson, MI: University Press of Mississippi.

Hyvärinen, M. (2008). Analyzing narratives and story-telling. *The SAGE Handbook of Social Research Methods*: 447–460.

Jefferson, A. Interview. (2017). May 12, 2017. *Be the Street* Archive. Ohio State University.

Jefferson, A. Interview. (2017). August 19, 2017. *Be the Street* Archive. Ohio State University.

Johnson, N. (1995). Cast in stone: monuments, geography, and nationalism. *Environment and Planning D: Society and Space* 13, 51–65.

Lindahl, C. (2012) Legends of hurricane Katrina: the right to be wrong, survivor-to-survivor storytelling, and healing." *The Journal of American Folklore 125* (496), 139–176.

Lowenthal, D. (1994). Identity, heritage, and history in R. Gillis (Ed.), *Commemorations: The Politics of National Identity*, Princeton, NJ: Princeton University Press, 41–57.

Maynes, M. J., J. L. Pierce, and B. Laslett (2012). *Telling Stories: The Use of Personal Narratives in the Social Sciences and History*. Ithaca, NY: Cornell University Press.

Mills, C. (1997). *The Racial Contract*. Ithaca, NY: Cornell University Press.

Modan, G. G. (2007). *Turf Wars: Discourse, Diversity, and the Politics of Place*. New York: John Wiley & Sons.

Modan, G. G. and A. Shuman (2011). Positioning the interviewer: strategic uses of embedded orientation in interview narratives," *Language and Society*, 40, 13–25.

Norkunas, M. (2004). Narratives of resistance and the consequences of resistance. *Journal of Folklore Research*, 41, 105–123.

Olick, J. K. (2007). *The Politics of Regret: On Collective Memory and Historical Responsibility*. New York: Routledge.

Palmenfelt, U. (2010). Narrating cultural heritage. *Journal of Ethnology and Folkloristics,* 4, 63–73.
Pickenpaugh, R. (2007). *Camp Chase and the Evolution of Union Prison Policy.* Tuscaloosa, AL: University of Alabama Press.
Portelli, A. (2003). The Order Has Been Carried Out: History, Memory, and Meaning of a Nazi Massacre in Rome. New York: Palgrave.
Romero, M. and A. J. Stewart, (Eds.) (1999) Women's Untold Stories: Breaking Silence, Talking Back, Voicing Complicity. New York: Routledge.
Rosenzweig, R. and D. Thelen (1998). *The Presence of the Past: Popular Uses of History in American Life.* New York: Columbia University Press.
Savage, K. (1994). The politics of memory: black emancipation and the Civil War monument, in *Commemorations: The Politics of National Identity* (Ed.) R Gillis, Princeton: Princeton, NJ: University Press, 127–149.
Schiffrin, D. (1996) Narrative as self-portrait: sociolinguistic constructions of identity. *Language in Society* 25, 167–203.
Shuman, A. (2006). Entitlement and empathy in personal narrative. *Narrative Inquiry,* 16, 148–155.
Shuman, A. (2005). *Other People's Stories: Entitlement Claims and the Critique of Empathy.* Urbana, IL: University of Illinois Press.
Thompson, E. (09/12/2017). With Confederate statues coming down nationwide, what should become of recently vandalized Camp Chase? *Columbus Dispatch.* Retrieved from www.columbusalive.com/entertainment/20170906/monumental-debate
Zombeck, A. M. (2011). Camp Chase prison: a study of power and resistance on the northern home front, 1863. *Oral History,* 118, 24–48.

25

"The big bang of chaotic masculine disruption"

A critical narrative analysis of the radical masculinity movement's counter-narrative strategies

Matias Nurminen

Introduction

The past decade has seen the rise of online communities and ideologies interested in masculinity. These intertwined groups, which dub themselves *the manosphere*, use narratives for recruitment and the ideological refinement of their agendas. This chapter studies the manosphere's strategic use of counter-narratives by examining how they are created and identifying the worldviews contested in these narratives. I show how the manosphere's radical antifeminist wing utilizes and re-utilizes narratives to build counter-narratives against feminism. The manosphere's narrative means employ the affordances of counter-narratives while at the same time challenging the very concept and its previous theoretical applications, not to mention the social context of interpretations.

Drawing from my literary expertise, I tackle the narrative strategies of the manosphere. I combine this knowledge with the study of narrative done in the field of the social sciences: discussions on positioning, narrative control, and, above all, counter- and master-narratives. In my analysis, I focus on a specific text titled "The Manosphere" (henceforth "M") produced by a movement called Men Going Their Own Way (MGTOW). "M" is an online manifesto for attracting new members to the movement. I examine how this text benefits from the use of counter-narratives and narrative-induced strategies to make it more approachable for the reader. To build a rapport with readers, the text alludes to the science-fiction movie *The Matrix* (1999), which is widely referenced by manosphere groups. At the core of the manosphere's ideology is *The Matrix* allusion to the "red pill", the antifeminist equivalent of the cultural-political term of "being woke", viz. becoming aware of a conspiracy against men. The red pill verges on becoming a conceptual metaphor and acts as a masterplot for resistance. It also embodies the antifeminist counter-narrative: to "red pill" oneself signifies accepting a counter-narrative. In "M", at least three different counter-narratives may be found – "the Lost Macho Man", "the Homeless Frontiers Man", and "the Middlebrow Renaissance Man" – representing different takes on masculinity and opposing the suggested feminist master narrative. Based on this material, I argue that the contested master narrative is always more or less constructed by counter-narratives.

"M" also provides the reader with hypothetical and generic stories that aim to address as many people as possible. As the text amplifies a male chorus while aggressively suppressing other voices, I suggest a dark aspect of polyphony to be at play in the text. I interpret these strategies as assuming narrative control to enforce what is true and false according to the manosphere's worldview.

The concept of *counter-narrative* refers to "the stories which people tell and live which offer resistance, either implicitly or explicitly, to dominant cultural narratives" that are in turn often called *master-narratives* (Andrews, 2004, p. 1). The theoretical claim of this chapter is that to create opposition, the manosphere projects a master narrative of feminism: the manosphere opposes this image of feminism with multiple counter-narratives that attempt to reclaim the uncontested male-orientation in Western societies. While the work on gender equality is all but done, the manosphere's claim of marginalization seems opportunistic, something that has been a discursive tactic of master-narratives (Gabriel, 2016, p. 212). The writers of the manosphere *position* themselves within these alleged binaries of master and counter in ways that portray them as righteous heroes. These writers seek to seize narrative control: sociologists Gubrium and Holstein see narrative control as "the sterner side of narrative collaboration" (2009, pp. 109–110). Control over the manosphere's online narrative environment makes it easier to promote increasingly radical counter-narratives.

This chapter draws attention to the lack of scope in earlier research on counter-narratives: the eminent work done, e.g., in *Considering Counter-narratives* (Bamberg & Andrews, 2004) unintentionally steers academia to see the spectrum of counter-narratives as positive. I suggest that seeing the texts themselves as the center of the discussion instead of the social realm might solve this unwanted evaluation (cf. Bamberg, 2004, p. 368; Piekut, 2017, p. 385). In contrast to social studies, literary studies and especially narratology concentrate more on narrative texture and technique than on the storytelling individual or society: they do not try to see narratives separate from their social realms but rather seek to identify narrative affordances and ways of storytelling in certain social realms. A focus on narrative strategies diminishes the unconscious dichotomy of hegemonic master narrative and its emancipating countering that was already disputed by Bamberg (2004, p. 361) but not followed through. As can be discerned from the chapter's tone, I do not support the manosphere's agendas, yet I seek to shed light on and demystify its narrative strategies in the spirit of charitable reading. Nevertheless, my notion is that the counter-narrative strategies of these groups are inspired and essential for understanding the darker side of a phenomenon we tend to see as benign.

The red pill: a metaphor and a masterplot for the antifeminist counter-narrative

The manosphere is a disjointed collection of masculinity communities, and it is challenging to define its boundaries exhaustively. It includes male-oriented self-improvement websites, the men's rights movement, and the seduction community that propagates advice on "picking up" women – there are hundreds of sites and communities depending on how they are counted. It has been suggested that due to its rapid growth, the manosphere would probably be hailed a "digital revolution" if the groups supported a different kind of cultural politics (Nagle, 2017, p. 86). For example, the biggest radical manosphere community, Reddit's discussion board /TheRedPill, has around 420,000 registered users, even though registration is not mandatory to read the material. The diversity of the manosphere is problematic: for example, constructive discussion groups spreading awareness about men's mental health issues are bundled with the radical antifeminist wing, such as groups like *neomasculinity*, who ascribe to an ideology openly hostile toward women, sexual minorities, and immigrants. This radical and vocal wing captures the media's attention and hosts groups like *the red pill* philosophy and the MGTOW movement: red pillers claim that men are secretly oppressed by gynocentric society and MGTOW antagonizes the concept of marriage. Misogyny and antifeminism seem to be visible undertones throughout the manosphere, but for the radical groups, they are the prevalent modus operandi (see also Ging, 2017; Nurminen, 2019).

It is often claimed the manosphere has no clear-cut agenda or leaders, but most factions share the aspiration to become better, even superior males. Many of the groups are aligned with the alt-right – also a vague bulk term for a complex phenomenon of far-right thinking – and the Gamergate incident, as in addition to feminism, they oppose immigration and liberal values. These groups isolate themselves from society with claims of entitlement for their stories and, as Amy Shuman suggests, "entitlement claims are alibis for a failure of empathy" (2005, p. 7). Under the guise of defending the masculine position they are entitled to, the manosphere groups attack people seen as conflicting with their position. The manosphere is mainly a Western phenomenon that attracts mostly young ethnically Caucasian males – white heterosexual maleness, while not exclusive, is not an exaggerated depiction. For example, the discussion forum on mgtow.com is "for men only": for "men-bers" instead of members.

Interestingly enough from the perspective of a literary scholar, radical manosphere movements find common ground in embracing literary fiction. For example, the title of neomasculinity's website, returnofkings.com, is an allusion to the title of the final volume in J.R.R. Tolkien's *The Lord of the Rings* (1954–1955). The website also holds a variety of neomasculinist readings of novels, like Tolstoy's *Anna Karenina* (1877) and Harper Lee's *To Kill a Mockingbird* (1960). The core narrative for the manosphere is *The Matrix* (1999), a science fiction movie directed by the Wachowski siblings, and its concept of "the red pill" that unites different manosphere groups. *The Matrix* tells the story of a hacker called Thomas Anderson – or, as he is known by his screen name, Neo – who finds out that the world he thinks is real is a simulation run by intelligent machines. In the real world, the machines grow people in tanks to be used as a power source, and the simulation Matrix keeps the people ignorant of their condition. Neo is recruited to participate in a rebellion against this conspiracy and soon learns he is "The One", the prophesized savior of humankind. The red pill alludes to a scene where Neo chooses between a red and a blue pill: the red one signifies the will to leave the Matrix and thus confront the evil conspiracy, while the blue pill allows one to forget the uncomfortable state of the world and to keep living in ignorance in the Matrix.

The radical movements in the manosphere exploit the narrative of *The Matrix* to allegorize their ideology and to justify their antifeminism and misogyny.[1] The red pill is interpreted differently between the movements, but the undertone is similar: a conspiracy against men that can be perceived through the red pill. Allusions to *The Matrix* connect the manosphere to a narrative of a righteous struggle. The red pill becomes a metaphor for revealing and upholding cultural oppositions. The claimed antagonists vary from gynocentric society and women in general to feminists and men not willing to red pill themselves.

Since *The Matrix* gained critical acclaim and was a financial success, allusions to the movie are easily accessible and memetic. *The Matrix* also relies on the stereotype of science fiction as a male-oriented genre: the film is considered a common ground for men who might interest themselves in the pro-male agenda. While the interpretation may seem harsh, one cannot help but offer the comparison between the protagonist Neo, who leads a secret life online after working his office job, and someone in danger of online radicalization. Relatability to Neo is the key to using *The Matrix* to recruit new members, but the intertextuality in itself is intriguing: as in the movie, where Neo is recruited with a combination of persuasion and allusions to Lewis Carroll's

Alice in Wonderland (1865), the antifeminist movements use *The Matrix* as part of their recruitment drive. The red pill signifies rebelling against a conspiracy, and it can be memetically shared with the phrase.

Gregory Machacek suggests that allusions can be used to "to divide an audience into those who have a cultural kinship with the author and those who do not" (2007, p. 526). Alluding to the metaphorical "red pill" activates *The Matrix* in the manosphere's texts. The film's righteous struggle is projected onto the manosphere's attacks on feminism. The allusion compares feminists with the monstrous machines in *The Matrix*. Furthermore, it enables the red pillers to see themselves as messianic saviors with the right to fight to save everyone else caught up in their version of the Matrix simulation. *The Matrix* is an underdog story par excellence: Lois Presser notes these stories are well-suited "to insurgencies and protest movements of all kinds, where adversaries have more resources" and that "the virtuous protagonist in the underdog story takes morally weighty action against the odds" and triumphs over a threat that might not be even real (Presser, 2018, pp. 88–89). The underdog position foreshadows a seemingly imminent victory over its adversaries.

While the red pill is an allusion, it manages to reach further: the depth of meanings activated is greater than the movie's narrative or its interpretation, since the term moves beyond language use and entices connections. The red pill verges on becoming a conceptual metaphor for righteous resistance, and these connotations make the allusion more appealing.

Hence, I suggest that talking about an allusion is not enough. To help define the red pill, I turn to H. Porter Abbott's (2002/2008, p. 43) notion of "more skeletal and adaptable" *masterplots* that are the supportive basis for our narratives and "often work in secret, influencing us without our wholly realizing it". Masterplot is not to be confused with the term master narrative, although Abbott, for example, views the terms as synonymous. However, I suggest that masterplots are covert cultural storylines that we abide by more or less consciously in our everyday lives. Sometimes these masterplots arouse resistance that can be addressed with counter-narratives. Master-narratives, in turn, are created in order to mirror the counter-narratives and only come into existence in relation to counter-narratives. In this sense, the red pill epitomizes the masterplot of resistance that enables the antifeminist counter-narrative. The counter-narrative contests the masterplot of gender equality in Western society by creating a master narrative of feminism that is, in a sense, a straw man. As the following text analysis shows, the manosphere utilizes multiple counter-narratives that are interrelated yet take different angles on masculinity, hoping to bring down the master narrative they themselves have created.

Positioning misogyny as tellable

The social sciences have tended to think unconsciously of counter-narratives as being well-intentioned. Recent studies discuss challenging hegemonic master-narratives of parenting (Eerola & Mykkänen, 2015; Kerrick & Henry, 2017; Símonardóttir & Gíslason, 2018), illness and disabilities (Okigbo & Ezumah, 2017) and ethnicity (Aspinall, 2015) with constructive counter-narratives. This positive mindset is not an innate quality of the social sciences, but rather a bias created for multiple reasons: gathering narratives in interviews that require trust between the interviewer and interviewees on how the data will be handled, difficulties in attaining interviews from supporters of radical groups, and viewing grass-roots movements' and individuals' countering narratives as noble vis-à-vis organized establishments' narratives (see also Gair & Moloney, 2013). Master-narratives are seen to be "often oppressive" and to "exclude experiences" (Piekut, 2017, p. 384). In addition, much-referenced academic studies on the subject (cf. Bamberg & Andrews, 2004) do not address the potentially harmful ways counter-narratives can be used. While the eminent studies do not deny the possibility of ill-willed counter-narratives, the lack of example cases has steered academia to see counter-narratives in a certain way.

There are exceptions to this positive bias: Ruth Page's article on Wikipedia counter-narratives sees these narratives as instrumental and more neutral means for discussing differing views and ideologies (Page, 2014; see also Perrino, 2018). The recent book *Counter-narratives and Organization* (Frandsen, Kuhn & Lundholt, 2017) offers a welcomed addition to the theoretical discussion from an organizational context: however, I find Yiannis Gabriel's article on conspiracy theories in the book to be particularly thought-provoking. He sees conspiracy theories varying from harmless to harmful counter-narratives, as going against the official account, and notes "effective conspiracy theories combine iconoclasm with plausibility, fancy with factuality, absurdity with logic" (Gabriel, 2016, p. 217).

The text "M" from mgtow.com is an exemplary conspiracy theory and, thus, a counter-narrative: it applies and combines the effective traits described by Gabriel. If not outright harmful, "M" exposes darker aspects of the use of counter-narratives. In "M" the multiple counter-narratives – which I have differentiated and tentatively named here "the Lost Macho Man", "the Homeless Frontiers Man", and "the Middlebrow Renaissance Man", and to which I will return to – ascertain narrative control. The control is achieved through strategic positioning and shifting between different counter-narratives.

"M" is a manifesto-like text that can be found on mgtow.com in the "About" section. It starts as follows:

> Slowly but surely, the Manosphere is gaining steam and extending its reach. Men in their late 30s and beyond who had the luxury of semi-rejecting the red pill while still finding moderate success are being outnumbered by a younger generation who realize they really don't have a choice in the matter. Unlike the older men, these men didn't choose to unplug; they were unplugged. Yet they thrive.
>
> *("M")*[2]

Although the "About" section is usually informational, the speaker uses this space to persuade the reader to join the movement. The text makes drastic claims about men, women, and the state of Western society. The red pill is mentioned at the beginning and it is followed through with another metaphorically coherent allusion to *The Matrix* – "unplugging", meaning the concrete act of separating oneself from the Matrix simulation. Unplugging is a highly embodied word and it too advocates how the red pill reaches beyond language. These allusions activate the red pill masterplot to set the tone of the text, and what is reproduced is the dystopian conspiracy-ridden world of *The Matrix*.

I suggest "M" seeks to convince those sympathetic to or at least curious about radical masculinity who are already – in manosphere terms – seeking to "unplug" or "red pill" themselves. When *The Matrix* becomes thus merged with other narratives, such as exemplary stories about men – hypothetical stories that pose as actual events, as I proceed to show – fiction starts to blur with reality. The manosphere's online narrative environment, which I have noted is peculiarly intertwined with the literary, makes the readers more susceptible to narrative influence.

The red pill activates the masterplot of resistance. While women and feminists are the main antagonists in "M", the text also attacks institutions such as the church:

> The companies they work for demand loyalty, but will fire them or lay them off without a second thought if profits dip one tenth of one percent. ... The women they encounter demand attention, loyalty, resources and undue privilege, while offering very little in return.

> ... Sunday after Sunday they listen as the same Bible used to preemptively absolve women of all past, current and future transgressions is used to condemn men.
>
> *("M")*

In "M", women and feminism are portrayed as dishonest, companies are unjust or inhumane, and the church is seen as partial to women and supporting the gynocentric status quo. The passages cited here portray men as victims, and this can also be understood in terms of positioning. Michael Bamberg notes that analyzing positioning grants "more centrality to the speaker's active engagement in the construction process of narratives" (1997, p. 341). Thus, to understand what is attempted by the manosphere's counter-narratives, one must analyze the positions taken in these narratives. I rely here on Bamberg's suggestion that there are three different levels of positioning: the first level is the level of storyworld, as in "how are the characters positioned in relation to one another within the reported events"; the second is the level of discourse, as in "how does the speaker position him- or herself to the audience"; and the third level is the level of self in contrast to the world, as in "how do narrators position themselves to themselves" (Bamberg, 1997, p. 337). Anna De Fina notes that it not easy to distinguish especially the second and third levels of positioning, as narrators have the ability – and often willingness – to "represent themselves as certain kinds of persons beyond the limits of the current interaction" (2015, p. 360). This is apparent when the narrator likely recognizes that there is something precarious in what he or she is about to tell and still keeps to it, as is in the case of "M".

In "M", the first-level positioning takes place when men are positioned as victims and feminist society and women are positioned as the antagonists. Of course, the position of victim is not something with which all the supporters of the manosphere identify. Francesca Polletta points out that people seeking social change to mend some disadvantage tend to "try to capitalize on familiar conventions of storytelling", yet there are risks in trying to "elicit sympathy": for example, giving personal accounts of injustice might come across as playing the part of the victim and "alienate potential recruits who are unwilling to see themselves as passive victims" (Polletta, 2006, pp. 2–3). In "M", the speaker takes up the position of victim, but it resolves the unwanted alienation by shifting between the positions from victim to martyr and from there to a conqueror in control. As Arnulf Depperman points out, with positioning the narrator can do the "moral work in storytelling" and share a point of view, even to "call for empathy and affiliation" (2015, p. 375). As the text holds that men are being cuckolded by a feminist society, it offers multiple positions for the readers to address this issue. These shifts in position also maneuvre between the different counter-narratives, and they make "M" more tellable: the changing position and counter-narrative increase variation and breach the expectations created by the previous positions taken by the narrator.

The three counter-narratives of "M"

A counter-narrative proposes a master narrative, shows what is wrong with it, and then offers a different narrative perspective. It is a "political intervention" into the ideological positions of the master narrative. Counter-narratives utilize "a formidable range of tropes involving irony, intertextuality, inversion, reframing, double entendres, killer facts and many other techniques to lend them credibility and plausibility" (Gabriel, 2016, p. 210). "M" is a compilation of counter-narratives that addresses the reader by using different tones, vocabularies, and narratives – or fragments of them. In the relatively short text, tropes such as intertextuality, inversion, and reframing are used avidly. Bamberg notes that instead of one counter-narrative, speakers shift between several stories: counter-narratives "operate on the edge of disputability" and hence require from the speaker what Bamberg calls "interactional subtlety and rhetorical finessing" (2004, p. 363). This rhetorical finesse is seen in "M" even at the level of language and vocabulary. On the one hand, the text is riddled with banal idioms, like "slowly but surely", while on the other hand the register keeps changing even in the middle of a sentence: "We now provide for ourselves and our immediate families, protect our interests, make selective sacrifices when the situation warrants, and conquer mountains of poon" ("M"). The language fluctuates between the use of online jargon and obscene slang words, like "poon", and what can only be described as a dignified, patriotic tone.

Gabriel proposes that master-narratives only form themselves as narratives in relation to counter-narratives, in the sense of Hegel's master–slave dialectic: "master-narratives need counter-narratives in order to recognize themselves as narratives, and counter-narratives need master-narratives in order to be recognized as counter-narratives" (Gabriel, 2016, p. 208). I would take this one step further by arguing that master-narratives are always more or less manufactured to oppose the countering narrative, and they are not necessarily genuine or depicted fairly. Counter-narrative is a powerful tool of persuasion that requires an opposing side, yet it does not call for fair treatment. Thus, counter-narratives are told against constructed master-narratives: my suggestion is that the more radical the counter-narrative, the more complex the constructed master narrative needs to be.

In "M", different voices collide through the text but all revolve around the same nucleus, which is the constructed master narrative of feminism. This master narrative is antagonistic, yet it is approached from multiple countering positions that accommodate competing takes on masculinity. These positions are part of the narrator's third-level positioning that involves masculinity (see Bamberg & Georgakopoulou, 2008, p. 391) while at the same time tying in the discursive posing of the second-level positioning. Thus, what we get in "M" are multiple narrative avatars of masculinity that I divide into three main counter-narratives: 1) the Lost Macho Man, 2) the Homeless Frontiers Man, and 3) the Middlebrow Renaissance Man.

The Lost Macho Man counter-narrative

The Lost Macho Man counter-narrative is the most prominently antifeminist, as it fosters traditional gender roles and hegemonic masculinity and attacks those women and men the speaker sees as opposing this narrative. The speaker antagonizes the "modern feminist" and "ungrateful women", and even "the average young woman" who only cares about men retweeting "a photo of her breasts". He also mentions "white knights" and "turning betas into men": "white knight" is a term used to describe men who defend gender equality or consider themselves feminist, and "betas" are weak men who are subordinate to the strong alpha males that are adored in the manosphere. The speaker dreams in this counter-narrative about the good old times and "conquering poon" after he walks away from society ("M"). The use of vulgar vocabulary stems from the Lost Macho Man counter-narrative, which, even though using online jargon, is purposefully ignorant about social media, as the mention of retweeting indicates: Twitter is far from the most used social media for sharing photographs, yet addressing social media ignorantly creates a tellability-inducing breach that catches one's attention. This reinforces the sense that the world is changing and leaving the Macho man behind. The aim, it seems, is to create relatability: if the reader still understands the means of social media and, thus, the fault in Macho man's statement about Twitter, maybe in a few years he too might not be able to keep up with the changing world.

The Homeless Frontiers Man counter-narrative

The Homeless Frontiers Man counter-narrative uses a variety of masterplots, metaphors, and comparisons connected to the ideas of nature and the natural, the most prominent example being the simile-narrative that starts with picturing happiness as an eagle "soaring through the air, because that's what it was made to" ("M"). The narrative then continues to picture happiness as a fish, a tree, and, lastly, a man. The simile-narrative utilizes the rhetoric tricks of the threefold list and structural repetition, which increases the tellability. The counter-narrative addresses the connection to nature and the natural. Nature is often thought of as attributing order, balance, or some sort of truth and design. The speaker utilizes this to make claims of his rights to, for example, to conquer, "because that's what he was made to do" ("M"). The references to nature and individualist freedom activate the American philosophical tradition of transcendentalism that sees the system and society as the cause of the individual's degradation – something that is strongly argued also in "M": the Homeless Frontiers Man counter-narrative opposes corporations and the system as obstructing men from being truly free. This counter-narrative shares the Macho Man's anti-modernist position and his longing for the past: distaste for organized society speaks volumes about "aggressive nostalgia" entailing "xenophobic and chauvinistic overtones" (Gabriel, 2016, p. 215; see also Ivanova, 2000).

The Middlebrow Renaissance Man counter-narrative

The Middlebrow Renaissance Man counter-narrative is almost inseparable from the Homeless Frontiers Man, but it emphasizes science and learnedness. The speaker tries to take authority and explain the ways of the world to the reader and even to pose as a reasonable voice. Here, the refined language creates an eloquent backdrop for blatant generalizations about the "natural hypergamous nature" of society and how "men and women share the same inherent character flaws, but not the same consequences" ("M"). I argue that this counter-narrative is middlebrow, as it strives to be learned and uses vivid language to capture the attention of the reader while at the same time seeking to be easily accessible. In doing so, it aims to make the reader feel erudite without effort. In the text, all negative comments are justified with appeals to the greater cause, which absolves the narrator and the reader of their misogyny. This can be seen in the patronizing segment that is clearly part of the Middlebrow Renaissance Man counter-narrative:

> He doesn't hate his corporation; he hates the system. He doesn't hate God; he hates what the church does in God's name. He doesn't hate women; he hates the unforgiving female support machine. He doesn't hate feminists or White Knights; he hates navigating the environment they create.
>
> *("M")*

This segment in "M" breaches all counter-narratives with its contrast to the hateful and bitter claims made before and after. By denying the blatant misogyny and antifeminism in both "M" and the community, and by claiming to be after the gynocentric system as a whole and not the individuals within it, the text delivers the readers from their aggression. This is also a combination of second- and third-level positioning as the narrator temporarily poses as one of the good guys and distances himself from the message of the manosphere. The narrator contradicts himself, but this positioning works as a retreat tactic if confronted. The sense of righteous struggle is activated once more and attacking feminists – women and men – is shown to be a normal act of rebellion against a corrupt system.

The dark polyphony of generic happenings

The counter-narratives of "M" seem to come together in the ending, which highlights the overlapping of these three narratives. The longing for the lost frontier and masculinity joins with the discourse of science: "The Manosphere is the Big Bang of chaotic masculine disruption that will eventually bring into existence a new personal world of freedom for those who choose to be free" ("M"). The manosphere is depicted as "the Big Bang", suggesting it is the beginning of something greater, and the use of aggressive discourse is muddled by referring to a "disruption". A new frontier is promised to those "who choose to be free", creating a resonance with the American credo of freedom. The choice of freedom is linked also to *The Matrix* and choosing the red pill. As attempts to discredit and silence conspiratorial counter-narratives tend only to fuel the counter-narratives' fire (Gabriel, 2016, p. 212), the coupling to freedom hinders counterclaims even further. Resistance is an attack on the right to be free. The antifeminist counter-narrative is shown as the only way to fight and be free.

At least three counter-narratives alternate to occupy "M". The text becomes a chorus of masculine voices that sing from the same hymn sheet of male superiority. This approach resonates with Mikhail Bakhtin's work on polyphony, yet the multitude of voices is discriminating. Counter-narratives have been discussed from a dialogical perspective, taking note of the polyphony between master and counter-narratives (e.g., Humle & Frandsen, 2016; Jensen, Maagard & Rasmussen, 2016), but the interaction in "M" is introverted. The chorus in "M" is one of dark polyphony: in supporting traditional male voices and counter-narratives, the chorus ridicules and dismisses other voices. The male chorus is dialogical, but the opposing spectrum of voices is represented as a caricature. I suggest that the dark polyphony enables greater maintenance of narrative control: there is a collaborating multitude of voices with a common enemy. I would argue that to interpret narrative control in texts like "M", one must turn to implicit ways of control, like activation: even the simplest inquiries control the way a "person responding might construct his or her story" (Gubrium & Holstein, 2009, pp. 109–110). While texts like "M" do not offer the opportunity for a direct dialogue, they do tempt the reader to construct – or at least revise – his or her own story. This is done through different activation cues that include intertextual referencing, using tones and vocabularies, and employing generic narrative fragments.

Laura Karttunen has studied hypotheticality and suggests that "even if the focus of the narrative is on the counterfactual scenario, entertaining such scenarios at least implicitly comments on the actual state of affairs" (2013, p. 124). In "M" the narrative fragments comment not only what actually is, but also what might be:

> They have best friends from childhood who disappear six months after the wedding, because the new bride doesn't want her hubby hanging out with single losers.
>
> They have to pick up the tab for dad's dinner, because his going broke trying to support mom, her new live-in boyfriend, and a 12 year old he's not certain is even his. The young man watches as middle-management dad making $70k per year tries to crank the engine in his 11 year old car to no avail, and then has to give him a ride back to his apartment on the seedy side of town.
>
> *("M")*

Instead of fixing its aim to one specific relatable narrative of hardship, the text tackles a variety of possible scenarios or exempla, from having to support former spouses to losing touch with a married friend. The exemplum is a tool for argumentative discourse: it is evoked to exemplify a generic claim and, on the other hand, from exempla one can derive and attempt to verify a claim (De Fina & Georgakopoulou, 2012, p. 98). While the events seem they could be real, they move beyond factual and counterfactual by being typical; they deal with what is hypothetical and what could be (see Karttunen, 2013, pp. 120–122). The exempla in "M" sway between universal and highly exact as they are, for example, filled with numbers: the exact numbers make the hypothesis of a reality more concrete. The use of numbers is related to the Middlebrow Renaissance Man counter-narrative and to the stereotype of men as good with numbers.

The narrative fragments pose as experienced events. As De Fina and Georgakopoulou point out, evidence of something experienced is "much more difficult to reject than rational argumentation" (2012, p. 98). The possibility of agency behind the experiences depicted makes them more real, while the stereotypicality allows one to imagine the agent more easily. What the speaker tries to achieve with stereotypical exempla is a cascade approach that seeks to give as many people as possible something relatable. The events in "M" are bound to resonate with the reader's experience, and this premeditated coincidence creates the sense of the narrator understanding the reader's hardships. The cascade approach pools supporters from different backgrounds. One revealing example is the "dad with the 11-year-old car": eleven years is about the average age of a car in the United States, so it is not at all unfathomable that one's father would drive a car this old. In addition, those whose car is close to this critical age can start to worry. Eleven years is a safe bet and it makes everyone driving cars older than this – or owning no car at all – seem worse off.

The generic exempla pose as personal accounts and mask that the experiences in "M" are stereotypical. The events depicted act as a platform for the hypothetical thoughts of the audience. These narrative fragments invite readers to join the chorus – the readers' voices to complement the exempla with their own experiences. In "M", the personal pronouns also keep changing from the distant "they" and "s/he" to the committed "we" and "you". These work as a tool for the second-level positioning, as the narrator's use of personal pronouns creates oppositions. While the exempla cited here seem to defy classification under one certain counter-narrative, they enable the dark polyphony of counter-narratives. Instead of one countering narrative, there is a multitude, and instead of one narrator, the text conjures up a feeling of a horde of men telling their stories – voices of the masculine Big Bang with no room for any other voices.

Conclusion

The three counter-narratives in "M" challenge our conceptions of master and counter-narratives: the theoretical discussion and its application have been hindered by the unconscious mindset that sees counter-narratives as a positive spectrum. In "M", the narrator takes advantage of the fruitful narrative position that the counter-narrative offers and serves readers a multitude of countering positions to offer relatability to as many men as possible. Relying on the intertextual red pill and its conspiratorial connotations makes the views memetic, shareable, and difficult to deny. The masterplot of resistance enables the manosphere's radical counter-narratives, which manufacture the master narrative of feminism. By constant positioning, the narrator promotes antifeminism and gives a misogynistic commentary while still attempting to absolve himself. "M" is riddled with dark polyphony that encourages certain voices yet silences others.

The material at hand also raises questions about positioning oneself as a scholar of a research subject that defies theories and is aggressive towards critical examinations. The social sciences seem not to favor disapproving positions to study subjects, and one may question whether this limits the scope of research. Furthermore, online narratives such as "M" are wholly different from narratives gathered in interviews, where issues of trust and confidentiality have to be considered. It is my conviction that the online aspect of counter-narratives should be studied thoroughly, as it enables the formation of radical communities.

Alice Marwick and Rebecca Lewis note how the strategic use of the red pill has spread to an arsenal of different radical groups, like the alt-right, white supremacists, and conspiracy theorists (2017, p. 29). Many of these groups share ideological views and, as I have analyzed, the red pill is an easily accessible reference point for radical communities. Angela Nagle calls the lively sharing of ideas between the manosphere and the alt-right "cross-pollination" (2017, p. 98). Therefore, we should consider the utilization of counter-narratives in ways that cannot be described as benign: the red pill is easily dismantled by a narrative analysis, but counter-narratives have complex power dynamics that are not so easily grasped, as this case shows. If the intertextual strategy of the red pill has taken root in the radical groups' discourse, their take on counter-narratives is probably tomorrow's headline. Advancing and broadening our theoretical scope on counter-narratives serves not just academia; it offers ways to confront radicalization and narrative strategies in the service of ideological work.

Notes

1 Some irony can be found it the fact that the directors of *The Matrix*, who were known as the Wachowski brothers (Larry and Andy), have had gender reassignment since directing the movie and are now women, Lana and Lilly Wachowski.

2 As of October 2018, the website www.mgtow.com has gone through changes and "M" was also edited. The only change is that the first paragraph cited here has been removed, but the original text can be found here: https://web.archive.org/web/20171115034613/www.mgtow.com/manosphere. While this editing is unfortunate, it does not affect my analysis. Furthermore, I find it interesting that references to the red pill were removed. I speculate that this is due to increasing strife between different manosphere groups. By distancing itself from the red pill discourse, MGTOW is trying to be a movement in its own right.

Literature

Abbott, H.P. (2002/2008). *The Cambridge Introduction to Narrative*. Cambridge: Cambridge University Press

Andrews, M. (2004). Opening to original contributions. Counter-narratives and the power to oppose. In M. Bamberg & M. Andrews (Eds.), *Considering Counter-Narratives. Narrating, Resisting, Making Sense* (pp. 1–6). Amsterdam & Philadelphia: John Benjamins.

Aspinall, P.J. (2015). Social representations of "mixed-race" in early twenty-first-century Britain: Content, limitations, and counter-narratives. *Ethnic and Racial Studies*, 38(7), 1067–1083.

Bamberg, M. (1997). Positioning between structure and performance. *Journal of Narrative and Life History*, 7(1–4), 335–342.

Bamberg, M. (2004). Considering counter narratives. In M. Bamberg & M. Andrews (Eds.), *Considering Counter-Narratives. Narrating, Resisting, Making Sense* (pp. 351–371). Amsterdam & Philadelphia: John Benjamins.

Bamberg, M. & Andrews, M. (Eds.) (2004). *Considering Counter-Narratives. Narrating, Resisting, Making Sense.* Amsterdam & Philadelphia: John Benjamins.

Bamberg, M. & Georgakopoulou, A. (2008). Small stories as a new perspective in narrative and identity analysis. *Text and Talk*, 28(3), 377–396.

De Fina, A. & Georgakopoulou, A. (2012). *Analyzing Narrative. Discourse and Sociolinguistic Perspectives.* Cambridge: Cambridge University Press.

De Fina, A. (2015). Narrative and identities. In A. De Fina & A. Georgakopoulou (Eds.), *The Handbook of Narrative Analysis* (pp. 351–368). Chichester: John Wiley & Sons.

Depperman, A. (2015). Positioning. In A. De Fina & A. Georgakopoulou (Eds.), *The Handbook of Narrative Analysis* (pp. 369–387). Chichester: John Wiley & Sons.

Frandsen, S., Kuhn, T. & Lundholt, M.W. (Eds.) (2017). *Counter-narratives and Organization*. London: Routledge.

Eerola, P. & Mykkänen J. (2015). Paternal masculinities in early fatherhood: Dominant and counter narratives by Finnish first-time fathers. *Journal of Family Issues,* 36(12), 1674–1701.

Gabriel, Y. (2016). Narrative ecologies and the role of counter-narratives: The case of nostalgic stories and conspiracy theories. In S. Frandsen, T. Kuhn, & M.W. Lundholt (Eds.), *Counter-narratives and Organization* (pp. 208–226). London: Routledge.

Gair, S. & Moloney, S. (2013). Unspeakable stories: When counter narratives are deemed unacceptable. *Qualitative Research Journal,* 13(1), 49–61.

Ging, D. (2017). Alphas, betas, and incels: Theorizing the masculinities of the manosphere. *Men and Masculinities*, 1–20. DOI: 10.1177/1097184X17706401

Gubrium, J.F. & Holstein, J.A. (2009). *Analyzing Narrative Reality*. Thousand Oaks, CA: Sage.

Humle, D.M. & Frandsen, S. (2016). Organizational identity negotiations through dominant and counter-narratives. In S. Frandsen, T. Kuhn, & M.W. Lundholt (Eds.), *Counter-narratives and Organization* (pp. 105–128). London: Routledge.

Ivanova, N. (2000). The nostalgic present. Retrospectives on the (post-)Soviet TV screen. *Russian Studies in Literature,* 36(2), 55–72.

Jensen, A., Maagaard, C.A. & Rasmussen, R.K. (2016). "Speaking through the other." Countering counter-narratives through stakeholders' stories. In S. Frandsen, T. Kuhn, & M.W. Lundholt (Eds.), *Counter-narratives and Organization* (pp. 83–102). London: Routledge.

Karttunen, L. (2013). How to distinguish hypothetical from actual speech in fiction. *Language and Dialogue,* 3(1), 108–128.

Kerrick, M.R. & Henry, R.L. (2017). "Totally in love": Evidence of a master narrative for how new mothers should feel about their babies. *Sex Roles*, 76(1–2), 1–16.

Machacek, G. (2007). Allusion. *PMLA,* 122(2), 522–536.

Marwick, A. & Lewis, R. (2017). *Media Manipulation and Disinformation Online.* New York: Data & Society Research Institute.

Nagle, A. (2017). *Kill All Normies. The Online Culture Wars from Tumblr and 4chan to the Alt-right and Trump.* Winchester, UK & Washington, US: Zero Books.

Nurminen, M. (2019). Narrative warfare. The "careless" reinterpretation of literary canon in online antifeminism. (Special Issue: *Real Fictions: Fictionality, factuality and narrative strategies in contemporary story-telling.*) *Narrative Inquiry,* 29(2), 312–331.

Okigbo, A.C. & Ezumah, B.A. (2017). Media health images of Africa and the politics of representation: A South African AIDS choir counter-narrative. *Journal of Asian and African Studies*, 52(5), 705–721.

Page, R. (2014). Counter narratives and controversial crimes in Wikipedia. *Language and Literature,* 23(1), 61–76.

Perrino, S. (2018). Narrative aftershocks: Digital retellings of an earthquake in Emilia-Romagna, Northern Italy. *Discourse, Context & Media,* 25(1), 88–97.

Piekut, A. (2017). "Brown eyes are not the same as blue eyes." Educational narratives, identities and positioning in adult education in Denmark. *Narrative Inquiry,* 27(2), 381–400.

Polletta, F. (2006). *It Was Like a Fever. Storytelling in Protest and Politics.* London: University of Chicago Press.

Presser, L. (2018). *Inside Story: How Narratives Drive Mass Harm.* Oakland: University of California Press.

Símonardóttir, S. & Gíslason, I.V. (2018). When breast is not best: Opposing dominant discourses on breastfeeding. *The Sociological Review*, 66(3), 665–681.

Shuman, A. (2005). Other People's Stories. Entitlement Claims and the Critique of *Empathy*. Urbana & Chicago: University of Illinois Press.

26

Othering and belonging in education

Master and counter-narratives of education and ethnicity

Anke Piekut

How do students with an ethnically diverse background narrate sameness, difference and otherness in an otherwise ethnically homogeneous educational context in Denmark? Exploring three migrant Danish students in Danish as a second language subject through one year, their educational narratives of both the subject and of ethnicity as an identity marker show ambivalence in relation to master and counter-narratives. Therefore, a prevalent feature is a complicated dialogue between otherness as part of the students' identity and the concept of master and counter-narratives. Focusing on three student participants, their educational narratives and the relation between othering and belonging, master and counter-narratives of ethnicity and education will be explored. Arguing that master-narratives of students with a migration background as "other" from the majority of students can be powerful means of creating personal and cultural detrimental identities, the aspect between othering and master and counter-narratives is, nevertheless, not clear-cut and needs further inquiry.

The three students in focus are enrolled in Danish as a second language, henceforth L2, as part of acquiring an upper secondary degree at an adult education center. Since the adult education centers in Denmark are linked to adverse master-narratives, the students have to navigate in a complex and conflicting educational context.

By being in an adult education context, the students are on the same trajectory as their Danish fellow students, but at the same time different regarding enrolment in the L2 subject. By being in the L2 class, the three students Abir, Faisal and Salma express both belonging as part of an ethnic minority group and at the same time being "othered" as an L2 student for the same reason of ethnicity. How the students identify and position themselves in the L2 subject as same, different and "othered" in master and counter-narratives of the subject will be in focus in this chapter.

Since both the theoretical and empirical angle are likewise important, the chapter is organized around an explanation of the educational context, a presentation of the method and theoretical concepts, followed by the analysis of the students' educational narratives and summing up in a tentative conclusion about the relation between master and counter-narratives and "otherness".

The context – the L2 subject and adult education in Denmark

Since the context in which the educational narratives emerge become important, I will outline the purpose and framework of values for adult education in Denmark. In Denmark, primary and lower secondary school is integrated as one continuous educational program, ranging from year 0 to 9 (and, voluntarily, year 10). After compulsory education, years 0–9, adolescents can choose between four different upper secondary programs or vocational training. Students at the adult centers are either taking continuing education or recommencing abandoned or interrupted lower or upper secondary education. Most students at the centers are between 19 to 30 years of age and have a variety of social and ethnic backgrounds, though the majority are students without a migration background. The centers are the only institutions in Denmark that provide qualifying upper secondary L2 courses. The L2 subject is designed to meet the needs of bilingual students, bringing grammar and an appropriate selection of texts into focus. Students who enroll in the L2 course are primarily 1st and 2nd generation immigrants and refugees. In other subjects, migrant and non-migrant students participate in the same subject. The adult education centers do have a "sweeper" function for young adults who need to acquire an upper secondary degree, as the students enrolled in adult education often carry with them experiences of former education connected to e.g. failure, bullying or academic and social marginalization. In the context of adult education, there seems to be two different overarching master-narratives: the centers' own narratives and the vernacular narratives about the centers. The common institutional narrative is that the centers offer students the opportunity to grow and develop in both academic and personal ways with high academic standards and well-educated teachers. The adult centers' dominant narratives are explicit and coherent and position the institutions as responsible, caring and professional. The vernacular narratives, on the other hand, shared by many students and the population in general, identify the centers as academic "parking-lots" and hang-outs for people with different problems and without motivation and effort in their own lives (Piekut, 2017). Students at the center must navigate between the institutions' master-narratives of "prosperity" and the detrimental vernacular narratives of "waste". Navigating in this educational landscape seems complicated for Abir, Faisal and Selma who are aiming for an upper secondary degree. All of them have experiences with migration; Faisal coming to Denmark as a young adult, whereas both Abir and Selma followed the Danish compulsory education program from year 0.

The method – the narrative interview

The student participants' educational narratives are part of a larger study on narratives in and about adult education. The background data for this study derives from four different adult centers in Denmark and consists of observations of L2 courses (about 30 hours over the academic year 2015–2016), semi-structured interviews with the teachers of the courses and informal talks with the students. As this is background data, guiding and informing my key data, the narrative interviews with three L2 students at one adult education center in a large Danish town, the background data also serves as implicit "thick description" (Geertz, 1973). Thick description highlights the importance of understanding the educational narratives as embedded in specialized and contextual institutional cultures. While the interviews were taken during the students' one-year L2 course, I had three in-depth interviews (Alheit, 1984; Alheit & Dausien, 2006; Horsdal, 2012) with each of them, supplemented with informal talks and text messages about e.g. exams. The duration of each interview was about one hour. By approaching the participants in a narrative interview, the methodology is interactional and understood as a dynamic co-construction of these narratives (Bamberg, 2011; Clandinin, 2007; Horsdal 2012; Mishler, 1999). Employing the narrative interview in research, Horsdal (2012) accentuates the interpersonal interaction and points to the attentive and responsive co-construction of meaning in the interview. As such, the interviewer is part of the meaning-making process, as both the interviewer and the interviewee collaboratively construct narratives in the narrative encounter. Gubrium and Holstein also accentuate the interactional aspect of narration:

> The theme and content of a story cannot be divorced from its interactional development and the ongoing construction of meaningful contexts. [...] who do we know who owns a story? Perhaps a text does, or the interaction or situation from which a story emerges.
>
> *(2009, p. 107)*

Following this line of thinking, we can't analyze the students' narratives as isolated phenomena, but must take the context and situation into account.

Mishler (1999) also emphasizes the narrative interview as a dialogical meaning-negotiating process and a way to perform identities. This accentuates the importance of aspects of identities and positioning in the students' educational narratives: how do they confirm, contest or relate to master-narratives of education in their own storied life? In the interviews, the three students reveal individual, group and institutional aspects that shape their experience with the adult center. That encouraged the theoretical approach to studying "otherness" in relation to the concept of master and counter-narratives, since aspects of "otherness" and "othering" were prevalent in the interviews.

The theoretical framework: master and counter-narratives and "otherness"

Master and counter-narratives

As the concept of master and counter-narratives in an educational setting calls for definitions and explanations, I want to direct attention to an important and fundamental concept, namely that counter-narratives are a means for resisting socially and culturally-informed master-narratives, often oppressive or excluding experiences that diverge from those conveyed through master-narratives (Amah, 2012; Harper, 2009; Matias, 2013; Solórzano & Yosso, 2002; Stanley, 2007). In this perspective, counter- or challenging narratives play a role in how students identify themselves as same, different or "othered" regarding the ideologies or values of master-narratives. Master-narratives as "majoritarian stories" (Solórzano & Yosso, 2002, p. 28) are in that perception characterized by conforming to a dominant, national and non-migrant Dane perspective on education and subject choice, thereby supporting master-narratives as a "script that specifies and controls how some social processes are carried out" (Stanley, 2007, p. 14). Characteristics not conforming to "majoritarian stories" are at risk of being defined as different, deviant or even defiant and as such "othered". Counter-narratives refer to "the stories which people tell and live, which offer resistance, either implicitly or explicitly, to dominant cultural narratives" (Andrews, 2004, p. 1). Solórzano and Yosso (2002) point to counter-narratives as tools for resisting "deficit" stories and thereby challenging racism, for instance. In education, counter-narratives can potentially expose institutional prejudices that disadvantage students of a minority group.

But what are counter-narratives countering? Matti Hyvärinen (2008) suggests that counter-narratives are *tellable*, thereby not simply recounting the normal or expected like the cultural script – the master-narratives – they are connected too. Following Hyvärinen, master-narratives are not tellable as they are tacit cultural conventions we are embedded in as they embody (implicit) expectations about how to act and value people and circumstances. That may be true in many contexts. In adult education, though, the master-narratives about the institution and about the subjects are more rather than less explicit and "told". In adult education, the students' counter-narratives make visible the majoritarian stories, cultural scripts or master-narratives of the institution by giving voice to minoritized experiences and explanations and in doing so deconstructing and challenging the dominant narrative (Howard, 2008; Piekut, 2017). As such, master and counter-narratives are relational concepts. The countering of a dominant master narrative makes the framework or the tacit understanding of the "master narrative" visible (Lundholt, Aagaard & Piekut, 2018).

Other, otherness and othering

Even though there are noticeable differences between attributing or adopting a presumably stable position in the noun "otherness" in relation to actively doing or being exposed to "othering" as a process of alienation or deviation, I will theorize the concept of otherness and othering as interconnected. However, in the analyses of the narratives of education I will distinguish between otherness and othering.

There are different definitions and approaches to the concept of otherness and I will briefly present some of them in the following. Fludernik (2007, p. 260) points to postcolonial studies showing important connections between identity and "alterity" (or otherness) as difference or deviation from cultural or societal norms that are constitutive of storytelling. Bakhtin's notion of otherness is tied to a philosophical understanding of *aesthetic empathizing* and to communication and the dialogical principal: all utterances between people emerge in an "I-thou" relation in a dialogic environment (Riessman, 2008). All utterances are saturated with meaning and ideologies from past, present and future communicative practices. Bakhtin writes that aesthetic empathizing is an act of

> empathizing into an individual object of seeing – seeing it from inside in its own essence. This moment of empathizing is always followed by the moment of objectification, that is, a placing outside oneself of the individuality understood through empathizing, a separating of it from oneself, a return into oneself.
>
> *(1993, p. 14)*

Bakhtin understands aesthetic empathizing as a space (in a metaphorical sense) where an individual empathizes with another individual and in doing so comprehends the self through the backdrop of others. That comprehension doesn't exist outside empathizing, or seeing the other as an individual, as active empathy simultaneously requires a turn toward the other and back to the self. Through that activity, we can enter into an alternative understanding. In a Bakhtinian sense, in interaction with others we can consciously understand the experience of others and in doing so contribute to an expansion or new comprehension of our own experience. The same interaction between our own and others' words is seen in Bakhtin's idea of communication:

> Our speech, that is, all our utterances (including our creative works), is filled with others' words, varying degrees of otherness or varying degrees of "our-own-ness" ... These words of others carry with them their own expression, their own evaluative tone, which we assimilate, rework, and re-accentuate.
>
> *(Bakhtin, 1986, p. 89)*

The reworking and re-accentuating of the words of others is an objective that is interesting to pursue in the analysis of the narratives of education, as it seems that the representation of the words of others are not only reworked or re-accentuated, but at times also misinterpreted and even distorted while not empathizing, accepting or understanding the interaction with an other.

In Dervin (2016), othering is described as discourses in which people or groups are hierarchically marginalized and discriminated by using stereotypes and prejudices against them. The concept of identity is closely related to the idea of othering. Identity markers such as nationality, race, language, religion etc. as essentializing identities restrict the other from representing him or herself, as these identity markers create boundaries between different and same, being inside or outside or being superior or inferior. As such, the concept is closely linked to power and knowledge, as the other is often described through a deficit understanding, thereby stereotyping the other as inferior. Dervin also describes processes of self-othering as "... *a way of defending oneself, claiming authority, and even asking for special rights – which is not always a good thing, especially if other rights are violated*" (2016: 46). As self-othering seems to be an important perspective in the student participants' narratives of education, I will pursue this concept in the following analysis. Since the students both express individual and group identification regarding ethnicity, subject and education, Powell and Menendian's (2016) definition of group identities seems important to accentuate, as they define group "othering" as: "... *a set of dynamics, processes, and structures that engender marginality and persist inequality across any of the full range of human differences based on group identities*" (2016, p. 17). In Powell and Menendian, othering is seen as an enduring and systematically (oppressive) attribution, based on group identity and belonging.

Othering seems to be a broad yet cogent term, pointing to a restrictive and exclusionary view of groups or persons with an immigration history, for instance. The term also implicitly addresses the opposite of its meaning, namely "belonging". Belonging and othering are closely connected to identity, being insider/outsider, same/different and to power structures in society and institutions. "Othering" points to fundamental perceptions of inclusion and exclusion and is often part of master or counter-narratives that segregate groups of students as part of an ethnocentric normative view. As such the concept can enter into a close dialogue with the idea of master and counter-narratives.

Abir, Faisal and Salma: the three student participants

All three participants, Abir, Faisal and Salma are pursuing an upper secondary degree and are enrolled in the same L2 course as part of their education. All of them had previously registered in different Danish (as L1) subjects and had problematic experiences with "the regular subject", as they call it. The L2 subject is formally an equivalent but alternative to the L1 (Danish) subject, and all students in the L2 course are, as mentioned, migrant students.

Abir was 19 when I met her, coming to Denmark from Iraq as a two-year-old and going to Danish Kindergarten and public school until year 10. Then, she went to a vocational training center, but could not find the required internship and had to interrupt her education. Growing up in a multicultural area in a larger Danish town, she moved into an apartment with some friends as she enrolled in the adult education center. At the center, she was assigned to the L2 course as her academic outcomes in the subject of Danish were not sufficient for Danish as L1.

Faisal was 22 and came from Afghanistan to Denmark with his parents and siblings four years before the interviews. Throughout his childhood and youth, he moved back and forth from Afghanistan to Pakistan, due to more qualifying educational opportunities in Pakistan. After completing the compulsory language school in Denmark with the highest marks, he had to enroll on the L2 course for an upper secondary degree. He lives in his own apartment, close to his parents and siblings.

Salma was also 19 when I met her and came from Iraq at age six together with her family. They moved between different cities in Denmark until Salma was in year 6, when they moved and stayed in a larger Danish town. She went to public school until year 10 and, like Abir, she went to vocational training to be a dental assistant but was not able to get an internship and had to interrupt her education. As a transfer, and waiting to turn 18 to enroll in adult education, she went to a production school. After an unsuccessful Danish as L1 course, she enrolled in the L2 course at the adult center.

Abir, Faisal and Salma – master and counter-narratives of othering and belonging

In the following analysis of the three student participants' narratives of education, it is crucial to emphasize that the L2 subject is designed to meet the needs of migrant Danish-speaking students but at the same time is criticized for not being able to notably qualify 1st or 2nd generation immigrants' or refugees' academic skills. In the narratives of being a student in a L2 course, the inherent and often tacit institutional prejudices based on ethnicity and language seem to become more visible. The dynamics of othering and belonging and master and counter-narratives uncover the relationship between identity, education and ethnicity in the context of adult education and the L2 subject.

Abir and public school

Abir went to adult education and enrolled in L2 as she couldn't find an internship for her education as a neurophysiological assistant at a vocational training center. In general, she is content with taking an upper secondary degree at an adult center because "*it is my future*", as she stated it. When restorying her childhood experiences with public school, she positions herself as a "foreigner" living in a multicultural area and visiting a school that differed from other schools in the same city regarding socioeconomic background and ethnicity, since "*there where almost only foreigners in my school*". Asked about the L1 subject in her public school, she tells: "*... there was a lot of disturbance in the classroom ... our teachers were far too nice ... our Danish teacher never scolded us for not doing our homework or assignments. And he never called my parents. [...]*" At the same time, she highlights the enjoyable social aspect of her public school. In her childhood restorying, the aspect of feeling different and othered by visiting a multicultural school is prevalent, as is the teachers' laissez faire approach to children belonging to an ethnic minority. There are no academic expectations or motivation, and the "far too nice" teachers enter into a dialogue with a master narrative of the relation between academic deficiency and ethnicity (Holmen, 2008; Holmen, 2011; Piekut, 2017). The mandatory two-week internship in year 8 as part of the pupils' study preparation becomes an adverse landmark event regarding othering for Abir. Abir recounts the school counsellor at public school referring Abir and her year group to vocational training, as: "*[...] she didn't find us suitable for upper secondary...*" Asking the counsellor for a reason, she stated: "*Because brown eyes are not the same as blue eyes*". By narrating her experiences from public school, the ethnic perspective at her school is highlighted, positioning Abir and the pupils as academic low achievers and inferior compared to the majority of non-migrant pupils. Accounts of positioning minorities or ethnically diverse groups as low achievers and without academic expectations (Amah, 2012; Harper, 2009; Matias, 2013; Solórzano & Yosso, 2002) seems to be an implicit cultural script or master narrative, including in the Danish school system. The pupils' attempts to contest the implicit master narrative by asking why they were not "suitable" for upper secondary can be understood as a counter-narrating strategy, resisting this "deficit" story. As a complex part of this, Abir identifies with being a "foreigner" and being an other as part of a minority, but rejects being othered by the school's counsellor. Being a foreigner and thereby an other for Abir is intrinsically related to belonging to a minority and enjoying the social life in school. The school counsellors' "evaluative tone" distorts the perspective of the other (Bakhtin, 1986), thereby authoritatively reworking a master narrative of deficiency. The counsellor's essentializing of ethnicity as a marker for academic outcomes restricts the other from representing herself (Dervin, 2016) or raising an "owned" voice against marginalization and exclusion. Othering and implicit master-narratives of ethnocentric normativity are at play in Abirs' restorying of public school experiences.

Abir – L2 in adult education

In describing the L2 course in adult education, the clashing of contrasting narratives is prevalent. On the one hand, Abir resists the culturally-informed, oppressive narrative about L2 students as "inferior" and lacking academic skills by underlining that "*Upper secondary is the right choice. And I am learning a lot in the L2 class*". On the other hand, she recognizes the dominant narratives about adult education and L2 as an academic hang-out for "unfit" immigrants taking a substandard exam compared to the Danish as a first language subject. All three students refer to vicarious – but incorrect – small stories about being rejected at universities because of an exam based on Danish as second language. Enrolling in an L2 course calls for explanations: "*You always have to argue for why you are enrolling in L2 and not a standard course to friends and some family members*" (Piekut, 2017). Abir talks about "*us in the L2 course*" as a temporary shared majority in an otherwise non-migrant Danish environment. The aspect of othering appears in different ways in Abir's narrative about education; she identifies herself as different from her Danish friends, but not alienated. She has a feeling of belonging to some of her peers in the L2 course and with her family, referring to them as an ethnic "us" in the interviews. The othering seems to be tied to the L2 course in an ambivalent way; Abir's friends who share the same migrant background and the more distant family advise against L2 courses: "*You won't learn anything if you are in a course with only foreigners*", and "*why do you want to join the L2 course? You are speaking normal Danish*". Enrolling in the course seems to confirm an ethnic and academic otherness, approving the master narrative about the course as inferior and adversely different from other courses at the centers. The ambivalent aspect of othering and being othered points to its counterpart in Abir's narrative of education, namely belonging. Abir follows the same educational trajectory as her older brothers. They too started in upper secondary, dropped out, enrolled in adult education and unsuccessfully in L1 and thereafter in L2 and are now successfully studying at universities. Linde (2009) talks about "narrative induction" when an existing set of stories are relevant to the shaping of one's own story. Abir belongs to the same "learning career" track (Merill & West, 2009) as her brothers: "*Yeah, you have to go that way and then eventually learn what you want to do*" and is narratively inducted by their learning career.

Abir actively engages in her education, rejecting or challenging processes of othering, but identifying as other in an educational context. But being "other" is not paramount in Abir's life; asked about her imagined future three years from now she replies: "*In three years … maybe I am taking further education. Maybe I am married and have kids. I want to be a nurse*". Abir doesn't construct an imagined future based on ethnicity and inequality, she claims the same possibilities and capabilities for education and family life as the majority of young people in Denmark. She and her roommates "*talk a lot about education, the future and so on ... what we want to become*". Belonging to a minority and identifying as an ethnic other in education is not incompatible with an academic and personally fulfilling career. Abir's self-othering in the L2 subject is closely connected to belonging to an other minority. Resisting the institutional othering is combined with countering a master narrative of academic deficiencies, but at the same time allowing the adult centers' master narrative of prosperity to resonate in her narrative of education.

Faisal's narrative of education

In the interviews, Faisal rejects being identified as ethnically different and thereby othered. Faisal is in his early twenties and came from Afghanistan to Denmark with his parents and siblings four years before the interviews. He had no option but to enroll in the L2 course. Like Abir, he acknowledges the learning potential of the course, but is disappointed in being referred to a course "with only foreigners". As he quotes: "*We as foreigners don't want to enroll in the L2 course. We want to be together with Danes*". In the interviews, Faisal positions himself as different from his ethnic peers due to his academic abilities:

> I almost always get 12 [highest grade in Denmark, author]. In language school I made a presentation on LEGO [for the final exam]. I had 34 slides, whereas the others had maybe five. When time was gone I still had 4–5 slides to go, but the examiner told me: "what are you doing here?". He said it outright! "This is not your place – you have to move on, to university and such...". That was so motivating.

Faisal is partially confirming the vernacular narrative about the centers as an academic hangout. Even though his migrant background and being part of an ethnic minority makes him the "same" as his peers in the L2 course, he identifies as different and constructs a self-othering narrative in relation to his peers, defending his identity as a student and claiming academic authority: "*... the students in my course where about 30 or 40 years old and had no educational basis. I felt I was wasting my time, taking L2 at the lower secondary level*". He feels othered through the L2 course and he is othering himself in relation to the uneducated, older peers in the L2 secondary course. In the interviews, he is persistent in recognizing himself and being recognized – as an academically interested "learner", deserting ethnicity as an identity marker. As part of that productive identity, he repeatedly uses metaphors and sayings about movement and change as part of his educational trajectories. On being referred to L2, instead of L1 as he applied to, he says: "*I know I have to push myself ... I would have moved on being in the normal subject [L1]. You have to push yourself or you will be stuck*". Faisal counters the vernacular narrative of the centers as an academic "parking lot" and "waste", not by rejecting the narrative, but by installing personal agency and will as part of his narrative. Following Bakhtin's notion of aesthetic empathizing, Faisal is empathizing into the others in the L2 course, placing himself outside his individuality and returning back into himself with an alternative or extended understanding of both himself in the L2 course and the others: agency and persistence are key for your future exam, and overrule ethnicity and difference, at least theoretically.

But acknowledging agency and academic potential in his narrative involves difficulties as the L2 course and the centers are embedded in dominant cultural narratives about ethnicity and academic ability. But neither the aspect of othering nor the concept of master and counter-narratives is unequivocal in Faisal's narrative. He is countering the detrimental perspective of the L2 subject at lower secondary when talking about L2 at upper secondary level:

> I am learning a lot there [the L2 course], but it is a problem for the teacher that there are 25–30 students in the course. The others have lived in Denmark maybe 10–20 years, and some were even born here. [...] The language level varies a lot.

As Faisal conceals that he is taking his upper secondary degree at an adult center from friends and distant family, because it is linked to disgrace, he underlines his position as a student taking an upper secondary degree – "same" as other students. Being aware of processes of othering, the articulation of his otherness is not unambiguous in his educational path. Regarding the basic vocational course that he passed with honors before taking his upper secondary at the adult center, he states "*It was easy. At the basic vocational course, I learned a lot... in the whole class I was the only one with black hair. That was good because I've learned the language*". Being an other is not the same as being othered, on the contrary, being an other in a homogeneous context leads to learning at a fast pace for Faisal, adding coherence to his narrative of education.

Salma – in and between L2

As for Salma, she was 19 when I met her for the interviews. She came to Denmark from Iraq at six years old. She lives in an apartment with her older sister in a large Danish town. Her parents and younger siblings live nearby the apartment. In the interviews, she repeats that she went to "normal schools" (her words) in Denmark and refers to herself as an "immigrant". After an unsuccessful Danish as L1 course at the adult center, she enrolled voluntarily in the L2 course:

> I choose the L2 course ... as it doesn't influence my education later on? Some people say it does mean a lot when there is an L2 course on your examination paper... well, what it tells about me is that I do have an ethnic background, so never mind!

She is identifying herself as a participant in the L2 course and as such part of an ethnically diverse group, "same" as the others in the group. She counters the deficiency narrative of the L2 course and accentuates that the course meets her needs. Only in the aforementioned L1 course, she felt different as the only migrant student; at the same time, the identification as different is connected to learning at a fast pace in the L1 course, but nevertheless not succeeding in taking the final exam. In the quote, she is articulating a widespread (but incorrect) assumption about the disqualifying aspect of having L2 as your subject on the upper secondary certificate. All three students mentioned that they heard vicarious stories about the L2 subject being inferior to L1 on their certificate, but they were uncertain about the truth of it. It seems that master scripts or master-narratives about minorities, ethnicity and education outcomes defies, or at least suspends, reason. Even though Salma is uncertain about the formal status of L2, she is pleased to be taking classes at the adult center:

> It is a really cool school. I'm happy being here. The teachers are really nice and even though I am young, I feel comfortable with many of the older students. My way of thinking is probably more mature than many other 19-year-olds.

Salma is not governed by the vernacular narratives about the centers. She acknowledges the academic and social conditions at the centers. But being in the context of adult education and L2, you have to navigate the powerful master-narratives and Salma, too, is surrounded by culturally dominant narratives about the L2 course:

> A lot of people think you shouldn't take the L2 course. It is linked to failure. Some girls don't tell that they are in the L2 course ... they just mention taking the subject Danish. Some brag about taking Danish but end up with the grade D ... it is kind of a competition.

The competition about succeeding in the L2 courses or keeping your enrolment in it a secret seems to favor two different aspects of othering. Competing by succeeding in L2 in spite of being an other is a countering endeavor for academic appreciation, simultaneously implicitly and discursively constructing the master narrative about L2 as a course for academically underprivileged minorities. The concealment about being in the course seems to be another way out of essentializing identities as part of othering. Bakhtin's (1986; 1993) notion of the interaction between one's own and others' words, assuming that all utterances are filled with others' words, is profound here: to defy the demeaning words of others, expressed in master-narratives about L2 as a substandard course, some students defend themselves against the evaluative and harmful words by competing in or concealing being an L2 student. Salma is putting her own positioning in perspective by distancing herself from both competing and concealing. She is not identifying herself as othered but recounts her experiences with ethnicity as being different in a Danish context, and the same in an ethnically diverse context. She faces other personal and educational problems, as in the last interview she is in doubt about finishing her upper secondary degree.

The students' narratives of education – a brief outline

As for many of the L2 students, Abir, Faisal and Salma's educational paths are neither linear nor smooth. Being in transition in and between educational contexts, the renegotiations of identities seem to be linked to both ethnicity and the degree of affiliation with the subjects and centers. Migrant Danish students seem to have different opportunities and constraints afforded to them regarding L2 compared to non-migrant students as master-narratives about the course are linked to disadvantages and yet meeting the needs of bilingual students. As a minority, the students experience a greater pressure to take a position on their ethnic identity and belonging, and they meet structural barriers such as forced enrolment in the L2 course, for instance. For Abir, processes of "othering" are answered with counter-narratives on both academic inferiority and ethnic group identification labels. Faisal dynamically rejects being identified by ethnicity and thereby "othered"; he sees himself as an academically interested student but is met with setbacks when he involves himself with (too) much engagement in his educational path. He both confirms master-narratives about the L2 course and counters aspects of the narratives by not accepting that ethnicity is an unequivocally internalized identity. Salma feels serene regarding the meaning of ethnicity in her life. She identifies in terms of "belonging" to a minority and feeling "othered" from a majority perspective; the othering is at the same time tied to acknowledgeable disciplinary learning, making the emotional aspects of othering ambivalent. She counters the narrative of L2 as inferior but expresses frustration about the course being slow.

Othering and the concept of master and counter-narratives

What does the concept of othering provide to the concept of counter- and master-narratives? First, it seems that the two concepts are intertwined in several ways. Othering can be an ambiguous affair since it sometimes implies its opposite, namely belonging, but the relational aspect between othering and belonging is not as unequivocal as it is for master and counter-narratives. The ambiguity also counts for the marginalizing aspects of othering, since being an "other" is not by definition as much a part of marginalization or essentializing as "othering" is;

being an "other" in the perspective of Bakhtin's (1993) aesthetic empathizing can potentially be liberating, comprehending both the self and the other, while "othering" as part of marginalizing individuals or groups weakens the empathy and understanding of those being othered. The same counts for master-narratives. Master-narratives of "deficient students" or master-narratives of excluded minorities can be resisted by counter-narratives, renegotiating and critically evaluating the oppressive cultural script. Both processes of othering and master-narratives can be linked to reproduction of power structures in society, thereby marginalizing minority groups and individuals. As an aspect where the two concepts differ, othering is part of a more explicit moral or social judgment, pointing to inferiority or difference, while master-narratives often appear more tacit or implicit, pointing to a majoritarian perspective. Master-narratives are overarching cultural scripts with including or excluding characteristics, where otherness or othering can take different paths in the overriding (master) narratives. Othering can be part of master or counter-narratives but doesn't have to be. Not all master-narratives are predictably oppressive, but all processes of othering are. As othering can be part of oppressive master-narratives, belonging can be part of counter-narratives.

As a rationale for this chapter was to understand how ethnic identity refers to individual and group identity and education, an interesting launchpad was to explore the relationship to and between otherness and master and counter-narratives. In the narratives of the students, we come closer to a sense of clarity regarding ethnicity and belonging to a minority in their educational life. And it seems evident that belonging to an ethnic group or minority is not tantamount to ethnic identity, as we can see in Faisal's narrative. It seems that the students' narratives of education reveal links between othering and master and counter-narratives, especially the power to connect processes of othering to master-narratives and belonging to countering narratives. But this relationship does not emerge as a clear-cut dichotomy, as self-othering can be part of counter-narratives and belonging can appear as an aspect of being part of an "othered" minority, as we see in Salma's narrative. The complexity between the two concepts is rich and encourages further inquiry.

As othering is a broad term in the way it seems to embrace structural dynamics, identifications and exclusions in both individuals and groups, "belonging" seems to be a productive counterpart to othering: belonging in a minority group as Abir and Salma or as part of a dynamic identity in a community of "learners" as Faisal. The students' narratives of education and the L2 course expose hegemonic power structures; the countering of master-narratives seems to question the assumption (or the master narrative) that education is the most important social equalizing agent, as processes of othering in adult education orchestrate socio-cultural disparity and contribute to inequality and ethnocentric normativity.

The students' counter-narratives seem to foster variance and subjectivity in relation to otherness. Counter-narratives have the potential to be a means of empowerment and inclusion, giving voice to individualized versions of the all-ethnic or detrimental narratives of the L2 course. The students' counter-narratives and narratives of otherness can have both a stabilizing and destabilizing aspect, depending on a variety of contextual affordances and constraints. Generating counter-narratives of inclusion could potentially reframe the L2 course, claiming the possibility of multiple identities other than ethnicity as an essentializing agent.

References

Alheit, P. (1984). *Das narrative Interview*. Eine Instruktion für "Anfänger". Arbeitspapiere des Forschungsprojekts "Arbeiterbiographien", 8, Bremen: Universität Bremen.

Alheit, P., & Dausien, B. (2006). Biographieforschung in der Erwachsenenbildung. In H.H. Krüger & W. Marotzki (Eds.), *Handbuch Erziehungswissenschaftliche Biographieforschung*. Wiesbaden: VS Verlag für Sozialwissenschaften.

Amah, I.A. (2012). Counter-narratives of non-high performing African American students. *International Review of Qualitative Research*, 5 (2), 225–250.

Andrews, M. (2004). Counter-narratives and the power to oppose. In M. Bamberg & M. Andrews (eds.), *Considering counter-narratives. Narrating, resisting, making sense* (pp. 1–7). Amsterdam: John Benjamins.

Bakhtin, M.M. (1993). Toward a philosophy of the act. In Liapunov V. & Holquist M. (eds.) *Toward a philosophy of the act*. Austin: University of Texas Press.

Bakhtin, M.M. (1986). The problem of speech genres. In Emerson, C. & Holquist M. (eds.) *Speech genres and other late essays*. Austin: University of Texas Press.

Bamberg, M. (2011) Who am I? Narration and its contribution to self and identity. *Theory & Psychology*, 21 (1), 3–24.

Clandinin, D.J. (Ed.) (2007). *Handbook of narrative inquiry: Mapping a methodology*. London: SAGE Publications.

Dervin, F. (2016). *Interculturality in education. A theoretical and methodological toolbox*. Palgrave Macmillan UK: London.

Fludernik, M. (2007). Identity/alterity. In Herman. D. (eds.) *The Cambridge companion to narrative*. New York: Cambridge University Press.

Geertz, C. (1973), *The interpretation of cultures*. New York: Basic Books, Inc., Publishers.

Gubrium J.F. & Holstein J.A. (2009). *Analyzing narrative reality*. SAGE UK: London.

Harper, S.R. (2009). Niggers no more: A critical race counternarrative on Black male student achievement at predominantly White colleges and universities. *International Journal of Qualitative Studies in Education*, 2(6).

Holmen, A. (2008). Dansk som andetsprog i den flerkulturelle skole. *Cursiv*, 2, 59–76. Aarhus: Aarhus Universitet.

Holmen, A. (2011). Den gode gartner og ukrudtet – Om minoritetselever I grundskolens danskfag. In C. Haas, C. Holmen, A., Horts, C. & Bergthóra, K. (Eds.), *Ret til dansk – uddannelse, sprog og kulturarv*. Aarhus: Aarhus Universitetsforlag.

Horsdal, M. (2012). *Telling lives. Exploring dimensions of narratives*. Routledge: New York.

Howard, T.C. (2008). The disenfranchisement of African American males in prek-12 schools: a critical race theory perspective. *Teachers College Record*, 110(5), 954–985.

Hyvärinen, M. (2008). Narrative form and narrative content. In Järventie I. & Lähde, M. (eds.) *Methodological challenges in childhood and family research*, Tampere University Press, Childhood and Family Research Unit Net Series Finland: Tampere.

Linde, C. (2009). *Working the past. Narrative and institutional memory*. New York: Oxford University UK: London.

Lundholt, M., Aagaard, C.M., & Piekut, A. (2018) Counter-narratives. In L. Heath & W. Johansen (Eds.), *The international encyclopedia of strategic communication*. Wiley: Boston.

Matias, C.E. (2013). Who you callin' white?! A critical counter-story on colouring identity. *Race Ethnicity and Education*, 16(3), 291–315.

Merill, B., & West, L. (2009). *Using biographical methods in social research*. London: SAGE Publishing.

Mishler, E.G. (1999). *Storylines. Craftartists' narratives of identity*. Cambridge: Harvard University Press.

Piekut, A. (2017). "Brown eyes are not the same as blue eyes". Educational narratives, identities and positioning in adult education in Denmark. *Narrative Inquiry*, 27(2), 378–397.

Powell, J.A. & Menendian, S. (2016). The problem of othering: towards inclusiveness and belonging. In *Othering & Belonging. Expanding the Circle of Human Concern*, Issue 1. Berkeley: Haas Institute for a Fair and Inclusive Society at the University of California.

Riessman, C.K. (2008). *Narrative methods for the human sciences*. Sage: Thousand Oaks.

Solórzano, D.G., & Yosso, T.J. (2002). Critical race methodology: Counter-storytelling as an analytical framework for educational research. *Qualitative Inquiry*, 8(1), 23–44.

Stanley, C.A. (2007). When counter-narratives meet master-narratives in the journal editorial-review process. *Educational Researcher*, 36(1), 14–24.

27

The functions of master and counter-narratives in biographical interviews

Self-positionings of German-Iranians in relation to discourses on self-optimization and migration

Niels Uhlendorf

Introduction

Individuals use master and counter narratives in biographical interviews to present themselves in relation to predominant discourses and social norms. The purpose of this chapter is to frame this topic theoretically and to outline one approach to empirical analysis using the example of a discourse on self-optimization in the context of migration. This involves a master narrative, in which migrants are expected to work extensively on themselves in order to be included in the host society, and despite the existence of structural discrimination, it suggests the promise of advancement through outstanding performance. On the other hand, the counter narrative questions this implicit promise, suggesting that it is an illusion. Therefore, the question arises as to *how* the master and counter narratives are used in biographical interviews to construct a sense of self. To answer this question, the results of a study will be presented, in which public representations of, and biographical interviews with German-Iranians were examined. Based on the analysis of this interrelationship, two ideal types of self-positionings are contrasted: an affirmation of the master narrative in contrast to an orientation towards the counter narrative. The conclusion presents a critical reflection on the power of optimization discourse, factors affecting the emergence of counter narratives in biographical self-presentations, and methodological strategies to capture the interrelations between public narratives and practices of biographical self-exploration.

Biography and narrative

Sociolinguistic theories conceive of narratives as a means of self-exploration. They serve to interpret biographical experiences and to create coherence among heterogeneous memories (Labov &

Waletzky, 1967; Schütze, 2016). The notion of coherence, however, has been criticized because it tends to reduce the performative, processual, fluid, and sometimes contradictory character of self and identity. Hence, some scholars claim one needs to pay more attention to the "constructions of self and identity as necessarily dialogical and relational, fashioned and refashioned in local interactive practices" (Bamberg, 2014, p. 140). Nevertheless, narratives are frequently used to make sense of different identity fragments and to offer presentations of the self and others. They are conceived as "rhetorical tools" to appear to be "intelligible" within a social environment.

In a set of unconscious processes, such narratives become part of the "fabric of memory" (Freeman, 2004, p. 289), which is influenced, to a great extent, by collective discourses (Bogner & Rosenthal, 2017). As Hahn (1998) pointed out, biographies and the practices of self-narration are structured by common discursive patterns in a specific historical-cultural setting. Individuals do not talk about themselves in a certain fashion because of natural instinct, but because ways of talking about oneself have been institutionalized in a given cultural context. In such processes, different institutions can have a considerable influence on the way we perceive ourselves in relation to others. Hahn coined the term "biography generators" for such "socially institutionalized devices that generate special kinds of discourse [...] where the main topic is the biography of at least one of the participants" (Hahn, 1998, p. 27). For example, speaking to a psychoanalytic therapist or confessing one's sins in the Christian Church generated specific patterns of talking about oneself. Hence, biographical identity (and the process of constructing one) is based on "historically and culturally varying forms of biography-generators" (ibid.), while individuals in complex societies are confronted with the challenge of creating different biographies for themselves:

> These biographies must be synchronized from time to time when incompatibilities and disturbances develop. The acts and motivations that enter these partial biographies depend on the criteria relevant to the sphere of life to which the individual is to be coordinated. The biography that is reconstructed from someone's medical history is based on factors that differ from those in the dossier representing the individual's vita before an employer [...].
>
> *(Hahn, 1998, p. 48)*

A similar argument was made by poststructuralists who emphasized the plurality of voices in every biography. People use a heterogeneous set of narratives and discourses to describe and interpret themselves and to make their experiences plausible to an (imagined) audience. From this perspective, a biographical narrative is always embedded in a variety of storylines, which are accessible and dominant in their cultural contexts. Consciously and unconsciously, individuals develop patterns and strategies to adopt predominant master-narratives or to use and further develop counter narratives and alternative interpretations of reality. Therefore, it seems helpful to take a deeper look into the theoretical implications of master and counter narratives in relation to biographies.

Master and counter narratives in biographies

Bamberg described two ideal types of narratives: *master-narratives*, which can be understood in two possible ways: (a) as a narrative that delineates how narrators position themselves with their story; and (b) predominant cultural narratives that tend to offer "frames according to which courses of events can easily be plotted, simply because one's audience is taken to 'know' and accept these courses" (Bamberg, 2004, p. 360). They give guidance and direction, and they tend to "structure how the world is intelligible" (ibid., p. 361). Master-narratives, in this second sense, tend to use heuristic ideas of "normal" or "natural" constructs. They may also conceal power relations and reproduce ideologies by offering what Bourdieu called an "illusio," i.e., discursive promises whereby individuals are "taken in and by the game" (Bourdieu & Wacquant, 1992, p. 210) in a hegemonically structured social field. Legitimizing and sometimes enchanting illusions within master-narratives may encourage the strong engagement of individuals, despite experiences of discrimination or unequal treatment.

A *counter narrative*, in contrast, criticizes, deconstructs, or challenges the normative structure of master-narratives with the objective of "emancipat[ing] individuals from what has been socially regulated and thus assumed 'natural' or 'normal'" (Martínez-Alemán et al., 2015, p. 8). It is related to hegemonic structures, and it may refer to individual and collective experiences with the power of normalizing ascriptions. While one of the key functions of master-narratives is to offer a way of identifying "what is assumed to be a normative experience" (Andrews, 2004, p. 1), the main function of a counter narrative in biographical self-descriptions is to deal and cope with non-normative experiences. Phoenix (2010) offers different examples in her study on identity claims by adults who attempted to make sense of apparently non-normative childhood experiences (e.g., being deprived of their parents or living in poverty). The participants described how they experienced powerful norms of what is discursively constructed as an "unbearable" or "unintelligible" biography. However, they reclaimed agency in the narrative process in an "attempt to craft liveable lives for themselves" (Phoenix, 2019, p. 2324).

While master and counter narratives serve as vocabularies for ideal types, Bamberg also emphasized that individuals in everyday life continuously oscillate between them (Bamberg, 2004, p. 364). He proposed the term "small stories" to look at the way in which people manage to link competing and sometimes contradictory narrative segments. Such acts entail people positioning themselves in relation to others and, in doing so they "'produce' one another (and themselves) situationally as 'social beings'" (Bamberg, 1997, p. 336). The narratives are usually developed by powerful discursive practices (e.g., in public media or scientific journals). In this process, subject models are constructed (e.g., idealistic heroes or damnable antagonists) and identified with certain collectives (e.g., migrants, non-migrants, occupational groups, political movements, and their members). Individuals, in turn, use such models when they interpret themselves and assume their own subjectivity. Judith Butler described this process as an interplay of interpellation and subjection (or subjectification). *Interpellation* means to be addressed, hailed, or named as a subject within an ideology, a discourse, or a knowledge regime. It can imply being confronted with different "legitimate" and "illegitimate" subject models (Butler, 1997). *Subjection* describes the act of processing these interpellations and appropriating subject positions. Therefore, "[s]ubjection consists precisely in this fundamental dependency on a discourse we never chose but that, paradoxically, initiates and sustains our agency" (ibid., p. 2). Individuals use existing subject models from discourses in order to be able to describe or explain themselves within a social sphere, as Hall (1995) argued: "You only discover who you are because of the identities you are required to take on, into which you are interpellated: but you must take up those positionalities, however temporarily, in order to act at all " (p. 65). In this context, Butler also described the power of discourse when people only find a limited number of identifications and possible ways of constructing a self (e.g., only two genders). According to that perspective, we are

> living in a world of categories and descriptions way before we start to sort them critically and endeavor to change or make them on our own. In this way we are [...] vulnerable to, and affected by, discourses we never chose.
>
> *(Butler, 2016, p. 24)*

However, as Butler argued, subject models are not only adopted, but also transformed or recombined in (unconscious) reiterative processes. Whereas complete resistance against an interpellation is hardly possible, people are able to position themselves in different ways, and every appropriation implies (at least) a (slight) subversion by constantly creating new versions of the original interpellation.

Narratives of self-optimization in the context of migration

Based on these considerations, narratives of self-optimization in the context of migration and biographical ways of appropriating such discourses will be examined. This research focus is based on analyses of contemporary Western societies as socially accelerated entities, which require permanent growth and include pressure for institutions, organizations, and individuals to optimize their outcomes constantly (Rosa, 2013). While norms of perfection (e.g., regulative and mostly unachievable ideals) have been prominent throughout human history, contemporary, neoliberal societies tend to come along with an

> optimization bid geared to a species of logic that we can accurately term "instrumental." To an increasing degree, optimization pressure is brought to bear on areas of life that by their constitution resist such instrumental treatment [...]. Body and soul or education and care, psychic growth and coping processes can hardly be optimized in an instrumental sense without incurring major harm [...].
>
> *(King, Gerisch, and Rosa, 2018, p. 3)*

Hence, the pressure of all-encompassing optimization results in different paradoxes and dilemmas, which must be dealt with individually. This goes hand in hand with neoliberal ideals of social competition, and "perfectionism mutates into a more or less absolute norm that first has to be fulfilled and then immediately and repeatedly exceeded" (ibid.; see also Bröckling, 2018). Self-optimization ideals, however, do not only appear as coercion, but – positively formulated – they also promise belonging, recognition, and power in the "imagined community" of a nation state.[1] Therefore, discourses on self-optimization are central in the context of migration, when questions like "*who belongs to the imagined community of a nation state?*" are negotiated. In this context, optimization norms are accompanied by a specific view about migration, in particular, a focus on the economic benefits and risks associated with it. For instance, discourse analyses have discovered a rhetoric that builds on extreme contrasts between only a few "ideal or model" migrants (e.g., highly qualified workers) (Sætermo, 2016), in contrast to a mass of "those cast beyond the pale" (Erel, Murji, & Nahaboo, 2016, p. 1348), i.e., migrants who apparently do not seem to fit into a meritocratic society (Friedrich & Schultes, 2011). This is associated with descriptions of a nation that is permanently in global competition and is, therefore, dependent on the best possible migration. Hence, there is a tendency to frame migration as a risk for the nation, while the structures of discrimination remain relatively invisible. A lack of success is, then, regarded as self-inflicted, since individuals are "invited to police their own legitimacy by actively demonstrating that they are no burden on a public that, depending on the national context, has been unsettled, diluted or eviscerated" (Lentin & Titley, 2011, p. 163). This focus on the nation's progress leads to interlocking securitarian, culturalist, and utilitarian rationalities that are directed towards collectives of migrants in different ways. Therefore, the norms of competition and self-optimization tend to be accompanied by a degradation of groups, which are perceived as "unproductive," and migrants are affected to an above-average extent by such attributions (Hövermann & Messner, 2019). Negative subject models that stand in the way of national progress are highlighted and present different "folk devils," i.e., "visible reminders of what we should not be" (Cohen, 2002, p. 2) in order to guarantee progress for the imagined community of the nation. Therefore, migrants from specific regions are often expected to position themselves as an exception from such stereotypes.

Method(olog)ical approach

The interplay of public discourse and biographical appropriation in the context of self-optimization and migration is examined here in reference to discourses on and the experience of "educationally successful" German-Iranians. In general, statistical analyses report high educational and professional success among the "collective" of German-Iranians: around 65 percent have a university entrance qualification, and an above-average number of individuals work in so-called "trusted professions" (i.e., as doctors, teachers, or lawyers) (Statistisches Bundesamt, 2016; Woellert & Klingholz, 2014). On the other hand, there are discourses on apparent threat (e.g., in reference to the Islamic Republic or to 9/11), exoticism, and unproductiveness (Said, 1997). Such extremes in public perception raise the question of which subject models of German-Iranians are represented publicly, and how individuals deal with such attributions. In order to discuss this mutual constitution, I will present a methodological approach that combines discourse analysis and biography analysis.

On the one hand, the *Sociology of Knowledge Approach to Discourse* (Keller, 2011) was used for the analysis of discursive representations of German-Iranians. It does not serve as a "fixed" method, but rather as a research program based on theoretical and methodological pillars. Discourse, in this context, is understood as "performative statement practices which constitute reality orders and also produce power effects in a conflict-ridden network of social actors, institutional dispositifs, and knowledge systems" (p. 48). This understanding allows one to look at the embedding of discourse in institutional arrangements and settings, as well as in individual strategies of appropriating discourses. In a circular sampling process, representations of German-Iranians were collected, which appeared in German-speaking public media between 2000 and 2014. In total, 168 texts from major newspapers and magazines were collected. In the process of analysis, *interpretative schemes* were examined, i.e., "fundamental meaning and action-generating schemata" (p. 57) of the subject models. Based on these interpretations, theoretical categories were discovered through a mixture of sequential analysis and the coding-like development of concepts.

On the other hand, biographical-narrative interviews (Schütze, 2016) were conducted, in which individuals who migrated from Iran to Germany during their childhood or early adolescence were asked to tell me their (comprehensive) life-story. In total, 11 in-depth interviews were conducted with individuals between 25 and 40 years old, all of whom had a university entrance qualification. The sampling process followed the principle of minimal and maximal contrasts (Glaser & Strauss, 1967), and the interviews were reconstructed sequentially, i.e., the segments were interpreted one after the other and related to each other. There were no predefined categories before the analysis; the categories were developed in the process of interpretation and comparison of the (narrative) segments. However, the subject models that emerged in advance from the discourse analysis were used as sensitizing constructs for the interpretation of the interviews.

Subject models in media representations

Four discursive subject models were discovered in the process of analyzing media representations:

- *Self-optimization in the mode of productivity.* The central characteristic of this subject model was outstanding productivity. If possible, subjects were presented as *more* productive than the average member of the host society and seemed to outperform what appeared to be average in the imagined community of the host society. For example, in reference to the question what "good integration" means, one article quoted a German-Iranian as saying: "Adapting is the first step. Being better is the second" (Cicero, 2012, Translation from German). Adaptation, thus, appeared to be a prerequisite for "good" integration, but it seemed even more desirable to be better than average or even irreplaceable. Such strong forms of productivity followed an idea of migration as an economic factor (as it is one characteristic of "Human Capital" approaches). The focus was on the value that can be created and enhanced by (exceptional) migrants. At the same time, this productivity might also appear threatening if members of the host society could lose privileges as a result of the "productive newcomers."

- *Self-optimization in the mode of assimilation.* In the second model, strong efforts were described to meet the standards of the imagined community in the most accurate way. In contrast to the first subject model, which contained a rather distinctive and competitive logic (being better than others), this one was about fulfilling existing standards but not surpassing them. In this respect, the (ideal) self-image of the host society is the standard by which migrants were measured. This contains an implicit promise that discrimination, stigmatization, and "othering" can be overcome through comprehensively working on one's self and one's abilities. The aim was to come as close as possible to the ideal social image of the host society. According to that logic, it seems worth aspiring to disappear behind normalized constructs: "Iranians in Germany were always proud not to attract attention. […] The majority […] of immigrants from Iran is coping with the new situation so well that they are not even perceived as a group" (Die Zeit, 2006, Translation from German).
- *Inability to fit into the competitive host society.* This subject model can be understood as a negative model or "folk devil" (Cohen, 2002), in which represented individuals appeared to be unable to adapt to a late-modern, competitive society. Rather, they tended to conserve their traditional culture, which seemed to be non-competitive and not adaptable to ideal models of contemporary life-conduct. For example: "I never understood people who come to a country like Germany, who don't follow the rules here, and instead, want to preserve their own culture and home in the new place" (Cicero, 2012, Translation from German).
  Apparently, the represented subjects do not "want' to optimize themselves, or they do not seem to be able to do so. Hence, this pattern of representation does not express a promise, but rather a warning: do not to be useless or even a burden for the host society; otherwise exclusive practices may be inevitable. In its extreme form, this constructs the opposition between a seemingly perfect human being of late modernity and an inflexible, deficient other.
- *Danger, threat, or hostility.* The fourth model was constructed as a disruption of social order. It also represented an anti-model or "folk devil," but not only in the sense of an apparent inadaptability. Furthermore, the represented subjects posed a danger or threat to members of the host society. Subjects might appear as hostile to the "imagined community" of the host society and are associated with crime, terrorism, or other forms of violence. Another example is an image of self-harm that can pose a threat to members of the host society, for example, self-burnings on the ground of the "imagined community" of the host society: "In several European cities, protesting Iranians used suicidal means. Several protestors […] burned themselves to object to the action of French authorities against Iranian Mujahideen" (Spiegel Online, 2003, Translation from German).

To sum up, the master narrative of self-optimization and migration builds on ideal-models as well anti-models in representations of German-Iranians. In this context, a certain life-conduct is constructed as an ideal, while others are condemned and subject models are constructed as "folk devils." At the same time, these models are also contradictory on different levels: while there is a claim for productivity, too much productivity is considered a threat and creates the fear that German-Iranians will take positions from members of the host society. In addition, demands of assimilation – of not being "visible" as a migrant anymore – can contradict the demands of late-modern capitalism to be "your authentic self" as a foundation of good self-marketing. Another contradiction can be seen in the ideal to not show oneself as a "victim," but appear to be a successful, powerful subject instead. In the logic of the discourse, this tends to mute voices that criticize discrimination or express suffering.

Self-positionings of biography narrators to the master narrative

I will now discuss two contrasting cases of how individuals appropriate such subject models in the process of narrating their own life-story. Since the narratives are embedded in self-descriptions, the logic of the respective biography is first laid out and then discussed in terms of the uses of the master and/or counter narratives.

Jamshed: affirmative appropriation

Jamshed,[2] a 33-year-old interview participant, spent his childhood in Iran and migrated to Germany at the age of eleven, where his father and two of his four siblings had already been living for three years. After arriving, he attended integrational and preparatory class for two years before he could go to secondary school. He was admitted to a grammar school ("Gymnasium") and wanted to obtain a university entrance qualification ("Abitur"). However, his math teacher advised him to give up higher education as he would not be suitable for an academic career. This feedback was described in Jamshed's narrative as resulting in a personal crisis, and he initially decided to quit school. Nevertheless, a few weeks later, after a period of disorientation, he decided to enroll in another school so that he could obtain his university entrance degree at the age of 21.

After spending some time in other occupations and subjects, he enrolled in mathematics and was about to finish his master's degree at the time of the interview. The fact that he needed a longer than average amount of time to finish his studies was justified several times in the interview. It was obviously important for him not to appear as a supposedly unproductive long-term student. Possibly, this was triggered even more by his interaction with an interviewer whose outer appearance and name indicated he has no experience of migration himself. Furthermore, the achievement of a degree was not only introduced as an important individual goal for Jamshed, but also as a family obligation:

> All five children have somehow (1 sec. pause) made something of themselves and have gone their way and are also successful. And I am – so to speak – the (*J. laughs*) the last child to finish education … or in this case: a university degree, and bring it home.

Jamshed introduced himself and his life in relation to his siblings and their occupations and degrees. He made it clear that he is expected to keep up the family standard, and therefore, he interpreted himself in relation to the expectations and norms of his family of origin. Within this narrative, he appeared to be "the last child" to "finish education," which implied there was pressure to enhance his performance. In the rest of the interview, the implicit family obligation also played an important role and seemed to be important for the image that Jamshed created of himself. His father, especially, served as a role model for him:

> My father … had to be independent from an early age and also had to work and has made something out of his life without much support. He finished job-training back in the time of the Shah, and worked his way up … he didn't have an academic education, but he said he was highly appreciated because of his experience and his reliability … Therefore, he was always promoted into higher positions.

While his father was presented as an absent figure in other segments, the narrative of his merits had a key position in Jamshed's biographical self-construction. The strong and productive image of his father comes along with the high expectations Jamshed has for himself. For instance, he described his diploma in mathematics as a "present" for his father, as something he can "give back to him."

While performance and social advancement, thus, played a major role in his biographical self-presentation, they were challenged by experiences of being underestimated by others due to implicit expectations of migrants:

> What all of us, I mean with a migrant background, have to struggle with are these low expectations … And therefore, I try to exert myself more … when someone gives 100 per cent, I have to give 120, you know? For example, at the university – we had to deliver some presentations … and I received some good feedback from fellow students … I also received a pat on the back … All of these are experiences of success, and I think that motivates me … to work even more … to contribute to change the bad image of immigrants, which is true in many cases, of course – not to (2 sec pause) beautify that image, but to enrich it.

Noticeable in this excerpt, was his effort to actively work against a "bad image," a reputation Jamshed wanted to disprove through his actions, especially since the image seemed to be "true" in "many cases." Therefore, his actions appeared to be an attempt to change the image of migrants, in general, and productivity seemed to be important in order to "enrich" the image of migrants and prove that negative stereotypes were wrong. Hence, the incorporated gaze of the host society resulted in an attempt "to present [his] outer appearance as optimal as possible." In his narrative, this even led to extended reflections on whether it was appropriate to grow a full beard, even though this might be associated with an image of non-integrated Muslim extremists. Even strong antipathy against him resulted in reflections on how to act in public in the most appropriate way to avoid such attributions.

In this sense, his biographical self-description clearly fit into the reconstructed master narrative. Jamshed tried to present himself, as far as possible, in images close to reconstructed subject models, and he distinguished himself from anti-models or "folk devils." Finally, Jamshed even claimed "self-optimization" would be the first and foremost task in his life:

> In my opinion, the whole life should be an optimization, eh – of one's personality (1 sec pause) and one's resources … That is something I realized from an early age on. A process of maturation must take place in any case, because otherwise one would go down, and one wouldn't be able to reach goals.

This affirmation of a logic of optimization, however, was not only introduced as a self-commitment, but also as something that he linked to his future children: "For me, this self-optimization is not the highest goal. I also have to pass it on – that means to a/ to my children … so that the carousel of life always keeps spinning." Hence, constant improvement not only takes an existential, life-giving and life-saving function. It also appears as a precondition of transgenerational advancement and appears in a constant analogy: *from his father*, who worked his way up without an academic background, *to himself*, who struggles to accomplish an academic degree, *to a potential (not yet born) descendant*, to whom "the fire" might be passed on. Overall, the narrative of his life was related in many ways to subject models of the master narrative: he described attempts to appear extraordinarily productive by "giving 120 percent while others give 100." At the same time, his narrative was structured by positioning against negative ascriptions of non-adaptability or of posing a threat to others. The master narrative was, therefore, appropriated, but also translated, and adapted for Jamshed's own biography.

Gisou: resistance and subversion

Gisou is a 36-year-old woman who spent the first seven years of her life in Iran, where her father owned a hotel, and her mother worked as an accountant. The family decided to leave Iran and seek refuge in Germany when the Iranian army attempted to make Gisou's brother a child soldier during the Gulf War. After migrating, Gisou's father kept the hotel and tried to run it from abroad, while Gisou's mother started to work in Germany as a saleswoman and social worker. Meanwhile, Gisou attended primary school and, afterwards, a German grammar school. She described personal crises during her childhood and adolescence (e.g., attacks of bulimia), especially due to her rather detached relationship with her parents. Therefore, she described a strong desire to move out of her parents' house, and after she obtained her high-school diploma, she enrolled in different subjects at a university in a faraway metropolis. She quit the university some years later, but settled there, met her future husband and started working in different (non-academic) jobs. The conflict with her parents was repeatedly emphasized in her biographical narrative, and she describes multiple experiences of disrespect because of her gender:

> My brother … was always allowed to … express his opinion, but I was like (1 sec. pause) I wasn't allowed to … first of all, I was not asked, and in case I said something, I wasn't taken seriously … [And nowadays,] it's already a sign of disrespect when they say … oh, these are just the thoughts of your husband or, like, you're under his thumb … when you're, eh … not recognized as a human being, as someone who has an opinion, that's problematic.

Her narrative was accompanied by rhetorical generalizations and argumentations, which reemphasized the hurtful experience of disrespect and misrecognition. Her family was described as lacking the ability to communication and support one another. This was expressed in her narrative through many negations ("I wasn't allowed," "I wasn't taken seriously," "not recognized," "I never had"), by which she developed the image of an (emotionally) absent family. Based on these experiences, she once tried to build a stronger relationship with her mother and convince her to oppose the male hegemony in their family. However, since her mother did not take her side, the feeling of being an outsider in the family grew even stronger: "The worst thing was … that my mother … didn't stand with me at all … she just kept supporting my father, eh, and my brother." Such experiences of disrespect led her to seek distance from her family. In the city far away from her parents, she described attempts at starting anew, and, recently, she decided to break off contact with them completely.

While she described the lack of parental respect for her (mostly) good performance in school, she also emphasized that she was confronted with high obstacles to a "good education." In this respect, she anticipated their disappointment for not obtaining an academic degree: "I don't have the kind of professional qualifications (1 sec. pause) my parents were hoping for." Based on such experiences of lacking recognition of her performance, Gisou could hardly identify with the master narrative of self-optimization. Instead, she focused on life-conduct that was based less on material possessions than on idealistic and sometimes hedonistic norms, accompanied by a sense of social bonding. In this sense, Gisou distinguished herself from the normative construction of the master narrative and its inherent subject models. For example, she described her working life, as follows:

> Work (*G. laughs*), it's good to earn money, but my life takes place in my leisure time. I mean, eh, I work to live, but I definitely don't live for my work – not at all. That counts for both of us ... my husband is the same (2 sec. pause) We like to be on vacation (*G. laughs*), and we like to be outside and ... we like to do cultural stuff.

In her narrative, she stressed the irrelevance of material wealth in many respects: "The main thing is, that we can go on vacation somehow (2 sec. pause), and that we can put some money in our pension fund, and then it's fine." In this description, she changed the perspective, and mainly narrated the story from the point of view of her (newly funded) family. In this respect, she constructed the private sphere of her family as being reliable and honest, in contrast to the ideal of working hard to gain material riches and social status ("material things are not very important for me"). In her narrative, this expression is combined with an (ironic) culturalization of "Persians in Germany," whom she constructed as mainly aiming for material wealth. Mostly, this stereotype was associated with her family of origin, and it was used to distance herself from them ("well, I'm quite an unt/ untypical Persian (*G. laughs*)"). Hence, the counter narrative against ideals of constant self-optimization was embedded in narratives of being distinct from her family of origin. In this sense, she attempted to emancipate herself from a norm of extraordinary productivity, and instead, deconstructed the assumptions behind this promise. In contrast to Jamshed, Gisou developed a biography claiming her life as intelligible, despite not fulfilling the norms of constant self-improvement.

Discussion

These two biographical cases show how a powerful master narrative is processed differently during self-narration and leads to different forms of appropriation based on the previous experiences of the interviewees. In the reconstructed representations, conceptions of normality, categories of intelligible and non-intelligible, reasonable and unreasonable life-conduct, as well as fortunate and unfortunate subject models were proposed. The ideal of appearing to be outstandingly productive was accompanied by promises to legitimize oneself in the imagined community of the host society. At the same time, too much productivity can also be constructed as a threat to members of the host society, and master-narratives must often reconcile contradictory story lines. Such opposing discourses can also serve as an "illusio" (Bourdieu & Wacquant, 1992) and disguise existing hegemonic structures behind a promise of social advancement through comprehensive self-optimization. Therefore, representations of subject models appear as powerful means to influence human beings in the way they construct a sense of their own self. As the example of Jamshed illustrates, representations can result in a strong affirmation of implicit subject models in the master narrative when they fit into previous biographical experiences. The practices of self-exploration and self-presentation are, then, strongly "institutionalized" (Hahn, 1998) by the construct of "ideal" migration and by promises of social advancement. However, as the example of Gisou illustrates, the contradictory nature of such interpellations may also lead to resistance or subversion, when the main story line of the master narrative is mainly associated with hurtful personal experiences. Though the strategies in both cases were directed towards agency in a hegemonically structured field (either through affirmation of a productivity regime or through resistance against it), they were both confronted with their own vulnerability. The master and counter narratives were, therefore, also appropriated to compensate for this.

From a methodological perspective, the question arises about what can be gained by combining discourse analysis with biographical interviews. Based on the presented material, it can be argued that it provides a helpful tool to understand biographical narratives in relation to predominant master and counter narratives. Biography narrators constantly deal with discursive constructions of normality, and an interview can be understood as the testimony of an individual's way of dealing with such subject models. Therefore, during the analysis of interviews, the question can be posed to what extent an orientation towards subject models enables or prevents the agency of the narrators.

Notes

1 Anderson (2016) describes the construct of a nation as an "imagined political community" (p. 6). He analyzes different practices of inventing a nation and imagining a shared identity among diverse members. Despite "inequality and exploitation that may prevail in each, the nation is always conceived as a deep, horizontal comradeship" (p. 7). In the context of migration research, such a view helps one to understand the powerful practices of differentiating between people who (naturally) seem to belong to a nation and people who first need to prove themselves.
2 Information by which the interviewees could easily be identified was anonymized (e.g., names and cities).

Works cited

Anderson, B. (2016). *Imagined Communities: Reflections on the Origin and Spread of Nationalism*. London: Verso.

Andrews, M. (2004). Opening to the original contributions: Counter-narratives and the power to oppose. In M. Bamberg & M. Andrews (Eds.), *Considering Counter-Narratives: Narrating, Resisting, Making Sense* (pp. 1–6). Amsterdam: John Benjamins.

Bamberg, M. (1997). Positioning between structure and performance. *Journal of Narrative and Life History*, 7 *(1–4)*, 335–342.

Bamberg, M. (2004). Considering counter narratives. In M. Bamberg & M. Andrews (Eds.), *Considering Counter-Narratives: Narrating, Resisting, Making Sense* (pp. 351–372). Amsterdam: John Benjamins Publishing Company.

Bamberg, M. (2014). Identity and narration. In P. Hühn, J. C. Meister, J. Pier, & W. Schmid (Eds.), *Handbook of Narratology* (pp. 241–252). Berlin: de Gruyter.

Bogner, A., & Rosenthal, G. (2017). Biographies - discourses - figurations: Methodological considerations from the perspectives of social constructivism and figurational sociology. In G. Rosenthal & A. Bogner (Eds.), *Biographies in the Global South: Life Stories Embedded in Figurations and Discourses* (pp. 15–49). Frankfurt/New York: Campus.

Bourdieu, P., & Wacquant, L. J. D. (1992). *An Invitation to Reflexive Sociology*. Cambridge: Polity Press.

Bröckling, U. (2018). The subject in the marketplace, the subject as a marketplace. In V. King, B. Gerisch, & H. Rosa (Eds.), *"Lost in Perfection": Impacts of Optimisation on Culture and Psyche* (pp. 24–25). London: Routledge.

Butler, J. (1997). *The Psychic Life of Power*. Stanford: Stanford University Press.

Butler, J. (2016). Rethinking vulnerability and resistance. In J. Butler, Z. Gambetti, & L. Sabsay (Eds.), *Vulnerability in Resistance* (pp. 12–27). Durham/London: Duke University Press.

Cicero (2012, June 15). Iranischer Werbezar: "Die Deutschen sind zu weich mit Migranten." *Cicero. Magazin Für Politische Kultur*. Retrieved from www.cicero.de/wirtschaft/die-deutschen-sind-zu-weich-mit-migranten/49722

Cohen, S. (2002). *Folk Devils and Moral Panics. The Creation of the Mods and Rockers*. London/ New York: Routledge.

Die Zeit (2006, March 16). Iran: "So ein nichts vertritt unser Land." *Die Zeit*. Retrieved from www.zeit.de/ 2006/12/Iran_Einwanderer

Erel, U., Murji, K., & Nahaboo, Z. (2016). Understanding the contemporary race-migration nexus. *Ethnic and Racial Studies, 39 (8)*, 1339–1360.

Freeman, M. (2004). Charting the narrative unconscious: Cultural memory and the challenge of autobiography. In M. Bamberg & M. Andrews (Eds.), *Considering Counter-Narratives: Narrating, Resisting, Making Sense* (pp. 289–306). Amsterdam: John Benjamins Publishing Company.

Friedrich, S., & Schultes, H. (2011). Von "Musterbeispielen" und "Integrationsverweigerern": Repräsentatio nen von Migrant_innen in der "Sarrazindebatte." In S. Friedrich (Ed.), *Rassismus in der Leistungsgesellschaft* (pp. 77–96). Münster: Edition Assemblage.

Glaser, B. G., & Strauss, A. L. (1967). *The Discovery of Grounded Theory: Strategies for Qualitative Research*. New Brunswick/London: AldineTransaction.

Hahn, A. (1998). Narrative identity and auricular confession as biography-generators. In A. I. Baumgarten, J. Assmann, G. A. G. Stroumsa, & G. G. Stroumsa (Eds.), *Self, Soul and Body in Religious Experience* (pp. 27–52). Leiden: Brill.

Hall, S. (1995). Fantasy, identity, politics. In E. Carter, J. Donald, J. Squires (Eds.), *Cultural Remix. Theories of Politics and the Popular* (pp. 63–69). London: Lawrence & Wishart.

Hövermann, A., & Messner, S. (2019). Marketization and anti-immigrant attitudes in cross-national perspective. *Social Science Research*, 84, doi:10.1016/j.ssresearch.2019.06.017.

Keller, R. (2011). The sociology of knowledge approach to discourse. *Human Studies, 34 (1)*, 43–65.

King, V., Gerisch, B., & Rosa, H. (2018). Introduction: "Lost in perfection" - ideals and performances. In V. King, B. Gerisch, & H. Rosa (Eds.), *"Lost in Perfection": Impacts of Optimisation on Culture and Psyche* (pp. 1–10). London: Routledge.

Labov, W., & Waletzky, J. (1967). Narrative analysis. Oral versions of personal experiences. In J. Helm (Ed.), *Essays on the Verbal and Visual Arts* (pp. 12–44). Seattle: University of Washington Press.

Lentin, A., & Titley, G. (2011). *The Crises of Multiculturalism. Racism in a Neoliberal Age*. London/ New York: Zed Books.

Martínez-Alemán, A. M., Pusser, B., & Bensimon, E. M. (2015). *Critical Approaches to the Study of Higher Education: A Practical Introduction*. Baltimore: John Hopkins University Press.

Phoenix, A. (2019). Situating children's family troubles: Poverty and serial migration. *Journal of Family* Issues, 40 *(16)*, 2310–2329.

Phoenix, A. (2010). Adult retrospective narratives of childhood experiences of serial migration and reunification with mothers. *Finnish Journal of Ethnicity and Migration, 5 (2)*, 70–78.

Rosa, H. (2013). *Social Acceleration: A New Theory of Modernity*. New York: Cambridge University Press.

Said, E. (1997). *Covering Islam. How the Media and the Experts Determine How We See the Rest of the World*. New York: Vintage Books.

Said, E. (1978). *Orientalism*. New York: Pantheon.

Sætermo, T. F. (2016). Negotiating Belonging as 'Ideal Migrants'. An Ethnographic Study of Skilled Migration from Venezuela to Canada. (Doctoral dissertation, Norwegian University of Science and Technology, Trondheim, Norway). Retrieved from http://hdl.handle.net/11250/2421024.

Schütze, F. (2016). Biographical analysis on the empirical base of autobiographical narratives: How to analyse autobiographical narratives. In W. Fiedler & H.-H. Krüger (Eds.), *Sozialwissenschaftliche Prozessanalyse: Grundlagen der qualitativen Sozialforschung* (pp. 75–116). Opladen: Barbara Budrich.

Spiegel Online (2003, June 19). Welle versuchter Selbstverbrennungen in Europa. *Spiegel Online*. Retrieved from www.spiegel.de/politik/ausland/iranische-opposition-welle-versuchter-selbstverbrennungen-in-europa-a-253763.html

Statistisches Bundesamt (2016). Bevölkerung mit Migrationshintergrund – Ergebnisse des Mikrozensus. Fachserie 1 Reihe 2.2 – 2016. Retrieved from www.destatis.de/GPStatistik/receive/ DEHeft_heft_00070829

Woellert, F., & Klingholz, R. (2014). *Neue Potenziale. Zur Lage der Integration in Deutschland*. Berlin: Berlin-Institut.

Part VII

Counter-narratives and the political sphere

28

Through the cracks in the safety net

Narratives of personal experience countering the welfare system in social media and human interest journalism[1]

Maria Mäkelä

Introduction: a countering masterplot

Personal stories going viral in social media is a contemporary phenomenon highlighting both the rhetorical potential and the risk of misrepresentation in public storytelling that *counters* some allegedly widely held notion. Positioning one's story as a counter-narrative challenging a socio-political doxa is a rhetorical gesture that maximizes visibility in contemporary, social media-dominated narrative environments. A case in point is stories of individual socio-economic hardship that construct the "system" as the antagonist. Stories countering the Nordic welfare state in particular call for an analysis of the logic of master and counter-narratives. References to the foolproof national welfare system as an ideologically dominant, rarely contested master narrative keep recurring in personal narratives spreading across social media in Finland and other Nordic countries.

I suggest that this binary logic of narrative truth formation in this particular socio-political setup can be approached from two points of view that are pertinent for contemporary narrative theory in general: (1) the affinity between the cognitive narrative prototype and the rhetorical repertoire of paradigmatic counter-narratives in social media; and (2) these stories' potential for virality and an afterlife as canonized, rarely contested narratives creating affective consensus. These viral narratives exemplify the normative functions and influence of counter-narratives, not simply as stories that may have a moral, but as narrative acts that construct the hegemonic narrative norm (the alleged "master narrative" of the foolproof national welfare system) through the gesture of countering. From a societal perspective, the study of this particular counter-narrative genre is crucial, as it may contribute to a general mistrust of public health care and social services, vital structures that remain unnarratable at heart. As Matti Hyvärinen notes in this volume, master-narratives are rarely told as they are essentially more script- than story-like; they lack the necessary world disruption to become tellable. This chapter provides some empirical evidence and qualitative analysis of this dynamic of (un)narratability. I will illustrate with a couple of exemplary viral narratives and popular news stories the rhetoric of these highly narratable counter-narratives on public welfare, and the difficulty in actively promoting a positively laden master narrative of a well-functioning social structure in the story economy of social media.

The examples are derived from a corpus of "dubious narratives" crowdsourced and publicly discussed and analyzed in Finnish social media (mainly Facebook and Twitter) in the research project *Dangers of Narrative* (Kone Foundation, 2017–2020). Several of the ideas presented here are moreover inspired by discussions with the stakeholders of the project. The project aims at mapping the dominant cultural and societal ways of instrumentalizing the narrative form, particularly stories of personal experience. Inspired by the work already done on the instrumentalization of narrative and the "storytelling boom" in narrative studies (e.g. Shuman, 2005; Polletta, 2006; Salmon, 2010; Fernandes, 2017), our aim is to provide both academic and non-academic audiences with narratology-based tools for "story-critical" reading, distribution and production of narratives. In January 2017, my research group sent out an open call on Facebook and Twitter to the Finnish audience, asking them to report "interesting, funny or dubious examples of instrumental storytelling." Thus far we have archived approximately 700 reported cases, as well as the prefatory words by the informants elaborating on their own opinions and interpretations. This corpus, originally thought of as an informal method for popularization, consists of pieces of narrative journalism, social media updates that have gone viral, as well as advertisement and charity campaigns. In our preliminary analysis of the material, we have been able to trace some culturally dominant *masterplots*, defined by Porter Abbott as "recurrent skeletal stories, belonging to cultures and individuals that play a powerful role in questions of identity, values, and the understanding of life" (Abbott, 2002, p. 192). This chapter is not, however, based on solid quantitative analysis of masterplots as the collection and consistent analysis of data is still in progress (see Mäkelä, 2018). Instead, I will focus on the qualitative analysis of the cognitive prototypicality and the ensuing potential for virality of masterplots countering the Finnish welfare system in social media. The *Dangers of Narrative* corpus of reported stories and reports by informants, as it stands now, serves merely as a springboard for more general reflections on the rhetoric and risks of personal storytelling in contemporary narrative environments.

Abbott (2002, pp. 42–46) does not equate masterplot with master narrative. Whereas "master narrative" commonly denotes dominant ideologies and discourses, Abbott understands masterplots more in terms of highly tellable, self-replicating story genres. Following Hyvärinen's and Abbott's emphasis on concrete, verbalized and situated narrative accounts, I aim to demonstrate how social media as narrative environments mould personal counter-narratives into influential masterplots that have a significant potential for self-multiplication with regard to both content and form. I hope that this analysis will shed light on the ongoing, social media fuelled revolution of storytelling authority. When H. Porter Abbott wrote his *Cambridge Introduction to Narrative* in 2002, masterplot-regulating individuals playing "a powerful role in questions of identity, values, and the understanding of life" could more or less be identified as the "elite" of gate keepers, whereas in the contemporary social media story economy, increasingly dominated by anti-elite agendas, narrative authority is essentially an *emergent* phenomenon, determined by likes and shares (Dawson & Mäkelä, 2020). In such narrative environments, as I will demonstrate, counter-narratives have a considerable potential to become masterplots modeled according to "skeletal" story templates that audiences recognize practically without reading and, moreover, share on their own social media profiles without much critical reflection. The teller's ability to position themselves as countering a commonly held elite consensus promotes significantly the social media tellability and authority of a narrative. With such contemporary narrative environments, I think that it is justifiable to speak of a "countering masterplot."

I will first describe in short the popular understanding of master and counter-narratives reflected in public discussions and informants' comments in the context of the *Dangers of Narrative* project. I will also provide my methodological rationale for diverging from the positively laden common use of the term counter-narrative. Then I will move on to describing the prominent masterplots countering the dialectically self-constructed master narrative of the foolproof Finnish welfare system. I will focus on a very limited set of narratives to highlight the formal features emblematic of these countering masterplots. A commentary on viral social media stories is accompanied with analyses of human-interest stories in the mainstream media. The reason for my bringing up some news stories while emphasizing social media storytelling is that the cases discussed demonstrate how mainstream media piggybacks on the personal narrative's potential for countering and virality.

The primary theoretical and methodological contexts for my analyses are cognitive narratology and recent critical social scientific approaches to instrumental storytelling. I argue that more narratological attention to the instrumentalization of personal counter-narratives is needed both in narrative and social media studies. Following Habermas (1989), the notions of the Nordic welfare state applied in this chapter are more rooted in the *public sphere* of the Nordic welfare state as separate from the actual socioeconomic model. More precisely, the macro-level narrative environment giving rise to instrumentalized personal stories of the failing "safety net" is what Zizi Papahcarissi calls *affective publics*, "public formations that are textually rendered into being through emotive expressions that spread virally through networked crowds" (Papacharissi, 2015, p. 14). Papacharissi, as several other eminent social media scholars, speak incessantly of "storytelling" as a key feature of the public sphere formed through social media sharing, but do not ground their argument on an elaborate understanding of narrativity (see also Dawson & Mäkelä, 2020). With the following qualitative analysis of some exemplary narratives, I wish to increase the scholarship's understanding of the viral-affective potential of specific kinds of narrative – those dealing with disruptive personal experience and explicitly countering an alleged master narrative.

The most vital consequence of the Nordic Welfare state has been political stability during the recent decades (e.g. Goodin, 1988; Piketty, 2014). This is not to say that the system itself was, indeed, foolproof; moreover, several studies and socioeconomic analyses provide ample evidence of the downfall of the Nordic welfare system caused by global neoliberalism (e.g. Veggeland [ed.], 2016). Narrative scholars can contribute to this pertinent discussion by studying the narrativization of the public sphere in this alleged socioeconomic paradigm shift: do, for example, viral personal stories of "falling through the cracks in the safety net" intensify the downfall of the system that remains, in essence, untellable?

Popular understanding of master and counter-narratives in the *Dangers of Narrative* crowdsourcing project

The discussions provoked by our popularizing analyses of "instrumental storytelling" on the *Dangers of Narrative* Facebook page (with its currently 7300 followers) have made it possible for us to observe how narrative-theoretical vocabulary catches on in social media discussions and journalistic use. Concepts that have been particularly communicable and even contagious are *master narrative, counter-narrative* and *masterplot*. Generally speaking, informants, social media users and journalists tend to use counter-narrative in complimentary terms, pointing to narrative practices that challenge conventional, clichéd story genres that appear as omnipresent in contemporary narrative environments; the dominant narrative formulae are, in turn, typically referred to as either master-narratives or masterplots. The one clichéd narrative formula most frequently labelled by our project's followers as either master narrative or masterplot is *inspirational conversion story*. One of its recurring subgenres is "illness as a hero's journey," such as wellbeing entrepreneurs' branding of their own survival from burnout, or the miraculous recovery narratives of advocates of alternative diets and anti-medicine lifestyle. The socio-economic variant of this masterplot is the story of the creation of a unique business model through the business owner's formative personal epiphany.

The reports received via crowdsourcing reflect a general saturation with the inspirational conversion story as well as a concern over their tendency to limit the scale of "shareable" experiences, foreground individual performance, and expand into a teachable exemplum, particularly when shared extensively online. Accordingly, the project also receives positive reports on narratives countering this masterplot, and in these reports, the term counter-narrative appears frequently. A case in point are stories of grieving, depression or illness that manage to highlight the nonlinearity of experience or the lack of an epiphany or other decisive turning point on one's "journey."

The project's informants and followers have not however been active in pointing out that counter-narratives also have a tendency to become formulaic and recursive in the story economy of social media – even in their very essence as *countering*. This is a hypothesis that differs from the common understanding of counter-narratives gradually gaining dominance and stabilizing as conventional discursive frameworks, that is, master-narratives (Bamberg, 2004a). One example of this development is the current omnipresence of anti-self-help personal stories undermining sarcastically the inspirational conversion story, reporting lessons left unlearned when going through loss, illness or other personal hardship. Thus far, we have received only positive reports on this countering masterplot.

Social scientific narrative studies dwelling on personal stories have typically assumed an uncritical perspective on the narratives themselves. One obvious reason for this is the intimate collaboration between narrative researchers and interviewees and the discretion needed in collecting, analysing and publicly discussing personal stories whose tellers are not themselves actively seeking publicity (see Plummer, 2001, pp. 204–231; Riessman, 2008, pp. 196–199). The other, related explanation has its roots in the mid-twentieth century civil rights movements and critical theories celebrating the "voicing" of the marginalized (see, e.g. Fernandes, 2017). Similar kind of sensitivity has fed into discussions on counter-narratives. Michael Bamberg discusses counter-narratives mostly in terms of invoking "potentially liberating and emancipating agenda" (Bamberg, 2004a, p. 362); by the same token, Molly Andrews maintains that by way of reframing our experience with counter-narratives, "[w]e become aware of new possibilities" (Andrews, 2004, p. 1). Counter-narratives seem to be good by definition as they provide individuals with less trodden paths for experience and identity formation (see, however, Nurminen in this volume). The combative notion of countering has thus acquired a one-sidedly positive association with scholars attributing it to internal, private struggles and mostly ignoring the strategic and political public uses of counter-narratives that may have all kinds of psychological and societal consequences – from healthy empowerment of oppressed groups to dangerous political destabilization.

A less recognized phenomenon in research are stories of individual experience that gain their rhetorical power by actively constructing their own opponent, a strawman type of "master narrative" that will never materialize and thus can never "narrate back," so to speak. This narrative setup is, moreover, prone to dehumanizing the alleged proponents of the master narrative. As Francesca Polletta (2006) notes in her study on storytelling in social movements, positioning oneself in the social and cultural margin is in itself a narrative gesture, inviting narrative responses. Conversely, representing the mainstream invites narrative countering, not narrative echoing or support. In media environments foregrounding "compelling" storytelling, master-narratives to be countered by personal storytelling appear as "official truths" forced upon the people by the elite. Next, I will move on to stories countering the master narrative of the foolproof Nordic welfare system reported to and discussed in the context of the *Dangers of Narrative* project. This set of examples demonstrates how social media fuelled counter-narratives conform closely to the cognitive narratological definitions of a prototypical and thus highly tellable narrative, and how they survive and flourish in social media even when apparently limited with regard to the phenomenon the tellers, and more importantly, the sharers of the stories insist they illustrate.

Popular and viral narratives countering the Nordic welfare system

Whether in public discourse or in research, referring to the "story of the welfare state" presupposes a rather general definition of narrative, reminiscent of Lyotard's (1979) *grands récits*. Both popular and academic discourses revolving around the alleged "success story" of the Nordic welfare system often suggest that an ideological groundwork of a political system is a master narrative that the inhabitants of the system find difficult to counter. Furthermore, the spatiotemporal exclusiveness of the *Nordic* welfare system makes its narrativization somewhat intelligible: this "success story" as a historical account concerns only the post World War II twentieth century Scandinavia and Finland.

Yet when can one actually witness this story told as a full-blown, compelling narrative? Anticipating the centennial of Finland's independence, novelist and theatrical director Aino Kivi launched a social media campaign with a hashtag #IWouldntBeHere, prompting users to share their stories of how the welfare state has made them who they are, in order to highlight the importance of government safety nets for different life situations and histories. The hashtag did not take off, and the ensuing storytelling was only moderately covered by the media, while being sarcastically attacked by right-wing liberals. This is no wonder, as the #IWouldntBeHere stories tended to be poor in experientiality, mostly listing infrastructures and benefits the updaters had used in the course of their lives. The campaign resulted in storytelling that only reinforced the stereotype of social democratic naiveté – citizens expressing their gratitude toward the state while appearing ignorant about the sources of government income – an element that the storytellers probably just had difficulties with factoring in, when social media prompts the user to foreground personal experience (Mäkelä, 2019), not economic-structural analysis. The example of the failure of #IwouldntBeHere attests to the ultimate untellability of the "story of the welfare state"; it may be a narrative in the extensive sense of a master-narrative, or a *grand récit*, but it does not lend itself easily to local manifestations of "compelling" – that is, prototypical – stories.

One of the key preliminary findings of the *Dangers of Narrative* project is an empirical confirmation of the cognitive narratological prototype model of narrative, emerging from the work of theorists such as David Herman, Monika Fludernik and Marie Laure Ryan. According to Herman's intelligible and easily popularizable definition, a representation most commonly framed as a narrative by the receiver's cognition is

> a situated account that conveys an ordered temporal and causal sequence of events, a storyworld with particulars, an event that disrupts this storyworld, and the experience of what it is like for a particular individual to live through this disruption.
>
> *(Herman, 2009, p. 14)*

The masterplots that most clearly emerge from the *Dangers of Narrative* corpus display the features listed by Herman; the master genre of the conversion story being a case in point. With Herman's definition, we can easily see what is lacking in the commendatory narratives of the welfare state and the foolproof government safety net: spatiotemporal embeddedness and disruptive experience. The cognitive narrative prototype is not at all useful in representing structures, systems, or routines. Rather, the description of structures, systems and routines comes close to the definition of master-narrative as a background structure that prompts storytelling only if it crumbles, as argued in this volume by Hyvärinen. Conversely, the common theoretical understanding of *counter-narratives*, as well as most of the examples used in scholarship analysing counter-narratives, conform closely to the cognitive prototype model. In cognitive-narratological terms, a counter-narrative is often a prototypical narrative; it urges the audience to *narrativize* (cf. Fludernik, 1996).

Hyvärinen demonstrates in his chapter how already the very act of countering fulfils the criterion of "world disruption," or "breach," highlighted by both narratological (Herman, 2009) and narrative-psychological (Bruner, 1991) definitions. Moreover, the gist of counter-narrativity dovetails with what Monika Fludernik (1996) calls *experientiality*. For Fludernik, mediated experientiality is the minimum criterion for narrativity. Eminent theorists of counter-narratives such as Andrews and Bamberg, in turn, emphasize the experiential facet in telling counter-narratives: counter-narrativity emerges from the disparity between a dominant discourse and the teller's experience. Consequently, from a cognitive-narratologically informed perspective, prototypical counter-narrativity manifests itself as experiential to a second degree: it materializes an individual's experience of a lack of matching experiential framework.

Several socio-politically charged stories of individual hardship have provoked heated discussion on the comments sections of our analyses, with some followers even attacking our research project for taking such a critical and analytical stance toward personal stories striving to concretize social injustice and bureaucratic malpractice. At the same time, however, our narrative-theoretical criticism of some of the dominant counter-genres is firmly based on a concern expressed via crowdsourcing over the dominance of the personal story in public discussions on the (mal) functioning of social services and healthcare. Stories questioning the validity of the master narrative of the Nordic welfare system provoke suspicion in our informants mainly for six reasons:

1. unverifiability of the subjective account;
2. the storyteller's self-positioning as morally superior (as a soldier of justice, a Good Samaritan, the sole speaker of truth, or as giving voice to the marginalized);
3. misrepresentation of general procedures and regulations of social service and healthcare professionals;
4. the caricaturization of public officers, authorities and other professionals;
5. the usurpation of other people's stories to serve the teller's own agenda (see Shuman, 2005 on "story ownership"); and
6. the disparity between the story's virality and its statistical representativeness.

The cases reported to us and the ensuing discussions with different audiences have helped our research team to locate the perceived risks precisely in the narrative gesture of countering an untellable master-narrative. On a more general level, we have located many of the "dangers of narrative" reported or hinted at by our informants and discussants precisely at the cognitive-prototypical elements: experientiality, particularity, world disruption and moral positioning (Mäkelä, 2018). The above listed dangers of narratives countering the master-narrative of a solid welfare system are thus masterplot specific manifestations of the general cognitive flipside of a compelling, prototypical narrative.

One meta level danger, in particular, emerges from the corpus, reports and discussions, yet it often remains unvoiced by the discussants and manifests merely in the defensive reactions of the storytellers: the social media immunity of the counter-narrative to falsification and criticism. The shield mechanism is a direct result of the story's anatomy as cognitive-experientially prototypical narratives: the primary reason for sharing a prototypical story is to convey "what it's like" to be a particular person going through a disruptive experience (Herman, 2009). How does one falsify – or, for that matter, confirm – another person's experience? A frequent line with which social services and healthcare professionals answer to story-shaped allegations of negligence starts with the phrasing "We do not want to dispute this person's experience ..." Moreover, if we are to believe Monika Fludernik when she writes that "there can [...] be narratives without plot, but there cannot be any narratives without (a) human [...] experiencer of some sort at some narrative level" (Fludernik, 1996, p. 13), it becomes evident that fact-checking is often an inconsequential measure when applied to personal stories. At the same time, however, these stories have the power to impose *moral positioning* on different actors (see, e.g. De Fina & Georgakopoulou, 2012, p. 98; also Bamberg, 1997 and 2004b on the three levels of positioning: story, interaction and social norms).

The conspicuous clickbait quality of the headlines of some of the reported news stories attests to the familiarity of the masterplot of "individual versus the faceless system," albeit the examples vary with regard to the gravity of the embedded allegations:

> The Social Insurance Institution gave conflicting advice – without welfare, 18 year old girl was forced to cancel her graduation party.
>
> (News website of the national broadcasting company *Yle*, June 6, 2017)

> Employment agency urged a dead woman to get a job.
>
> (Tabloid *Iltalehti*, November 16, 2017)

> Wrong medicine took a boy into psychiatric ward for years – at the age of 16, he managed to expose the nationwide oppression and humiliation of children in institutions.
>
> (News website of the national broadcasting company Yle, September 15, 2018)

These and many other similar stories have been reported in crowdsourcing by members of the very same professional groups that are positioned as antagonists in them: social services and healthcare professionals. In their anonymous reports, they often point out the constant disparity in such narrative setups as an inevitable result of professional confidentiality. The discredited professionals in these stories will have no narrative way of their own to counter such confrontational representations of their work. Doctors and social workers are not allowed to share stories that would provide affective ground for social media users and material for "case" and feature journalism. What is more, they are not even able to comment on individual cases in public.

One illustrative case reported via crowdsourcing is a web column with a fair amount of social media shares entitled "My ill friend" and written by a celebrity journalist of the national broadcasting company Yle. The story consists of a long quotation from the anonymous "friend," recounting her ample and in every way horrendous experience with public healthcare. The editorial framing by the journalist consists merely of informing the readers about the friend's condition (type one diabetes) and the given consent to publish the story. The previously listed problems of unverifiability, self-positioning, misrepresentation of general procedures, caricaturization of healthcare professionals, story ownership and claims for representativeness loom large here.

> Doctors at the public health-care centre are somehow more scatterbrained, not focusing on the patient at all. They don't have a clue who I am and what's wrong with me. Often the schedules are made so tight that they have barely looked at my patient file before I enter the examination room. Most of the short, 15 minute session is spent by my recounting the facts about myself. And time's up!
>
> The same evening, the same physician can be much more competent at the private clinic. Value for money. [...]

> In the public healthcare, I've witnessed this "that one has money, she should use the private clinic" attitude. So I've actually started to style myself to look poorer when I go to see a doctor. Better not carry a Chanel bag on your shoulder. [...]
>
> I gave my blanked to this old lady, when she was praying for a warmer. I was scolded for doing this because it was forbidden. [...] An angry glare at me, angry yelling at the granny. That's quite embarrassing, no matter how old or demented you are.
>
> *(Translation MM)*

Although published on the website of the publicly funded national media company, the story is framed and presented similarly to a social media share, inviting further shares – in fact, it is even likely that the text has originally been a Facebook post. The crushing critique of the public welfare is from time to time interrupted by intensely emotional passages focusing on the teller's loneliness and fear of death as a person who suffers from several grave illnesses and has no family to support and comfort her.

The whole is a disturbing mixture of strong normativity, sweeping generalizations and intense subjectivity, yet precisely because of that it steers clear from criticism and falsification. It is difficult to imagine a readerly position from which the teller's experience could be outrightly disapproved. Yet the story positions if not all, then at least most doctors working in the private sector as ignorant opportunists, the teller herself as a Good Samaritan, the system itself as generally corrupt, and moreover, takes the liberty of interpreting the experiences of several other patients whose stories are embedded in the teller's. Details of embodied experience, prompting affective response in the audience, mix with iterative narration and normative claims, resulting in a story that suggests every visit to the public healthcare to be a traumatic experience, and not just to the teller, but for others as well. The case is exemplary of an argumentative use of narrative: a normative claim is presented through an exemplum (or in this case, exempla), which, mutatis mutandis, is again used to verify the normative claim, as if the "lesson" would be a natural consequence of the story that was selected to illustrate the claim in the first place. Anna De Fina and Alexandra Georgakopoulou maintain that precisely because of this narrative's double standard, it is often more difficult to argue against an exemplum than against rational argumentation (De Fina & Georgakopoulou, 2012, p. 98). Then what is the teller opposing, finally – and how might the journalist justify the sharing of the story? The time of publishing for this column four years ago dates back to time when the new Finnish government started to plan a new healthcare reformation that would include a lot of privatization, a project that was immediately countered by strong opposition that appealed repeatedly to the master-narrative of the foolproof, equal public welfare system. This context, and the master narrative along with it, is implied in the "Story of my ill friend."

How could the healthcare professionals ever reply to these story-shaped allegations? Whenever a viral social media story reaches the news, the officials and welfare professionals repeatedly play the stock role of reiterators of the same comment: "I/we cannot comment on this particular case, but normally we ..." Against the backdrop of these storytelling limitations, viral social media narratives and journalistic "human interest" stories foreground the disruptive experience of the individual. This happens to such a degree that any attempt at elaborating on the routine procedures or setting this one case in proportion to its representativeness, or the moral lessons derived from it in a larger, systemic context, will fizzle out.

The personal counter-narrative's virality and resistance in social media

All this is not to say that stories of individual experience could not contribute to much-needed changes in societies today as they have always done (see also Fernandes, 2017, p. 3). The question that I am concerned with here is that the story logic of social media crucially alters the dynamics between established, dominant master-narratives and private, particular counter-narratives as commonly conceptualized in narrative studies. Researcher of social politics Sujatha Fernandes discusses strategic and often carefully planned ("curated") campaigns that feed on individuals' life-stories and harness them for promoting political agendas in the age of affect-driven social media "consumption of others" (ibid., p. 2). Her critical approach to the general story positivity and her attempt at demonstrating the "affinity between stories and late capitalist culture" (ibid., p. 3) is highly compatible with mine, yet the focus is slightly different. Fernandes provides a comprehensive genealogy of the storytelling boom and analyses the multiple ways with which charitable attempts at "giving voice" in the contemporary story economy are consumed by a neoliberal ideology. The "dubious" narratives crowdsourced in the *Dangers of Narrative* strongly support the claims made by Fernandes: celebration of individual virtues, empowerment, ethics of encounter and entrepreneurship overshadows such political aspects as class and other supra-individual structures in the masterplots under which the majority of reported stories fall. The social political concern of my analysis, the undermining of the Nordic welfare model, is thus closely related to the overall development that Fernandes openly criticizes. Yet unlike Fernandes who focuses on carefully curated storytelling as a contrived voicing imposed on the marginalized by the elite, my own approach here is an attempt to complement Fernandes' story-critical approach by paying attention to the seemingly spontaneous grassroots political storytelling and the somewhat haphazard activism emerging around these stories in social media.

An insufficiently researched feature of contemporary storytelling is the effects of virality on narrative rhetoric and ethics. The strong public resonance with the experiential narrative prototype is at least partly compatible with Tony Sampson's definition of virality emphasizing "vibratory events" created by shared affect: "small, unpredictable events can be nudged into becoming big, monstrous contagions without a guiding hand" (Sampson, 2012, p. 6). Although stories of personal experience that counter the alleged master narrative of the flawless welfare safety net highlight the dramatic experiential "breach," or "world disruption," in the life of an individual, they are originally "small" in terms of representativity and authority. They are "unpredictable" in terms of narrative agency – virality can turn *anyone* into a national narrative authority on social services within a few minutes (see also Munster, 2013, pp. 100–103). Moreover, the narrative hype around one singular story is short-lived (see Nahon & Hemsley, 2013, 28). These countering masterplots become representative and authorial mostly "without a guiding hand", and as they aim to represent the social margin, their virality is not primarily dependent on public influencers (see also Vosoughi et al., 2018; cf. Nahon & Hemsley, 2013). Admittedly, however, and as demonstrated by some of my previous examples, gatekeepers such as news media have a crucial role in reinforcing the countering masterplot.

Now I will look a bit more closely at a recent social media post that was not directly reported to us via crowdsourcing but encapsulates effectively the affinity between the experiential narrative prototype, a personal narrative's strategic positioning as a counter-narrative, and the viral potential of these narrative elements. The story's exceptional, and from the perspective of the storyteller herself, probably also somewhat unprecedented virality aptly demonstrates how the story logic of social media makes small stories big, makes them resistant to criticism and contributes to counter-narratives' building up into masterplots. Another reason for my singling out a story outside the original crowdsourced material is that it was extensively discussed on our Facebook page after I published a popularizing analysis of it. The third reason for selecting this particular story is its self-positioning as a "shareable story" (Page, 2018) with a campaigning element, as well as the fact that it received some news coverage.

Ethically speaking, public posts by private citizens gaining unprecedented social media visibility issue a serious challenge to narrative research. Should they be regarded and conceptualized as public discourse, comparable to opinion pieces in the gate-kept media? Or should the researcher rather be extra sensitive with regard to the story logic of social media where stories get out of proportion so quick and unexpectedly? I think that both stances are fathomable, and therefore every case requires individual evaluation. In the *Dangers of Narrative* crowdsourcing project, the public posts that we comment on will need to have gone viral and gained unexceptional visibility or media coverage. Typically, these are the stories that provoke the most heated discussions on the comments section, reflecting, among other social and cultural aspects, the viral personal story's immunity to criticism, established by the story logic of social media. We have preferred not to cite the comments section directly as one can never be sure if the commentator is fully aware of the publicity of the comments. This exemplary story ends with an explicit prompt to share ("Feel free to share"). As a literary scholar, I analyse and comment on the text, not the teller behind it; moreover, our project is not doing fact-checking, but mainly pointing out the possible pitfalls (or sometimes benefits) of a narrative's rhetoric and afterlife in social media.

This Facebook story that received 6300 shares has a title "This is how the Finnish welfare state cares for its youth in Anno Domini 2019," explicitly marking the master-narrative to be countered by the personal story. The "evaluation" part of the story (Labov, 1972) is thus foregrounded, while at the same time the narrative is framed as best fits the genre of a personal Facebook post: it conveys an immediate experience, its "what it's like" quality. This happens in the very first sentence after the title: "I'm just so confused about the officials' actions concerning a minor, that I really need to tell this to you as well." The narrative recounts in a detailed manner a one night episode during which the teller ends up accommodating two teenagers returning from a party, the other one having allegedly been kicked out of his/her parents' house and being a frequent resident in a Red Cross reformatory. First, the teller recounts in a poignantly sarcastic manner her experiences with a Red Cross worker who refuses shelter from the teenager due to a curfew. Then the teller moves on to describe in length the interaction with a social services emergency duty officer over the phone:

> The duty officer said that all children and young have a home to go to in Finland. We drifted into a discussion on how this in fact is not the case. This took a long time and really started to stretch my patience. That was after all a social worker on the line, shouldn't every officer know people have problems. [...]
>
> I asked if the duty officer really didn't know what to do in this situation. I asked the officer how it was possible not to have a protocol for this and not having experience of similar situations. The duty officer replied, that [s/he] didn't know how to proceed and had never encountered anything like this.
>
> The phone conversation resulted in the conclusion that the only option was for me to take the youth to stay over. I was wondering how can it go like this? [...]
>
> Just when the teens had gotten into bed, the officer calls me back to inform me that child welfare is working on this. So they are actually calling me at 1 am to let me know that the child welfare will be calling me back during the same night. I told them that here's where I'm drawing the line. [...] The duty officer sounded surprised after hearing I wasn't willing to stay up all night.
>
> One more time, to be clear, I tell the officer that I'm just a random innocent aunt, not working in a night shift, unlike you guys at the other end of the line. [...]
>
> Anyway, I just wanted to sleep, and now I'm alone responsible for this teen, a stranger, abandoned by the world, in Finland, and it's 2019.

> How abandoned can the youth be in this country? [...] There are so many stories of vulnerable young people ending up being abused or mistreated in one way or another. Is that the point when the officers eagerly rush to help? Oh well, I sure know that this is just daydreaming. (Who would even tell about maltreatment if the adults haven't been interested in the first place?)
>
> *(Translation MM)*

Toward the end of the long story, the reader gradually learns that the post has been written during the same night as the events took place, and the post ends with an intensely emotional paragraph, switching from a moral register to an experiential one: "I'm so tired I'm crying. [...] If I'm the only adult who a youth can ask help from, I just can't turn my back and sleep. That's for sure." In social media storytelling, experientiality, simultaneity and testing the limits of tellability ("I shouldn't be telling you this"; "I don't know why I'm telling this to you") together form the core parameters of narrative rhetoric. The "art" of social media storytelling results from a careful manipulation of these parameters, all the while coming across as a completely spontaneous urge to "share." (Mäkelä, 2019) The teller of this viral narrative succeeds precisely in this.

Accordingly, the reception of the story in social media and also in a news report was overwhelmingly positive, and the teller received more than 1600 thank you notes for being a Good Samaritan from Facebook users on the post's comments section. Several commentators recounted their own, similar experiences or hinted at such. I tracked down a couple of shares that were critical, mostly concentrating on the problematic issues of verifiability, caricaturization, misrepresentation of protocols, moral self-positioning and the case's representativeness with regard to the general state of the Finnish child welfare services. I will argue neither against nor for the story's representativeness with regard to social workers or the welfare services, but rather flesh out shortly the social media fuelled narrative dynamic that turns experientiality into representativeness and further into normativity. The cognitive prototypicality is key to the story's social media success, but it is also key to its rhetorical pitfalls in a larger sociopolitical context.

Due to the particularizing nature of prototypical narrativity, the story focuses on individuals and the ethics of encounter – not structures, procedures and their possible underlying deficiencies. The post comes across as targeted against, not only one duty officer, but a Red Cross worker and all the other parents who are not "there" for the teenagers – "there" being limited to the spatio-temporal coordinates of this particular story. The story disambiguates the multifaceted problems related to issues such as custody, or the rights and duties of child welfare officials by drawing sympathy for the teller and antipathy for the social worker, in an affectively irresistible and unequivocal manner. The ethics of encounter are streamlined into an allegory of the welfare state that leaves its youth to the predators. The plethora of comments that the post received reflect a general disenchantment with the welfare system, while inspiring scarcely any suggestions on how to improve the system – in all its ethical complexities and variations in the customer base. Yet this is a problem we might have with any story conveying what it's like to live through a world-disrupting experience. It is the social media likes and shares that feed into a disproportionate exemplarity. In this allegory constructed primarily in the reception of the story, an exceptional, exemplary individual saves the day when the public welfare system in its entirety fails.

I have labeled this type of "shared story" the *viral exemplum* (Mäkelä, 2018; Dawson and Mäkelä, 2020). The logic of the viral exemplum is that of a chain reaction from experientiality through representativeness to normativity. When shared, a relatable individual experience becomes representative in a concrete, material sense. As Anna Munster points out, the virality of a random experience may be explained by its "singular generality": the experience is attached to a singular agent, yet the experience is easily generalizable – it could have befallen anyone (Munster, 2013, p. 101).

Thus, although some sharers of the story had similar stories of their own, the "representativeness" of the story primarily results from the affective prompt to share. Furthermore, representativeness creates normativity as the affective consensus created by liking and sharing sets up an ethical norm. In this process, repetition replaces authority. My tentative hypothesis is that the viral exemplum generates *emergent authority*, and as such, it is always already an act of countering some allegedly established authority. The narrative-rhetorical dynamics of experientiality-representativeness-normativity establishes viral emotional stories as normative exempla. Their ultimate "truth" lies in the affirmation of affective doxa instead of, or beyond, referentiality. Therefore even a falsified "original" experience in social media may lead to normative conclusions and political action. Many viral exempla in social media attest that a (prototypical, compelling) narrative's natural dynamic is from the margin to the centre; therefore the story logic of social media favours a spiralling movement, outward from a small centre – the (countering) personal story.

Conclusion

Then what are the sharers of these stories actually sharing? I find it hard to believe that all sharers of the story actually maintain that the lives of Finnish youth are depending on individual charity. As argued by José Van Dijck (2013, pp. 44–45), sharing is the new norm, marketed by Facebook as a development toward more empathetic societies. As evinced also in linguistic-narratological research by Ruth Page, "shared stories" are based on "an assumption of commonly held beliefs" (Page, 2018, p. 18 *et passim*). Yet these beliefs, manifesting as, and even generated by affective responses, can be surprisingly contingent on one singular story. Therefore the common moral ground of social media storytelling is not always to be located at a dominant master-narrative but can, in fact, be found in the very narrative act of countering. The sharer of the story does not share information, but rather a righteous ethical response to the narrative act of countering.

The ideal of the foolproof, solid welfare system is almost by definition anti-narrative. It lacks moral positioning reducible to individual agents: the blind system does not tell a deserving individual from a non-deserving. It is not interested in the taxpayers' good will or character. When working, it lacks world disruption – indeed, it strives to be its opposite. Citizens countering the master-narrative of a foolproof welfare system are not, in most of the cases, willing to get rid of the system altogether. Nevertheless positioning oneself as the underdog facing an inhumane system is what works in narrative terms, particularly in social media. The strong, individuating experientiality and stark moral positioning in these stories risk representing the society as a battle between the good (us) and the bad (them), a story that is difficult to re-counter with a compelling narrative.

Note

1 This article was written in the context of research projects *Dangers of Narrative* (Kone Foundation 2017–2020) and *Instrumental Narratives: The Limits of Storytelling and New Story-Critical Narrative Theory* (no. 314768), both directed by the author. I wish to thank the anonymous reviewer of this manuscript for some extremely helpful comments and suggestions.

References

Abbott, Porter (2002). *Cambridge Introduction to Narrative*. Cambridge: Cambridge University Press.

Andrews, Molly (2004). "Opening to original contributions: Counter narratives and the power to oppose." In M. Bamberg & M. Andrews (eds.), Considering Counter Narratives. Narrating, Resisting, Making Sense. Amsterdam: John Benjamins. 1–6.

Bamberg, Michael (1997). "Positioning between structure and performance". *Journal of Narrative and Life History*, 7(1–4), 335–42.

Bamberg, Michael (2004a). "Considering counter narratives." In M. Bamberg & M. Andrews (eds.), Considering Counter Narratives. Narrating, Resisting, Making Sense. Amsterdam: John Benjamins. 351–371.

Bamberg, Michael (2004b). Positioning with Davie Hogan. Stories, tellings, and identities. In C. Daiute & C. Lightfoot (eds.), *Narrative Analysis. Studying the Development of Individuals in Society* (pp. 135–157). Thousand Oaks, CA: Sage.

Bruner, Jerome (1991). "The narrative construction of reality." *Critical Inquiry, 18*(1), 1–21.

Dawson, Paul & Maria Mäkelä (2020). "The story logic of social media: co-construction and emergent narrative authority." *Style,* 54(1).

De Fina, Anna & Alexandra Georgakopoulou (2012). *Analyzing Narrative. Discourse and Sociolinguistic Perspectives.* Cambridge: Cambridge University Press.

Fernandes, Sujatha (2017). *Curated Stories: The Uses and Misuses of Storytelling.* Oxford: Oxford University Press.

Fludernik, Monika (1996). Toward a Natural Narratology. New York & London: Routledge.

Goodin, Robert E. (1988). *Reasons for Welfare. The Political Theory of the Welfare State.* Princeton: Princeton University Press.

Habermas, Jürgen (1989). *The Structural Transformation of the Public Sphere: An Inquiry into a Category of Bourgeois Society.* Trans. by Burger, T. with the Assistance of Lawrence F., Cambridge: Polity Press.

Herman, David (2009). *Basic Elements of Narrative.* Oxford and Malden, MA: Wiley Blackwell.

Labov, William (1972). *Language in the Inner City: Studies in the Black English Vernacular.* Philadelphia: University of Pennsylvania Press.

Lyotard, François (1979). *La Condition postmoderne.* Paris: Minuit.

Mäkelä, Maria (2018). "Lessons from the dangers of narrative project: toward a story-critical narratology." *Tekstualia, 4,* 175–186.

Mäkelä, Maria (2019). "Literary facebook narratology: experientiality, simultaneity, tellability." *Partial Answers, 17*(1), 159–182.

Munster, Anna (2013). *An Aesthesia of Networks. Conjunctive Experience in Art and Technology.* Cambridge, MA: MIT Press.

Nahon, Karine & Jeff Hemsley (2013). *Going Viral.* New York: Polity Press.

Page, Ruth (2018). *Narratives Online: Shared Stories in Social Media.* Cambridge: Cambridge University Press.

Papacharissi, Zizi (2015). *Affective Publics. Sentiment, Technology, and Politics.* New York: Oxford University Press.

Piketty, Thomas (2014). *Capital in the Twenty-First Century.* Cambridge, MA: Harvard University Press.

Plummer, Ken (2001). *Documents of Life 2: An Invitation to a Critical Humanism,* London, Thousand Oaks, New Delhi: Sage.

Polletta, Francesca (2006). *It Was Like a Fever. Storytelling in Protest and Politics.* London: University of Chicago Press.

Riessman, Catherine Kohler (2008). *Narrative Methods for the Human Sciences.* Los Angeles, London, New Delhi & Singapore: Sage.

Salmon, Christian (2010). *Storytelling: Bewitching the Modern Mind,* Trans. by D. Macey. London and New York: Verso.

Sampson, Tony D. (2012). *Virality: Contagion Theory in the Age of Networks.* Minneapolis, MN: University of Minnesota Press.

Shuman, Amy (2005). *Other People's Stories: Entitlement Claims and the Critique of Empathy.* Champaign, IL: University of Illinois Press.

Van Dijck, José (2013). *The Culture of Connectivity: A Critical History of Social Media.* Oxford: Oxford University Press.

Veggeland, Norald, ed. (2016). *The Current Nordic Welfare State Model.* New York: Nova Science Publishers.

Vosoughi, Soroush, Deb Roy & Sinan Aral (2018). "The spread of true and false news online." *Science 359*(6380), 1146–1151.

29

Understanding food sovereignty

Exploring counter-narrative and Foucault's genealogy

Thore Prien

Introduction

At the World Food Summit organized by the FAO in Rome in 1996, La Via Campesina (LVC), an association of more than 100 farmers, indigenous and landless associations from the Americas, Africa, Europe and Asia, presented the concept of food sovereignty, which aims at increasing ecological and locally organized agriculture. Food sovereignty then developed into an influential counter-narrative to food security, a narrative that LVC and other critical voices see as consistent with the maintenance of industrialized agriculture and the global dominance of agrobusiness.

The World Food Summit in Rome was preceded by a decade in which the course was set for a neoliberally framed global corporate food regime (McMichael 2013a). Land and seeds of small peasants and indigenous peoples came under the influence of global institutions, first and foremost the WTO and the IMF, whose policies prepared the ground for increasingly aggressive agrobusiness companies. Governments and transnational corporations of the North thus renewed the colonial order by taking over the global South with a contractually regulated accumulation by dispossession (Harvey 2003). This neoliberal turn in agriculture meant that the states of the global South were forced to discontinue subsidies and public support for agriculture, for example by the IMF debt regime and the so-called structural adjustment programmes, but also by the WTO Agreement on Agriculture (McMichael 2012). At the same time, they had to open their markets to imports, which was all the more devastating because the European Union and the United States were able to use the Uruguay Round negotiations to maintain subsidies for their agriculture and finally export their products cheaply to the countries of the South. Seventy per cent of the countries of the global South were then exposed to food importers and thus price fluctuations on the world market, as were many farmers who had to grow cash crops such as coffee, cocoa or sugar. For example, McMichael (2012) notes for Kenya that "forty percent of Kenya´s children work on plantations, which export pineapple, coffee, tea, and sugar. While these foodstuffs supply European markets, 4 million Kenyans face starvation" (p.140). In addition, due to competitive pressure and aggressive agrobusiness practices, millions of small peasants were driven from their ancestral lands. "Global Peasantries (...)", says Araghi (2009), "are caught in a storm of violent forces that uproot, dispossess, and propel them into emerging vast spaces of informal labor in the global slums, spaces outside the traditionally rural but even past the margins of urbanity" (p. 112).

Governments and agribusiness corporations, which strengthen their market power through mergers (ETC Group 2018), are at the same time forcing a capitalist production of nature (Smith 2010; Castree 2001). The concept of food sovereignty is also directed against this. The IPBES report on the disappearance of biodiversity (2019) and the most recent IPCC report (2019) have highlighted the urgent need to abandon industrialized agriculture. Monocultures, massive use of pesticides and chemical fertilizers, biopiracy legalized by patent rights, land and water grabbing lead to existential dangers to the livelihoods. Alongside the warming of the climate, the consequences of these agrobusiness techniques are the destruction of agro- and biodiversity, the devastation of soil, the poisoning of the environment by pesticides and an increasing water shortage.

To many, this seems to be the price to be paid, for better or for worse, for feeding the world's population. But it is precisely here that the advocates of the concept of food sovereignty can cite an amazing fact: the just described disastrous social and ecological consequences of industrialized agriculture do not even lead to higher productivity. The majority of humanity is still fed by small peasants beyond the world market, who earn more yield per hectare on their small areas than the monocultures of industrialized agriculture (GRAIN 2014). To give just one example, Ethiopia can be shown to have "a positive association between yield and land fragmentation" (Paul & wa Gĩthĩnji 2018, 757).

To what extent can we understand Food Sovereignty as a counter-narrative? The concept of counter-narrative has been well researched recently (Bamberg & Andrews 2004; Lundholdt et al. 2018; Lueg, Bager & Lundholdt in this volume) and initial considerations have been made as to the extent to which peasant movements can position food sovereignty as counter narrative (Patel 2009; Martínez-Torres & Rosset 2010; Juárez et al. 2018). In this chapter I use the term counter-narrative against the background of Foucault's genealogy and his concept of subjugated knowledge. I regard food sovereignty as a counter-narrative, since it is the narrative, world-covering form of subjugated peasant knowledge and thus the form of narrative that arises from the resistance of the oppressed peasants. Analogously, however, the dominant neoliberal discourse of nutrition also creates its own narrative. The connection between Foucault's theory and the concept of narrative is intended in the following to prove on the one hand the necessity of connecting discourse and genealogy with the concept of the narrative (Viehöver 2002; 2010), but also questions as to how the chances of the counter-narrative "food sovereignty" as understood in this way are to assert themselves in the truth games of globalized agriculture.[1] In combining Foucault´s theory with the concept of counter-narrative this chapter contributes to an ongoing debate on food-sovereignty as an effective counter-narrative and seeks to explore the productivity of such a combined approach.

I structure this account as follows: first, I describe the two competing narratives of food security and food sovereignty already mentioned above. I begin by outlining how food security could become hegemonic as a neoliberal concept and describe what food sovereignty, as counter-narrative to food security, means. In a second step, I address the reasons for the dominance of the food security narrative. There is no doubt that its hegemony is explained by the strategic selectivity of states and governments, by the lobbying work of agrobusiness and supermarket chains, and not least by the unquestioned everyday conviction in the metropolises that the world can only be fed with industrialized agriculture. But behind these power relations and hegemonies lies the success of what I would like to analyze with Foucault as truth games of global agriculture. Foucault's tools can be used to show how a truth of global agriculture is produced confirming the neoliberal paradigm of food security. With a view to Foucault's archaeological discourse analysis, I show which rules determine the truth of the discourse on agriculture. Then I turn to Foucault's later genealogical phase, to show how this discourse and the social practice of agriculture are interwoven. For Foucault, the real meaning of archaeology and genealogy was ultimately to expose how subjugated knowledge can become a means of resistance. Only then, in a third step, do I come to the question of what it means not only to start from discourses but to analyze the effect of narratives and counter-narratives. Understanding food security as narrative and food sovereignty as counter-narrative, adds an important dimension to the analysis of discourses, practices and subjugated knowledge. While with Foucault we can understand which rules and practices determine the truth games of discourses and can reflect with the concept of subjugated knowledge about resistance, with these public narratives and the concept of the (counter-)narrative a possibility seems to open up that Foucault did not take into account. The counter-narrative, so my thesis of the respective section, could show a further effect of subjugated knowledge. Finally, I ask what research perspectives this opens up.

Food security and food sovereignty

Food security as a neoliberal concept

The critical agro-studies largely agree that food security is not a neutral concept, but serves as a Trojan horse for neoliberal ideology (Patel 2009; Mooney & Hunt 2009; Koc 2013). But food security was by no means a part of the neoliberal framework from the outset. When the concept began its triumphal march in the 1970s as the successor to the terms "Right to Food" and "Freedom from Hunger", it was still regarded as the desirable result of state support (Fairnbairn 2010). This could be understood as the semantic equivalent of an already crisis-ridden but still dominant US-centred global food regime, in which the USA had succeeded since the end of the Second World War in using its Food for Peace (Public Law 480) programme to exchange surpluses for influence, thus influencing the conditions of agriculture worldwide (McMichael & Friedmann 1989). The concept of food security was first prominently presented at the 1974 World Food Summit, while the first signs of the crisis of the US-centred food regime were already evident. Agricultural subsidies were seen by many as too high a burden on national budgets, and exacerbated the production surpluses on which this food regime was based, competition and growth opportunities of large transnational companies were hampered by stagnating export and import figures, e.g. for grain and meat. This pointed a way from a US-centred food regime to a WTO-centred-food-regime/corporate-food-regime (McMichael 2013a), where the Uruguay Round of the GATT created the WTO with its turn towards unequal free trade.

From now on, this turning away from Keynesianism was transferred to the concept of food security, which proclaims the market as a solution to food insecurity and shifts from state and community solutions to the actions of individuals and households. The World Bank's well-known definition of food security is thus free of all influences that point to the social complexity of food: "Access by all people at all times to enough food for an active and healthy life" (World Bank 1986).

Food security thus becomes "agnostic about food production systems" (Vanhaute & Van Den Abeele 2015, p.33) and ignores

> notions of power and control, questions about how a population will earn money to be able to purchase the food that has been made available, or whether indeed a country will be permitted to produce within its borders the food that will be fed to its population.
>
> *(Patel & McMichael 2009, 10)*

The genealogy of the semantics of food security can therefore be analyzed as an interaction with the political economy, but this, however, does not mean that capital simply determines this semantics. As Patel (2009) notes,

> "food security" moved from being simply about producing and distributing food, to a whole nexus of concerns around nutrition, social control and public health. In no small part, that broadening was a direct result of the leadership taken by Via Campesina to introduce at the World Food Summit in 1996 the idea of "food sovereignty", a term that was very specifically intended as a foil to the prevailing notions of food security (665).

Food sovereignty

La Via Campesina, the Nyéléni-movement, human rights and the scientific community

Although still marginal in global terms, food sovereignty has achieved a number of successes in the decades since its development. This is due to the successful work of LVC, which is considered the largest social movement in the world and has through persistent work succeeded in putting the concerns of small peasants, agricultural workers and indigenous peoples on the agenda of world politics, without allowing itself to be taken in by it (Gaarde 2017). For example, LVC made a significant contribution to the UN General Assembly's inclusion of the declaration "Rights of small farmers and other people working in rural areas" in the internationally binding human rights record on 17 December 2018. What is more, some states, such as Venezuela, Senegal and Nepal, have already given constitutional status to the concept of food sovereignty, while others, such as Mali or Bolivia, are ready to do so. In addition, and this can also be regarded as a success of the concept, a global network of activists in the North and South has joined forces in the Nyéléni movement. Last but not least, a broad debate among scientists from various disciplines has developed in order to investigate the social conditions of food sovereignty (Patel 2009; Edelman et al. 2014; Shattuck et al. 2015; Alonso-Fradejas et al. 2015).

A list of claims

Food sovereignty aims to organize food and agriculture beyond the capitalist world market and to oppose the pressure of agrobusiness and institutions of neoliberal global governance outlined above. The implementation of food sovereignty involves a number of conditions that are clearly opposed to the prevailing corporate food regime (Martinez-Torres & Rosset 2010, pp. 169–170):

- food and agriculture must not be part of international free trade agreements;
- the distribution of food should take place on local markets with fair, regulated prices, so that farmers are no longer separated from marketing;
- substantial subsidies must be linked to the needs of smallholder production and not, as the EU and the USA do, benefit agrobusiness;
- the aim is to give farmers sufficient, healthy nutrition and the opportunity to produce their own food themselves the status of a human right;
- land, water and forests are to be transferred to municipal administration through land reforms;
- chemical fertilizers, pesticides and monocultures are to be replaced by agroecology;
- instead of patents and Plant Breeders' Rights, seeds should be freely accessible;
- instead of mere producers of goods, farmers and small peasants are to be recognized in their role as "guardians of culture and crop germplasm" and "stewards of productive resources" (Martinez-Torres & Rosset 2010, 170).

The meaning of "food" and "sovereignty" in food sovereignty

Food sovereignty aims at radical political renewal of contexts in which food is produced, distributed and consumed. The "food" in food sovereignty refers to the distinction between "Food from Nowhere" and "Food from Somewhere". "Food from Nowhere" lies on supermarket shelves, while the origin and conditions of its production remain largely in the dark. By analogy with Marx's (1887, pp. 47–59) famous chapter on the fetish character of commodity, producers have lost control over the "Food from Nowhere", while consumers cannot even take note of the geographical power relations inscribed in it (McMichael 2013a, p. 106). "Food from Somewhere" is food that is not traded on anonymous markets. In local community production, the concrete quality of the work, nature and soil remains visible, producers and consumers meet each other. This does not necessarily mean that global trade is completely excluded in a society shaped by food sovereignty (Burnett & Murphy 2014), even though it is currently disputed in the food regime debate whether a character of "Food from Somewhere" can be achieved in supermarkets through seals and producer guarantees (Campbell 2009).

To what understanding of sovereignty does the second word of the concept refer? At first glance, "sovereignty" here is simply directed against the loss of state-sovereignty within the globalization-process. As described above, the states of the global South add up to give a large part of their room for manoeuvre. In this light, food sovereignty does indeed begin with the demand to give back to the states of the South the legislation on their agriculture. La Via Campesina (1996) states: "Food Sovereignty is the right of each nation to maintain and develop its own capacity to produce its basic foods respecting cultural and productive diversity". But sovereignty here means more than in classical political theory. The territoriality implied by this concept, which Max Weber and Georg Jellinek consider essential, is here connected with the materiality of the soil. By resorting to Polanyi (2010) it can be recalled that sovereignty has always been bound to the land and the food produced on it (McMichael 2014, p. 934) and it is the peasants who work the territory. La Via Campesina therefore extend the concept of sovereignty:

> We should exchange the industrial agroexport food system for a system based on food sovereignty, that returns the land to its social function as the producer of food and sustainer of life, that puts local production of food at the center, as well as the local market and local processing (...).
>
> *(La Via Campesina 2012)*

This allows for reinterpretation of the claim to sovereignty. If the state fails to guarantee the above-mentioned social function, then sovereignty must also be won by local communities of small peasants and consumers against their respective states. The goal is therefore not only to regain state sovereignty against global institutions such as the IMF and the WTO. Rather, food sovereignty means "a *process* of social transformation and a reformulation of states from within" (McMichael 2014). The movement for food sovereignty can make strategic use of the "multiple and competing sovereignties" that globalization has created, as Shattuck et al. (2015) explain:

> Indeed, food sovereignty activists have long worked simultaneously for political change at multiple scales: for national agrarian reform; for international recognition of peasant´s rights; for the creation of local markets; for the development of agroecological farming practices and for transnational farmer-to-farmer-networks to disseminate and share them.
>
> *(p. 425)*

Sovereignty, which in the history of political ideas was aimed at the representation of the people, is reinterpreted in the concept of food sovereignty rather to that global networking of manifold objections against the ruling order that Hardt and Negri (2001) described as multitude. The proposal of food sovereignty in analogy to Baumann's (2012) "Liquid Modernity" as a version of a "Liquid Sovereignty" (Conversi 2016) is certainly difficult to reconcile with the ideological content of sovereignty, but it makes the character of the search for a new understanding of sovereignty clear.

Overcoming the urban/rural and South/North difference

La Via Campesina has repeatedly pointed out that the concept of food sovereignty is not limited to agriculture alone, but concerns the entire social organization between urban and rural areas. Just as the negative effects of the corporate food regime, such as land grabbing, can only be understood in the totality of city and countryside (Zoomers et al. 2017), so food sovereignty is also described as a perspective that unmakes the contrast between city and countryside by establishing a "direct, solidarity-based relationship between producers and consumers" (Edelman et al. 2014, p. 918). Thus, food-sovereignty "is not simply a peasant movement - one might say it is a movement informed by a peasant perspective underlining the importance of revaluing farming for domestic food provisioning and for addressing social inequalities" (McMichael 2014, p. 935). Analogously, it must also be possible to successfully balance the inequalities and contrasts between South and North by understanding and changing the rich consumers of the North through the character of their "imperial way of life" (Brand & Wissen 2018).

Gender awareness

Food sovereignty as a mode of production would also mean ending the burden, and exploitation and violence against women that is structurally inherent in the current food regime. La Via Campesina in particular has put the question of the exploitation of women in globalized agriculture at the top of their agenda.

Food sovereignty in response to the crisis of the corporate food regime

One argument of the supporters of the concept is that the crisis of the current food regime, visible, for example, in the increase in landgrabbing and the recurring price crises for food – especially the price peak of 2007/2008 and the subsequent food riots (McMichael & Patel 2009; Bello & Baviera 2010) – is almost challenging protest and the search for alternatives, as McMichael (2014) stresses:

> While the twentieth-century agrarian crisis has been expressed in various forms of peasant resistance (...) and movements for reform of the agri-food system (...), it is only now, as a final enclosure ensues in the shadow of ´the nemesis effect´, (...) rising energy and food prices and destablisation of human populations, that an ontological alternative is universally meaningful and necessary.
>
> *(p. 19)*

Critique

The concept of food sovereignty has certainly been met with criticism (Bernstein 2014; Jansen 2015; Agarwal 2014). In addition to the question of whether the food regime as a whole can even perceive the assumed crisis, the criticism can be limited to the following points: 1) the adherents did not differentiate the peasantry sufficiently; 2) adherents celebrated the peasant-farmers as quasi-natural resistance against capitalism, without realizing how much they are also integrated in capitalist value chains; 3) and the approach of food sovereignty adopts a relationship that is too affirmative towards agroecology and a merely assumed peasant wisdom, so that the subsequent rejection of any industrial technology denies the small peasants the opportunities associated with it; 4) can also be asked to what extent food-sovereignty produces exclusions by addressing only certain farmers (Jones & Eshleman 2018). These criticisms come from friendly scientific contexts. The political and scientific mainstream, however, remains in the process of ignoring food sovereignty as a possible political solution to the crises of world food supply, bio- and agro-diversity and climate catastrophe.

The discourses of world nutrition: archaeology, genealogy and the resistance of subjected knowledge

Archaeology of discourses: agriculture in development discourse

This observation leads us back to the above-mentioned question of the causes of the still marginal position of food sovereignty in the discourse on global agriculture. Foucault (1972) worked out certain rules of formation with which the sayable is separated from the unsayable in discourses. The structuralism of early Foucault explains these rules of discourse solely "as practices obeying certain rules" (Foucault 1972, 138), which constantly reproduce the discourses themselves. With reference to this archaeology of discourses, theorists of critical post-development theory have been able to show how, since the beginning of modernity, a certain model of development policy, which also encompasses industrial agriculture since the Green Revolution (Patel 2013), was able to assert itself as the undisputed game of truth (Ziai 2015). The effects of development discourse can be described by the dominance of development discourses that construct a difference between lifestyles that are acceptable and lifestyles that are not and therefore have yet to "develop". This means that a difference is created between unacceptable ways of dealing with nature [e.g. subsistence farming by small peasants or agro-ecological agriculture] and the acceptable ways in which industrialized agriculture prevails. With this archaeological perspective it also becomes clear how competing discourses such as that on food sovereignty remain excluded from this order of discourse. The formation rules, which Foucault (1972) distinguishes work in the discourse on development (Ziai 2015, pp. 39–45):

- the formation of objects: the subject of discourse is "underdevelopment" as a deficient form of the societies of the South. Other objects, such as a possible superiority of the indigenous and small peasants' relations to nature, remain outside the discourse;
- the formation of enunciative modalities: in the development discourse, legitimacy and claim to truth belong to the experts, mostly white experts, the institutions and NGOs of the West;
- the formation of concepts: the term "development" defines Western industrialization as the goal. The dualistic basic structure of the discourse is shown by the fact that the associated term "underdevelopment" is associated with a number of terms which are automatically connotated as negative, namely as deviating from the western mode of development, such as "overpopulation". In the discourse of development, the smallholder farmer is also conceived as a deficient embodiment of underdevelopment: she undermines the developed state of the art by neither being integrated into the value chain nor willingly using GMOs and pesticides;
- the formation of strategies: this rule allows the discourse to pick out from the multitude and often contradictory elements those which guarantee its unity. In addition, the discourse can thus govern changes in society and react to non-discursive practices. Ziai leads the critiques of development theories and the transition from the Cold War to the ideology of good governance.

> Despite these changes, the discourse maintained its identity as a "development discourse" by strategically selecting from the new contents.

These formation rules of the development discourse, however, do not remain unbroken. Ziai (2015, pp. 91–97) points out, the undermining of the development discourse of its own goals, which had become increasingly apparent since the 1980s, and revealed its crisis in the 1990s. From then on, the discourse integrated topics such as sustainability, good governance, democratization, global social policy and empowerment. With this intensified reference to problem areas that can hardly be separated from the role of the North in the discourse, such as ecological sustainability, the first cracks in the clear layout of the North-South dichotomy appeared. In the end the discourse still remained framed in such a way that it shifted the problem situation to the South, e.g. by making it necessary for small peasants to become entrepreneurs, through schemes like microcredits (Ziai 2015, pp. 91–97). The development discourse thus systematically leads to the naturalization of the Western development model and at the same time has a depoliticizing effect.

Genealogy of practices: agriculture as biopolitics

After archaeology and its study of discourse formations, Foucault turned to genealogy. To ask genealogical questions means to examine the effect of dispositives, e.g. the interplay of discourses with the materiality producing them (architecture, technology, landscape). The focus is on the question of how people are subjectivized by a certain form of government. For Foucault, the concept of bio-power is essential, the form of power with which the government looks at the whole of the population, not just in order to control them, but to release their potential through a liberal art of government. To govern liberally means to govern as efficiently and economically as possible and to trust in the forces of the market. In order to govern liberally, politics aligns its rationality with the fortune telling of the prize, the neoliberal veridiction (Foucault 2010). At the same time, this form of government aims at a subjectivation of people (Rose 2005), whose neoliberal form can be brought to the formula of the "entrepreneurial personality" (Bröckling 2016).

For research on how agriculture is governed, the advantage of this perspective is that "the lense of biopolitics adds a productive new dimension by focusing on how neoliberal intervention seeks to optimize rural peoples´ valuation and use of the resources in question" (Fletcher et al. 2018, 1071). I will now select two examples from the literature to show how the interplay of neoliberal veridiction, governmental subjectivation and science determines the practice of globalized agriculture:

- Scientific models and an Invisibility Spell: Leblond and Trottier (2016) were able to show how the models from which governments, global organizations and NGOs gain their knowledge about global agriculture are characterized by neoliberal assumptions about productivity, trade and growth. At the same time, these models make smallholder agriculture appear invisible, as the areas of small peasants are too small to be displayed in the pixel sizes chosen by many models. Small peasants are thus subject to an "Invisibility Spell" in the truth games of science. With these models, world food can then only be thought of with reference to increased production in industrial agriculture, while the performance of small peasants is ignored.

> Global models that rose to dominance proved very successful at constructing a representation of the world that legitimizes the activities of certain actors, such as foreign investors who claim to develop potential yields in places suffering from inefficient or inexistent agriculture.

> They also legitimize productivist policies and the promotion of deregulated international market of agricultural products.
>
> *(38)*

By being shared and reproduced within the scientific community, these models give the appearance of objectivity and indisputable technical knowledge. Behind this, however, there are power effects that make the world of small peasants and indigenous people superfluous:

- Entrepreneurship and Nutrition: from a geneaological perspective it can also be shown how philanthropic initiatives like "A New Green Revolution for Africa" and the "New Alliance for Food Security" exert neoliberal governmentality as a joint project of science, politics and business, "more biopolitical - more focused on the management of individual bodies - than the original Green Revolution" (Patel 2013, 5). This is where private economic influence, the social image of the entrepreneur and scientific theories of nutrition come together in favour of the supremacy of agribusiness. This development is not new – the World Bank and AGRA have long been working on a "Value-chain Agriculture" (McMichael 2013b) transforming the small peasants of the global South into subordinate, namely indebted entrepreneurs –, but with the global hunger crisis in 2009, when the number of people starving worldwide exceeded one billion, the actors of the corporate food regime saw the opportunity for an expansion of "nutrition ideology". At their meeting in L'Aquila, Italy, the G8 countries announced the allocation of US$22 billion for action against hunger over the next three years. The G8 relied on the development of new policies and founded the New Alliance for Food Security and Nutrition in 2012 under the US presidency (cf. Patel et al. 2015). The New Alliance, which initially entered into partnerships with Ghana, Ethiopia, Tanzania, Côte d'Ivoire, Burkina Faso and Mozambique, consistently focused on private-sector investment and, in addressing the issue of hunger, oriented itself to the measurement of "nutrition", a term that "pulls the locus of policy action toward the individual body, rather than on the relations that humans have to one another, and the world around them" (Patel 2013, p. 47). This definition can be understood as a mere scientific enumeration of vitamins, minerals and calories. The social conditions for healthy food and its production are ignored. For example, access to land would be indispensable for the elimination of vitamin A and iron deficiency. Instead, the New Alliance is focusing on fortifying foods such as iodized salt or the infamous rice enriched with vitamin A in order to open up new markets for the private sector. It is no coincidence that this kind of knowledge about nutrition is closely interwoven with companies that are virtually dependent on knowing that questions of legitimacy are ignored. For example, the World Bank has launched the Business Alliance for Food Fortification, chaired by companies such as Coca-Cola, Unilever and Danone (Patel et al. 2015).

Resistance and subjugated knowledge

But how can smallholders defend themselves against this kind of government? According to Foucault (2003), criticism is effective if it is able to highlight the fragility of institutions, as "discontinuous, particular, and local critiques" (p.6). Subjugated knowledges, Foucault continues, are on the one hand "historical contents that have been buried or masked in functional coherences or formal systematizations" (p. 7) and on the other hand "whole series of knowledges that have been disqualified as nonconceptual knowledges, as insufficiently elaborated knowledges: naive knowledges, hierarchical inferior knowledges, knowledges that are below the required level of erudition or scientificity" (p. 7).

For the discussion of possible resistance to the dominant food regime, the appeal that Foucault's description of subjugated knowledge constitutes is obvious. The local knowledge of small peasants about other cultivation methods, the various researches on agroecology and finally the indigenous knowledge correspond exactly to the conditions that Foucault formulates for subjugated knowledge (even if he himself had other phenomena in mind). The local organizational form, with which projects of food sovereignty rebel against industrialized agriculture, also is in line with Foucault's considerations of the many local resistances (Foucault 1977). The above examples are not the only way to show how cracks open up in the dispositives and discourses of the global food regime and how resistant, subjugated knowledge penetrates there. For food sovereignty, this is currently particularly evident in the discourses in which the climate catastrophe and the extinction of species mean that the discourse formation and practices of industrial agriculture can no longer be effortlessly maintained. More and more, knowledges are being shaken and the protagonists of food sovereignty are penetrating the discourses with their knowledge of the soil, nature and healthy nutrition.

On the added value of the narrative: food sovereignty as a counter-narrative

A world to win: narrative as explanation of the globalized world, counter-narrative as bundling of protest

The analytical added value of the concept of narratives and counter-narratives comes to light precisely with a view to the relationship between power and resistance through the subjugated knowledge that Foucault examines in his genealogy. While archaeology of discourses and genealogy of power are important for understanding the current food regime, here the dimension of narrative mediation of the world remains peculiarly underexposed. The world-enclosing power of narratives can provide an answer to the question that has been increasingly posed since the 1990s at the latest, namely how the concept of subjugated knowledge can be combined into a global counter-movement (Hardt & Negri 2001). In recent years, the issue of how social movements make use of counter-narratives has attracted increased attention (Wittmayer et al. 2019), and La Via Campesina's struggle for food sovereignty has already received well-founded empirical discussions on the strategic use of its narratives (Juarez 2018).

At this point I ask how the conditions of the narrative following Ricœur (2009) can be translated into the counter-narrative of food sovereignty. Departing from Ricœur´s concept of narrative I aim at demonstrating that Foucault´s conceptualization of discourse lacks considering the idea that narratives are constitutive for the existence of discourses and thus for social order as a whole. There are two arguments for this (Viehöfer 2002). The formation rules of discourses require a flexible structure in order to be updated in speech. At the same time, the practices need an overarching form that transforms the scattered data, episodes, facts into a unified story so that people can access it at all. Both are performed by narratives. Thus, discourses such as those on climate catastrophe (Viehöfer 2010) and on nutrition have always been based on narratives.

Plot, space and time structures: characteristics of narratives

Following up on Viehöfer (2002; 2010), I will elaborate on some characteristics of public narratives and then ask what this means for the narrative of food security and the counter-narrative of food sovereignty.

- Narratives obey a formal principle, the narrative configuration. This ensures that the individual data, facts, episodes, etc. are transformed into a unified story. Narratives obey a fable composition, i.e. they create a plot in which persons, events and coincidences are brought together to form a meaningful story that has a beginning and an end. The surface semantics of the events are combined with a deep semantics of the plot;
- Narratives create their own time compared to chronological time. Episodes and events are thus classified into temporality;
- The narrative also unfolds its own spatial structures;
- Epic, drama and novel create possibilities of thinking to inhabit the world and let us confront reality with these possibilities. Behind this lies the possibility of explaining cultural change through the reorganization of plot structures, but also of trying out new forms of social organization within these plot structures. Viehöfer (2010) has now put forward the fascinating thesis with reference to the climate catastrophe that today the natural sciences form analogous plot structures.

Change the plot: farewell to the entrepreneur

The perspectives for the understanding of food security and food sovereignty opening with this turn to Ricœur become clear with two examples. Consider as an example for the food security narrative the self-portrayal of A New Green Revolution for Africa (AGRA 2017). It reveals a plot in which African small peasants initially inhabit a non-capitalist outside, and are then integrated into the markets through measures of AGRA and investments from the global economy. The objective of the plot is food security on a thriving African continent whose small peasants are integrated into the world of capital through global value chains. Their wishes, needs and hardships are combined at AGRA together with agrobusiness and the global market under the hand to create a success story that has been laid out in the depth structure of the plot. The world that is thought of here is a world populated by liberal entrepreneurs beyond crises and scarcity. What is crucial here is that AGRA's plot is relying on the postmodern neoliberal concept of time and spatial structures as described by Frederik Jameson (1991; 2003). Here, time is perpetual present time detached from past and future, while space is conceived of as a network of global availability. In order for AGRA's food security plot to function, the new small peasants-entrepreneurs are dependent on being integrated into this neoliberal spatio-temporal fix (Jessop 2006).

The elements of the narrative are quite different in the counter-narrative of food sovereignty, if one looks at the writings of La Via Campesina, such as the Marabá Declaration (La Via Campesina 2016). Here, too, small peasants are the protagonists of the plot, albeit in much more differentiated roles. Here the small peasants a priori have the power to create the world of food sovereignty themselves and do not have to be equipped with capital funds first, as in the plot of AGRA. The beginning and end of the plot and the entire configuration with which data and events are inserted differ massively: the beginning of their history lies before colonization and describes neoliberalism as a break, while the end of the plot visualizes a world without exploitation and agrobusiness. In addition, time and space in the narratives of food sovereignty differ fundamentally from time and spatial concepts in the plot of the narrative of food security. Space is no longer the quality-less space created by capital, but the space in which the peculiarities of nature, soil and history have left their traces. Here, time does not step back behind space, but is connected with the events of the Globalization Project, with the rhythms of nature and agriculture, and finally with the time that soil and nature have before the destruction of species and climate catastrophe becomes irreversible.

Conclusion

This juxtaposition of Foucault's concept of power with the concept of counter-narrative could bring the following gain: while on the one hand genealogy and archaeology, as just seen, help to understand the dominance of a neoliberal concept of food security, the concept of the counter-narrative expands the arsenal of social movements such as La Via Campesina. Foucault is right when he writes how the subjugated knowledge penetrates into the cracks of the practices of domination. But if it is true that he underestimates the extent to which archaeology and genealogy are constituted by narratives and that the subjugated knowledge designs its own narratives then this could lead to a new picture of the connection between subjugated knowledge and the fragility of institutions. La Via Campesina and the movement for food sovereignty, as I had argued in the last section, create counter-narratives with their own plots, and notions of time, and space. If the counter-narrative prevails, the constitution of discourses through the narratives of neoliberalism becomes increasingly unlikely. The climate catastrophe now promotes an understanding of time and space that corresponds to food sovereignty: time escapes its neoliberal uniformity (Malm 2018, pp.1–11) and there is little doubt that agroecology and soil valuation must be sustainable. The task should now be to show how the counter-narratives therefore complicate the genealogy and archaeology of the ruling corporate food regime by replacing the plot of faceless value chains with a different understanding of time and space.

Note

1 To distinguish Foucault and the concept of narrative from each other is naturally a heuristic decision. For an understanding of the (counter-)narrative that uses Foucault's concept of power, see the article by Antoinette Fage-Butler in this volume.

References

Agarwal, B. (2014). Food sovereignty, food security and democratic choice: critical contradictions, difficult conciliations, *The Journal of Peasant Studies*, 41:6, 1247–1268, doi: 10.1080/03066150.2013.876996

Alonso-Fradejas, A., Borras, S., Holmes, T., Holt-Giménez, E., & Robbins, M. (2015). Food sovereignty: convergence and contradictions, conditions and challenges, *Third World Quarterly*, 36:3, 431–448, doi: 10.1080/01436597.2015.1023567

AGRA (2017). Strategy overview for 2017 – 2021. Inclusive agricultural transformation in Africa, Available at https://agra.org/wp-content/uploads/2018/02/AGRA-Corporate-Strategy-Doc-3.-2.pdf

Araghi, F. (2009). The invisible hand and the visible foot: Peasants, dispossession and globalization. In A. Akram-Lodhi & K. Christobal (eds.), *Peasants and Globalization: Political Economy, Rural Transformation and the Agrarian Question* (pp. 111–147). London: Routledge.

Bamberg, M. & Andrews, M. (eds.) (2004). *Considering Counter-Narratives: Narrating, Resisting, Making Sense.* Amsterdam: Benjamins.

Bauman, Z. (2012). *Liquid Modernity*. Cambridge: Polity Press.

Bello W. & Baviera, M. (2010). Capitalist agriculture, the food price crisis & peasant resistance, in: Wittman, H., Desmarais, A. A. & Wiebe, N., *Food Sovereignty. Reconnecting Food, Nature & Community*, Halifax: Fernwood Publishing, 62–75.

Bernstein, H. (2014). Food sovereignty via the 'peasant way': a sceptical view, *Journal of Peasant Studies*, 41:6, 1031–1063, doi: 10.1080/03066150.2013.852082

Brand, U. & Wissen, M. (2018). *The Limits to Capitalist Nature: Theorizing and Overcoming the Imperial Mode of Living.* London: Rowman & Littlefield International.

Bröckling, U. (2016). *The Entrepreneurial Self: Fabricating a New Type of Subject.* Los Angeles: SAGE.

Burnett, K. & Murphy, S. (2014). What place for international trade in food sovereignty?, *The Journal of Peasant Studies*, 41:6, 1065–1084, doi: 10.1080/03066150.2013.876995

Campbell, H. (2009). Breaking new ground in food regime theory: corporate environmentalism, ecological feedbacks and the "food from somewhere" regime? *Agric Hum Values* 26:309. https://doi.org/10.1007/s10460-009-9215-8

Castree, N. (2001). Marxism, capitalism, and the production of nature, in: N. Castree & B. Brown (eds.), *Social Nature. Theory, Practice, and Politics*, Malden Ms.: Blackwell Publishers, 189–207.

Conversi, D. (2016). Sovereignty in a changing world: From Westphalia to food sovereignty, *Globalizations*, 13:4, 484–498, doi: 10.1080/14747731.2016.1150570

Edelman, M., Weis, T., Baviskar, A., Borras, S., Holt-Giménez, E., Kandiyoti, D., & Wolford, W. (2014). Introduction: Critical perspectives on food sovereignty, in: *The Journal of Peasant Studies*, 41:6, 911–931. doi: 10.1080/03066150.2014.963568

ETC Group (2018). Too big to feed: The short report. Mega-mergers and the concentration of power in the agri-food sector. Available at www.etcgroup.org/content/too-big-feed-short-report

Fairnbairn, M. (2010). Framing resistance: International food regimes & the roots of food sovereignty, in: Wittman, H., Desmarais, A., & Wiebe, N. (eds.), *Food Sovereignty. Reconnecting Food, Nature & Community* (pp. 15–32). Halifax: Fernwood Publishing.

Fletcher, R., Dressler, W., Anderson, Z., & Büscher, B. (2018). Natural capital must be defended: Green growth as neoliberal biopolitics, in: *The Journal of Peasant Studies*, 46:5, 1068–1095, doi: 10.1080/03066150.2018.1428953.

Foucault, M. (1972). *The Archaeology of Knowledge*. New York: Pantheon.

Foucault, M. (1977). Intellectuals and power. A conversation with Gilles Deleuze, in: D. F. Bouchard (ed.). *Language, Counter-Memory, Practice: Selected Essays and Interviews by Michel Foucault*, Ithaca, New York: Cornell University Press, 205–217.

Foucault, M. (2003). *Society Must be Defended. Lectures at the College de France 1975–1976*, London: Penguin.

Foucault, M. (2010). *The Birth of Biopolitics: Lectures at the Collège de France, 1978–1979*, New York, NY: Palgrave Macmillan.

Friedmann, H. & McMichael, P. (1989). Agriculture and the state system. The rise and decline of national agricultures, 1870 to the present, in: *Sociologia Ruralis*, Vol. XXIX-2, 93–117.

Gaarde, I. (2017). *Peasants Negotiating a Global Policy Space: La Via Campesina in the Committee on World Food Security*. Abingdon: Routledge.

GRAIN (2014). Hungry for land: small farmers feed the world with less than a quarter of all farmland. Available at www.grain.org/article/entries/4929-hungry-for-land-small-farmers-feed-the-world-with-less-than-a-quarter-of-all-farmland

Hardt, M. & Negri, A. (2001). *Empire*. Cambridge, MA: Harvard University Press.

Harvey, D. (2003). *The New Imperialism*. Oxford: Oxford University Press.

IPBES (2019). Global assessment report on biodiversity and ecosystem services of the Intergovernmental Science-Policy Platform on Biodiversity and Ecosystem Services. Available at https://ipbes.net/global-assessment

IPCC (2019). Climate Change and Land: an IPCC special report on climate change, desertification, land degradation, sustainable land management, food security, and greenhouse gas fluxes in terrestrial ecosystems. Available at www.ipcc.ch/srccl/cite-report/

Jameson, F. (1991). *Postmodernism, or, The Cultural Logic of Late Capitalism*, London: Verso.

Jameson, F. (2003). The end of temporality, in: *Critical Inquiry*, 29, 695–718.

Jansen, K. (2015). The debate on food sovereignty theory: Agrarian capitalism, dispossession and agroecology, in: *The Journal of Peasant Studies*, 1, 213–232. doi: 10.1080/03066150.2014.945166

Jessop, B. (2006). Spatial fixes, temporal fixes and spatio-temporal fixes, in: Castree, G. (eds.), *David Harvey. A Critical Reader*, Malden: Blackwell Publishing, pp.142–166.

Jones, K. & Eshleman, J. (2018). Food sovereignty: Governance and exclusion in an alternative social movement, in: Kennedy, A. & Liljeblad, J. (eds.), *Food System Governance. Challenges for Justice, Equality and Human Rights*, London: Routledge.

Juárez, P., Trentini, F. & Becerra, L. (2018). Transformative social innovation for food sovereignty: The disruptive alternative. In: *International Journal of Sociology of Agriculture & Food*, 24: 3, 318–335.

Koc, M. (2013). Discourses of food security. In B. Kraagac (ed.), *Accumulations, Crises, Struggles: Capital and Labour in Contemporary Capitalism* (pp. 245–265). Berlin: LIT Verlag.

La Via Campesina (1996). *The Right to Produce and Access to Land*. Rome: Via Campesina.

La Via Campesina (2012). The people of the world confront the advance of capitalism: Rio +20 and beyond. Available at: https://viacampesina.org/en/the-people-of-the-world-confront-the-advance-of-capitalism-rio-20-and-beyond/

LaVia Campesina (2016). Marabá Declaration International Conference of Agrarian Reform. Available at https://viacampesina.org/en/wp-content/uploads/sites/2/2016/04/2016-06-20%20Marab%20Declaration%20PDF%20EN.pdf

Leblond, N. & Trottier, J. (2016). Performing an invisibility spell: Global models, food regimes and smallholders. In: *The International Journal of Sociology of Agriculture and Food*, 23:1, 21–40.

Lundholt, M. W., Maagaard, C. A., & Piekut, A. (2018). Counternarratives. I. R. L. Heath, & W. Johansen (red.), *The International Encyclopedia of Strategic Communication*. Hoboken, NJ: Wiley-Blackwell. https://doi.org/10.1002/9781119010722.iesc0201

Malm, A. (2018). *The Progress of This Storm. Nature and Society in a Warming World*, London: Verso.

Martínez-Torres, M. & Rosset, P. (2010). La Vía Campesina: the birth and evolution of a transnational social movement, *The Journal of Peasant Studies*, 37:1, 149–175, doi: 10.1080/03066150903498804

Marx, K. (1887). *Capital: A Critique of Political Economy* Volume I. Available at: www.marxists.org/archive/marx/works/download/pdf/Capital-Volume-I.pdf

McMichael, P. (2012). *Development and Social Change, A Global Perspective*. London: Sage.

McMichael, P. (2013a). *Food Regimes and Agrarian Questions*. Halifax: Fernwood Publishing.

McMichael, P. (2013b). Value-chain agriculture and debt relations: Contradictory outcomes, in: *Third World Quarterly*, 34: 4, 671–690.

McMichael, P. (2014). Historicizing food sovereignty. *Journal of Peasant Studies*, 41:6, 933–957, doi: 10.1080/03066150.2013.876999

Mooney, P. & Hunt, S. (2009). Food security: The elaboration of contested claims to a consensus frame. *Rural Sociology*, 74:4, 469–497.

Patel, R. (2009). What does food sovereignty look like? The Journal of Peasant Studies, 36:3, 663–706, doi: 10.1080/03066150903143079

Patel, R. (2013). The Long Green Revolution. *The Journal of Peasant Studies*, 40:1, 1–63. doi: 10.1080/03066150.2012.719224

Patel, R. & McMichael, P. (2009). A political economy of the food riot. *Review: A Journal of the Fernand Braudel Center*, 32:1, 9–35.

Patel, R., Bezner Kerr, R., Shumba, L. & Dakishoni, L. (2015). Cook, eat, man, woman: Understanding the New Alliance for Food Security and Nutrition, nutritionism and its alternatives from Malawi, *The Journal of Peasant Studies*, 42:1, 21–44, doi: 10.1080/03066150.2014.971767

Paul, M. & wa Gĩthĩnji, M. (2018). Small farms, smaller plots: Land size, fragmentation, and productivity in Ethiopia. *The Journal of Peasant Studies*, 45:4, 757–775, doi: 10.1080/03066150.2016.1278365

Polanyi, K. (2010). *The Great Transformation: The Political and Economic Origins of Our Time*. Boston, MA: Beacon Press.

Ricœur, P. (2009). *Time and Narrative, I-III*, Chicago: University of Chicago Press.

Rose, N. (2005). *Governing the Soul: The Shaping of the Private Self*. London: Free Association Books.

Shattuck, A., Schiavoni, S. & VanGelder, Z. (2015). Translating the politics of food sovereignty: Digging into contradictions, *Uncovering New Dimensions, Globalizations*, 12:4, 421–433. doi: 10.1080/14747731.2015.1041243

Smith, N. (2010). *Uneven Development: Nature, Capital, and the Production of Space*. London: Verso.

Vanhaute, E. & Van Den Abeele, C. (2015). Peasant movements in the twentieth and twenty-first centuries: From parochial reactions to global struggle? In: Marung, S. & Middell, M. (eds.), *Transnational Actors, Crossing Borders : Transnational History Studies* (Vol. 8, pp. 17–33). Leipzig, Germany: Leipziger Universitätsverlag.

Viehöfer, W. (2002). "Menschen lesbarer machen": Narration, Diskurs, Referenz, in: M. Arnold, G. Dressler & W. Viehöfer (eds.), *Erzählungen im Öffentlichen. Über die Wirkung narrativer Diskurse*, Wiesbaden: Springer, 65–132.

Viehöver, W. (2010). Governing the planetary greenhouse in spite of scientific uncertainty. In: *Science, Technology & Innovation Studies*, 6:2, 127–154.

Wittmayer, J. M., Backhaus, J., Avelinoa, F., Pel, B., Strasser, T., Kunze, I. & Zuijderwijke, L. (2019). Narratives of change: How social innovation initiatives construct societal transformation. In: Futures, 112, September 2019, 102433 https://doi.org/10.1016/j.futures.2019.06.005

World Bank (1986). Poverty and hunger. *Issues and Options for Food Security in Developing Countries*. Available at http://documents.worldbank.org/curated/en/166331467990005748/pdf/multi-page.pdf

Ziai, A. (2015). *Development Discourse and Global History: From Colonialism to the Sustainable Development Goals*, London: Routledge.

Zoomers, A., van Noorloos, F., Otsuki, K., Steel, G. & van Westen, G. (2017). The rush for land in an urbanizing world: From land grabbing toward developing safe, resilient, and sustainable cities and landscapes, in: *World Development*, 92, 242–252. https://doi.org/10.1016/j.worlddev.2016.11.016

30

Counter-narratives of EU integration

Insights from a discourse analytical comparison of European referendum debates

Wolf J. Schünemann

Introduction

Just until quite recently, descriptions of European integration have been marked by a combination of resounding dominant narratives: the story of the EU as a peace project, as a guarantor of political stability and economic prosperity for all its peoples. What all those stories had in common was their progressive character. This is what Gilbert (2008) described as the "progressive narrative" of EU integration. While Gilbert's view is directed on historiography, the dominant discourse exerted power on political actors across the continent and still does so – though remarkably less forcefully. Those who had political responsibility for European affairs at the national or EU level have tended towards a shared knowledge on the inevitable progressivity of the European project. Those who were striving for such positions have felt the necessity to align with this discourse. Finally, anyone who questioned the shared belief that the EU "has the future on its side" (Gilbert, 2008) risked being excluded from serious and rational discourse and being flagged as a Eurosceptic (Taggart, 1998), which semantically more or less (hard vs. soft Euroscepticism) coincided with being backward-looking, old-fashioned, nationalist, affective and irrational. During the last decade, however, this dominant discourse seems to have considerably lost ground as we have seen a politicization of European politics (Grande & Hutter, 2016). From one crisis of the European project to the next, from national election to national election, voices and stories that openly question EU integration seem to have become much louder. At an early stage, Hooghe and Marks (2008) have grasped this development and therefrom derived the need to overcome dominant functionalist approaches and to move towards a post-functionalist theory of EU integration. Built upon this paradigmatic shift in EU integration theory, a number of empirical works have shed light on comparative patterns of politicization that European politics have undergone (Hutter, & Grande 2014; Statham & Trenz, 2013; Trenz & de Wilde, 2009). However, while those accounts indeed reveil the increased contestation of the European project and are sensitive to sociocultural specificities they have only partly covered the discursive dimension in general and narratives in particular. Thus, there is a need to apply interpretive techniques to study both master and counter-narratives of EU integration more profoundly.

As regards counter-narratives, it seems important to note that so-called Euroscepticism is no niche phenomenon anymore. The counter-narratives of European integration, which were never completely silenced and were sometimes quite present in national public discourses, are here to stay. While they have been articulated and driven by actors at the margins of the political spectrum and have only reluctantly, if at all, been channeled to the levels of decision-making in previous years, today they have more and more reached the center stage of politics. As for the actors, those who were marginalized as helpless Eurosceptics a few years ago are now serious competitors for political power in many European democracies or have already gained governmental offices and sustainably changed European politics and its certainties (Brack & Startin, 2015). The counter-narratives they (re)produce obviously follow discursive strands originating in the earlier days of European integration. Some of them work transnationally, others instead clearly reflect their national signature. In order to study these more general patterns, I take a look at a number of cases, namely countries that to varying degrees have shared an overall integrationist stance in EU history: France, the Netherlands and Ireland. During the 2000s, they all had their own direct democratic situations in which counter-narratives of European integration came up very prominently in public debates and revealed underlying contestation of the community project.

European developments in recent years with the Brexit vote at its dramatic core have made the discursive turn regarding EU integration again even clearer. True, it is important to note the special character of the United Kingdom in this regard. The overall British discourse on European politics has always been much more critical than in most countries in continental Europe (Risse, 2010). However, while certainly articulated in a specific and particularly hostile way, some elements similar to British anti-EU discourse are at work in most of the other member countries as well.

In the following sections, I will present recurrent counter-narratives of EU integration. The empirical results to be presented in sections 3 and 4 stem from a comparative study on EU referendum debates during the EU's constitutional process in the 2000s (Schünemann, 2014, 2018). Beforehand, the next section unfolds the conceptual field of narrativity as far as useful for this chapter. Moreover, it puts emphasis on the conceptual and empirical connections of (counter-) narratives, EU integration and the referendum situation. Finally, it sheds light on the methodology of the study referred to in the empirical parts.

Counter-narratives, narratives, discourse

One of the more recent indications of the interpretive turn in the social sciences (Rabinow & Sullivan, 1979) is the greater interest in narrativity shown by many scholars across the disciplines including political science (Gadinger et al., 2014; Patterson & Monroe, 1998; Roe, 1994). However, explicit analyses of narrativity in EU politics are still scarce (Biegón, 2013; Diez, 1999, Schünemann, 2017; Trenz & de Wilde, 2009). Interestingly, the greater scholarly attention has been flanked or followed by a remarkable arrival of the narrative as a category or even an objective in political communication. In this vein, more and more, politicians publicly plead and seek for narratives in support of policies or polities. In fact, especially EU integration has been an early and frequent case for politicians to derive the need of a certain (a new) narrative. In 2013, for instance, the former President of the EU Commission launched an initiative for a "new narrative for Europe" (Barroso, 2013), which can be interpreted as an attempt to heal the EU's so-called legitimacy deficit.

On the conceptual level, narratives can be understood as special patterns of discursive meaning making. As regards their inner structures, we define narratives as combinations of statements that are organized along a storyline or a plot, which effectively tell a story about something or someone developing in a temporal dimension: "A narrative is essentially a story" (Patterson & Monroe, 1998, p. 315; see also Viehöver, 2006, 2014). Narratives are crucial for human communication as they allow to overcome contingency due to the inherent plausibility of a story: "narrative also refers to the ways in which we construct disparate facts in our own worlds and weave them together cognitively in order to make sense of our reality" (Patterson & Monroe, 1998, p. 315; see also Gadinger et al., 2014, p. 9). More specifically, narratives are central to political communication as they serve basic functions of the political process such as the formation of collective identity, legitimation, argumentation and of course critique (Fisher, 1985).

This chapter is mainly interested in counter-narratives as defined by Andrews: "the stories which people tell and live which offer resistance, either implicitly or explicitly, to dominant cultural narratives" (Andrews, 2004, p. 1). The concept stems from critical theory and critical discourse analysis (Godwin, 2015). Narrative research is loaded with the ambition to contribute to a "liberating and emancipating agenda" (Bamberg, 2004, p. 351). Against this background, it is important to clarify that the research presented in this chapter is critical in the sense of empirical social research only. In contrast to the origins of the concept of counter-narratives in Critical Theory (Zamudio, Russell, Rios, & Bridgeman, 2011), it is not critical in the sense of normatively supporting certain stories or the actors telling them (e.g. the different camps in a campaign), at the expense of others, even if the latter is supposed to be dominant.

The discourse theoretical foundation of my research is taken from Foucault's archaeological and genealogical works (Foucault, 1981; see also Leclercq-Vandelannoitte, 2011, p. 1252). The empirical work presented here is greatly inspired by the Sociology of Knowledge Approach to Discourse (SKAD) developed by Reiner Keller in the late 1990s (Keller, 1998, 2005, 2008, 2013) and broadly applied in modified versions thereafter (Keller, Hornidge, & Schünemann, 2018). This includes applications for political debates and its special logic in general and for EU referendum debates in particular as exerted by Schünemann (2014; 2018). Following SKAD, the narrative is only one structural element that can be observed in discourses and in which knowledge and meaning are processed. A narrative is thus an interpretive scheme of a particular kind among others. What makes it special is its particular form, as it basically tells a story. Thus, it is at least marked by a consecutive line of events or in other words: "discrete sequences of symbolic actions" (Fisher, 1985, p. 358) and significant actor constellations: "individual characters emerge as protagonists versus antagonists, as good versus bad, as heroes versus villains" (Bamberg, 2004, p. 357).

Narrativity is of special interest for the study of political debates as the narrative paradigm revolves around the rhetorical function of "social influence" (Fisher, 1985, p. 354). Political speech in general is often directed towards the goal of building or affirming collective identities, which is even increased by the need for addressing populations (Charland, 2001, p. 617). EU political debates especially touch upon constitutive questions of (political) identities. Among discursive formats, one could argue with Bamberg (2004, p. 354), narratives have become "the privileged way of fashioning self and identity". Also according to the literature on new rhetoric (Perelman, 1980), rhetorical constitution is done by storytelling: "Narrative is fundamental to the rhetoric of constitution because narratives open diegetic spaces, story spaces, which are meaningful because they produce identification with a point of view" (Charland, 2001, p. 617; see also Kramer, 2014, p. 699; Patterson & Monroe, 1998). As in EU political debates, it is rather easy to depict the issue voted on as one on which the transformation of political communities, maybe even the successive loss of a collective identity, depends.

EU referendum debates are thus particularly well-suited for studying counter-narratives, as referendums serve as facilitating moments for dissenting voices to appear since they open up the usual discursive space that is structured by political competition (of office-seeking actors) to new kinds of actors, organizations and their stories. Direct democratic votes and the debates around them thus change the political and discursive opportunity structures (Koopmans & Statham, 1999; McCammon, 2014; Rucht, 1994; Schünemann, 2016; Trenz & de Wilde, 2009; Ullrich, 2013). Direct votes give political actors that find themselves normally at the margins of the political spectrum with less visibility the chance to speak up, to be seen and listened to in mainstream media, as they constitute the main opposition forces in a major and suddenly bipolar political conflict on EU integration.

From a comparative perspective, there is a clear advantage in orienting towards the constitutional process instead of studying, for instance, the recent Brexit referendum, as the cases chosen constitute a comparative selection. All of these referendums dealt with related treaties (Constitutional Treaty for France and the Netherlands in 2005; Lisbon Treaty for Ireland in 2008/2009). The treaty documents differed mostly in form but were very similar regarding the provisions enshrined. Moreover, the constitutional process must be seen as a turning period in European integration, as it represents the culmination of neo-federalist ambition. This ambition is important for our view on dominant narratives and counter-narratives, as the constitutional moment was the high time of the dominant progressive narrative. In effect, referendum campaigns and results considerably shook many well-conserved certainties that had worked as the foundation of dominant narratives beforehand.

For the empirical discourse analysis, a comprehensive data corpus was built, including large numbers (F: 620, NL: 294, IRL: 528) of campaign documents produced during the respective referendum campaigns and published on the publicly available websites of the relevant campaign actors. In addition, 29 background interviews with politicians and activists have been conducted in Amsterdam, Den Haag, Dublin and Paris in 2009 and 2010. I approached the data material with a strategy of open coding for a first round and then recoded the entire data set with a developed codebook a second time.

Progressive narratives of EU integration as the constitutive elements of a dominant discourse

In order to identify counter-narratives, it is important to clarify what can be considered a dominant discourse or dominant narrative, the "master-narrative" (Andrews, 2004; Bamberg, 2004, p. 359; Zamudio et al., 2011; "meta-narrative" in Patterson & Monroe, 1998. Indeed, as Trenz and de Wilde (2009, p. 2) rightly state: "The assessment of the worth of European integration [] takes place through narratives and counter-narratives". As to the dominant narrative, one can recur to what Gilbert (2008) dissects as a progressive narrative, which has been shared by Europhiles of all sorts, politicians, journalists and even academics, in empirical analysis turns out to be a combination of at least three constitutive elements: one is emphasizing peace, the other prosperity and the third teleology. While the first and second thus include important rationales for European integration, the third is a kind of integrationist metanarrative about the only available direction for the development of European integration.

The *historical narrative* for many countries focuses on the EU's quality as a peace project. At least, in the French and Dutch referendum debates, we can easily find a widely shared continental European story of peace and stability. After centuries of conflict and war between European national states (Poniatowski, 2005) it is the "peace project Europe" (Halsema, 2005) that suffices for many as a one-word-legitimation of continuing integration. In this sense, during the French debate on the Constitutional Treaty the PS politician and former prime minister Pierre Mauroy named peace in a Senate intervention as the primary reason to vote yes on the treaty and referred to the founding fathers of the Communities: "The prime goal of those who have engaged in the European construction after the Second World War, was to build peace" (Mauroy, 2005). The same narrative was also very present in the Dutch debate:

> The truth is that Europe is an unknown success story. Sixty years ago, Europe rose from the ashes produced by hate, intolerance and violence and it succeeded in living the dream of a free and peaceful continent. Never before, mankind had succeeded in such a gigantic project of freedom, democracy, human rights, equality, solidarity and prosperity.
>
> *(Veld, 2005)*

Despite its transnational character, the Irish case shows that the story of Europe as a peace project can be told (if at all) in a very country-specific manner. For the Irish debate, there are only rare instances in which the narrative was articulated, mostly in a very specific way referring to the Northern Ireland question: "Without the support and example of the EU it is difficult to imagine Northern Ireland at peace with itself, the Republic and the United Kingdom" (Costello, 2008). This argument has regained its importance in the current negotiations of the EU-British trade relations after Brexit, in which the available options for cross-border trade between the parts of the Irish Island are of central importance (Irish backstop).

The widely shared success stories of EU integration, however, are not only about peace, but also prosperity. So, there is a very frequently reproduced *economic narrative*, telling the economic success story of EU integration. Of course, this narrative frequently interferes with the peace story (see Veld, 2005). However, the two narratives can be analytically separated. First of all, it is fair to say that, until the Euro crisis, it was an easy task and frequent practice to frame European integration as an economic success story. In fact, economic growth and increasing prosperity in all corners of the European Union were the overall promises upon which the community had been more or less built. And indeed, while one could evaluate the achievements of the EU in specific policy fields very differently, the positive economic effects of regional integration for member states and their societies were taken for granted by many observers for a long time. Thus, not surprisingly, economic success stories did frequently appear in the referendum debates and served as a prime reason for why continued integration in general and the ratification of the treaty at hand in particular was good for Europe and the respective nation. The Dutch case is a good example in this regard. There was hardly a treaty proponent not making an economic argument by telling the economic success story of market integration and emphasizing the export-oriented position of the country as an "open economy" (Nicolaï, 2005) being particularly dependent on the economic exchange with their partner states within the Union: "Open borders, the Euro and the free competition on the European market constitute the lifeline of our economy" (Kroes, 2005). Given the widely shared knowledge on the meaning of the EU single market for the Dutch economy, it was easy for proponents – though not without danger in a democratic debate – to transform the argument into threatening narratives of isolation and damage in the case of a no vote. For instance, then-minister of economic affairs Laurens Jan Brinkhorst warned: "Then in the long run the lights will go down in the Netherlands" (cited in Voerman & Van de Walle, 2009, p. 110). This narrative pattern of course can also serve as an early example of what in the context of the British referendum has been widely criticized as so-called "project fear" (Daddow, 2016).

The narrative of the economic success story was very prominent in the Irish debates on the Lisbon Treaty as well. Also, Ireland is normally portrayed as a particularly open and globalized economy, "the best gateway to Europe" (Burke, 2008), which is heavily dependent on foreign direct investment. In this sense, Ireland's place as an "attractive location for FDI" (Whelan, 2008) or "a desirable location for both existing and future foreign direct investment by businesses seeking a foothold in the European market" (Power, 2008) was attributed to European market integration. Interestingly, the economic success story of European integration was told in a nationally specific way, as it appears combined with the ubiquitous narrative of the Celtic Tiger: "The historic economic and political developments in Ireland during our membership of the EU represent a European success story as well as an obviously Irish one" (Roche, 2007). The miraculous transformation of Ireland from the "poor man of Europe" to its "shining light" is clearly the prevalent narrative pattern in this context. Thus, European integration and the EU were not so much seen as a success story in and of themselves, but rather for having served as a facilitator of the country's economic development: "EU membership has been pivotal to Ireland's success story" (Kenny, 2008). The French case, in contrast, shows how the economic success story there had already lost its appeal in 2005. It appeared very seldom and in a very specific, i.e. sceptical, manner. The French case serves as a good example to show how EU integration can be associated with unfavourable restrictions on economic development and even industrial decline. These patterns have clearly become more and more visible in the course of the so-called Euro crisis and the resulting politicization of the EU's economic order (Kriesi & Grande, 2016).

Fitting into the context of constitutional debate, the *constitutional narrative* is a progressive narrative of a particular kind, as it articulates the vision enshrined in European treaties from the outset as the unspecified goal of integrationist efforts: an ever closer union (art. 1 EU Treaty). The basic narrative manifests its teleology therein that every new treaty was depicted as the necessary next step on the ladder of integration: "Now it is time for the next step, with the Lisbon Treaty" (Mitchell, 2008). Thus, in the statements of treaty proponents, it is not about a potentially controversial reform of the EU, nor about certain policies and their effects on Europe and the respective nation, but about timely development. In a rather technical sense, it is thus not a matter of politics but a matter of modernization (White, 2008). As with the bicycle metaphor, introduced so prominently by the first European Commission president Walter Hallstein and repeated so often ever since, speakers that articulate this argument suggest that any form of stagnation in institutional development would mean an existential risk to integration as such: "Timely and appropriate reform is the lifeblood of all successful organisations" (Cox, 2008). Against this background, the treaty at hand would bring the necessary institutional reforms for preserving the Union and its governability in the twenty-first century: "This new century requires a new Europe" (Lamassoure, 2005).

Counter-narratives of EU integration

What is true for the dominant or progressive narrative, namely that it must not be seen as singular but as a set of narratives, is also true for the opposite side. In contrast to the assumption that so-called Euroscepticism would need to be understood as "a counter-narrative" itself (Trenz & de Wilde, 2009, p. 4), I would argue that there is not one Euroscepticim and that EU critique manifests in a diverse set of counter-narratives of which frequently occuring examples are discussed in the following.

Anti-federalist narrative of the European superstate

The most fundamental counter-narrative of EU integration points to the essence of integrationist logic from another perspective. It is the equally progressive, anti-federalist narrative of the European superstate. EU integration is basically perceived as a creeping loss of political authority and national sovereignty through further competence transfers to the EU level with a superstate as its undeclared final goal. It is prominent in the discourses of treaty opponents in all cases examined. With the treaty at hand, as opponents told the story towards its inevitable end, the federalist move subsequently undermining national autonomy and transforming member states into provinces of a new federal state would be complete. Unsurprisingly, the narrative was told in a particularly dramatic fashion on the far right. "No to the European super state" (LPF, 2005), is, for example, one of the central slogans of LPF (Lijst Pim Frotuyn) in the Dutch debate. In the French debate, among many others, the leader of the French Front National (FN), Jean-Marie Le Pen, derived the supposed state quality of the new union directly from its constitutional symbolism: "A Constitution is the founding act of a state [...] the European Constitution is thus the founding act of the European Super-State" (Le Pen, 2005a). The sovereignist MPF (Mouvement pour la France) equally portrayed the Constitutional Treaty as "the supreme law [...] of a European superstate on its way to being finalized" (MPF, 2005). From the perspective of the critics, the tendency towards federalization has always been the hidden agenda behind European integration: "European integration has a history of creeping federalisation" (Rouvoet & van Middelkoop, 2005). In contrast, the nation state is depicted as being reduced to provincial status: "a province of Europe, governed by Brussels" (Labaune, 2005). In the Dutch case, right-wing populist Geert Wilders explained during a talk: "The European constitution abrogates the principle of primacy of national democracy and political independence of member states. Both, in a judicial and a political sense, the Netherlands become the province of a European super state" (Wilders, 2005a). Even the Dutch SP (Socialist Party) leader warned that the Netherlands would degenerate into a powerless province (Marijnissen, 2005). The term province, of course, has special connotations in the Dutch historical context (Republic of the Seven United Netherlands). Wilders, for instance, used the intertextual reference when naming the central document of his campaign "onafhankelijkheidsverklaring" ("independence declaration", Wilders, 2005b).

The special meaning of the terms "province" and even "union" gets very clear in the Irish case with the context of a more vivid post-colonial trauma. Speakers often combined and dramatized the fear of a European superstate with the warning against a new empire oppressing the young Irish nation. For instance, PANA-speaker (Peace and Neutrality Alliance) Cole said: "Of course Ireland was part of a militarised, centralised, neo-liberal Superstate before, it was called the British Union and Empire" (Cole, 2008). As regards the term province, it offers the opportunity for interesting intertextual references. So Cóir stated in a leaflet: "We'll be a province once again" (Cóir, 2008), thereby referring to the famous Irish rebel song "A nation once again". The anti-federalist narrative of the European superstate at least partly originates from British EU critique. Thus, it is not surprising that it also loomed large in the most recent case, the Brexit referendum. However, in the run-up to the referendum in 2016 the derived motive to "take back control" was linked to the issue of immigration and border control as well as the related newer counter-narratives of EU integration (Hobolt, 2016).

The narrative of the neoliberal project

Another recurrent counter-narrative traditionally voiced by the political left throughout Europe is not at all confined to such actors. However, it also shows clear repercussions for other camps across the political spectrum. It says that European integration was essentially driven by big business and big finance following their hidden neoliberal agenda. Market ideology is said to be the leading idea of integration and the whole construction was based upon it, hence leading to ruinous deregulation, undermined welfare states and substantial threats to democracy:

> For fifty years, in which the political elites have constructed Europe, their goal has been to create a market at the continental level wherein capital and products can freely move in order to respond to the expansion of the largest companies.
>
> *(Laguiller, 2005)*

This counter-narrative has traditionally been particularly strong in the French discourse. Here, hardly any treaty opponents existed who would not have told the story of European integration as driven by "the neoliberal ideology" (Hoang-Ngoc, 2005) or referring to the treaty at hand as the "neoliberal constitution" (Généreux, 2005). Especially given its pseudo-constitutional ambition, the treaty at hand was very suspicious to many observers, as it would cement liberal market ideology, which normally should be left open and modifiable to politics. With this special status, in a teleological sequence of neoliberal reforms of the EU, this treaty was depicted as a culmination point, as it would not only regulate an economic system but constitutionalize it: "No to neoliberalism forever" (MRC, 2005).

While it was central to the argumentation of all treaty opponents in the French debate, the narrative of the neoliberal project was not as present in the Dutch and Irish cases. Where it appeared at all, it was rather exclusively voiced by campaigners on the left. So, for instance, SP politician Van Bommel clarified: "In my opinion, with the more moderated Lisbon agenda, it is only confirmed what we knew for a long time anyway; the European Union is an economic union in the first place, predominantly oriented towards a liberal internal market" (van Bommel, 2005). In a central document of CAEUC (Campaign Against the EU Constitution), it becomes obvious how the Lisbon Treaty was portrayed as one element in a long series of treaty reforms dedicated to a neoliberal agenda: "Neo-liberalism is EU policy, and it is pushed further by this renamed constitution" (Burke, 2008). Many other campaigners in the Dutch and Irish debates criticized the "ultra-liberal character of the EU" (Kox, 2005) or the "neo-liberal EU superstate" (Cole, 2008). They pointed to the "primacy of the free market" in different provisions made by the treaty and rooted it in a "neoliberal economic agenda" (RSF, 2008).

In more detailed reasoning, some ingredients of the neoliberal project are the same and seem to work on a transnational basis, namely the sanctification and constitutionalization of free-market ideology as well as a warning against social dumping or the famous "race to the bottom" (CGN, 2005; Généreux, 2005; Higgins, 2008). However, other concerns or blind spots seem to be more country-specific. For instance, the problem of fiscal dumping played a central role in the French debate. However, not very surprising given the Irish economic position as a tax haven, it was completely missing in the Irish debate where economic success was largely attributed to low corporate tax rates attracting foreign direct investments. In contrast, the critique of enforced austerity through the Stability and Growth Pact was an important element, especially in the French debate where the "stupid pact" (Lecourieux, 2005) became a resounding dictum. It also appeared from time to time in the Irish debate (Allen, 2008). However, we found not one instance for the Dutch case, as the Netherlands is traditionally attached to a stability dogma in financial policy. Seen from today, the transnational quality of this narrative is however obvious given its appearance as a central discursive piece of public and political contestation of EU austerity programs in the countries affected by the so-called Euro crisis (Kriesi & Grande, 2016).

The narrative of the democratic deficit

The democratic deficit of the European Union is a constantly and transnationally debated concern regarding European integration, at least since the qualitative transformation of the Union with the Maastricht Treaty in the 1990s. It is also a key term of the referendum debates examined.

While proponents admitted the deficit but pointed to the respective institutional reforms enshrined in the treaty as potential remedies, opponents did not regard the reforms as sufficient. Moreover, every new competence transfer to the EU level was seen as happening at the expense of more authentic democracy at the national level. In stories on the democratic deficit, the Commission once more played the bugaboo role as an "unelected elite" (Cochrane, 2008), "a non-elected Brussels Commission" (NP, 2008), "the bureaucracy of Brussels" (DLR, 2005), "Brussels bureaucrats and politicians" (Herben, 2005), "a faceless bureaucracy" (Ó Snodaigh, 2008) and "the tyranny of bureaucrats" (Le Pen, 2005b). Based in Brussels, thus far away from the citizens and their needs, this Commission would, however, attract more powers. In the Dutch debate, it was not Geert Wilders alone who argued in very general terms: "Europe is not any more a Europe of the people, but a Europe of bureaucrats from Brussels" (Wilders, 2005b). The general story was very similarly told by the French MPF: "Europe is erected without and against its people" (MPF, 2005).

What is more, the treaty was depicted as an aggravation of the democratic deficit. Due to competence transfers to the European level, it would further erode national democracies without building a sufficient alternative: "They kill our national democracies without building a real European democracy" (DLR, 2005). Treaty provisions that prescribe a transfer of new competences from the national to the European level were thus placed within a trend of disempowerment of national institutions, particularly democratically elected parliaments. In this vein, the Lisbon Treaty, for instance, was depicted by opponents as a "further erosion of our democratic rights" (Voteno, 2008).

The narrative of the democratic deficit is of course a constant element of EU critique that appears and – supposedly – functions transnationally. Of course, it served as discursive cornerstone for so-called Brexiteers of all sorts in the case of the British referendum on EU membership. Moreover, it is central to EU-critique uttered across political spectrums in all member states, regardless of the referendum situation.

Conclusion: forget the bicycle – the EU can stand (and fall later)

During years of European integration, it has not been taken into account that the story of the European project can be told in different ways. Progressive narratives of peace, stability and prosperity were dominant in EU historiography as well as the discourses shared among elites at all levels of the multi-level system. In contrast, dissenting voices and the stories they told were marginalized as Eurosceptical. This has changed only recently with so-called Eurosceptics gaining ground in political conflicts on integration. This comes with political consequences, as the European project has seen many instances of public contestation that resulted in stagnation and even regression and disintegration (see Brexit). So, now, it is indeed time for a post-functionalist integration theory (Hooghe & Marks, 2008) as the neo-functionalist approach, illustrated by the metaphor of the bicycle that needs to move forward continuously, cannot explain recent developments convincingly.

However, while open contestation, especially by national political leaders, might be an unfamiliar phenomenon, contestation has been present before. We can find traces of the counter-narratives that are resounding today further back in integration history. Direct democratic votes on EU issues and the political debates leading up to them serve as good cases to study the threads of dissent, most of the time hidden behind a rather elitist permissive consensus. This chapter revealed some of the most persistent counter-narratives of European integration in the referendum debates on the ratification of the EU Constitutional Treaty and the Lisbon Treaty in 2005 and 2008/2009 respectively. By applying a methodology based on the Sociology of

Knowledge Approach to Discourse (SKAD), it tried to systematically dissect the prominent counter-narratives and to depict them in international comparison, thereby also pointing to their country-specific features.

Interestingly, when analyzing EU political debates and campaigns, the common perspective on (dominant) narratives and counter-narratives of EU integration must be reverted on the operational level. In fact, referendum debates on EU issues have mostly shown that EU-sceptics and critical forces came out earlier and articulated their statements and stories more forcefully, so that, more or less, Europhile mainstream actors had to react, and traditional progressive narratives of EU integration often appeared as counter-arguments against the critics. Today, the relation of forces seems to have reversed anyway, as many Eurosceptics have occupied central positions within their political systems or even made it into government offices. Moreover, the share of hard and soft critics of European integration in the European Parliament is likely to rise again after the European Parliament elections in May 2019. This will most probably have the effect that counter-narratives of European integration will further gain ground in EU politics.

References

Allen, K. (2008). *Reasons to Vote No to the Lisbon Treaty. EU Constitution Referendum 2008.* Retrieved from https://web.archive.org/web/20110311023827/http://www.voteno.ie/resources/reasons-to-vote-no-to-the-lisbon-treaty.pdf.

Andrews, M. (2004). Opening to the original contributions: Counter-narratives and the power to oppose. In M. G. W. Bamberg & M. Andrews (Eds.), *Studies in narrative: Vol. 4. Considering counter-narratives: Narrating, resisting, making sense* (pp. 1–6). Amsterdam: Benjamins.

Bamberg, M. G. W. (2004). Considering counter narratives. In M. G. W. Bamberg & M. Andrews (Eds.), *Studies in narrative: Vol. 4. Considering counter-narratives: Narrating, resisting, making sense* (pp. 351–371). Amsterdam: Benjamins.

Barroso, J. M. (2013). *A new narrative for Europe.* Retrieved from http://europa.eu/rapid/press-release_SPEECH-13-357_en.htm.

Biegón, D. (2013). Specifying the arena of possibilities: Post-structuralist narrative analysis and the European Commission's legitimation strategies. *Journal of Common Market Studies*, 51(2), 194–211.

Brack, N., & Startin, N. (2015). Introduction: Euroscepticism, from the margins to the mainstream. *International Political Science Review*, *36*, 239–249. https://doi.org/10.1177/0192512115577231

Burke, C. (2008). *Vote "Yes" for more jobs - Colm Burke MEP.* Retrieved from www.finegael.ie/news/y/1010565/article/ CAEUC. (2008). Lisbon Treaty. Vote No. Retrieved from www.campaign-against-eu-constitution.org/files/CAEUCpamphlet4Feb08.pdf.

CGN. (2005). *5 redenen om tegen te stemmen.* Retrieved from http://web.archive.org/web/20071114010337/http://www.grondwetnee.org:80/grondwetnee2.php?subaction=showfull&id=1115393004&archive=&start_from=&ucat=2&category=2.

Charland, M. (2001). Politics: Constitutive rhetoric. In T. O. Sloane (Ed.), *Encyclopedia of rhetoric* (pp. 616–619). Oxford [u.a.]: Oxford University Press.

Cochrane, D. (2008). *Libertas to Government: "We're Ready, Name the Date".* Retrieved from http://web.archive.org/web/20080302015400/www.libertas.org/content/view/241/127/.

Cóir. (2008). *See how Lisbon will cost you. 4 things you should know.* Retrieved from www.coircampaign.org/images/LeafletsPosters/leaflet_may08_final.pdf.

Cole, R. (2008). *Partnership Europe or Imperial Europe.* Retrieved from www.pana.ie/idn/240408.html.

Costello, J. (2008). *Defeat for Lisbon would rob workers north and south of major benefits.* Dublin. Retrieved from https://web.archive.org/web/20090504165752/http://www.labour.ie/press/listing/1211881008604603.html.

Cox, P. (2008). *Voting YES Will Consolidate and Enhance Ireland's European and Global Prospects into the Future.* Retrieved from http://web.archive.org/web/20080517070521/yestolisbon.ie/index.php/component/content/article/49?ed=1.

Daddow, O. (2016). *Project Fear is the legacy of decades of Euroscepticism. Dare Cameron make a positive case for the EU?* Retrieved from http://eprints.lse.ac.uk/73262/1/blogs.lse.ac.uk-Project%20Fear%20is%20the%20legacy%20of%20decades%20of%20Euroscepticism%20Dare%20Cameron%20make%20a%20positive%20case%20for%20the%20EU.pdf.

Diez, T. (1999). Speaking 'Europe': The politics of integration discourse. *Journal of European Public Policy*, 6(4), 598–613.

DLR. (2005). *L'Europe bureaucratique ou l'Europe des citoyens?* Retrieved from http://web.archive.org/web/20050408041105/http://www.lachainedunon.com/.

Fisher, W. R. (1985). The narrative paradigm: An elaboration. *Communication Monographs*, *52*, 347–367. https://doi.org/10.1080/03637758509376117

Foucault, M. (1981). *Archäologie des Wissens. Suhrkamp-Taschenbuch Wissenschaft: Vol. 356*. Frankfurt am Main: Suhrkamp.

Gadinger, F., Jarzebski, S. & Yildiz, T. (2014). Politische Narrative. Konturen einer politikwissenschaftlichen Erzähltheorie. In F. Gadinger, S. Jarzebski & T. Yildiz (Eds.): *Politische Narrative. Konzepte - Analysen - Forschungspraxis*. Wiesbaden: Springer VS (pp. 3–38).

Généreux, J. (2005). *Au nom de l'Europe, c'est NON*. Retrieved from http://web.archive.org/web/20051016001404/http://www.france.attac.org/a4910.

Gilbert, M. (2008). Narrating the process: Questioning the progressive story of European integration. *Journal of Common Market Studies*, *46*, 641–662.

Godwin, K. A. (2015). The counter narrative: Critical analysis of liberal education in global context. *New Global Studies*, *9*, 181. https://doi.org/10.1515/ngs-2015-0033

Grande, E. & Hutter, S. (2016). The politicisation of Europe in public debates on major integration steps. In S. Hutter, E. Grande, & H. Kriesi (Eds.), *Politicising Europe: Integration and mass politics* (pp. 63–89). Cambridge: Cambridge University Press.

Halsema, F. (2005). *De Europese Grondwet verdient een progressieve voorstem*. Retrieved from http://groenlinks.nl/nieuws/2006/09/19/de-europese-grondwet-verdient-een-progressieve-voorstem.

Herben, M. (2005). Pleidooi voor een Europa van de menselijke maat. In B. J. Spruyt & E. B. Stichting (Eds.), *Samen Zwak. Pleidooien tegen de Europese Grondwet* (pp. 53–59). Amsterdam.

Higgins, J. (2008). Why you should Vote No to Lisbon. *The Socialist, 35*.

Hoang-Ngoc, L. (2005). *L'idéologie néo-libérale du «gouvernement économique» européen*. Retrieved from http://web.archive.org/web/20050325005306/www.nonsocialiste.fr/article/articleview/453/1/318/.

Hobolt, S. B. (2016). The Brexit vote: A divided nation, a divided continent. *Journal of European Public Policy*, *23*(9), 1259–1277. https://doi.org/10.1080/13501763.2016.1225785

Hooghe, L. & Marks, G. (2008). A postfunctionalist theory of European integration: From permissive consensus to constraining dissensus. *British Journal of Political Science*, *39*, 1–23.

Hutter, S. & Grande, E. (2014). Politicizing Europe in the national electoral arena: A comparative analysis of five West European countries, 1970–2010. *Journal of Common Market Studies, 52*(5), 1002–1018. https://doi.org/10.1111/jcms.12133

Keller, R. (1998). *Müll - die gesellschaftliche Konstruktion des Wertvollen. Die öffentliche Diskussion über Abfall in Deutschland und Frankreich*. Opladen, Wiesbaden: Westdt. Verl.

Keller, R. (2005). Analysing discourse. An approach from the sociology of knowledge. *Forum: Qualitative Social Research (FQS)*, *6*, Art. 32.

Keller, R. (2008). *Wissenssoziologische Diskursanalyse Grundlegung eines Forschungsprogramms* (2. Aufl.). Wiesbaden: VS Verl. für Sozialwissenschaften.

Keller, R. (2013). *Doing discourse research: An introduction for social scientists*. London: SAGE Publications.

Keller, R., Hornidge, A.-K. & Schünemann, W. J. (Eds.). (2018). *Routledge advances in sociology. The sociology of knowledge approach to discourse: Investigating the politics of knowledge and meaning-making*. Abingdon, Oxon; New York, NY: Routledge.

Kenny, E. (2008). *Europe: Let's Be At The Heart Of It - Kenny*. Retrieved from www.finegael.ie/news/y/1009701/article/.

Koopmans, R. & Statham, P. (1999). Political claims analysis: Integrating protest event and political discourse approaches. *Mobilization: An International Quarterly*, *4*, 203–221. https://doi.org/10.17813/maiq.4.2.d7593370607l6756

Kox, T. (2005). *Frans nee heeft grote invloed op Nederlands euro-referendum*. Retrieved from https://web.archive.org/web/20120505230735/http://www.sp.nl/nieuwsberichten/2681/050415-frans_nee_heeft_grote_invloed_op_nederlands_euro_referendum.html.

Kramer, O. (2014). Politik zwischen Gegenwart und Zukunft: Das *genus deliberativum* in der Mediokratie. In G. Ueding & G. Kalivoda (Eds.), *Rhetorik-Forschungen: Vol. 21. Wege moderner Rhetorikforschung: Klassische Fundamente und interdisziplinäre Entwicklung* (pp. 681–701). Berlin: de Gruyter.

Kriesi, H., & Grande, E. (2016). The Euro crisis: A boost to the politicisation of European integration? In S. Hutter, E. Grande, & H. Kriesi (Eds.), *Politicising Europe: Integration and mass politics* (pp. 240–276). Cambridge: Cambridge University Press.

Kroes, N. (2005). *Neelie Kroes, Europees Commissaris voor de Mededinging*. Retrieved from http://web.archive.org/web/20061002111905/www.vvd.nl/index.aspx?FilterId=974&ChapterId=1147&ContentId=1790.

Labaune, P. (2005). *Le combat de la France*. Retrieved from http://web.archive.org/web/20061107031117if_/http://www.debout-la-republique.fr:80/.

Laguiller, A. (2005). Au référendum, c'est Non! *Lutte Ouvrière, 2005*.

Lamassoure, A. (2005). Ce siècle nouveau exige une Europe nouvelle. *Le Figaro*.

Le Pen, J.-M. (2005a). *Intervention Parlement Européen, Strasbourg*. Retrieved from http://web.archive.org/web/20050606103638/http://www.frontnational.com/doc_interventions_detail.php?id_inter=34.

Le Pen, J.-M. (2005b). *Déclaration de M. Jean-Marie Le Pen, président du Front national, sur les raisons de voter "non" au référendum sur la Constitution européenne du 29 mai*, Paris le 1er mai 2005. Retrieved from http://web.archive.org/web/20050606103605/http://www.frontnational.com/doc_interventions_detail.php?id_inter=72.

Leclercq-Vandelannoitte, A. (2011). Organizations as discursive constructions: A Foucauldian approach. *Organization Studies, 32*, 1247–1271. https://doi.org/10.1177/0170840611411395

Lecourieux, A. (2005). *L'Europe, espace pertinent face à la mondialisation*. Retrieved from http://web.archive.org/web/20051018051810/http://www.france.attac.org/a4644.

LPF. (2005). *Waarom "NEE" tegen de Europese Grondwet*. Retrieved from http://nederland.archipol.ub.rug.nl/content/lpf/20050607/www.lijstpimfortuyn.nl/article4e8c.html?id=980.

Marijnissen, J. (2005, May 21 2005). De ene Eurostaat komt er in een snel tempo aan. *Trouw*.

Mauroy, P. (2005). *Intervention de Pierre Mauroy: révision constitutionnelle*. Retrieved from http://web.archive.org/web/20050524180334/www.ouisocialiste.net/article.php3?id_article=358.

McCammon, H. (2014). Discursive opportunity structure. In D. A. Snow, D. Della Porta, B. Klandermans, & D. McAdam (Eds.), *Wiley-Blackwell encyclopedias in social science. The Wiley-Blackwell encyclopedia of social and political movements* (Vol. 14, p. 337). Hoboken, NJ: John Wiley & Sons. https://doi.org/10.1002/9780470674871.wbespm073

Mitchell, G. (2008). Treaty will prepare EU for challenges of 21st century. *Irish Times*.

MPF. (2005). *Constitution Europeenne*. Retrieved from http://web.archive.org/web/20050104011405/http://www.mpf-villiers.com/mcgi/cgi.exe?exec=PRJ&TYP=2#.

MRC. (2005). *Constitution européenne - C'est non!* Retrieved from http://web.archive.org/web/20050219230956/http://www.mrc-france.org/tr23.

Nicolaï, A. (2005). *Atzo Nicolaï: Een stem voor Europa is een stem voor jezelf!* Retrieved from http://web.archive.org/web/20061002124953/www.vvd.nl/index.aspx?FilterId=974&ChapterId=1147&ContentId=1793.

NP. (2008). **What the Lisbon Treaty would do... (Detailed Explanation)*. Retrieved from http://web.archive.org/web/20080529215339/http://www.nationalplatform.org:80/wordpress/?page_id=66.

Ó Snodaigh, A. (2008). *Fine Gael must tell truth on Ireland's loss of VETO*. Retrieved from www.sinnfein.ie/contents/12485.

Patterson, M., & Monroe, K. R. (1998). Narrative in Political Science. *Annual Review of Political Science, 1*(1), 315–331. https://doi.org/10.1146/annurev.polisci.1.1.315

Perelman, C. (1980). *Das Reich der Rhetorik: Rhetorik und Argumentation. Beck'sche schwarze Reihe: Bd. 212*. München: Beck.

Poniatowski, A. (2005, February 9 2005). Constitution européenne et la Turquie, parlons-en, justement. *Le Figaro*.

Power, J. (2008). *Irish Hotels Federation Calls for Yes Vote on the Lisbon Treaty*. Retrieved from http://web.archive.org/web/20080607043259/http://www.ihf.ie/press/documents/080506yesvote.htm.

Rabinow, P. & Sullivan, W. M. (1979). *Interpretive social science: A reader*. Berkeley: University of California Press.

Risse, T. (2010). A community of Europeans?: Transnational identities and public spheres. Cornell Paperbacks. Ithaca [N.Y.]: Cornell University Press.

Roche, D. (2007). *Dick addresses Seanad Eireann on Reform Treaty and Referendum*. Retrieved from http://web.archive.org/web/20080215113242/http://www.dickroche.com:80/?menu=14&PHPSESSID=a27225bccceecc75cbd284efc4328a33.

Roe, E. (1994). *Narrative policy analysis: Theory and practice*. Durham: Duke University Press.

Rouvoet, A., & van Middelkoop, E. (2005). Een Grondwet met een verborgen agenda. In B. J. Spruyt & E. B. Stichting (Eds.), *Samen Zwak. Pleidooien tegen de Europese Grondwet* (pp. 81–88). Amsterdam.

RSF. (2008). *Defend sovereignty, neutrality, democracy*. Retrieved from http://web.archive.org/web/20110726142506/http://www.rsf.ie/saoirse/current/may08.pdf.

Rucht, D. (1994). *Modernisierung und neue soziale Bewegungen: Deutschland, Frankreich und USA im Vergleich. Theorie und Gesellschaft: Bd. 32*. Frankfurt u.a.: Campus-Verl.

Schünemann, W. J. (2014). *Subversive Souveräne: Vergleichende Diskursanalyse der gescheiterten Referenden im europäischen Verfassungsprozess. Theorie und Praxis der Diskursforschung*. Wiesbaden: Springer VS.

Schünemann, W. J. (2016). Manifeste Deutungskämpfe: Die wissenssoziologisch-diskursanalytische Untersuchung politischer Debatten. In S. Bosancic & R. Keller (Eds.), *Perspektiven Wissenssoziologischer Diskursforschung*. Wiesbaden: Springer VS.

Schünemann, W. (2017). Almost the same stories: Narrative patterns in EU treaty referendums. *National Identities*. Advance online publication. https://doi.org/10.1080/14608944.2016.1255188

Schünemann, W. J. (2018). SKAD analysis of European multi-level political debates. In R. Keller, A.-K. Hornidge & W. J. Schünemann (Eds.), *Routledge advances in sociology. The sociology of knowledge approach to discourse: Investigating the politics of knowledge and meaning-making* (pp. 91–111). Abingdon, Oxon; New York, NY: Routledge.

Statham, P. & Trenz, H.-J. (2013). How European Union politicization can emerge through contestation: The constitution case. *Journal of Common Market Studies*, 51(5), 965–980. https://doi.org/10.1111/jcms.12032.

Taggart, P. (1998). A touchstone of dissent: Euroscepticism in contemporary Western European party systems. *European Journal of Political Research*, *33*, 363–388.

Trenz, H.-J. & Wilde, P. de. (2009). *Denouncing European integration: Euroscepticism as reactive identity formation*. Retrieved from www.sv.uio.no/arena/english/research/publications/arena-working-papers/2001–2010/2009/WP_1409.pdf.

Ullrich, P. (2013). Kulturvergleich, diskursive Gelegenheitsstrukturen und linke Nahostdiskurse: Entwurf einer wissenssoziologischen und diskurstheoretischen Perspektive für die Protestforschung. In R. Keller & I. Truschkat (eds.), *Theorie und Praxis der Diskursforschung. Methodologie und Praxis der Wissenssoziologischen Diskursanalyse. Band 1: Interdisziplinäre Perspektiven* (pp. 315–337). Wiesbaden: VS Verlag für Sozialwissenschaften.

Van Bommel, H. (2005, April 16 2005). *Referendum na een Frans "nee" afblazen schaadt vertrouwen in politiek. Friesch Dagblad*.

Veld, Sophie in 't. (2005). *Waarom ik voor de Europese grondwet stem*. Retrieved from www.d66.nl/europa/nieuws/20050521/congrestoespraak_sophie_in_t_veld?ctx=vhopg90lkduz.

Viehöver, W. (2006). Diskurse als Narrationen. In R. Keller, A. Hirseland, W. Schneider & W. Viehöver (Eds.), *Handbuch sozialwissenschaftliche Diskursanalyse* Bd. 1 Theorien und Methoden (2nd ed., pp. 179–208). Wiesbaden: VS Verl. für Sozialwiss.

Viehöver, W. (2014). Erzählungen im Feld der Politik, Politik durch Erzählungen: Überlegungen zur Rolle der Narrationen in den politischen Wissenschaften. In F. Gadinger, S. Jarzebski & T. Yildiz (Eds.), *Hofmann* (pp. 67–91). Wiesbaden: Springer VS.

Voerman, G. & Van de Walle, N. (op. 2009). *Met het oog op Europa: Affiches voor de Europese verkiezingen, 1979–2009*. Amsterdam: Boom.

Voteno. (2008). *Irish Leaders adopt increasing desperate tactics in effort to win Lisbon*. Retrieved from www.voteno.ie/html/press.htm#desperatetactics.

Whelan, J. (2008). *Lisbon Vote Critical for Export Industry*. Retrieved from www.irishexporters.ie/LisbonVoteCritical.shtml.

White, P. (2008, June 11 2008). *Yes vote required to prevent Ireland's isolation and a loss of jobs. Irish Times*.

Wilders, G. (2005a). *Eerste openbare speech Geert Wilders sinds de moord op Theo van Gogh*. Retrieved from http://web.archive.org/web/20050314020628/http://www.groepwilders.nl/.

Wilders, G. (2005b). *Onafhankelijkheidsverklaring - een boodschap van hoop en optimisme.* Retrieved from http://web.archive.org/web/20050326071758/http://www.geertwilders.nl:80/index.php?option=com_content&task=view&id=120&Itemid=71.

Zamudio, M., Russell, C., Rios, F. A. & Bridgeman, J. L. (2011). *Critical race theory matters: Education and ideology.* New York: Routledge. Retrieved from http://lib.myilibrary.com/detail.asp?id=289856.

31

Between convention and resistance

Counter-narrative strategies in political asylum claims

Abigail Stepnitz

Asylum-seekers, those individuals who flee their countries of origin because of persecution, are among the most disadvantaged participants in the legal process. Facing linguistic and cultural barriers, with limited access to the resources needed to effectively present themselves before the state, asylum seekers navigate the process with little more than their own life stories of persecution and fear.

Asylum stories are crucial: to seek asylum in the United States (US), as in many countries, individuals must present a credible narrative that shows either past experience or future fear of harm. That harm must be as a result of one of the protected categories laid out in the Geneva Convention on the Status of Refugees: race, nationality, religion, political opinion or membership in a particular social group (UNHCR, 1951).

A credible asylum narrative must do more than simply present facts, feelings or experiences. It must integrate those personal aspects with the necessary legal arguments that give the fears the weight of a refugee claim. If asylum seekers fail to do so, they risk being removed to a country where their life may well be at risk. The legal process itself is, in many countries, highly discretionary. In such a high-stakes legal process it seems obvious that most claimants would do everything in their power to narratively frame their experiences in a way that resonates with relevant decision-makers. As I discuss in detail below, adhering to legal requirements and reproducing dominant cultural and rhetorical tropes in asylum claims is likely to benefit claimants.

Some asylum seekers, however, have to navigate a balance between agency and persecution even more delicately than others, especially those whose claims arise as a result of oppositional political activities. Beyond claims based on persecution arising from a political opinion, political opposition claims are those raised by individuals whose political views or actions can be described, in the context of their countries of origin, as disruptive, dangerous or revolutionary, and sometimes violent.

These individuals run the risk of being seen as troublemakers or even terrorists. To overcome these assumptions and to frame their experiences in ways that resonate with asylum decision-makers, these claimants present a particular kind of counter-narrative. They narrate and explain their actions by invoking moral authority, stereotypical American values about the value of free speech, and the importance of resisting undemocratic leaders or attempts to supersede the rule of law. These claims speak to America's mainstream self-perception as a place welcoming of political protestors or revolutionaries, especially those who stood against regimes regarded by the American government as hostile or dangerous (Hing, 2000; Loescher & Scanlan, 1998; Zolberg, 2006.) This perception allows asylum seekers to make use of a dissident identity that makes them more desirable as an eventual American. Like many counter-narratives which are powerful because they articulate an alternative, rather than presenting direct challenges to master-narratives, asylum claims based on political opposition engage in subtle forms of resistance (Bamberg & Andrews, 2004; Ewick & Silbey, 2003, 1995). In doing so, those making political opposition claims engage in an oppositional construction of a political subject by appropriating dominant knowledge about who engages in political contestation and why.

Drawing on a sample of 30 first-person narratives submitted in political opposition asylum claims in the US from nationals of 11 countries between 1989 and 2011,[1] I show how claimants narrate their lives in a way that allows them to reframe a dissident identity as one that aligns with presumed American values and interests. My analysis reveals three emergent narrative themes in the sample: those where the claimant constructs themselves as on the right side of history, if even on the wrong side of the law; those who construct their actions and selves as embodying traditionally American values such as freedom of speech, tolerance and respect for the rule of law; and those who opposed Communism.

The question of authorship of asylum narratives is complex. In this research I engage only with narratives of claimants who had the benefit of legal representation. This means these narratives are not un-edited accounts, but have been prepared with the assistance of an attorney or another legal professional. That said, I refer to claimants as authors of these stories because fundamentally, the experiences that give rise to, and the consequences of decisions made about the asylum narrative, belong to the claimant.[2]

This chapter proceeds in four parts. In part one I situate my inquiry in the legal context of political asylum claims and in the literatures on asylum and narrative. In part two I discuss first the legal and cultural components that make up the political asylum master-narrative. In part three I will present the data relating to the emergence of counter-narratives. Lastly, in part four I conclude with a discussion of these emergent counter-narrative strategies with regard to the master narrative components and the nature of credible storytelling in asylum more broadly.

Asylum, political opinion and the machinery of the state

Asylum was developed as both an international legal category, and in many states as a particular legal process, at the end of the Second World War. The original impetus for developing a system of recognizing those unable or unwilling to return to their country of origin was a desire to avoid the kinds of atrocities that had happened in Europe, and provide safe and legal pathways for resettlement when individuals and communities could not be protected by their own governments. The 1951 Convention was in many ways more of a reaction to the events of WWII rather than a template for the management of future displacement. It most certainly was not designed to cope with contemporary social, political, economic and environmental factors that give rise to the current global levels of asylum seeking. As of summer 2018 there were 3.2 million pending asylum applications globally (UNHCR, 2019), and as pressures on asylum systems around the world mount under the weight of unprecedented displacement, and suspicions and fears surrounding migrants' intentions and impact are stoked by the rise of populism in destination countries, understanding how these claims are considered is crucial.

In the US individuals can claim asylum in two ways: affirmative claims are raised by people who are not facing removal from the country, and defensive claims are raised by those who are.

This research considers only affirmative claims. To make an affirmative claim an individual must submit a written application, and most submit a variety of corroborating evidence, including a first-person declaration describing their experiences, relevant medical or mental health records, expert evidence on conditions in their country of origin, and any other documents or materials that lend weight and credibility to their claims.[3]

At the heart of asylum claims based on political persecution is the question of whether or not the opinions held by claimants will meet the necessary legal tests to be considered political. Opinions, whether stated or imputed (Khudaverdyan v. Holder, 2015), are considered "political" for the purposes of asylum if they are sufficiently detailed articulations of "an ideal or conviction of sorts" (Saldarriaga v. Gonzales, 2005). However, the Refugee Convention has been interpreted such that applicants are not expected to be political philosophers (Grahl-Madsen, 1966), whose views are easily articulated along a recognized ideology or platform of a specific political party. Rather, a broadly-conceived notion of political opinions allows claimants to seek protection when they hold any opinion on any matter in the "machinery of the State or uncontrolled non-state actors may be engaged against" (Goodwin-Gill & McAdam, 2007, p. 87). Furthermore, applicants need only demonstrate, using direct or circumstantial evidence (INS v. Elias Zacarias, 1992) that it is reasonable to assume their political views, stated or imputed, are at least one reason they were persecuted. They are not expected to produce irrefutable proof of their persecutors' intentions (Matter of J-B-N- & S-M, 2007; Rivera-Barrientos v. Holder, 2012).

Outside of explicit political engagement in political activities, other common variations of political opinion claims in the US are women who are feminists (Fatin v. INS, 1993), including those who resist their own experience of gendered domestic or intimate violence, those who are union members or engage in union activities, journalists, whistleblowers, student activists and those targeted for remaining neutral during politically-charged times (Rivera-Moreno v. INS, 2000).

Law, counter-narrative and disjunctive realities

Recent decades have seen a "narrative turn" in many fields, and law is no exception. Increasingly, those who study legal processes are recognizing the significance and value of telling stories, and of looking to those stories as tools for theory building and as sources of data about experiences of and with the law. Socio-legal scholars, building from Goffman's assertion that the personal narrative is "an act of self-presentation" (1967, p. 247), have focused in particular on the role of narrative in identity construction, both for individuals and in the context of institutions and as a form of expression uniquely suited to exploring motives in collective action, such as social movements. Legal stories, scholars have come to see, are not just reflections of individual ideologies or beliefs, but are powerful cultural tools that work to provide cohesion, to frame and challenge public opinion, and to change policy (Bumiller, 1992; Ewick and Silbey, 1995; Nepstad, 2001; Benford, 2002; Ferree, 2003; Polletta, 2006; Loseke, 2007; Baillot, Cowan, and Munro, 2009.)

Legal narratives are ways of organizing and performing knowledge, which reveal and structure our relationships to each other and to the state. More than accounts or lists of events, they are strategically constructed and are deeply, interactively tied to action, both those of the narrators themselves, and those that are intended as a result of the narrative (Ochs and Capps, 2009; Gergen and Gergen, 2006; Blommaert, Bock, and McCormick, 2006.) For example, the sentencing of someone convicted of a crime is more than a verbal declaration, it is the beginning of a chain of events in which several actions are taken to deprive that person of their liberty (Cover, 1986) signatures on certain forms can establish or dissolve marriages, bind businesses contractually and create or terminate obligations. In this way, legal narratives are an especially salient site in which speakers and listeners can identify, generate, organize and affirm social meanings (Bearman and Stovel, 2000), shape identities and signify group memberships (Leary, 1977; Polletta, 2006).

As with all successful narratives, legal narratives that "work" are generally those in which the narrator and the audience share sufficient cultural and linguistic common ground for that meaning to be easily recognizable (Labov and Waletzky, 1967; Leary, 1977; Bearman and Stovel, 2000; Polletta, 2006). We build our own narratives out of the stuff of the stories that surround in dynamic and fluid ways (Ewick and Silbey, 2003, 1343).

In common law systems, such as in the US, this reliance on other people's stories happens in another defined way – through creation of and reliance upon legal precedent. Legal stories are reproduced not just culturally, but institutionally, and that reproduction can make it much harder to present credible alternatives. To present a counter-narrative in a legal context then, is to resist cultural and institutional pressures to tell familiar, recognizable stories.

Because counter-narratives are inherently relational they are also always interactional and performative. The narratives themselves are performative or hermeneutic actions, and counter-narratives politically so. Yet counter-narratives need not overtly refer to or critique the master narrative, and certainly do not need to be constructed as entirely dichotomous. Put simply and beautifully by Ochs and Capps "it is the voicing of a disjunctive reality itself that constitutes the counterpoint" (2009, 37.) All narratives are strategic, but counter-narratives even more so.

So what then does a legal counter-narrative have to do or be? Legal counter-narratives must contain all of the practical and normative world-building potential along with a positionality and a tension that makes them resistant, distinct and powerful enough to challenge beliefs held not just by other people, but by the state itself. Defining what is challenging to the state is not simple, however, as the very categories of dominant and resistant are fluid, not static (Bamberg and Andrews, 2004, 3).

Political asylum master-narratives

An asylum master-narrative is one produced in relation to "socially available and hegemonic discourses and practices" (Anthias, 2002, 511.) Despite the recognition that experiences of migration – especially forced migration – can lead to fractured identities, the importance of the force of both law and culture on the narrative resources that allow claimants to tap into an asylum-seeking master-narrative cannot be overstated. For asylum seekers the master-narrative is not a single narrative form, but rather a triangulated and evolving refraction of their reality, motives and potentials through a series of legal and political as well as cultural lenses. Different claimants will draw on different legal and cultural narrative resources depending on their own identity and on the nature of their legal claim. Below I offer concise descriptions of these legal and cultural forces that give shape to asylum master-narratives.

Law and policy

The law, and various policy and statutory forms of guidance, create the first building blocks for the asylum-seeker master-narrative. When seeking asylum, an individual must first indicate which of the convention grounds their claim invokes – race, nationality, religion, political opinion, and/or membership in a particular social group – and then explain how that intersects with both an objective risk and their unique, subjective experience or fear of harm. Many claims invoke more than one; in this sample 88% of claimants indicated at least two grounds, most commonly political opinion and membership in a particular social group.

The legal burden of proof rests on the asylum-seeker to establish eligibility, which can be based on a "reasonable possibility" of either past persecution or a well-founded fear of future persecution. Their narrative must express the legal concept of "nexus" by linking an objective basis for their fear with a subjective experience of risk or harm (USCIS, 2013). Claimants must also show that they are not prohibited from seeking or enjoying asylum because of any statutory "bars," including applying within 12 months of arrival in the US, and ensuring they do not have criminal or other questionable records. Finally, and crucially, narratives must convince an administrative decision maker that the case warrants a favorable exercise of discretion (USCIS, 2013).

But these specific contours of the system are not the only legal or policy considerations. Indeed, research shows that broader questions of narratives aligning with the social, political and economic positions and objectives of the country in which they are seeking protection can be as important as the individual claimant's own experience (Holzer, Schneider and Widmer, 2000; Rosenblum and Salehyan, 2004; Salehyan and Rosenblum, 2008). Telling an asylum story that lines up with US positions on human rights, sanctions, trading relationships or otherwise supports domestic or international policy positions is also part of the master-narrative.

Culture

After meeting these legal requirements, most asylum claims also rely on master-narrative forms involving the reproduction of stereotypes about their countries of origin or other identities they hold (such as racialized or gendered tropes.) This is not a coincidence; telling a reasonably familiar story about persecution, fear and danger, as well as presenting oneself as a person of good moral standing who can integrate into the US is an effective way of framing an asylum claim (Coutin, 2001; Blommaert, Bock, and McCormick, 2006). This is especially true for claims which fit comfortably into what decision-makers expect from asylum seekers; what some refer to even as a refugee "genre" (Watzlawik and Brescó de Luna, 2017). Specifically, the master-narrative expectations are that asylum-seekers tell clear, consistent, detailed stories (Cohen, 2001), which substantively link their own lived experiences to the material conditions in their countries of origin, which give rise to persecution (Bohmer and Schuman, 2013). They are also expected to "sell suffering" (Ticktin, 1999), to make the fear they experienced tangible for the decision-makers (Watzlawik and Brescó de Luna, 2017). These assumptions are reinforced by media, civil society and even academic portrayals of asylum seekers and refugees as desperate, weak and vulnerable (Malkki, 1995; Fiddian-Qasmiyeh, 2014; Sigona, 2014; Wright, 2014). They are also reinforced by the nature and volume of documentary evidence required in the asylum process, in particular evidence of torture or other physical "proof" of harm (Fassin and D'halluin, 2005; Bohmer and Shuman, 2018.) Lastly, asylum seekers are expected to offer "untempered gratitude" in return for safety (Buck, 2008: 49).

Certain groups face particular expectations as well, for example women seeking asylum are expected to express "appropriate" emotionality, especially shame (McKinnon, 2009) as women are expected to "communicate through their emotions" (Melloy, 2006: 654). Women are also expected to perform character traits and behaviors traditionally viewed as "feminine" such as a focus on domestic and family life, and feminine mannerisms and demeanor (Carlson, 2009; McKinnon, 2011).

As such, it is clear that legal and political considerations, as well as cultural ideas about deservingness and credibility, are crucial in understanding the contours of the typical asylum narrative. And yet there are those who need to seek asylum in the US who cannot avail themselves of these narrative strategies, often because the very nature of their experience of fear or violence precludes it. In these cases, counter-narrative strategies highlight important alternative legal and cultural pathways to protection.

Political asylum counter-narratives

In the data and discussion that follow I demonstrate how asylum seekers making political opposition claims in the US between 1989 and 2011 construct and rely on counter-narratives to present their life histories and political actions as consistent with, rather than a threat to, the values and identities considered desirable in the US.

Primary data analyzed below are part of a larger stratified random sample of asylum claims made in California between 1989 and 2011, for a project relating to credibility construction in more broadly. I collected 4,800 cases in 2018, which were then stratified by persecution type and randomly sampled (Seawright and Gerring, 2008). While this larger sample contains dozens of claims that invoke some kind of political action or opposition, this sample of 30 claims that link the claimant's views or activities directly to their experience of fear or persecution.

I then coded these narratives, using grounded-theory and abductive analysis techniques (Charmaz and Mitchell, 2001; Glaser and Strauss, 2009), and with reference to concepts drawn from relevant literatures on asylum and narrative (Miles, Huberman, and Saldaña, 2013) Specifically, I coded for narrative themes relating to both substance and structure of the narratives, which explained the kinds of political activities or views held by the claimants, and in particular, whether these could invoke suspicion rather than sympathy on the part of decision makers. This includes, for example, participating in and perpetrating violence and destruction of property, and being outspoken critics of social, political and economic policies in their countries of origin.

My analysis reveals how asylum seekers used counter-narrative strategies to make claims arising as a result of their oppositional political activities. Three types of examples of counter-narrative emerge from these claims: being on the right side of history, if even on the wrong side of the law; embodying traditionally American values such as freedom of speech, tolerance and respect for the rule of law, and opposing Communism. These are not distinct counter-narrative strategies, rather they are three different claim contexts in which similar counter-narrative strategies are employed to position political opposition as leading to the kind of fear or persecution that makes one eligible and desirable for asylum.

Many narratives rely on more than one of these themes. As such, the following vignettes demonstrate examples of the themes in action, rather than evidence of distinct narrative types. Vignettes are reproduced with as little editing as possible, beyond what was necessary to protect anonymity and occasionally to improve clarity. Original phrasing, syntax, grammar and spelling are retained and any changes to the original text are in brackets.

The right side of history, the wrong side of the law

The first set of counter-narratives is that which acknowledge the claimant's political opposition activities may have been illegal, but present them as morally just. Individuals making these claims seek to avoid being marked as a criminal, which could both legally exclude them from being recognized as a refugee,[4] and may culturally bias decision makers against them. In these counter-narratives people navigate the complexities of their actions both by taking responsibility for what they did, and by positioning those actions as morally sound, or as necessary in the face of corruption, illegitimate or undemocratic governments. These claims speak of deep, personal commitments to causes or ideals that animated actions, never to frenzied, careless participation in protests or riots. Most reflect a reasoned consideration of the risks involved, and a value-laden decision to participate, invoking frames similar to those of civil disobedience.

Some claimants must reckon with more than the radical nature of their views, but must also address and overcome participation in or passively condoning violence. This is particularly common in narratives of civil conflict. For some this takes the shape of focusing on what propelled them to join opposition groups. Many of the Central American narratives are similar, focusing on the violence and disregard for civilian life evidenced by the armed forces, and how this drove them to join the guerrillas. For example, this young man from Guatemala who states

> One day the army said everyone had to leave or they would be killed, and then they bombed the area. After this my whole family eventually became involved with the guerrillas. All five of my sisters collaborated, and the husband of one of them was a combatant throughout the 1980s.

Others who condoned violence choose to make it clear that they emerged as voices of reason, restraint or decency even when others in their group engaged in illegal or immoral activity. Such as this protestor who opposed the outcome of a contentious presidential election in West Africa:

> People poured into [the presidential candidate's] house and destroyed everything inside, eventually burning down the house. We, the campaign group members, including myself, tried to stop them from destroying the house, but it was impossible. Unfortunately, the two security guards who had shot at the crowd were killed in the riot. Finally, the police came and ended the demonstration [and] began arresting people. I ran away.

Recognizing that even if they engaged in violent or illegal behaviors, many claimants suggest that it was only because they were faced with forces within their country that did not respect the rule of law. In doing so, they present themselves as having no choice, in pursuit of justice and decency, other than to take the law into their own hands. One young man who was a member of a guerrilla organization in Central America states:

> I respect the laws but many times the government doesn't. For example the army causes many problems and they have done many things that show that they don't respect the laws. For example there were several peasants living in the mountains near a rich plantation. It was dangerous because there were guerrillas in the area and so these peasants left their houses to live lower down where there were more people. Later the army burned all the houses with all the peoples' things inside without investigating if they belonged to the guerrillas. But they did not destroy any property on the rich plantation. The army doesn't respect the Indians nor the poor people. But to the rich they don't do anything.

Embodying "American" values

A second trend in political opposition counter-narratives is that of invoking values that are stereotypically considered to align with the idea of "America" such as protecting freedom of speech, tolerance and respect for the rule of law. Focusing both on intention and outcome, these narratives position claimants as embodying these values, which both justifies their actions and helps them to overcome any assumptions about agency or for those whose proactive approach to political activities makes it difficult to construct themselves as weak.

A young man from the Horn of Africa, for example, describes how he became a pro-democracy campaigner after his cousin was murdered for opposing the government in power. He specifically characterizes his actions as designed to push back against a "barbaric" government that would suppress voting, and focuses on the fact that he was "open" and "vocal," invoking ideas tied to free speech. He writes

> I very publicly said that a government that kills and imprisons people because they oppose it is a barbaric government no different than Hitler. I said openly that in [my country] anyone who legitimately opposes the government is a target. I was open.

Similarly, a West African claimant characterized his party as dedicated to social progress and democracy, which made him willing to engage in anti-government protests. "I thought [it] was a unifying force for the country and that all the people would have a voice in government; especially people who had been denied access to political power for many years." Others focus less on their own actions and focus instead on praising the US, with many of these characterizations are clear and obvious, such as "Only here in the USA I will be safe, only here I will be free and have the protection and the liberty that I need."

Starting in the early 2000s, and likely as a result of the rise in Islamophobia in the US after the September 11th terror attacks in New York City, there is a marked increase in claims that address questions of faith and secularism from individuals who practice Islam or who come from countries with large Muslim populations. During a time in which Muslims were being characterized as perpetrators of violence as opposed to victims of persecution, these stories become counter-narratives because of the need to at once claim their Islamic faith, but simultaneously distance themselves from the aspects that could be read as un-American. These individuals go to particular lengths to distance themselves from ideas of theocracy and to advocate for secular approaches to government. As one young man stated "I have always been an advocate of secularism. Nobody should govern [my country] in the name of Allah because that will be the way to dictatorship, torture, and genocide."

Women in particular work to distance themselves from gendered assumptions about their faith, the treatment of women in Muslim-majority countries, and particular cultural practices. One young woman from Central Africa distances her Islamic faith from the practice of cutting young women's genitals.

> The way that I believe in Islam is different from my father. The Koran does not say that girls must be circumcised or not go to school. Girls must be able to learn the Koran and must practice Islam. My father believes that girls must cover their entire bodies, and not even show any hair. I do not believe that is the right way to practice Islam.

Another woman refers to the patriarchal views of all of the men in her "culture," which she defines as the members of a particular clan, and characterizes them in part as strictly adhering to Islamic law and upholding familial structures and practices which she resists. "All the men have the same attitude even as young boys," she writes, "Women are not worth anything. To me my father and brothers just represented the way men think in [my] culture, which seemed so wrong to me."

Fighting Communism

The last example of political opposition counter-narrative strategies is the most geographically and temporally bound. These claims come either from individuals who fled Central America during or after the civil conflicts in the late 1980s and early 1990s. These claims stress as opposition to Communism, an approach that is not counter-narrative in and of itself. However, in these cases we see anti-Communism elevated to more than a political belief, but to a justification for engagement in violence and oppression against civilians that would ordinarily complicate – if not render impossible – a claim for asylum.

The Central American claims occupy a densely articulated political space, given the role of US intervention in the region which both contributed to the rise of anti-capitalist movements, and supported regimes designed to suppress these uprisings. During the conflicts, which took place from 1980 to 1992, the US government provided nearly USD 6B in military aid as well as extensive and controversial training to Central American armed forces (Booth, Wade and Walker, 2006; Chomsky, 1985; D'Haeseleer, 2017). The police and armed forces in the region were known to engage in extrajudicial violence, forced disappearances and summary executions, both of Communist opposition fighters and of civilians, especially those suspected of supporting any rebel groups (Chomsky, 1985; Historical Clarification Commission, 1999.) As such, those who participated as members of the armed forces must frame their asylum counter-narratives in such a way as to position anti-communism as a discrete political belief that was under threat.

Most Central American claimants create counter-narratives that frame their own military service as part of a larger effort to combat Communism. Take for example the narrative of a young man who was drafted into the army in his Central American country of origin. He talks about why he served, despite the fact that he knew the army was involved in persecuting indigenous people and behaving in ways that are contrary to internationally-accepted rules of war, such as engaging in torture, mistreating civilians and using child soldiers. He writes about making this choice in part to protect his family, and invokes frames of national service and loyalty. He does not so much align his political views with that of the army, but makes it clear that his decision to serve was sacrificial as he believes it kept his family safer.

> In May, 1987, the Commissioners recruited me for military service. I was the only boy of age in my village, so I was the only one recruited. I only wanted to be happy, and I thought it was best for me to do my Military Service. With the army I felt happier. With the guerrillas I could never be happy, because they would oblige me to make my whole family support them. With the Army, I was serving my country.

Another former soldier talks not only about his rejection of the guerrillas' insistence that he take up arms against the government, but also rejects their characterization of American intervention:

> The Communist Guerrillas of my country tried to recruit me to fight with them. I was approached by a group of men, who had hidden fire-arms and told me I should join them to fight against the Government, to gain liberty in our Country. That our Country was under the control of the imperialist Americans. They told me if I did not join in the Liberation, I was a traitor and deserved to be eliminated (…) I told them no. I was frightened by the Guerrillas threats, I had to leave my parents and my country, in search of freedom and security in America.

Lastly, there are those who claim and account for their membership in Communist groups and explain it either by invoking the kinds of democratic values that they were promised after the revolution or by characterizing the guerillas as the lesser of two evils. Such an approach is illustrated in the narrative of a young guerilla fighter from Nicaragua "I never wanted the Communist system but the Somoza Government was killing the young people so, I joint the people to get out the regime."

Discussion and conclusion

These claimants cannot tap into the master-narrative components of traditional perceptions of vulnerability or worthiness, nor can they reflect behaviors consistent with US policy objectives – especially not those who supported guerrilla organizations. As such, when it comes to articulating this type of political asylum narrative claimants may need to use counter-narrative strategies to demonstrate personal identity characteristics other than those which may be assumed based on their own prior actions. These counter-narratives allow asylum seekers to navigate from an identity such as "dissident," "radical" or "trouble-maker" to one of "freedom-fighter" or "advocate" or "truth-seeker."

Perhaps the most important unifying facet of these claims, and that which makes them undeniably counter-narratives is the way they manage agency. All asylum seekers must strike a delicate balance when it comes to presenting themselves as sufficiently vulnerable to be subjected to persecution, whilst also self-sufficient, capable and competent enough to, firstly, have managed to flee, and secondly, to integrate as a citizen in the country where they seek protection. Many asylum seekers do this by performing their vulnerability through tropes about weakness, fear and violence.

Those making political opposition cannot suggest such a loss of agency, however. Indeed, some have to acknowledge that their specific political actions created their own vulnerability. It is the simultaneous presentation of that agency as both evidence of vulnerability and moral rectitude that makes distinct the political asylum counter-narrative. Given the malleable, even volatile nature of global politics, this process is one that is often in flux. Powerful counter-narrative strategies allow claims about resisting gendered social norms in Muslim-majority countries to take on a different political hue in the light of the US "war on terror," taking up arms against your own government shifts from being threatening to being laudable when that government had anti-democratic tendencies, and violence becomes resistance when the intentions align politically with those of the decision makers.

Those who are claiming asylum must do so in such a way as to frame their beliefs, activities and choices as warranting international protection. For those whose political alliances were to parties not recognized or respected by the US government, who espoused what could be considered anti-Western or even anti-American views, especially socialist or communist views, or those who engage in violent or other illegal forms of resistance, the challenge is both legal and rhetorical. They have to tell a story that presents their life and their choices as compatible with eventually being an American, making the narrative component of their claims as important as the legal arguments.

The counter-narratives analyzed herein provide a window into the ways that some asylum seekers strategically frame and present their experiences and beliefs, allowing them to retain needed political weight in their characterization of vulnerability to persecution, whilst also presenting themselves as embracing what it is to be American. These invocations of Americanness are not just a convenient shorthand or a form of intended flattery. When someone is recognized as a refugee they are nearly always able to eventually regularize that status and become a citizen. In that way, asylum seekers who are granted refugee status become American in waiting (Haas, 2017). Proving their suitability to that new civic role, that they are worth investing in as potential citizens, is as much a part of being recognized a refugee as meeting the conditions set out in the 1951 Convention.

Notes

1 The full list of countries in the sample is El Salvador, Guatemala, Eritrea, Ethiopia, Kenya, Mali, Nicaragua, Nigeria, Sudan, Turkmenistan and Yemen.
2 This is not intended to minimize the amount or significance of work done by interpreters and attorneys. Indeed, attorneys in particular play an incredibly powerful role in this process, and those asylum seekers in the US who are represented enjoy recognition rates five times higher than those who navigate the process without the benefit of legal counsel (TRAC, 2017)
3 All asylum claims are considered by Asylum Officers who are employees of United States Citizenship and Immigration Services (USCIS), part of the Department of Homeland Security (DHS.) These officers decide if the individual has a credible claim and meets all necessary legal tests for eligibility and if so, grant them refugee status. Cases not granted are referred to an immigration judge for further consideration. Cases that fail at that stage can be appealed through various levels of the US judicial system.
4 The Convention does allow for some claimants to be excluded under Article 1(F), which precludes from protection persons who committed war crimes or "serious, non-political crimes." Persons considered not to be deserving of international protection Article 1 F of the 1951.

Works cited

Anthias, F. (2002). Where do I belong?: Narrating collective identity and translocational positionality. *Ethnicities*, *2*(4), 491–514.

Baillot, H., Cowan, S., & Munro, V. E. (2009). Seen but not heard? Parallels and dissonances in the treatment of rape narratives across the asylum and criminal justice contexts. *Journal of Law and Society*, *36*(2), 195–219.

Bamberg, M., & Andrews, M. (2004). *Considering Counter-Narratives: Narrating, resisting, making sense*. John Benjamins Publishing.

Bearman, P. S., & Stovel, K. (2000). Becoming a Nazi: A model for narrative networks. *Poetics*, *27*(2–3), 69–90.

Benford, R. (2002). Controlling narratives and narratives as control within social movements. In J. E. Davis (Ed.), *Stories of Change: Narrative and social movements* (pp. 53–76). SUNY Press.

Blommaert, J., Bock, M., & McCormick, K. (2006). Narrative inequality in the TRC hearings: On the hearability of hidden transcripts. *Journal of Language and Politics*, *5*(1), 37–70.

Bohmer, C., & Shuman, A. (2013). Narrating Atrocity: Obstacles to Proving Credibility in Asylum Claims. *Refugee Law Initiative*, 21.

Bohmer, C., & Shuman, A. (2018). *Political Asylum Deceptions: The culture of suspicion*. Cham, Switzerland: Palgrave Macmillan.

Bumiller, K. (1992). *The Civil Rights Society: The social construction of victims*. Johns Hopkins University Press.

Charmaz, K., & Mitchell, R. G. (2001). Grounded theory in ethnography. In P. Atkinson, A. Coffey, S. Delamont, L. Lofland, & J. Lofland (Eds.), *Handbook of Ethnography*. SAGE.

Chomsky, N. (1985). *Turning the Tide: U.S. intervention in Central America and the struggle for peace*. Haymarket Books.

Cover, R. M. (1986). Violence and the word. *Yale Law Journal*, *95*(8), 1601–1630.

Ewick, P., & Silbey, S. (2003). Narrating social structure: Stories of resistance to legal authority. *American Journal of Sociology*, *108*(6), 1328–1372.

Ewick, P., & Silbey, S. S. (1995). Subversive stories and hegemonic tales: Toward a sociology of narrative. *Law & Society Review*, *29*(2), 197–226.

Fassin, D., & D'halluin, E. (2005). The truth from the body: Medical certificates as ultimate evidence for asylum seekers. *American Anthropologist*, *107*(4), 597–608.

Ferree, M. M. (2003). Resonance and radicalism: Feminist framing in the abortion debates of the United States and Germany. *American Journal of Sociology*, *109*(2), 304–344.

Gergen, M. M., & Gergen, K. J. (2006). Narratives in action. *Narrative Inquiry*, *16*(1), 112–121.

Glaser, B. G., & Strauss, A. L. (2009). *The Discovery of Grounded Theory: Strategies for qualitative research*. Transaction Publishers.

Goffman, E. (1967). *Interaction Ritual: Essays on face-to-face behavior* (1st ed.). Garden City, NY: Anchor Books.

Haas, B. M. (2017). Citizens-in-waiting, deportees-in-waiting: Power, temporality, and suffering in the U.S. asylum system. *Ethos*, *45*(1), 75–97.

Hing, B. O. (2000). No place for angels: In reaction to Kevin Johnson. *University of Illinois Law Review*, *2000*(2), 559–601.

Historical Clarification Commission. (1999). *Guatemala: Memory of silence.*
Holzer, T., Schneider, G., & Widmer, T. (2000). Discriminating decentralization: Federalism and the handling of asylum applications in Switzerland, 1988–1996. *Journal of Conflict Resolution, 44*(2), 250–276.
Labov, W., & Waletzky, J. (1967). Narrative analysis: Oral versions of personal experience. In J. Helms (Ed.), *Essays on the Verbal and Visual Arts* (pp. 74–104). Seattle: University of Washington Press.
Leary, J. P. (1977). White guys' stories of the night street. *Journal of the Folklore Institute, 14*(1/2), 59–71.
Loescher, G., & Scanlan, J. A. (1998). *Calculated Kindness.* New York: The Free Press.
Loseke, D. R. (2007). The study of identity as cultural, institutional, organizational, and personal narratives: Theoretical and empirical integrations. *The Sociological Quarterly, 48*(4), 661–688.
Miles, M. B., Huberman, A. M., & Saldaña, J. (2013). *Qualitative Data Analysis: A methods sourcebook* (Fourth edition). Los Angeles: SAGE.
Nepstad, S. (2001). Creating transnational solidarity: The use of narrative in the U.S.-Central America Peace Movement. *Mobilization: An international quarterly, 6*(1), 21–36.
Ochs, E., & Capps, L. (2009). *Living Narrative: Creating lives in everyday storytelling.* Cambridge: Harvard University Press.
Polletta, F. (2006). *It Was Like a Fever: Storytelling in protest and politics.* Chicago: University of Chicago Press.
Rosenblum, M. R., & Salehyan, I. (2004). Norms and interests in US asylum enforcement. *Journal of Peace Research, 41*(6), 677–697.
Salehyan, I., & Rosenblum, M. R. (2008). International relations, domestic politics, and asylum admissions in the United States. *Political Research Quarterly, 61*(1), 104–121.
Seawright, J., & Gerring, J. (2008). Case selection techniques in case study research: A menu of qualitative and quantitative options. *Political Research Quarterly, 61*(2), 294–308.
UNHCR. (1951). Convention and protocol relating to the status of refugees. Retrieved March 5, 2019, from UNHCR website: www.unhcr.org/protection/basic/3b66c2aa10/convention-protocol-relating-status-refugees.html
UNHCR. (2019). *Mid-year Trends 2018.* Geneva, Switzerland: United Nations.
USCIS. (2013, November 1). Asylum Procedures Manual 2013. Retrieved October 23, 2019, from www.uscis.gov/sites/default/files/files/nativedocuments/ Asylum_Procedures_Manual_2013.pdf
Watzlawik, M., & Brescó de Luna, I. (2017). The self in movement: Being identified and identifying oneself in the process of migration and asylum seeking. *Integrative Psychological and Behavioral Science, 51*(2), 244–260.
Zolberg, A. (2006). *A Nation by Design: Immigration policy in the fashioning of America.* Cambridge: Harvard University Press.

Cases Cited

Fatin v. INS, 12 F.3d 1233, 1242 (3rd Cir. 1993)
INS v. Elias Zacarias, 502 U.S. 478, 481–83 (1992)
Khudaverdyan v. Holder, 778 F.3d 1101, 1106 (9th Cir. 2015)
Rivera-Barrientos v. Holder, 666 F.3d 641, (CA10 2012)
Rivera-Moreno v. INS, 213 F.3d 481, (9th Cir. 2000)
Saldarriaga v. Gonzales, 402 F.3d 461, 466 (4th Cir. 2005)
Matter of J-B-N- & S-M-, 24 I&N Dec. 208, 211 (BIA 2007)

Concluding remarks

Narrative processuality and future research avenues for counter-narrative studies

Ann Starbæk Bager, Klarissa Lueg and Marianne Wolff Lundholt

In this concluding chapter we will sum up some of the main themes and debates in this book and look at future research avenues.

The chapters in the handbook clearly emphasise contemporary research on counter-narrative representing a vital, diverse, potent and promising field of study. The handbook features an impressive commitment by scholars from various research fields (e.g., from organisation and business studies, from sociology, from literature studies and from political science). Evidently, there are many diverse approaches to and applications of the concept of counter-narrative, depending on the particular research field, "objects"/topics of study as well as on theoretical, philosophical and empirical orientations. Nevertheless, there are innovative and similar trajectories or threads of thought that we will do our best to sum up here, knowing full well that we cannot embrace, and give sufficient credit to, all of the profound and inspiring nuances and discussions brought up, and initiated, in the book.

Common to perspectives adopted in this handbook are the following:

1. their stand on challenging more traditional BIG story approaches to canonical stories and narratives, including the beginning-middle-end (BME) viewpoint tuned to coherence, clear-cut plots and narrative structures (Bager, 2019);
2. their criticism of merely text and product-oriented perspectives not taking contextual circumstances into account, but redirecting focus to narrative processes and the interaction and relationships between various narrative resources, and
3. the favouring of social constructivist and postmodern assumptions over structuralist and functionalistic rationalities.

For these reasons, the contributions in this handbook are part of moving the traditional narrative field toward studying the complexities and contradictory aspects of social life, such as the struggles between resistive and controlling forces in and between various social groups and contexts by studying a *diversity* of narrative genres and representations. In this respect, counter-narrative studies are inherently critically oriented towards taking for granted knowledge, but aim at inquiring into how and which knowledge systems and forms gain dominance over others in social processes and at laying bare the implications of this for various groups, communities and contexts.

From this critical, social constructivist and pluralistic purview, the various authors discuss and challenge conceptualisations and studies of narratives and counter-narratives from different theoretical, methodological and empirical standpoints. We will comment on some of these debates in the chapter at hand.

The chapter is structured in six parts. First, we explain how the handbook represents a review of the last 16 years of studies on counter-narratives. In this section, we comment on how the perception of the relationship between narratives and counter-narratives has changed over time and how various scholars in the handbook contribute to enhancing earlier conceptions. The discussion reveals a change of course within counter-narrative studies: a strict narrative/counter-narrative duality gives way to narrative context sensitivity and processuality.

In section two we look at the most represented theoretical and analytical perspectives that various chapters draw on to deal with narrative processuality, polyphony and complexity, and discuss their implications for narrative and counter-narrative studies.

In section three we sum up some of the analyses in the handbook that reveal how narrative struggles play out and how some rationalities and master-narratives gain dominance over others in diverse contexts (such as higher education and European politics). In this section we argue how the turn to narrative processuality, for instance through the analogy of narrative ecologies as coined by Gabriel (2017), provides a contemporary framework and language enabling counter-narrative scholars to discuss societal change as ongoing dynamics between power/control and resistive forces on many levels in society spanning from the global to the local.

Section four comprises a review and a discussion of a range of methodological challenges and pitfalls within studies on (counter) narratives. Issues of this kind are raised in various chapters in the handbook across its seven subsections. We look at chapters that nuance and rethink narrative theories to meet some of the challenges and pitfalls. Then we turn to discourse studies from which numerous authors in the handbook draw inspiration to add conceptual and analytical rigour to the reflection and analysis of narrative/discursive processes.

In section five we discuss ethical and ideological concerns that the handbook gives rise to. We further discuss the potentials of taking a narrative and storytelling activist perspective where narrative scholars are actively involved in studying and helping new narrative structures along in situated practices.

In section six we present our concluding remarks and we outline avenues for future research. Among other things, we invite (counter) narrative scholars to intensify empirical attention to processuality, to interaction, and to multimodal and temporal multiplicity.

Review of the last 16 years of counter-narrative studies

The handbook comprises a review and nuancing of the last 16 years of studies on counter-narratives and it provides insights into contemporary and important studies of the dynamics between resistive and controlling forces in various social contexts. In particular, Bamberg and Wipff (in this handbook) in their chapter on *Re-considering counter-narratives*, from a retrospective position, review central texts that have played an important role in putting counter-narratives on the agenda as a significant and promising research topic. Similar to other chapters in the handbook (such as those authored by Bager & Lundholt; Bamberg & Wipff; Hyvärinen; Johansen; Lueg, Graf & Powel; Rehnberg & Grafström), they refer back to the publication by Bamberg and Andrews (2004) entitled *Considering counter narratives*. This publication proposed the concept of counter-narratives as an innovative way to reflect on and inquire into issues of resistance and control in diverse contexts. From then onwards, counter-narratives developed as a new, promising concept and research avenue for narrative scholars.

Back then, Bamberg and Andrews posited that "Counter narratives only make sense in relation to something else, that which they are countering. The very name identifies it as a positional category, in tension with another category" (Bamberg & Andrews, 2004, p. x). This assumedly dichotomic relationship between counter-narrative and dominant, hegemonic or master-narratives has been expounded widely, for instance by another key publication that is diligently referred to throughout the handbook: this handbook's predecessor *Counter narratives and organization* by Frandsen, Kuhn and Lundholt (2017). Here, the authors positioned the study of counter-narratives into a particular context – the organisation – and proposed more nuanced and complex ways of grasping the dichotomic narrative/counter-narrative relationship.

In Frandsen, Kuhn and Lundholt (2017), the concept of counter-narratives was unfolded and examined in order to challenge more traditional approaches to narrative studies within organisations. Here, diverse takes on counter-narratives were addressed as ways and means to study "how some narratives gain dominance over others; how narratives intersect, relate to, challenge and reinforce each other; and how actors 'inside' and 'outside' organisations co-construct narratives" (Frandsen, et al., 2017: 2). The concept of counter-narratives was presented as an alternative way of re-telling stories about the complexities inherent in organisational life that are being increasingly emphasised in contemporary organisational studies (Bager, 2019). One of the main arguments was that some, more traditional narrative scholars tend to overlook the complex, power-infused and often contradictory aspects of organisational life. Research into counter-narratives was highlighted to enable scholars to depict some of the political and social complexities and tensions faced in organisational life (Frandsen et al., 2017).

The authors discussed a binary relationship between narratives and counter-narratives in the sense that dominant narratives have the power to shape individuals and organisational worldviews, identities and values while the master-narrative can be destabilised and negotiated through counter-narrative processes. However, they complicated the strict dichotomic relationship in various ways, such as counter-narratives being viewed as a challenge to dominant narratives that can also themselves be countered by other counter-narratives in complex ways (Frandsen et al., 2017).

Bamberg and Andrews were already aware of such duality issues back in 2004 as they stated that "... what is dominant and what is resistant are not, of course, static questions, but rather are forever shifting placements ... the discussion of counter narratives is ultimately a consideration of multiple layers of positioning" (Bamberg & Andrews, 2004, p. x). From these trains of thoughts, both publications invited further scrutiny and critical discussion of the potential of counter-narrative studies and this handbook is evidence that such debate has been pertinaciously taken up by numerous authors representing various research fields and communities.

Beyond a strict narrative/counter-narrative duality and towards narrative context sensitivity and processuality

The nuancing debate on narrative/counter-narrative duality is taken up by numerous authors throughout this handbook, which suggests that scholars are studying how narrative resources are drawn on by certain actors in particular representations, contexts, times and situations. These studies challenge the assumption of narratives/counter-narratives as close-knit dichotomic pairs, which is often taken for granted, and show how narrative processes interact in less dualistically structured, more creative and much messier and entangled ways.

Hyvärinen (in this handbook), for instance, rethinking the position of rigid dichotomy from a theoretical perspective by revisiting Brunerian theory, proposes investigating how narrators creatively draw on diverse master and counter-narratives in particular contexts.

A similar view is applied by Johansen (in this handbook). Departing from studies of how Danish craft breweries construct collective organisational identities in autobiographies, Johansen challenges the narrative/counter-narrative duality and suggests that the inter-relation between the two notions is better reflected as centripetal and centrifugal processes of counter-narrativisations.

On the same note, Bager and Lundholt (in this handbook) invite us to study the dynamics between organisational narrative structures and representations in organisational change processes (cf. crystallised forms of knowledge and situated organisational story efforts in order to investigate aspects of complicit and countering forces and control vs. agency mechanisms)

Obviously, numerous chapters in this handbook represent a conceptual shift from studies of narrative/counter-narrative dualities to studies of narrative processes of counter-narrativisation (Johansen, in this handbook) or to the dynamics between diverse narrative recourses such as between narrative representations/structures and the small stories that circulate in situated practices (e.g. Bager & Lundholt; Bamberg & Wipff; Markussen & Knutz, in this handbook).

Several authors in this handbook (e. g. Holmgren & Strunck) propose thinking of the relationship between different kinds of narratives in terms of fluidity in which the connections between narratives and matters of dominance are constantly negotiated and (re)positioned. Hence, counter-narrative studies are based on how such processes of (counter) narrativisations or (counter) storying position themselves in relation to each other in a mix of resistive and countering forces.

Counter-narratives are not positive, conflictual or straightforward phenomena per se

In continuation of the critical review of the narrative/counter-narrative dichotomy, several chapters contest that counter-narratives are positive phenomena per se working in favour of minorities. Such chapters align with Rasmussen (2017) regarding how early studies of counter-narratives have emerged within critical humanistic methodological bodies that favour suppressed and marginalised groups, often with an emancipatory quest. Here, counter-narratives are often examined from a minority viewpoint that "tends to exclude complex power struggles in and around organisations which may exhibit more messy empirical configurations than the dichotomy allows for" (Rasmussen, 2017, p. 171).

As an example, Nurminen (in this handbook) discusses counter-narratives as serving to enable radical and extreme online communities in relation to the radical masculinity movement's use of counter-narrative strategies. The author demonstrates how such online groups and participants utilise counter-narratives to further their anti-women ideology. The practical use of counter-narratives thus works in subtle ways not always in favour of, or benign to, marginalised groups.

On another note, Borland and Shuman (in this handbook) draw attention to counter-narratives being deployed by people in power, especially as heritage discourse. Their case study unveils how heritage projects masquerading as counter-narratives serve crucially to protect an exclusionary white heritage discourse by purporting to be one narrative among many.

On a third note, Holmgren and Strunck (in this handbook) argue from a critical discourse and legitimation perspective how a bank's master and contesting narratives in a post-merger process in a Danish bank live side by side in harmony. Thus, counter-narratives are not always a negative and destructive phenomenon in opposition to master-narrative structures. They argue that such studies are a way to gain a deeper understanding of how narratives either hamper or support organisational strategies.

Rehnberg and Grafström (in this handbook) address how counter-narratives can emerge from surprising sources. From their studies of discursive struggles in the media landscape in times of radical reorganisation, involving negotiations of what is considered journalism, they show how counter-narratives in media texts are worked up as strategic devices by those that are representing and defending the master-narrative as part of a defensive act.

These chapters (and other chapters in the handbook), prove that narrative processes are indeed messy, tensional and contradictory affairs that provide important glimpses into identity creative processes and power-resistance dynamics in various contexts.

They further underline that we ought to study narrative/counter-narrative processes with an open mind and not merely from a minority viewpoint as well as from any other pre-disposed outlooks. As such, all chapters in the handbook share an interest in dynamic, complex and context-sensitive approaches to studying narrative representations and/or processes. In other words, the question about counter-narrative being emancipatory, progressive or liberating, is up for empirical scrutiny. Narrative processes are indeed polyphonic, complex and unpredictable affairs – leading us to discuss important issues of ideology and ethics, in relation to counter-narrative studies, later in the chapter.

Narrative inquiry – from diverse analytical, theoretical and methodological orientations

How do narrative scholars deal with issues of narrative processuality, complexity, entanglement and polyphony? Across the seven sections in the handbook, scholars turn to a range of theoretical and methodological bodies in order to work up narrative research designs. Some perspectives are oriented towards theoretical and conceptual issues, while others focus on working up context-sensitive analyses of diverse narrative processes. In the following we will sum up some of the most significant perspectives which are most represented in the handbook, and we will discuss their implications for narrative and counter-narrative studies. We will start by outlining important elements from the two most central frameworks: storytelling organisational theory and the narrative practice approach. Thereafter we turn to aspects of Bourdieusian field theory and the sociology of knowledge approach to discourse.

Storytelling organisation theory

Several chapters link up to storytelling organisation theory (SOT). SOT has evolved, mainly, within the works of Boje (Boje, 2001; Lundholt & Boje, 2018). His and other SOT scholars' works offer a strong ontological view of organisational narrative and storytelling practices and invite us to grasp organisations as continuously being (re)constituted through a variety of intense, chaotic and ambiguous storytelling practices (Bager & Lundholt, in this handbook; Boje, in this handbook; Svane, in this handbook; Rantakari & Vaara, 2017).

Boje and other SOT scholars prompted the much-cited division between narratives and living stories. Whereas narratives are made through retrospective sensemaking and represent crystallised forms of knowledge (often found in organisational strategy work), living stories are situated sensemaking efforts taking place in concrete encounters. Living stories are messy, tensional affairs that embed a manifold and often contradictory set of voices and narratives/discourses (Jørgensen, 2011; Bager, Mølbjerg & Raudaskoski, 2016; Jørgensen & Boje, 2010). Boje is also the originator of the concept of the antenarrative conceptualised as a bet on the future, which he presents as the bridge between narratives and situated living stories. The antenarrative approach also opens up an optimistic door for the creation and facilitation of new and more comprehensive narrative structures, to which we will return.

The concept of antenarrative is taken up by authors in the handbook (such as Lueg, Graf & Powell). Further, Svane combines the concept and other insights from SOT with Hegel's dialectics from which the author deduces four middles of storytelling. From a theoretical point of view, Svane proposes these middles as important managerial tasks in organisational practices and processes and thereby advances earlier work (such as Svane, Gergerich & Boje, 2017).

Boje draws on an extensive compilation of methodological and theoretical perspectives relevant to what he terms antenarrative inquiry strategies (Benjaminian dialogical foretelling method, Heideggerian dialectic of "negation of the negation" forenotions, Bakhtinian architectonic dialogism, Deleuzian rhizomatics, Butler's antinarrative and a Baradian sociomaterial antenarrative inquiry into actor routines and material actants). From this complex methodological tissue, he inquires into issues of sustainability and the Kolding pyramid, and he demonstrates how antenarrative strategies can work as parts of a storytelling inquiry method.

As stated by Bager and Lundholt (in this handbook), Boje's extensive body of work has provided important contributions to and a solid theoretical platform for counter-narrative studies, even though he just recently adopted the term. Earlier studies reflected concepts such as *hegemony* (i.e. privileged voices taken for granted or too subtle to be acknowledged (Boje, 2001, p. 35) and *story coercion* (i.e. the [un]conscious efforts to create universal meaning; Boje, Luhman, & Baack, 1999). From these, SOT scholars have studied ways in which dominant groups control others as well as ways in which local stories (cf. *microstoria*; Boje, 2001, p. 55) or living story webs (Svane et al., 2017) resist narratives.

Central to SOT is an anchoring in Bakhtinian thinking which is also evident in several other chapters in the handbook (such as Bager & Lundholt; Meretoja; Svane). The massive inspiration from Bakhtinian thinking will be continuously discussed throughout the rest of this chapter.

The narrative practice approach: counter-narrative as multiple layers of (re)positioning

Another central perspective that is heavily drawn on in the handbook is the narrative practice approach (NPA) that has mainly emerged from the works of Bamberg in his developments of the small story approach (Bamberg, 1997, 2004a), from the works of Geogakopoulou, as well as from co-authored publications (Bamberg & Georgakopoulou, 2008; De Fina & Georgakopoulou, 2019; Georgakopoulou, 2007). NPA has carried out narrative analysis in the direction of studying local identity formations as played out in situated practices through inquiring into multiple layers of positioning. It also had an important impact on the field of social psychology and identity research, as it was part of turning traditional identity studies into local meaning-making and the social co-production of professional identities (Bager, 2019).

The analysis starts off by studying *small stories* which are aligned with SOT's conceptualisation of *living stories*: narrators in the here and now use story efforts in the unfolding and co-creation of identity and meaning-making. Small stories represent how people work up stories to juggle claims about who they are that are hearable both as complicit with and as countering dominant discourses or narratives. Analysing small story efforts can reveal elements of positioning work and identity creation that would otherwise have remained unnoticed (Bamberg & Georgakopoulou, 2008). According to Bamberg and Georgakopoulou (2008), small story analysis offers a window into what they term the micro-genetic processes of identities as "in the making" or "coming into being" (Bamberg & Georgakopoulou, 2008, p.3). This turn towards practices and processuality is an important part in contemporary narrative studies as represented in the handbook (Rantakari & Vaara, 2017; De Fina & Georgakopoulou, 2019).

To NPA scholars, narratives and counter-narratives are not stable entities that people carry around and activate in certain situations unaffected by contextual circumstances. Rather, what counts and can be analysed as counter-narratives is worked up in co-creative processes of small story efforts between all participants involved, including the researcher in researcher-designed practices (e.g., interview settings). Also, the inspiration from Bakhtinian polyphonic and entangled thinking plays an important role. In this line of thoughts, the subject's meeting and entanglement with the co-present and distant others as well as alien perspectives affect meaning-making and the co-creation of identity and thereby the emergence of counter narratives (Bager, 2016, 2019; Bamberg & Wipff, in this handbook; Bakhtin, 1986, 1993).

NPA involves a three-layered positioning model. The model is inspired from discourse psychology, ethnomethodology and conversation analysis that invite scholars to inductively look at what takes place in interaction as the starting point of analysis of and reflection on identity work. This situated outlook represents an alternative to looking through deductive categories and searching for coherent life narratives. As Bamberg and Wipff (in this handbook) state, the NPA signified a shift from the analysis of narratives as texts or personal memories (i.e., as parts of people's or organisations' interior resources) to empirically analysable discursive activities taking place in interactions. Such analytical moves are, amongst other things, based on the argument that there tend to be crucial gaps between how people narrate themselves and their actions and what they actually perform in local situations, thereby underpinning ethnomethodological heritage.

Furthermore, NPA reflects a sort of middle position between structural and performative approaches to narrative studies as the model leads us to look at both interactional and content-oriented dimensions of narrative processes (Bager, 2019; Bamberg, 1997).

These situated and performance-based orientations and their implications explain why several authors in the handbook turn to NPA to deal with issues of narrative processuality and context sensitivity. It further allows the narrative analyst to span dimensions of concrete situated narration and the broader narrative and discursive structures that are regarded as surrounding and impacting on situated identity creative practices.

As an example, Bager and Lundholt (in this handbook) combine storytelling organisation theory (SOT) and NPA and apply small story analysis to the study of organisational identity creation in change processes in a Danish bank. The analysis is accomplished through the three levels of positioning model. The final step uncovers which broader narrative and discursive structures the organisational narrators link up to and make relevant in the co-production of professional identities. Applying this model makes the societal, organisational, historical and cultural backdrop of discourse formations (in relation to both societal, organisational and narrative structures) part of the narrative analysis (Bager, 2019; Bager & Lundholt, in this handbook). The analysis example of interview data shows traces of how bank counsellors experience identity dilemmas as an integral part of the processes of changing the bank's master-narratives to a new and more streamlined one. The authors state that the studies of dynamics between organisational discursive narrative structures and representations and the small story efforts provide an important glimpse into professional identity struggles in times of change that can help us navigate and design more comprehensive organisational change processes.

The NPA outlook also nuances the traditional quest for studying dynamics between narrative and counter-narrative resources. In this quest NPA invites us to look at how complicit and countering stories are entangled and natural parts of identity processes and of the creation of new narrative and counter-narrative structures. In NPA, small stories are seen as important sense-making activities that play out in a messy compilation of countering and supportive voices that local narrators co-create and invoke when making sense of self and others (cf. human, non-human, present and distant others) in situated practices.

Inspiration from Bourdieu's field theory

Other authors in the handbook link up to Bourdieu's field theory to discuss and show struggles between hegemonic field logics (e.g. Jensen & Ernst; Uhlendorff; Lueg, Graf & Powell). For instance, Jensen and Ernst conclude that combining narrative with Bourdieu's conceptual triad offers an innovative and valuable framework for reflecting narrative time and space in organisational processes.

Lueg, Graf and Powell contribute to contemporary Bourdieusian field studies, and to neo-institutionalist approaches by analysing hegemonic narratives of the academic field (see also Lueg, 2018). They suggest that contemporary university governance discourse is suspended between two poles: the Humboldtian perspective, favouring professorial power and authority relations, and the managerial perspective, subordinating faculty under market considerations. They propose bringing together Boje's notion of ante-narrative and the Bourdieusian notion of field struggle (Bourdieu, 1988, 1998): moments of ante-narratives were (and are) being used to secure professorial group privileges. The fight over privileges and ownership, the narrative clash was prone to be won by strong, external forces, that is, the managerial narrative.

Inspiration from the sociology of knowledge approach to discourse

Keller (in this handbook) introduces the sociology of knowledge approach to discourse (SKAD). Keller runs through an impressive gallery of sociological and discourse-based thoughts that inform the SKAD school and discusses its relevance to counter-narrative studies. One of the main points is that the field of discourse studies and in particular studies favouring the broad societal and historical dimensions of discourse (e.g. Foucauldian inspired studies of discourse formations) represent a general contextualisation for the analysis of narratives and counter-narratives, to which we will return.

So, various theoretical (and methodological) frameworks are required in order to deal with issues of narrative and counter-narrative processes and structures in various contexts. What ties these perspectives together is an aspiration to study how narrative struggles play out. Such studies are closely tied to power and hegemony and share an interest in how certain narratives gain dominance over others and how narrative struggles develop. In the following, we will posit some examples from the handbook on such narrative struggles in which certain master-narratives gain dominance over others. We will return to the multileveled character of narrative studies and processes later in the chapter.

Counter-narrative studies point towards "hegemonic" agendas and diverse narrative ecologies

Some chapters show how neoliberal master-narratives tend to overshadow other narratives by foregrounding certain knowledge systems in favour of market values, instrumentality and individuality (cf. masters of own faith). These neoliberal master-narratives tend to background and threaten more social/collective-oriented knowledge systems and narratives. For instance, Lueg, Graf and Powell (in this handbook) study narrative struggles in higher education and discuss how contemporary governance discourse is stretched out between two poles. These two poles are the Humboldtian, favouring professorial power and authority relationships on the one hand, and the managerial perspective, subordinating faculty to market considerations and continuous evaluation at the other. The authors elaborate on how a neoliberal managerial agenda seem to permeate European universities, thereby backgrounding and threatening the Humboldtian purview. They further discuss elements of elitism inherent to both, the Humboldtian and the managerial narrative.

In another context, Schünemann (in this handbook) looks at European discourse and shows how earlier counter-narratives have become dominant narratives on the political systems, gained ground and have become central themselves. The author discusses how earlier left-wing Eurosceptic counter-narratives have taken dominant positions within European governments and thereby on the European political scene in general as many Eurosceptics have occupied central positions within their political systems or even made it into government office.

These and other chapters in the handbook (e.g., by Prien) illustrate how the concepts of *master narrative* and *counter-narrative* can be employed to understand ongoing societal change in many areas. Such evolutionary narrative processes involve indeterminacy and unpredictability in the interplay between dominant and counter-narratives in various tension-filled practices detectable in diverse narrative resources.

Authors in the handbook (e.g. Rehnberg & Grafström) point to the analogy of "narrative ecologies" to explain such dynamics. The term "narrative ecologies" was coined by Gabriel (2017, p. 220) as denoting "spaces where, by analogy to natural ecologies, different elements and populations of narrative emerge, interact, compete, adapt, develop and die". To Gabriel (2017, p. 222) narratives and counter-narratives "can be thought of as co-constructing elements of narrative ecologies", and further proposes that "different types of narrative ecologies can be viewed as fostering different configurations of narrative patterns". Gabriel's (2017) narrative ecology analogy stems from studies of organisational narrative practices from which seven types of narrative ecologies are mapped out (narrative temperate regions, deserts, monocultures, mountains, marshlands, jungles, narrative allotments and gardens). Numerous chapters in this handbook prove that such diverse types of narrative ecologies are to be found in various contexts on diverse levels throughout society. As argued earlier, some narrative ecologies are played out wherein narratives and counter-narratives co-exist peacefully side by side resembling Gabriel's metaphor of *narrative monocultures.* Other narrative ecologies are more characterised by ambiguities and conflicts, coming closer to *narrative jungles.* A recurring trajectory of thought in the handbook is that the characteristics and effects of narrative processes are to be mapped out from diverse narrative resources in situated contexts.

As such, the narrative and discursive struggles that are reflected throughout the handbook can be understood as a rejection of a rather simple narrative/counter-narrative duality in favour of narrative ecologies (Gabriel, 2017, p. 220). We believe that the acceptance of narrative processuality and diverse types of narrative ecologies is a promising and interesting contemporary framework from which we can study and critically debate ongoing societal change consisting of dynamics between power/control and resistive forces and its effects in diverse contexts.

Methodological challenges and pitfalls within narrative studies

An ongoing debate in the handbook is the discussion on theoretical and methodological challenges and pitfalls within (counter) narrative studies. Bamberg and Wipff (in this handbook) draw our attention to blurriness in much master-narrative literature. Other authors point to the fact that the existence and characteristics of a master-narrative often lack analytical justification as well as documentation and are more often presumed and are therefore rather speculative affairs (e.g. Hyvärinen, in this handbook). Some posit a range of problems concerning lack of transparency in narrative literature together with theoretical and conceptual vagueness. Others posit that the literature on narrative structures often have little anchoring in narrative theory, which leads to confusing and varying use of terms and lack of clear definitions. Others focus on a lack of clear accounts of how to analyse narrative data (Fage-Butler) whilst others focus on how counter narrative analysis strategies can help narrative scholars and social scientists in general to present empirical data in more nuanced ways (Müller & Frandsen, in this handbook). The various chapters provide possible enhancements and solutions from diverse perspectives and we will now turn to some of these.

Nuancing narrative theories

Some of the handbook's authors turn to theories within narrative studies to challenge and sharpen their conceptual and analytical outlooks. For instance, Hyvärinen's (in this handbook) rethinking of Brunerian narrative theory from a theoretical perspective which tones it to embrace analysis of narrative processuality in the terms of how narrators draw on diverse master and counter-narrative recourses.

Klinge, Carlson and Kahle combine Bamberg's (2004a) works on counter-narrative with Schütze's (1983) idea of text structure analysis, more specifically by drawing on Schütze's distinction between the text genres of narrative, argumentation, evaluation and description. They thereby reconstruct counter-narratives via text structure analysis and argue how different forms of counter positioning affect not only the content but also the actual textual structure of interviewees' accounts.

Inspiration from discourse studies

It is worth noting that numerous authors in the handbook turn toward discourse studies in order to address and overcome methodological, theoretical and analytical vagueness in their (counter) narrative analyses. In the following we will discuss the inspiration for and relevance to discourse studies together with how narrative scholars in general can benefit from some of the metaphors, models and analytical tools which some discourse scholars draw on to deal with issues of, for instance, discursive processuality and the multilevelled nature of discourse.

It's no surprise that narrative scholars, also numerous authors in this handbook (e.g. Bager & Lundholt; Bamberg & Wipff; Fage-Butler; Holmgren & Strunck; Keller; Prien), increasingly turn to discourse studies as an obvious avenue to find inspiration for how to deal with methodological, conceptual and analytical vagueness within (counter) narrative studies. First of all, the field of discourse studies has close affinities with counter-narrative studies and as Keller (in this handbooks) posits, discourse represents a general contextualisation for the analysis of narratives and counter-narratives. Discourse studies also take a critical stance toward formations of discourses in which some power/knowledge systems gain hegemony over others (Bager & Mølholm, 2019). These discursive mechanisms and struggles are aligned by several of the handbook's authors with narrative-generating processes that tend to naturalise and legitimise certain power and knowledge structures in society (e. g. Bager & Lundholt, in this handbook; Bamberg & Wipff, in this handbook; Keller, in this handbook, Prien, in this handbook).

Second, studying discourse is aligned with studying processes (Bager, 2019; Heracleous, 2017) which mirrors the narrative turn towards processuality.

Third, various strands of discourse studies have a rich experience and well-developed methodological bodies for applying concepts for close analysis of manifold empirical representations related to diverse levels and processes of discursive configurations.

Multiple layers of narratives and discourses

What becomes evident throughout the handbook is a demand to study narrative processes in relation to multiple levels of narrative practices and meaning making. In the introduction (Lueg, Bager & Lundholt, in this handbook), we proposed distinguishing between micro, meso and macro levels of narrative inquiry and the relevance of studying the interplay between narrativisations on these multiple levels. This line of thought lives on in many chapters in the handbook (e. g. Bager & Lundholt; Bamberg & Wipff, Keller; Lueg; Graf & Powel).

Within discourse studies, there is a long and highly relevant tradition of thinking in terms of discourse on diverse levels that resembles the division between master-narratives and living or small stories. Like master-narratives, Discourses (with a capital D) point toward cultural evolutionary knowledge-creation processes in which some Discourses, understood as knowledge forms/systems, gain more ground and thereby tend to overshadow and background others. Similar to living or small stories, discourses (with a lower-case d) reflect situated meaning-making activities in which actors co-construct discourses and meaning (Bager, 2019). It is widely accepted that the Discourse/discourse levels are dialectically entangled in various subtle ways: the historically congealed Discourses affect and are drawn on and made relevant in situated contexts and the emergence of situated discourses impact broader discursive structures (Horsbøl & Raudaskoski, 2016; Gee, 2004, Iedema, 2003). Discourse studies are increasingly, and in various degrees, analysing how such discursive processes and dialectics are played out by looking at a range of discursive resources and data types (Bager, 2019; Nicolini, 2009a, 2009b).

Alvesson and Kärremann (2011) outline four levels of organisational discourse – micro, meso, macro and mega – and discuss how diverse discourse scholars tend to foreground certain layers and discursive dimensions in their analyses. These four layers have been widely cited within (organisational) discourse studies and have helped scholars add precision according to their focus on certain levels of discourse as well as positioning within the field of discourse studies in general. We believe that narrative scholars can benefit from such positioning activities to meet some of the methodological blurriness addressed in this handbook.

Bager (2019) elaborates a relevant three-layered model to illustrate the interrelatedness and entanglement between diverse layers of Discourse/discourse and narrative/story as part of an embodied discourse-based narrative analysis methodology. This methodological framework combines aspects from the narrative practice approach (NPA) and storytelling organisation theory (SOT), which underlines its relevance to this handbook. We believe that the model can inspire (counter) narrative scholars regardless of their inspiration from discourse theory in order to add precision to discussions on dynamics between diverse narrative representations, levels and features.

The model is composed of three layers of discursive/narrative dimensions that are shot through by entangled discursive and narrative features: the outer layer represents the societal level of narratives/Discourse that embed the historical crystallisation of formations of Discourse/narratives. The inner layer illustrates concrete situations in which discourse/living or small stories are worked up and co-created by situated participants. The middle layer reflects institutional or organisational Discourse and narratives and involves how these play out in a mix between elements from the outer societal layer and the inner situated layer.

Figure 32.1 also displays how narrative and discursive meaning-making is housed in a time-space continuum recognising how *temporal multiplicity* plays an important role when we continuously (re)create identity, stories/narratives and discourses (Bager, 2015, 2016; Bakhtin, 1986; Cunliffe et al., 2004). Voices, discourses and stories are made up by participants in situated practices

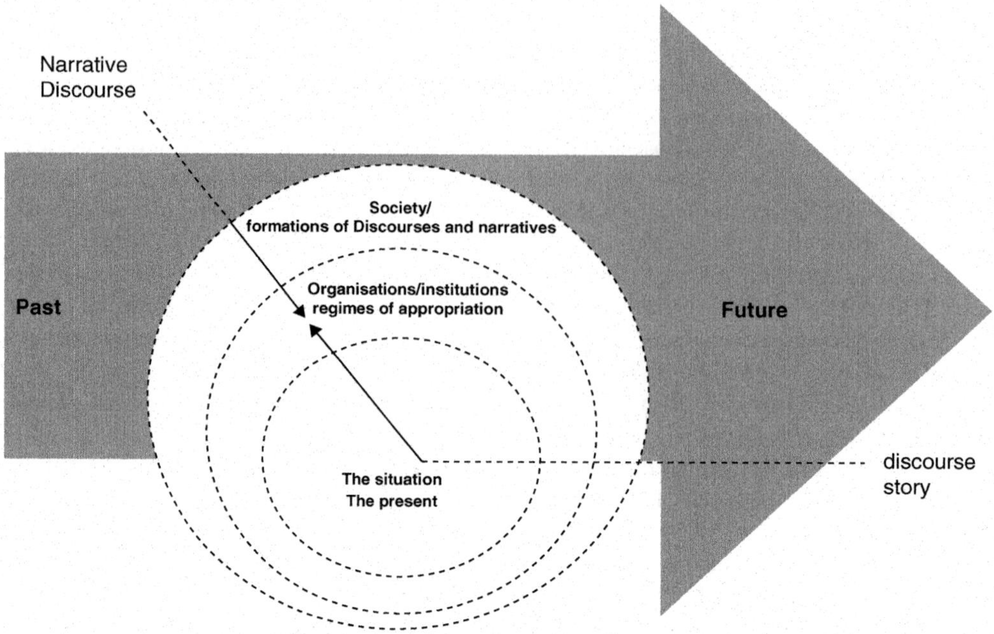

Figure 32.1 Multiple layers of discourse/discourse and narrative/story (with inspiration from Bager, 2019)

that draw on a diversity of voices/Discourse/narratives from outside and inside of dialogic events – from the past and the present and in anticipation of the future (Bager, 2015; Bakhtin, 1986, 1993). The diverse layers and timely configurations are all reflected as parts of overall narrative meaning-making and identity-creation processes.

Methodological metaphors of zooming in-and out and a toolkit logic

The model is accompanied by the methodological metaphors of *zooming in and out* together with a *toolkit logic* (Nicolini, 2009a, 2009b). The former invites scholars to zoom in and out between the diverse layers of narrative/discursive processes and the latter to activate multiple theories and perspectives in the process of analysis. The toolkit logic follows the rationale that in order to reflect the multilevelled, polyphonic and complex aspects of narrative/(D)discursive processes one must have a broad toolbox with a compilation of theories and concepts that reflects aspects on all of three discursive/narrative levels.

Bager emphasises that the model is an analytical construct and it's obvious that discursive/narrative processes do not play out in clear and tidy ways as the illustration may show, which is in accordance with key points in the handbook. Nevertheless, the model can help narrative scholars add precision according to which layers are under scrutiny in certain parts of the narrative analysis and from there discuss its entanglements and relationship to other narrative layers and elements.

The model's layers have the potential to be tailored to specific studies reflecting diverse layers of narrative practices and processes. Put in relation to the various chapters that link up to NPA, their analyses start by zooming in on the inner layer in agreement with the three-levelled positioning analytical model. From narrators' local positioning and small story activities and its content-oriented characteristics (positioning level 1) together with the interactional dimensions (positioning level 2), such analyses zoom out and discuss how the local small story efforts relate to broader narrative/discursive levels (positioning level 3). The model (Figure 32.1) invites the analyst to zoom out on broader narrative elements in relation to the institutional or organisational settings and further out to narrative structures on societal level in order to reflect and straddle the local and global aspects in the narrative analysis. From such zooming in and out activities, we achieve the basis for the discussion on narrative counter-narrative dynamics and its effects.

The Foucauldian-inspired analyses in the handbook mostly zoom out on the outer layer of the model and discuss how certain historically created discourse formations consisting of certain master-narratives are subjectivising people in certain directions (e.g., Prien). An argument made in several chapters in the handbook (e.g., by Keller; Prien) is that the Foucauldian perspective does not reflect situated narrative/discursive meaning-making in local settings together with its multimodal characteristics. Therefore, these analyses need to take other perspectives into account (cf. a toolkit logic) in order to extend the Foucauldtian perspective to study how discourse formations on a historical and broad societal level subjectivise participants in concrete situations (Bager et al., 2016; Bager & Mølholm, 2019). SKAD is a perfect example of how a compilation of discursive tools is applied for close analysis of a wide range of empirical representations straddling all three levels, as shown in Figure 32.1 (Keller, in this handbook).

Holmgren and Strunck mainly zoom in on the inner layer (Figure 32.1) and study linguistic structures using a combination of critical discourse analysis and legitimation. As a means to support precision in the narrative analysis, they analyse how linguistic features of identity work in interview data with middle managers on recruitment policies and practices in a post-merger process in a Danish bank. From there they zoom out on the organisational layer and discuss how contesting narratives co-exist peacefully alongside the master-narrative that the bank wishes to implement. They conclude that the approach contributes to a deeper understanding of how narratives either impede or support organisational strategies.

Jensen and Ernst (in this handbook) argue for similar ideas as they seek to achieve a multilevelled theorisation of narrative processes by drawing on Bourdieu's affiliated field theory. They link the narrative micro analytical level of everyday practices (inner layer in Figure 32.1) with the macro analytical level of the wider field (Layer 2 + 3 in Figure 32.1), through Bourdieu's concepts of field, habitus and capital.

In Markussen's and Knutz's (in this handbook) analysis of family narratives concerning incarcerated fathers and their children in the challenging prison context, they argue for a theoretical and analytical distinction between personal, family and master-narratives. The three-layered model (Figure 32.1) can be tailored to reflect such theoretical and analytical distinctions and helps provide precision in the analysis.

To sum up, the model and the division between several layers of narrative and discourse can help narrative scholars add precision according to which narrative levels they zoom in and out of in diverse stages of their analyses. More importantly, it can help facilitate discussions on which diverse narrative (and discursive) perspectives and theories are drawn on in order to reflect and discuss dynamics between diverse levels of (counter) narrative processes.

However, we should be careful in making such assumptive categorisations of levels prior to actual studies and analyses as, for instance Latour, reminds us that the micro elements are to be found in the macro and vice versa. We suggest that the levels emerge in the process of performing analysis according to what becomes relevant in analyses of concrete narrative representations and processes (cf. the NPA three positioning model).

Diverse counter-narrative strategies for gathering, analysing and representing data

Several chapters in the handbook address methodological issues of data gathering and decoding processes from plurivocal and pluralistic counter-narrative perspectives.

Müller and Frandsen (in this handbook) problematise the accessibility to data from which counter-narratives can be derived in respect to 1) what researchers are able to gain access to and 2) how researchers make sense of the data in the process of analysis. They argue that counter-narrative scholars may design the research process in a way that increases the sensitivity towards counter-narratives. As part of this quest, they propose ethnographically inspired studies of "deep hanging out" with references to Geertz (1998).

The authors discuss the potential of bringing three diverse counter-narratives analysis strategies to complement traditional categorising and coding strategies; what they term "common sense coding", which many social scientists rely on when making sense of empirical data. They argue that such common-sense coding might limit the possibilities for analysing social situations involving various participants, interests, viewpoints, perceptions and experiences, as the laws of logic do not easily apply. They discuss the theoretical and methodological implications of a counter-narrative perspective and illustrate how it enables scholars to analyse and represent empirical data in more nuanced ways that embrace narrative ambiguities. Their counter-narrative strategies involve looking at aspects such as untold stories and deconstruction, multiplicity and ambiguity, together with tensions and paradoxes (Müller & Frandsen, in this handbook).

They focus on organisational data and stress its inherent ambiguities, for instance how the management in a particular organisational setting can both help and exploit employees at one and the same time. Furthermore, they portray how employees can both be motivated and de-motivated at the same time. Such ambiguities are supported by other analyses in the handbook that also link up to NPA (e.g. Bager & Lundholt; Bamberg & Wipff). Such analyses prove how polyphony and paradoxes mark the ongoing simultaneous presence of contradicting truths (Fairhurst, Cooren, & Cahill, 2002).

Avoidance of drawing out common sense analytical findings and performing (counter) narrative tautologic studies

We applaud the proposal to think of alternative ways of gathering multiple data types and applying diverse counter-narrative analytical strategies, which match the turn towards narrative processuality and the analytical involvement of multiple narrative levels, representations and features. However, we see a need for narrative scholars to critically reflect on how we design such processes, from which ideological perspectives and with what aims.

If we for instance design our narrative data collection and analytical manoeuvres toward unveiling and addressing narrative/counter-narrative dynamics, we need to consider how we avoid performing "tautologic narrative studies", in the sense that we merely justify our theoretical and ideology-saturated assumptions and thereby risk only finding what we are looking for. If we for instance assume that certain master (counter) narrative dynamics are repressing certain groups and minorities that we favour in accordance with our ideological assumptions, we may very well risk looking for situations and narrative representations that support such assumptions and support counter-narrative strategies that have the potential to shake and transform such repressive narrative structures into what we assume to have the potential to become more egalitarian and comprehensive ones. A similar discussion is well known in literature that addresses war games within organisational culture studies (e. g. Martin & Frost, 2011). Here, the authors debate how diverse strands within culture studies are performing tautologic analyses and data representation in their battles regarding which perceptions of organisational culture is the best suited. For instance, scholars that represent an integration perspective tend to look for and foreground data that confirms univocal and harmonious organisational cultures whose values can be shared by all organisational members (cf. an organisation *has* a culture). Whereas representatives of the differentiation or fragmentation culture perspectives tend to find and spotlight data that supports their basic assumptions of how organisational cultures come about and are maintained – the former foregrounds data that posits organisational cultures as shared within subgroups and teams. The latter enhances data that depicts organisational cultures as consisting of ambiguities and paradoxes and shows that organisational culture cannot be shared but is performed through processes involving multiple and often contradicting interpretations and continuous negotiations of meaning (cf. organisations perform cultures).

This discussion complies with the arguments in the handbook that draw connections with Rasmussen's (2017) critique of how traditional counter-narrative studies tend to favour and support minorities and suppressed groups as an inherently positive feature. Because, from which rationales and basic assumptions are we to decide which narrative/counter-narrative structures we ought to support? And which ones are we to oppose? And are narrative scholars the ones to decide on such issues anyway? Such question raises important questions concerning narrative ethics.

The emancipation paradox and the Achilles heel of narrative polyphony

The questions and studies as brought forward in this handbook prove how counter-narratives can play out in unpredictable ways. This new focus calls for a debate on issues of (counter) narrative ideology and ethics. Earlier in this concluding chapter we provided examples for the unpredictable positioning of counter-narratives: they *can* be viewed as favouring suppressed minorities, but they may also favour extremist groups. They may work in favour of those in power, and they may be representing dominant master-narratives, and serve as a means of control. Moreover, they can in some instances be reflected as diverse narrative ecologies such as, for instance, narrative jungles or at other times as harmonious narrative monocultures.

Such analyses tap into what can be seen as the Achilles heel of narrative polyphony. If we, first, propose plurality and if we, second, propose that repressed voices or collectives take a more central position within society, who is to decide which voices are to be silenced and which ones are to be fostered. As Bakhtinian thinking is massively represented in the handbook, it is obvious to take these considerations into account. A Bakhtinian ethics of dialogue invites us to foster the centrifugal and diversifying forces of social life, and to contest centripetal and monologising forces that historically tend to close down diversity (cf. non-alibi in being and answerability; Bager, Svane & Jørgensen, 2018; Bakhtin, 1993). Nevertheless, when forms of counter-narrative knowledge are fostered in order to suppress monologising master-narratives, we cannot predict the effects of the new emerging ones even though we anticipate more comprehensive and less repressive narrative structures. Such points call for reflexivity and critical awareness in designing data processing (e.g., data collection, decoding and representation).

The discussion triggers aspects of what scholars address as the emancipation paradox (Bager & Moelholm, 2019; Clegg et al., 2006). The emancipation paradox points toward how some dialogic-oriented scholars tend to push their own theoretical and methodological idiosyncrasies onto the people they are researching on or with. For instance, the discussion can be seen within participatory studies such as Action Research (AR) or Organisational Discourse Activism (ODAc) and other participatory approaches in which scholars take performative researcher positions. In such participatory studies, scholars carry out research together with co-researchers and contribute to a change in local practices and/or communities (Bager & Moelholm, 2019). Here, scholars call for critical reflexivity and awareness of which ideological means and ends researchers are serving and in whose favour. A basic idea in AR and ODAc is the ambition to involve co-researchers in the field of study to co-produce important decisions and inductively co-develop theories in the research process based on everyday experiences and forms of knowledge. In such studies it can be an ongoing element to try to avoid giving voice to participants or collectives that do not wish to be emancipated or benefit from emancipation.

More scholars in the handbook reason for more participatory and performative narrative methodologies in which innovative and more involved relations between researchers can be tried out (such as Bager & Lundholt; Boje; Markussen & Knutz). In such participatory narrative studies, scholars and co-researchers can discuss and negotiate how inquiries and studies of (counter) narratives can help foster change of narrative practices on diverse levels and co-produce new narrative structures and engage in closer, more practice-based and less researcher-controlled researcher-researched relationships.

So, we argue that narrative scholars ought to watch their step and not glorify the use of counter-narratives on a preset liberating and emancipatory agenda and we invite them to engage in the practice of critical reflexivity to try and avoid the pitfall of the emancipation paradox in a desire to critically address the Achilles heel of narrative polyphony.

Summing up and outline of future counter-narrative research avenues

Several of the handbook's discussions and analyses of narrative practices and processes prove how a binary and clear-cut division between narratives and counter-narratives does not suffice when looking at various narrative processes. Central to these discussions is the proposal to study narrative and storytelling practices and processes in its contextual embeddedness together with how diverse participants render narrative resources (such as dominant/master-narratives, counter-narratives, antenarratives, small stories, living stories etc.) relevant in and across particular representations, situations, times and contexts. Here, a key aspect is that pointing out implications of and the dynamics between narrative and counter-narrative (or counter story) structures and representations must be a matter of context-sensitive analyses that reveal the many ways in which various countering and complicit narrative resources interact, collide and sometimes co-exist.

The narrative and discursive struggles reflected throughout this handbook can be understood as turning away from a rather simple narrative/counter-narrative duality in favour of narrative ecologies (Gabriel, 2017, p. 220). We believe that this turn to narrative processuality and diverse types of narrative ecologies is a promising and interesting contemporary framework. Narrative scholars can capitalise on this framework by critically debating ongoing societal change, dynamics between controlling and resistive forces, and the effects of these processes.

Throughout the handbook, a range of narrative methodological challenges and pitfalls are addressed concerning issues of theoretical, conceptual and methodological vagueness and imprecision in (counter) narrative studies. In this respect, numerous theoretical and methodological perspectives are employed in the reflection on and debate of such challenges and in the desire to overcome them in various ways. What binds these works together is their shared focus on narrative processuality, context sensitivity and a demand to study narrative processuality according to several narrative (and discursive) layers.

Multiple frameworks are provided that invite narrative scholars to study centripetal (unifying) and centrifugal (diversifying) forces on several narrative levels found in a variety of data types in society spanning from the global to the local – spanning societal, political, institutional, organisational and more or less informal and digital communities and practices. In many chapters we argue that in order to study overall narrative meaning-making and knowledge-producing processes, we need to consider their multilevelled, polyphonic, multimodal and multiple temporal features. From here, narrative scholars can engage with how the narratives and/or stories people (and material, nature) enact unmask structures of power and ideology that shape our communities and tend to foreground some rationalities and knowledge systems at the expense of others. Such analyses thereby allow us to gain a deeper understanding of the dynamics behind emerging master-narratives – not least counter-narratives – in transforming narrative ecologies and social arenas. The handbook thereby proves the potential and rigour of applying counter-narrative strategies to reflect various issues of power-control mechanism throughout society.

Future counter-narrative research avenues

Analyses and points in the handbook together with recent activities within the broad field of narrative studies (as conducted by the Center for Narratological Studies) point toward several interesting future avenues for research. In the following, we will firstly, briefly summarise our invitation for narrative scholars to engage with and try out new practices of critical narrative reflexivity. Second, in an attempt to turn this into an applicable endeavour, we propose approaches favouring narrative activism that moves beyond a descriptive approach. Finally, we will propose further studies of narrative processuality in respect to issues of narrative temporality, multimodality and sociomateriality.

Critical narrative reflexivity

The unpredictable and subtle nature of (counter) narrative processes and its implications for practice also invites narrative scholars to carefully consider ethical and ideology-saturated issues. For instance, we appeal to narrative scholars to engage in critical reflexivity concerning how to design, collect, handle and represent data in order to avoid drawing out common sense analytical findings and to avoid the pitfall of performing tautologic narrative analyses that risk supporting the narrative scholars' preset idiosyncrasies and merely finding what they are looking for. Moreover, we propose critical awareness and methodological transparency on how narrative scholars deal with the Achilles heel of narrative polyphony and seek to avoid the emancipation paradox so that narrative scholars do not push their own idiosyncrasies onto the people and practices that they are researching into or with.

Narrative and storytelling activism

We can see how narrative scholars are increasingly turning toward narrative activist approaches in the sense that (counter) narrative inquiries are used to fuel changes in local practices. This tendency is visible in CNS activities such as our annual conferences together with recent and ongoing publications. The topics of the last two conferences have among other things highlighted discourse activist approaches where narrative scholars engage in fostering a change in practices such as in organisational contexts.

Some of the perspectives have linked up to Boje's work with narrative therapy, centring on helping new stories along (e.g. Boje's work with helping veterans overcome war traumas and PTSD issues; Bager & Lundholt, in this handbook). In this respect, Boje, Larsen & Bruun (2017) are developing the concept of true storytelling that centres on helping new organisational stories and antenarratives along in relation to matters of sustainability. Other perspectives have linked up to discourse studies and the new approach of organisational discourse activism (ODAc; Bager &

Mølholm, 2019). As mentioned earlier, it might not be down to narrative scholars to decide which forms of narrative knowledge we ought to give voice to and which ones we should tone down. In the aforementioned narrative and storytelling activist approaches, the research participant(s) are involved with taking such important decisions.

Narrative multimodality and temporal multiplicity

Discussions in the handbook propose further studies that resemble recent suggestions on future narrative studies concerning issues of multimodality and temporal multiplicity (Bager, 2019; Rantakari & Varaa, 2017).

In regard to narrative multimodality, several chapters touch on issues of data accessibility and the potential of gathering diverse multimodal data types in order to reflect and analyse (counter) narrative processes. Jensen & Ernst (in this handbook) use a range of data types in their analyses of organisational post-merger (counter) narrative processes. Bager & Lundholt (in this handbook) argue that in order to really understand issues of organisational change processes in contemporary times of technologisation, narrative scholars must also take material, digital and other multimodal aspects into account in narrative analyses, a point which is also supported by the main theoretical bodies that are represented in the handbook. In Bakhtinian thinking, NPA, SOT, Bourdieu's field theory as well as SKAD narrative processes are enmeshed in embodied and multimodal ways of co-performing narrative structures which also calls for narrative analyses that take such multimodal aspects more into account.

A few chapters mention temporal features of (counter) narrative processes but they do not study such aspects in detail. In line with many of the approaches represented in the handbook, narrative temporality is moved away from strict and functionalistic beginning-middle-end assumptions where universal temporal features can be deduced. Instead, the handbook taps into more complex ways of perceiving narrative timeliness, where multiple temporal features are entangled and present in every situation (Bager, 2016, 2019, Cunliffe et al., 2004). As mentioned in relation to the three-layered model, in line with Bakhtinian thinking, situated narrative practices always embed temporal features from the past, re(configured) in the now in anticipation of future narrative responses.

With this handbook, we hope to contribute to further conceptualisations and detailed studies of narrative multimodality, multiple narrative features and their implications for social practices.

References

Alvesson, M., & Karreman, D. (2000). Varieties of discourse: On the study of organizations through discourse analysis. *Human Relations*, *53*(9), 1125–1149.

Alvesson, M., & Kärreman, D. (2011). Decolonializing discourse: Critical reflections on organizational discourse analysis. *Human Relations*, *64*(9), 1121–1146.

Bager, A. S. (2015). Organizational (auto)-ethnography: An interaction analysis of identity work through the study of other-orientation and storytelling practices in a leadership development forum. *Tamara Special Issue on Organizational Ethnographies*, *13*(3), 35–56.

Bager, A.S. (2016). Små fortællinger: Diskursanalyse af fortællinger i praksis. (Eng: Small Stories: Discourse Analysis of situated narratives) In Raudaskoski, P, & Horsbøl, A. (Eds.), *Diskurs Og Praksis* (pp. 135–166). København, Samfundslitteratur.

Bager, A.S. (2019). A multimodal discourse analysis of positioning and identity work in a leadership development practice. *Communication & Language at Work*, *6*(1), 40–62.

Bager, A. S., Mølbjerg, K. J. & Raudaskoski, P. L. (2016). Dialogue and governmentality-in-action: A discourse analysis of a leadership forum. In P. McIlvenny, J.Z. Klausen & L.B. Lindegaard (Eds.), *New Perspectives on Discourse and Governmentality*. Amsterdam, John Benjamins Publishing.

Bager, A.S., Svane, M., & Jørgensen, K.M. (2018). Ethics perspective on entrepreneurship. In *The Palgrave Handbook of Multidisciplinary Perspectives on Entrepreneurship* (pp. 457–477). Cham: Palgrave Macmillan.

Bager, A.S. & Mølholm, M. (2019). A methodological framework for organizational discourse activism: An ethics of dispositif and dialogue. *Philosophy of Management*, 1–28.

Bakhtin, M. M. (1986). *Speech Genres & Other Late Essays*. Austin, TX: University of Texas Press.

Bakhtin, M. M. (1993). *Toward a Philosophy of the Act*. Austin, TX: University of Texas Press.

Bamberg, M. (1997). Positioning between structure and performance. *Journal of Narrative and Life History*, 7(1–4), 335–342.

Bamberg, M. (2004a). Considering counter-narratives. In M. Bamberg & M. Andrews (Eds.), *Considering Counter-narratives: Narrating, Resisting, Making Sense* (Studies in Narrative, 4; 351–371). Philadelphia, PA: John Benjamins Publishing.

Bamberg, M. (2004b). Talk, small stories, and adolescent identities. *Human Development*, *47*, 366–369.

Bamberg, M. (2011). Who am I? Narration and its contribution to self and identity. *Theory & Psychology*, *21*(1), 3–24.

Bamberg, M., & Andrews, M. (Eds.). (2004). *Considering Counter-Narratives: Narrating, Resisting, Making Sense* (Studies in Narrative, 4). Philadelphia, PA: John Benjamins Publishing.

Bamberg, M., & Georgakopoulou, A. (2008). Small stories as a new perspective in narrative and identity analysis. *Text & Talk*, *28*(3), 377–396.

Boje, D. M. (2001). *Narrative Methods for Organizational & Communication Research*. London, UK: Sage Publications.

Boje, D. M., Luhman, J. T., & Baack, D. E. (1999). Stories and encounters between storytelling organizations. *Journal of Management Inquiry*, *8*(4), 340–360.

Boje, D.M., Larsen, J., & Brunn, L. (2017). *True Storytelling. How to Succeed with your Implementation*. Working Paper. Available at: oldfriendsindustries.com.

Bourdieu, P. (1988). *Homo Academicus*. Stanford: Stanford University Press.

Bourdieu, P. (1998). *The State Nobility: Elite Schools in the Field of Power*. Stanford: Stanford University Press.

Clegg, S., Courpasson, D. and Phillips, N. (2006). *Power and Organizations*. London: Sage Publications.

Cunliffe, A.L., Luhman, J.T., & Boje, D.M. (2004). Narrative temporality: Implications for organizational research. *Organization Studies*, *25*(2), 261–286.

De Fina, A., & Georgakopoulou, A. (2019). *The Handbook of Narrative Analysis*. John Wiley & Sons.

Fairhurst, G.T., Cooren, F., & Cahill, D.J. (2002). Discursiveness, contradiction, and unintended consequences in successive downsizings. *Management Communication Quarterly*, *15*(4), 501–540.

Frandsen, S., Lundholt, M.W., & Kuhn, T. (2017). Introduction. In S. Frandsen, T. Kuhn, & M.W. Lundholt (Eds.), *Counter-Narratives and Organization* (pp. 208–226). London: Routledge.

Gabriel, Y. (2017). 10 narrative ecologies and the role of counter-narratives. In Frandsen, S., Kuhn, T. & Lundholt, M. (Eds.), *Counter-narratives and Organization*, 208–226. London: Routledge.

Gee, J.P. (2004). *An Introduction to Discourse Analysis: Theory and Method*. London: Routledge.

Geertz, C. (1998). Deep hanging out. *The New York Review of Books*, *45*(16), 69–72.

Heracleous, L., (2017). Discourse theory. In Langley, A. & Tsoukas, H. (Eds.), *The Sage Handbook of Process Organization Studies*. London: Sage, pp. 190–203.

Georgakopoulou, A. (2015). Small stories research. In De Fina, A. & Georgakopoulou, A. (Eds.), *The Handbook of Narrative Analysis*, 255–271.

Georgakopoulou, A. (2007). *Small stories, interaction and identities* (Vol. 8). John Benjamins Publishing.

Horsbøl, A., & Raudaskoski, P. (2016). *Diskurs og praksis: Teori, metode og analyse*. (Eng: Discourse and Practice: Theory, method and analysis). København: *Samfundslitteratur*.

Iedema, R. (2003). *Discourses of Post-Bureaucratic Organization* (Vol. 5). John Benjamins Publishing.

Jørgensen, K.M. (2011). Antenarrative writing - tracing and representing living stories. In Boje, D. (Eds.) *Storytelling and the Future of Organizations: An Antenarrative Handbook*, 284–297. London: Routledge

Jørgensen, K. M., & Boje, D. M. (2010). Resituating narrative and story in business ethics. *Business Ethics: A European Review*, *19*(3), 253–264.

Lueg, K. (2018). Organizational changes towards a European academic field: A case study of frictions in the narratives of Europeanization at a German University from an institutional perspective. *Innovation: The European Journal of Social Science Research*, *31*(4), 484–503.

Lundholt, M.W., & Boje, D. (2018). Understanding organizational narrative-counter-narratives dynamics: An overview of Communication Constitutes Organization (CCO) and Storytelling Organization Theory (SOT) approaches. *Communication and Language at Work*, *5*(1), 18–29.

Martin, J & Frost, P. (2011). The Organizational Culture War Games, in M. Godwyn & J.H., Gittell (Eds.), *Sociology of Organizations: Structures and Relations*, Pine Forge Press, pp. 315–336.
Nicolini, D. (2009a). Zooming in and out: Studying practices by switching theoretical lenses and trailing connections. *Organization Studies*, *30*(12), 1391–1418.
Nicolini, D. (2009b). Zooming in and zooming out: A package of method and theory to study work practices. In S. Ybema, D. Yanow, & H. Wels (Eds.), *Organizational Ethnography: Studying the Complexities of Everyday Life* (pp. 120–138). London: Sage.
Rantakari, A., & Vaara, E. (2017). Narratives and processuality. In A. Langley & H. Tsoukas (Eds.), *The SAGE Handbook of Process Organizational Studies* (pp. 271–285). Los Angeles, CA: Sage Publications.
Rasmussen, R.K. (2017). Rethinking counter-narratives in studies of organizational texts and practices. *Counter-Narratives and Organization*, 293–332.
Schütze, F. (1983). Biographieforschung und narratives Interview. *Neue Praxis*, *13*(3), 283–293.
Svane, C.C.C.M., Gergerich, E., & Boje, D.M. (2017). Fractal change management and counter-narrative in cross-cultural change. In *Counter-Narratives and Organization* (pp. 137–162). New York: Routledge.

Index

Note: Locators in *italics* refer to figures and those in **bold** to tables.